Mathematics *for* GCSE

Mark Bindley

John Mansfield School, Peterborough

$$C = \frac{5(f - 32)}{9}$$

SIMON & SCHUSTER
EDUCATION

First published in 1990 by
Basil Blackwell Ltd
108 Cowley Road
Oxford OX4 1JF

Reprinted in 1992, 1994 by
Simon and Schuster Education

Simon and Schuster Education
Campus 400
Maylands Avenue
Hemel Hempstead
Herts HP2 7EZ

British Library Cataloguing in Publication Data

Bindley, Mark
    Mathematics for GCSE: an instruction manual
    for students
    1. Mathematics
    1. Title
    510

ISBN 0 7501 0386 8 net edition
ISBN 0 7501 0510 0 non-net edition

Phototypeset by
Dobbie Typesetting Limited, Plymouth, Devon

Printed in Great Britain by
Butler and Tanner Ltd, Frome

Contents

P1 70% → C & 45% P2. + 55% A

P1 83% → B 55% P2 65% A.

Introduction

About this Instruction Manual

This book is designed to help students pass GCSE Mathematics with a Grade A, B or C. It is also conceived for Key Stage 4 of the National Mathamatics Curriculum. Pages vi to xi show how the book almost completely covers the Programmes of Study for Attainment Levels 5 to 10.

It can be used:

- as a one- or two-year course for students in classes preparing to take the examination for the first time;

- as a one-year course for students in classes re-sitting the examination to improve their grades;

- as a self-study manual for external students;

- as a teaching and revision aid for parents and private tutors helping students to prepare for the examination.

It features:

- a contents organisation which matches the proposed National Mathematics Curriculum and the present GCSE syllabuses offered by the five examination groups;

- very extensive explanations and worked examples, which support individual learning programmes in mathematics classes, and self-study for external students;

- frequent Checkpoint exercises to test a student's understanding and to provide reinforcement of skills and techniques;

- practice and revision exercises at the end of each unit;

- extended problems for coursework at the end of each unit;

- a wide range of past paper questions from each of the five GCSE examining boards.

This book assumes that:

- students aiming for Grades A, B and C will not need extensive teaching material dealing with basic arithmetic (although the necessary syllabus content is still covered in review sections at the start of the book);

- students will own and use a scientific calculator (unless it is specifically indicated otherwise, all exercises should be completed with a calculator);

- students will obtain a copy of the individual GCSE syllabus they are studying. This will indicate the exact coverage required and dictate the sections of the book that must be studied.

Some advice to students

There is no 'correct' way to succeed in examinations and everybody has their own special ideas and study methods.

I will however offer the following general advice which I hope you may find helpful in developing your own failsafe route to success.

- As you work through the Checkpoints, try to keep your solutions in an organised folder or exercise book. These can form a valuable revision aid during the final weeks, days and hours before the examination.

- Working through the Practice and Revision exercises during the final weeks of your course is a very good way to revise. You can make a note of all the questions that cause difficulty and repeat them after a few days to make certain that you have mastered the necessary techniques.

- Most GCSE examinations include a page giving formulae etc. Make sure you obtain a copy of this so you do not waste time memorising unnecessary information.

- Obtain as many past papers for your particular syllabus as you possibly can and work through them using the teaching notes in this book to help you.

- During the final revision period, try to work through as many of the examples in this book as possible. Don't just read the examples, cover the solution with a piece of paper and try to solve the problem. If you cannot solve the problem study the solution and then try again. If you are really serious about that grade A, you need to master every worked example in this book!

- Go into the examination feeling prepared. Make sure you have calculator, spare calculator, pencils, pens, geometrical instruments, sweets, tissues, mascots, cushions and everything else you need.

Good luck! Remember, everything is possible with enough effort. The greater the pain, the greater the gain!

Mark Bindley

Using this book for the National Curriculum

Entries preceded by a bracketed letter are statements of attainment. Subsequent entries are the programme of study associated with this statement of attainment.

Level 5	Programme of Study	Page No
	To achieve level 5 within the attainment targets students should:	
Number	(a) *Use an appropriate non-calculator method to multiply or divide two numbers.*	
	• understanding and using non-calculator methods by which a three-digit number is multiplied by a two-digit number and a three-digit number is divided by a two-digit number.	5
	• multiplying and dividing mentally single-digit numbers of powers of 10 with whole number answers.	19
	(b) *Find fractions or percentages of quantities.*	
	• calculating fractions and percentages of quantities using a calculator where necessary.	8–11
	• using unitary ratios.	15
	• understanding the notion of scale in maps and drawings.	205
	(c) *Refine estimations by 'trial and improvement' methods.*	
	• using 'trial and improvement' methods.	107
	• approximating, using significant figures or decimal places.	5
	(d) *Use units in context.*	
	• using Imperial units still in daily use and knowing their rough metric equivalents.	*throughout*
	• converting one metric unit to another.	*throughout*
	• using negative numbers in context, including ordering, addition, subtraction and simple multiplication and division.	16–17
	• using index notation to express powers of whole numbers.	3, 17
Algebra	(a) *Follow instructions to generate sequences.*	
	• generating sequences.	103–7
	• recognising patterns in numbers through spatial arrangements.	4, 105
	• understanding and using terms such as 'prime', 'cube', 'square root' and 'cube root'.	2, 4, 17, 272
	• recognising patterns in equivalent fractions.	9, 50
	(b) *Express a simple function symbolically.*	
	• expressing simple functions symbolically.	108
	• understanding and using simple formulae or equations expressed in symbolic form.	78, 89
	• understanding and using co-ordinates in all four quadrants.	127
Shape and space	(a) *Use accurate measurement and drawing in constructing 3-D models.*	
	• measuring and drawing angles to the nearest degree.	205–6
	(b) *Use properties of shape to justify explanations.*	
	• explaining and using properties associated with intersecting and parallel lines and triangles, and knowing associated language.	191–9
	• identifying the symmetries of various shapes.	234
	(c) *Use networks to solve problems.*	
	• using networks to solve problems.	372
	• specifying location by means of co-ordinates in four quadrants.	127
	(d) *Find areas of plane shapes or volumes of simple solids.*	
	• finding areas of plane figures (excluding circles), using appropriate formulae.	23–34
	• finding volumes of simple solids (excluding cylinders), using appropriate formulae.	39–41
	• finding the circumference of circles, practically, introducing the ratio π.	35–6

Level 5	Programme of Study	Page No

Handling data

(a) *Use a computer database to draw conclusions.*

• inserting and interrogating data in computer database; drawing conclusions.

(b) *Design and use an observation sheet to collect data.*

• designing and using an observation sheet to collect data; collating and analysing results. — 323

• collecting, ordering and grouping continuous data using equal class intervals and creating frequency tables. — 324

(c) *Interpret statistical diagrams.*

• constructing and interpreting pie charts from a collection of data with a few variables. — 329

• constructing and interpreting conversion graphs. — 134–7

• constructing and interpreting frequency diagrams and choosing class intervals for a continuous variable. — 326–31

(d) *Use an appropriate method for estimating probabilities.*

• understanding that different outcomes may result from repeating an experiment. — 365

• recognising situations where estimates of probability can be based on equally likely outcomes, and others where estimates must be based on statistical evidence. — 363–5

• knowing that if each of *n* events is assumed to be equally likely, the probability of one occurring is 1/*n*. — 364

Level 6	Programme of Study	Page No

To achieve level 6 within the attainment targets students should:

Number

(a) *Calculate with fractions, decimals, percentages or ratio, as appropriate.*

• ordering decimals and appreciating place values. — 5

• understanding and using equivalent fractions and equivalent ratios and relating these to decimals and percentages. — 5, 14

• working out fractional and percentage changes. — 12, 14

• converting fractions to decimals and percentages and finding one number as a percentage of another. — 14

• calculating, using ratios in a variety of situations. — 15

(b) *Use estimation to check calculations.*

• using estimation and approximation to check that answers to multiplication and division problems involving whole numbers are of the right order. — *throughout*

Algebra

(a) *Explore number patterns using computer facilities or otherwise.*

• using spreadsheets or other computer facilities to explore number patterns.

• suggesting possible rules for generating sequences. — 103–7

(b) *Solve simple equations.*

• solving linear equations; solving simple polynomial equations by 'trial and improvement' methods. — 89

(c) *Use and plot Cartesian co-ordinates to represent mappings.*

• drawing and interpreting simple mappings in context, recognising their general features. — 126–51

Shape and space

(a) *Use 2-D representation of 3-D objects.*

• recognising and using common 2-D representation of 3-D objects. — 24, 210

(b) *Transform shapes using a computer, or otherwise.*

• enlarging a shape by a whole number scale factor. — 222

• classifying and defining types of quadrilaterals. — 147

• knowing and using angle and symmetry properties of quadrilaterals and polygons. — 194–6

• using computers to generate and transform 2-D shapes.

• devising instructions for a computer to produce desired shapes and paths.

(c) *Understand and use bearings to define direction.*

• Understanding and using bearings to define directions. — 207

(d) *Demonstrate that they know and can use the formulae for finding the areas and circumferences of circles.*

• finding areas of circles using the formulae. — 36

Level 6	Programme of Study	Page No

Handling data

(a) *Design and use a questionnaire to survey opinion.*

- specifying an issue for which data are needed; designing and using observation sheets to collect data; collating and analysing results. — 326

- designing and using a questionnaire to survey opinion (taking account of bias); collating and analysing results. — 322–5

(b) *Understand and use the basic ideas of correlation.*

- creating scatter graphs for discrete and continuous variables and having a basic understanding of correlation. — 361–3

- constructing and interpreting information through two-way tables and network diagrams. — 366–9

(c) *Identifying all the outcomes of combining two independent events.*

- identifying all the outcomes when dealing with two combined events which are independent, using diagrammatic, tabular or other forms. — 366

(d) *Know that the total probability of all the mutually exclusive outcomes of any event is 1.*

- appreciating that the total sum of the probabilities of mutually exclusive events is 1 and that the probability of something happening is 1 minus the probability of it not happening. — 364

Level 7	Programme of Study	Page No

To achieve level 7 within the attainment targets students should:

Number

(a) *Multiply and divide mentally single-digit multiples of any power of 10.*

- multiplying and dividing mentally single-digit multiples of any power of 10, realising that with a number less than one, multiplication has a decreasing effect and division has an increasing effect. — *throughout*

(b) *Use a calculator efficiently when solving problems.*

- solving problems and using multiplication and division with numbers of any size. — 17

- expressing positive integers as a product of primes. — 2

- using the memory and bracket facilities of a calculator to plan a calculation and evaluate expressions. — 80–2

(c) *Recognise that measurement is approximate and choose the degree of accuracy appropriate for a practical purpose.*

- recognising that measurement is approximate; and choosing the degree of accuracy appropriate for a particular purpose. — 5–7

- recognising that a measurement expressed to a given unit is in possible error of half a unit. — 7

- understanding and using compound measures, e.g. speed, density. — 162–6

Algebra

(a) *Use symbolic notation to express the rules of sequences.*

- using symbolic notation to express the rules of sequences. — 104

- exploring complex number patterns generated by a computer.

- using the rules of indices for positive integer values. — 17

- understanding the meaning of reciprocals and exploring relationships. — 148

(b) *Solve equations or simple inequalities.*

- solving a range of polynomial equations by 'trial and improvement' methods.

- using algebraic and graphical methods to solve simultaneous equations in two variables. — 96

- drawing and interpreting the graphs of linear functions. — 139

- generating various types of graph on a computer or calculator and interpreting them.

- constructing and interpreting flow diagrams with and without loops. — 370–2

Shape and space

(a) *Use coordinates (x,y,z) to locate position in 3-D.*

- using coordinates to locate position in 3-D. — 127–8

(b) *Determine the locus of an object which is moving subject to a rule.*

- determining the locus of an object moving subject to a rule. — 212

(c) *Use Pythagoras' Theorem.*

- Understanding and applying Pythagoras' Theorem. — 272

(d) *Carry out calculations in plane and solid shapes.*

- using knowledge and skills in length, area and volume to carry out calculations in plane and solid shapes. — 23–42

- enlarging a shape by a fractional scale factor. — 224

Level 7	Programme of Study	Page No

Handling data

(a) *Organise and analyse data.*

- specifying a simple hypothesis; designing and using an appropriate questionnaire or method to test it; collecting and analysing results to see whether a hypothesis is valid. — 322–5
- using and recording grouped data with class intervals suitably defined; producing a frequency table; calculating the mean using a calculator. — 323
- comparing the mean, median, mode and range of a frequency distribution, where appropriate, for given sets of data, and interpreting the results. — 342–56
- drawing a frequency polygon as a line graph from a frequency distribution for grouped data; making comparisons between two frequency distributions. — 334
- constructing and interpreting flow diagrams with and without loops. — 370–2
- drawing a line of 'best fit' by inspection on a scatter diagram.

(b) *Understand and use relative frequency as an estimate of probability.*

- understanding and using relative frequency as an estimate of probability. — 366
- appreciating, when assigning probabilities, that relative frequency and equally likely considerations may not be appropriate and 'subjective' estimates of probability have to be made. — 364

(c) *Given the probability of exclusive events, calculate the probability of a combined event.*

- understanding and applying the addition of probabilities for mutually exclusive events. — 366–9

Level 8	Programme of Study	Page No

To achieve level 8 within the attainment targets students should:

Number

(a) *Calculate with numbers expressed in standard form.*

- expressing and using numbers in standard index form, with positive and negative integer powers of 10. — 18
- using index notations to represent powers and roots. — 2, 17

(b) *Evaluate formulae, including the use of fractions or negative numbers.*

- substituting negative numbers into formulae involving addition, subtraction, multiplication and division. — 80
- calculating with fractions. — 9

(c) *Solve numerical problems, checking that the results are of the right order of magnitude.*

- estimating and approximating to check that the results of calculations are of the right order. — *throughout*

Algebra

(a) *Manipulate algebraic formulae, equations or expressions.*

- manipulating algebraic expressions. — 81–9
- understanding and using a range of formulae and functions. — 80–110
- understanding the relationship between powers and roots. — 273
- understanding direct and inverse proportions. — 148
- interpreting and using m and c in $y = mx + c$. — 133–9

(b) *Solve inequalities.*

- solving a variety of linear and other inequalities. — 92
- using straight-line graphs to locate regions given by linear inequalities. — 155–62

(c) *Interpret graphs which represent particular relationships.*

- knowing the form of graphs of simple functions, e.g. quadratic, cubic, reciprocal. — 140–51
- interpreting graphs which describe real-life situations and contexts. — 134–7, 167–8

Shape and space

(a) *Use mathematical similarity to solve problems.*

- understanding and using mathematical similarity; knowing that angles remain unchanged and corresponding sides are in the same ratio. — 279

(b) *Use sine, cosine or tangent in right-angled triangles.*

- using sine, cosine and tangent in right-angled triangles, in 2-D. — 279–90

(c) *Distinguish between formulae by considering dimensions.*

- distinguishing between formulae for perimeter, area and volume by considering dimensions. — 23–42
- understanding and using vector notation, including its use in describing translations. — 237

Level 9	Programme of Study	Page No
Handling data	(a) *Use diagrams, graphs or computer packages to analyse a set of complex data.*	
	• constructing and interpreting a histogram with understanding of the connection between area and frequency.	333
	• presenting a set of complex data in a simplified form using a variety of diagrams and graphs and computer statistical packages.	*throughout*
	(b) *Use sampling to investigate a 'population'.*	
	• using sampling to investigate a 'population' and recognising the reliability of different methods in relation to different sizes of population.	
	(c) *Use conditional probabilities.*	
	• producing a tree diagram to illustrate the combined probability of several events which are not independent.	368

Level 10	Programme of Study	Page No
	To achieve level 10 within the attainment targets students should:	
Number	(a) *Determine the possible effects of errors on calculations.*	
	• calculating the upper and lower bounds in the addition, subtraction, multiplication and division of numbers expressed to a given degree of accuracy.	7
	• determining the possible effects of error on calculations involving measurements.	7
Algebra	(a) *Use a calculator or computer to investigate sequences.*	
	• using a calculator or computer to investigate whether a sequence given iteratively converges or diverges.	
	(b) *Manipulate algebraic expressions where necessary when solving problems.*	
	• manipulating a range of algebraic expressions in a variety of contexts.	*throughout*
	(c) *Find the approximate area between a curve and the horizontal axis between two limits, and interpret the result.*	
	• finding the approximate area between a curve and the horizontal axis between two limits, and interpreting the result.	171
	(d) *Sketch and compare the graphs of functions.*	
	• sketching the graph of functions derived from other functions, e.g. $y = f(x-a)$, $y = f(kx)$, $y = f(x) + a$ from the graph of $y = f(x)$ for different values of a and k.	
	• interpreting and using coefficients in quadratics.	101–3
Shape and space	(a) *Solve problems in 2-D or 3-D.*	
	• knowing and using angle and tangent properties of circles.	201
	• using sine and cosine rules to solve problems including simple cases in 3-D.	296
	• understanding how transformations are related by combinations and inverses.	227–31
	• using matrices to define transformations in 2-D.	228
Handling data	(a) *Describe the dispersion of a set of data.*	
	• describing the dispersion of a set of data; calculating the standard deviation of a set of data.	358
	• considering different shapes of histograms representing distributions, with special reference to mean and dispersion, including the normal distribution.	
	(b) *Interpret diagrams such as those used in critical-path analysis or linear programming.*	
	• interpreting various types of diagram, such as those used in the analysis of critical-path and linear programming.	372
	(c) *Calculate the probability of any two events happening.*	
	• understanding the probability for any two events happening.	366

Numbers and Measures

The need for mathematics

The history of mathematics goes back to the very beginnings of the human race. As soon as our ancient ancestors evolved above the level of animals, they **needed** mathematics.

- They needed to **count** their possessions.
- They needed to **measure time** and, since the sun and stars were the our first clocks, this meant **measuring angles**, as these bodies moved across the sky.
- They needed to **measure** the **lengths** and **area** of the land that they owned or farmed.
- As trade developed, they needed to **measure weight** and **volume.**

At first, people only used whole numbers.

'I own 7 cows, 5 goats and 24 sheep.'
'There are 200 people living in our settlement.'

You cannot, however, solve all problems with whole numbers and, as human societies developed, **fractions** were invented and used. By 470 AD, when the Hindu mathematician Aryabhata wrote a famous mathematics book called the Lilavati, all the rules for calculating with fractions were well established. Decimals gradually evolved during the 13th, 14th and 15th centuries as a standardised system of fractions based on powers of 10. The Muslim mathematician Al Kashi gave the value of 3 14159 for π in 1430 AD, but did not use a decimal point. The first person to use a decimal point was the Italian mathematician Pelazzi, in 1492 AD. France, after the revolution, was the first country to introduce a fully decimalised system of numbers and measures and, over the last two hundred years, almost all other countries have copied the French.

Natural numbers, integers, rationals and irrationals

When numbers were first invented, only whole numbers were used and a number line might have looked like this.

```
1   2   3   4   5
●   ●   ●   ●   ●
```

There was no number between 1 and 2, or between 2 and 3. There was no number less than 1. Because these are the simplest and earliest numbers to have been used, they are called the **natural** numbers.

When subtraction was invented, some problems could not be answered using the set of natural numbers. For example,

$$3 - 3 \text{ and } 5 - 7$$

Mathematicians had to invent the number 0 and the **negative** numbers to answer these problems.

The number line now looked like this.

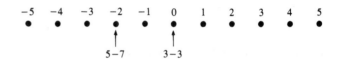

These numbers are called the **integers**. Any subtraction problem using integers can always be answered by another integer. However, there were still no numbers between the successive integers and, when division was invented, some problems could not be answered using the set of integers. For example,

$$12 \div 5 \text{ and } 9 \div -2$$

Mathematicians had to invent fractions and decimals to answer these problems.

The number line now looked like this.

Any fraction or decimal is represented by a point somewhere on the line. The set of every possible fraction or decimal number is called the set of **rational numbers**.

You may well think that any point on the number line must be a rational number but in fact this is not the case. Greek mathematicians experimented with square roots and tried very hard to find the square root of two, which they knew must be some point on the number line between 1 and 2.

1

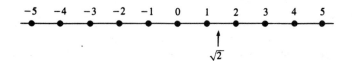

Eventually they proved that no rational number could possibly be multiplied by itself and produce an answer of exactly 2. They then discovered that many other square roots could not be expressed as exact rational numbers. The Greeks were puzzled that a simple quantity like $\sqrt{2}$ could not be written down as a rational number. They called numbers like $\sqrt{2}$ **irrational** numbers. Some other examples of irrational numbers are $\sqrt{3}$, $\sqrt{17}$, and π, all of which are points on the number line, but cannot be written down as exact fractions or decimals.

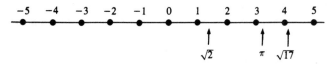

The complete set of numbers, both rational and irrational, which can be represented by points on a number line is called the set of **real** numbers.

Numbers

Factors, multiples and primes

12 can be divided exactly by 3.

$$12 \div 3 = 4$$

12 **cannot** be divided exactly by 5.

$$12 \div 5 = 2 \text{ remainder } 2$$

This is a list of all the numbers which divide exactly into 12.

$$1, 2, 3, 4, 6, 12.$$

Any number which divides exactly into 12 is called a **factor** of 12. So, we can write

the factors of 12 are 1, 2, 3, 4, 6 and 12.

If a number has 2 as one of its factors, it is called an **even** number. In other words, an **even** number is a number which divides exactly by 2.

So, we can write

14 is an even number because it divides exactly by 2.

If a number does not have 2 as one of its factors, it is called an **odd** number. In other words, an **odd** number is a number which does not divide exactly by 2.

So, we can write

9 is an odd number because it does not divide exactly by 2.

If a number has exactly two factors, it is called a **prime** number. In other words, a **prime** number is a number which can only be divided exactly by itself and the number 1.

So, we can write

7 is a prime number because it has only two factors, the numbers 7 and 1.

9 is not a prime number because it has three factors, the numbers 9, 3 and 1.

When we multiply 12 by the numbers 1, 2, 3, 4, 5, ..., we produce the answers 12, 24, 36, 48, 60, ... These numbers all divide exactly by 12. Any number which divides exactly by 12 is called a **multiple** of 12.

So, we can write

the first 5 multiples of 12 are 12, 24, 36, 48 and 60.

CHECKPOINT 1

Copy and complete the following.

1 The factors of 8 are .....
2 The factors of 25 are .....
3 The factors of 13 are .....
4 The first 10 even numbers are 2, 4, ...
5 The first 10 odd numbers are 1, 3, ...
6 The first 10 prime numbers are 2, 3, 5, 7, 11, ...
7 The first 7 multiples of 6 are .....
8 The first 6 multiples of 7 are .....

Prime factors

1, 2, 3, 4, 6 and 12 are all factors of the number 12. 2 and 3 are called the **prime factors** of 12 because they are **factors** of 12 and also **prime numbers**. Any number which is not prime can be written as a chain multiplication of its prime factors.

So, we can write

$$12 = 2 \times 2 \times 3$$

Large numbers, like 360, may take a long time to break down into a chain multiplication of prime factors. Here is a quick method we can use with large numbers.

First, we break 360 into **any** multiplication.

$$360 = 10 \times 36$$

Now, we keep breaking each part of this multiplication until only prime numbers are left.

$$360 = 10 \times 36$$
$$360 = 2 \times 5 \times 36$$
$$360 = 2 \times 5 \times 6 \times 6$$
$$360 = 2 \times 5 \times 2 \times 3 \times 6$$
$$360 = 2 \times 5 \times 2 \times 3 \times 2 \times 3$$

More neatly, we can write

$$360 = 2 \times 2 \times 2 \times 3 \times 3 \times 5$$

There is a special way to write chain multiplications of the same number.

$$2 \times 2 \times 2 \text{ can be written as } 2^3$$

$$3 \times 3 \text{ can be written as } 3^2$$

$$4 \times 4 \times 4 \times 4 \times 4 \times 4 \text{ can be written as } 4^6$$

So, we can write

$$360 = 2^3 \times 3^2 \times 5$$

CHECKPOINT 2

Copy and complete the following.

1 The factors of 50 are .....

2 The prime factors of 50 are .....

3 50 can be written as a chain multiplication of its prime factors as follows ......

4 400 can be broken down into a chain multiplication of prime factors as follows.

$$400 = 10 \times 40$$

$$400 = 2 \times 5 \times 40$$

....

5 126 can be broken down into a chain multiplication of prime factors as follows .....

HCF and LCM

3 and 6 are **common factors** of 12 and 18 because they divide into both numbers. 6 is the **highest common factor** of 12 and 18 because it is the **largest** number which divides into both 12 and 18.

So, we can write

the highest common factor of 12 and 18 is 6.

24, 48 and 72 are **common multiples** of 6 and 8 because they divide by both numbers. 24 is the **lowest common multiple** of 6 and 8 because it is the smallest number which divides by both numbers.

So, we can write

the lowest common multiple of 6 and 8 is 24.

With a set of large numbers like 360, 420 and 600, it can be difficult to spot the highest common factor (**HCF**).

Here is a method we can use with large numbers.

First, we write each number as a chain multiplication of prime factors.

$$360 = 2 \times 2 \times 2 \times 3 \times 3 \times 5$$

$$420 = 2 \times 2 \times 3 \times 5 \times 7$$

$$600 = 2 \times 2 \times 2 \times 3 \times 5 \times 5$$

Now, we pick out all the prime factors which are included in **every** chain.

$$360 = \underline{2} \times \underline{2} \times 2 \times \underline{3} \times 3 \times \underline{5}$$

$$420 = \underline{2} \times \underline{2} \times \underline{3} \times \underline{5} \times 7$$

$$600 = \underline{2} \times \underline{2} \times 2 \times \underline{3} \times \underline{5} \times 5$$

Multiplying these common prime factors together gives the HCF of the set of numbers.

$$2 \times 2 \times 3 \times 5 = 60$$

So, we can write

the HCF of 360, 420 and 600 is 60.

With a set of large numbers like 360, 420 and 600, it can also be difficult to spot the lowest common multiple (**LCM**).

Here is a method we can use with large numbers.

First, we write each number as a chain multiplication of prime factors.

3

$$360 = 2 \times 2 \times 2 \times 3 \times 3 \times 5$$

$$420 = 2 \times 2 \times 3 \times 5 \times 7$$

$$600 = 2 \times 2 \times 2 \times 3 \times 5 \times 5$$

Now, we form the simplest chain multiplication which contains each of these chains.

$$2 \times 2 \times 2 \times 3 \times 3 \times 5 \times 5 \times 7$$

Multiplying this chain gives the LCM of the set of numbers.

$$2 \times 2 \times 2 \times 3 \times 3 \times 5 \times 5 \times 7 = 12\,600$$

So, we can write

the LCM of 360, 420 and 600 is 12 600.

CHECKPOINT 3

Copy and complete the following.

1 The highest common factor of 27 and 36 is ......
2 The highest common factor of 24, 16 and 32 is .....
3 The lowest common multiple of 8 and 14 is .....
4 The lowest common multiple of 2, 5 and 7 is .....
5 Find the HCF of 36, 90 and 126.
6 Find the HCF of 300, 450 and 700.
7 Find the LCM of 36, 90 and 126.
8 Find the LCM of 300, 450 and 700.
9 Find the HCF and LCM of 45, 99 and 18.
10 Find the HCF and LCM of 147, 105 and 84.

Square, rectangular and triangular numbers

Any number can be represented by a group of dots.

Some sets of numbers are given special names because of the patterns into which that number of dots can be arranged. For example, these are the first five **square numbers**.

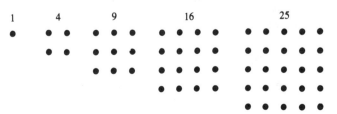

These are the **rectangular numbers**.

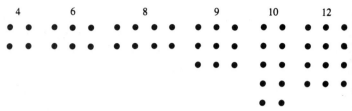

(The pattern of dots must have at least two rows and two columns and squares count as special rectangles.)

These are the first five **triangular numbers**.

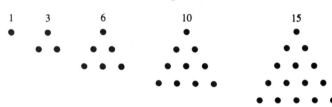

CHECKPOINT 4

1 Write down the first ten square numbers.
2 Write down the first 20 rectangular numbers.
3 Write down the first ten triangular numbers.
4 What could these numbers be called? Draw diagrams of the next three numbers in the set.

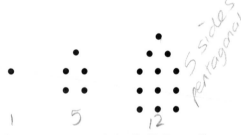

5 What could these numbers be called? Draw diagrams of the next three numbers in the set.

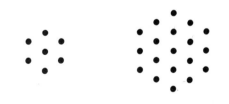

6 What could **cube** numbers be? What would the first five **cube** numbers be?

7 What could **pyramid** numbers be? What would the first five pyramid numbers be? Could there be more than one type of pyramid number?

Decimals

This text assumes that you can already add, subtract, multiply and divide decimals, either in your head or using pencil and paper or calculator. The following reviews are provided for you to check and revise those skills.

Addition and subtraction of decimals

CHECKPOINT 5

1 Calculate, without written calculations or a calculator.

a $73 + 5.0$	**b** $7.3 + 5$	**c** $7.3 + 0.5$	**d** $7.3 + 50$
e $2.1 + 3.2$	**f** $23.5 + 2.5$	**g** $1.35 + 5$	**h** $1.35 + 0.5$
i $1.35 + 0.05$	**j** $12.7 + 7.2$	**k** $3.7 - 2$	**l** $3.7 - 0.2$
m $3.7 - 0.02$	**n** $45.69 - 32$	**o** $45.69 - 3.2$	**p** $45.69 - 0.32$
q $102 - 0.9$	**r** $5.3 - 2.7$	**s** $5.3 - 0.27$	**t** $53 - 2.7$

2 Calculate, without a calculator.

a $34.67 + 23.89$	**b** $123 + 67.9$	**c** $234.7 + 34.93$
d $23.89 + 27.4$	**e** $1345 + 234.56$	**f** $13.45 + 234.56$
g $134.5 + 2345.6$	**h** $1.345 + 23456$	**i** $1.345 + 23.456$
j $986.7 + 78.96$	**k** $34.5 - 14.93$	**l** $123.89 - 17.76$
m $123.45 - 34.73$	**n** $12.345 - 3.473$	**o** $123.45 - 3.473$
p $234.5 - 127.9$	**q** $9112.5 - 758.6$	**r** $1.7003 - 0.067$
s $12.05 - 9.99$	**t** $234.7 - 167$	

3 Calculate with a calculator.

a $34.5 + 23.7 + 234.6$ **b** $456.1 + 678.9 + 234.9$
c $124.56 + 456.78 + 123.89$ **d** $4590.8 + 3400.73$
e $1.00234 + 12.3406$ **f** $98.456 + 29.6543$
g $67.048 + 523.336$ **h** $34.987 + 34.67 + 67.49$
i $23.8 + 84.9 + 58.2 + 41.9 + 34.8 + 87.3 + 78.9 + 99.9$
j $234.89 + 555.57 + 56 + 68 + 89.3 + 0.06 + 234.567$
k $3456.8 - 234.9$ **l** $345.67 - 234.89$
m $78.93 - 18.564$ **n** $233.75 - 231.99$
o $4008.09 - 3678.54$ **p** $5916.34 - 4563.29$
q $98.456 - 38.439$ **r** $10\,000.67 - 999.99$
s $(23.45 + 67.89) - 23.67$

Multiplication and division of decimals

CHECKPOINT 6

1 Calculate, without written calculations or a calculator.

a 3×0.3	**b** 0.5×5	**c** 0.4×0.4	**d** 0.8×7
e 0.8×0.1	**f** 27×0.2	**g** 16×0.2	**h** 80×0.5
i 250×0.4	**j** $5 \times 0.2 \times 0.5$	**k** 10×0.34	**l** 10×3.4
m 10×0.034	**n** 5.567×10		**o** 5.567×100
p $5.567 \times 10\,000$	**q** 0.5567×1000		**r** $56.45 \div 10$
s $56.45 \div 100$	**t** $56.45 \div 1000$		**u** $0.45 \div 10$
v $234 \div 100$	**w** $879 \div 1000$	**x** $53.09 \div 10$	**y** $53.09 \div 100$

2 Calculate without a calculator.

a 34.5×3	**b** 89.4×19	**c** 405.3×47
d 34.5×0.3	**e** 89.4×1.9	**f** 40.53×4.7
g $12.3 \div 5$	**h** $45.65 \div 2$	**i** $127 \div 8$
j $459.6 \div 4$	**k** $345.98 \div 5$	**l** $1 \div 8$

3 Calculate with a calculator.

a 34.67×23	**b** 56.7×45	**c** 90.98×1.04
d $34.5 \div 3$	**e** $23.89 \div 7$	**f** $23.78 \div 3.7$
g $78.95 - 34.7$	**h** $13 \div 19$	**i** $1 \div 11$ **j** $0.56 \div 0.7$

Decimal places and significant figures

Many decimal calculations produce answers with a long string of decimal places. For example,

$$34.568 \times 13.439 = 464.559\,352$$

Sometimes these calculations do not even produce answers that are possible. For example, to find the cost of 13.4 metres of cloth at £9.99 a metre, we calculate

$$\text{cost} = 13.4 \times 9.99 = £133.866$$

But the answer is not a possible amount of money.

Sometimes our calculations produce decimals which repeat the same pattern of digits again and again. These are called **recurring decimals**. For example,

$$23 \div 6 = 3.833\,333\,333\,333\,3\ldots\ldots$$

$$12.4 \div 7 = 1.771\,428\,571\,428\,571\,428\,571\,428\,57\ldots\ldots$$

We usually write these answers with dots on the first and last recurring digits. So,

$$3.833\,333\,333\,333\,3\ldots\ldots \text{ is written } 3.8\dot{3}$$

and

$$1.771\,428\,571\,428\,571\,428\,571\,428\,57\ldots\ldots \text{ is written } 1.77\dot{1}\,428\,\dot{5}$$

To solve all these problems, decimals answers are often given **correct to a given number of decimal places**. For example,

$$464.559\,352 \text{ correct to } \textbf{1 decimal place} \text{ is } 464.6$$

$$£133.866 \text{ correct to } \textbf{2 decimal places} \text{ is } £133.87$$

$$3.833\,333\,333\,333\,3 \text{ correct to } \textbf{3 decimal places} \text{ is } 3.833$$

$$1.771\,428\,571 \text{ correct to } \textbf{4 decimal places} \text{ is } 1.771\,4$$

To correct a decimal to a given number of decimal places.

● Count out, to the right of the decimal point, the number of places you require.

● Look at the digit immediately to the right of the last one you require.

If it is 4 or less, chop it off with all the digits which follow it.

If it is a 5 or more, chop it off with all the digits which follow it **but add 1 to the last digit you require.**

Examples

1 Write 34.548 37 correct to 2 decimal places.

We count out the two places we require, and the next digit to the right is an 8.

$$34.548\ 37$$
$$\uparrow$$

We chop the 837 off, but because 8 is greater than 5, we add 1 to the last digit we require.

34.548 37 correct to 2 decimal places is 34.55

2 Write 34.548 37 correct to 3 decimal places.

We count out the three places we require, and the next digit to the right is a 3.

$$34.548\ 37$$
$$\uparrow$$

We chop the 37 off, but because 3 is less than 5, we do not add 1 to the last digit we require.

34.548 37 correct to 3 decimal places is 34.548

Sometimes, the result of adding 1 will 'carry' along the decimal.

Example

Write 25.999 547 correct to 3 decimal places.

Counting places gives

$$25.999\ 547$$
$$\uparrow$$

Cutting off and adding 1 gives
26.000

Correcting a value to a number of **significant figures** is a way to approximate both whole numbers and decimals. The technique is very similar to that used to correct to a given number of decimal places, but you start counting digits at **the first significant figure, not at the decimal point.** The **first significant figure** is the first digit from the left of the number which is **not** a zero. When approximating whole numbers, you cannot simply chop off the digits after the number of significant figures you want; they must be replaced with zeros.

Examples

1 Write 345 278 correct to 3 significant figures.

We count out three digits, starting at the 3. The next digit after these digits is a 2, so we replace 278 with 000.

345 278 correct to 3 significant figures is 345 000.

2 Write 345 278 correct to 4 significant figures.

We count out four digits, starting at the 3. The next digit after these digits is a 7, so we replace 78 with 00 **and add 1 to the last significant figure.**

345 278 correct to 4 significant figures is 345 300.

3 Write 25.683 correct to 3 significant figures.

We count out three digits, starting at the 2. The next digit after these digits is an 8. Because we are to the right of the decimal point, we do not need to add any zeros, but because 8 is greater than 5 we add 1 to the 6 as we chop off the 83.

25.683 correct to 3 significant figures is 25.7.

4 Write 0.000 034 621 0 correct to 2 significant figures.

We count out two digits **starting at the 3 because it is the first non-zero digit.** The next digit after these digits is a 6.

0.000 034 621 0 correct to 2 significant figures is 0.000 035.

5 23 407 correct to 4 significant figures is 23 410.

6 234.07 correct to 4 significant figures 234.1.

7 0.003 278 07 correct to 2 significant figures is 0.0033.

1 Calculate correct to 1 decimal place.

a $12 \div 9$ **b** 6.7×9.8 **c** $15 \div 8$ **d** $27.3 \div 12.9$
e $66.7 \div 6.6$ **f** 12.58×11 **g** 6.9×5.3 **h** 5.6×1.78

2 Write down all the answers to question 1, correct to 2 significant figures.

3 Calculate correct to 2 decimal places.

a 23.45×45.67 **b** $23 \div 7$ **c** $0.67 \div 9$ **d** $1.49 \div 1.7$
e $1.5 \times 1.5 \times 1.5$ **f** $3.4 \times 3.4 \times 3.4$ **g** $250 \div 157$
h $12.31 \div 13.56$

4 Write down all the answers to question 3, correct to 1 significant figure.

5 Calculate, giving each answer to a sensible number of decimal places.

a The cost of 3.7 metres of cloth at £5.99 a metre.
b The amount each person should pay if 7 people are sharing equally a restaurant bill of £94.89.
c The weight, in grams, of one marble if 25 marbles weight 580 grams on a scale which is accurate to the nearest gram.
d The area of a square with a side length of 1.5 cm (correct to the nearest millimetre).
e The volume of a cube with an edge length of 1.25 m (correct to the nearest centimetre).

6 The turnstiles at a football club show that the following numbers attended their last five home games: 17 893, 21 557, 26 299, 34 307 and 44 619. How do you think these attendance numbers might be reported in the local paper?

Limits of Accuracy

When each number in a calculation is given correct to a certain number of decimal places, we can establish **limits of accuracy** for the answer.

Examples

1 The side length of a square is measured as 12 cm, correct to the nearest centimetre. What are the limits within which the perimeter and the area of the square must lie?

12 cm correct to the nearest centimetre could be any length between

$$11.5 \text{ cm and } 12.49 \text{ cm}$$

We usually treat this range of numbers as 11.5 cm to 12.5 cm.

This means that the **smallest** possible value for the perimeter is

$$11.5 + 11.5 + 11.5 + 11.5 = 46 \text{ cm}$$

The **greatest** possible value for the perimeter is

$$12.5 + 12.5 + 12.5 + 12.5 = 50 \text{ cm}$$

The **smallest** possible value for the area is

$$11.5 \times 11.5 = 132.25 \text{ cm}^2$$

The **greatest** possible value for the area is

$$12.5 \times 12.5 = 156.25 \text{ cm}^2$$

2 What are the least and greatest possible values of this calculation, if all the numbers are correct to 1 decimal place?

$$\frac{16.3 \times 2.8}{0.7}$$

The least value will occur when we make the top of the division as **small** as possible and the bottom of the division as **large** as possible.

The least value is

$$\frac{6.25 \times 2.75}{0.75} = 22.9 \text{ (to 1 d.p.)}$$

The greatest value will occur when we make the top of the division as **large** as possible and the bottom of the division as **small** as possible.

The greatest value is

$$\frac{6.35 \times 2.85}{0.65} = 27.8 \text{ (to 1 d.p.)}$$

1 If all the numbers in the following calculations are correct to the nearest whole number, what are the least and greatest possible values for the answer?

a $34 + 12$ **b** $34 - 12$ **c** 34×12 **d** $34 \div 12$
e $25 + 17$ **f** $25 - 17$ **g** 25×17 **h** $25 \div 17$
i $\dfrac{36 + 74}{18}$ **j** $\dfrac{56 \div 19}{12 + 5}$ **k** $\dfrac{45 \times 45}{57 - 2}$ **l** $\dfrac{56 \div 12}{13 \div 9}$

2 If all the numbers in the following calculations are correct to 1 decimal place, what are the least and greatest possible values for the answer?

a $3.4 + 1.2$ **b** $3.4 - 1.2$ **c** 3.4×1.2 **d** $3.4 \div 1.2$

e $53.7 + 30.3$ **f** $53.7 - 30.3$ **g** 53.7×30.3 **h** $53.7 \div 30.3$

i $\dfrac{3.6 + 5.4}{0.2}$ **j** $\dfrac{8.1 - 0.7}{2.5}$ **k** $\dfrac{3.1 \times 5.5}{9.9}$ **l** $\dfrac{3.1 \times 2.5}{0.1}$

3 Sally is taking her husband and his parents out to lunch. She estimates that the restaurant meal will cost between £8 and £20 a head. What is the greatest and the least amount that Sally should expect to pay?

4 The sides of a rectangle are measured as 12.6 cm and 4.7 cm, correct to the nearest millimetre. What are the least and greatest values for the perimeter and area of the rectangle?

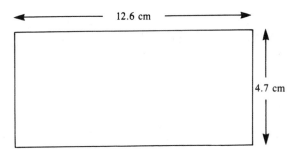

5 The edge length of a cube is measured as 1.25 metres, correct to the nearest centimetre. What are the least and greatest possible values for the volume and surface area of the cube?

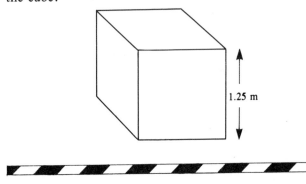

Fractions

Fractions (sometimes called common fractions) were once an important method of calculation. Calculators, computers and metric measurements have made decimal arithmetic so easy that fraction arithmetic is now rarely required. An understanding of fractions is still, however, important because fractions form a part of our everyday language.

'**Half** our students own a computer.'

'**Nine tenths** of the crowd were well behaved.'

'She is entitled to **one fifth** of the profits.'

Basic skills

A common fraction is written as one number (the **numerator**) over another number (the **denominator**). Examples are

$$\frac{1}{2} \qquad \frac{3}{4} \qquad \frac{5}{6} \qquad \text{and} \qquad \frac{13}{56}$$

An **improper fraction** is one in which the top number is larger than the bottom. It is called an improper fraction because it is greater than 1 and should therefore normally be simplified.

An example is $\frac{12}{7}$, which should be written as $1\frac{5}{7}$.

A number like $1\frac{5}{7}$, which has both a whole number and a fractional part, is called a **mixed number**.

Two fractions which represent the same part of a quantity are called **equivalent fractions**. An example of a pair of equivalent fractions is

$$\frac{2}{3} \qquad \text{and} \qquad \frac{10}{15}$$

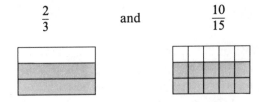

There are four basic skills which we must master when we work with fractions. These skills are demonstrated in the following examples.

Examples

1 Change the improper fractions 13/4 and 17/7 into mixed numbers.

$$\frac{13}{4} = 3\frac{1}{4} \qquad \frac{17}{7} = 2\frac{3}{7}$$

2 Change the mixed numbers $5\frac{1}{2}$ and $7\frac{3}{8}$ into improper fractions.

$$5\frac{1}{2} = \frac{11}{2} \qquad 7\frac{3}{8} = \frac{59}{8}$$

3 Simplify $\frac{24}{48}$ and $\frac{45}{85}$.

We simplify fractions by spotting common factors of the top and bottom numbers. Dividing by these common factors simplies the fraction. In this case, the fractions have 24 and 5 as common factors so we can simplify like this.

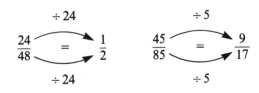

4 Complete these pairs of equivalent fractions.

$$\frac{3}{4} = \frac{?}{20} \qquad \frac{5}{6} = \frac{?}{42}$$

We replace the question marks by spotting that the bottom numbers have been multiplied by 5 and by 7. The top numbers must also be multiplied by 5 and by 7.

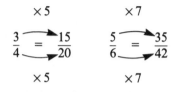

We then change each fraction into an equivalent one with this new number at the bottom.

In this case, both 3 and 4 divide exactly into 12. So we have

$$\frac{2}{3} = \frac{8}{12}$$

$$\frac{3}{4} = \frac{9}{12}$$

It is now obvious that $\frac{3}{4}$ is the larger fraction.

CHECKPOINT 9

1 Change each of the following improper fractions into a mixed number.

a $\frac{23}{5}$ **b** $\frac{9}{7}$ **c** $\frac{15}{2}$ **d** $\frac{17}{3}$

e $\frac{19}{4}$ **f** $\frac{27}{5}$ **g** $\frac{19}{11}$ **h** $\frac{27}{8}$

i $\frac{33}{12}$ **j** $\frac{99}{5}$ **k** $\frac{67}{4}$ **m** $\frac{200}{99}$

2 Change each of the following mixed numbers into an improper fraction.

a $3\frac{3}{4}$ **b** $9\frac{1}{2}$ **c** $8\frac{2}{3}$ **d** $1\frac{1}{4}$

e $7\frac{3}{4}$ **f** $9\frac{5}{8}$ **g** $2\frac{13}{16}$ **h** $5\frac{5}{32}$

i $11\frac{2}{3}$ **j** $10\frac{3}{4}$ **k** $1\frac{19}{20}$ **l** $2\frac{4}{99}$

3 Copy and complete the following.

a $\frac{2}{5} = \frac{?}{10}$ **b** $\frac{5}{8} = \frac{?}{24}$ **c** $\frac{7}{6} = \frac{?}{18}$ **d** $\frac{3}{7} = \frac{?}{21}$

e $\frac{12}{17} = \frac{?}{51}$ **f** $\frac{1}{9} = \frac{?}{27}$ **g** $\frac{11}{12} = \frac{?}{48}$ **h** $\frac{4}{5} = \frac{?}{35}$

i $\frac{5}{9} = \frac{?}{45}$ **j** $\frac{8}{11} = \frac{?}{55}$ **k** $\frac{7}{10} = \frac{?}{100}$ **l** $\frac{1}{9} = \frac{?}{99}$

4 Simplify the following.

a $\frac{50}{70}$ **b** $\frac{25}{60}$ **c** $\frac{6}{9}$ **d** $\frac{12}{15}$ **e** $\frac{24}{30}$ **f** $\frac{35}{65}$ **g** $\frac{65}{90}$ **h** $\frac{45}{63}$

i $\frac{27}{81}$ **j** $\frac{44}{66}$ **k** $\frac{26}{52}$ **l** $\frac{39}{52}$

Comparing fractions

Which is the bigger fraction, $\frac{2}{3}$ or $\frac{3}{4}$?

To answer a question like this, we first find a number that both bottom numbers will divide into.

CHECKPOINT 10

1 Which is the larger of each of the following pairs of fractions?

a $\frac{1}{3}$ and $\frac{1}{4}$ **b** $\frac{3}{4}$ and $\frac{4}{5}$ **c** $\frac{3}{5}$ and $\frac{5}{6}$

d $\frac{3}{7}$ and $\frac{5}{9}$ **e** $\frac{1}{2}$ and $\frac{4}{6}$ **f** $\frac{2}{3}$ and $\frac{5}{7}$

g $\frac{4}{7}$ and $\frac{7}{10}$ **h** $\frac{1}{2}$ and $\frac{3}{7}$ **i** $\frac{5}{8}$ and $\frac{2}{3}$

j $\frac{3}{7}$ and $\frac{5}{11}$ **k** $\frac{4}{5}$ and $\frac{9}{11}$ **l** $\frac{3}{5}$ and $\frac{7}{12}$

2 Bill scored 8 out of 25 in a Maths test and 6 out of 20 in an English test. In which test did he do best?

3 Jane scored 93 out of 100 in an Art exam and 19 out of 20 in a Biology exam. In which exam did she do best?

4 In one bag of sweets, there are 4 red sweets out of a total of 25. In another bag there are 5 red sweets out of a total of 30. Which bag has the biggest fraction of red sweets?

5 Susan takes 8 cards from a pack of 5 of these are picture cards. Siloben takes 12 cards and gets 7 picture cards. Which girl got the biggest fraction of picture cards?

6 In class 5A, 3 students out of 20 are absent. In class 5B, 5 students out of 24 are absent. Which class has the biggest fraction of absent students?

7 Liverpool have played 10 games and won 7 of them. Arsenal have played 12 games and won 9 of them. Which team has won the biggest fraction of their games?

8 In one batch of 10 television sets, 3 are faulty. In another batch of 24 sets, 7 are faulty. Which is the worst batch?

9 When shooting at a target, John hit the bull with 19 arrows out of 25, Bill hit the bull with 15 arrows out of 20 and Shafiq hit the bull with 37 arrows out of 50. Who is the best shot?

Examples

1 What fraction of 1 hour is 25 minutes?

$$25 \text{ minutes is } \frac{25}{60} \text{ or } \frac{5}{12} \text{ of one hour.}$$

2 What fraction of £1 is 64p?

$$64\text{p is } \frac{64}{100} \text{ or } \frac{16}{25} \text{ of £1}$$

3 If $\frac{3}{5}$ of the 240 apples in a barrel are bad, how many good apples are there?

To calculate $\frac{3}{5}$ of 240, we first divide by 5 to find $\frac{1}{5}$ and then multiply by 3 to find $\frac{3}{5}$.

$$\frac{1}{5} \text{ of } 240 = 240 - 5 = 48$$

$$\frac{3}{5} \text{ of } 240 = 48 \times 3 = 144$$

So, 144 apples are bad, and therefore 96 are good (240−144).

CHECKPOINT 11

1 Look carefully at this diagram.

What fraction of the shapes are

a triangles
b quadrilaterals (4 sides)
c pentagons (5 sides)
d hexagons (6 sides)
e circles
f drawn with straight lines
g either 3-sided or 4-sided
h shaded
i not shaded
j drawn with curved sides?

2 What fraction of 1 minute is

a 10 seconds **b** 25 seconds **c** 12 seconds **d** 40 seconds
e 30 seconds **f** 15 seconds?

3 What fraction of 1 hour is

a 6 minutes **b** 50 minutes **c** 42 minutes **d** 35 minutes
e 45 minutes **f** 20 minutes?

4 What fraction of a 24-hour day is

a 1 hour **b** 4 hours **c** 6 hours **d** 8 hours
e 2 hours **f** 12 hours **g** 16 hours **h** 18 hours
i 13 and a half hours **j** 5 and a quarter hours?

5 What fraction of £1 is

a 25p **b** 40p **c** 10p **d** 50p **e** 85p **f** 75p **g** 48p
h 4p **i** 2p **j** 27p?

6 Calculate

a $\frac{2}{5}$ of 250 **b** $\frac{1}{2}$ of 90 **c** $\frac{3}{4}$ of 48 **d** $\frac{3}{7}$ of 91

e $\frac{4}{5}$ of 100 **f** $\frac{2}{3}$ of 24 **g** $\frac{3}{8}$ of 24 **h** $\frac{7}{9}$ of 81

i $\frac{35}{40}$ of 160 **j** $\frac{27}{80}$ of 360

7 There are 25 000 football supporters at a game and the police estimate that $\frac{7}{8}$ of them support the home team. Estimate the number who support the away team.

8 Jean-Paul rents 2 videos a week and estimates that $\frac{2}{5}$ of the videos he rents are boring. How many boring videos does he hire in one year?

Percentages

Percentages and fractions

We know that fractions are used to express parts of a quantity. For example, we may say

'If I earned half as much again I could afford a house'

or

'Japanese imports have captured two thirds of the market'.

Percentages are used in the same way. For example, we may say

'If I received a 50% pay rise I might be happy'

or

'66% of the market has been lost to Japan'.

Percentages are simply a special way of writing fractions. Each percentage is a fraction with 100 as the bottom number.

For example,

$$25\% \text{ is the same as } \frac{25}{100}$$

$$\text{and } 66\% \text{ is the same as } \frac{66}{100}$$

Examples

1 Write 66% and 20% as fractions.

$$66\% = \frac{66}{100} = \frac{33}{50}$$

$$20\% = \frac{20}{100} = \frac{1}{5}$$

2 Write $\frac{4}{5}$ and $\frac{3}{4}$ as percentages.

To do this, we must change the bottom numbers of the fraction to 100.

$$\frac{4}{5} \xrightarrow{\times 20} \frac{80}{100} \quad \text{and} \quad \frac{3}{4} \xrightarrow{\times 25} \frac{75}{100}$$

So, $\frac{4}{5} = 80\%$ and $\frac{3}{4} = 75\%$.

CHECKPOINT 12

1 Write each of the following percentages as a fraction in its simplest form.

a 25%   **b** 60%   **c** 68%   **d** 90%   **e** 64%
f 99%   **g** 40%   **h** 15%   **i** 32%   **j** 95%

2 Write each fraction as a percentage.

a $\frac{1}{2}$ **b** $\frac{17}{20}$ **c** $\frac{7}{10}$ **d** $\frac{11}{20}$ **e** $\frac{12}{25}$

f $\frac{1}{10}$ **g** $\frac{6}{25}$ **h** $\frac{3}{25}$ **i** $\frac{5}{10}$ **j** $\frac{11}{25}$

3 By what fraction has the price been reduced in this special offer?

GIFT SETS
COTY, YARDLEY, LENTHÉRIC
UP TO 30% OFF
SELECTED LINES

Calculating a percentage of a quantity

Examples

1 There were 160 questions in a Maths test and Mary Jones obtained a mark of 45%. How many questions did she get right? We must calculate 45% of 160.

To do this, we remember that 45% is the same as $\frac{45}{100}$.

$$45\% \text{ of } 160 = \frac{45}{100} \text{ of } 160$$

$$45\% \text{ of } 160 = \frac{45 \times 160}{100} = \frac{7200}{100} = 72$$

So, Mary got 72 answers correct out of 160.

2 A garage adds 15% VAT to the marked price on all the tyres that it sells. How much will a tyre marked with a price of £25.70 actually cost?

$$15\% \text{ of } 25.7 = \frac{15}{100} \text{ of } 25.7$$

$$15\% \text{ of } 25.7 = \frac{15 \times 25.7}{100} = 3.855$$

£3.855 to the nearest penny is £3.86, so the tyre costs

$$£25.70 + £3.86 = £29.56$$

CHECKPOINT 13

1 Calculate

a 25% of 156   **b** 60% of 145   **c** 68% of 275
d 90% of 855   **e** 64% of 64   **f** 99% of 2500
g 40% of £56.80   **h** 15% of £45   **i** 32% of 45
j 95% of 120 minutes

2 If 28% of Ms Mutton's monthly income of £870 goes on mortgage repayments, how much does she pay each month?

3 Mr Asquith, the Labour Party candidate, received 44% of the 28 000 votes cast. How many people voted for Mr Asquith?

4 A year ago, Ms Fox's house was worth £85 500. During the last year house prices have risen by an average of 12%. Estimate the increase in the value of Ms Fox's house.

5 Find the amount of VAT (at 15%) which will be added to the cost of the replacement window in this advertisement.

> ## REPLACEMENT WINDOWS
> ### EXAMPLE:
> 4ft × 3ft 6in Double Glazed Window with single top opening in attractive maintenance-free uPVC.
> ### FULLY FITTED (including sill)
> ## ONLY £184 PLUS VAT
> ★ *With Full 10 Year Guarantee.*

6 If prices are increasing by 5% each year, what will a coat which now costs £40 cost in 4 years time?

Increasing and decreasing by a percentage

Increasing and decreasing quantities by a percentage are common calculations. In both cases there are two alternative methods to find our answers.

Examples

1 15% VAT must be added to the £34.00 price of a radio. What does the radio actually cost?

METHOD 1

$$15\% \text{ of } 34 = \frac{15 \times 34}{100} = 5.1$$

Cost of radio = £34.00 + £5.10 = £39.10

METHOD 2

15% added to any quantity increases it to 115% of its original value. So, our actual cost will be 115% of £34.

$$115\% \text{ of } 34 = \frac{115 \times 34}{100} = 39.1$$

Cost of radio = £39.10

2 The prices of all the items in a shop are reduced by 20% in a sale. Find the sale price of a suit previously sold for £140.

METHOD 1

$$20\% \text{ of } 140 = \frac{20 \times 140}{100} = 28$$

Sale price = £140 − £28 = £112

METHOD 2

20% subtracted from any quantity reduces it to 80% of its previous value. So our sale price will be 80% of £140.

$$80\% \text{ of } 140 = \frac{80 \times 140}{100} = 112$$

Sale price = £112

CHECKPOINT 14

1 Increase

a 145 by 20%   **b** £50 by 15%   **c** £348 by 15%
d £45 000 by 5%   **e** £18 000 by 8%.

2 At this time last year, Gafar Khan was earning £198 a week. Inflation for the past year has been 5.4%. Calculate the new weekly wage that Gafar needs to keep up with inflation.

3 Copy this table and fill in the three missing numbers.

31st Issue Certificates
Value and yield of £25 Certificate

YEARS AFTER PURCHASE	VALUE AT END OF YEAR	YIELD FOR YEAR TAX-FREE
1	£26.44	5.76%
2	£28.20	6.66%
3		7.80%
4		8.95%
5		10.14%

4 A shop buys food mixers for £15. To work out a selling price for the mixers, a profit mark-up of 25% is added to the cost price. 15% VAT is then addded to obtain the price the mixers must be sold for. Find the selling price for the mixers.

5 Decrease

a 145 by 20%   **b** £50 by 15%   **c** £348 by 20%
d £45 000 by 5%   **e** £18 000 by 8%.

6 A firm used 3500 litres of heating oil last year. This year it hopes to reduce its heating oil bill by 12%. How much oil are they planning to use this year?

7 At this time last year, Gafar Khan was earning £198 a week. Business has been bad, however, and he now earns 30% less than he did. Calculate his new wage.

8 Copy this table and fill in the missing numbers.

COUNTY COUNCIL MANPOWER

	31.3.87 FTE	31.3.88 FTE	Change %
Education	7,722.7	7707.2 ✓	−0.2
Public Protection	761.1	779.2	2.4
Social Services	2,116.4	2175.8 ✓	2.8
Transportation & Planning	821.3	813.4 ✓	−1.0
Leisure & Recreation	311.2	316.1	1.6
Police	1,526.8	1,557.3	2.0
Policy & Resources	311.7	310.1 ✓	−0.5
Property Management	265.5	272.0	2.4
Magistrates Courts	80.8	81.8	1.2
Probation	123.6	130.2	5.3
	14,041.1	14,140.5	0.7

FTE = Full Time Equivalent: hours worked by part-time employees are amalgamated to reflect the number of full-time employees needed to work the same hours.

Expressing one number as a percentage of another

Suppose we know that Kim Ashton scored 72 correct marks out of a possible 80 in a Science test, what was Kim's percentage score?

As a fraction, Kim scored $\frac{72}{80}$.

To find the percentage score, we must change the bottom number of the fraction into 100.

$$\frac{72}{80} = \frac{?}{100}$$

100 divided by 80 is 1.25, so to change 80 into 100, we need to multiply by 1.25. Multiplying 72 by 1.25 to find the new top number gives

$$\frac{72}{80} \xrightarrow[\times 1.25]{\times 1.25} = \frac{90}{100}$$

So, Kim scored 90% in the test.

If you study this example, you will see that in order to change our fraction into a percentage we

• divided 100 by the bottom number.
• multiplied the top number by the result of this division.

This is exactly the result obtained when a fraction is multiplied by 100.

$$\frac{72}{80} \times 100 = \frac{72 \times 100}{80} = 90$$

Studying calculations like this gives us a simple rule.

> **To write one number as a percentage of another.**
>
> • To write one number as a percentage of another, form a fraction with the two numbers and then multiply this fraction by 100.

Examples

1 Write 45 as a percentage of 190.

This is the required calculation.

$$\frac{45}{190} \times 100 = \frac{45 \times 100}{190} = 23.7\% \text{ (to 1 d.p.)}$$

2 In one box of 240 apples, 36 are bad. In another box of 200 apples, 26 are bad. Which box has the better apples? In the first box, the percentage of bad apples is

$$\frac{36}{240} \times 100 = \frac{36 \times 100}{240} = 15\%$$

In the second box the percentage of bad apples is

$$\frac{26}{200} \times 100 = \frac{26 \times 100}{200} = 13\%$$

Our conclusion is that the second box has the better apples.

3 What is the percentage reduction in price on this workshop kit?

BLACK & DECKER
BDK202 Workshop Kit.
Cat. No. 710/4215.
~~£87.95~~
Sale Price
£77.95

The kit originally cost £87.95 and has been reduced to £77.95, a cash reduction of £10.
The percentage reduction is

$$\frac{10}{87.95} \times 100 = \frac{10 \times 100}{87.95} = 11.4\% \text{ (approximately)}$$

1 Write

a 8 as a percentage of 25   **b** 34 as a percentage of 85

c £1.25 as a percentage of £50

d 42 as a percentage of 120

e £5.25 as a percentage of £35

f 48p as a percentage of 64p

g £8.50 as a percentage of £25

h 45 minutes as a percentage of 1 hour

i 36p as a percentage of 45p

j 14 grams as a percentage of 35 grams

k 12 minutes as a percentage of 1 hour 36 minutes

l 5.1 cm as a percentage of 6.8 cm.

2 These are the marks that a group of 20 pupils scored in a test with a maximum mark of 120. Convert them to percentage marks, correct to the nearest 1%.

43	56	78	89	94	96	102	112	65	105
84	22	17	68	72	118	88	71	59	60

3 In one bag of potatoes, 3 out of 20 are rotten, in a second bag 5 out of 30 potatoes are rotten and in a third bag 7 out of 40 potatoes are rotten. What is the percentage of rotten potatoes in each bag? Which is the best bag?

4 In one school, 6 out of 10 teachers are female, in a second school, 14 out of 25 teachers are female, and in a third school, 22 out of 50 teachers are male. Which school has the largest percentage of female staff?

5 Calculate the percentage reductions in price on each of these items.

BRITAX
"Babysure" Car Seat.
Cat. No. 375/2582.
~~£27.99~~
Sale Price

£22.99

SWAN
Compact
Microwave Oven.
Cat. No. 420/8341.
~~£144.95~~
Sale Price

£134.95

OLYMPUS
Supertrip Compact.
35 mm Camera.
Cat. No. 560/6100.
~~£54.95~~
Sale Price

£44.95

Fractions, percentages and decimals

Fractions, percentages and decimals are all ways of representing part of a quantity.

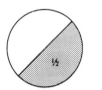

Any given fraction, percentage or decimal can always be converted to each of the other systems.

Examples

1 FRACTION TO PERCENTAGE
Change $\frac{5}{8}$ to a percentage.

$$\frac{5}{8} \times 100 = \frac{5 \times 100}{8} = 62.5\%$$

2 FRACTION TO DECIMAL
Change $\frac{5}{8}$ to a decimal.
We treat the fraction as $5 \div 8$ and using a calculator, obtain $5 \div 8 = 0.625$.

$$\frac{5}{8} = 0.625$$

3 DECIMAL TO PERCENTAGE
Change 0.85 to a percentage.
Just like fractions, we multiply by 100.

$$0.85 = 85\%$$

4 DECIMAL TO FRACTION
Change 0.76 to a fraction.

$$0.76 = \frac{7}{10} + \frac{6}{100} = \frac{76}{100} = \frac{19}{25}$$

5 PERCENTAGE TO FRACTION
Change 65% to a fraction.

$$65\% = \frac{65}{100} = \frac{13}{20}$$

6 PERCENTAGE TO DECIMAL

Change 65% to a decimal.

$$65\% = \frac{65}{100} = 0.65$$

1 Change each of these fractions into percentages.

a $\frac{3}{4}$　　**b** $\frac{4}{5}$　　**c** $\frac{7}{8}$　　**d** $\frac{9}{10}$　　**e** $\frac{1}{2}$　　**f** $\frac{1}{5}$

g $\frac{1}{4}$　　**h** $\frac{3}{16}$　　**i** $\frac{2}{3}$　　**j** $\frac{1}{12}$　　**k** $\frac{5}{6}$　　**l** $\frac{5}{9}$

2 Change each of these fractions into decimals.

a $\frac{3}{4}$　　**b** $\frac{4}{5}$　　**c** $\frac{7}{8}$　　**d** $\frac{9}{10}$　　**e** $\frac{1}{2}$　　**f** $\frac{1}{5}$

g $\frac{1}{4}$　　**h** $\frac{3}{16}$　　**i** $\frac{2}{3}$　　**j** $\frac{1}{12}$　　**k** $\frac{5}{6}$　　**l** $\frac{5}{9}$

3 Change each of these decimals into fractions.

a 0.1　　**b** 0.8　　**c** 0.3　　**d** 0.35　　**e** 0.64　　**f** 0.08
g 0.005　**h** 0.05　**i** 0.5　　**j** 0.375　**k** 0.45　　**l** 0.25

4 Change each of these decimals into percentages.

a 0.1　　**b** 0.8　　**c** 0.3　　**d** 0.35　　**e** 0.64　　**f** 0.08
g 0.005　**h** 0.05　**i** 0.5　　**j** 0.375　**k** 0.45　　**l** 0.25

5 Change each of these percentages into fractions.

a 80%　**b** 32%　**c** 25%　**d** 70%　**e** 98%　**f** 55%
g 40%　**h** 48%　**i** 65%　**j** 50%　**k** 75%　**l** 99%

6 Change each of these percentages into decimals.

a 80%　**b** 32%　**c** 25%　**d** 70%　**e** 98%　**f** 55%
g 40%　**h** 48%　**i** 65%　**j** 50%　**k** 75%　**l** 99%

Ratios

Establishing and simplifying a ratio

A ratio is used to compare two or more numbers. For example, we may say

'The ratio of girls to boys in the top set is 5 to 4'.

By this we mean that for every five girls in the group there are four boys.

This is equivalent to saying that the **fraction** of girls in the top set is $\frac{5}{9}$. Fractions compare the separate parts into which an object is divided with the **whole object**. Ratios compare the separate parts into which an object is divided **with each other**. Ratios can be simplified in the same way as fractions.

Examples

1 Simplify the ratio 24 to 90.

24 and 90 both divide by 6, so we can write

24 to 90 = 4 to 15

2 To make shortcrust pastry, we mix 400 g of plain flour with 100 grams of butter and 50 grams of fat. What is the ratio of these ingredients in its simplest form?

The basic ratio is

400 to 100 to 100

We can divide by 100 and simplify the ratio to

4 to 1 to 1

The symbol ':' is often used to represent 'to' in ratios; in the last example, the final ratio could be written

4 : 1 : 1

1 Simplify each of the following ratios.

a 4 : 6　　**b** 12 : 16　　**c** 6 : 30　　**d** 15 : 18　　**e** 30 : 35
f 112 : 64　**g** 54 : 90　　**h** 24 : 84　**i** 20 : 200　**j** 96 : 204
k 1 cm to 1 metre　　**l** £2.50 : £3.00　　**m** £2.50 : £3.50
n 40 days : 1 year　**o** 45 minutes : 3 hours　**p** 60° : 300°

2 In a school there are 273 boys and 219 girls. What, in its simplest form, is the ratio of boys to girls?

3 Harry Losealot likes to bet on horses. Last year, out of 250 bets, Harry won 45 times. What is the ratio of Harry's winning bets to his losing bets?

4 Out of 96 students in a school taking GCSE Mathematics, 12 fail. What is the ratio of passes to fails?

Dividing a quantity in a ratio

Ratios are often used to divide a quantity into parts.

Examples

1 To make concrete, Bill mixes gravel, sand and cement powder in the ratio $9:5:2$. How much of each ingredient should he use to make 80 kg of concrete?

To answer the question, we first add up the total number of **'shares'** in the ratio. This comes to $9+5+2$, or 16 **'shares'**. Since we require 80 kg of concrete, each one of these **'shares'** must weigh $80 \div 16 = 5$ kg. So, Bill must use

$9 \times 5 = 45$ kg of gravel
$5 \times 5 = 25$ kg of sand
$2 \times 5 = 10$ kg of cement powder

2 Divide 24 sweets between Bill and Belinda in the ratio $5:7$.

We require $5+7$ or 12 'shares'.

$$24 \div 12 = 2$$

Therefore, Bill gets 5×2 sweets and Belinda gets 7×2 sweets.

Bill gets 10 sweets and Belinda gets 14 sweets (which adds up correctly to 24).

CHECKPOINT 18

1 Divide 36 kg in the ratios

a $1:2$ **b** $3:1$ **c** $5:1$ **d** $5:4$ **e** $2:7$
f $8:1$ **g** $1:11$ **h** $5:7$ **i** $17:1$ **j** $5:13$

2 Divide £100 in the ratios

a $3:1$ **b** $2:3$ **c** $1:4$ **d** $5:3$ **e** $7:1$
f $1:1$ **g** $1:9$ **h** $7:3$ **i** $19:1$ **j** $3:17$

3 Mr Bilson has £300 worth of premium bonds and Mrs Bilson has £500 worth of premium bonds. They agree to share any winnings in the same ratio as the number of bonds they hold. How do they share a win of £25 000?

4 One sunny day, Jane and Jessica decide to sell squash and cakes from a stall. Jane buys £1.20 worth of ingredients and Jessica buys £1.80 worth of ingredients. They agree to share the takings in the same ratio as their contributions to the costs. How do they share total takings of £15.50? Do you think this is a fair way to share the takings?

5 Sam, Sanjay and Susan all club together to buy a packet of sweets costing 48p. Sam contributes 12p. Sanjay contributes 16p and Susan contributes 20p. They find there are 36 sweets in the packet. What is a fair way to share the sweets?

Directed numbers

This text assumes that you can already add, subtract, multiply and divide directed numbers, either in your head or using pencil and paper or scientific calculator. The following reviews are provided for you to check and revise those skills.

> Addition and subtraction of directed numbers
>
> **Remember that to subtract a negative number, you add the corresponding positive number.**
>
> So, $18 - -7 = 18 + 7 = 25$
>
> and $-18 - -7 = -18 + 7 = -11$

Examples

$18 + 7 = 25$	$18 + -7 = 11$
$-18 + 7 = -11$	$-18 + -7 = -25$
$18 - 7 = 11$	$18 - -7 = 25$
$-18 - 7 = -25$	$-18 - -7 = -11$

CHECKPOINT 19

1 Copy and complete the following.

$8 + 5 =$ $8 + -5 =$
$-8 + 5 =$ $-8 + -5 =$
$8 - 5 =$ $8 - -5 =$
$-8 - 5 =$ $-8 - -5 =$

2 Copy and complete the following.

$3 + 7 =$ $3 + -7 =$
$-3 + 7 =$ $-3 + -7 =$
$3 - 7 =$ $3 - -7 =$
$-3 - 7 =$ $-3 - -7 =$

3 Copy and complete the following.

$13 + 9 =$ $13 + -9 =$
$-13 + 9 =$ $-13 + -9 =$
$13 - 9 =$ $13 - -9 =$
$-13 - 9 =$ $-13 - -9 =$

4 Copy and complete the following.

$11 + 11 =$ $11 + -11 =$
$-11 + 11 =$ $-11 + -11 =$
$11 - 11 =$ $11 - -11 =$
$-11 - 11 =$ $-11 - -11 =$

5 Copy and complete the following.

$$5 + 23 =$$
$$-5 + 23 =$$
$$5 - 23 =$$
$$-5 - 23 =$$

$$5 + {}^-23 =$$
$$-5 + {}^-23 =$$
$$5 - {}^-23 =$$
$$-5 - {}^-23 =$$

Multiplication and division of
directed numbers

**If the signs of the two numbers are the same, your answer
will be positive; if the signs are different your answer will
be negative.**

Remember this and you can't go wrong but **don't** try to
apply the rule to addition and subtraction!

Examples

$$18 \times 6 = 108$$
$$-18 \times 6 = -108$$
$$18 \times -6 = -108$$
$$-18 \times -6 = 108$$

$$18 \div 6 = 3$$
$$-18 \div 6 = -3$$
$$18 \div -6 = -3$$
$$-18 \div -6 = 3$$

CHECKPOINT 20

1 Copy and complete the following.

$$10 \times 5 =$$
$$-10 \times 5 =$$
$$10 \times -5 =$$
$$-10 \times -5 =$$

$$10 \div 5 =$$
$$-10 \div 5 =$$
$$10 \div -5 =$$
$$-10 \div -5 =$$

2 Copy and complete the following.

$$12 \times 8 =$$
$$-12 \times 8 =$$
$$12 \times -8 =$$
$$-12 \times -8 =$$

$$12 \div 8 =$$
$$-12 \div 8 =$$
$$12 \div -8 =$$
$$-12 \div -8 =$$

3 Copy and complete the following.

$$6.5 \times 5 =$$
$$-6.5 \times 5 =$$
$$6.5 \times -5 =$$
$$-6.5 \times -5 =$$

$$6.5 \div 5 =$$
$$-6.5 \div 5 =$$
$$6.5 \div -5 =$$
$$-6.5 \div -5 =$$

4 Copy and complete the following.

$$1.2 \times 0.4 =$$
$$-1.2 \times 0.4 =$$
$$1.2 \times -0.4 =$$
$$-1.2 \times -0.4 =$$

$$1.2 \div 0.4 =$$
$$-1.2 \div 0.4 =$$
$$1.2 \div -0.4 =$$
$$-1.2 \div -0.4 =$$

Powers and standard form

Powers of numbers

We already know that there is a special way to write chain
multiplications of the same number.

$2 \times 2 \times 2$ can be written as 2^3.

3×3 can be written as 3^2.

$4 \times 4 \times 4 \times 4 \times 4 \times 4$ can be written as 4^6.

2^3 is read as **'2 to the power 3'**.

3^2 is read as **'3 to the power 2'**.

4^6 is read as **'4 to the power 6'**.

The power notation can be extended to zero and negative
powers. The definitions of zero and negative powers can be
deduced from the patterns in a reducing list of powers of
a number. For example, this is a table of reducing powers
of 2.

$$2^5 = 32$$
$$2^4 = 16$$
$$2^3 = 8$$
$$2^2 = 4$$

We see that as the powers reduce by 1 on the left hand side,
the values on the right hand side are divided by 2.

If we continue this pattern we obtain

$$2^1 = 2$$
$$2^0 = 1$$
$$2^{-1} = \frac{1}{2}$$
$$2^{-2} = \frac{1}{4}$$
$$2^{-3} = \frac{1}{8}$$
$$2^{-4} = \frac{1}{16}$$

A similar pattern for powers of 3 is

$$3^5 = 243$$
$$3^4 = 81$$
$$3^3 = 27$$
$$3^2 = 9$$
$$3^1 = 3$$
$$3^0 = 1$$
$$3^{-1} = \frac{1}{3}$$
$$3^{-2} = \frac{1}{9}$$
$$3^{-3} = \frac{1}{27}$$

These patterns suggest these rules for powers.

Powers of numbers

- Any number to the power 1 is equal to itself.
- Any number to the power zero is equal to 1.
- Any number to a negative power is equal to 1 over the corresponding positive power.

Example

Evaluate 5^1, 17^0 and 8^{-3}.

$$5^1 = 5$$
$$17^0 = 1$$

$$8^{-3} = \frac{1}{8^3} = \frac{1}{512}$$

When powers of a number are multiplied the effect is to **add** the powers together.

Examples

1 Write as a single power of 3, $3^3 \times 3^2$.

The calculation $3^3 \times 3^2$ means $(3 \times 3 \times 3) \times (3 \times 3)$.

This can be written as the single power 3^5.

2 Write as a single power of 10, $10^5 \times 10^{-3}$.

The calculation means

$$(10 \times 10 \times 10 \times 10 \times 10) \times \frac{1}{(10 \times 10 \times 10)} \text{ or } 10^2.$$

Multiplying powers of the same number

- $a^m \times a^n = a^{m+n}$

CHECKPOINT 21

1 Find the value of

a 5^6	**b** 6^5	**c** 10^2	**d** 10^3	**e** 10^4	**f** 2^7
g 4^{-2}	**h** 5^{-1}	**i** 10^1	**j** 12^0	**k** 8^{-2}	**l** 1^{-1}
m 7^0	**n** 35^1	**o** 2^{-8}	**p** 6^{-3}	**q** 10^{-3}	**r** 10^{-5}

2 Write each of the following calculations as a single power of the number.

a $2^2 \times 2^3$	**b** $3^5 \times 3^4$	**c** $4^7 \times 4^3$	**d** $2^9 \times 2^2$
e $10^3 \times 10^2$	**f** $10^5 \times 10^1$	**g** $3^4 \times 3^0$	**h** $5^0 \times 5^5$
i $3^2 \times 3^{-2}$	**j** $4^3 \times 4^{-3}$	**k** $2^5 \times 2^{-2}$	**l** $10^3 \times 10^{-2}$

Standard form

Very large and very small numbers are common in Science. For example, the average distance of the Earth from the Sun is 150 000 000 km and a human blood cell is 0.000 01 m long. These numbers are very difficult to write down without mistakes and to read and compare. Mathematicians have developed a shorthand way to write down very large and very small numbers, called **standard form**. The numbers are written as a number between 1 and 10, multiplied by a power of 10.

Examples

1 Write 150 000 000 in standard form.

$$150\,000\,000 = 1.5 \times 100\,000\,000 \text{ or } 1.5 \times 10^8$$

2 Write 0.000 01 in standard form.

$$0.000\,01 = 1 \div 100\,000 \text{ or } 1 \times 10^{-5}$$

3 Write 1.3×10^5 as a normal number.

$$1.3 \times 10^5 \text{ means } 1.3 \times 100\,000 \text{ or } 130\,000$$

4 Write 1.67×10^{-5} as a normal number.

$$1.67 \times 10^{-5} \text{ means } 1.67 \div 100\,000 \text{ or } 0.000\,016\,7$$

CHECKPOINT 22

1 Write the following in the standard form.

a 37 000   **b** 3700   **c** 370 000   **d** 150 000   **e** 650 000 000
f 65 000 000   **g** 6 500 000   **h** 650 000   **i** 65 000   **j** 6500
k 650   **l** 65

2 Write the following as normal numbers.

a 2×10^5 **b** 3×10^8 **c** 1.7×10^4 **d** 3.45×10^9
e 1.6×10^9 **f** 3.8×10^3 **g** 8.3×10^3 **h** 4.72×10^5
i 6.73×10^6 **j** 1.99×10^{12} **k** 7.3×10^2 **l** 8.09×10^{10}

3 Write the following in the standard form.

a 0.37   **b** 0.004   **c** 0.000 004 50   **d** 0.000 000 056
e 0.000 578   **f** 0.000 000 1   **g** 0.65   **h** 0.065
i 0.0065   **j** 0.000 65   **k** 0.000 065   **l** 0.000 006 5

4 Write the following as normal numbers.

a 2×10^{-5} **b** 3×10^{-8} **c** 1.7×10^{-4} **d** 3.45×10^{-9}
e 1.6×10^{-9} **f** 3.8×10^{-3} **g** 8.3×10^{-3} **h** 4.72×10^{-5}
i 6.73×10^{-6} **j** 1.99×10^{-12} **k** 7.3×10^{-2} **l** 8.09×10^{-10}

5 Rewrite each of the following statements using the standard form.

a The lifetime of an omega particle is 0.000 000 000 11 seconds.

b The mass of the Earth is 5 967 000 000 000 000 000 000 000 kg.

c The average distance of Uranus from the Sun is 2 869 000 000 km.

d A large orange contains 0.016 grams of vitamin C.

e The moon orbits at an average distance of 384 000 km from the Earth.

f A light-year, which is the distance travelled by light in one year, is equal to 9 460 500 000 000 000 metres.

Calculations with numbers in the standard form

Examples

1 Calculate $8 \times (3.1 \times 10^5)$.

$$8 \times 3.1 \times 10^5 = 24.8 \times 10^5$$

In standard form this is 2.48×10^6.

2 Calculate $(1.3 \times 10^7) \times (5.6 \times 10^4)$.

$$1.3 \times 10^7 \times 5.6 \times 10^4 = 1.3 \times 5.6 \times 10^7 \times 10^4$$
$$= 7.28 \times 10^{11}$$

3 Calculate $(1.3 \times 10^5) \div (5.8 \times 10^2)$.

$$\frac{1.3 \times 10^5}{5.8 \times 10^2} = \frac{1.3}{5.8} \times \frac{10^5}{10^2} = 0.22 \times 10^3$$

In standard form this is 2.2×10^2.

4 Calculate $(7.4 \times 10^5) \div (2.8 \times 10^{-4})$.

$$\frac{7.4 \times 10^5}{2.8 \times 10^{-4}} = \frac{7.4}{2.8} \times \frac{10^5}{10^{-4}} = 2.6 \times 10^9$$

Answers in standard form

CHECKPOINT 23

1 Calculate

a $5 \times (1.7 \times 10^4)$ **b** $9 \times (2.5 \times 10^7)$
c $15 \times (3.25 \times 10^6)$ **d** $40 \times (2.8 \times 10^{-4})$

on divisions always cancel out.

e $65 \times (7.1 \times 10^{-6})$ **f** $(3.2 \times 10^7) \times (1.9 \times 10^6)$ *+7x+6 = +13*
g $(1.78 \times 10^6) \times (1.94 \times 10^2)$ **h** $(2.5 \times 10^5) \times (1.9 \times 10^{-2})$ *+5 x -2 = +3*
i $(8.3 \times 10^{-3}) \times (1.0 \times 10^8)$ **j** $(1.89 \times 10^{-7}) \times (1.95 \times 10^{-3})$ *-7x-3 = -10*
k $(3.2 \times 10^7) \div (1.9 \times 10^6)$ *subtract* *=2*   **l** $(1.78 \times 10^6) \div (1.94 \times 10^2)$ *subtract.*
m $(2.5 \times 10^5) \div (1.9 \times 10^{-2})$ *add*   **n** $(8.3 \times 10^{-3}) \div (1.0 \times 10^8)$ *add*
o $(1.89 \times 10^{-7}) \div (1.95 \times 10^{-3})$ *subtract.*

Matrix arithmetic

Addition and subtraction of matrices

A **matrix** is a rectangular array of numbers. Matrices are a very common way to organise and record information. For example, this matrix records the number of home games won, drawn and lost by four teams.

| | Home Games | | |
	Won	Drawn	Lost
Liverpool	5	2	2
Manchester United	4	4	1
Norwich	6	0	3
Arsenal	3	6	0

Mathematicians usually write matrices inside brackets, often with no headings. The matrix above might appear as

$$\begin{pmatrix} 5 & 2 & 2 \\ 4 & 4 & 1 \\ 6 & 0 & 3 \\ 3 & 6 & 0 \end{pmatrix}$$

This matrix stores the teams' away games record.

$$\begin{pmatrix} 3 & 1 & 4 \\ 5 & 0 & 3 \\ 6 & 0 & 2 \\ 4 & 0 & 4 \end{pmatrix}$$

These matrices can be combined to produce an overall record for the teams.

$$\begin{pmatrix} 5 & 2 & 2 \\ 4 & 4 & 1 \\ 6 & 0 & 3 \\ 3 & 6 & 0 \end{pmatrix} + \begin{pmatrix} 3 & 1 & 4 \\ 5 & 0 & 3 \\ 6 & 0 & 2 \\ 4 & 0 & 4 \end{pmatrix} = \begin{pmatrix} 8 & 3 & 6 \\ 9 & 4 & 4 \\ 12 & 0 & 5 \\ 7 & 6 & 4 \end{pmatrix}$$

This process of combining two matrices is called **matrix addition**. As we have seen, it is quite easy. We simply add together corresponding pairs of numbers in the two matrices.

We can also subtract matrices. For example, these matrices store the total points of four football teams after weeks 18 and 19 of the season.

19

	Week 19		Week 18
Derby	$\begin{pmatrix} 21 \\ 17 \\ 11 \\ 15 \end{pmatrix}$	Derby	$\begin{pmatrix} 18 \\ 17 \\ 10 \\ 12 \end{pmatrix}$
Millwall		Millwall	
Newcastle		Newcastle	
Watford		Watford	

By subtracting the matrices we can work out the points scored in week 19.

$$\begin{pmatrix} 21 \\ 17 \\ 11 \\ 15 \end{pmatrix} - \begin{pmatrix} 18 \\ 17 \\ 10 \\ 12 \end{pmatrix} = \begin{pmatrix} 3 \\ 0 \\ 1 \\ 3 \end{pmatrix}$$

Matrices can be multiplied by normal numbers. For example, this matrix stores the number of newspapers, magazines and comics taken each week by three different households.

	Browns	Smiths	Patels
Newspapers	7	6	14
Magazines	4	1	2
Comics	2	4	0

To calculate the numbers taken during a year, we can multiply this matrix by 52.

$$52 \times \begin{pmatrix} 7 & 6 & 14 \\ 4 & 1 & 2 \\ 2 & 4 & 0 \end{pmatrix} = \begin{pmatrix} 364 & 312 & 728 \\ 208 & 52 & 104 \\ 104 & 208 & 0 \end{pmatrix}$$

Letters are often used to represent matrices.

Example

$$A = \begin{pmatrix} 3 & 0 \\ -1 & 3 \end{pmatrix} \quad B = \begin{pmatrix} 2 & -2 \\ 6 & 0 \end{pmatrix} \quad C = \begin{pmatrix} 5 & 0 \\ -2 & 7 \end{pmatrix}$$

Calculate $A + B$, $B - C$, $5A$, and $2B + 3C$.

$$A + B = \begin{pmatrix} 3 + 2 & 0 + -2 \\ -1 + 6 & 3 + 0 \end{pmatrix} = \begin{pmatrix} 5 & -2 \\ 5 & 3 \end{pmatrix}$$

$$B - C = \begin{pmatrix} 2 - 5 & -2 - 0 \\ 6 - -2 & 0 - 7 \end{pmatrix} = \begin{pmatrix} -3 & -2 \\ 8 & -7 \end{pmatrix}$$

$$5A = \begin{pmatrix} 5 \times 3 & 5 \times 0 \\ 5 \times -1 & 5 \times 3 \end{pmatrix} = \begin{pmatrix} 15 & 0 \\ -5 & 15 \end{pmatrix}$$

$$2B + 3C = \begin{pmatrix} 4 & -4 \\ 12 & 0 \end{pmatrix} + \begin{pmatrix} 15 & 0 \\ -6 & 21 \end{pmatrix} = \begin{pmatrix} 19 & -4 \\ 6 & 21 \end{pmatrix}$$

CHECKPOINT 24

1

$$A = \begin{pmatrix} 5 & 6 \\ 3 & 2 \end{pmatrix} \quad B = \begin{pmatrix} 3 & 0 \\ 3 & 2 \end{pmatrix}$$

Calculate the following.

a $A + B$ **b** $A - B$ **c** $3A$ **d** $5B$
e $3A + 5B$ **f** $10B$ **g** $2A$ **h** $10B - 2A$

2

$$X = \begin{pmatrix} 7 \\ 5 \\ 0 \end{pmatrix} \quad Y = \begin{pmatrix} 8 \\ -7 \\ 6 \end{pmatrix} \quad Z = \begin{pmatrix} -4 \\ 15 \\ 11 \end{pmatrix}$$

Calculate the following.

a $X + Y$ **b** $X + Z$ **c** $Y + Z$ **d** $X + Y + Z$
e $X - Y$ **f** $3Z$ **g** $25Y$ **h** $5X + 8Z$

3

$$P = \begin{pmatrix} 2 & 3 & 4 \\ 4 & 0 & -1 \\ 5 & 2 & 0 \end{pmatrix} Q = \begin{pmatrix} 7 & 8 & 0 \\ 2 & -1 & 3 \\ -3 & 3 & 0 \end{pmatrix} R = \begin{pmatrix} -2 & 1 & -3 \\ 1 & 2 & 3 \\ 5 & 7 & 9 \end{pmatrix}$$

Calculate the following.

a $P + Q$ **b** $R - Q$ **c** $5R$ **d** $6P$
e $8P$ **f** $2P + 3Q$ **g** $P + 2Q + 3R$ **h** $5R - 2P$

4

$$A = \begin{pmatrix} 5 & -4 & -1 & 0 \\ 3 & 2 & 0 & 1 \end{pmatrix} \quad B = \begin{pmatrix} 9 & 2 & -3 & 0 \\ 8 & -2 & 5 & -5 \end{pmatrix}$$

Calculate the following.

a $A + B$ **b** $A - B$ **c** $B - A$ **d** $10A$
e $3A + 2B$ **f** $5A - 3B$ **g** $4A - B$ **h** $5A + 7B$

5 Fifth year students in a school take a mixture of GCSE and RSA exams. These matrices show the number of examinations taken for the four fifth year forms.

FORM 5W	GCSE	RSA
Boys	75	22
Girls	82	12

FORM 5R	GCSE	RSA
Boys	63	31
Girls	61	35

FORM 5A	GCSE	RSA
Boys	81	11
Girls	85	10

FORM 5F	GCSE	RSA
Boys	55	23
Girls	72	29

Combine these matrices to produce a single matrix for

a 5A and 5W **b** 5F and 5R **c** The girls
d The boys **e** The whole school
f Each GCSE exam cost £12.50 to enter and each RSA exam cost £9.00 to enter. What was the total cost of the examinations?

Multiplication of matrices

It is possible to multiply one matrix by another matrix. For example, this matrix shows the points system used now for football and the old system which was in earlier use.

	Points	
	New System	Old System
Win	3	2
Draw	1	1
Loss	0	0

We can combine this matrix with a matrix showing the number of games won, drawn and lost.

$$\begin{pmatrix} 5 & 2 & 2 \\ 4 & 4 & 1 \\ 6 & 0 & 3 \\ 3 & 6 & 0 \end{pmatrix} \begin{pmatrix} 3 & 2 \\ 1 & 1 \\ 0 & 0 \end{pmatrix} = \begin{pmatrix} 17 & 12 \\ 16 & 12 \\ 18 & 12 \\ 15 & 12 \end{pmatrix}$$

The result is a matrix which shows the effects of the 3, 1, 0 points system. We see that under the old system all the teams would have been level but under the 3, 1, 0 system they all have a different number of points.

If you study the example, you will see that each **row** of the first matrix has been combined with each **column** of the second matrix. The columns have been combined by a process of multiplying the numbers in pairs and then adding the results.

$$(5 \quad 2 \quad 2) \begin{pmatrix} 3 \\ 1 \\ 0 \end{pmatrix} = (5 \times 3) + (2 \times 1) + (2 \times 0) = 17$$

All matrix multiplication is completed in this way. There are occasions when the rows and columns do not match, for example when the rows have 4 numbers and the columns only have 3 numbers. In this case, **matrix multiplication is not possible.**

Example

$$A = \begin{pmatrix} 3 & 2 & 0 \\ 2 & 1 & 1 \end{pmatrix} \quad B = \begin{pmatrix} 4 & 5 & 8 \\ 1 & 0 & 9 \end{pmatrix} \quad C = \begin{pmatrix} 5 & 3 & 3 & 0 \\ 2 & 4 & 2 & 4 \\ 2 & 1 & 2 & 4 \end{pmatrix}$$

Calculate AC and AB.

To find AC, we first divide A into rows and C into columns. It is helpful to number these rows and columns.

Our answer will have as many rows as A and as many columns as C.

The next step is to prepare a blank answer matrix of this size.

This blank answer matrix is very useful, because it tells us which row to combine with which column. For example, to obtain the top left hand number in our answer we combine R1 with C1 and to obtain the bottom right hand number in our answer we combine R2 with C4.

The second number in the top row of our answer is obtained by a combination of R1 and C2 like this.

$$(3 \quad 2 \quad 0) \begin{pmatrix} 3 \\ 4 \\ 1 \end{pmatrix} = (3 \times 3) + (2 \times 4) + (0 \times 1) = 17$$

When we have completed all the other row and column combinations, our answer looks like this.

$$\begin{array}{c} R1 \\ R2 \end{array} \begin{pmatrix} 3 & 2 & 0 \\ \hline 2 & 1 & 1 \end{pmatrix} \quad \begin{array}{cccc} C1 & C2 & C3 & C4 \end{array} \\ \begin{pmatrix} 5 & 3 & 3 & 0 \\ 2 & 4 & 2 & 4 \\ 2 & 1 & 2 & 4 \end{pmatrix} =$$

$$\begin{array}{c} \\ R1 \\ R2 \end{array} \begin{array}{cccc} C1 & C2 & C3 & C4 \\ \begin{pmatrix} 19 & 17 & 13 & 8 \\ 14 & 11 & 10 & 8 \end{pmatrix} \end{array}$$

We have now completed the calculation of AC. It is not possible to calculate AB, because the rows and columns do not match. The rows of A have 3 numbers and the columns of B only have 2 numbers.

Unlike normal numbers, when we multiply two matrices A and B, AB is usually not equal to BA.

Example

$$A = \begin{pmatrix} 2 & 3 \\ -1 & 5 \end{pmatrix} \quad B = \begin{pmatrix} 3 & 6 \\ 0 & -2 \end{pmatrix}$$

Calculate AB and BA.

$$AB = \begin{array}{c} R1 \\ R2 \end{array} \begin{pmatrix} 2 & 3 \\ \hline -1 & 5 \end{pmatrix} \begin{array}{cc} C1 & C2 \end{array} \begin{pmatrix} 3 & 6 \\ 0 & -2 \end{pmatrix} = \begin{array}{c} R1 \\ R2 \end{array} \begin{array}{cc} C1 & C2 \end{array} \begin{pmatrix} 6 & 6 \\ -3 & -16 \end{pmatrix}$$

$$BA = \begin{array}{c} R1 \\ R2 \end{array} \begin{pmatrix} 3 & 6 \\ \hline 0 & -2 \end{pmatrix} \begin{array}{cc} C1 & C2 \end{array} \begin{pmatrix} 2 & 3 \\ -1 & 5 \end{pmatrix} = \begin{array}{c} R1 \\ R2 \end{array} \begin{array}{cc} C1 & C2 \end{array} \begin{pmatrix} 0 & 39 \\ 2 & -10 \end{pmatrix}$$

1

$$A = \begin{pmatrix} 3 & 4 \\ 2 & 1 \end{pmatrix} \quad B = \begin{pmatrix} 5 & 0 \\ 0 & 5 \end{pmatrix} \quad C = \begin{pmatrix} 6 & 3 \\ 3 & 6 \end{pmatrix} \quad D = \begin{pmatrix} 0 & 5 \\ 5 & 0 \end{pmatrix}$$

Calculate the following.

a AB **b** BA **c** AC **d** CA **e** AD **f** DA
g BC **h** CB **i** BD **j** DB **k** CD **l** DC

2

$$A = \begin{pmatrix} 2 & 3 \\ 0 & 1 \end{pmatrix} \quad B = \begin{pmatrix} 3 & 5 \\ 0 & 1 \end{pmatrix} \quad C = \begin{pmatrix} 4 & 4 \\ 0 & 1 \end{pmatrix} \quad D = \begin{pmatrix} 2 & 1 \\ 1 & 2 \end{pmatrix}$$

Calculate the following.

a AB **b** BA **c** AC **d** CA **e** AD **f** DA
g BC **h** CB **i** BD **j** DB **k** CD **l** DC

3

$$A = \begin{pmatrix} -2 & 3 \\ 0 & -1 \end{pmatrix} \quad B = \begin{pmatrix} -3 & 3 \\ 0 & -1 \end{pmatrix} \quad C = \begin{pmatrix} -1 & 0 \\ 0 & 1 \end{pmatrix} \quad D = \begin{pmatrix} -2 & 0 \\ 1 & 2 \end{pmatrix}$$

Calculate the following.

a AB **b** BA **c** AC **d** CA **e** AD **f** DA
g BC **h** CB **i** BD **j** DB **k** CD **l** DC

4

$$A = \begin{pmatrix} 3 & -2 & 1 \\ 1 & 3 & 0 \end{pmatrix} \quad W = \begin{pmatrix} -1 & 0 \\ 0 & 1 \end{pmatrix} \quad X = \begin{pmatrix} 0 & -1 \\ 1 & 0 \end{pmatrix}$$

$$Y = \begin{pmatrix} 0 & -1 \\ -1 & 0 \end{pmatrix} \quad Z = \begin{pmatrix} 1 & 0 \\ 0 & 1 \end{pmatrix}$$

Calculate the following.

a WA **b** XA **c** YA **d** ZA **e** AZ **f** WX **g** YZ **h** ZY

5

$$M = \begin{pmatrix} 5 & -6 & 2 \\ 3 & 0 & -3 \\ 3 & 4 & 1 \end{pmatrix} \quad N = \begin{pmatrix} 3 & 4 & 0 \\ 7 & -5 & 2 \\ -1 & 2 & 0 \end{pmatrix}$$

Calculate MN and NM.

Area and volume

How area and volume measurement began

The need to measure lengths, areas and volumes is very ancient. Over 5000 years ago, the Egyptians lived in a country which was flooded each year by the overflowing waters of the Nile. After each flood, surveyors had to mark out field boundaries which had been washed away by the flood waters. They measured the **area** of each field because the taxes that the farmers paid to the Pharaoh were based on the area of land they owned. To do this, Egyptian mathematicians had to discover how to measure the areas of **rectangles** and **triangles**. At about the same point in history these skills were also known to Chinese mathematicians.

As trade grew, the need to measure **volume** developed. Three thousand years ago, Phoenician traders were already sailing North to trade with the communities living in what is now Northern France, Devon and Cornwall.

Much of this trade was in metals, grain and liquids like oil and wine. All these commodities were traded by **volume**, and the mathematicians of the time had to discover how to measure the volumes of the containers in which they were stored. Many of the containers were circular in shape and their volume could not be calculated until mathematicians had discovered how to measure the **area of a circle**.

In the following sections we will learn how to measure the areas of these basic shapes.

Rectangle

Parallelogram

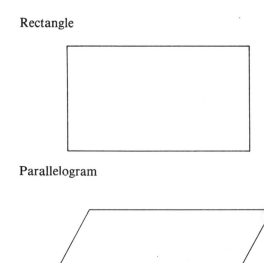

Triangle

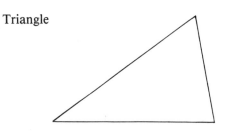

Trapezium
(a quadrilateral with one pair of parallel sides)

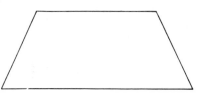

Circle

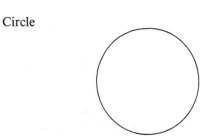

Compound shapes, made up from two or more basic shapes

We will also learn how to measure the volumes of the following basic solids. When you are making drawings of solid objects, **isometric** (or dotty) graph paper is very useful.

Cube

Cuboid

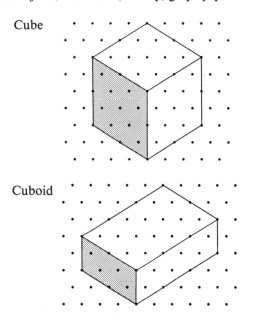

Prism (any solid which has the same shape along its whole length)

Triangular prism

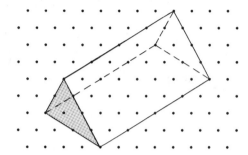

Hexagonal prism

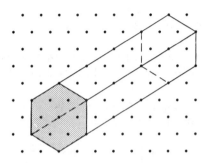

Irregular prism

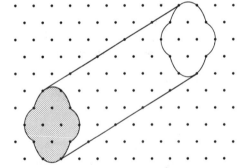

Pyramid

Cylinder

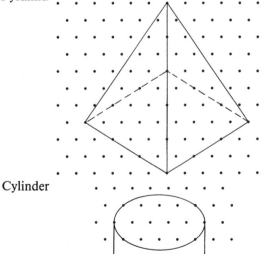

Cone

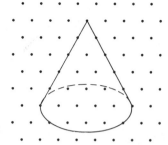

Sphere

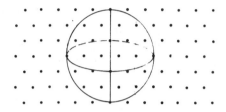

Compound solids, made up from two or more basic solids

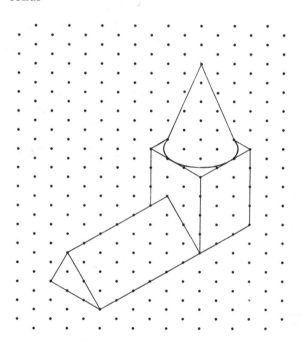

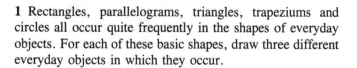

CHECKPOINT 26

1 Rectangles, parallelograms, triangles, trapeziums and circles all occur quite frequently in the shapes of everyday objects. For each of these basic shapes, draw three different everyday objects in which they occur.

2 Use isometric paper to copy the diagram at the top of the next page. On your copy write the names of each basic solid which has been used to build up the diagram.

24

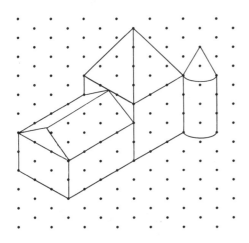

3 On isometric paper, draw sketches of everyday objects which are cubes, cuboids, prisms, pyramids, cylinders cones and spheres.

4 a Why are sugar lumps cubes?

b Why are wheels cylinders?

c Why are bricks cuboids, rather than cubes?

d Why are dice usually cubes? Could you use any other solid to make dice? What would these dice look like?

e Why are cornflake packet cuboids? Are any other shapes used to make packets?

f Why are tins usually cylinders? Are any other shapes used to make tins?

g Why are golf balls, footballs, tennis balls and hockey balls spheres? Why are rugby balls and American footballs not spheres? What shape are ice-hockey pucks?

Areas and perimeters

The **area** of a shape is a measurement of size of its surface. The **perimeter** of a shape is a measurement of the distance around the outside of the shape.

For the past 5000 years, the square has been used as the basic shape with which we measure areas. We do not know exactly why this should be so, but it is probably because the square is the simplest shape which fits together to completely fill a flat area, without overlapping or leaving gaps.

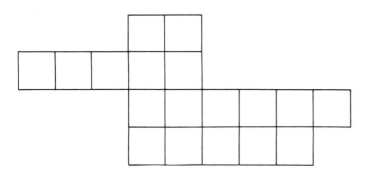

Many different standard squares have been used, like the square inch, the square foot, the square yard and the acre. In our metric system of measurements, the standard squares used to measure area are the square millimetre, the square centimetre, the square metre and the hectare.

Here are a square millimetre and a square centimetre. The abbreviations for these are mm^2 and cm^2.

1 mm^2 1 cm^2

A square metre (a square 1 metre by 1 metre) is obviously too large to draw in this book. A hectare is a square 100 metres by 100 metres (10 000 square metres). The abbreviations for these are m^2 and ha.

We measure the area of a shape by finding the number of standard squares which would have an equal area.

Some area measurements can be made directly by dividing a shape into square units. For example, this shape

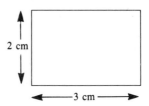

has an area of 6 cm^2.

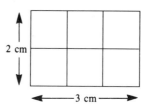

Other shapes cannot be divided into standard squares, but mathematicians have discovered ways to calculate the number of standard squares which have the same area.

For example, we can calculate that this shape

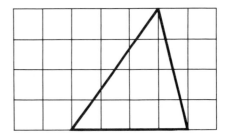

has an area of 8 cm^2. This means that it has an area **equivalent** to 8 centimetre squares.

25

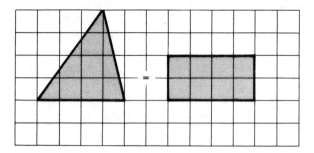

Mathematicians have discovered ways to calculate the area of many different shapes and some of these are explained in the following sections.

Area and perimeter of a rectangle

The area of a rectangle is calculated by multiplying the base length by the height.

This is obviously true for whole number measurements as this diagram shows.

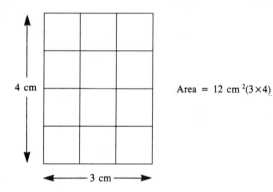

Area = 12 cm^2 (3×4)

It is also true for decimal measurements as this diagram shows.

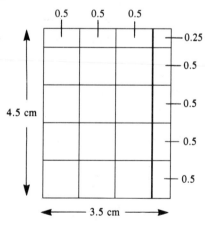

Area = 15.75 cm^2 (3.5×4.5)

Examples

---

1 Find the perimeter and area of this rectangle.

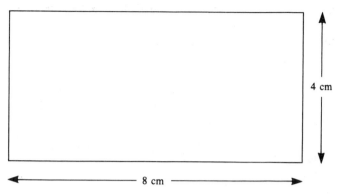

Perimeter = 4 + 8 + 4 + 8 = 24 cm   Area = 4 × 8 = 32 cm^2

2 Find the perimeter and area of this rectangle.

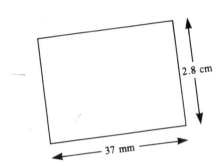

There is a mixture of units in the measurements given. We must therefore first convert all the measurements into either centimetres or millimetres. Using centimetres, we have

Perimeter = 3.7 + 2.8 + 3.7 + 2.8 = 13 cm

Area = 3.7 × 2.8 = 10.36 cm^2

3 Find the perimeter and area of this shape.

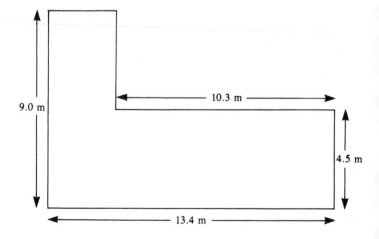

First, we must fill in all the missing measurements. This is quite easy to do. For example, by comparing the length of 13.4 m and 10.3 m, we can deduce that the missing length

is 3.1 m. In the same way, comparing the 9 m and the 4.5 m allows us to deduce that the missing height is 4.5 m. The perimeter can now be found by adding all these measurements.

The area is found by dividing the shape into rectangles, calculating their areas and then adding these areas together to find the area of the whole shape.

This diagram shows the completed calculations.

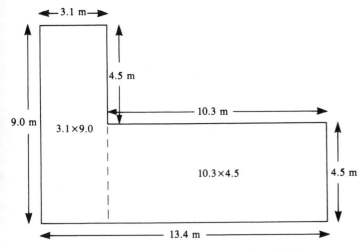

Perimeter $= 3.1 + 4.5 + 10.3 + 4.5 + 13.4 + 9.0 = 44.8$ m

Area $= (3.1 \times 9.0) + (10.3 \times 4.5) = 27.9 + 46.35 = 74.25$ m^2

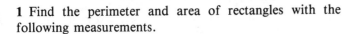

CHECKPOINT 27

1 Find the perimeter and area of rectangles with the following measurements.

a 2 cm by 16 cm   **b** 23 m by 60 m
c 165 mm by 113 mm   **d** 8.9 cm by 4.0 cm
e 2.1 m by 4.5 m   **f** 34 mm by 7.3 cm (in cm and cm^2)
g 125 cm by 2.7 m (in m and m^2)
h 24 cm by 0.89 m (in cm and cm^2)

2 By making measurements correct to the nearest tenth of a centimetre, find the perimeter and area of each of the following shapes.

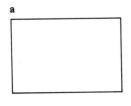

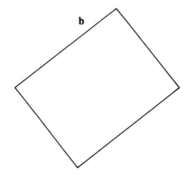

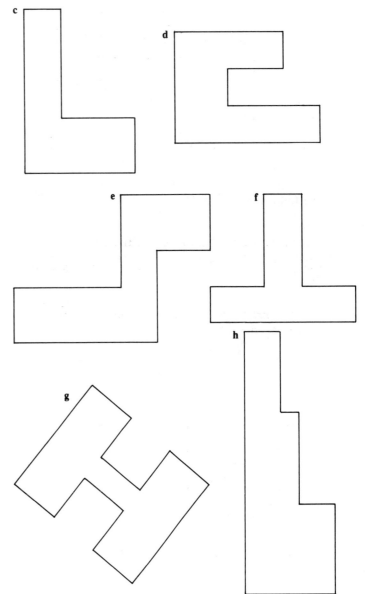

3 Find the perimeter and area of each of the following shapes.

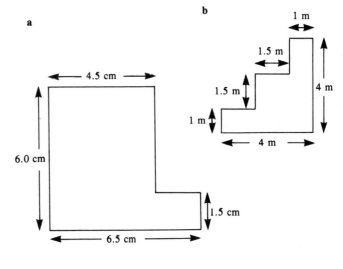

27

d

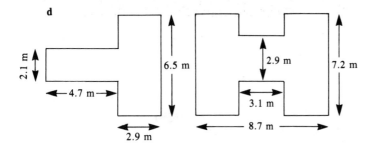

4 The carpet that Julie Hasdell wants to buy for her lounge is only available from a roll with a width of 4 metres. The carpet shop will only sell a length cut from this roll; they will not sell carpet cut to any particular shape. These diagrams show the carpet roll and the measurements of Julie's lounge.

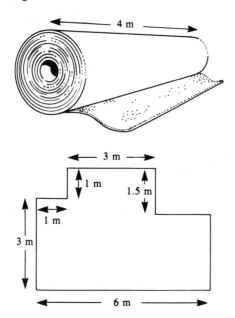

a What length of carpet does Julie need to buy?

b If the carpet costs £9.99 per square metre, how much will Julie pay?

c What area of the carpet will be wasted after it has been cut to fit Julie's lounge?

d What is the cost of this wasted carpet?

Area and perimeter of a parallelogram

The area of a parallelogram is also calculated by multiplying the base length by the height.

This is because any parallelogram has the same area as a rectangle with the same base length and height. These diagrams show a simple 'scissors and glue' demonstration that any parallelogram can be converted to a rectangle with the same base, height and area.

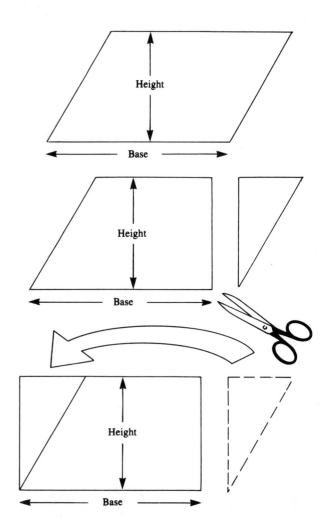

Any side of a parallelogram can be selected as the 'base'. When a base side has been selected, the 'height' **must** be measured at right angles to the base side. The following diagrams show two different ways to select the base side of the same parallelograms.

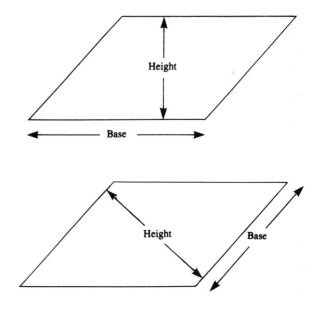

28

Examples

1 Find the perimeter and area of this parallelogram.

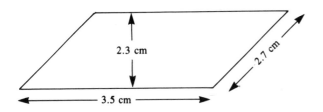

Perimeter = $3.5 + 2.7 + 3.5 + 2.7 = 12.4$ cm

Area = $3.5 \times 2.3 = 8.05$ cm^2

2 This is the plan for the entrance of a hotel. Find the perimeter and the floor area of the entrance.

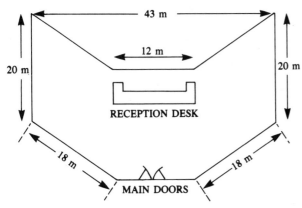

First, we must fill in all the missing measurements.

The area is found by dividing the shape into rectangles and parallelograms, calculating their areas and then adding these areas together to find the area of the whole shape. This diagram shows the completed calculations.

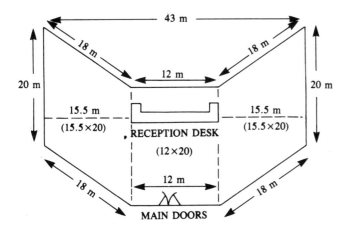

Perimeter = $18 + 12 + 18 + 20 + 18 + 12 + 18 + 20 = 136$ m

Area = $(15.5 \times 20) + (15.5 \times 20) + (12 \times 20)$

Area = $310 + 310 + 240 = 860$ m^2

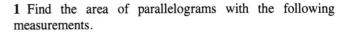

CHECKPOINT 28

1 Find the area of parallelograms with the following measurements.

a base = 5 cm, height = 8 cm

b base = 5.4 m, height = 9.4 m

c base = 3.7 mm, height = 8.9 mm

d base = 5.4 m, height = 94 cm (in m^2)

e base = 456 mm, height = 0.89 m (in cm^2)

2 By making measurements correct to the nearest tenth of a centimetre, find the perimeter and area of each of the following shapes.

a

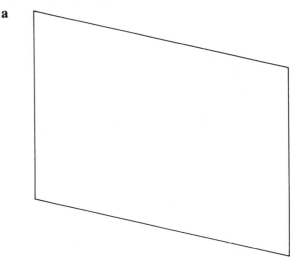

b

c

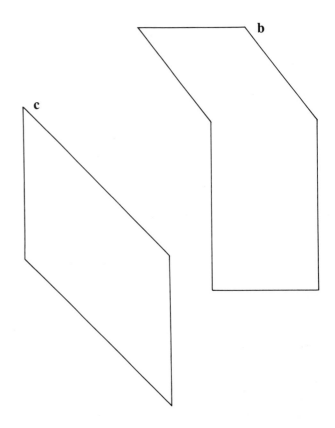

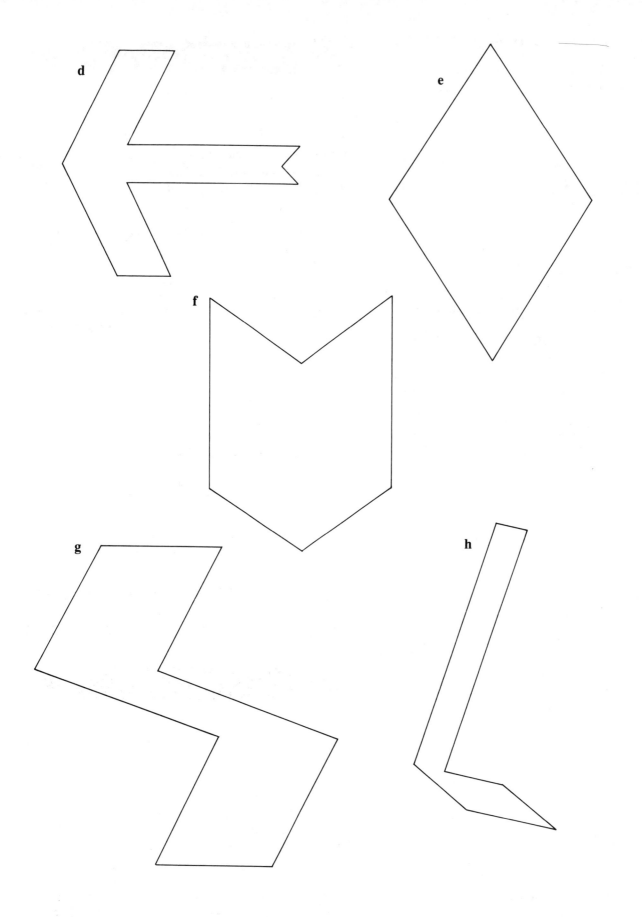

d

e

f

g

h

Area and perimeter of a triangle

Any triangle with a base b and a height h

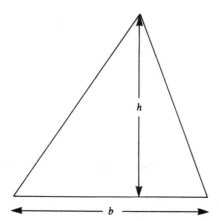

is half of a parallelogram with a base b and a height h.

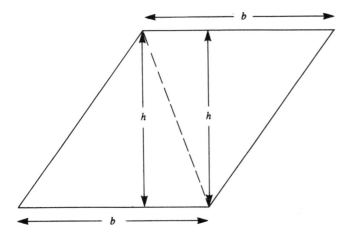

So, since the area of the parallelogram is $b \times h$, the area of the triangle is

$$\frac{b \times h}{2} \quad \text{or} \quad \frac{bh}{2}$$

Examples

1 Find the perimeter and area of this triangle.

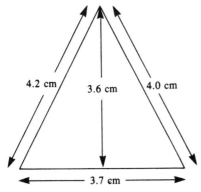

Perimeter $= 4.2 + 4.0 + 3.7 = 11.9$ cm

Area $= \dfrac{3.6 \times 3.7}{2} = \dfrac{13.32}{2} = 6.66$ cm^2

2 Find the area of this shape.

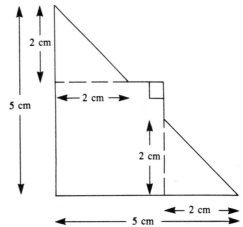

Filling in the missing measurements and dividing the shape into triangles and rectangles gives us this diagram.

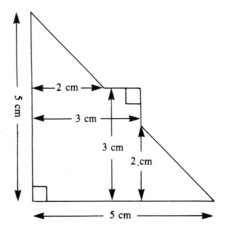

Area $= (3 \times 3) + \dfrac{(2 \times 2)}{2} + \dfrac{(2 \times 2)}{2} = 9 + 2 + 2 = 13$ cm^2

CHECKPOINT 29

1 Find the area of triangles with the following measurements.

a base $= 5$ cm, height $= 8$ cm
b base $= 5.4$ m, height $= 9.4$ m
c base $= 3.7$ mm, height $= 8.9$ mm
d base $= 5.4$ m, height $= 94$ cm (in m^2)
e base $= 456$ mm, height $= 0.89$ m (in cm^2)

2 By making measurements correct to the nearest tenth of a centimetre, find the perimeter and area of each of the following shapes.

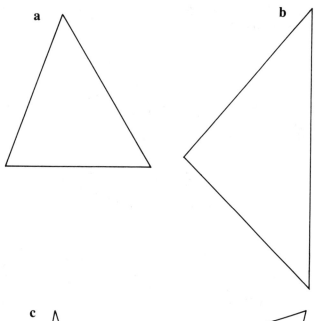

a

b

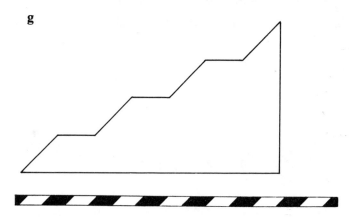

g

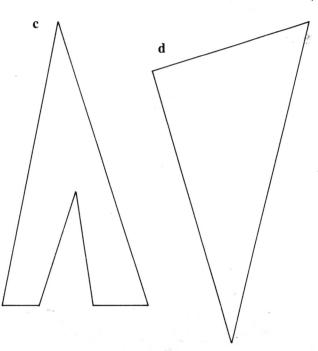

c

d

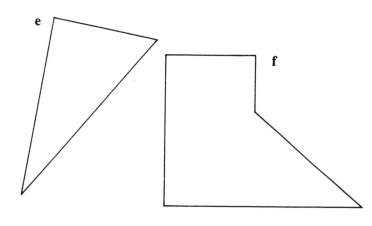

e

f

Area and perimeter of a trapezium

A trapezium with parallel sides *a* and *b* and height *h*

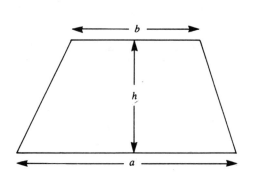

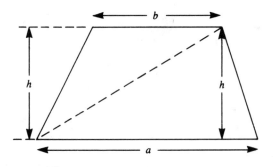

can be divided into two triangles, one with base *a* and height *h*, the other with base *b* and height *h*. The areas of these triangles are

$$\frac{a \times h}{2} \text{ and } \frac{b \times h}{2}$$

So the area of the trapezium is

$$\frac{a \times h}{2} + \frac{b \times h}{2}$$

This can be simplified to give this area formula for **any** trapezium.

$$\text{Area} = \frac{h(a+b)}{2}$$

32

Examples

1 Find the area and perimeter of this trapezium.

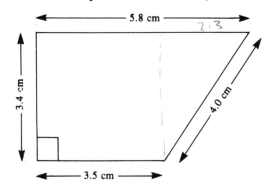

Perimeter = 3.4 + 5.8 + 4.0 + 3.5 = 16.7 cm

$$\text{Area} = \frac{3.4(5.8 + 3.5)}{2} = \frac{3.4 \times 9.3}{2} = \frac{31.62}{2} = 15.81 \text{ cm}^2$$

2 This diagram shows a plan for the wing of an aircraft. Calculate the surface area of the top of the wing.

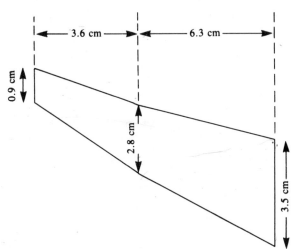

$$\text{Surface area} = \frac{6.3(3.5 + 2.8)}{2} + \frac{3.6(2.8 + 0.9)}{2}$$

$$\text{Surface area} = \frac{39.69}{2} + \frac{13.32}{2} = 26.505 \text{ cm}^2$$

CHECKPOINT 30

1 Find the area of trapeziums with the following measurements.

a $h = 5$ cm, $a = 3$ cm, $b = 2$ cm
b $h = 11.3$ m, $a = 7.9$ m, $b = 2$ m
c $h = 4$ mm, $a = 3.9$ mm, $b = 8.7$ mm
d $h = 5$ cm, $a = 33$ mm, $b = 24$ mm (in cm^2)
e $h = 15.4$ m, $a = 398$ cm, $b = 897$ cm (in m^2)

2 By making measurements correct to the nearest tenth of a centimetre, find the perimeter and area of each of the following shapes.

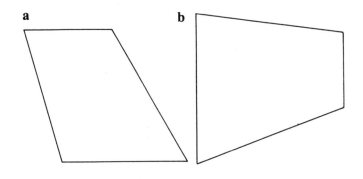

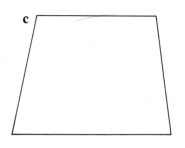

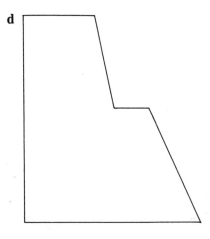

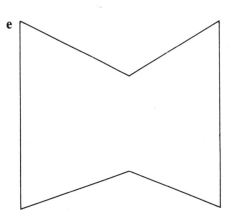

33

f

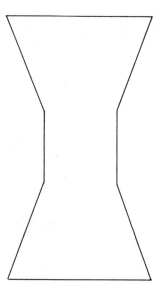

3 Find the area of each of the following shapes.

a

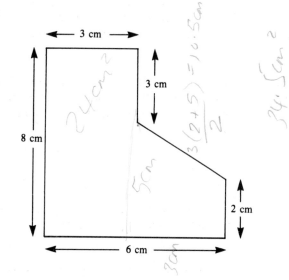

b

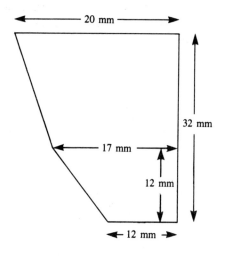

c

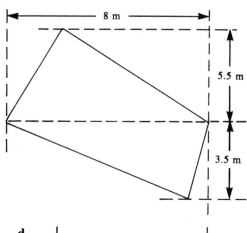

d

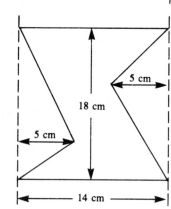

e

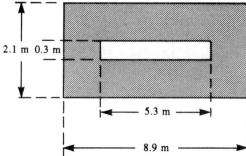

f

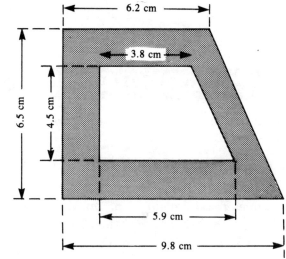

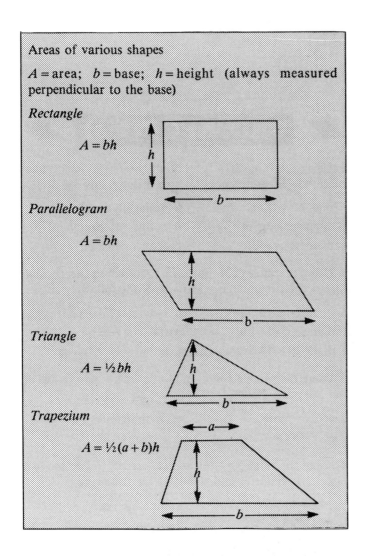

Areas of various shapes

A = area; b = base; h = height (always measured perpendicular to the base)

Rectangle

$A = bh$

Parallelogram

$A = bh$

Triangle

$A = \frac{1}{2}bh$

Trapezium

$A = \frac{1}{2}(a + b)h$

The circumference and area of a circle

Terms used in referring to a circle

A **radius** of a circle is a line joining the centre to a point on the circle.

A **diameter** of a circle is a line which joins two points on the circle **and** passes through the centre.

The **circumference** of a circle is its perimeter, the distance along its boundary.

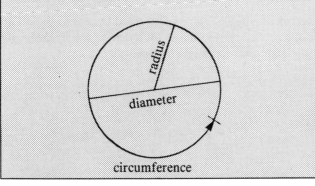

The first use that humans made of this very useful shape was in the construction of wheels. Nobody knows how long ago the wheel was invented, but it has certainly been around for a very long time.

As soon as you have made a wheel, you are tempted to ask the question

'What is the connection between the size of the wheel and the distance it rolls in a single turn?' (This distance is of course equal to the **circumference** of the wheel.)

Ancient mathematicians investigating this problem discovered that an approximate value for the circumference of a circle could be calculated by multiplying the diameter by 3.

Better approximations could be calculated by multiplying the diameter by a number between 3 and 3.2. Some of the different multipliers worked out by ancient mathematicians are

Egyptians   3.16 (1500 BC)
Archimedes   between 3.1409 and 3.1416 (287–212 BC)
Tsu Chung Chih (Chinese)   3.1415926 (480 AD)

The Greek letter π (pi) is used to stand for all these different multipliers. This allows us to write the formula

$$C = \pi d$$

to calculate the circumference of a circle, where π can be 3 or 3.1 or 3.14 or 3.142 and so on, depending on the accuracy we require. In most examination questions you will be told which value of π to use.

Example

Find the circumference of this circle using the value 3.14 for π.

2.5 m

Circumference $= 3.14 \times 2.5 = 7.85$ m

If you have a scientific calculator, it may have a special button to give a value for π. A button on an eight digit calculator gives the value 3.1415927. In an examination, be very careful not to use the button of your calculator if the question gives a different value for π.

You may be wondering what the **exact value of π is. There is no exact value for π.** It is an example of an **irrational number.** Irrational numbers cannot be written down exactly. All the values you may see for π, even those used by calculators and computers, are approximations.

Values for π can also be used to calculate the area of a circle. The formula to calculate the area of a circle is

$$A = \pi r^2 \ (= \pi \times r \times r)$$

Example

Find the area of this circle using the value 3.142 for π.

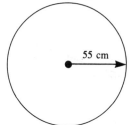

55 cm

Area $= 3.142 \times 55 \times 55 = 9504.55 \, \text{cm}^2$

We can of course use the formulas in reverse to find the radius or diameter, given the area or circumference. The reverse formulas are

$$d = \frac{C}{\pi}$$

and

$$r = \sqrt{\frac{A}{\pi}}$$

Examples

1 Find, correct to one decimal place, the diameter of a circle with a circumference of 36.5 cm ($\pi = 3.1$).

Diameter $= \dfrac{36.5}{3.1} = 11.8 \, \text{cm}$ (to one decimal place)

2 Find, correct to two decimal places, the radius of a circle with an area of 49.55 m² ($\pi = 3.14$).

Radius $= \sqrt{\dfrac{49.55}{3.14}} = 3.97 \, \text{m}$ (to two decimal places)

3 Find the circumference of a circle with area of 192 mm² ($\pi = 3$).

Radius $= \sqrt{\dfrac{192}{3}} = \sqrt{64} = 8 \, \text{mm}$

Circumference $= 3 \times (8 \times 2) = 48 \, \text{mm}$

CHECKPOINT 31

1 Using the value 3.14 for π find, correct to one decimal place, the circumference and area of the following circles.

a diameter = 8 cm
b radius = 8 cm
c diameter = 3.5 m
d radius = 10.8 mm
e diameter = 240 m
f radius = 43 mm

2 Using the value 3.142 for π find, correct to two decimal places, the circumference and area of the following circles.

a diameter = 10 cm
b radius = 12.3 cm
c diameter = 13.1 m
d radius = 32.3 mm
e diameter = 14.5 mm
f radius = 11.9 mm

3 Using the value 3 for π find the diameter and radius of the following circles.

a area = 75 cm²
b circumference = 300 cm
c area = 48 m²
d circumference = 99 mm

4 Using the value 3.14 for π find, correct to one decimal place, the diameter and radius of the following circles.

a area = 80 cm²
b circumference = 59.5 cm
c area = 5.5 m²
d circumference = 37.2 mm

5 A bicycle is fitted with wheels which have a diameter of 65 cm. How far would you expect the bike to travel as the wheels turn 10 times?

6 The instruction for a garden fertilizer states

'Apply 100 grams per square metre'.

How many kilograms of fertilizer should be applied to a circular flower bed with a diameter of 12 metres?

Area and Perimeter of a Sector of a Circle

A **sector** of a circle is a shape formed by two radii and an arc of a circle. The size of a sector is determined by the length of the radii and the angle between them.

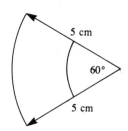

5 cm

60°

5 cm

Any sector represents a fraction of a whole circle with the same radius. For example, the sector above is $\frac{60}{360}$ or $\frac{1}{6}$ of a circle with a radius of 5 cm.

We find the perimeter or area of a sector by calculating the appropriate fraction of the circumference or area of a whole circle with the same radius.

Example

Find the area and perimeter of this sector ($\pi = 3.14$).

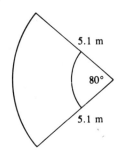

This sector represents 80/360 or 2/9 of a circle with the same radius.

The area of the sector is therefore

$$\frac{2}{9} \times 3.14 \times 5.1 \times 5.1 = \frac{2 \times 3.14 \times 5.1 \times 5.1}{9} = 18.1 \text{ m}^2 \text{ (to 1 d.p.)}$$

To find the perimeter we first calculate the length of the circular arc. This is

$$\frac{2}{9} \times 3.14 \times 10.2 = \frac{2 \times 3.14 \times 10.2}{9} = 7.1 \text{ m (to 1 d.p.)}$$

To this answer, we must add the lengths of the two radii to find the **total** perimeter of the sector.

Total perimeter $= 5.1 + 5.1 + 7.1 = 17.3$ m (to 1 d.p.)

CHECKPOINT 32

1 Find, correct to one decimal place, the area and perimeter of the following sectors ($\pi = 3.14$).

a radius $= 5$ cm, sector angle $= 45°$
b radius $= 12.7$ cm, sector angle $= 90°$
c radius $= 60$ m, sector angle $= 36°$
d radius $= 125$ mm, sector angle $= 144°$
e radius $= 85$ cm, sector angle $= 225°$
f radius $= 14.9$ m, sector angle $= 180°$

2 Calculate, correct to two decimal places, the area and total perimeter of each of the following shapes ($\pi = 3.142$).

a

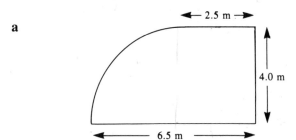

b

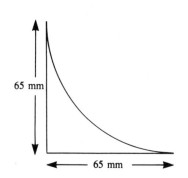

c

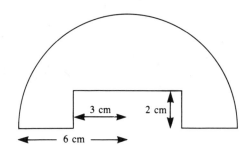

d

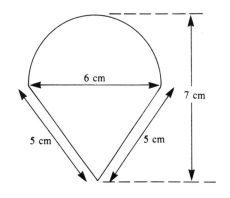

e

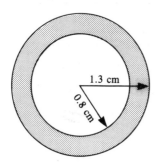

1.3 cm

0.8 cm

f

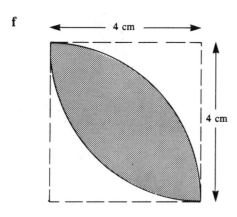

4 cm

4 cm

g (area only)

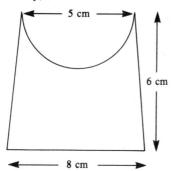

5 cm

6 cm

8 cm

h

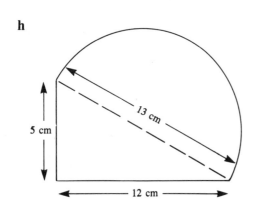

13 cm

5 cm

12 cm

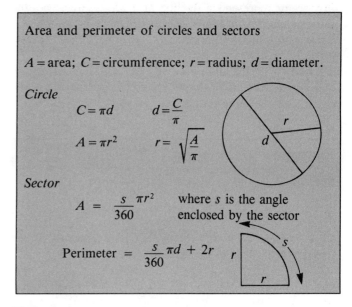

Area and perimeter of circles and sectors

A = area; C = circumference; r = radius; d = diameter.

Circle

$$C = \pi d \qquad d = \frac{C}{\pi}$$

$$A = \pi r^2 \qquad r = \sqrt{\frac{A}{\pi}}$$

Sector

$$A = \frac{s}{360} \pi r^2 \qquad \text{where } s \text{ is the angle enclosed by the sector}$$

$$\text{Perimeter} = \frac{s}{360} \pi d + 2r$$

Volumes

The **volume** of an object is a measurement of the space that it occupies. The cube is the basic solid with which we measure volumes. In our metric system of measurements, the standard cubes used to measure volume are the cubic millimetre (mm^3), the cubic centimetre (cm^3) and the cubic metre (m^3). **Liquid** volumes are often measured in **litres** (l). A litre is 1000 cubic centimetres. When working with liquids, the cubic centimetre is often called a **millilitre** (ml). In a supermarket, you will find that the volume of many jars and bottles is shown in millilitres.

We measure the volume of a solid by finding the number of standard cubes which would have an equal volume. Some volume measurements can be made directly by dividing a solid into cubic units. For example, this solid

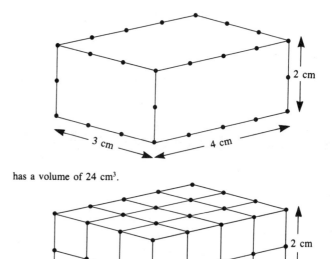

2 cm

3 cm

4 cm

has a volume of 24 cm^3.

2 cm

3 cm

4 cm

Other solids cannot be divided into standard cubes, but mathematicians have discovered ways to calculate the number of standard cubes which have the same volume. For example, we can calculate that this solid

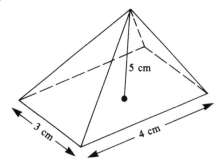

has a volume of 20 cm³. This means that it has a volume **equivalent** to 20 centimetre cubes.

Mathematicians have discovered ways to calculate the volumes of many different solids and some of these are explained in the following sections, together with ways to calculate their surface areas.

Surface area and volume of a prism

A prism is a solid which has the same shape along its whole length.

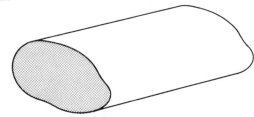

Cuboids and cylinders are special cases.

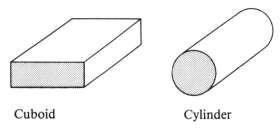

Cuboid   Cylinder

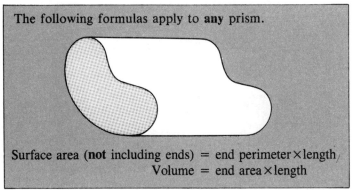

The following formulas apply to **any** prism.

Surface area (**not** including ends) = end perimeter × length
Volume = end area × length

Examples

1 Find the surface area and volume of this cornflake packet.

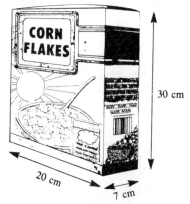

Surface area (**not** including top and bottom)
$$= \text{end perimeter} \times \text{length}$$
$$= (20 + 7 + 20 + 7) \times 30$$
$$= 1620 \text{ cm}^2$$
Total surface area $= 1620 + (20 \times 7) + (20 \times 7) = 1900 \text{ cm}^2$
Volume $= \text{end area} \times \text{length}$
$$= 7 \times 20 \times 30$$
$$= 4200 \text{ cm}^3$$

Note. These calculations are worked out in this way in order to be consistent with the calculations for other types of prism. You may, however, prefer to calculate the volume of a cuboid by using the formula

$$\text{Volume} = \text{height} \times \text{width} \times \text{depth}$$

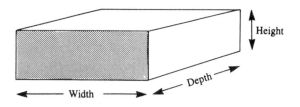

You can then calculate the surface area by adding together the areas of each of the faces.

2 Find the volume of this tent and the area of nylon required to make it.

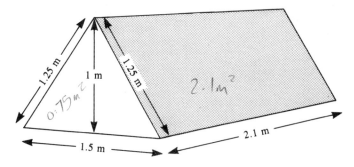

Volume $= \text{end area} \times \text{length}$

39

$$\text{Volume} = \frac{1.5 \times 1}{2} \times 2.1 = 1.575 \text{ m}^3$$

Surface area (**not** including ends) = end perimeter $\times$ length
$$= (1.5 + 1.25 + 1.25) \times 2.1$$
$$= 8.4 \text{ m}^2$$
$$\text{Total surface area} = 2 \times \frac{(1.5 \times 1)}{2} + 8.4$$
$$= 9.9 \text{ m}^2$$

3 This diagram shows a tin of beans. Calculate the volume, correct to 1 cm³, of the can and the area, correct to 1 cm², of the label stuck round it ($\pi = 3.14$).

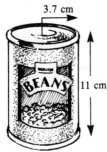

3.7 cm

11 cm

Volume = end area $\times$ length
Volume = $3.14 \times 3.7 \times 3.7 \times 11 = 473$ cm³ (nearest cm³)
Area of label = end perimeter $\times$ length
Area of label = $3.14 \times 7.4 \times 11 = 256$ cm² (nearest cm²)

CHECKPOINT 33

1 Find the volume and total surface area of each of the following prisms ($\pi = 3.14$).

a

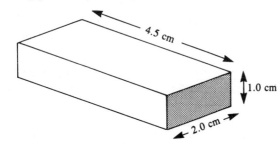

4.5 cm

1.0 cm

2.0 cm

b

30 cm   30 cm   30 cm

30 cm

20 cm

160 cm

90 cm

c

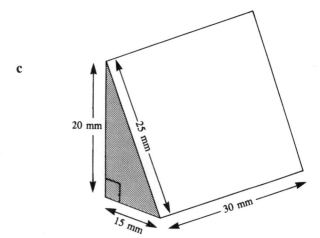

20 mm   25 mm

15 mm   30 mm

d

10 cm   8.7 cm   10 cm

20 cm

10 cm

e

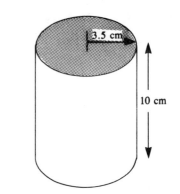

3.5 cm

10 cm

f

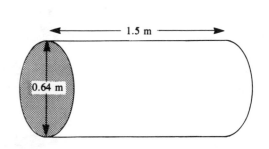

1.5 m

0.64 m

g

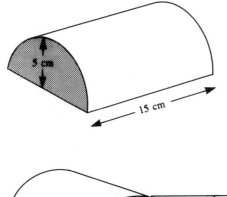

5 cm

15 cm

h

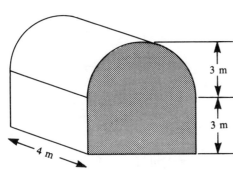

3 m

3 m

4 m

2 Calculate the volume and weight of this gold ingot, given that 1 cubic centimetre of gold weighs 19.29 grams.

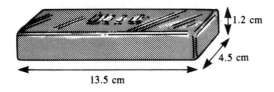

1.2 cm

4.5 cm

13.5 cm

3 This diagram shows a concrete girder. Calculate the volume of the girder and its weight in tonnes (1000 kg = 1 tonne), given that 1 cubic centimetre of the concrete weighs 2.2 grams.

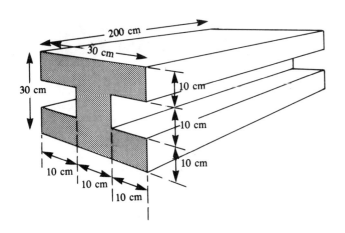

200 cm

30 cm

30 cm

10 cm

10 cm

10 cm

10 cm

10 cm

10 cm

4 This diagram shows a swimming pool is in the shape of a prism with a length of 25 m and a cross-section in the form of a trapezium.

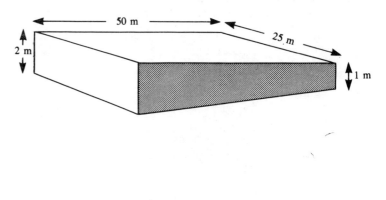

50 m

25 m

2 m

1 m

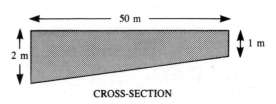

50 m

2 m

1 m

CROSS-SECTION

a Calculate the surface area of the water in the pool.

b If the pool is filled within 30 cm of the top, calculate the volume of water in the pool.

c If the empty pool is filled by water flowing at the rate of 5 m³ per minute, how long will it take to fill the pool to within 30 cm of the top?

5 A granite pillar, in the form of a cylinder with a length of 4.5 m and a radius of 0.25 m is to be transported from the quarry by helicopter, unless it is too heavy, in which case it will travel on a lorry. One cubic metre of granite weighs 2640 kg. The helicopter has a maximum lifting capacity of 2500 kg.

a Calculate the volume of the pillar in cubic metres.

b Calculate the weight of the pillar in kilograms.

c Does the pillar travel by road or helicopter?

Surface areas and volumes of pyramids, cones and spheres

Mathematicians have discovered these area and volume formulas.

Pyramid (any shape of base)

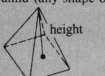

$$\text{Volume} = \frac{\text{area of base} \times \text{height}}{3}$$

Cone (a pyramid with a circular base)

$$\text{Volume} = \frac{\text{area of base} \times \text{height}}{3} = \frac{\pi r^2 h}{3} \left(\frac{\pi \times r \times r \times h}{3} \right)$$

$$\text{Surface area (excluding the base)} = \pi r l \ (\pi \times r \times l)$$

Sphere

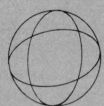

$$\text{Volume} = \frac{4\pi r^3}{3} \left(\frac{4 \times \pi \times r \times r \times r}{3} \right)$$

$$\text{Surface area} = 4\pi r^2 \ (4 \times \pi \times r \times r)$$

Example

1 Find the volume of this pyramid

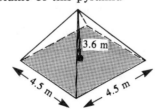

$$\text{Volume} = \frac{\text{area of base} \times \text{height}}{3}$$

$$\text{Volume} = \frac{4.5 \times 4.5 \times 3.6}{3} = 24.3 \text{ m}^3$$

2 Find the volume and total surface area of this cone ($\pi = 3.14$).

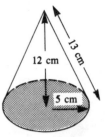

$$\text{Volume} = \frac{\text{area of base} \times \text{height}}{3} = \frac{\pi r^2 h}{3}$$

$$\text{Volume} = \frac{3.14 \times 5 \times 5 \times 12}{3} = 314 \text{ cm}^3$$

Surface area (excluding the base) $= \pi r l$
Surface area (excluding the base) $= 3.14 \times 5 \times 13$
$\qquad\qquad\qquad\qquad\qquad\qquad = 204.1 \text{ cm}^2$
Area of base $= 3.14 \times 5 \times 5 = 78.5 \text{ cm}^2$
Total surface area $= 204.1 + 78.5 = 282.6 \text{ cm}^2$

3 Find the volume and total surface area of a beachball with a radius of 15 cm ($\pi = 3.14$).

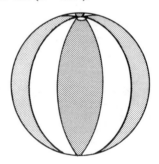

$$\text{Volume} = \frac{4\pi r^3}{3} = \frac{3.14 \times 4 \times 15 \times 15 \times 15}{3} = 14\,130 \text{ cm}^3$$

$$\text{Surface area} = 4\pi r^2 = 4 \times 3.14 \times 15 \times 15 = 2826 \text{ cm}^2$$

CHECKPOINT 34

1 Find the volume of each of the following solids ($\pi = 3.14$).

a

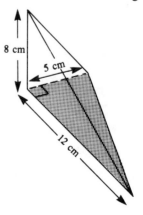

b

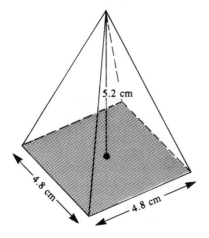

c

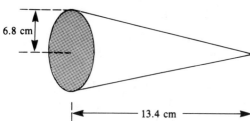

d

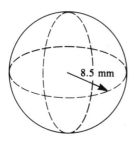

e

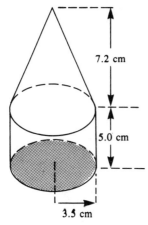

f

Hemisphere (half a sphere)

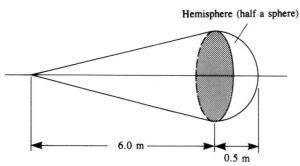

2 The roof of a house is constructed in the shape of a square based pyramid, with sides 4 metres long and a height of 3 metres. Find the volume of the space inside the roof.

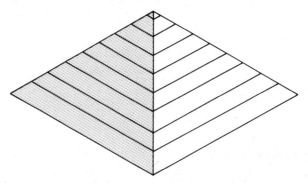

3 A circular concrete pipe of length 5 m has an internal radius of 0.5 m and an external radius of 0.6 m.

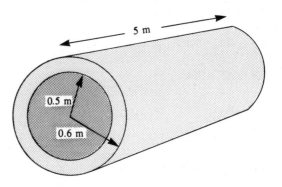

a Calculate the volume of a cylinder of radius 0.5 m and length 5 metres.

b Calculate the volume of a cylinder of radius 0.6 m and length 5 metres.

c Calculate the volume of concrete in the pipe.

d Calculate the weight of the pipe, correct to the nearest kilogram, given that 1 cubic metre of concrete weighs 2160 kg.

4 A grain hopper is in the form of a cone, with a radius of 1.5 metres and a height of 4 metres.

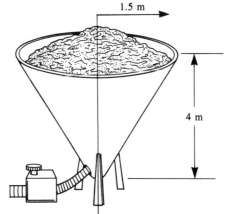

a Calculate the volume of the hopper.

b How long will it take to empty the hopper at a rate of 15 litres per second?

Practice and revision exercise (arithmetic)

1 One way to find all the prime numbers less than 100 was invented by the Ancient Greek mathematician Eratosthenes. His method is called 'the sieve of Eratosthenes'. Follow these steps which show how his method works.

a Make a copy of this diagram.

1	2	3	4	5	6	7	8	9	10
11	12	13	14	15	16	17	18	19	20
21	22	23	24	25	26	27	28	29	30
31	32	33	34	35	36	37	38	39	40
41	42	43	44	45	46	47	48	49	50
51	52	53	54	55	56	57	58	59	60
61	62	63	64	65	66	67	68	69	70
71	72	73	74	75	76	77	78	79	80
81	82	83	84	85	86	87	88	89	90
91	92	93	94	95	96	97	98	99	100

b Cross out the number 1, which is not prime because it has only one factor.

c Cross out all the multiples of 2, except 2 itself, ie 4, 6, 8, 10 ...

d Cross out all the multiples of 3, except 3 itself.

e Cross out all the multiples of 5, except 5 itself.

f Cross out all the multiples of 7, except 7 itself.

g Make a list of the remaining numbers. These are all the prime numbers less than 100.

2 List all the factors of
a 24   **b** 51   **c** 100

3 List all the prime factors of
a 30   **b** 84   **c** 105

4 Write these numbers as a chain multiplication of prime factors.
a 60   **b** 210   **c** 2808

5 Find the HCF and the LCM of each of the following sets of numbers.
a 8 and 10   **b** 8, 12 and 18   **c** 26, 65 and 130

6 Write down the first 12 square numbers.

7 Write down the first 12 rectangular numbers.

8 Write down the first 12 triangular numbers.

9 Calculate, **without written calculations or a calculator**.
a $89 + 3.0$ **b** $8.9 + 3$ **c** $8.9 + 0.3$ **d** $8.9 + 30$
e $7.5 - 4.2$ **f** $7.9 - 1.4$ **g** $11.5 - 0.6$ **h** $20 - 17.5$

10 Calculate, **without a calculator**.
a $44.67 + 73.86$ **b** $523 + 97.9$ **c** $114.7 + 75.93$
d $33.89 - 13.4$ **e** $1376 - 754.56$ **f** $5431.45 - 476.56$

11 Calculate **with** a calculator.
a $77.5 + 25.9 + 703.6$ **b** $300.1 + 296.9 + 456.9$
c $(13.956 + 7834.78) - 561.67$
d $(19.65 + 45.78) - (25.65 - 11.97)$

12 Calculate, **without written calculations or a calculator**.
a 3×0.7 **b** 0.8×4 **c** 0.6×0.6 **d** 0.9×2
e 0.5×0.2 **f** 10×0.2 **g** 100×0.2 **h** 1000×0.5
i $34.7 \div 1000$ **j** $0.96 \div 10$ **k** $473 \div 100$ **l** $803 \div 1000$
m $27.94 \div 10$ **n** $0.012 \div 100$

13 Calculate **without a calculator**.
a 55.5×3 **b** 23.4×19 **c** 300.5×4.7
d 36.7×0.34 **e** $17.5 \div 8$ **f** $34.3 \div 7$
g $0.347 \div 5$ **h** $234.1 \div 4$

14 Calculate **with** a calculator.
a 34.67×23 **b** 56.7×45 **c** 90.98×1.04
d $34.5 \div 3$ **e** $23.89 \div 7.1$ **f** $23.78 \div 3.7$

15 Calculate correct to 1 decimal place.
a $232 \div 7$ **b** 3.4×5.7 **c** $1.5 \div 6$ **d** $38.9 \div 10.4$

16 Calculate correct to 2 decimal places.
a 67.67×23.07 **b** $232 \div 7$
c $0.127 \div 0.12$ **d** $2.34 \div 3.2$

17 If all the numbers in the following calculations are correct to the nearest whole number, what are the least and greatest possible values for the answer?
a 4×5 **b** 34×27 **c** $45 \div 9$
d $\dfrac{25 \times 25 \times 3}{4 \times 7}$

18 If all the numbers in the following calculations are correct to one decimal place, what are the least and greatest possible values for the answer?

a 5.1×5.1 **b** $7.3 \div 2.6$ **c** $\dfrac{3.7 \times 5.6}{2.9}$

19 The sides of a rectangle are measured as 9.5 cm and 8.5 cm, correct to the nearest millimetre. What are the least and greatest values for the perimeter and area of the rectangle?

20 Change each of the following improper fractions into a mixed number.

a $\dfrac{12}{5}$ **b** $\dfrac{31}{10}$ **c** $\dfrac{34}{7}$ **d** $\dfrac{7}{3}$ **e** $\dfrac{7}{4}$

21 Change each of the following mixed numbers into an improper fraction.

a $1\dfrac{3}{4}$ **b** $3\dfrac{2}{3}$ **c** $7\dfrac{1}{2}$ **d** $12\dfrac{1}{11}$ **e** $6\dfrac{5}{6}$

22 Copy and complete the following.

a $\dfrac{2}{5} = \dfrac{?}{15}$ **b** $\dfrac{5}{8} = \dfrac{?}{16}$ **c** $\dfrac{7}{6} = \dfrac{?}{24}$ **d** $\dfrac{3}{7} = \dfrac{?}{28}$

e $\dfrac{12}{17} = \dfrac{?}{68}$ **f** $\dfrac{1}{9} = \dfrac{?}{18}$ **g** $\dfrac{11}{12} = \dfrac{?}{60}$ **h** $\dfrac{4}{5} = \dfrac{?}{65}$

23 Simplify the following.

a $\dfrac{50}{60}$ **b** $\dfrac{25}{70}$ **c** $\dfrac{6}{15}$ **d** $\dfrac{12}{18}$ **e** $\dfrac{24}{36}$ **f** $\dfrac{35}{75}$ **g** $\dfrac{65}{75}$

24 Which is the larger of each of the following pairs of fractions?

a $\dfrac{2}{7}$ and $\dfrac{3}{8}$ **b** $\dfrac{3}{5}$ and $\dfrac{4}{7}$ **c** $\dfrac{3}{50}$ and $\dfrac{5}{60}$

25 Jane scored 93 out of 120 in an Art exam and 39 out of 50 in a Biology exam. In which exam did she do best?

26 What fraction of a 24 hour day is

a 3 hour   **b** 5 hours   **c** 6 hours   **d** 9 hours
e 10 hours   **f** 12 hours   **g** 14 hours   **h** 20 hours
i 9 and a half hours   **j** 8 and a quarter hours

27 What fraction of £1 is

a 25p   **b** 50p   **c** 95p   **d** 75p   **e** 84p   **f** 8p?

28 Calculate the following.

a $\dfrac{3}{5}$ of 250   **b** $\dfrac{1}{2}$ of 70   **c** $\dfrac{3}{4}$ of 144   **d** $\dfrac{3}{7}$ of 21

e $\dfrac{4}{5}$ of 250   **f** $\dfrac{2}{3}$ of 48   **g** $\dfrac{3}{8}$ of 96   **h** $\dfrac{7}{9}$ of 108

29 Write each of the following percentages as a fraction in its simplest form.

a 25%   **b** 50%   **c** 56%   **d** 94%   **e** 32%

30 Write each fraction as a percentage.

a $\dfrac{1}{2}$ **b** $\dfrac{3}{4}$ **c** $\dfrac{3}{10}$ **d** $\dfrac{17}{20}$ **e** $\dfrac{18}{25}$

31 Calculate the following.

a 25% of 144   **b** 60% of 230   **c** 68% of 325
d 90% of 600   **e** 72% of 72   **f** 99% of 10 000
g 40% of £49.60

32 Increase

a 300 by 20%   **b** £80 by 15%   **c** £297 by 15%
d £25 000 by 5%   **e** £18 493 by 8%.

33 Decrease

a 380 by 20%   **b** £95 by 15%   **c** £310 by 20%
d £39 000 by 5%   **e** £47 000 by 8%.

34 Write

a 16 as a percentage of 25
b 51 as a percentage of 85
c £12.25 as a percentage of £50
d 36 as a percentage of 120
e £5.25 as a percentage of £75
f 60p as a percentage of 64p
g £11.30 as a percentage of £25
h 15 minutes as a percentage of 1 hour
i 18p as a percentage of 45p
j 21 grams as a percentage of 35 grams.

35 Copy and complete this table.

FRACTION	PERCENTAGE	DECIMAL
$\frac{1}{2}$	50%	0.5
		0.25
	75%	
$\frac{1}{5}$		
		0.1
	15%	
$\frac{3}{5}$		
		0.52
	4%	
$\frac{1}{20}$		

36 Simplify each of the following ratios.

a 4 : 10   **b** 12 : 18   **c** 6 : 36   **d** 15 : 21   **e** 20 : 35
f 144 : 64   **g** 45 : 90   **h** 44 : 84   **i** 0.1 : 1   **j** 33 : 187

37 Divide 40 kg in the ratios

a 1 : 3   **b** 4 : 1   **c** 5 : 3   **d** 7 : 1   **e** 7 : 3.

38 Divide £120 in the ratios

a 3 : 1   **b** 2 : 3   **c** 1 : 4   **d** 15 : 9   **e** 5 : 2 : 1.

39 Copy and complete the following.

$8 + 15 =$ $8 + -15 =$ $7 + 12 =$ $7 + -12 =$
$-8 + 15 =$ $-8 + -15 =$ $-7 + 12 =$ $-7 + -12 =$
$8 - 15 =$ $8 - -15 =$ $7 - 12 =$ $7 - -12 =$
$-8 - 15 =$ $-8 - -15 =$ $-7 - 12 =$ $-7 - -12 =$

40 Copy and complete the following.

$2 \times 5 =$ $2 \div 5 =$ $2.5 \times 10 =$ $2.5 \div 10 =$
$-2 \times 5 =$ $-2 \div 5 =$ $-2.5 \times 10 =$ $-2.5 \div 10 =$
$2 \times -5 =$ $2 \div -5 =$ $2.5 \times -10 =$ $2.5 \div -10 =$
$2 \times -5 =$ $-2 \div -5 =$ $-2.5 \times -10 =$ $-2.5 \div -10 =$

41 Find the value of

a 4^6 **b** 2^5 **c** 10^5 **d** 10^4 **e** 10^{-1} **f** 2^{-7}
g 3^{-2} **h** 10^{-4} **i** 10^1 **j** 12^0 **k** 8^{-2} **l** 1^{-1}

42 Write each of the following calculations as a single power of the number.

a $2^4 \times 2^3$ **b** $3^7 \times 3^2$ **c** $4^5 \times 4^0$ **d** $2^{-9} \times 2^7$
e $10^5 \times 10^4$ **f** $10^8 \times 10^0$ **g** $5^2 \times 5^{-2}$ **h** $10^3 \times 10^{-3}$
k $2^{15} \times 2^{-12}$ **l** $10^8 \times 10^{-7}$

43 Write in the standard form.

a 3000   **b** 45 000   **c** 346   **d** 367.9   **e** 23 400 000 000

44 Write as a normal number.

a 3.1×10^6 **b** 5.67×10^4 **c** 1.91×10^8 **d** 5.067×10^{10}

45 Write in the standard form.

a 0.000 03   **b** 0.017   **c** 0.000 001   **d** 0.000 053
e 0.009 009

46 Write as a normal number.

a 3.1×10^{-6} **b** 5.67×10^{-4} **c** 1.91×10^{-8}
d 5.067×10^{-10}

47 Calculate the following.

a $50 \times (1.38 \times 10^{-4})$
b $700 \times (9.03 \times 10^{-6})$
c $(3.8 \times 10^{-3}) \times (1.5 \times 10^8)$
d $(5.76 \times 10^{-7}) \times (8.93 \times 10^{-3})$
e $(7.04 \times 10^{-3}) \div (1.21 \times 10^8)$
f $(1.5 \times 10^{-7}) \div (8.7 \times 10^{-3})$

48

$$A = \begin{pmatrix} 3 & 2 \\ 0 & 7 \end{pmatrix} \qquad B = \begin{pmatrix} 13 & 0 \\ 5 & 7 \end{pmatrix}$$

Calculate the following.

a $A + B$ **b** $A - B$ **c** $3A$ **d** $5B$ **e** $3A + 5B$

49

$$P = \begin{pmatrix} 3 & 4 & 5 \\ 3 & -1 & -2 \\ 6 & 3 & 1 \end{pmatrix} \quad Q = \begin{pmatrix} 8 & 9 & 1 \\ 1 & -2 & 2 \\ -4 & 0 & -1 \end{pmatrix} \quad R = \begin{pmatrix} -3 & 0 & -4 \\ 0 & 3 & 4 \\ 6 & 8 & 7 \end{pmatrix}$$

Calculate the following.

a $P + Q$ **b** $R - Q$ **c** $5R$ **d** $6P$
e $8P$ **f** $2P + 3Q$ **g** $P + 2Q + 3R$ **h** $5R - 2P$

50

$$A = \begin{pmatrix} 2 & 5 \\ 3 & 2 \end{pmatrix} \quad B = \begin{pmatrix} 3 & 0 \\ 0 & 2 \end{pmatrix} \quad C = \begin{pmatrix} 4 & 2 \\ 1 & 7 \end{pmatrix} \quad D = \begin{pmatrix} 2 & 2 \\ 7 & 1 \end{pmatrix}$$

Calculate the following.

a AB **b** BA **c** AC **d** CA **e** AD **f** DA
g BC **h** CB **i** BD **j** DB **k** CD **l** DC

51

$$A = \begin{pmatrix} -3 & 2 \\ 0 & -4 \end{pmatrix} B = \begin{pmatrix} -5 & 4 \\ 0 & -1 \end{pmatrix} C = \begin{pmatrix} -3 & 2 \\ 0 & 1 \end{pmatrix} D = \begin{pmatrix} -1 & 0 \\ 1 & 5 \end{pmatrix}$$

Calculate the following

a AB **b** BA **c** AC **d** CA **e** AD **f** DA
g BC **h** CB **i** BD **j** DB **k** CD **l** DC

52

$$A = \begin{pmatrix} 4 & -3 & 0 \\ 0 & 2 & 5 \end{pmatrix} \quad W = \begin{pmatrix} -1 & 0 \\ 0 & -1 \end{pmatrix} \quad X = \begin{pmatrix} 0 & 1 \\ 1 & 0 \end{pmatrix}$$

$$Y = \begin{pmatrix} 0 & 1 \\ -1 & 0 \end{pmatrix} \quad Z = \begin{pmatrix} 1 & 0 \\ 0 & 1 \end{pmatrix}$$

Calculate the following.

a WA **b** XA **c** YA **d** ZA **e** AZ
f WX **g** YZ **h** ZY

Practice and revision exercise (area and volume)

1 Use isometric paper to copy this diagram. On your copy write the names of each basic solid which has been used to build up the diagram.

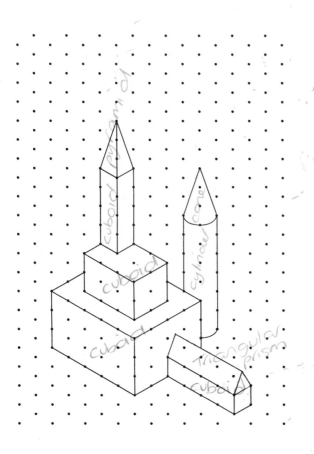

2 Find the perimeter and area of a rectangle with a height of 5 cm and a base of 6.5 cm.

3 Find the perimeter and area of this shape.

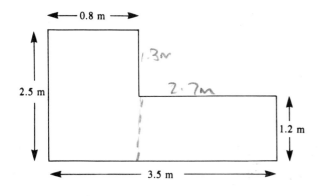

4 By making measurements correct to the nearest tenth of a centimetre, find the perimeter and area of this shape.

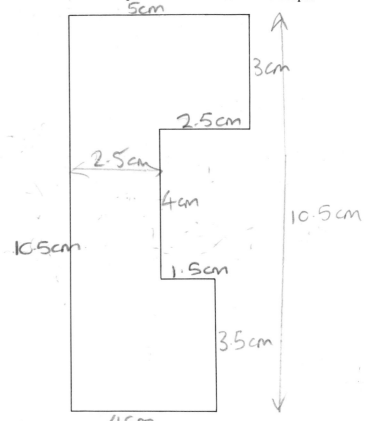

5 Find the area of a parallelogram with a height of 5.3 cm and a base of 7.55 cm.

6 Find the perimeter and area of this shape.

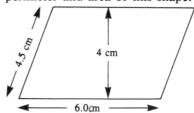

7 By making measurements correct to the nearest tenth of a centimetre, find the perimeter and area of this shape.

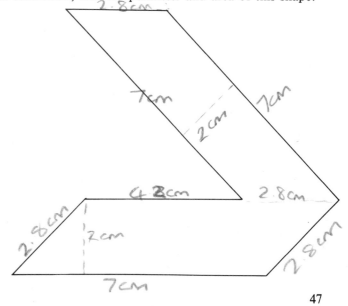

47

8 Find the area of a triangle with a height of 8 m and a base of 7.5 m.

9 Find the perimeter and area of this shape.

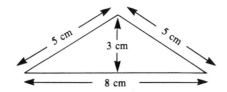

10 By making measurements correct to the nearest tenth of a centimetre, find the perimeter and area of this shape.

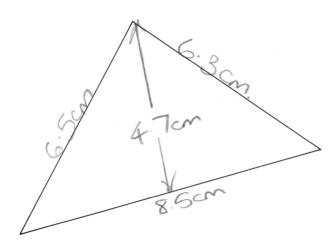

11 Find the area of a trapezium with a height of 5.3 cm, and parallel sides of 7.5 cm and 8.0 cm.

12 By making measurements correct to the nearest tenth of a centimetre, find the perimeter and area of this shape.

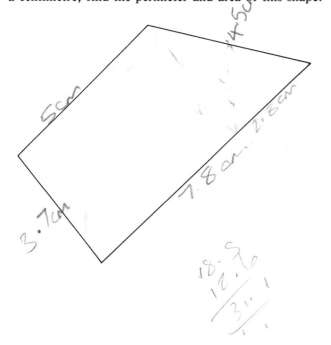

13 Find the area and circumference of a circle with a radius of 5.3 cm ($\pi = 3.1$).

14 Find the area and circumference of a circle with a diameter of 4.25 m ($\pi = 3.14$).

15 Find the radius and circumference of a circle with an area of 507 mm² ($\pi = 3$).

16 Find the diameter and area of a circle with a circumference of 37.68 cm ($\pi = 3.14$).

17 Find the total perimeter and area of a sector with an angle of 80° cut from a circle of radius 1.25 m ($\pi = 3.14$).

18 Find the perimeter and area of this shape ($\pi = 3.14$).

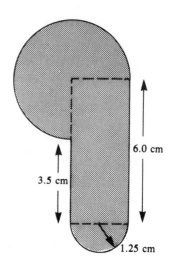

19 Find the volumes and surface areas of each of these prisms ($\pi = 3.14$).

a

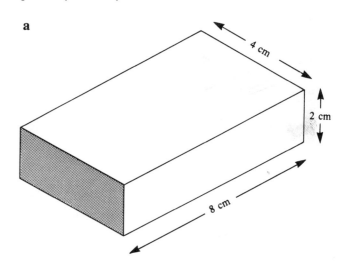

b

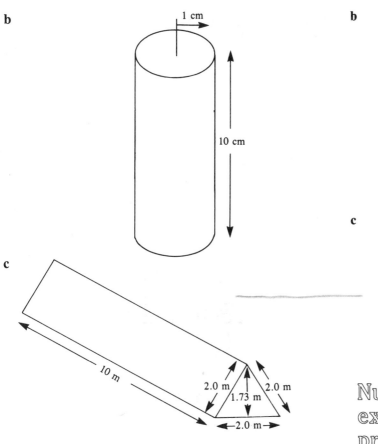

1 cm

10 cm

c

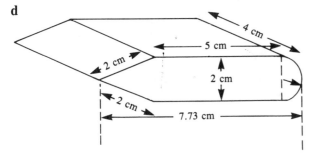

10 m

2.0 m   2.0 m

1.73 m

2.0 m

d

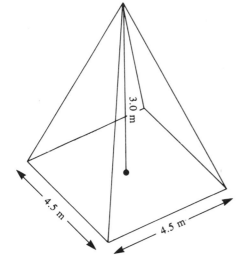

4 cm

5 cm

2 cm

2 cm

2 cm

2 cm

7.73 cm

20 Find the volume of each of the following solids ($\pi = 3.14$).

a

3.0 m

4.5 m   4.5 m

b

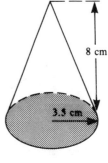

8 cm

3.5 cm

c

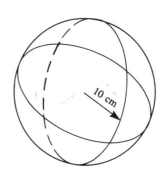

10 cm

Numbers and measures – extended problems for project work

1 This diagram shows a disco light.

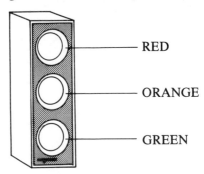

RED

ORANGE

GREEN

- The red light flashes every 4 seconds.
- The orange light flashes every 5 seconds.
- The green light flashes every 6 seconds.
- The lights have just all flashed together.

How long will it be before

a the red and orange lights flash together?

b the orange and green lights flash together?

c all the lights flash together?

The lights will repeat a fixed pattern of flashes. What is this pattern and how many times will it be repeated during a three hour disco?

Design your own set of lights and predict the pattern it will produce.

2 Each number has a fixed number of factors. For example, the number 8 has 4 factors (1, 2, 4 and 8) and the number 9 has 3 factors (1, 3 and 9).

a If you double the number 9, you produce the number 18 which has 6 factors (1, 2, 3, 6, 9 and 18). So, doubling the number has also doubled the number of factors. Find some other numbers for which this also works. Can you establish a rule?

b If you multiply the number 8 by 3, you produce the number 24 which has 8 factors (1, 2, 3, 4, 6, 8, 12 and 24). So, multiplying the number by 3 has doubled the number of factors. Find some other numbers for which this also works. Can you establish a rule?

c If you know the prime factors of a number, how can you use them to predict all the other factors of the number?

d How can your answer to part **c** be used to explain your answers to parts **a** and **b**?

3 A circle is drawn with 8 points marked around the circumference.

Starting on one point, a line is drawn to the point 3 further round the circle in the clockwise direction. From this point a line is drawn to the next point 3 further round the circle in the clockwise direction. This is continued until all the points on the circle have been connected.

a The start of the diagram is shown below. Copy and complete it.

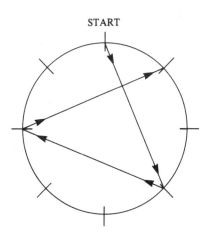

START

b Draw a second diagram to show what happens if you connect each new point to the point 2 further round the circle. Explain why, in this case, every point will not be connected.

c Investigate other possibilities for this circle with 8 points. Can you establish a rule which will predict if every point will be connected?

d Investigate other circles with different numbers of points marked around the circumference.

e Can you establish any general rules for a circle with any number of points marked around the circumference?

4 One way to see if a large number is prime is to test-divide it by all smaller numbers. For example, if we wanted to know if 211 is a prime number we could test-divide like this.

$$211 \div 2 = 105 \text{ remainder } 1$$

$$211 \div 3 = 70 \text{ remainder } 1$$

$$211 \div 4 = 52 \text{ remainder } 3$$

_____

_____

Eventually we will either find a number that divides exactly into 211 or, when we reach $211 \div 211$, decide that it definitely is a prime number.

a This is of course an incredibly tedious method! Find the simplest and quickest method you can to replace this long-winded test. Explain why your method works.

b If you have access to a microcomputer, write a program to test for prime numbers.

5 This is a problem which is at least 500 years old. An old woman is selling eggs. When asked how many eggs she has, she replies, 'Taken in groups of 11, 5 eggs are left over, but taken in groups of 23, 3 are left over.' What is the least number of eggs the old lady has for sale?

a Solve the problem. Why is the word **least** used?

b Solve this variation of the problem.

A man is selling onions. When asked how many onions he has for sale he replies, 'Taken in groups of 2, 3, 4, 5, 6 and 7 there are 1, 2, 3, 4, 5 and no onions left over.' What is the least number of onions the old man has for sale?

c Make up some simple examples of this type of puzzle. Can you discover some which have no solution? Is it possible to predict whether a problem will have a solution?

6 Obtain the final league table for the last football season and investigate the change that took place some years ago, from 2 points for a win, 1 for a draw and 0 for a loss; to 3 points for a win, 1 for a draw and 0 for a loss. If last season's matches had been played under the old points system, what effect would this have had on league positions, championships and relegations?

7 A **Farey lattice** is a graph which is used to show fractions. It has one axis for the numerator (top number) and one axis for the denominator (bottom number). Fractions are shown as points on the graph.

This is a Farey lattice with the fractions $\frac{1}{2}$, $\frac{2}{3}$ and $\frac{3}{5}$ on it.

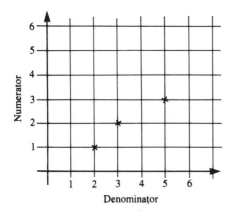

a Draw a Farey lattice with numbers up to 12 on both the axes. Mark on the fractions 2/3, 4/6, 6/9 and 8/12. What do you notice?

b Add to your lattice the fractions 1/2, 2/4, 3/6 and 4/8. What do you notice?

c Can you make up a rule about sets of **equivalent** fractions plotted on a Farey lattice? Add at least two more sets of fractions to your lattice to show that your rule works.

d Arrange the following fractions into order of size, starting with the smallest: 3/8, 5/6, 9/10, 1/2, 1/5, 4/7 and 1/8.

e The point (0,0) on a graph is called the **origin**. Draw a Farey lattice and plot each of the fractions from part **d**. Join each point to the origin with a straight line. What do you notice?

f Explain how a Farey lattice can be used to sort fractions into size. Demonstrate your answer by drawing a lattice and sorting these fractions, 3/4, 1/12, 1/2, 3/5, 1/9, 2/11, 9/10, 2/3, 1/4, 3/7, 3/8 and 1/3.

g The **Farey sequence** of fractions of order four is the set of all simplified fractions with denominators of **4 or less**. The fractions should be arranged in order of size, so the Farey sequence of order four is 1/4, 1/3, 1/2, 2/3 and 3/4.
Find the Farey sequences of order 5, 6 and 7.

8 Paper comes in various standard sizes, like A0, A1, A2, A3 and A4. These sizes decrease as the 'A' number increases, so an A3 sheet is smaller than an A2 sheet.

a Obtain sheets of A3, A4 and A5 paper. Measure their heights and widths, correct to the nearest millimetre, and calculate their areas. What do you notice?

b Can you predict the measurements of all paper sizes from A0 to A6? Organise your predictions into a table showing the length and width of each paper size. Obtain as many different sizes as you can to check your predictions.

c If you had one sheet of each size of paper from A0 to A6, how could they be fitted together without overlapping? Draw a diagram to illustrate your answer.

d What would happen if you had one sheet of each size piled on top of one another, so that one bottom corner of each size was aligned? Draw a diagram to illustrate your answer.

e What is the relationship between the height and the width of any 'A' size paper?

9 a If a gardener has 36 metres of fencing, she can form many different rectangular enclosures. For example, she could form a 6 metre by 12 metre enclosure or an 8 metre by 10 metre enclosure.

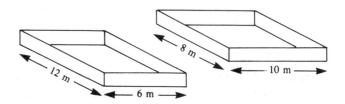

Investigate the areas of some of the different rectangular enclosures that can be formed. What is the length and width of the rectangle which encloses the maximum area?

b This sheet of card is to be made into an open topped box by removing four corner sections, folding and glueing. What is the maximum volume that the box can have? What size corners must be cut out to give this maximum volume?

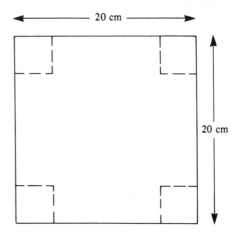

c This sheet of paper is to be made into a hollow triangular prism with open ends by folding and glueing. What is the maximum volume that the triangular prism can have? Where must the paper be folded to give this maximum volume?

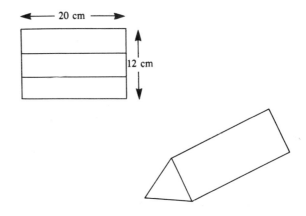

d This circle of card is to be made into a cone by cutting out a sector, folding and glueing. What is the maximum volume that the cone can have? What is the angle of the sector cut out to give this maximum volume?

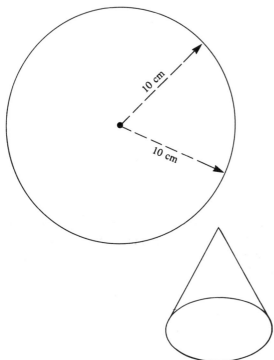

10 cm

10 cm

Numbers and measures
Past paper questions

Numbers

1 The following are the first six numbers in a pattern:

$$13 \quad 21 \quad 34 \quad 55 \quad 89 \quad 144$$

a Which of these numbers are

(i) even,
(ii) square,
(iii) prime?

b The difference between the first and second numbers is $21 - 13 = 8$. Write down the difference between

(i) the fourth and fifth numbers,
(ii) the fifth and sixth numbers.

c (i) Write down the seventh number of the pattern.
(ii) Explain how you arrived at this answer.

d Write as decimals, showing every figure on your calculator display,

(i) $\dfrac{89}{55}$ (ii) $\dfrac{144}{89}$

What do you notice about these two answers? (SEG)

52

2 What is the next number in each of the following sequences? Give reasons for your answers.

a   1, 1, 2, 3, 5, . . .

b   64, 49, 36, 25, . . .   (SEG)

3 a Express as a product of its prime factors

(i) 126
(ii) 420

b Find the smallest number of which 126 and 420 are factors. (SEG)

4 a Write down all the positive whole numbers which divide exactly into 24. (These are called the factors of 24.)

b Write down all the factors of 60.

c Write down the highest common factor of 24 and 60. (SEG)

5   8   9   10   11   12

a Which of the five numbers is a square number?

b Which of the five numbers is a factor of 27?

c Which of the five numbers is a multiple of six?

d Which of the five numbers is a prime number? (LEAG)

6   8, 12, 15, 16, 18, 19, 20, 21, 24, 32

From the ten numbers listed above select

a a prime number,

b a perfect square,

c a multiple of 7,

d the square root of 64,

e a factor of 30,

f the next term in the sequence 3, 4, 6, 9, 13, ...(MEG)

7   6, 8, 37, 289, 444, 464

From the list of numbers above, write down

a a prime number,

b a square number,

c a number which is a multiple of two other numbers in the list. (MEG)

8 The table shows all the factors of the numbers from 1 to 9.

Number	Factors
1	1
2	1,2
3	1,3
4	1,2,4
5	1,5
6	1,2,3,6
7	1,7
8	1,2,4,8
9	1,3,9

a What is the next number to have exactly two factors?
b What name do we give to all those numbers with exactly two factors?
c Find the next number after 9 with exactly three factors (this will be the third such number).
d The fourth number with exactly three factors is 49. Find the fifth such number. (NEA)

9 6, 12, 15, 18, 25, 30, 35
From the list of numbers

a write down the smallest odd number,
b write down the number that has an exact square root,
c find the sum of the even numbers. (LEAG)

10 0 1 2 3 4 5 6 7 8 9
10 11 12 13 14 15 16 17 18 19
20 21 22 23 24 25 26 27 28 29
30 31 32 33 34 35 36 37 38 39
40 41 42 43 . . . . . .

Look at this number pattern.

2
12 13

This is called the **12L** because 12 is the middle number.

To find the value of **12L** you multiply the end numbers and add the middle number, as follows:

$$(2 \times 13) + 12$$

Therefore the value of **12L** is 38.

a What is the value of **27L**?

b
?
x ?

(i) Write the numbers missing from this **L** in terms of x.
(ii) Find the value of this **L** in terms of x.

c Which **L** has a value of 998? (WJEC)

11 a Work out $5^2 + 12^2$.
b Work out $(5 + 12)^2$. (MEG)

12

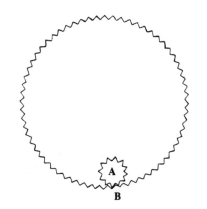

A small circular wheel has teeth on the outside of its circumference. These teeth match the teeth on the inside of a larger wheel as the smaller wheel rotates around inside the fixed larger one.

At the start, the point marked **A** on the smaller wheel is alongside the point marked **B** on the larger wheel. The small wheel is now rotated around the inside of the larger wheel.

a If there are 12 teeth on the small wheel and 108 teeth on the large one, how many times will the point **A** on the small wheel come round to touch the circumference of the large one by the time it has returned to the start position?

b Write down a different number of teeth for the small and large wheels so that question (a) would still have the same answer as before.

c Write down what you think is the rule connecting the number of teeth on the small and large wheels for this to happen. (WJEC)

13 A gardener buys roses and decides to plant them one metre apart in triangles.

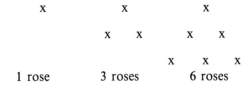

1 rose   3 roses   6 roses

a Draw a picture of the similar pattern using 10 roses.

b How many roses would he need if the triangle had 5 roses along each side?

He decides to form the triangular pattern using 15 roses.

c How long is each side of his triangle?
d Draw an accurate scale diagram of this pattern. (Use 1 cm to represent 1 metre.)

His son, who is keen on patterns, counts the number of equilateral triangles that can be drawn.

Five roses on each side—1 arrangement

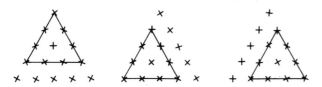

Four roses on each side—3 arrangements

He continues by counting triangles with 3 roses on each side.

e How many equilateral triangles can be drawn with 3 roses on each side? (SEG)

Decimals, fractions and percentages

1

CASH PRICE £275
or Hire Purchase 20% deposit of cash price followed by 24 equal monthly instalments of £13
or £7.50 per month rental.

22 inch colour T.V.
Full guarantee on parts and labour for 4 years.

a How much deposit is required for the Hire Purchase agreement?
b What is the total cost of buying the television on Hire Purchase?
c How much is required for 6 months rental?
d What is the total cost of renting the television for 4 complete years? (SEG)

2 Use your calculator to convert $\frac{5}{8}$ to a decimal fraction.

3 Messrs RENTHEM TV and Video Rental Company advertises the following rates for renting TV and video:

20″ TV   £10.51 per month
Video   £14.72 per month.

a Mr Shafi rents a 20″ TV. How much rental does he pay in twelve months?
b Mrs Ali also rents a 20″ TV. Because she pays 12 months in advance the firm charges her £114 for the year. How much does Mrs Ali save each year by paying in advance?
c Mr Brown rents a 20″ TV and a video and the firm has a special offer of £25 per month to rent them both. How much does Mr Brown save each month on this special offer?
d RENTHEM'S also offer the 20″ TV for sale at a cash price of £280 plus VAT. If VAT is charged at 15% calculate the total cash price. (SEG)

4 a Use your calculator to find the value of

$$\frac{730 \times 8.45 \times 7}{83 \times 9}$$

and write down the full calculator display.
b Express your answer correct to one place of decimals. (NEA)

5 a A girl earns £1.56 an hour as a part-time waitress. If she works for 5 hours, how much does she earn?
b A boy works in a shop on one day from 9.30 a.m. to 12.30 p.m. and from 1.15 p.m. to 4.45 p.m. He is paid £9.62.
  (i) How long does he work?
  (ii) How much is he paid per hour? (MEG)

6 In a factory, 214 of the workers all earn the same weekly wage. If their total weekly wage bill is £31 532.90, how much does each worker earn? (MEG)

7 John, Mary and Majid charge for baby-sitting. Their charges are given in the table.

For each hour (or part of an hour) before midnight	For each hour (or part of an hour) after midnight
£0.75	£1.05

Work out the amount earned when
a John sat for 3 hours before midnight.
b Mary sat from 9 o'clock at night until 1 o'clock the following morning.
c Majid sat from 18.00 to 21.20. (LEAG)

8 Packing cases weigh 28 kg each. 25 of the cases are loaded onto a lift. The weight limit for the lift is 750 kg. How much short of the limit is the load on the lift? (LEAG)

9

```
┌─────────────────────────────────────────────┐
│              FLOWER'S GARAGE                  │
│   Phone Carmouth 2345        Main Rd.         │
│                              Carmouth         │
│                                      £        │
│                                               │
│ Parts   4 spark plugs at 79p each   (a)......... │
│         (b)........brake pads at £4.52 each  9.04 │
│         4 tyres at (c).........each    98.00  │
│         1 only exhaust system          41.30  │
│         Total cost of parts         (d)........ │
│                                               │
│ Labour 4½ hours at £11.00 per hour  (e)........ │
│         Total cost of parts and labour (f)..... │
│ VAT at 15%                             30.15  │
│         TOTAL TO PAY                (g)........ │
└─────────────────────────────────────────────┘
```

A customer received a bill from Flower's Garage.

Some of the figures could not be read.

Fill in the spaces marked (a) to (g) with the correct figures.

(LEAG)

10

Write the price reduction as a fraction.   (LEAG)

11 The picture shows a 5 litre can of oil. 1 litre is about 1¾ pints.

a Write 1¾ as a decimal.

b Find the number of pints of oil in the 5 litre can.

(MEG)

12 ⅞ of an iceberg is under water.

a What is this as a decimal?

b What percentage of an iceberg can be seen?

(MEG)

13 A school has 840 pupils. $\frac{3}{10}$ of them live less than 1 mile from school.

45% of them live between 1 mile and 3 miles from school. The rest live more than 3 miles from school.

a How many pupils live less than 1 mile from school?

b What percentage of the pupils live more than 3 miles from school?

(LEAG)

14 In a sequence of fractions, the next term after

$\frac{x}{y}$ is $\frac{x+y}{2x+y}$. The first term is $\frac{2}{3}$.

a Write down the first six terms of the sequence $\frac{2}{3}, \frac{5}{7}, \ldots$

b Find the **squares** of the values of these six terms to as many decimal places as your calculator will give. What do you notice about these squares of values?

c Find the term in the sequence which comes immediately before

$$\frac{2378}{3363}$$

d One term in the sequence is $\frac{p}{q}$. Find, in terms of p and q, the term which comes immediately before $\frac{p}{q}$.

(MEG)

15 Copy and complete the following weekly wage slip.

Name: M. J. Thomas	Date:6/5/88
Wages	£
40 hours at £4.60 per hour	....
Overtime	
6 hours at £6.90 per hour	....
Total Wage (gross)	....

Deductions	
National Insurance	16.56
Superannuation	11.04
Income Tax	48.76
Total Deductions	....
Wage (net amount)	
Take-home pay	....

(WJEC)

16

The sweets in a box are classed as creams, caramels or toffees. In a box of Keely's Choice, ⅜ of the contents are creams, ¼ of them are caramels and the remainder are toffees.

a Work out the fraction of the sweets in the box that are either creams or caramels.
b What fraction of the sweets in the box are toffees?
c There are 24 sweets in the box. Work out the number of caramels in the box.

(LEAG)

17 Jane is going on holiday to France and needs to buy some films for her camera. If she buys them in England before she goes, they will cost her £2.25 each. If she waits until she gets to France and buys them there, they will cost her 20.16 francs each.

If the exchange rate is £1 to 9.60 francs, find out how much, in English currency, she can save on each film by buying them in France. (MEG)

18

A saline drip in a hospital releases 0.1 ml every 3 seconds. How long does it take to empty a 500 ml bag?

(WJEC)

19 The readings on Mr. Power's electricity meter were as follows.

Beginning of first quarter	End of first quarter (beginning of second)
0 2 3 4 7	0 2 8 2 6

a How many units of electricity did Mr Power use during the first quarter?

b Mr Power uses 435 units of electricity during the second quarter. What is the reading on Mr Power's meter at the end of the second quarter?

c Complete Mr Power's electricity bill for the second quarter.

	£
435 units at 5.2p per unit	....
Quarterly standing charge	8.15
Total	_____

(WJEC)

20 Margaret and David want to find out how much petrol their car uses in miles per gallon. They fill the car with petrol when the reading on the milometer is

| 0 | 2 | 8 | 3 | 4 | 0 |

After a few days they stop at a garage selling petrol at £1.70 per gallon. They fill the car up again and the cost of the petrol is £13.60.

By this time the milometer reading is

| 0 | 2 | 8 | 6 | 2 | 0 |

How many miles per gallon does the car do over this period?

(WJEC)

21 Taking 8 kilometres per hour to be 5 miles per hour, find

a the speed in kilometres per hour equivalent to the British speed limit of 30 miles per hour,

b the speed in miles per hour equivalent to the French speed limit of 60 kilometres per hour.

(MEG)

22

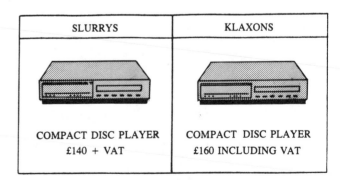

SLURRYS	KLAXONS
COMPACT DISC PLAYER £140 + VAT	COMPACT DISC PLAYER £160 INCLUDING VAT

VAT is 15%

Slurrys and Klaxons are selling the same model of compact disc player. Slurry's price is £140 plus 15% VAT. Klaxon's price is £160 (including VAT).

a What is Slurry's total price (including VAT)?

At sale time Klaxons cut their prices by 15%.

b What is Klaxons' sale price?

After the sale the prices return to normal. Slurrys offer special credit arrangements on their disc players.

SLURRYS SPECIAL OFFER

NO DEPOSIT

£4 per week for 52 weeks

---

c How much would you pay altogether under Slurrys' offer?

A compact disc player measures 25 cm by 30 cm by 10 cm. Each one is packed in a cardboard box which allows 5 cm space all round the disc player for internal packaging.

d What are the dimensions of the cardboard box?

(SEG)

23 A machine always works at the same rate. It produces 150 rods in 5 minutes. How long will it take to produce 375 rods?

(SEG)

24 'Alpha Cars' offers a Sierra for hire at £15 a day plus 5p per kilometre. How much would it cost Mr Jones to hire the Sierra for a day and drive 240 kilometres?

(SEG)

25 Zenka wants to buy her father a packet of electric drill bits for his birthday.

In the first packet that she looks at, there are four different drills and their sizes are marked in inches.

 The sizes are ⅜, ¼, ½ and ⅛.

a Which is the larger size drill bit, ⅜ or ¼?
b Write the four sizes in order, starting with the smallest.

(NEA)

26 Peter earns £5 per week by working on Saturday mornings. He saves 60% of his wage.

a How much does he save each week?
b Given that he spends ¼ of the rest on a weekly magazine, how much does this magazine cost him?

(SEG)

27 Bill Jones's salary was £950 per month. His boss gave him a salary increase of 8%.

a Calculate 8% of £950.
b What was his new salary per month?

(SEG)

28 Use your calculator to complete the following calculations:

a $\dfrac{7.2 \times 2.9}{14.4} = \dfrac{}{14.4} = \ldots\ldots\ldots\ldots$

b $(8.1)^2 \div 24 = \ldots\ldots\ldots \div 24 = \ldots\ldots\ldots$

(SEG)

29 In 1987 the rate of exchange was 2.95 German Marks to £1 sterling.

a A tourist changes £25 into Marks. How many Marks would she receive?
b She pays 42 Marks for a gift to bring home. What is the cost of the gift in pounds and pence to the nearest penny?

(SEG)

30 Joan divides her pocket money into three parts. She spends one third of it on makeup. She spends three-fifths of it on magazines. The rest is saved.

a What fraction of her pocket money is saved?
b If she saves 6p each week, how much pocket money does she receive?

(SEG)

31 a Use your calculator to write as decimals

  (i) $\dfrac{1}{10}$,

  (ii) $\sqrt{2}$,
  (iii) π .

The following is a list of numbers, written in order of size:

$$\frac{1}{10} \, , \, \sqrt{2}, \, 2, \, \sqrt{9}, \, \pi \, , \, 4.25.$$

b Write down
  (i) all the natural numbers,
  (ii) all the irrational numbers in this list.

(SEG)

32 Mr. Ng's telephone bill consists of two parts: a standing charge of £15 and 5p per unit used. Calculate

a the total bill if 125 units are used,
b the number of units used if the total bill is £25.00.

(SEG)

33 In an election, the votes cast for the candidates of the various parties were as follows:

SMP Alliance Party	11 997
Calculator Freedom Party	5 126
Euclid Revival Party	2 567
Others	320

a Write down to the nearest thousand
  (i) the number of votes cast for the winning candidate,
  (ii) the total number of votes cast in the election.
b (i) Use your answers to write down the fraction

$$\frac{\text{number of votes cast for the winning candidate}}{\text{total number of votes cast}}$$

(ii) Use this fraction to estimate the percentage share of the votes obtained by the winning candidate.
(MEG)

34 A video-recorder sells in the shop for £414. This price is obtained by increasing the net value by 15% to account for Value Added Tax. Calculate its net value.
(MEG)

35 The basic price of a camera is £35. VAT is added at the rate of 15%. Calculate the amount to be paid for the camera. (MEG)

36 a In June 1980 the retail price index was 265.7. In June 1981 it was 295.8. The rate of inflation is the percentage increase in the retail price index over the previous year. Calculate the rate of inflation in June 1981.
b A garage offers second-hand cars for sale at a price which gives them a 40% profit on the amount they paid.
  (i) The garage pays £1575 for a mini. At what price will it be offered for sale?
  (ii) A family car is offered for sale at £4130. What did the garage pay for it?
c The 15.36 train from Exeter arrives in London at 18.08. The distance from Exeter to London is 173¾ miles.
Calculate the average speed of the train in miles per hour correct to three significant figures.
(MEG)

37 Mr. and Mrs. Williams invest £1000 in an investment account which pays 10.5% per annum interest.

a How much interest do they get in a year?
b They have to pay tax on this interest at the rate of 27p in the £1. How much tax do they pay? How much of the interest is left after paying tax?
c What percentage is this 'after tax' interest of their £1000 investment?
(WJEC)

38 A trade union negotiates the following rise in wages on behalf of its members:

5% of weekly wage or £6 per week, whichever is greater.

One employee finds that, for him, there is no difference between a rise of 5% and a rise of £6 per week. Calculate this employee's weekly wage before the rise.
(NEA)

SALE
35 mm Camera
was £39.95
Now £31.96

a Calculate the reduction in the price of the camera.
b What is this reduction as a percentage of the normal price? (NEA)

40 At the beginning of 1987 a house was valued at £49 500. During 1987 the prices of houses in the area went up by 13%. What was the house worth at the end of 1987?
(NEA)

41 An advertisement contains the following statement.
'The 32nd Issue offers a guaranteed return of 52% after five years. This is equivalent to 8.75% a year over the five years.'

a Investigate the truth of this statement by completing the following table to show the year by year growth of an initial investment of £100 at 8.75% a year.

	Amount at end of year
Year 1	
Year 2	
Year 3	
Year 4	
Year 5	

From this table, write down, correct to one place of decimals, the total percentage increase over the five years.
b Given that National Savings Certificates are bought in multiples of £25, find the minimum amount of money which would have to be invested initially in order to produce a total of at least £1000 at the end of the five years. (NEA)

42 Sarah Jones earns £720 per month.

a Calculate how much Sarah earns in a year.
b Her tax allowances for the year are £3400. Calculate her taxable income for the year.
c The rate of tax is 27% of her taxable income. Calculate the amount of income tax Sarah pays in a year.

(WJEC)

43 An advertisement for double-glazing reads:

'We guarantee 5 windows (opening out) and a front or back door in uPVC or Aluminium, supplied and fitted for only—
£1750.00 + VAT (at 15%)'.

Gwen buys five windows and a front door. What is the total amount Gwen has to pay?

(WJEC)

44 David wants to buy a television. He can buy a Beovision (the best set there is) for £345 with 12 months free credit or a basic Flan for £295.

SUPPOSE he pays £59 deposit on the Beovision and then 11 equal monthly instalments.

a How much is left to pay after the deposit?
b How much is each of the 11 instalments?

IF he wants to buy the Flan, he has to pay 20% deposit.
c What is 20% of £295?
d How much is left to pay?

Interest is charged on the balance at 16½%.
e How much is left to pay including the interest?

This has to be paid in 11 instalments.
f How much is each instalment?
g Which television would you advise David to buy, and why?

(MEG)

45 John has a full-time job and lives with his parents. He pays them one-fifth of his wages for housekeeping.

a How much does he pay his parents if he earns £80 a week?
b John receives a 7% pay rise.
  (i) How much extra will he earn each week?
  (ii) What is the total weekly amount that he will now pay to his parents?

(MEG)

46 Rachel is to buy a new stereo system, costing £240, on an interest free credit scheme.

a She must pay a 25% deposit. How much is this?
b How much is left to pay after she has paid the deposit?
c How much are her monthly payments, if she pays the remainder in six equal monthly payments?

(LEAG)

47 'Electric Kettle: Special Offer 15% off marked price.' The marked price is £27.95. How much would you pay, to the nearest penny, at the 'special offer' price?

(LEAG)

48 Of the total land area of Belgium, 1.4 million hectares is cultivated and six hundred thousand hectares is forest.

a Write both these numbers in figures.

b The total land area of Belgium is 3 million hectares. What area of land is neither cultivated nor forest?

(MEG)

49   PARKES TYRES

Tyres	Cost
145 × 12	£19.85 each
155 × 13	£16.50 each
185/60	£37.50 each

Work out the cost of four 155 × 13 tyres.

(LEAG)

50 In 1972 India had 100 251 000 houses and a population of 638 389 000. How many people were there to each house? Give your answer to the nearest whole number.

(MEG)

51 Three friends are using their calculators.

a Mari multiples two numbers. The answer is 3.6. Write down **two** numbers she could have multiplied together.
b John subtracts one number from another. The answer is 4.2. Write down **two** numbers he could have used.
c Lena divides £14.30 by 3. The answer appears as:

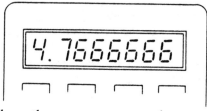

Write down the answer correct to the nearest penny.

(WJEC)

52 In 1985 Mr. Whettam's water bill for the whole year was £69.40. For this one payment his family could use as much water as they liked.

a How many pence per day, to the nearest penny, did this payment of £69.40 represent?

b During 1985 Mr. Whettam's family used 40 gallons of water each day. What was the cost of each gallon of water? Give your answer in pence, to two decimal places.

In 1986 Mr. Whettam's water bill was again £69.40, but the family used 25% more water each day than in 1985.

c (i) How much water each day did the family use in 1986?
  (ii) How much did each gallon of water cost in 1986?

In 1987 the water company put a water meter into Mr. Whettam's house. Then he had to pay 0.5 pence for each gallon of water used.

d (i) How much did he have to pay in 1987 if the family used 40 gallons of water each day?

(ii) How much water should the family use each day if the bill for the year is to be £69.40?

(SEG)

53 Because of bad weather, my journey from Norwich to Nottingham took 5½ hours instead of the usual 3½ hours.

a Calculate the percentage increase in my travel time, correct to one decimal place.

The distance from Norwich to Nottingham is about 135 miles.

b Calculate the approximate percentage decrease in my average speed.

(LEAG)

54 Supergrowth Unit Trust claims that the value of its units is likely to grow by 21% compound interest per annum. Assuming that this claim is true, calculate the value, after 5 years, of an investment of £1000 in Supergrowth Unit Trust.

(MEG)

55 Each member of Melchester Diners' Club has to pay an annual subscription of £45 and a fee of £5.50 at each meeting attended. The Club has 42 meetings each year.

a Find the total cost of a year's membership for a member who attends all 42 meetings.

b To retain membership, a member must attend at least 60% of the year's meetings. Find the minimum number of meetings that a member can attend in a year and still retain membership.

c Calculate to the nearest penny, the average cost per meeting for a member who attends 32 meetings in the year.

(MEG)

Ratio

1 A recipe for blackcurrant ice cream to serve 4 people is

400 g blackcurrants
160 g sugar
140 ml cream
90 ml water

Write down the amounts that you would require to make a similar ice cream to serve 6 people.

(MEG)

2

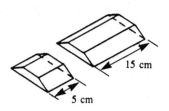

A 20 cm ruler is cut into two pieces 5 cm and 15 cm long. The piece 5 cm long weighs 3 grams. What is the weight of the 15 cm piece?

(SEG)

3

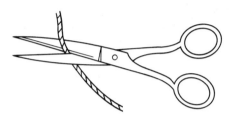

A piece of string is 36 cm long. John cuts it into two pieces, making one piece twice as long as the other. What are the lengths of the two pieces?

(SEG)

4 Don has 120 records. The ratio of the number of Don's records to the number of Phil's records is 3:5. How many records does Phil have?

(LEAG)

5 Select from the set 6, 9, 14, 18 to complete correctly each of the following:

a .... times three is ....

b .... is five more than ....

c The ratio of .... to .... is 3:2.

(MEG)

6 There are 180 pupils in the first year at Bronglais Comprehensive School. The ratio of the number of boys to the number of girls in the first year is 5:4. How many girls are in the first year?

(WJEC)

7 To make a shade of orange paint, a decorator mixes yellow and red paint in the ratio of 1 to 3.

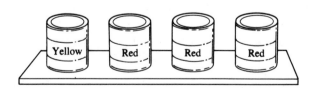

How many tins of yellow paint are needed to mix with 12 tins of red paint?

(MEG)

60

8 Jill has 40 pence and Dave has 60 pence. They agree to spend all the money on sweets and to share them in the same ratio as their money.

They buy 30 toffee-lumps. How many toffee-lumps should each have?

(LEAG)

9 Ms Woosnam is planning her GCSE Social Studies course. The marks for the course are divided in the ratio 3:2 between coursework and the written examination. She has 65 lessons to teach and decides to allocate them in the same ratio as the marks.

Find the number of lessons that she should devote to coursework and to preparing for the written examination.

(MEG)

10 A greengrocer sells oranges according to their size. Oranges of 4 cm radius are sold at 10 for £1; oranges of 5 cm radius are sold at 6 for £1.

a Calculate the ratio of the volumes of these two sizes of oranges.

b Assuming that all the oranges are of the same quality, state which purchase would give the better value, giving a reason for your decision.

(SEG)

11 A gang of workers is digging a trench. When there are six workers they manage to dig a trench 18 m long in one day. All the workers dig at the same rate.

a Work out the length of trench that one worker could dig in one day.

b A group of workers digs 12 m in one day. How many workers are there in the group?

(LEAG)

12 a In her will Mrs Hannah Pennypincher left half her money to the SMP, a third to the SDP, a tenth to the SNP, and the remainder to her husband, Simon Alan Pennypincher (SAP). What fraction of her money would he inherit?

b If she changed her will to share the money between the SMP and SAP only, in the ratio 4 to 1 respectively, what fraction would her husband now inherit?

(MEG)

13 A photocopier can print copies smaller or larger than the original. The ratio of lengths in the original to lengths in the copies must be one of the following:

    1:0.5   1:0.7   1:1   1:14   1:2

A firm has always used the ratio 1:1, but now wishes to reduce the area of paper used for each copy by about one half. Which ratio should the firm choose? Explain your answer.

(SEG)

14 George and his sister Mildred both collect coins. Just before Christmas, George had four times as many coins as Mildred had. For Christmas, Mildred was given a collection of 60 coins, but George did not receive any.

If Mildred had x coins before Christmas,

a how many coins did George have?

b how many coins did Mildred have after Christmas? After Christmas George and Mildred both had the same number of coins.

c Form an equation from your answers to **a** and **b** and solve it to find how many coins Mildred had before Christmas.

d Some time later Aunt Florence decided to give her collection of 125 coins to George and Mildred, dividing them between them in the ratio 2:3, with George getting the smaller number of coins. How many coins did Mildred receive from Aunt Florence?

(LEAG)

15 If the following ingredients are mixed together, there will be enough dough to make eight pizzas.

> # PIZZA RECIPE
> ### (MAKES EIGHT)
>
> 16 ounces of flour
>
> 4 ounces of butter
>
> 3 eggs
>
> ¼ pint of milk
>
> 1 ounce of yeast

a How much flour is needed to make one pizza?

b How much butter would be needed for six pizzas?

c Ahmed makes twelve pizzas to store in his freezer. What is the total weight in pounds and ounces of all the ingredients, excluding milk and eggs?
(16 ounces = 1 pound.)

(NEA)

Directed numbers

1 On Monday at 0600 the temperature was $-6°C$. At 0800 it was $-1°C$ and by 1000 it was 12 degrees higher than at 0600.

a By how much had the temperature risen at 0800?

b What was the temperature at 1000?

(SEG)

2 In Wiltshire during one day in February the lowest temperature recorded was $-7°C$ and the highest temperature was $8°C$. What was the temperature difference?

(SEG)

3 At 2 a.m., the temperature was $-10°C$ Celsius. At 5 a.m., the temperature was $-3°$ Celsius.

a At which time was the temperature higher?

b What is the difference between the two temperatures?

(MEG)

4 a At noon on a January day the temperature was $3°C$. By 6 p.m. it had fallen by $5°C$. What was the temperature at 6 p.m.?

b At midnight the temperature was $-7°C$. By how many degrees had the temperature fallen between noon and midnight?

(MEG)

5

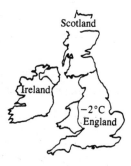

A freezer is switched off at 0900 in order to defrost it. The diagrams show the temperatures in the freezer at 0900 and one hour later at 1000.

a What is the temperature in the freezer when it is switched off?

b By how much does the temperature rise in the hour between 0900 and 1000?

c The temperature rises by the same amount in the next hour. What is the temperature at 1100?

(WJEC)

6

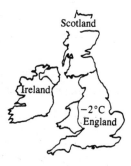

The weather map shows that the temperature in England is $-2°C$.

a Calculate the temperature in Scotland if it is $5°C$ colder than in England.

b Calculate the temperature in Ireland if it is $6°C$ warmer than in England.

(LEAG)

7 This table gives the temperature in Sheffield during one week in January 1987.

Day	Sun	Mon	Tues	Wed	Thurs	Fri	Sat
Noon	$-3°C$	$-2°C$	$1°C$	$-3°C$	$2°C$	$3°C$	$-2°C$
Midnight	$-8°C$	$-8°C$	$-6°C$	$-10°C$	$-6°C$	$-3°C$	$-5°C$

a What is the lowest temperature in the table?

b On which day was there the biggest drop in temperature between noon and midnight?

c How much was this drop?

d What was the least rise in temperature between midnight one day and noon the following day?

e On the next Sunday the temperature was $8°$ higher at noon than at midnight the previous night. What was the temperature at noon?

(MEG)

Powers and standard form

1 a

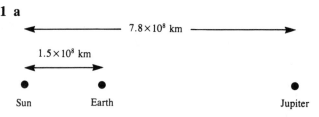

Not to scale

The distance of the Earth from the Sun is 1.5×10^8 km and of Jupiter from the Sun is 7.8×10^8 km. When these three bodies are in a straight line, as shown in the diagram above, what is the distance between the Earth and Jupiter?

b Use the formula

$$M = kv$$

to find the value of M, in standard form, when $k = 7.4 \times 10^{22}$ and $v = 9.9 \times 10^2$.

(MEG)

2 a Using index notation, express each of the following numbers as the product of its prime factors:
   (i) 150,
   (ii) 252.

b (i) Find the largest number which is a factor of both 150 and 252.
   (ii) Find the smallest number which, when divided by each of 150 and 252, leaves a remainder of 1.

(SEG)

3

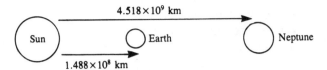

Sun — 4.518×10⁹ km → Neptune

Earth

1.488×10⁸ km →

Not drawn to scale

The Earth is 1.488×10^8 km from the Sun. Neptune is 4.518×10^9 km from the Sun.

Calculate the distance from the Earth to Neptune, when they are in line, as in the diagram. Write the answer in standard form, correct to four significant figures.

(LEAG)

4 The time, T minutes, taken by the moon to eclipse the sun totally is given by the formula

$$T = \frac{1}{v}\left(\frac{rD}{R} - d\right)$$

d and D are the diameters, in kilometres, of the moon and sun respectively;

r and R are the distances, in kilometres, of the moon and sun respectively from the earth;

v is the speed of the moon in kilometres per minute.

Given that

$$d = 3.48 \times 10^3$$
$$D = 1.41 \times 10^6$$
$$r = 3.82 \times 10^5$$
$$R = 1.48 \times 10^8$$
$$v = 59.5$$

calculate the time taken for a total eclipse, giving your answer in minutes, correct to 2 significant figures.

(MEG)

5 a Calculate

$$\frac{2.43}{0.046 \times 19.7}$$

giving your answer to 2 significant figures.

b For any radio wave, the frequency, f, measured in hertz, and the wavelength, λ, measured in metres, are related by the formula

$$f\lambda = 3 \times 10^8$$

A radio station is broadcasting on a frequency of 6.4×10^7 hertz. Calculate the wavelength in metres correct to 2 significant figures.

c

A word-processor is advertised at a price of '£399 + VAT'. The rate of VAT is 15%. How much does the word-processor cost to buy?

(MEG)

6 The distance light travels in one year is called a 'light year'. One light year equals 9.46×10^{12} km to three significant figures. The most distant object from Earth is 1.5×10^{10} light years away. How far is this in kilometres? Give your answer in standard form to two significant figures.

(MEG)

7 Find the value of x in each of the following equations:

a $2^x = 8$

b $2^x = \frac{1}{8}$

c $8^x = \frac{1}{2}$

(SEG)

8 Given that $a^x = 1616$, calculate

a a when $x = 2$,

b x when $a = 256$,

c x when $a = \frac{1}{4}$

(SEG)

9 Which is the larger of these numbers?

$$9.8 \times 10^{-3} \qquad 1.21 \times 10^{-2}$$

Explain how you came to your decision.

(SEG)

10 The table below gives some information about some of the planets in our solar system.

Planet	Radius (km)	Mass (kg)	Distance from the Sun (km)
Mercury	2.43×10^3	2.30×10^{23}	5.97×10^7
Earth	6.38×10^3	5.98×10^{24}	1.50×10^8
Saturn	6.04×10^4	5.69×10^{26}	1.43×10^9
Jupiter	7.14×10^4	1.90×10^{27}	7.78×10^8

Using the table, write down the name of

a the planet with greatest mass,

b the planet with the smallest radius,

c the planet which is just over 5 times as far away from the Sun as the Earth.

(NEA)

Matrix arithmetic

1 Given that

$$a = \begin{pmatrix} 4 \\ -5 \end{pmatrix} \text{ and } b = \begin{pmatrix} -3 \\ 2 \end{pmatrix} \text{ find } a - 2b.$$

(LEAG)

2

The map shows the main roads between five villages P, Q, R, S and T. X is merely a road junction. The numbers on the map are distances in kilometres. A wholesaler wishes to site his warehouse so that he can best serve the small shops in each village. The wholesaler takes the goods to the shops visiting a different village each day.

a Copy and complete the matrix **D** which shows the least road distance between any pair of villages.

	P	Q	R	S	T
P	0	9	9	12	7
Q	9	0	6	11	16
R					
S					
T					

$D = $ (above)

b The running costs for the wholesaler depend on both the bulk of goods to be transported and the distance to be travelled. He therefore considers the product of distance and population (assuming that bulk of goods is proportional to population). The matrix, **N**, of populations (in hundreds) is

$$N = \begin{array}{c} P \\ Q \\ R \\ S \\ T \end{array} \begin{bmatrix} 12 \\ 16 \\ 7 \\ 6 \\ 20 \end{bmatrix}$$

Form the matrix **DN** and, on the basis of your result, advise the wholesaler in which village he should place his warehouses.

c A suitable site becomes available at X. Investigate whether the wholesaler should be advised to take this site.

(MEG)

3 Trackpaks of various sorts are sold for model railways. Trackpak C contains 5 Straights, 2 Points and 4 Curves. Trackpak D contains 2 Straights, 1 Points and 8 Curves.

a The contents of Trackpak C may be represented by the matrix

$$C = \begin{pmatrix} 5 \\ 2 \\ 4 \end{pmatrix}$$

Give a similar matrix **D** for the contents of Trackpak D.

b (i) Evaluate the expression $3C + 2D$.
   (ii) Explain clearly what your answer to **b** (i) represents.

c The cost of the components is as follows: Straights 95p each, Points £2.15 each, Curves £1 each.
   (i) Evaluate the product

$$(0.95 \quad 2.15 \quad 1.00) \times \begin{pmatrix} 5 & 2 \\ 2 & 1 \\ 4 & 8 \end{pmatrix}$$

   (ii) Explain clearly what your answer to **c** (i) represents.

(MEG)

Area and volume

1 A double-glazing firm advertised the fact that its sales had doubled. It used this diagram:

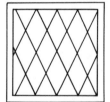

The side of the smaller square is 2 cm long. The side of the larger square is double this length.

a Calculate the area of the smaller square.
b Calculate the area of the larger square.
c Why is the advertisement misleading?

(SEG)

2 To answer this question use a centimetre square grid.

a Rectangle A is 7 cm long. Its perimeter is 20 cm. Complete a drawing of rectangle A.
b Rectangle B is 4 cm wide. Its area is 32 cm². Complete a drawing of rectangle B.
c Rectangle D has the same area as square C, which is 6 cm by 6 cm. Complete a drawing of rectangle D, if it has a height of 4 cm.

(WJEC)

3

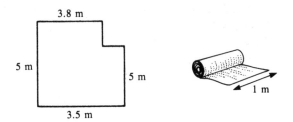

3.8 m

5 m

5 m

3.5 m

The figure represents the floor of the living room of a house and a roll of carpet.

a Calculate the perimeter of the room.

b Calculate the area of the floor of the room.

c The carpet is sold in strips, 1 m wide, to any required length.

  (i) Copy the figure and draw lines to show how you would completely cover the floor of the room with carpet, using as few strips of carpet as possible.

  (ii) Calculate the total length of carpet you would use. Any part width strips must be counted as full width.

(LEAG)

4

The picture is in a square of area 25 cm². Calculate

a the length of a side of the square,

b the perimeter of the square.

(NEA)

5 The diagram below represents the end view of a garden shed. The edges *AB* and *AE* are equal in length, *CD* = 2.6 m and angle *BAE* = 66°.

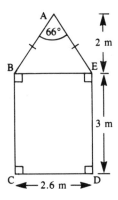

a Calculate the size of angle *ABE*.

b Calculate the size of angle *ABC*.

c Calculate the area of triangle *ABE*.

d Calculate the total area of the end of the shed.

(NEA)

6

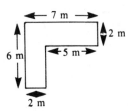

7 m

2 m

6 m

5 m

2 m

a The diagram shows a corridor 2 m wide. Calculate the area of the floor of the corridor.

b The floor of this corridor is covered with square carpet tiles which have a side of 0.5 m as shown.

0.5 m

0.5 m

  (i) How many carpet tiles are needed to cover 1 square metre?

  (ii) How many tiles are needed to cover the corridor?

(SEG)

7

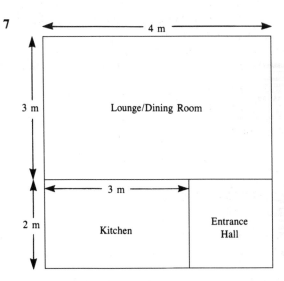

4 m

3 m

Lounge/Dining Room

3 m

2 m

Kitchen

Entrance Hall

The above diagram, which has not been drawn to scale, shows the ground floor of a house.

a What is the floor area of the lounge/dining room?

b David covers the floor of the kitchen using ½ m by ½ m carpet tiles. How many of these tiles are needed?

c Write down the length and breadth of the entrance hall of the house.

(MEG)

8

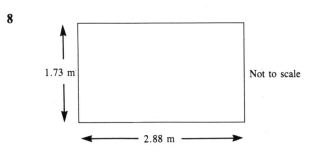

1.73 m

Not to scale

2.88 m

The diagram is of a sheet of glass which has been cut to fit a large rectangular window.

a Calculate the exact value of
  (i) the perimeter of the glass (in m),
  (ii) the area of one side of the glass (in m²).

b Write down your answers to part (a) correct to the nearest whole number.

(MEG)

9

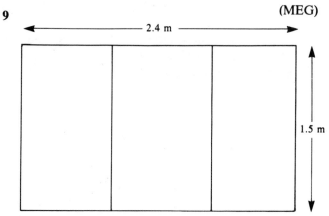

The rectangular window in the diagram (width 2.4 m and length 1.5 m) has to be glazed with three pieces of glass. Each of the pieces is the same size.

a Work out the width and length of one of the pieces of glass needed.

b Work out the area of the piece of glass whose dimensions you found in **a**.

c Glass costs £2.40 a square metre.

Calculate the total cost of the glass needed to glaze the window.

(LEAG)

10 A college sells tickets for a show.

a Tickets cost either £1 or £2. Mr. Patel bought 10 tickets costing a total of £18. How many of each kind did he buy?

b Each ticket measures 5 cm × 2 cm. The tickets are cut from sheets of card, 26 cm × 24 cm. Mrs Smith cuts out the tickets with their longer sides parallel to the longer sides of the card, as shown in the diagram:

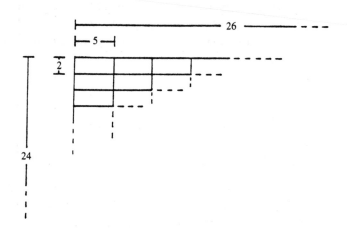

What is the largest number of tickets she can cut from one sheet of card?

(SEG)

11 A compact disc player measures 26 cm × 36 cm × 6 cm. The player is first totally surrounded by polystyrene, which is 2 cm thick, and then the whole is packed tightly into a cardboard box.

a What are the dimensions of the cardboard box?

b What is the volume of the polystyrene used?

c Using a scale of 1 cm to represent 5 cm draw a scale diagram of a suitable net for this cardboard box. (Ignore any overlap necessary to fix the box together.)

Eight of these boxes are packed into a case. The manufacturer wishes to pack them in such a way that he uses the least possible amount of cardboard for each case. One possible arrangement is shown in the diagram.

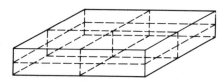

d Calculate the area of cardboard for a case with the eight players arranged as above.

e Consider two other possible arrangements for packing eight boxes into a case. Which of your two arrangements uses the smaller amount of cardboard?

f From your answers to **d** and **e** deduce which is the most economical arrangement for packing boxes into a case.

(SEG)

12 A rectangle has an area of 48 cm².

a The length of each side is a whole number of centimetres. One possible rectangle would be 1 cm wide by 48 cm long.

(Note: 48 cm wide by 1 cm long is **not** a different rectangle).

  (i) Write down the sizes of all the other possible rectangles.
  (ii) Which of these answers gives the least perimeter for the rectangle?

b Another rectangle with the same area has a width of ½ cm.
  (i) What is the length of this rectangle?
  (ii) What is the perimeter of this rectangle?

(SEG)

13 The diagram below shows a triangle which is used in a design. The marked angle is 90°.

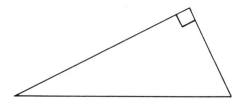

a Measure and write down the sides of the triangle to the nearest millimetre.

b Write down the perimeter of the triangle.

c Calculate the area of the triangle.

d Complete the diagram to show how two of these triangles can be used to make a rectangle.

(SEG)

14

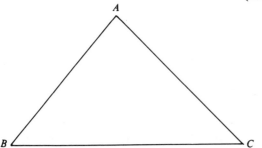

ABC is an accurately drawn triangle.

a Measure and write down the size of
  (i) angle *A*,
  (ii) angle *B*.

b Find the length of the perimeter of the triangle, in mm.

c Find the area of the triangle in mm².

(LEAG)

15

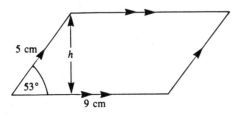

The diagram represents a parallelogram with a base of 9 cm.

a Calculate the height (*h*) of the parallelogram.

b Calculate the area of the parallelogram.

(NEA)

16

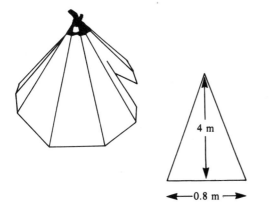

The Nez Perce Indians lived in tepees. A tepee was made from 10 triangles of hide like this. How many square metres of hide were needed to make a tepee?

(MEG)

17 This is a sketch of Brian's garden.

The measurements are in metres.

a Calculate the area of the garden.

b Brian is going to sow grass seed over the whole garden. He uses 45 g of seed for each square metre. He can buy seed in 2 kg bags.

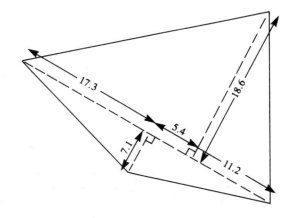

How many bags should he buy?

(MEG)

18 *ABCDE* represents the shape of the end wall of a house. It is drawn accurately on a 1 cm square grid.

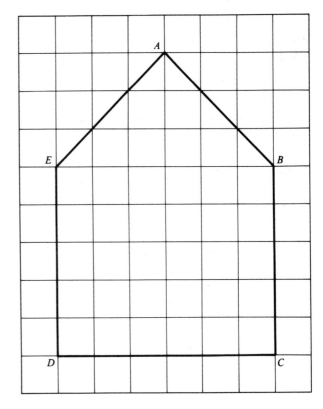

a (i) Name two edges of the shape that are parallel.
  (ii) Name two edges of the shape that are perpendicular.

b (i) Measure and write down the length of *AB*.
  (ii) Find the perimeter of the shape *ABCDE*.

c Find the area of the shape *ABCDE*.

(MEG)

19

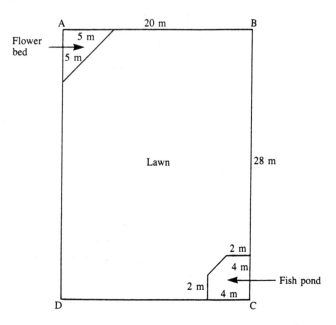

The above diagram represents a rectangular garden *ABCD* which measures 20 m by 28 m.

There is a flower bed at corner *A* and a fish pond at corner *C*.

a On squared paper, draw a scale drawing of the garden using a scale of 1 cm to represent 2 metres.

b Calculate the area of the garden which is covered by lawn.

(WJEC)

20 The material for a lampshade is cut from a trapezium as illustrated in the diagram.

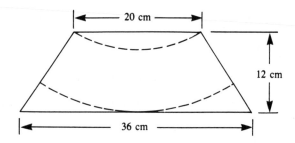

Calculate the area of the trapezium

a in cm²,

b in m².

(SEG)

21 This sketch shows Ralph's garden. It is 8 m wide. One side is 12 m long. The other side is 16 m long. There is a flower bed 6 m by 2 m and a pond. The rest of the garden is grass.

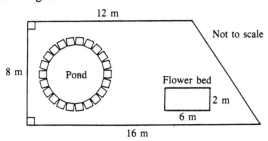

a What is the area of the garden (in m²)?

Each autumn Ralph covers the flower bed with mushroom compost 15 cm deep.

b What volume of compost does he use (in m³)?

The edge of the circular pond is made from 22 paving slabs. Each paving slab is a 50 cm square.

c About how wide is the pond? Give your answer in metres.

The pond and paving slabs take up about 16 m².

d What is the area of the grass in the garden (in m²)?

(MEG)

22

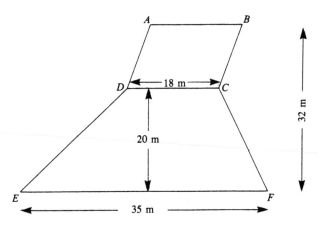

In the diagram, *ABCDEF* represents a plot of land. *ABCF* is a parallelogram and *FCDE* is a trapezium with *FC* parallel to *ED*. The perpendicular distance between *ED* and *FC* is 20 m and the perpendicular distance between *ED* and *AB* is 32 m.

a Calculate the area of the plot in m².

b The ground is to be prepared for a car park. In order to do this, the earth is dug away to a depth of 35 cm over the whole plot. What volume of earth, in m³, is removed?

c This earth is used to cover two rectangular gardens, one measuring 17 m by 25 m and the other measuring 15 m by 16 m, both to the same depth throughout. Find this depth to the nearest centimetre.

(WJEC)

23 A circle has a radius of 9 cm.

a Work out, to the nearest centimetre, the circumference of the circle.

b An equilateral triangle is drawn with the same perimeter as the circle. Work out the length, to the nearest centimetre, of one of the sides of the triangle.

(LEAG)

24 The diameter of a bicycle wheel is 40 cm.

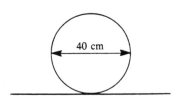

a Calculate the circumference of the wheel. Give your answer in centimetres.

b Calculate how far along a road the bicycle travels while the wheel is making 50 complete turns. Give your answer in metres, to the nearest metre. (You may use $\pi = 3.14$.)

(MEG)

25

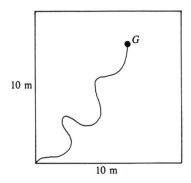

A square field has sides of length 10 m. A goat is tied by a rope of length 8 m to a post in one corner of the field.

a What area of the field can the goat graze?

b What percentage of the field can the goat graze? (Take π to be 3.14 or use the π button on your calculator.)

(SEG)

26

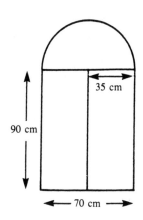

A metal frame, shown in the diagram, is made for a window. The lower part consists of two rectangles, each 90 cm by 35 cm, and the upper part is a semi-circle with radius 35 cm. Calculate the length of metal used in making

a the straight pieces,

b the curved piece. (Take π to be 3.14 or use the π button on your calculator. Give your answer correct to the nearest whole number.)

c the total frame.

(SEG)

27

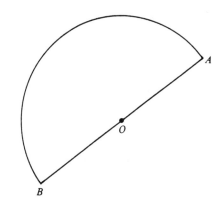

The diagram shows a semi-circular shape.

a Measure and write down the length in cm of the radius *OA*.

b Use the formula

$$\text{perimeter} = (\pi + 2) \times \text{radius}$$

and $\pi = 3.14$ to find the perimeter of the semi-circular shape.

Give your answer in centimetres correct to the nearest whole number.

(NEA)

28 For breeding purposes, fish are kept to an area of a lake enclosed by two concentric circles as shown by the shaded area in the diagram.

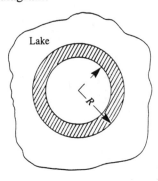

Lake

a Write down an expression for the shaded area in terms of R and r, the radii of the circles, and π.

b If the shaded area is 1180 m² and $(R+r)$ is 25 metres, calculate the value of $(R-r)$ to the nearest whole number of metres.

c Using the rounded value of $(R-r)$ found in part **b**, calculate the values of R and r.

(NEA)

29

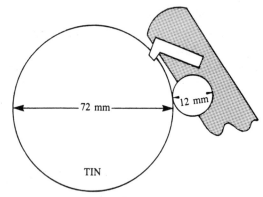

An electric can opener has a small wheel of diameter 12 mm. This is held firmly against the edge of a tin, and turns at a speed of 1 revolution per second. The tin is a cyclinder of diameter 72 mm.

a The circumference of a circle is calculated using the formula:

$$\text{circumference} = 3.14 \times \text{diameter}$$

Calculate the circumference of
 (i) the small wheel,
 (ii) the tin.

b How many seconds does it take to open the tin completely?

(NEA)

30 The two circles in this diagram both have the same centre O. The smaller circle represents a lake in a park. The circumference of the bigger circle is the outer edge of a path around the lake. The radius of the lake is 17 m. The width of the path is 1 metre.

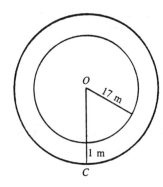

a Calculate the circumference of the lake. (Either take π as 3.14, or use the π button on your calculator.)

b Write down the length of OC.

c Calculate the circumference of the outer edge of the path, giving your answer to the nearest whole number.

d The outer edge of the path is to be painted white. It costs 20p per metre to paint it.
 (i) How many metres can be painted for £1?
 (ii) How much does it cost to paint the whole of the outer edge of the path?

(SEG)

31

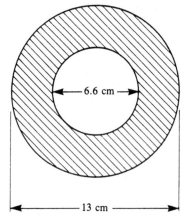

This is a floppy disk for a microcomputer. The useful area is shaded. Find the percentage of the area of the disk that is useful.

(MEG)

32

A circle is contained within a square as shown in the diagram. The radius of the circle is 5 cm. Estimate the area of the shaded part of the diagram. (Take the value of π to be 3.)

(SEG)

33 The diagram shows the plan of a concrete drive that Mr. Fraser intends to lay in his garden.

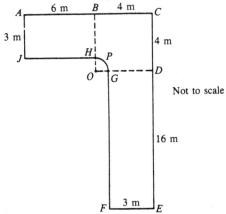

ABC and *CDE* are perpendicular straight lines and both *DEFG* and *ABHJ* are rectangles. The arc *HPG* is part of a circle, of radius 1 m, with centre at *O*.

$AJ = EF = 3$ m. $AB = 6$ m, $BC = CD = 4$ m and $DE = 16$ m. $OB = OD = 4$ m.

Taking π to be 3.14, find the total area of the drive, correct to the nearest square metre.

(MEG)

34 It is suggested that a new thirty-pence coin is to be introduced. It would be based on an equilateral triangle *ABC* of side 1.50 cm. Arcs of circles of radius 1.50 cm are centred at *A*, *B* and *C*. This is shown in Figure 1.

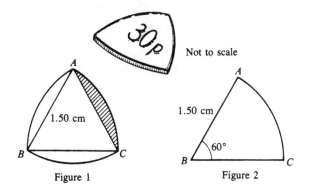

a What fraction of the area of the complete circle is the area shown in Figure 2?

In Figure 1 you may assume that the area of triangle *ABC* is 0.974 cm².

b Calculate the shaded area in Figure 1 correct to 3 significant figures.

c Calculate the area of the top face of the coin correct to 3 significant figures.

(MEG)

35 A flat metal component is to be made in the shape shown in the figure. The curves *AB* and *DC* are both arcs of circles with centre *O*. The radius of the arc *AB* is *r*, the radius of the arc *DC* is *R*. The angle $AOB = 60°$.

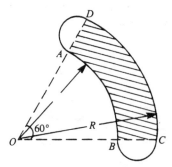

a (i) Write down a formula for the area of sector *ODC* in terms of *R*.
  (ii) Show that the area of the shaded region *ABCD* is

$$\frac{1}{6}\pi(R^2 - r^2).$$

The unshaded ends of the shape are both semi-circles.

b (i) Write down the length of the diameter *BC* in terms of *R* and *r*.
  (ii) Find the total area of the two semi-circles in terms of *R* and *r*.

c Find the area, in mm², to the nearest mm², of metal sheet required to make the component when $OD = 39$ mm and $OA = 27$ mm.

d The metal sheet is 1.4 mm thick. Find the volume, in mm³, to the nearest mm³, of the component.

(LEAG)

36

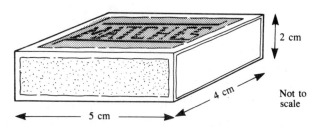

The diagram shows a matchbox measuring 5 cm by 4 cm by 2 cm.
a Calculate the volume of the matchbox.

12 similar matchboxes fill a carton with base dimensions of 10 cm by 8 cm.

Calculate

b the volume of the carton,
c the height of the carton,
d the total number of matches in the carton, if each box contains 48 matches.

(MEG)

37 Below are five familar objects, all shaped differently.

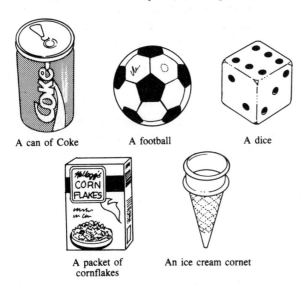

A can of Coke   A football   A dice

A packet of cornflakes   An ice cream cornet

a Which of the above objects is a sphere?

b What mathematical shape is the can of coke?

c Which one of the following shapes is *not* shown amongst the objects above?

    a cone; a cuboid; a square-based pyramid; a cube.

(NEA)

38

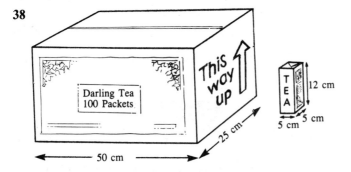

The box in the diagram is filled with packets of tea. Each packet of tea is 5 cm by 5 cm by 12 cm. When full, the box contains 100 packets of tea. The packets of tea are stacked upright in the box.

a How many packets of tea fit onto the base of the box?

b How many layers of packets of tea are there in a full box?

c What is the height of the box?

(LEAG)

39

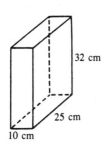

The figure is a drawing of a rectangular petrol can. How many litres of petrol does it hold when full?

(LEAG)

40

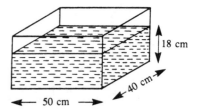

The diagram shows a perspex fish-tank. It is 50 cm long, 40 cm wide and contains water 18 cm deep.

a What area of perspex is needed to make the base of the tank?

b What is the volume of the water in the tank? Give your answer in litres.

Wilf pours another 6 litres of water into the tank.

c How much does the water rise?

(MEG)

41 The diagram shows a solid tower made by stacking 10 child's building bricks on the floor. Each brick is a coloured cube of side 10 cm. Some of the bricks are hidden from view in this diagram.

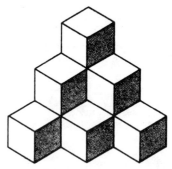

a (i) How many bricks can be seen in this diagram?
   (ii) How many bricks are there in the bottom layer?
  (iii) How many bricks are hidden from view?

b (i) Calculate the volume of one brick.
   (ii) Calculate the volume of the tower.

c (i) How many square faces can be seen in this diagram?
   (ii) How many square faces are there on one of the hidden sides of the tower?
  (iii) A child walks round the tower. How many square faces can be counted altogether?

(MEG)

42 A certain type of chocolate is sold in cartons which are in the form of triangular prisms. The ends are equilateral triangles, with 6 cm sides. The prisms are 15 cm long.

a On a sheet of paper using a scale of 1 cm to represent 2 cm of the prism, draw an accurate net which could be folded to make the prism.

b Measure and write down the height of one of the triangles of your net.

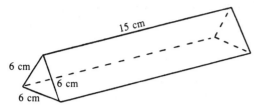

c What is the height of each triangular end of the full-size prism?

d Calculate for the full-size prism
  (i) the area of each end,
  (ii) the area of each rectangular face,
  (iii) the total area of card needed to make each carton, ignoring any overlaps.

(SEG)

43

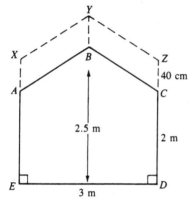

The diagram shows the end view of a greenhouse.

> B is 2.5 m above ED
> $AB = BC$
> $AE = CD = 2$ m
> $ED = 3$ m

Last winter, 40 cm of snow settled on the roof.

a Calculate the area, in m², of
  (i) the end of the greenhouse, $ABCDE$,
  (ii) the end, $XYZDE$, **including** the layer of snow.

b Hence find the area of the snow section, $XYZCBA$.

c Explain why the answer to **b** should equal the width of the greenhouse multiplied by the depth of snow.

(LEAG)

44

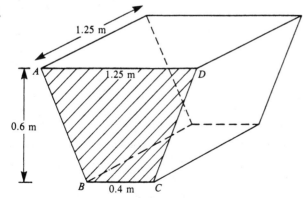

The diagram above shows a container used at a lime-kiln.

It is in the shape of an open-top prism. Its cross-section $ABCD$ (shown shaded in the diagram) is a trapezium. The edges BC and AD are horizontal, $BC = 0.4$ m and $AD = 1.35$ m. The vertical height of the container is 0.6 m and its length is 1.25 m.

Find

a the area, in square metres, of the cross-section $ABCD$,

b the capacity, in cubic metres, of the container, if it is filled level with the top of the sides. Give your answer correct to 2 decimal places.

(MEG)

45

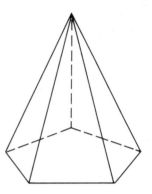

A glass paperweight is a pyramid with a five-sided base. How many edges has it?

(SEG)

46 a Write down the mathematical name given to the shape of the following objects.
  (i) A can of baked beans.
  (ii) An ordinary dice with 6 faces.

b Give an example of an everyday use of a sphere.

(MEG)

47 A fruit cake is a cylinder of height 7 cm and radius 9 cm. It is to have its top and sides covered in marzipan.

a (i) The top covering is 0.7 cm thick. Calculate this volume of marzipan.
  (ii) A strip of marzipan 7.7 cm wide is to be wrapped round the side of the cake. Show that it must be about 57 cm long.
  (iii) This strip is 0.5 cm thick. Calculate the volume of marzipan needed for the whole cake.

b A family baker makes 12 such cakes. He buys marzipan in 500 g packs. Each pack has a volume of 180 cm³. How many packs will he need to cover the 12 cakes?

(MEG)

48 Alex buys himself a new mug.

The mug is in the form of a cylinder, with internal radius 3.5 cm and height 8 cm. Taking π to be 3.14 or by using the π key on your calculator, calculate

a the volume of water, correct to the nearest cm³, the mug will hold,

b the depth of water in the mug, correct to the nearest cm, when 200 cm³ of water has been poured into the mug.

(MEG)

49

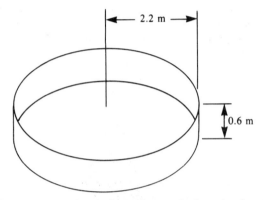

The figure shows the design of a sand-pit to be dug in a children's playground. It is in the shape of a circular cylinder with radius 2.2 m and depth 0.6 m. The wall of the sand-pit is to be lined with firm plastic sheets. The sheets to be used are 1.5 m long and 0.6 m wide.

a Find
  (i) the circumference, in metres, to the nearest 0.1 m, of the sand-pit,
  (ii) the number of sheets of plastic which must be bought.
b Calculate the volume, in m³, to the nearest 0.01 m³, of sand required.
The mass of 1 m³ of the sand is approximately 1.2 tonnes.
c Find the mass, in tonnes, to the nearest tonne, of sand required.

It is decided to order the plastic sheets and the sand, to the nearest tonne, from a local builder's yard. The charges at this yard are:

Loose sand:	£11.50 per tonne
Plastic sheets (1.5 m × 0.6 m):	£2.58 each
Delivery charge:	£5 (fixed rate)

(All prices include VAT)

d Find the total cost of the materials, including the delivery charge.

(LEAG)

50 A solid cone of ice-cream has a circular top of radius 3.5 cm and a height of 14 cm. Calculate the volume of ice-cream, correct to two significant figures.

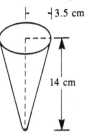

(NEA)

51

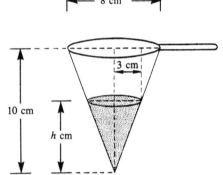

The drawing shows a measuring scoop used for measuring soap powder for a washing machine. It has a diameter of 8 cm and a height of 10 cm. Calculate the height of the powder (h cm) in the scoop when the radius of the soap powder surface is 3 cm.

(NEA)

52

a Calculate the volume of a cylindrical can with diameter 7.4 cm and height 10.6 cm.

b Calculate the area of sheet metal used to make this can.

(NEA)

53 Soup can be bought in cylindrical cans of radius 3.4 cm and length 10 cm.

a Find the volume of a can, to three significant figures. (Use $\pi = 3.142$ or the π button on your calculator.)

b Each can contains 350 cm³ of soup.
  (i) Write down the volume of each can which is not filled with soup.
  (ii) What percentage of the volume of each can is not filled with soup?

(SEG)

54 The volume of a cone is approximately $1.05r^2h$.

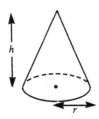

Calculate the volume of a cone when $r = 5$, $h = 12$.

(SEG)

55 The volume, V cm^3, of a cone whose height is fixed varies with r^2, where r cm is the radius of the base of the cone.

a Given that $V = 100$ when $r = 5$, obtain a formula for V in terms of r.

b Calculate the volume of the cone with base-radius 3 cm.

c Calculate the value of r when $V = 50$.

d Calculate the percentage change in r when V increases from 50 to 75.

(SEG)

56 Phiz is sold in cylindrical cans of radius 3 cm.

a A standard can contains 350 cm^3. Find its height. (Use 3.14 as the value of π or use the π button on your calculator.)

b A large can has the same radius, but has height 22 cm. Small cans cost 20p each. If large cans are to be better value for money, calculate the maximum cost for a large can.

(SEG)

57 A drinking chocolate tin is in the shape of a cylinder with a radius of 4 cm and a height of 12 cm.

a (i) Calculate the volume of this tin of drinking chocolate. (Give your answer to the nearest cm^3.)

 (ii) Calculate the volume of drinking chocolate in a *new* tin, if the drinking chocolate occupies ¾ of the space inside the tin.

b Every day a family of four each have a drink for supper. Each drink is made from 1 teaspoon of drinking chocolate, which is approximately 3 cm^3. How many days would you expect a *new* tin of drinking chocolate to last the family of four?

(NEA)

58 To estimate the volume of timber in the trunk of a conifer, a pupil considered the trunk to be a cone and measured the circumference of the base to be 68 cm. To find the height she walked back 30 m from the base of the tree and took a sighting of the top of the tree. From her eye level (1.2 m above the ground), the angle of elevation of the top of the tree was 26°.

a Calculate the height of the tree.

b Calculate the volume of timber (in m^3) in the trunk of the tree.

(NEA)

59 Fred has to make a cone of base radius 3.5 cm and vertical height 12 cm. To do this he uses a sector of a circle as shown in the diagram below.

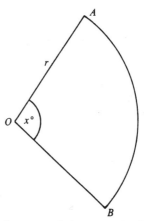

a Draw a diagram of the cone, indicating clearly the positions of O, A and B.

b Calculate
  (i) the radius, r cm, of the sector,
  (ii) the angle, $x°$, at the centre of the sector.
(MEG)

60 Shops selling Tony's ice cream have concrete displays outside the premises. Each one is a hemisphere, radius 35 cm, on top of a cone, of height 60 cm, on a cylindrical base of height 20 cm and diameter 70 cm. Concrete weighs 2.2 g per cm³.

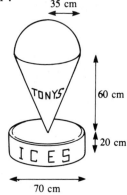

35 cm

TONYS

60 cm

20 cm

I C E S

70 cm

a What is the weight of the concrete display in kilograms?

b Similar concrete displays half as high and half as wide are placed inside the shops. What is the weight of one of the half-sized displays?
(WJEC)

61 *In this question, give answers correct to 3 significant figures.*

Petrol is stored in a cylindrical tank. The axis of the cylinder is horizontal, the circular ends have radius 1.3 m, and the length of the cylinder is 4.6 m. The depth of the petrol is 0.8 m, as shown in the diagram (in which O is the centre of the circle, and ADC is the level of the petrol).

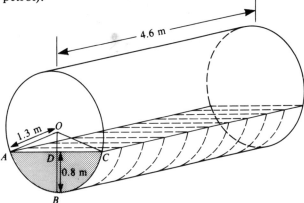

4.6 m

1.3 m O

A D C

0.8 m

B

Calculate

a the length of OD,

b the angle AOD,

c the area of the triangle OAC,

d the area of the sector $OABC$,

e the cross-sectional area of the petrol (the area of the shaded region $ABCD$),

f the volume of petrol in the tank.

Another cylindrical tank also has length 4.6 m, but its radius is 2.6 m and it contains petrol to a depth of 1.6 m.

g Calculate the volume of petrol in this second tank.
(MEG)

62 a The formula $A = 4\pi r^2$ gives the surface area A of a sphere with radius r. Taking r as 6370 km find the corresponding value of A, showing all the figures from your calculator. You may use $\pi = 3.142$.

b Give your answer to (a) in standard form correct to one significant figure.
(MEG)

63 The pressure needed to blow up a balloon varies as the cube of its radius. When the radius is 5 cm, the pressure needed is 80 g/cm².

a What pressure is required when the radius is 15 cm?

b What is the radius of the balloon when the pressure needed is 640 g/cm²?
(WJEC)

64 A plastic cup has base diameter 5.0 cm, top diameter 7.5 cm and depth 7.0 cm. Consider this as being formed by removing a cone OXY from a cone OAB as shown in the figure.

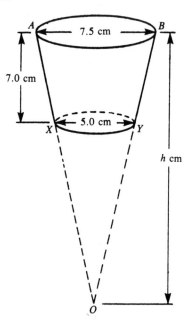

A 7.5 cm B

7.0 cm

X 5.0 cm Y

h cm

O

a State the scale factor of the enlargement mapping XY onto AB.

b Explain why the volume of cone OXY is $\frac{8}{27}$ that of cone OAB.

c State the height, h centimetres, of cone OAB.

d Calculate the volume of liquid which the cup will hold.

(MEG)

65 (In this question, take π to be 3.142 and give each answer correct to three significant figures.)

a The ice cream in a 'Conetti' is in the shape of a circular cone with base radius 3.6 cm and vertical height 11.4 cm. The curved surface is completely covered with wafer of negligible thickness.

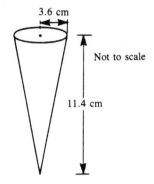

3.6 cm

Not to scale

11.4 cm

(i) Calculate the volume of the ice cream.
(ii) Calculate the area of the wafer.

b

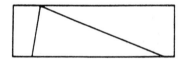

The 'Conettis' are packed in a rectangular box with their curved surfaces in contact with the base of the box. A vertical cross-section through the axis of one Conetti is shown in the diagram above. Calculate the least possible height of the box.

c The ice cream is also sold in containers in which the ice cream has the shape of a circular cylinder of height 3.6 cm. The volume of ice cream in each container is the same as in one Conetti. Calculate the radius of the cylinder.

(MEG)

66 (In this question, take π to be 3.142 and give each answer correct to three significant figures.)

a

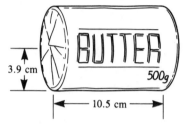

3.9 cm

10.5 cm

A firm sells 500 g packs of butter in the form of a circular cylinder with radius 3.9 cm and length 10.5 cm. Calculate the volume of the cylinder.

b

6.5 cm

6.5 cm

The firm also sells 500 g packs of butter in the form of a rectangular block with a square cross-section of side 6.5 cm. Calculate the length of the rectangular block.

c The firm decides to sell 250 g packs of butter in the form of a circular cylinder.
   (i) If the radius of the (250 g) cylinder is 3.9 cm, find the length of the cylinder.
   (ii) If the length of the (250 g) cylinder is 10.5 cm, calculate the radius of the cylinder.

(MEG)

Algebra

How algebra began

An unknown Hindu mathematician, working in India sometime between 100 BC and 150 AD, invented the counting system based on the number 10 which is now used in every country in the world. This system differed from all earlier systems in that it had a symbol for zero. This symbol was at first a dot and later a circle.

This allowed the Hindu mathematicians to introduce the very powerful concept of **place value**. Their new numbers were organised under the now familiar column headings of units, tens, hundreds, thousands, etc. A symbol could represent different values, depending on its **place** in a number. The symbols Z and Ƶ were already in use to represent two and three (they had developed from = and ≡. With the addition of the symbol ○ for a blank column, these symbols could now represent a whole range of numbers, for example:

- Thirty ƵO
- Thirty-two ƵZ
- Three hundred and two ƵOZ
- Three hundred and thirty ƵƵO
- Three hundred and thirty-two ƵƵZ

Earlier number systems, without a zero, caused many problems for ancient mathematicians. The main problem with these systems was that arithmetic with the numbers was very difficult. Calculations were not worked out on paper; they had to be physically worked out on a counting frame or **abacus**.

The new Hindu number system made calculations much easier. New rules of arithmetic were developed for both whole numbers and fractions. The *Lilavati*, written by the Hindu mathematician Aryabhata about 470 AD, sets out rules for calculation that are very similar to modern methods. (It also gives a table of trigonometrical ratios and an estimate for π of 3.1416.)

The Hindu number system was adopted by Arab traders because of the ease with which it allowed them to calculate. It was studied and developed at the Arab university in Baghdad, and in the universities established in Spain and Southern France as part of the Moorish occupation of these countries. An English monk, Adelard of Bath, disguised himself as a Moslem and studied at Cordova in Spain in about 1120 AD. He and others helped spread the new number system into the mathematically backward countries of Northern Europe.

Because calculation with the new numbers was so much easier, three areas of mathematics were much advanced by Indian and Arab mathematicians. First, they became interested in establishing and proving general rules about the way numbers behave. Second, they became interested in solving practical problems involving numbers. Third, they became interested in the study of number patterns and series.

The modern name for these studies is **Algebra**, a word first used by the Arab mathematician Alkarismi in the ninth century. The three main branches of Algebra are studied in the following sections.

Establishing rules (simplification and substitution)

The language of algebra

One important feature of the new Hindu numbers was their use of a set of ten special symbols. Earlier systems had used letters of the alphabet to also represent numbers. For instance, the Romans used V for five and C for one hundred.

Because the letters of the alphabet no longer represented any **particular** numbers, they could be used to represent **generalised** numbers. For example, instead of writing down a long-winded explanation of how to multiply two fractions, they could now just write:

$$\frac{a}{b} \times \frac{c}{d} = \frac{ac}{bd}$$

where the letters a, b, c and d represented **any** number you cared to think of. This provided the Hindu and Arab mathematicians with a powerful way to communicate their discoveries.

Over the centuries, a standard shorthand has been developed to write down mathematical statements.

For example, in 1464, Regiomontanus might have written the statement:

5 census et 7 demptis 9 rebus aequatur zero

In 1591, Vieta would have written the same statement:

5 in A quad − 7 in A plano + 9 aequatur 0

In 1637, Descartes wrote:

$$5x^2 - 7x + 9 = 0$$

You should already be familiar with the following standard mathematical shorthand.

$=$	is equal to
$<$	is less than
$>$	is greater than
$\leqslant$	is less than or equal to
$\geqslant$	is greater than or equal to
$m + 9$	9 added to the number represented by the letter m
$m - 9$	9 subtracted from the number represented by the letter m
$9m$	9 times the number represented by the letter m
$\dfrac{m}{9}$	the number represented by the letter m divided by 9
$\dfrac{9}{m}$	9 divided by the number represented by the letter m
m^2	the number represented by the letter m, squared; that is $m \times m$
m^5	the number represented by the letter m, raised to the power 5; that is $m \times m \times m \times m \times m$
ab	the number represented by the letter a multiplied by the number represented by the letter b

Brackets have a special function in this mathematical shorthand; they indicate **priorities**. That is to say, they show the order in which a calculation should be worked out. The part of the calculation in brackets is **always** worked out first.

$a - (b + c)$	First add the numbers represented by the letters b and c, then subtract this result from the number represented by the letter a
$(a - b) + c$	First subtract the number represented by the letter b from the number represented by the letter a, then add the number represented by the letter c.

Using this shorthand, we can quickly and simply express many different mathematical statements.

Examples

The area of a triangle can be found by multiplying the height by the base and then dividing the result by 2.
    This can be written:

$$A = \frac{hb}{2}$$

where it is understood that A represents the area, h the height and b the base.

The number m is 4 times the number n, plus 7.
    This can be written:

$$m = 4n + 7$$

Four times the number y, minus 6 times the number x is equal to 14.
    This can be written:

$$4y - 6x = 14$$

The total cost of g geraniums at 80p each and m marigolds at 20p each must be less than £9.
    This can be written:

$$80g + 20m < 900$$

Five times the square of the number x, plus 7 times the number x, minus 9 is equal to zero.
    This can be written:

$$5x^2 + 7x - 9 = 0$$

CHECKPOINT 1

1 Write each of the following statements in standard mathematical shorthand.

a The area of a circle can be found by multiplying π by the square of the radius.

b To convert a temperature in degrees Fahrenheit (F) into degrees Celcius (C), first subtract 32, then multiply by 5, then divide by 9.

c The number p is 3 times the number q, minus 11.

d The number y is 7 times the number x plus 23.

e 2 times the number j, plus 3 times the number k, equals 16.

f The cost of f pieces of fish at 85p each, plus c portions of chips at 40p each came to £8.25.

g 7 times the number y, minus 4 times the number x is always greater than 20.

h The cost of m marigolds at 25p each, plus p petunias at 35p each plus n nasturtiums at 10p each must be less than £25.

i 5 times the square of the number m, plus 4 times the number m, minus 11 is equal to zero.

j This diagram shows a solid steel cube of side length d cm, plated with chrome.

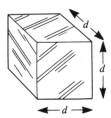

The cost in pennies (C) of manufacturing the cube is $5\times$ the volume in cubic centimetres, plus $2\times$ the total surface area in square centimetres, plus 75.

Substitution

Mastering the meaning of mathematical shorthand allows us to substitute particular values into general expressions. For example, if we know the meaning of:

$$ab + a + b$$

we can quickly find the value of the expression for any particular value of a and b. For example, if $a=2$ and $b=3$:

$$ab + a + b = 2 \times 3 + 2 + 3 = 11$$

Examples

If $m=5$ and $n=8$, then:

$m+n=5+8=13$ $\qquad$ $n-m=8-5=3$
$3m=3\times5=15$ $\qquad$ $3m+2n=3\times5+2\times8=31$
$mn=5\times8=40$ $\qquad$ $n^2=8\times8=64$
$m^3=5\times5\times5=125$ $\qquad$ $3mn^2=3\times5\times8\times8=960$
$3m^2n=3\times5\times5\times8=600$ $\qquad$ $3m^2n^2=3\times5\times5\times8\times8=4800$

CHECKPOINT 2

If $a=4$, $b=5$ and $c=2$, find the value of:

a $a+b$ $\qquad$ **b** $b-c$ $\qquad$ **c** $a+b+c$
d $2a+3b$ $\qquad$ **e** $5c-2b$ $\qquad$ **f** ab
g abc $\qquad$ **h** $2ac$ $\qquad$ **i** ab^2
j a^3b $\qquad$ **k** a^2+c^2 $\qquad$ **l** $17+2cb^2$
m $a(b+c)$ $\qquad$ **n** $ab+c$ $\qquad$ **o** $ab+ac$

Negative numbers may be involved in substitution, in which case all the rules for negative number arithmetic must be carefully observed.

Examples

If $m=-5$ and $n=8$, then:

$m+n=-5+8=3$ $\qquad$ $n-m=8--5=13$
$3m=3\times-5=-15$ $\qquad$ $3m+2n=3\times-5+2\times8=1$
$mn=-5\times8=-40$ $\qquad$ $n^2=8\times8=64$
$m^3=-5\times-5\times-5=-125$ $\quad$ $3mn^2=3\times-5\times8\times8=-960$
$3m^2n=3\times-5\times-5\times8=600$
$3m^2n^2=3\times-5\times-5\times8\times8=4800$

CHECKPOINT 3

If $a=-4$, $b=5$ and $c=-2$, find the value of:

a $a+b$ $\qquad$ **b** $b-c$ $\qquad$ **c** $a+b+c$
d $2a+3b$ $\qquad$ **e** $5c-2b$ $\qquad$ **f** ab
g abc $\qquad$ **h** $2ac$ $\qquad$ **i** ab^2
j a^3b $\qquad$ **k** a^2+c^2 $\qquad$ **l** $17+2cb^2$
m $a(b+c)$ $\qquad$ **n** $ab+c$ $\qquad$ **o** $ab+ac$

Using a formula

The practical application of the skills of substitution is in the use of a formula to solve a problem. Many different formulas have been worked out by mathematicians and others to solve a whole range of problems.

Example

A formula used to calculate the correct dose of medicine for a child older than 12 months is:

$$C = \frac{An}{n+12}$$

where A is the adult dose, n is the child's age in years and C is the child's dose.

What is the correct dose of medicine for a child aged 8 years if the adult's dose is 50 ml?

Substituting these values in the formula, we have:

$$C = \frac{50 \times 8}{8+12}$$

which gives $C=20$ ml.

CHECKPOINT 4

1 If a car is travelling at v miles per hour, its stopping distance, d metres, is given by the formula:

$$d = \frac{v^2 + 20v}{60}$$

(This formula calculates a total stopping distance, including the time taken for a driver to react and apply the brakes.)

a Draw up a table of values showing the stopping distances for speeds from 10 mph to 70 mph in steps of 10 mph.
b Does the car travel twice as far when stopping from 60 mph as it does when stopping from 30 mph?
2 The number of rolls of wallpaper required to decorate a room can be calculated with the formula:

$$n = \frac{dh}{5}$$

where n is the number of rolls required, d is the distance round the room in metres and h is the height of the room in metres.

Since wallpaper can only be bought in complete rolls, all answers must be rounded up to the next whole number.

Copy and complete this table showing the number of rolls of wallpaper required for rooms of various sizes.

Height of room (metres)	Distance round room (metres)							
	6	8	10	12	14	16	18	20
3	4	5	6	8				
3.5								
4								

3 A formula used to calculate the dose of medicine suitable for an infant (a child less than twelve months old) is:

$$I = \frac{Am}{150}$$

where I is the infant's dose, A is the adult's dose and m is the infant's age in months.

Draw up a table of values that a doctor could use to prescribe a dose for infants of a drug with an adult's dose of 75 ml.
4 When a body is dropped from a height, the distance it has fallen and its velocity are given by the formulae:

$$s = \frac{9.8t^2}{2} \text{ and } v = 9.8t$$

where s is the distance fallen (in metres), v is the velocity (in metres per second) and t is the time (in seconds) the body has been falling.

a An observer watches as a stone is dropped from the top of a cliff. The stone takes 2.5 seconds to hit the beach. How high is the cliff?
b An apple falls from a tree and hits a man on the head travelling at a speed of 4.9 metres per second. How far had the apple fallen?
c If a flowerpot knocked from a windowledge has fallen 19.6 metres, how fast is it travelling?

Simplifying an expression

A piece of mathematical shorthand like $3x + 4y$, or $7m^2 + 9m$, is called an **expression**. The separate parts of an expression, such as $3x$ or $4y$, are called the **terms** of the expression. So,

$$3x^2 + 7x + 5$$

is an **expression** with three **terms**.

Some expressions can be simplified. For example, the expression

$$7x + 3x$$

means 7 times the number x, plus 3 times the number x. It is clear that this expression is equivalent to 10 times the number x, whatever value x might take. So, $7x + 3x$ can be more simply written as $10x$. In the same way:

$$3p + 2p = 5p$$
$$12a - 3a = 9a$$
$$x^2 + x^2 = 2x^2$$
$$17p^3 - 12p^3 = 5p^3$$

When an expression has many terms, some may combine with others to simplify the expression. For example:

$$5p + 7q - 2p + 8q$$

can be simplified because $5p - 2p = 3p$ and $7q + 8q = 15q$. So,

$$5p + 7q - 2p + 8q = 3p + 15q$$

We must be careful not to combine terms which do not sensibly combine. For example, it makes perfect sense to say that 7 times the number x plus 3 times the number x is equal to 10 times the number x:

$$7x + 3x = 10x$$

However, it makes no sense at all to try to combine 7 times the square of the number x with 3 times the number x. We cannot simplify:

$$7x^2 + 3x$$

Examples

$$4p + 3e + 7p + 18e = 11p + 21e$$
$$5t - 6r - 3t + 8r = 2t + 2r$$
$$5t - 6r + 3t - 8r = 8t - 14r$$
$$a^2 + 3a - 5a + 7 = a^2 - 2a + 7$$
$$x^2 + xy + xy + y^2 = x^2 + 2xy + y^2$$

As a general rule, two terms can only be combined if the letter parts are **identical**. That is to say, $3a^2b$ can be combined with $5a^2b$ but **not** with $5ab^2$, $5a^2b^2$ or $5ab$.

The only exception to this rule is when a slight rearrangement can make two terms identical. This usually happens when a multiplication of letters is written in two different ways, for example, mn and nm. We know that whatever the values of the letters m and n, mn will always have the same value as nm, so we **can** combine an mn term with an nm term. For example:

$$2mn + nm = 3mn$$

or, if you prefer, $3nm$.

Simplify each of the following expressions.

a $11x + 12y + 7x + 5y$ **b** $11x + 12y - 7x + 5y$
c $11x + 12y + 7x - 5y$ **d** $11x - 12y + 7x + 5y$
e $-11x + 12y + 7x + 5y$ **f** $11x - 12y - 7x - 5y$
g $m^2 + 3m + 5m + 15$ **h** $b^2 + 5b - 2b - 10$
i $2a^2 - 12a - 2a + 12$ **j** $3v^3 + 3v^2 + 2v^2 + 2v$
k $12ab^3 - 8a^2b + 15ba^2 - 10ab$
l $5st - 5s^2t + 10t^2s - 7st^2 + 8ts^2$

Brackets

We already know that brackets are included in expressions to indicate the **order** in which calculations should be completed. When a bracket indicates that a multiplication is to be performed after an addition or subtraction, there is always an alternative calculation that allows multiplication to be performed first. For example, the expression:

$$8 \times (5 - 2)$$

indicates that 2 is to be subtracted from 5 and then the result multiplied by 8, giving a final answer of 24. The multiplication sign is normally missed out in our mathematical shorthand, so this result would be written:

$$8(5 - 2) = 8(3) = 24$$

An alternative way to calculate this result, doing the multiplication **first**, is to multiply both numbers inside the bracket by the number outside **before** subtracting.

$$8(5 - 2) = 40 - 16 = 24$$

The process of removing a bracket is called **expanding** the bracket. It is a useful technique when we wish to simplify an expression containing brackets.

Examples

$$4(2m + 6) = 8m + 24$$
$$3(5 - x^2) = 15 - 3x^2$$
$$-2(3e - 5f) = -6e + 10f$$
$$3c(4c + 5d - 3) = 12c^2 + 15cd - 9c$$
$$-4x(2x^3 - 3x + 5 - 7y) = -8x^4 + 12x^2 - 20x + 28xy$$

Two special cases, where there is no term written outside the bracket, can be dealt with by placing either 1 or -1 outside the bracket.

$$(2x - 7) = 1(2x - 7) = 2x - 7$$
$$-(2x - 7) = -1(2x - 7) = -2x + 7$$

Expand each of the following brackets.

a $3(4r + 7)$ **b** $5(6g - 9)$ **c** $-6(6r + 6)$
d $-6(6r - 6)$ **e** $(4m - 3n)$ **f** $-(4m - 3n)$
g $s(s - 1)$ **h** $-s(s - 1)$ **i** $-s(1 - s)$
j $5n(3n - 2n^2 + 6)$ **k** $-5n(3n - 2n^2 + 6)$ **l** $-5n^2(3n - 2n^2 - 6)$

Now we have mastered the skill of expanding brackets, we can simplify expressions that contain brackets.

Examples

$$4(x + 1) + 5(2x + 3) = 4x + 4 + 10x + 15 = 14x + 19$$
$$5(a + b) - 2(a - b) = 5a + 5b - 2a + 2b = 3a + 7b$$
$$y(2y - 1) + 4(2y - 1) = 2y^2 - y + 8y - 4 = 2y^2 + 7y - 4$$
$$x(x + y) - y(x + y) = x^2 + xy - yx - y^2 = x^2 - y^2$$

Expand brackets and then simplify.

a $3(4r + 7) + 2(2r - 6)$ **b** $5(6g - 9) - 4(g + 7)$
c $-6(6r + 6) - 6(6 - 6r)$ **d** $-6(6r - 6) - 6(6 + 6r)$
e $(4m - 3n) - (3n - 4m)$ **f** $-(4m - 3n) + 4m + 11n$
g $s(s - 1) + (s - 1)$ **h** $-s(s - 1) + (s - 1)$
i $-s(1 - s) + (1 - s)$ **j** $5n(3n - 2n^2 + 6) + 5(n^2 - 1)$
k $5n(2n + 1) - 3(2n + 1)$ **l** $x(2x + y) - y(2x + y)$

Extra complications are caused when a bracket is multiplied by another bracket. We can deduce a rule to deal with the problem by considering a simple example:

$$(3 + 5)(7 - 2)$$

Doing the addition and subtraction first, we have:

$$(3 + 5)(7 - 2) = (8)(5) = 40$$

If we want to do the multiplication first, we must multiply each term in the second bracket by each term in the first bracket. The easiest way to ensure that we do this is to draw up a small table like this:

$\times$	7	-2
3	21	-6
5	35	-10

So,

$$(3 + 5)(7 - 2) = 21 - 6 + 35 - 10 = 40$$

This result is true for any multiplication of two brackets.

The general rule to multiply brackets is to multiply each term in the second bracket by each term in the first bracket. In symbols this rule is expressed like this:

$$(a+b)(c+d) = ac + ad + bc + bd$$

The second method would not normally be used to complete this calculation, but it demonstrates a method we can use to simplify brackets multiplied by brackets. The use of a small multiplication table is your author's personal preference. It is not taught by all teachers, but of all the methods I have used over the years to teach this skill, it has produced the most success.

Examples

$(2x+1)(x+3)$

$\times$	x	$+3$
$2x$	$2x^2$	$6x$
$+1$	x	3

So,
$$(2x+1)(x+3) = 2x^2 + 6x + x + 3 = 2x^2 + 7x + 3$$

$(a+b)(a-b)$

$\times$	a	$-b$
a	a^2	$-ab$
b	ba	$-b^2$

So,
$$(a+b)(a-b) = a^2 - ab + ba - b^2 = a^2 - b^2$$

CHECKPOINT 8

Expand the following expressions.

a $(x+3)(x+5)$ **b** $(x+5)(x-7)$ **c** $(a-9)^2$
d $(2w+3)(w-1)$ **e** $(a+b)(a+b)$ **f** $(a-b)(a-b)$
g $(x-y)(y-x)$ **h** $(3x+5)(x-3)$ **i** $(2x-3)(x+2)$
j $(2x+3y)(3x-2y)$ **k** $(3x-4)(2x-5)$ **l** $(2x+y)^2$

Standard expansions

Three bracket expansions may be included on your syllabus as **standard results**; that is results that you should have memorised. If you completed the last checkpoint, you have already evaluated these results. They are:

$$(a+b)(a+b) = a^2 + b^2 + 2ab$$
$$(a-b)(a-b) = a^2 + b^2 - 2ab$$
$$(a-b)(a+b) = a^2 - b^2$$

To check the understanding of these results in an examination, an examiner usually makes up a calculation that can be quickly answered by using one of them.

Examples

Evaluate $98.5^2 + 1.5^2 + 2(98.5)(1.5)$.

If we spot that this calculation is of the form

$$a^2 + b^2 + 2ab$$

we can use the fact that

$$a^2 + b^2 + 2ab = (a+b)(a+b)$$

and write

$$98.5^2 + 1.5^2 + 2(98.5)(1.5) = (98.5 + 1.5)(98.5 + 1.5)$$
$$= (100)(100)$$
$$= 10\ 000$$

Sometimes, to prevent the use of a calculator to solve the problem, very large numbers are used.

Evaluate $10000000005^2 - 5^2$

If we spot that this calculation is of the form $a^2 - b^2$, we can use the fact that $a^2 - b^2 = (a+b)(a-b)$ and write;

$$10000000005^2 - 5^2 = (10000000005 + 5)(10000000005 - 5)$$
$$= (10000000010)(10000000000)$$
$$= 100000000100000000000$$

CHECKPOINT 9

Evaluate the following.

a $23^2 + 77^2 + 2(23)(77)$ **b** $1001^2 - 1^2$
c $123^2 + 23^2 - 2(123)(23)$ **d** $9.95^2 + 0.05^2 + 2(9.95)(0.05)$
e $9.95^2 - 0.05^2$ **f** $10.05^2 + 0.05^2 - 2(10.05)(0.05)$
g $1021^2 + 21^2 - (42)(1021)$ **h** $67.5^2 + 32.5^2 + (65)(67.5)$
i $100000000008^2 - 8^2$
j $1000000055^2 + 55^2 - (110)(1000000055)$

Algebraic fractions

The expression we are simplifying may include fractions, in which case we will need to apply all the normal rules for fraction arithmetic.

Examples

1 Simplify

$$\frac{x}{2} + \frac{y}{3}$$

The common denominator is 6. Applying the usual rules, we get

$$\frac{3x + 2y}{6}$$

2 Simplify

$$\frac{3}{a} - \frac{4}{b}$$

The common denominator is ab. a goes into ab b times and b goes into ab a times, so applying the usual rules we get

$$\frac{3b-4a}{ab}$$

3 Simplify

$$\frac{a}{2x} + \frac{b}{y}$$

The common denominator is $2xy$. $2x$ goes into this y times, and y goes into this $2x$ times; so applying the usual rules we get

$$\frac{ay+2bx}{2xy}$$

4 Simplify

$$\frac{ab}{ce} \times \frac{cb}{ad}$$

Letters can 'cancel' in exactly the same way that numbers do in a normal fraction multiplication. The 'cancelling' here is

$$\frac{\not{a}b}{\not{c}e} \times \frac{\not{c}b}{\not{a}d}$$

which gives

$$\frac{b^2}{de}$$

5 Simplify

$$\frac{6a^2}{b} \div ab^2$$

As usual in fraction arithmetic, we start by making any non-fractional expression into a fraction by placing it over 1. This gives us

$$\frac{6a^2}{b} \div \frac{ab^2}{1}$$

Then, applying the usual rules we get

$$\frac{6a^2}{b} \times \frac{1}{ab^2}$$

We can now cancel:

$$\frac{6a^{\not{2}}}{b} \times \frac{1}{\not{a}b^2}$$

which gives

$$\frac{6a}{b^3}$$

CHECKPOINT 10

1 Simplify

a $\dfrac{x}{4} + \dfrac{v}{5}$ **b** $\dfrac{a}{3} - \dfrac{b}{7}$ **c** $\dfrac{p}{3} - 4$ **d** $\dfrac{2}{x} + \dfrac{3}{4}$

e $\dfrac{1}{2} - \dfrac{7}{x}$ **f** $\dfrac{3}{2c} + \dfrac{5}{d}$ **g** $\dfrac{7}{3e} - \dfrac{5}{2f}$ **h** $\dfrac{w}{y} + \dfrac{x}{z}$

i $\dfrac{2w}{3m} - \dfrac{5r}{6n}$ **j** $\dfrac{a}{x} + \dfrac{bc}{yz} - \dfrac{t}{z}$

2 Simplify

a $\dfrac{a}{c} \times \dfrac{b}{d}$ **b** $\dfrac{2}{b} \times \dfrac{4b}{3a}$ **c** $\dfrac{c(a-b)}{6} \times \dfrac{3c}{2d}$

d $\left(\dfrac{3e+1}{ad}\right)^2$ **e** $\dfrac{x^3y^2}{4uv} \times \dfrac{8uv^2}{x^2y}$ **f** $\dfrac{3ab}{4c} \div 9$

g $25 \div \dfrac{5}{ef}$ **h** $\dfrac{abc}{e^2} \div \dfrac{bf}{ef}$ **i** $\dfrac{r^2(e+f)}{5e} \div \dfrac{3(e+f)}{25}$

j $\dfrac{12xy^2}{5z} \div x^2y$

Practical applications

The practical application of the skills of simplification is in constructing and simplifying mathematical statements. For example, suppose a professional gardener always plants a 12 foot diameter circular flower bed with 36 marigolds, 36 lobelias and 60 begonias. An 18 foot diameter bed is planted with 50 marigolds, 50 lobelias and 160 begonias. This can be expressed mathematically as follows.

For a 12 foot bed we need . . . . $36m + 36l + 60b$

For an 18 foot bed we need . . . . $50m + 50l + 160b$

Now, if the gardener is off in her van to plant out a garden with five 12 foot beds and two 18 foot beds, she needs to take:

$$5(36m + 36l + 60b) + 2(50m + 50l + 160b)$$

or

$$180m + 180l + 300b + 100m + 100l + 320b$$

or

$$280m + 280l + 620b$$

This is 280 marigolds, 280 lobelias and 620 begonias.

Examples

A 'think of a number' trick goes as follows.

Think of a number, add 6, multiply by 3, add 3, divide by 3, take away your original number. (The answer will always be 7.)

a Explain how this trick works.

b Make up a similar trick of your own.

To answer part **a**, let us use x to represent the starting number. The set of instructions can then be written in mathematical shorthand like this:

$$\frac{3(x+6)+3}{3} - x$$

Expanding and simplifying above the division line gives

$$\frac{3x + 21}{3} - x$$

The fraction simplifies to give

$$x + 7 - x$$

It now becomes obvious that whatever number we start with, our final answer must always be 7.

To answer part **b**, we can start with a similar expression and work backwards. Suppose we want our answer to always be 5. We can start with

$$x + 5 - x$$

Now, if we multiply and divide the $x + 5$ by 4, we can write

$$\frac{4(x + 5)}{4} - x$$

Now, to confuse things we can take part of the number term (20) outside the bracket, like this:

$$\frac{4(x + 3) + 8}{4} - x$$

Our final 'trick' is, therefore,

• think of a number, add 3, multiply by 4, add 8, divide by 4, take away the original number. (The answer will always be 5.)

![CHECKPOINT 11]

1 A toy manufacturer sells construction kits. Each kit contains parts of four different types: angle brackets, long rods, short rods and base plates. Three different kits are sold. Kit A contains 20 angle brackets, 10 short rods, 20 long rods and 5 base plates. Kit B contains 30 angle brackets, 15 short rods, 30 long rods and 8 base plates. Kit C contains 50 angle brackets, 30 short rods, 40 long rods and 12 base plates.

a Write down a mathematical shorthand for the contents of the three kits.

b Write down and simplify an expression for the components necessary to manufacture 500 A kits, 200 B kits and 50 C kits.

2 A 'think of a number' trick goes like this.
Think of a number, add 9, multiply by 6, add 12, divide by 6, take away your original number.

a What number will these calculations always produce as an answer?

b Explain how this trick works.
c Make up a similar trick of your own.

3 A farmer has 200 fencing panels, each 1 m long, to make this rectangular enclosure against a straight hedge. He uses x panels to make both of the two equal sides.

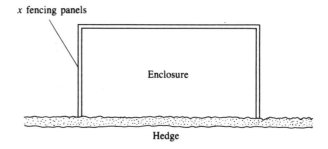

a Write down an expression for the width of the enclosure (in metres).

b Write down and simplify an expression for the area of the enclosure (in square metres).

c Draw up a table of values for the area of the enclosure as x takes values from 10 panels to 100 panels in steps of 5 panels.

4 An open box is made from a sheet of aluminium 24 cm by 24 cm. To do this, a square x cm by x cm is cut from each corner of the sheet and the resulting projections are then folded up to make the sides of the box. This is the construction plan.

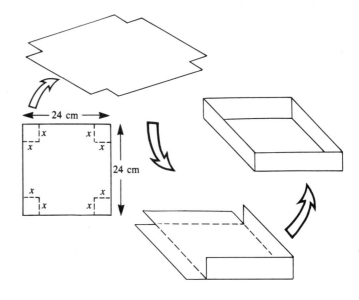

a Write down an expression for the side length of the box.

b Write down and simplify an expression for the volume of the box.

c Draw up a table of values showing the volume of the box as x takes values from 1 cm to 11 cm, in steps of 1 cm.

d Which value of x should be selected to produce a box with the maximum possible volume?

5 a Write down an expression for the area of this shape.

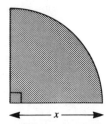

b Write down an expression for the area of this shape.

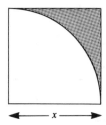

c Write down and simplify an expression for the area of this shape.

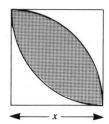

6 A river is flowing at a speed of y km per hour. A canoeist can paddle at a speed of x km per hour in still water.

a Write down an expression for the speed of the canoeist as she paddles downstream.

b Write down an expression for the speed of the canoeist as she paddles upstream.

c Write down an expression for the time taken for the canoeist to travel 6 km downstream.

d Write down an expression for the time taken for the canoeist to travel 6 km upstream.

e Write down and simplify an expression for the total time taken for the canoeist to paddle 6 km downstream and then to return.

Factorisation

The **factors** of a number are those numbers which divide exactly into the number. For example, the factors of 12 are 1, 2, 3, 4, 6 and 12.

In the same way, the factors of an expression are those numbers or expressions which divide exactly into the expression. For example, the factors of $4x$ are 1, 2, 4, x, $2x$ and $4x$.

Factorisation is the reverse process to expanding a bracket. To factorise an expression means to spot that the terms have a common factor and then to extract this factor outside a bracket. For example, when we look at the expression

$$3x + 12$$

we can spot that each term has 3 as a factor. Therefore, we can extract 3 outside a bracket and write

$$3x + 12 = 3(x + 4)$$

There are often many different ways in which an expression can be factorised. For example, the expression

$$8m - 4m^2$$

can be factorised in all the following ways:

$$8m - 4m^2 = 2(4m - 2m^2)$$
$$8m - 4m^2 = 4(2m - m^2)$$
$$8m - 4m^2 = m(8 - 4m)$$
$$8m - 4m^2 = 2m(4 - 2m)$$
$$8m - 4m^2 = 4m(2 - m)$$

In the last case, we have extracted the **highest common factor** of the terms in the expression. When we do this, we say we have **factorised the expression completely.**

Examples

Each of the following expressions has been factorised completely.

$$12w - 9 = 3(4w - 3)$$
$$a + 2ab = a(1 + 2b)$$
$$21x - 7x^2 = 7x(3 - x)$$
$$ab^2 + a^2b + ab = ab(b + a + 1)$$
$$8y^3 - 6y^2 + 10y = 2y(4y^2 - 3y + 5)$$

CHECKPOINT 12

Factorise completely each of the following expressions.

a $30p + 15$ **b** $27 - 12e$ **c** $q + 3qr$
d $6mn - m$ **e** $13e^2 - 5e$ **f** $9f^2 - 7f^3$
g $pq^2 + p^2q + pq$ **h** $abcd + acd + bcd$
i $12m^2n - 4mn^2 + 6mn$ **j** $25f^2g^3 + 15f^2g^2 - 10f^3g^2$

A practical application of the skills of factorisation is in simplifying formulas to produce the easiest method of calculation.

Example

Find the simplest possible calculation formula for working out the volume of concrete needed to manufacture this pipe.

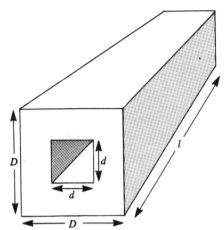

To calculate the volume, we will need to subtract the volume of the inner cuboid from the volume of the outer cuboid. That is, subtract the volume of the 'hole in the middle' from the volume the pipe would have if it were solid. The volume of a cuboid is found by multiplying the end area by the length, so we have:

$$\text{Volume of pipe} = D^2l - d^2l$$

Now, if we use this as a calculation formula, each specific calculation will require 5 steps: working out D^2 and d^2, multiplying each by l and finally subtracting. If, on the other hand, we factorise our formula like this,

$$\text{Volume of pipe} = l(D^2 - d^2)$$

we produce a calculation formula which requires only 4 steps: working out D^2 and d^2, subtracting and finally multiplying by l.

CHECKPOINT 13

1 Find the simplest possible calculation formula for working out the volume of concrete needed to manufacture this pipe.

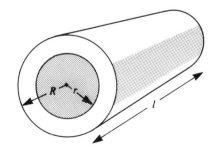

2 Find the simplest possible calculation formula for working out the volume of metal needed to cast a hollow brass sphere with an internal radius of m cm and an external radius of n cm.

3 This diagram shows a trapezium.

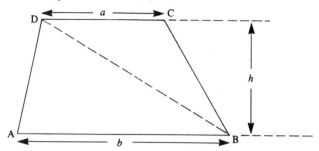

a Write down an expression for the area of triangle ABD.
b Write down an expression for the area of triangle BCD.
c Write down and simplify a formula for the area of the trapezium.

4 This diagram shows a segment formed in a 60° sector of a circle. Write down and simplify an expression for the area of the segment.

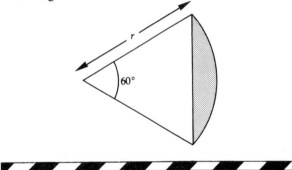

Factorisation of a quadratic

The expression $x^2 + 7x + 10$ cannot be factorised by the extraction of a common factor because the terms do not have one. The expression does, however, look rather like the results obtained when two brackets are multiplied together. It may be possible therefore to factorise the expression into a bracket multiplied by another bracket. The only problem is finding the two brackets!

Let's look at what we know. If this expression is two brackets multiplied together, it must be the result of a small multiplication table like the one below.

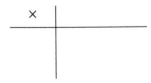

Now, we know that x^2 can only be the result of multiplying x by x. This fills in two gaps in the table.

×	x
x	x^2

87

The number term, $+10$, can only have come from the bottom right hand corner, because it could not have resulted from a multiplication on either of the x terms we have filled in. This fills in one more gap in the table.

$\times$	x
x	x^2
	10

To complete the table we need a little trial and error. We must fill in two numbers next to the x terms which meet two conditions:

- They multiply to produce 10.

- They produce two x terms which combine to a total of $7x$.

We could, for example, try 10 and 1. They meet the first condition, but when we try them in the table we get

$\times$	x	$+1$
x	x^2	x
$+10$	$10x$	10

which gives $x^2 + 11x + 10$, so the second condition has not been met.

If, on the other hand, we try 5 and 2, they meet both conditions.

$\times$	x	$+5$
x	x^2	$5x$
$+2$	$2x$	10

So, we can factorise $x^2 + 7x + 10$ into two brackets:

$$x^2 + 7x + 10 = (x+5)(x+2)$$

That explanation might seem a little long-winded, but we can now summarise it like this:

A scheme for factorising a quadratic
1 If you are asked to factorise an expression like $2x^2 + x - 6$, with no obvious common factors, try to factorise it into a bracket multipled by another bracket.
2 Draw up a blank multiplication table and insert the x^2 term in the top left hand corner. You should then be able to fill in the two x terms outside the table.
3 Insert the number term in the bottom right hand corner.
4 Try to find two numbers to fill in outside the table which meet the following conditions:

- They multiply to produce the number term.
- They combine to produce the correct x term.

Examples

1 Factorise $x^2 + 10x + 24$.
Steps 1, 2 and 3 give:

$\times$	x
x	x^2
	24

Step 4 could involve any pair of numbers that multiply to produce 24. The only pair that combine to also produce $10x$ is 4 and 6.

$\times$	x	$+4$
x	x^2	$4x$
$+6$	$6x$	24

So,
$$x^2 + 10x + 24 = (x+4)(x+6)$$

2 Factorise $2x^2 + x - 6$.
Steps 1, 2 and 3 give:

$\times$	x
$2x$	$2x^2$
	-6

Step 4 could involve any pair of numbers that multiply to produce -6. That makes this problem more difficult, both because we are dealing with a negative and because there is a $2x$ term outside the table. There are no tricks here, we must just slog away with trial and error until we come up with the correct numbers. The solution is

$\times$	x	$+2$
$2x$	$2x^2$	$4x$
-3	$-3x$	-6

So,

$$2x^2 + x - 6 = (2x-3)(x+2)$$

To help you get the feel of this kind of factorisation, you are given one factor of the expression in each part of question 1.

1 Copy and complete the following.

a $x^2 + 8x + 15 = (x+3)(x+5)$

b $x^2 + 7x + 12 = (x+3)(x+4)$

c $x^2 + x - 12 = (x-3)(x+4)$

d $x^2 + 3x - 10 = (x+5)(x-2)$

e $x^2 - 10x + 21 = (x-3)(x-7)$

f $x^2 - 7x + 10 = (x-2)(x-5)$

g $2x^2 + 7x + 3 = (2x+1)(x+3)$

h $2x^2 + 17x - 9 = (x+9)(2x-1)$

i $2x^2 + 5x - 12 = (x+4)(2x-3)$

j $3x^2 - 26x + 35 = (x-7)(3x-5)$

2 Factorise the following expressions.

a $x^2 + 9x + 18$ $(x+6)(x+3)$

b $x^2 + 6x + 5$ $(x+1)(x+5)$

c $x^2 + 4x - 5$ $(x+5)(x-1)$

d $x^2 - 4x - 5$ $(x-5)(x+1)$

e $x^2 - 6x + 5$ $(x-5)(x-1)$

f $x^2 - 11x + 28$ $(x-7)(x-4)$

g $2x^2 + 5x + 3$ $(2x+3)(x+3)$

h $3x^2 + 13x + 4$ $(3x+1)(x+4)$

i $2x^2 + 11x - 6$ $(2x-1)(x+6)$

j $2x^2 - 14x + 20$ $(2x-10)(x-2)$
$(2x-4)(x-5)$

Solving problems (equations)

Simple equations

Having developed a shorthand for writing mathematical statements, Hindu, Muslim and European mathematicians developed methods to solve a range of problems. For example, look at this problem.

A new employee of a company starts on a salary of £8,000 per year and then recieves a yearly increase of £500 each year for 10 years. How many years must an employee work before earning £12,500 a year?

If we let the number of years be represented by the letter n, we can write down this equation.

$$12\,500 = 8\,000 + 500n$$

A mathematical statement like this is called an **equation**. **Solving an equation** means working out the actual value of the unknown letter. The left hand side and right hand side of an equation are equal.

> The left hand and right hand sides of an equation will therefore still be equal if we choose to:
> - add any number to **both** sides of the equation
> - subtract any number from **both** sides of the equation
> - multiply **both** sides of the equation by any number
> - divide **both** sides of the equation by any number.

We can solve simple equations by selecting the correct numbers to add to, subtract from, multiply or divide both sides until we are left with the unknown number by itself on one side of the equation.

So, starting with

$$12\,500 = 8000 + 500n$$

we can decide to subtract 8000 from both sides of the equation. This gives us

$$12\,500 - 8000 = 8000 + 500n - 8000$$

or, simplifying,

$$4500 = 500n$$

Now, if we decide to divide both sides by 500 we get

$$\frac{4500}{500} = \frac{500n}{500}$$

or, simplifying,

$$9 = n$$

We have of course now solved the equation, because we know that n is equal to 9 years.

With a little practice you can rapidly spot the correct arithmetic to apply to both sides of the equation to produce a solution. It is simply a case of asking yourself what arithmetic is being applied to the unknown letter, and then applying the inverse steps. That is to say, because in our example n was being **multiplied** by 500 and **added** to 8000, we decided to **subtract** 8000 and **divide** by 500.

Examples

1 Solve $3e - 7 = 11$.

$$3e - 7 = 11$$

Add 7 to both sides:

$$3e - 7 + 7 = 11 + 7$$

which gives

$$3e = 18$$

Divide both sides by 3:

$$\frac{3e}{3} = \frac{18}{3}$$

which gives the answer

$$e = 6$$

2 Sally gives half her mints to Siloben and then gives 3 mints to Afzal. She has 7 mints left. How many did she start with? If we let s represent the number of sweets, we can write this equation

$$\frac{s}{2} - 3 = 7$$

Add 3 to both sides:

$$\frac{s}{2} - 3 + 3 = 7 + 3$$

which gives

$$\frac{s}{2} = 10$$

Multiply both sides by 2:

$$2 \times \frac{s}{2} = 2 \times 10$$

which gives

$$s = 20$$

3 A boat which can move at a speed of 5 km an hour in still water is travelling upstream. It takes 3 hours to travel 10.5 km. At what speed is the water flowing in the river.

If we let x represent the speed of the river, the speed of the boat upstream must be $5 - x$. In 3 hours it will travel a distance of 3 times this speed, or $3(5 - x)$ km.

So, we can write this equation:

$$3(5 - x) = 10.5$$

Divide both sides by 3:

$$\frac{3(5 - x)}{3} = \frac{10.5}{3}$$

which gives

$$5 - x = 3.5$$

Subtracting 5 from both sides:

$$5 - x - 5 = 3.5 - 5$$

which gives

$$-x = -1.5 \text{ or } x = 1.5$$

CHECKPOINT 15

1 Solve the following equations.

a $5m = 25$ **b** $21 = 7t$ **c** $9x = -81$

d $t + 4 = 24$ **e** $17 = r - 4$ **f** $17 = 4 - r$

g $\frac{x}{2} = 6$ **h** $\frac{t}{5} = -5$ **i** $-12 = \frac{v}{6}$

j $2w + 1 = 3$ **k** $4 + 7m = 32$ **l** $4 - 7m = 32$

m $\frac{x}{5} - 1 = 13$ **n** $3(x + 1) = 51$ **o** $4(2x - 1) = 8$

p $3(2x - 1) + 2(3x + 1) = 7$

2 One side of a triangle is x cm long. One of the other sides is 2 cm longer than x and one is 5 cm longer than x. If the perimeter of the triangle is 17 cm, what is the value of x?

3 A man in a betting shop doubles his stake money of £x with his first bet. He then loses £10 on his second bet and half the money he has left on his third bet. If after the three bets he has £4 left, what was his stake money?

4 When three women share out the profits from their car boot stall, Liz always takes £5 more than Marge because they use her car. Betty takes twice as much as Liz because she provides most of the stock. Find how much each woman will get as her share of a £60 profit.

Some equations may have x terms on both side of the equals sign. In this case, we must simplify to a single x term as part of the solution.

Examples

1 $4t - 5 = 3t + 12$

Start with

$$4t - 5 = 3t + 12$$

Subtract $3t$ from both sides:

$$4t - 5 - 3t = 3t + 12 - 3t$$

which gives

$$t - 5 = 12$$

Add 5 to both sides:

$$t - 5 + 5 = 12 + 5$$

which gives the answer

$$t = 17$$

2 At the races, Julie and Sharon both start off with the same stake money. Julie bets twice, doubling her money on the first race and losing £4 on the second. Sharon bets three times: she loses £3 on the first race, trebles what she has left on the second and loses £8 on the third. If Julie and Sharon have won the same amount by the end of the day, how much did each start with?

If we let £x represent the amount they start with, the amount that Julie has left can be expressed as

$$2x - 4$$

The amount that Sharon has left can be expressed as

$$3(x - 3) - 8$$

Since these amounts are equal, we can write

$$2x - 4 = 3(x - 3) - 8$$

Expanding the bracket gives

$$2x - 4 = 3x - 9 - 8$$

Simplifying gives

$$2x - 4 = 3x - 17$$

We can subtract $2x$ from both sides:

$$2x - 4 - 2x = 3x - 17 - 2x$$

which gives

$$-4 = x - 17$$

If we add 17 to both sides,

$$-4 + 17 = x - 17 + 17$$

we get the answer

$$x = 13$$

So, Julie and Sharon each started with £13. It is easy to work out that they finished with £22!

CHECKPOINT 16

1 Solve

a $8p + 4 = 7p - 3$ **b** $x - 15 = 9 - 2x$ **c** $4 - p = 15 - 2p$

d $3e = 18 - 6e$ **e** $5w - 17 = 7 - 3w$ **f** $3m + 3 - m = 3m - 8$

g $\dfrac{x}{2} + 3 = x + 5$ **h** $7 + \dfrac{a}{3} = a - 6$

i $3(x - 5) + 2 = x - 1$ **j** $12 - x = 5(x + 3) - 3(x + 5)$

k $3(2p - 1) = 5(p + 1)$ **l** $3(x + 7) - 1 = 7x$

m $5(2s - 1) + 4 = 6s + 1$ **n** $4 + 5(2x + 3) = 8(3 - x)$

2 I am 39 years old and my daughter is 7 years old. In n years time I will be three times older than my daughter. What is the value of n?

3 N is the first of three consecutive whole numbers whose sum is 85 more than N. Find the three numbers.

4 Julie and Sharon have been to the races again. Sharon lost half her money on her first bet and £10 on her second bet. Julie lost £6 on her first bet, but doubled the money she had left on her second bet. They both started with £x, but Julie now has £35.50 more than Sharon. How much money did they start with?

Equations like the ones we have been dealing with can be made as complicated as you, I, or an examiner pleases. The most difficult you are likely to meet are ones which contain several fractional terms, like this:

$$\frac{(x + 9)}{4} - \frac{(2x - 3)}{5} = 7$$

There is a simple technique to simplify equations like this. We multiply every term in the equation by the common denominator of all the bottom numbers in the fractional terms. In the example above, 4 and 5 have a common

denominator of 20. So, we would solve the equation like this:

$$\frac{20(x + 9)}{4} - \frac{20(2x - 3)}{5} = 20 \times 7$$

Cancelling the 4 and the 5 into their common denominator removes the fractions and gives us

$$5(x + 9) - 4(2x - 3) = 140$$

Expanding the brackets:

$$5x + 45 - 8x + 12 = 140$$

Simplifying:

$$57 - 3x = 140$$

If we subtract 57 from both sides,

$$57 - 3x - 57 = 140 - 57$$

we get

$$-3x = 83$$

Dividing by -3:

$$\frac{-3x}{-3} = \frac{83}{-3}$$

gives us

$$x = -27.67 \text{ (to 2 d.p.)}$$

Most of the equations we have dealt with so far have been rather contrived, in that they were designed to have nice neat whole number solutions. In the past, most examination problems have been of this kind. This is changing and, as in the last example, you may need a calculator to help you solve some of the equations on your examination papers.

CHECKPOINT 17

1 Solve, giving answers correct to 2 decimal places.

a $1.8x + 16.7 = 23.4$ **b** $23.6 - 5c = 11.3$

c $5x - 7.25 = 2.5x$ **d** $3(y - 3.5) + 1.2 = 9.6$

e $\dfrac{p - 2}{4} + \dfrac{p + 4}{5} = 8$ **f** $\dfrac{2y + 1}{3} + \dfrac{y - 7}{4} = 6$

g $\dfrac{3(u + 1)}{2} + \dfrac{2(u - 3)}{3} = 15$ **h** $\dfrac{7s}{2} - \dfrac{4(2s + 5)}{3} = \dfrac{s}{4}$

i $\dfrac{2w + 1}{2} - \dfrac{5 - w}{7} = 1.5$ **j** $\dfrac{e + 9}{3} - \dfrac{2 - e}{2} = 3$

2 The Grabensqueeze Building Society will lend you nine tenths of the value of the house you want to buy, up to a limit of 2.5 times your annual salary. How much does somebody need to be earning to buy a £100,000 house with a Grabensqueeze mortgage?

3 Afzal is x years old. His wife is six years younger than him and one seventh of his age is equal to one sixth of her age. How old is Afzal?

4 The volume of this food tin can be calculated with the formula

$$V = 3.14r^2h$$

A tin is designed with a base radius of 3.6 cm. What height must it have to give it a volume of 500 cm²?

Inequalities

The equation

$$3x - 12 = 3$$

is a mathematical **statement** about the number x.

It means three times the number x, minus 12 gives an answer of 3. We have learnt how to 'solve' such equations by applying the rules of algebra to produce the simpler mathematical statement

$$x = 5$$

An **inequality** is also a mathematical statement about a number. For example,

$$3x - 12 < 3$$

This means three times the number x, minus 12 gives an answer less than 3. Just as with equations, we can apply the rules of algebra to obtain a simpler statement.

Starting with

$$3x - 12 < 3$$

and adding 12 to both sides of the inequality:

$$3x - 12 + 12 < 3 + 12$$

gives

$$3x < 15$$

Dividing both sides of the inequality by 3:

$$\frac{3x}{3} < \frac{15}{3}$$

gives us the answer

$$x < 5$$

92

So, the statement 'three times the number x, minus 12 gives an answer less than 3' can be simplified to the statement 'the number x is less than 5'.

The simplification or solution of an inequality is often illustrated on a number line. A number line drawn to illustrate $x < 5$ would look like this:

A number line drawn to illustrate $x \geqslant -2$ would look like this:

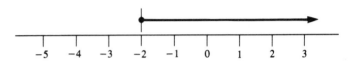

Notice that a solid 'blob' on the end of the line indicates that the last number is included in the solution and a hollow 'blob' indicates that it is not.

Examples

1 Solve the inequality and illustrate your solution on a number line.

$$\frac{2w}{3} - 4 \geqslant 2$$

Adding 4 to both sides of the inequality gives

$$\frac{2w}{3} \geqslant 6$$

Multiplying both sides of the inequality by 3 gives

$$2w \geqslant 18$$

Dividing both sides of the inequality by 2 gives

$$w \geqslant 9$$

We can illustrate the solution with this number line.

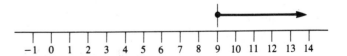

2 To buy a house, Sally James would need a deposit of one tenth of the selling price and a mortgage of 2.5 times her salary. If she can't afford to buy an £80,000 house, write down and simplify a statement about Sally's salary and illustrate the statement with a number line.

Letting s represent Sally's salary, we can write

$$2.5s + 8000 < 80\,000$$

Subtracting 8000 from both sides of the inequality gives

$$2.5s < 72\,000$$

Dividing both sides of the inequality by 2.5 gives

$$s < 28\,800$$

In other words, Sally must earn a salary less than £28,800. We can illustrate this statement with this number line.

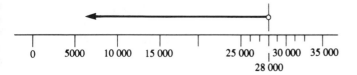

So far, we have just assumed that all the rules for simplifying equations can also be applied to inequalities. It certainly seems sensible to argue that if the left hand side of an inequality is greater (or less) than the right hand side of an inequality, then this will still be true if we choose to:

- add any number to both sides of the inequality
- subtract any number from both sides of the inequality
- multiply both sides of the inequality by any number
- divide both sides of the inequality by any number.

Unfortunately, these statements are **not** completely true. There is a problem if we either multiply or divide both sides of an inequality by a negative number. To illustrate this problem, look at this inequality, which is certainly true:

$$8 > 5$$

If we now multiply both sides of the inequality by -2, we have

$$-16 > -10$$

which is **not** a true statement. The correct statement would be $-16 < -10$.

In the same way, if we start with the true statement

$$-100 < 20$$

and divide both sides of the inequality by -5, we have

$$20 < -4$$

which is **not** a true statement. The correct statement is $20 > -4$.

This problem is caused by the difference between positive and negative numbers. With positive numbers like $+2$, $+4$ and $+8$, we have the ordering

$$+2 < +4 < +8$$

But, with negative numbers like -2, -4 and -8, we have the ordering

$$-2 > -4 > -8$$

To solve the problem, we need to add one extra rule for the simplification of inequalities. Our rules thus become:

> To simplify an inequality you can:
> - add any number to both sides of the inequality
> - subtract any number from both sides of the inequality
> - multiply both sides of the inequality by any number
> - divide both sides of the inequality by any number.
> - If you divide or multiply by a **negative** number, you must reverse the direction of the inequality.

CHECKPOINT 18

1 Solve these inequalities and illustrate your solution with a number line.

a $x + 4 \leqslant 7$ **b** $y - 7 > -10$

c $3e < -21$ **d** $\dfrac{y}{8} \geqslant 1.5$

e $5x - 2 > 38$

f $6.2 + \dfrac{w}{4} < 4.8$ **g** $\dfrac{3e}{4} + 7 \geqslant 19$

h $8(x - 7) \leqslant 28$ **i** $4(3x + 20) > 50$

j $\dfrac{3x + 2}{4} + 5 \geqslant 13$

2 This is the design for a greenhouse. It is to be 4 m long, have walls 2 m high, a centre roof height of 0.8 m and a width of x m. If the volume of the greenhouse must be at least 24 m³, write down and simplify an inequality for x. Illustrate the inequality with a number line.

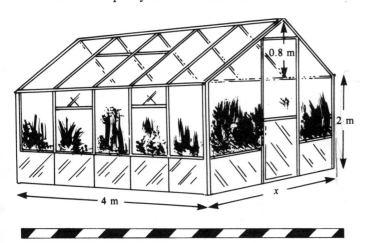

Examples

1 Solve the inequality $13 - x \geqslant 20$ and illustrate the solution with a number line.

Starting with

$$13 - x \geqslant 20$$

subtracting 13 from both sides of the inequality gives

$$-x \geqslant 7$$

Multiplying both sides by -1 and reversing the sign gives

$$x \leqslant -7$$

We can illustrate the solution with this number line.

2 Solve this inequality and illustrate the solution with a number line.

$$18 - \frac{5x}{2} > 12$$

Subtracting 18 from both sides of the inequality gives

$$-\frac{5x}{2} > -6$$

Multiplying both sides of the inequality by 2 gives

$$-5x > -12$$

Dividing both sides of the inequality by -5 and reversing the direction of the inequality gives

$$x < 2.4$$

We can illustrate the solution with this number line.

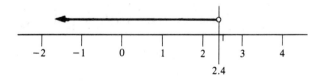

1 Solve these inequalities and illustrate the solution with a number line.

a $9 - x \leqslant 17$ **b** $9 - x \geqslant 7$

c $8 - 2x < 14$ **d** $8 - \frac{y}{2} < 9$

e $2(3 - 4x) \leqslant 4$

2 Gurmit is sent to the shop with a £10 note to buy a box of chocolates that costs £2.20. He is also told to buy as many 45p chocolate bars as he likes, so long as he brings back at least £6 change. Write down and simplify an inequality for x, the number of bars of chocolate that he buys. Illustrate the inequality with a number line.

Rearranging a formula

A formula represents a fixed set of rules for solving a problem. For example, the formula

$$t_{\text{thaw}} = 90w + 90$$

can be used to calculate the thawing time (t_{thaw}) in minutes needed to defrost a frozen turkey of weight w pounds. The value that a formula is designed to calculate is called the **subject** of the formula. In the case of the turkey formula, t_{thaw} is the subject of the formula.

We can use the rules of equation-solving to rearrange a formula and to change the subject. For example, we could take our turkey formula and rearrange as follows.

$$t_{\text{thaw}} = 90w + 90$$

Subtract 90 from both sides:

$$t_{\text{thaw}} - 90 = 90w + 90 - 90$$

which gives

$$t_{\text{thaw}} - 90 = 90w$$

Divide both sides by 90:

$$\frac{t_{\text{thaw}} - 90}{90} = \frac{90w}{90}$$

gives the answer

$$\frac{t_{\text{thaw}} - 90}{90} = w$$

The subject is usually written on the left, so our rearranged formula is

$$w = \frac{t_{\text{thaw}} - 90}{90}$$

This formula can now be used to answer a question like: 'If I have 24 hours available to defrost a turkey before I start to cook it, what is the heaviest turkey I can buy?'

Examples

1 Make F the subject of the formula

$$C = \frac{5(F-32)}{9}$$

Multiply both sides by 9:

$$9 \times C = 9 \times \frac{5(F-32)}{9}$$

which gives

$$9C = 5(F-32)$$

Divide both sides by 5:

$$\frac{9C}{5} = \frac{5(F-32)}{5}$$

which gives

$$\frac{9C}{5} = F-32$$

Adding 32 to both sides gives

$$\frac{9C}{5} + 32 = F$$

or

$$F = \frac{9C}{5} + 32$$

2 Make r the subject of the formula

$$V = \frac{\pi r^2 h}{3}$$

Multiply both sides by 3:

$$3 \times V = 3 \times \frac{\pi r^2 h}{3}$$

which gives

$$3V = \pi r^2 h$$

Divide both sides by πh:

$$\frac{3V}{\pi h} = \frac{\pi r^2 h}{\pi h}$$

which gives

$$\frac{3V}{\pi h} = r^2$$

Finally, taking the square root of both sides

$$\sqrt{\frac{3V}{\pi h}} = \sqrt{r^2}$$

or

$$r = \sqrt{\frac{3V}{\pi h}}$$

CHECKPOINT 20

1 Rearrange each of these formulae to make the letter given in brackets the subject.

a $t = e + 5$ (e) **b** $m = r - 4$ (r) **c** $C = \pi d$ (d)

d $y = 2x + 3$ (x) **e** $y = tx - r$ (r) **f** $s = u + vt$ (v)

g $y = \frac{3x}{2}$ (x) **h** $A = \frac{h(a+b)}{2}$ (h) **i** $s = \frac{t(u+v)}{2}$ (v)

j $R = \frac{V}{I}$ (V) **k** $s = ut + \frac{at^2}{2}$ (u) **l** $s = ut + \frac{at^2}{2}$ (a)

m $v^2 = u^2 + 2as$ (s) **n** $v^2 = u^2 + 2as$ (u)

o $s = 4\pi r^2$ (r) **p** $V = \pi l(R^2 - r^2)$ (R)

2 The formula $t_{cook} = 20w + 20$ can be used to calculate the cooking time (t_{cook}) in minutes needed to cook a defrosted turkey of weight w pounds.

a Use this formula and the defrosting formula given earlier in the text to produce a formula for t_{total}, the total time in minutes to thaw and cook a turkey of weight w pounds.

b Make w the subject of your formula.

c It is 9 pm, and Scott's mother-in-law is coming to dinner tomorrow, expecting to eat at about 7 pm. What is the heaviest turkey that Scott has time to defrost and cook?

If a formula involves a square root, it will be necessary to square both sides to remove it.

Examples

Make A the subject of the formula

$$r = \sqrt{\frac{A}{\pi}}$$

Square both sides:

$$r^2 = \left(\sqrt{\frac{A}{\pi}}\right)^2 = \frac{A}{\pi}$$

Multiply both sides by π:

$$\pi \times r^2 = \pi \times \frac{A}{\pi}$$

which gives

$$A = \pi r^2$$

CHECKPOINT 21

1 Rearrange each of these formulas to make the letter given in brackets the subject.

a $r = \sqrt{\frac{V}{\pi h}}$ (V) **b** $u = \sqrt{v^2 - 2as}$ (v)

c $V = \sqrt{\frac{2(E - mgh)}{m}}$ (E) **d** $t = 2\pi \sqrt{\frac{l}{g}}$ (g)

The letter we require as the new subject of a formula may occur more than once in our starting formula. In this case, we will need to factorise at some point in our rearrangement to obtain a single occurrence of the letter.

Examples

1 Make h the subject of the formula

$$V = \pi R^2 h - \pi r^2 h$$

Factorising gives

$$V = h\,(\pi R^2 - \pi r^2)$$

Dividing both sides by $(\pi R^2 - \pi r^2)$ gives

$$h = \frac{V}{(\pi R^2 - \pi r^2)}$$

2 Make p the subject of the formula

$$T = \frac{pq}{p+q}$$

Multiplying both sides by $p+q$ gives

$$T(p+q) = pq$$

or

$$Tp + Tq = pq$$

Subtracting pq from both sides gives

$$Tp + Tq - pq = 0$$

Factorising gives

$$p(T-q) + Tq = 0$$

Subtracting Tq from both sides gives

$$p(T-q) = -Tq$$

Dividing both sides by $T-q$ gives

$$p = \frac{-Tq}{T-q}$$

CHECKPOINT 22

Rearrange each of these formulas to make the letter given in brackets the subject.

a $V = ID^2 - Id^2$ (I) **b** $V = \dfrac{R^2h - r^2h}{3}$ (h)

c $f = \dfrac{a}{a+b}$ (a) **d** $T = \sqrt{\dfrac{p+q}{p-q}}$ (q)

Simultaneous equations

All the equation problems we have tackled so far have involved finding the value of a single letter which is contained in a single equation. **Simultaneous equations** ask us to find the value of more than one letter and give us more than one equation. For example, we might be given the pair of equations:

$$x + y = 9$$

$$x - y = 3$$

To solve this pair of simultaneous equations, we must find values of x and y which satisfy both equations.

A solution can be found by combining the equations in such a way that one letter disappears. Remember, in each equation the left hand side is equal to the right hand side. It follows that if we add the two left hand sides the result must be equal to adding the two right hand sides. So, starting with

$$x + y = 9$$

$$x - y = 3$$

if we add the left hand sides and the right hand sides we get

$$x + y + x - y = 9 + 3$$

which gives

$$2x = 12$$

So,

$$x = 6$$

Now, the first equation told us that

$$x + y = 9$$

and we now know that $x = 6$; therefore

$$6 + y = 9$$

So,

$$y = 3$$

Our solution is $x = 6$ and $y = 3$.

There are many pairs of values for x and y which make **one** of the equations true, for example $x = 4$, $y = 5$ makes the first equation true and $x = 7$, $y = 4$ makes the second equation true. The word **simultaneous** means 'at the same time'. Our solution, $x = 6$, $y = 3$ is the only pair of values that make both equations true **simultaneously**.

We can also subtract corresponding sides of simultaneous equations to produce a new equation. Starting with

$$2a + b = 5.7 \qquad \text{(Equation 1)}$$

$$a + b = 4 \qquad \text{(Equation 2)}$$

subtracting Equation 2 from Equation 1 gives

$$a = 1.7$$

Substituting 1.7 for a in Equation 2 gives

$$1.7 + b = 4$$

So,

$$b = 2.3$$

Our solution is $a = 1.7$ and $b = 2.3$.

Numbering the equations like this in your solutions and writing down the steps as you apply them will help both you and the examiner marking your script. Remember these are not normal 'sums' and you do not have to subtract Equation 2 from Equation 1 just because it is below it. If the algebra is easier, subtract 'upwards' and take Equation 1 from Equation 2. In the same way, having found the value of one letter, always pick the easiest equation to substitute back into.

Example

Solve

$$m + 4t = 12$$

$$m + 8t = 17$$

Call the equations 1 and 2 as follows:

$$m + 4t = 12 \qquad \text{(Equation 1)}$$

$$m + 8t = 17 \qquad \text{(Equation 2)}$$

Subtracting Equation 1 from Equation 2 gives

$$4t = 5$$

So,

$$t = 1.25$$

Substituting 1.25 for t in Equation 1 gives

$$m + 5 = 12$$

So,

$$m = 7$$

Our solution is $t = 1.25$ and $m = 7$.

Solve the following simultaneous equations:

a $x + y = 8$
$x - y = 3.4$

b $2x + y = 17$
$x + y = 11$

c $3p + 5q = 21$
$7p - 5q = -1$

d $5 + 3m = 2n$
$3 + 5m = 2n$

e $3x = 27 + 7y$
$12x = 3 - 7y$

f $p = 1 + q$
$2p = 20 - q$

g $5a + 3b = 32$
$8a + 3b = 44$

h $a + b = 0$
$5a - b = 6$

i $7x + 3y = 14$
$9x + 3y = 18$

j $5m - 13 = q$
$m + 3 = q$

The next examples demonstrate problems where we need to be particularly careful with plus and minus signs.

Examples

1 Solve

$$3u - 4w = 14$$

$$3u - 7w = 20$$

Call the equations

$$3u - 4w = 14 \qquad \text{(Equation 1)}$$

$$3u - 7w = 20 \qquad \text{(Equation 2)}$$

Subtract Equation 1 from Equation 2:

$$-3w = 6$$

(The $-3w$ term comes from $-7w - -4w$; this is equivalent to $-7w + 4w$, or $-3w$.)

Dividing by -3 gives

$$w = -2$$

Substituting $w = -2$ in Equation 1 gives

$$3u - (4 \times -2) = 14$$

$$3u - -8 = 14$$

$$3u + 8 = 14$$

$$3u = 6$$

$$u = 2$$

Our solution is $w = -2$ and $u = 2$.

2 Solve

$$2y - 3x = 17$$

$$7y - 3x = 37$$

Call the equations

$$2y - 3x = 17 \qquad \text{(Equation 1)}$$

$$7y - 3x = 37 \qquad \text{(Equation 2)}$$

Subtract Equation 1 from Equation 2:

$$5y = 20$$

(We subtract because this is the only way to eliminate the x terms. $-3x - -3x$ is equivalent to $-3x + 3x$ or 0. Adding the equations would give us $-3x + -3x$ which is $-6x$.) Dividing by 5 gives

$$y = 4$$

Substituting 4 for y in Equation 1 gives

$$8 - 3x = 17$$
$$-3x = 9$$
$$x = -3$$

Our solution is $y = 4$ and $x = -3$.

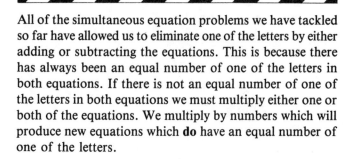

CHECKPOINT 24

1 Solve the following.

a $4a + 3b = 17$
   $4a - 2b = 2$

b $2x - q = 3$
   $2x + 3q = 23$

c $7t = 14.5 - 2w$
   $7t = 8w + 29.5$

d $8x + 2y = -15$
   $8x - 2y = 15$

e $3e - 2f = 11$
   $2e - 2f = 4$

f $r - 4s = -6$
   $3r - 4s = 6$

g $6m - 2n = -10$
   $8m - 2n = -16$

h $-39.2 = 4x - 7y$
   $-18.2 = x - 7y$

i $8 = q - p$
   $20 = 5q - p$

j $3x - 5y = 17$
   $8x - 5y = 37$

2 Bill is in a generous mood. He bought the first round of drinks and paid £5.10 for 3 pints of beer and 2 sherries. He then insisted on buying the second round and paid £7.30 for 5 pints of beer and 2 sheries. How must does each type of drink cost?

3 A fairground stallholder gives cash prizes on her rifle range. Each customer pays £x for a go and can win a prize of £y if he or she is lucky. On a day when she has 200 customers and pays out 7 prizes, the stallholder makes £65 profit. On a day when she has 300 customers and pays out 7 prizes, the stallholder makes £115 profit. How much does each customer pay and what is the value of each prize?

All of the simultaneous equation problems we have tackled so far have allowed us to eliminate one of the letters by either adding or subtracting the equations. This is because there has always been an equal number of one of the letters in both equations. If there is not an equal number of one of the letters in both equations we must multiply either one or both of the equations. We multiply by numbers which will produce new equations which **do** have an equal number of one of the letters.

Examples

Solve

$$4r - 3e = 50$$
$$r + 6e = -1$$

Call the equations 1 and 2:

$$4r - 3e = 50 \qquad \text{(Equation 1)}$$
$$r + 6e = -1 \qquad \text{(Equation 2)}$$

Multiply Equation 2 by 4 to produce Equation 3:

$$4r + 24e = -4 \qquad \text{(Equation 3)}$$

(We now have two equations, Equation 1 and Equation 3, which both contain a $4r$ term).

Subtracting Equation 1 from Equation 3 gives

$$27e = -54$$
$$e = -2$$

Substituting -2 for e in Equation 2 gives

$$r + -12 = -1$$
$$r = 11$$

Our solution is $e = -2$ and $r = 11$.

In the last example was it was quite easy to multiply Equation 2 by 4, thus producing Equation 3, which contained the same r term as Equation 1. Other examples may not be so straightforward and a double multiplication may be needed.

Example

Two kilograms of butter and five kilograms of sugar cost £7.55. Three kilograms of butter and four kilograms of sugar cost £9.12. Find the cost per kilogram of butter and sugar.

Let b and s represents the cost per kilogram of butter and sugar. We can then write down two equations:

$$2b + 5s = 7.55 \qquad \text{(Equation 1)}$$
$$3b + 4s = 9.12 \qquad \text{(Equation 2)}$$

Studying these equations, we see that no simple multiplication of one equation can produce the b term or s term contained in the other equation. We will therefore have to multiply **both** equations to produce **two** new equations which do have either the same b term or the same *s* term. We have a choice: we must decide whether we intend to eliminate the *b* terms or the *s* terms. If we decide to eliminate the *b* terms we need two equations with the same *b* term. If we decide to eliminate the *s* terms we need two equations with the same *s* term. Let's assume we have decided to eliminate the *b* terms. In the first equation we have $2b$ and in the second equation we have $3b$. If we multiply the first equation by 3 and the second equation by 2, we will produce two new equations which both contain a $6b$ term.

$$2b + 5s = 7.55 \qquad \text{(Equation 1)}$$
$$3b + 4s = 9.12 \qquad \text{(Equation 2)}$$

Multiplying Equation 1 by 3 and Equation 2 by 2 gives

$$6b + 15s = 22.65 \qquad \text{(Equation 3)}$$
$$6b + 8s = 18.24 \qquad \text{(Equation 4)}$$

Subtracting Equation 4 from Equation 3 gives

$$7s = 4.41$$
$$s = 0.63$$

Substituting 0.63 for *s* in Equation 1 gives

$$2b + 3.15 = 7.55$$
$$2b = 4.4$$
$$b = 2.2$$

Our solution is butter costs £2.20 a kilogram and sugar costs £0.63 a kilogram.

CHECKPOINT 25

1 Solve the following:

a $m + 5n = 13$
   $3m + n = 11$

b $m + 4n = 9$
   $6m - 3n = 27$

c $4x - 3y = 30$
   $x + y = 4$

d $8t = 4s - 40$
   $2t = 3m - 18$

e $5e - f = 64$
   $2e - 5f = 54$

f $4x + 4y = 26$
   $3x + 6y = 27$

g $4m + 2n = -2$
   $3m - 2n = -5$

h $8x - 3y = 9$
   $5x + 4y = 35$

i $5t - 7s = -5$
   $7t - 5s = 17$

j $8a - 3b = 21$
   $7a - 7b = 49$

2 Janice paid £6.40 for 4 adults and 2 children at the cinema. Later, talking to her friend Raj who also saw the film, she finds that Raj paid the same amount for 2 adults and 5 children. How much does an adult ticket and a child's ticket cost?

3 Arthur Fowler earns £*x* a week, of which he saves £*y* and spends the rest. Pete Beal earns twice as much as Arthur and saves three times as much; he spends £150 a week.

Denis Watts earns three times as much as Arthur and saves twice as much; he spends £250 a week. How much do all three earn and save?

Quadratic equations

Early Hindu and Arab mathematicians were interested in all kinds of number puzzles and riddles and discovered many new properties of numbers by solving them. We have already learned to solve quite a range of these puzzles or equations, but one type we cannot yet solve is illustrated by the following riddle.

'I think of a number and square it. I add six, then take away five times the number. The result is zero, what number did I think of ?'

If we let *x* represent the number, we can write this mathematical statement about *x*:

$$x^2 - 5x + 6 = 0$$

An equation like this, which contains a square, is called a **quadratic equation**.

There are several techniques for solving quadratic equations. The two techniques most likely to be included in your syllabus are:

- solution by factorisation
- solution by formula

These are covered in the next two sections and checkpoints. You should consult your syllabus to see whether you need to study one or both of the sections.

Solution by **factorisation** is a rather old-fashioned method in the days of computers and calculators and only works if the quadratic expression **can** be factorised. In fact most questions solved by this method are carefully contrived so that they do have simple factors. This is true of the example given earlier:

$$x^2 - 5x + 6 = 0$$

This can be factorised into

$$(x - 3)(x - 2) = 0$$

We now argue that, since $(x - 3)$ multiplied by $(x - 2)$ is zero, either $(x - 3)$ or $(x - 2)$ must be zero.

Either

$$(x - 3) = 0$$

or

$$(x - 2) = 0$$

In which case, it is clear that either $x = 2$ or $x = 3$.

It may surprise you that we appear to have produced **two different answers for one problem**. We can easily check that both are correct by substituting the values in the original equation; substituting $x = 2$ in the lefthand expression gives

$$2^2 - (5 \times 2) + 6$$

or

$$4 - 10 + 6,$$ which is certainly equal to zero.

Substituting $x = 3$ gives

$$3^2 - (5 \times 3) + 6$$

or

$$9 - 15 + 6,$$ which is also equal to zero.

So, the quadratic equation has two equally valid solutions. If you go back over the solution to the equation, you will see that the whole technique hinges on the argument that if two numbers or expressions multiply to produce zero, at least one of them must be equal to zero. It follows that the starting point to this technique must be an equation with zero on one side.

Example

A carpet is 2 metres longer than it is wide. If it has an area of $15\,\text{m}^2$, how wide is it?

If we let x represent the width of the carpet, we have this diagram:

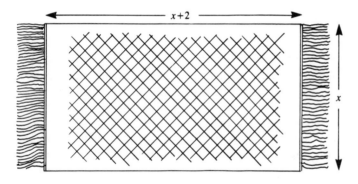

and this equation:

$$x(x + 2) = 15$$

If we are to solve this by factorisation, we must first make one side of the equation zero.

Subtracting 15 from both sides gives

$$x(x + 2) - 15 = 0$$

or

$$x^2 + 2x - 15 = 0$$

Factorising gives

$$(x + 5)(x - 3) = 0$$

Therefore

$$\text{either } x + 5 = 0 \text{ or } x - 3 = 0$$

$$\text{either } x = -5 \text{ or } x = 3$$

Both these numbers satisfy the equation, but a carpet cannot have a width of -5 metres, so in practical terms, the solution is that the carpet is 3 metres wide.

We can summarise this section as follows.

> To solve a quadratic equation by factorisation:
> 1 Rearrange if necessary until one side of the equation is zero.
> 2 Factorise the quadratic expression.
> 3 Set each factor equal to zero to produce the solutions to the equation.

Examples

1 Solve

$$x^2 - 8x = 0$$

Factorising gives

$$x(x - 8) = 0$$

Therefore

$$\text{either } x = 0 \text{ or } x - 8 = 0$$

$$\text{either } x = 0 \text{ or } x = 8$$

2 Solve

$$x^2 + 10x = 39$$

Rearranging gives

$$x^2 + 10x - 39 = 0$$

Factorising gives

$$(x + 13)(x - 3) = 0$$

Therefore

$$\text{either } x + 13 = 0 \text{ or } x - 3 = 0$$

$$\text{either } x = -13 \text{ or } x = 3$$

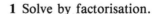

CHECKPOINT 26

1 Solve by factorisation.

a $x^2 + 4x + 3 = 0$ b $x^2 - 7x = 0$
c $x^2 + 9x + 18 = 0$ d $x^2 - 4x - 5 = 0$
e $x^2 - 6x = -5$ f $x^2 - x = 12$
g $2x^2 + 7x = 30$ h $x^2 = 12 - 4x$
i $2x^2 = 5x - 3$ j $m^2 - 8 = 2m$

2 The base of this triangle is x cm long. The height is 3 cm longer than the base.

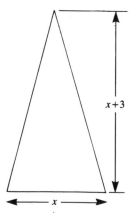

If the triangle has an area of 14 cm², find the value of x.

3 If you hit a cricket ball vertically upwards with your bat 4 feet above the ground and it leaves your bat with a speed of 36 feet per second, a formula for its height (in feet) above the ground after t seconds is

$$h = 4 + 36t - 16t^2$$

Find the two times when the ball will be 12 feet above the ground.

4 A rectangle has a base length of $2x + 3$ cm and a height of $x + 5$ cm.

a Write down and simplify an expression for the area of the rectangle.

b If the area of the rectangle is 49 cm², find the value of x.

The solutions of a quadratic equation are called the **roots** of the equation. The Muslim mathematician Alkarismi, working in the ninth century, discovered a formula for finding the roots of any quadratic equation. This formula applies to the general quadratic equation:

$$ax^2 + bx + c = 0$$

and states that the roots of this equation will be

$$x = \frac{-b + \sqrt{b^2 - 4ac}}{2a} \quad \text{or} \quad x = \frac{-b - \sqrt{b^2 - 4ac}}{2a}$$

One of the questions in the problem exercise explores the methods by which Alkarismi discovered this formula.

We will use the formula to find the roots of the equation

$$3x^2 - 5x + 2 = 0$$

First, we must compare the equation with the general equation $ax^2 + bx + c = 0$ and carefully write down the values of a, b and c. These are:

$$a = 3, \ b = -5 \text{ and } c = 2$$

Substituting these values for a, b and c in the formula for the roots gives

$$x = \frac{-(-5) + \sqrt{(-5^2) - 4 \times 3 \times 2}}{2 \times 3}$$

or

$$x = \frac{-(-5) - \sqrt{(-5^2) - 4 \times 3 \times 2}}{2 \times 3}$$

$$x = \frac{5 + \sqrt{25 - 24}}{6} \quad \text{or} \quad x = \frac{5 - \sqrt{25 - 24}}{6}$$

$$x = \frac{5 + 1}{6} \quad \text{or} \quad x = \frac{5 - 1}{6}$$

$$x = 1 \text{ or } x = 0.67 \text{ (to 2 d.p.)}$$

If you study the two parts of the formula, you will notice that they only differ by one minus sign instead of a plus sign. The two parts are often combined using this special double sign ± which means 'plus or minus'. The general formula can then be expressed like this.

If

$$ax^2 + bx + c = 0$$

then the roots of the equation will be

$$x = \frac{-b \pm \sqrt{b^2 - 4ac}}{2a}$$

Some quadratic equations have no solutions. For example, consider the equation

$$x^2 + x + 5 = 0$$

We can draw up this table of values for $x^2 + x + 5$.

Value of x	−3	−2	−1	0	1	2	3
Value of x^2	9	4	1	0	1	4	9
Value of $x^2 + x + 5$	11	7	5	5	7	11	17

If the table were extended to the right, it is quite clear that the value of $x^2 + x + 5$ will continue to increase. But, if the table is extended to the left, the value of $x^2 + x + 5$ will also increase because x^2 will always be positive even when x is negative. So, we can see from the table that there are no values of x which can make the equation $x^2 + x + 5 = 0$ true. If you attempt to solve such an equation by factorisation, you will find that you simply cannot factorise it. If we attempt to find the roots of $x^2 + x + 5 = 0$ by the formula method, a problem occurs.

First, we must compare the equation with the general equation:

$$ax^2 + bx + c = 0$$

and carefully write down the values of a, b and c.

These are

$$a=1, \ b=1 \text{ and } c=5$$

Substituting these values for a, b and c in the formula for the roots gives

$$x = \frac{-1 \pm \sqrt{1^2 - 4 \times 1 \times 5}}{2 \times 1}$$

$$x = \frac{-1 \pm \sqrt{1 - 20}}{2}$$

$$x = \frac{-1 \pm \sqrt{-19}}{2}$$

$$x = \frac{-1 + \sqrt{-19}}{2} \quad \text{or} \quad x = \frac{-1 - \sqrt{-19}}{2}$$

This is as far as we can go with the formula. The square of a positive number is a positive number and the square of a negative number is also a positive number. Therefore, no number can be squared and produce a negative answer. So, -19 does not have a square root and we cannot obtain solutions to the equation from the formula. With this exception, the formula can quickly and easily produce the roots of a quadratic equation.

To solve a quadratic equation by formula:

1 Rearrange the equation, if necessary, to make the right hand side equal to zero.
2 Carefully compare the equation to the general equation $ax^2 + bx + c = 0$ and write down the values of a, b and c.
3 Substitute the values of a, b and c in the general formula for the roots:
$$x = \frac{-b \pm \sqrt{b^2 - 4ac}}{2a}$$

Examples

1 Solve $3x^2 - 4x + 1 = 0$.

Comparing to $ax^2 + bx + c$ gives $a=3$, $b=-4$, $c=1$.

Substituting these values for a, b and c in the formula gives

$$x = \frac{-(-4) \pm \sqrt{(-4)^2 - 4 \times 3 \times 1}}{2 \times 3}$$

$$x = \frac{4 \pm \sqrt{16 - 12}}{6}$$

$$x = \frac{4 \pm \sqrt{4}}{6}$$

$$x = \frac{4 + 2}{6} \text{ or } x = \frac{4 - 2}{6}$$

$$x = 1 \text{ or } 0.33 \text{ (to 2 d.p.)}$$

2 Solve $x^2 + 4x + 4 = 0$.

Comparing to $ax^2 + bx + c$ gives $a=1$, $b=4$, $c=4$.

Substituting these values for a, b and c in the formula gives

$$x = \frac{-4 \pm \sqrt{4^2 - 4 \times 1 \times 4}}{2 \times 1}$$

$$x = \frac{-4 \pm \sqrt{16 - 16}}{2}$$

$$x = \frac{-4 \pm 0}{2}$$

$$x = \frac{-4 + 0}{2} \text{ or } x = \frac{-4 - 0}{2}$$

$$x = -2$$

3 Solve $2x^2 - 3 = 7x$.

Rearranging gives

$$2x^2 - 7x - 3 = 0$$

Comparing with $ax^2 + bx + c$ gives $a=2$, $b=-7$, $c=-3$.

Substituting these values for a, b and c in the formula gives

$$x = \frac{-(-7) \pm \sqrt{(-7)^2 - 4 \times 2 \times -3}}{2 \times 2}$$

$$x = \frac{7 \pm \sqrt{49 - -24}}{4}$$

$$x = \frac{7 \pm \sqrt{73}}{4}$$

$$x = \frac{7 + 8.54}{4} \text{ or } x = \frac{7 - 8.54}{4}$$

$$x = 3.89 \text{ or } -0.39 \text{ (to 2 d.p.)}$$

1 Solve the following quadratic equations by use of the formula.

a $x^2 + 6x + 6 = 0$ **b** $x^2 - 5x + 1 = 0$
c $x^2 + 5x - 3 = 0$ **d** $x^2 + 7x + 10 = 0$
e $x^2 - 7x - 5 = 0$ **f** $4x^2 + 3x - 2 = 0$
g $5x^2 - 9x + 1 = 0$ **h** $3x^2 - 5x - 4 = 0$
i $3x = 7 - 4x^2$ **j** $90 = 15t - 4.9t^2$

2 The sides of any right-angled triangle ABC are related by the formula

$$AB^2 = BC^2 + CA^2$$

where AB is the longest side.

If the sides of this right-angled triangle are x cm, $x+4$ cm and $x+5$ cm, find the value of x.

3 Solve

$$\frac{14}{(x+3)} + \frac{15}{(x+4)} = 6$$

(Hint. Start by multiplying the whole equation by $(x+3)(x+4)$.)

4 A rectangular lawn is 12 m by 15 m. A path of constant width makes a border all the way round the lawn as this diagram shows. If the path has an area of 150 m², how wide is it?

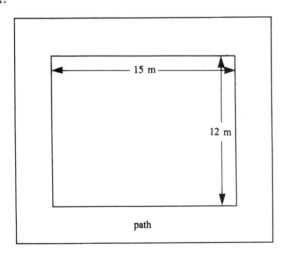

15 m
12 m
path

Number patterns and number sequences

The Hindu Mathematician Aryabhata revived the ancient interest in number patterns and sequences of numbers.

Working with the new numbers based on groups of ten, he and other Hindu and Arab mathematicians made many new discoveries. Many of these discoveries concerned **sequences** of numbers. A sequence is a set of numbers arranged into an order. The simplest example is the set of positive whole numbers.

$$1, 2, 3, 4, 5, 6, 7, 8, \ldots$$

Because this sequence is the most simple and basic of all, these numbers are given a special name. They are called the set of **natural numbers**.

Other sequences can be developed from the set of natural numbers. For example, if we multiply all the natural numbers by 2, we produce the set of **even numbers**.

1,	2,	3,	4,	5,	6,	7,	8,	...
↓	↓	↓	↓	↓	↓	↓	↓	
2,	4,	6,	8,	10,	12,	14,	16,	...

Each number in a sequence is called a **term** of the sequence. We use the basic sequence of natural numbers to number the terms in all other sequences. The first 8 terms in the sequence of odd numbers are numbered like this:

Term number	1	2	3	4	5	6	7	8
Term	1	3	5	7	9	11	13	15

Using this notation, we can write:

9 is the 5th term in the sequence of odd numbers.

Copy and complete the following.
a The 10th term of the sequence of even numbers is . . .
b The 50th term of the sequence of even numbers is . . .
c The 50th term of the sequence of odd numbers is . . .
d The 7th term of the sequence of prime numbers is . . .

Describing sequences

We can use mathematical shorthand to describe sequences. The terms of a sequence are represented by a letter, with a small suffix to denote each individual term. For example, if we decide to use the letter A to represent a sequence, A_1 is the first term, A_2 is the second term, A_3 is the third term and so on.

If we use the letter U to represent the sequence of even numbers, we have:

U_1	U_2	U_3	U_4	U_5	U_6	U_7	U_8
2	4	6	8	10	12	14	16

If you wanted to know what the 200th even number is, you could write down the first 200 terms of the sequence, 2, 4, 6, 8, 10, 12 . . . You would however probably spot that since U_1 is 2, U_2 is 4 and U_3 is 6, it follows that U_{200} must be 400. In other words, if you want to know the nth even number, multiply n by 2. We can summarise this rule for working out even numbers with a formula like this:

$$U_n = 2n$$

where n can be any natural number.

Similar formulas can be found to work out the terms of many other sequences. For example, the formula $T_n = 3n + 1$ produces the sequence:

$$T_1 = 3 \times 1 + 1 = 4$$
$$T_2 = 3 \times 2 + 1 = 7$$
$$T_3 = 3 \times 3 + 1 = 10$$

Examples

Write down the first four terms and the tenth term of the sequence produced by the following formula:

$$U_n = 3 \times 2^{n-1}$$

The first four terms are:

$$U_1 = 3 \times 2^{1-1} = 3 \times 2^0 = 3 \times 1 = 3$$
$$U_2 = 3 \times 2^{2-1} = 3 \times 2^1 = 3 \times 2 = 6$$
$$U_3 = 3 \times 2^{3-1} = 3 \times 2^2 = 3 \times 4 = 12$$
$$U_4 = 3 \times 2^{4-1} = 3 \times 2^3 = 3 \times 8 = 24$$

The tenth term is:

$$U_{10} = 3 \times 2^{10-1} = 3 \times 2^9 = 3 \times 512 = 1536$$

CHECKPOINT 29

Write down the first four terms and the tenth term of the sequences produced by the following formulas.

a $T_n = 2n - 1$

b $T_n = 5n + 3$

c $T_n = n^2$

d $T_n = n^2 + n$

e $T_n = \dfrac{n^2 + n}{2}$

f $T_n = 102 - 2n$

g $T_n = 2^{n-1}$

h $T_n = 5 \times 4^{n-1}$

Producing the terms of a series if you are given the formula is relatively easy. It is more difficult to reverse this process and to find a formula that produces the terms of a given series.

Examples

1 Find a formula for the nth term of the sequence:

$$3, \quad 7, \quad 11, \quad 15, \quad 19, \ldots$$

It is best to start by constructing a table like this;

T_1	T_2	T_3	T_4	T_5
3	7	11	15	19

Examining the table we can see that the sequence starts with 3 and that each new term is produced by adding 4 to the previous term. So, we can write

$$T_1 = 3$$
$$T_2 = 3 + 4$$
$$T_3 = 3 + 2 \times 4$$
$$T_4 = 3 + 3 \times 4$$
$$T_5 = 3 + 4 \times 4$$

So, T_n can be expressed as

$$T_n = 3 + (n - 1) \times 4$$

which can be simplified to

$$T_n = 3 + 4n - 4$$
$$T_n = 4n - 1$$

A sequence like this, in which each new term is formed by adding a constant amount to the previous term is called an **arithmetic sequence**.

2 Find a formula for the nth term of the sequence:

$$5, \quad 10, \quad 20, \quad 40, \quad 80, \quad \ldots$$

It is best to start by constructing a table like this:

T_1	T_2	T_3	T_4	T_5
5	10	20	40	80

Examining the table we can see that the sequence starts with 5 and that each new term is produced by multiplying the previous term by 2. So, we can write

$$T_1 = 5$$
$$T_2 = 5 \times 2$$
$$T_3 = 5 \times 2 \times 2$$
$$T_4 = 5 \times 2 \times 2 \times 2$$
$$T_5 = 5 \times 2 \times 2 \times 2 \times 2$$

or, using power notation,

$$T_1 = 5 \times 2^0$$

$$T_2 = 5 \times 2^1$$

$$T_3 = 5 \times 2^2$$

$$T_4 = 5 \times 2^3$$

$$T_5 = 5 \times 2^4$$

So, T_n can be expressed as

$$T_n = 5 \times 2^{n-1}$$

A sequence like this, in which each new term is formed by multiplying the previous term by a constant amount, is called a **geometric sequence**.

CHECKPOINT 30

1 Find a formula for the nth term of each of the following sequences:

a 1, 3, 5, 7, 9, ...

b 5, 17, 29, 41, 53, ...

c 120, 112, 104, 96, 88, ...

d 2, 10, 50, 250, 1250, ...

e 3, 12, 48, 192, 768, ...

f 4000, 2000, 1000, 500, 250, ...

2 A gardener always plants flower beds with red geraniums, blue ageratums and yellow marigolds. Her planting plans for 1, 2 and 3 geraniums are:

```
A M A          A M A M          A M A M A
M G M          M G G A          M G G G M
A M A          A M A M          A M A M A
1 geranium     2 geraniums      3 geraniums
```

Find a formula for the number of ageratums and marigolds needed if n geraniums are planted.

3 An ancient story tells of a boy who did a king a great favour. For his reward, the boy asked for a chessboard full of rice. He wanted 1 grain on the first square, 2 grains on the second square, 4 grains on the third square, 8 grains on the fourth square, 16 grains on the fifth square and so on. The king laughed at this simple request, but in fact it proved impossible to grant.

a Find a formula for the number of grains of rice on the nth square of the board.

b Why was the request impossible to grant?

Square and triangular numbers

Two sequences that are neither arithmetic nor geometric are the **square numbers** and the **triangular numbers**.

The sequence of square numbers is 1, 4, 9, 16, 25, ... They are called square numbers because the terms of the sequence can be represented by square patterns of dots like this:

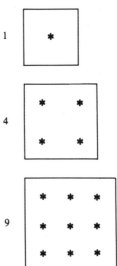

If we use the letter S to represent the sequence of square numbers, we have

S_1	S_2	S_3	S_4	S_n
1	4	9	16	n^2

The sequence of triangular numbers is 1, 3, 6, 10, 15, ... They are called triangular numbers because the terms of the sequence can be represented by triangular patterns of dots like this:

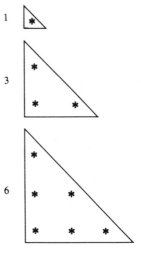

The next checkpoint invites you to find a formula for the nth triangular number.

1 Two identical numbers can be placed together to form a rectangle.

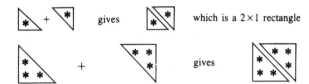

which is a 2×1 rectangle

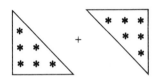

which is a 2×3 rectangle

which is a 3×4 rectangle

a Copy this pattern and continue it for 2 more triangular numbers.

b A rectangle is formed from the 10th triangular number. How many dots high and how many dots wide will this rectangle be?

c A rectangle is formed from the 50th triangular number. How many dots will this rectangle contain? Use your answer to calculate the 50th triangular number.

d A rectangle is formed from the nth triangular number. Write down a formula for the number of dots in this rectangle. Use your answer to write down a formula for the nth triangular number.

2 Find a formula for the nth term of the sequences illustrated in these diagrams:

a The 'pentagonal numbers'

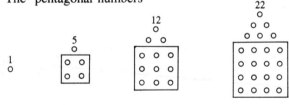

b The 'stellate' numbers

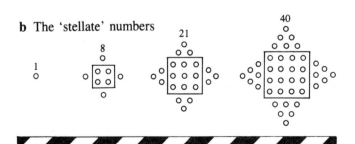

Iteration

There is often a simple rule which links each term in a sequence with the term that follows it. For example, each new term in the sequence of even numbers can be formed by adding 2 to the previous term.

$$2 \xrightarrow{+2} 4 \xrightarrow{+2} 6 \xrightarrow{+2} 8 \xrightarrow{+2} 10 \xrightarrow{+2} 12 \xrightarrow{+2} 14 \xrightarrow{+2} 16 \xrightarrow{+2} \ldots\ldots$$

We can express the rule with the formula

$$T_{n+1} = T_n + 2$$

All the previous formulas we have dealt with have established a link between a value of n and the nth term of a sequence. This formula establishes a link between the nth term in a sequence and the term which follows it, the $(n+1)$th term. With a formula like this, we can produce all the terms of a sequence if we know the first term.

Example

The first term in a sequence is 5. The formula linking the terms in the sequence is

$$U_{n+1} = 2U_n + 1$$

What are the next 4 terms of the sequence?
We can generate the terms like this:

$$U_1 = 5$$
$$U_2 = 2U_1 + 1 = 11$$
$$U_3 = 2U_2 + 1 = 23$$
$$U_4 = 2U_3 + 1 = 47$$
$$U_5 = 2U_4 + 1 = 95$$

A formula which establishes a link between the nth term and the $(n+1)$th term of a sequence is called an **iteration formula**.

CHECKPOINT 32

1 In each case, you are given the first term of a sequence and the iteration formula which links the terms. Write down the next four terms of the sequence.

a $U_1 = 4$, $U_{n+1} = U_n + 4$ **b** $U_1 = 1$, $U_{n+1} = 5U_n$

c $U_1 = 100$, $U_{n+1} = \dfrac{U_n}{2}$ **d** $U_1 = 1$, $U_{n+1} = 2U_n + 3$

e $U_1 = 1$, $U_2 = 1$, $U_{n+1} = U_n + U_{n-1}$

2 Find the iteration formula which links each term in the following sequences. Use the formula to write down the next 2 numbers in each sequence.

a 14, 17, 20, 23, . . .   **b** 101, 99, 97, 95, . . .
c 1, 2, 4, 8, . . .   **d** 1458, 486, 162, 54, . . .
e 3, 7, 15, 31, 63, . . .   **f** 2, 2, 4, 6, 10, 16, . . .

The sequence:

1, 1.4, 1.41, 1.414, 1.4142, 1.41421, 1.414214, 1.4142136, . . .

is formed from successively more accurate approximations for the square root of 2. It is sometimes possible to develop an iteration formula to produce successively more accurate approximations for a required result.

For example, suppose we wished to find a value for $\sqrt{12}$. We could start with a guess of 4. This is of course very inaccurate because 4^2 is 16, so we know that our guess is too large.

Now, $12 \div 4 = 3$, so we know that 4 is too large and 3 is too small.

A more accurate value for $\sqrt{12}$ must lie somewhere between 3 and 4. We can therefore obtain a better approximation by taking an average of 3 and 4. This gives us

$$\frac{3+4}{2} \text{ or } \frac{7}{2} \text{ or } 3.5$$

So, starting with a guess of 4 for $\sqrt{12}$, we have produced a better approximation of 3.5.

Now, we can repeat the process with 3.5 as our starting guess. 3.5^2 is 12.25, so we know that our guess is too large. Now, $12 \div 3.5 = 3.43$ (to 2 d.p.), so we know that 3.5 is too large and 3.43 is too small.

A more accurate value for $\sqrt{12}$ must lie somewhere between 3.5 and 3.43. We can therefore obtain a better approximation by taking an average of 3.5 and 3.43. This gives us

$$\frac{3.5+3.43}{2} \text{ or } \frac{6.93}{2} \text{ or } 3.465$$

So, starting with a guess of 3.5 for $\sqrt{12}$, we have produced a better approximation of 3.465.

3.465^2 is 12.006225, and our approximation is accurate to within less than one hundredth. We could of course carry on with 3.465 as our starting guess and obtain better and better approximations for $\sqrt{12}$. A summary of this technique is:

- Make a guess at the square root of 12. Call this guess n.

- Divide 12 by the guess, giving a value of $\frac{12}{n}$.

- Find the average of n and $\frac{12}{n}$.

- Use the average as an improved value of n and repeat these steps.

These rules can be more neatly expressed as an iteration formula. If U_n is our first approximation and U_{n+1} is our next approximation, we can write

$$U_{n+1} = \frac{U_n + \dfrac{12}{U_n}}{2}$$

We can of course use an identical technique to find successive approximations to the square root of any number, and an iteration formula to find approximations for the square root of the number x is

$$U_{n+1} = \frac{U_n + \dfrac{x}{U_n}}{2}$$

Example

Use the iteration formula to produce four successive approximations for $\sqrt{2}$, starting with a guess of 1. Calculate the square of each approximation to check its accuracy.

We can organise our results in this table, writing down all the figures produced on an 8-digit calculator.

U_n	$2 \div U_n$	U_{n+1}	$(U_{n+1})^2$
1	2	1.5	2.25
1.5	1.3333333	1.4166666	2.0069442
1.4166666	1.4117647	1.4142156	2.0000057

The four approximations are:

1, 1.5, 1.4166666, 1.4142156

CHECKPOINT 33

Use the iteration formula to produce four successive approximations for each of the following numbers, starting with a suitable guess. Calculate the square of each approximation to check its accuracy.

a $\sqrt{8}$ **b** $\sqrt{33}$ **c** $\sqrt{207}$
d $\sqrt{36}$ (start with a guess of 5)

Functions

Mathematical relationships like $y = 2x + 1$ or $T_n = 4n - 1$ can be thought of as a set of instructions to transform one sequence of numbers into another sequence of numbers. For example, if we apply the relationship $y = 2x + 1$ to all the numbers in the set 1, 2, 3, 4, 5, we transform these numbers into 3, 5, 7, 9, 11. This transformation can be illustrated with a diagram like this:

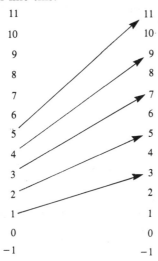

A diagram like this is called a **mapping diagram** or **arrow diagram**. When dealing with these numerical transformations, a new type of notation is often introduced. Instead of writing $y = 2x + 1$ to describe the mapping, we write

$$x \rightarrow 2x + 1$$

This is read as 'x becomes $2x + 1$'.

Example

Draw a mapping diagram to illustrate the transformation $x \rightarrow 8 - x$, applied to the set of numbers -2, -1, 0, 1, 2, 3, 4, 5, 6, 7, 8, 9, 10.
This is the required diagram.

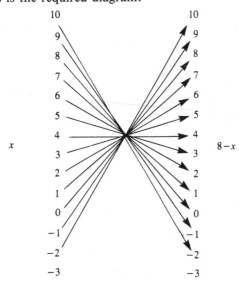

Numerical transformations of this kind are called **functions**. To be strict, a function must map each member of a set of numbers onto only **one** new number. Therefore, an arrow diagram of this kind, illustrating the mapping $x \rightarrow \sqrt{x}$, applied to the set of number 0, 1, 4 does not represent a function because some members in the set are mapped onto **two** answers.

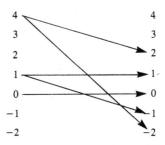

The set of numbers that are transformed by a function is called the **domain** of the function. The set of numbers that are produced is called the **range** of the function.

Example

Draw a mapping diagram to illustrate the application of the function $x \rightarrow x^2 + 3$ to the domain -3, -2, -1, 0, 1, 2, 3. State the range of the function.
This is the required diagram.

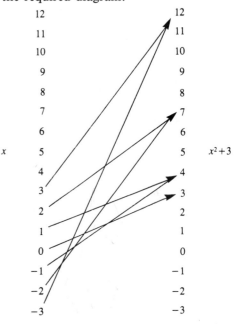

The range is 3, 4, 7, 12.

CHECKPOINT 34

Draw diagrams to show each of the following functions applied to the domain -3, -2, -1, 0, 1, 2, 3. In each case state the range.

a $x \rightarrow x + 4$ b $x \rightarrow 2x$ c $x \rightarrow x^2 + 3x - 4$

d $x \rightarrow \dfrac{x}{2}$ e $x \rightarrow x^2$ f $x \rightarrow \dfrac{12}{x}$

Function shorthand

There are two shorthand ways to show that a letter has been selected to represent a function. For example, if we select the letter f to represent the function $x \rightarrow x^2 - 2x$, we can write either

$$f(x) = x^2 - 2x$$

'x becomes $x^2 - 2x$ if you apply function f'

or

$$f: x \rightarrow x^2 - 2x$$

'f is a function such that the number x becomes $x^2 - 2x$'.

If x is 4, for example, then applying function f would give us $f(4) = 4^2 - 8 = 8$.

CHECKPOINT 35

1   Given that

$$f(x) = x^2 - 2x, \quad g(x) = 2x, \quad h(x) = \frac{36}{x}, \quad k(x) = 36 - x,$$

find the value of

a $f(5)$ **b** $g(7)$ **c** $h(12)$ **d** $k(36)$ **e** $g(-4)$
f $h(-18)$ **g** $f(-3)$ **h** $k(-11)$ **i** $h(0.5)$ **j** $f(1.5)$

2   Given the functions

$$r: x \rightarrow 3x, \quad s: x \rightarrow 3-x, \quad t: x \rightarrow \frac{x}{3}, \quad u: x \rightarrow \frac{3}{x}$$

find the value of

a $r(5)$ **b** $s(5)$ **c** $t(5)$ **d** $u(5)$ **e** $r(-5)$
f $s(-5)$ **g** $t(-5)$ **h** $u(-5)$ **i** $t(0.6)$ **j** $u(0.6)$

Functions of functions

Several functions in succession can be applied to a number. For example, if we have the two functions

$$f: x \rightarrow 2x \text{ and } g: x \rightarrow x+2$$

we can apply first f and then g to the number 4.

Applying function f to 4 will give us 8. If we then apply function g to 8 we obtain a final answer of 10.

In mathematical shorthand we write

$$gf(4) = 10$$

Notice the reversed order of the letter in this shorthand. $gf(4)$ means $g(f(4))$, that is function f followed by function g. In the same way, $fg(4)$ means $f(g(4))$, that is function g followed by function f. In this case,

$$fg(4) = 12$$

Example

Given that

$$p(x) = 2x + 1 \text{ and } q(x) = 2x - 1$$

find the value of

a $p(5)$ **b** $q(5)$ **c** $pq(5)$ **d** $qp(5)$

We have

$$p(5) = 11$$

$$q(5) = 9$$

$$pq(5) = p(q(5)) = p(9) = 19$$

$$qp(5) = q(p(5)) = q(11) = 21$$

CHECKPOINT 36

1 Given that

$$f(x) = x^2 - 2x, \quad g(x) = 2x, \quad h(x) = \frac{36}{x}, \quad k(x) = 36 - x,$$

find the value of

a $fg(5)$ **b** $gf(5)$ **c** $hk(12)$ **d** $kh(12)$ **e** $gh(-4)$
f $hg(-4)$ **g** $ff(1)$ **h** $gg(-5)$ **i** $kk(15)$ **j** $hh(18)$

2 Given the functions
$$r: \rightarrow 3x, \quad s: x \rightarrow 3-x, \quad t: x \rightarrow \frac{x}{3}, \quad u: x \rightarrow \frac{3}{x}$$

find the value of

a $rs(5)$ **b** $sr(5)$ **c** $tu(5)$ **d** $ut(5)$ **e** $ur(-5)$
f $ru(-4)$ **g** $ts(-5)$ **h** $st(-5)$ **i** $tt(0.6)$ **j** $uu(0.6)$

We can use the rules of algebra to find a function equivalent to the application of two other functions.

Example

Given that

$$p(x) = 2x + 1 \text{ and } q(x) = x^2 + 1$$

find an expression for

a $pq(x)$ **b** $qp(x)$

For **a** we have

$$pq(x) = p(q(x))$$
$$pq(x) = p(x^2 + 1)$$
$$pq(x) = 2(x^2 + 1) + 1$$
$$pq(x) = 2x^2 + 3$$

For **b** we have

$$qp(x) = q(p(x))$$
$$qp(x) = q(2x + 1)$$
$$qp(x) = (2x + 1)^2 + 1$$
$$qp(x) = 4x^2 + 4x + 2$$

CHECKPOINT 37

1 Given that

$$f(x) = x + 2, \qquad g(x) = 2x, \qquad h(x) = x^2, \qquad k(x) = (x + 2)^2$$

find an expression for

a $fg(x)$ **b** $gf(x)$ **c** $hf(x)$ **d** $kf(x)$ **e** $gk(x)$

2 Given the functions

$$r: x \to 3x, \qquad s: x \to 3 - x, \qquad t: x \to \frac{x}{3}, \qquad u: x \to \frac{3}{x},$$

find an expression for

a $rs(x)$ **b** $sr(x)$ **c** $ss(x)$ **d** $st(x)$ **e** $uu(x)$

Inverse functions

The **inverse** of a function f is the function which will reverse the effects of f. That is to say, a function which will map $f(x)$ back onto x. The shorthand for the inverse of the function represented by the letter f is f^{-1}.

In some cases, the inverse of a function is 'common sense'. For example, if f is the function

$$f: x \to x + 2$$

it is 'common sense' that the inverse function which will reverse the effects of f is

$$f^{-1}: x \to x - 2$$

We can easily test to see if our 'common sense' is correct. Remember f^{-1} must map $f(x)$ back onto x. So, we simply select a suitable value of x, and apply first f and then f^{-1}. If our inverse function is correct, our final result will be equal to the original value selected for x. So, selecting $x = 4$ we have

$$f(4) = 4 + 2 = 6$$

and

$$f^{-1}(6) = 6 - 2 = 4$$

> When a function is more complicated, the usual strategy for finding an inverse function is as follows.
> 1 Write down in the correct order the arithmetical steps performed by a function.
> 2 Write down the reverse arithmetical steps **in reverse order**.
> 3 Build up a function which performs the reverse order of reverse arithmetical steps.

Example

Find the inverse of the function

$$f: x \to \frac{2x - 3}{4}$$

The steps in this function are:

multiply by 2, subtract 3, divide by 4.

The reverse steps, in reverse order are therefore:

multiply by 4, add 3, divide by 2.

The inverse function is therefore

$$f^{-1}: x \to \frac{4x + 3}{2}$$

Testing with $x = 5$, we have

$$f(5) = \frac{2 \times 5 - 3}{4} = \frac{7}{4} = 1.75$$

and

$$f^{-1}(1.75) = \frac{4 \times 1.75 + 3}{2} = \frac{10}{2} = 5$$

CHECKPOINT 38

Find the inverse of each of the following functions. Test each answer with a suitable value of x.

a $f: x \to 3x - 2$ **b** $g: x \to 3(x - 2)$

c $h: x \to \dfrac{2x}{3}$ **d** $f: x \to \dfrac{x - 7}{6}$

e $m: x \to \dfrac{x}{6} - 7$ **f** $g: x \to \dfrac{3x - 5}{4}$

g $f: x \to \dfrac{5 + 4x}{3}$ **h** $k: x \to 3(2x - 7)$

There are two reverse arithmetical steps which are far from being a matter of 'common sense'. The first is the step of 'subtracting from' a number. In other words, what is the inverse of a function like $x \to 8 - x$?

This is the mapping diagram for the function.

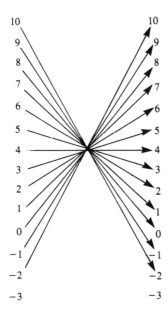

We need an inverse function that will reverse all these arrows. Experiment will show that the only way to reverse all the arrows is to apply the same function again. That is to say, subtracting all the numbers from 8 again. This can be demonstrated with this 'double' mapping diagram.

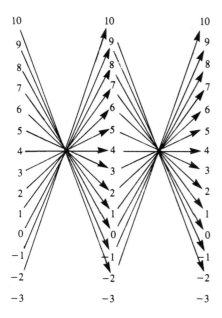

Inverse functions – a special case

In general terms, if f is any function of the form

$$f : x \rightarrow K - x$$

then the inverse function f^{-1} is

$$f^{-1} : x \rightarrow K - x$$

The second reverse step which is far from obvious is the step of 'dividing into' a number. In other words, what is the inverse of a function like

$$x \rightarrow \frac{12}{x} \quad ?$$

Experiment will show that this is also a function which is its own inverse.

Inverse functions—a special case

In general terms, if f is any function of the form

$$f : x \rightarrow \frac{K}{x}$$

then the inverse function f^{-1} is

$$f^{-1} : x \rightarrow \frac{K}{x}$$

Example

Find the inverse of this function and test your answer with a suitable value of x.

$$f : x \rightarrow \frac{12}{8 - 2x}$$

The steps in this function are:

multiply by 2, subtract from 8, divide into 12.

The reverse steps, in reverse order are:

divide into 12, subtract from 8, divide by 2.

The inverse function is therefore

$$f^{-1} : x \rightarrow \frac{8 - \dfrac{12}{x}}{2}$$

Testing with $x = 3$, we have

$$f(3) = \frac{12}{8 - 6} = \frac{12}{2} = 6$$

$$f^{-1}(6) = \frac{8 - \dfrac{12}{6}}{2} = \frac{8 - 2}{2} = 3$$

CHECKPOINT 39

Find the inverse of each of the following functions. Test your answer with a suitable value of x.

a $f : x \rightarrow 2 - x$ **b** $g : x \rightarrow 8 - 2x$ **c** $h : x \rightarrow \dfrac{2}{3x}$

d $f : x \rightarrow \dfrac{7 - x}{6}$ **e** $m : x \rightarrow 7 - \dfrac{x}{6}$ **f** $g : x \rightarrow 7 - \dfrac{6}{x}$

g $f : x \rightarrow \dfrac{1}{1 - x}$ **h** $k : x \rightarrow \dfrac{36}{12 - 4x}$

Algebra – Practice and revision exercise

1 Write each of the following statements in standard mathematical shorthand.

a The number y is always 5 more than the number x.

b 3 times the number t, minus 4 times the number s is equal to the number r.

c To convert a temperature in degrees Celsius (C) into a temperature in degrees Fahrenheit (F), multiply by 9, divide by 5 and then add 32.

d The final velocity (v) of an object which accelerates is equal to its initial velocity (u) plus the product of its acceleration (a) and the time for which it accelerates (t).

2 If $a = 6$, $b = 3$ and $c = 5$, find the value of:

a $a+b$	**b** $b-c$	**c** $2a+3b$
d $5c-2b$	**e** ab	**f** $2ac-ab$
g ab^2	**h** a^3b	**i** $17+2cb^2$
j $a(b+c)$		

3 If $a = -2$, $b = -1$ and $c = 5$, find the value of:

a $a+b$	**b** $b-c$	**c** $2a+3b$
d $5c-2b$	**e** ab	**f** $2ac-ab$
g ab^2	**h** a^3b	**i** $17+2cb^2$
j $a(b+c)$		

4 When an electrical appliance of W watts power is used for h hours, in an area where eletricity costs c pence per unit, the price of the electricity used P pence is given by

$$P = \frac{Whc}{1000}$$

Find the cost of running a 750 watt iron for 4 hours in an area where electricity costs 12p per unit.

5 Simplify each of the following expressions.

a $17x+y+3x+5y$ **b** $3x+2y-2x+6y$

c $x-12y+7x+9y$ **d** $-x+2y+7x+5y$

e $2m^2+8m-5m+27$ **f** $2a^2-14a-2a+14$

g $9v^3+5v^2-3v^2+2v$ **h** $14s^2t+3t^2s-4st^2-7ts^2$

6 Expand the brackets and simplify.

a $4(3r+5)$ **b** $-4(7r-5)$

c $-(3m-5n)$ **d** $-a(1-b)$

e $4r(3r-2r^2+9)$ **f** $5(8r+5)+3(4r-9)$

g $(4m-3n)-(3n-4m)$ **h** $a(b-1)-(ab-1)$

i $4n(3n+2)-5(6n+1)$ **j** $x(2y-x)-y(2y-x)$

7 Expand.

a $(x+4)(x+1)$ **b** $(x-3)(x+9)$

c $(5x+3)(x-3)$ **d** $(b-1)^2$

e $(x+y)(x-y)$ **f** $(x+3y)^2$

8 Simplify.

a $\dfrac{x}{5} + \dfrac{y}{6}$ **b** $\dfrac{7}{x} + \dfrac{3}{5}$

c $\dfrac{2}{3} + \dfrac{3}{x}$ **d** $\dfrac{7}{z} + \dfrac{5}{y}$

e $\dfrac{w}{ef} + \dfrac{x}{5e}$ **f** $\dfrac{2}{b} \times \dfrac{5a}{7b}$

g $\dfrac{x^2y^3}{6uv} \times \dfrac{8v^2}{x^2y^2}$ **h** $\dfrac{3pq}{11c} \div 9$

i $\dfrac{pqr}{f^2} \div \dfrac{p^2q}{ef}$ **j** $ab\left(\dfrac{1}{a} + \dfrac{c}{b}\right)$

9 A 'think of a number' trick goes like this: think of a number, add 8, multiply by 5, add 10, divide by 5, take away your original number.

a What number will these calculations always produce as an answer?

b Explain how this trick works.

10 This advertisement for conifers states that a 20 tree pack will provide a hedge 38 ft long.

a What length of hedge would a 30 tree pack provide?

b Write down a formula for the length of hedge (in feet) provided by a pack containing n trees.

c Write down a formula for the length of hedge (in metres) provided by a pack containing n trees.

11 A boat leaves harbour with 12 000 litres of fuel oil on board. Each day the engines use 800 litres of oil. Write down a formula to calculate the oil that is left after the boat has been at sea for t days.

12 Factorise completely each of the following expressions.

a $20x + 35$

c $15e^2 - 5ef$

e $abcd + acd + bcd$

b $b - 6ab$

d $xy^2 + x^2y + xy$

f $14m^2n - 21mn^2 + 7mn$

13 A landscape gardener always surrounds rectangular lawns with a 2 metre wide concrete path. Write down and simplify a formula for the area of a path which surrounds a rectangular lawn which is x metres by y metres.

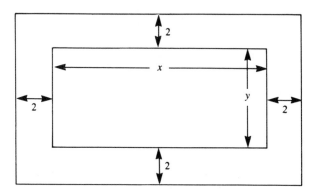

14 Copy and complete:

a $x^2 + 9x + 14 = (x + 2)($ $)$

b $x^2 + x - 42 = (x - 6)($ $)$

c $x^2 - 13x + 40 = (x - 8)($ $)$

d $2x^2 + 14x + 24 = (2x + 8)($ $)$

e $3x^2 - 2x - 8 = (x - 2)($ $)$

15 Factorise:

a $x^2 + 11x + 18$

c $x^2 - 8x - 9$

e $2x^2 - 15x - 8$

b $x^2 + 11x - 12$

d $2x^2 + 15x + 7$

f $2x^2 - 8x + 10$

16 Solve:

a $6m = 36$

d $t + 45 = 104$

g $\dfrac{x}{4} = 12.5$

j $2x + 7 = 11$

m $\dfrac{x}{4} - 5 = 1$

b $108 = 12t$

e $18 = r - 7$

h $\dfrac{t}{5} = -13$

k $13 + 7m = 48$

n $3(2x - 1) = 51$

c $12x = -26$

f $15 = 5 - r$

i $-21 = \dfrac{7v}{2}$

l $9 - 8m = 49$

o $4(1 - 2x) = 8$

p $2(2x - 1) - 3(2x + 1) = 7$

17 In 1976, a new bakery opened in Market Grunting. By 1978, the cost of a loaf had increased by 2 pence. Between 1978 and 1984, the price doubled. Since 1984, the price has increased by a further 13 pence. If the loaf now costs 43 pence, how much did it cost in 1976?

18 Solve:

a $9p + 4 = 5p - 12$

c $5m + 13 - m = 3m - 23$

e $9 + \dfrac{a}{2} = a - 7$

g $5(1 - 2p) = 5(p + 2) - 5$

b $x - 25 = 5 - 5x$

d $\dfrac{x}{5} + 4 = x - 6$

f $7(x - 2) + 2 = x - 6$

h $4 + 9(2x + 8) = 3(8 + 2x) - x$

19 Solve, giving answers correct to 2 decimal places.

a $2.3x + 11.9 = 23.4$

b $3(y - 4.6) + 5.2 = 7.6$

c $\dfrac{p - 3}{3} + \dfrac{p + 4}{4} = 28$

d $\dfrac{2y + 1}{7} + \dfrac{y - 7}{3} = 7$

e $\dfrac{3(u + 1)}{4} + \dfrac{2(u - 3)}{5} = 3$

f $\dfrac{e + 5}{6} - \dfrac{5 - e}{4} = \dfrac{5}{12}$

20 Solve these inequalities and illustrate your solution on a number line.

a $x + 5 < 11$

c $9e \leqslant -72$

e $5x - 7 > 53$

g $\dfrac{5e}{3} + 9 \geqslant -2$

i $4(5x + 20) > 120$

k $13 - x \leqslant 21$

m $12 - 2x < 32$

o $7(3 - 5x) < 91$

b $y - 8 > -23$

d $\dfrac{y}{8} \geqslant 3.25$

f $8.5 + \dfrac{w}{4} < 4.75$

h $7(2x - 7) \leqslant 0$

j $\dfrac{3x + 2}{5} + 5 > 9$

l $11 - x \geqslant 4$

n $9 - \dfrac{y}{2} < 9$

21 Rearrange each of these formulas to make the letter given in brackets the subject.

a $y = x + 5$ (x)

c $C = 2\pi r$ (r)

e $y = 4x - 1$ (x)

g $s = u + vt$ (u)

i $A = \dfrac{h(a + b)}{2}$ (a)

k $E = mc^2$ (c)

m $v^2 = u^2 + 2as$ (a)

o $V = \dfrac{4\pi r^3}{3}$ (r)

b $p = t - 7$ (t)

d $d = \dfrac{C}{\pi}$ (C)

f $m = tx - tr$ (r)

h $y = \dfrac{7x}{8}$ (x)

j $s = \dfrac{t(u + v)}{2}$ (t)

l $P = \dfrac{kI}{d^2}$ (d)

n $A = 180 - \dfrac{360}{n}$ (n)

p $V = \dfrac{4\pi(R^2 - r^2)}{3}$ (R)

22 Rearrange each of these formulas to make the letter given in brackets the subject.

a $Q = \sqrt{\dfrac{s}{t}}$ (s) **b** $a = b\sqrt{\dfrac{d}{e}}$ (e)

c $F = \sqrt{\dfrac{m+n}{m}}$ (n) **d** $t = R\sqrt{\dfrac{2d}{s}}$ (d)

23 Rearrange each of these formulas to make the letter given in brackets the subject.

a $A = \dfrac{ah+bh}{2}$ (h) **b** $T = \dfrac{m+n}{mn}$ (m)

c $y = \dfrac{p-a}{q-a}$ (a) **d** $F = \sqrt{\dfrac{mn}{m+n}}$ (m)

24 Solve the following simultaneous equations.

a $x+y=9$
$x-y=1$
     b $2x+y=10$
$x+y=7$

c $p=7+q$
$2p=44-q$
     d $5a+3b=7$
$5a+8b=2$

e $3p-2q=0$
$3p+2q=30$

25 Solve the following simultaneous equations.

a $4a-3b=6$
$4a-2b=8$
     b $7t=24-2w$
$7t=8w-26$

c $3e-2f=10$
$2e-2f=8$
     d $6m-2n=-4$
$8m-2n=6$

e $-3=q-p$
$27=5q-p$

26 Solve the following simultaneous equations.

a $m+5n=9$
$3m+n=13$
     b $m+4n=10$
$6m-3n=-21$

c $4x-3y=15$
$5x+2y=13$
     d $4x+4y=30$
$3x+6y=30$

e $5t-7s=25$
$7t-5s=11$

27 Seven kilograms of butter and two kilograms of sugar cost £17.18. Three kilograms of butter and five kilograms of sugar cost £10.47. Find the cost per kilogram of butter and sugar.

28 Solve by factorisation the following quadratic equations.

a $x^2+5x+4=0$ **b** $x^2+2x-35=0$

c $x^2+12=7x$ **d** $2x^2+11x+15=0$

e $2x^2-x=21$ **f** $3x^2-19x+28=0$

29 Solve by using the formula the following quadratic equations.

a $x^2+7x+2=0$ **b** $x^2+5x=3$

c $x^2-6x+7=0$ **d** $2x^2+3x+1=0$

e $3x^2+5=9x$

30 These luxury placemats are made from heavy embroidered cloth which costs 0.5 pence per square centimetre. They are stitched along all edges with silver thread, at a cost of 0.8 pence per centimetre of stitching. The designer label which is fixed to the placemats costs 2 pence.

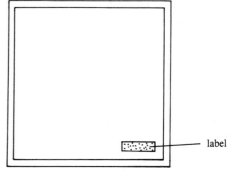

label

a Write down a formula for the total cost of manufacturing a placemat which measures x cm by x cm.
b Find the size of a placemat which costs 84p to manufacture.

31 Copy and complete.
a The 11th term in the sequence of even numbers is . . .
b The 2000th term in the sequence of even numbers is . . .
c The 2000th term in the sequence of odd numbers is . . .
d The 10th term in the sequence of prime numbers is . . .

32 Write down the first five terms and the tenth term of the sequences produced by the following formulas.

a $T_n=3n-1$ **b** $T_n=4n+5$

c $T_n=\dfrac{360}{n}$ **d** $T_n=n^3$

e $T_n=\dfrac{n^2}{2}+\dfrac{n}{2}$ **f** $T_n=1000-5n$

g $T_n=3^{n-1}$ **h** $T_n=4\times5^{n-1}$

33 Find a formula for the nth term of the following sequences.

a 1, 5, 9, 13, 17, . . .   **b** 6, 17, 28, 39, 50, . . .
c 205, 190, 175, 160, 145, . . . **d** 9, 18, 36, 72, 144, . . .

34 Simon is betting on the cut of a deck of cards with his wife Afifa. Their first bet is 10p, and Simon loses and pays Afifa the 10p. He figures that if he doubles the stake to 20p, and wins, he will recover his losses and be 10p up. Simon does this, but loses again and has to pay Afifa 20p. He figures that if he doubles the stake to 40p, and wins, he will recover his losses and still be 10p up . . .

a What bet will Simon have to make after he has lost 5 times?
b Write down a formula for the bet that Simon will have to make after he has lost n times.

35 In each case, you are given the first term of a sequence and the iteration formula which links the terms. Write down the next four terms of the sequence.

a $U_1 = 1$, $U_{n+1} = U_n + 2$ **b** $U_1 = 1$, $U_{n+1} = 2U_n$

c $U_1 = 1$, $U_{n+1} = \dfrac{U_n}{10}$ **d** $U_1 = 6$, $U_{n+1} = \dfrac{24}{U_n}$

e $U_1 = 1$, $U_2 = -1$, $U_{n+1} = U_n \times U_{n-1}$

36 Find the iteration formula which links each term in the following sequences. Use the formula to write down the next 2 numbers in each sequence.

a 24, 27, 30, 33, ...   **b** 360, 180, 90, 45, ...
c 1, 2, 1, 2, 1, ...   **d** 5, 16, 49, 148, ...
e 3, 4, 7, 11, 18, ...

37 Draw mapping diagrams to show each of the following transformations applied to the set of numbers -3, -2, -1, 0, 1, 2, 3.

a $x \to x + 5$ **b** $x \to 3x$

c $x \to \dfrac{x}{2} + 3$ **d** $x \to x(x+1)$

e $x \to x^2 - 3x + 4$ **f** $x \to \dfrac{6}{x}$

38 Given that

$f(x) = x + 12$, $g(x) = 12x$, $h(x) = \dfrac{12}{x}$, $k(x) = 12 - x$,

find the value of

a $f(5)$ **b** $g(7)$ **c** $h(12)$ **d** $k(36)$ **e** $g(-4)$
f $h(-4)$ **g** $f(-3)$ **h** $k(-11)$ **i** $h(0.5)$ **j** $f(1.5)$

39 Given the functions

$r: x \to 3x^2$, $s: x \to 2x + 3$, $t: x \to \dfrac{x}{3} + 2$, $u: x \to (3 - x)^2$,

find the value of

a $r(5)$ **b** $s(5)$ **c** $t(5)$ **d** $u(5)$ **e** $r(-5)$
f $s(-5)$ **g** $t(-5)$ **h** $u(-5)$ **i** $t(0.6)$ **j** $u(0.6)$

40 Given that

$f(x) = x^2 - x$, $g(x) = 5x$, $h(x) = \dfrac{24}{x}$, $k(x) = 8 - x$,

find the value of

a $fg(5)$ **b** $gf(5)$ **c** $hk(12)$ **d** $kh(12)$ **e** $gh(-4)$
f $hg(-4)$ **g** $ff(1)$ **h** $gg(-5)$ **i** $kk(3)$ **j** $hh(6)$

41 Given the functions

$r: x \to 8x$, $s: x \to 8 - x$, $t: x \to \dfrac{x}{8} + 8$, $u: x \to 8 + \dfrac{8}{x}$,

find the value of

a $rs(2)$ **b** $sr(2)$ **c** $tu(2)$ **d** $ut(2)$ **e** $ur(-2)$
f $ru(-2)$ **g** $ts(-2)$ **h** $st(-2)$ **i** $tt(16)$ **j** $uu(1)$

42 Given that

$f(x) = x + 5$, $g(x) = 5x$, $h(x) = x^2$, $k(x) = (x + 5)^2$,

find an expression for

a $fg(x)$ **b** $gf(x)$ **c** $hf(x)$ **d** $kf(x)$ **e** $gk(x)$

43 Given the functions

$r: x \to 8x$, $s: x \to 8 - x$, $t: x \to \dfrac{x}{8}$, $u: x \to \dfrac{8}{x}$,

find an expression for

a $rs(x)$ **b** $sr(x)$ **c** $ss(x)$ **d** $st(x)$ **e** $uu(x)$

44 Find the inverse of each of the following functions. Test each answer with a suitable value of x.

a $f: x \to 2x - 3$ **b** $g: x \to 2(x - 3)$

c $h: x \to \dfrac{5x}{4}$ **d** $f: x \to \dfrac{x - 8}{7}$

e $m: x \to \dfrac{x}{9} + 13$ **f** $g: x \to \dfrac{2x - 7}{9}$

g $f: x \to \dfrac{3 + 7x}{11}$ **h** $k: x \to 9(7x - 13)$

45 Find the inverse of each of the following functions. Test your answer with a suitable value of x.

a $f: x \to 8 - x$ **b** $g: x \to 10 - 5x$

c $h: x \to \dfrac{5}{4x}$ **d** $f: x \to \dfrac{1 - x}{2}$

e $m: x \to 1 - \dfrac{x}{2}$ **f** $g: x \to 1 - \dfrac{2}{x}$

g $f: x \to \dfrac{12}{12 - x}$ **h** $k: x \to \dfrac{1}{3(2 - x)}$

Algebra – extended problems for project work

1 Asked to solve the equation $x^2 + 10x = 39$, the great ninth-century mathematician Alkarismi came up with the following solution.

First, he drew a square with a side x units along. The area of this square is x^2.

Second, he extended two sides of the square by an extra 5 units.

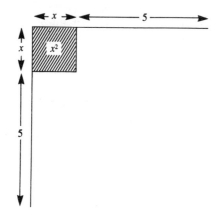

Third, he made rectangles between the extended sides and the square. The area of the L-shaped figure he formed is $x^2 + 5x + 5x$, or $x^2 + 10x$. This of course is the left hand side of the equation to be solved.

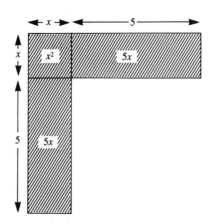

Fourth, he completed a large square with sides $x + 5$ units long. The area of this figure is $x^2 + 10x + 25$, or $(x + 5)^2$.

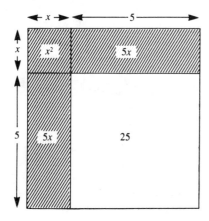

Returning to the original equation, Alkarismi could now solve it like this.

$$x^2 + 10x = 39$$

Adding 25 to both sides gives

$$x^2 + 10x + 25 = 64$$

But the diagrams have shown that $x^2 + 10x + 25$ is the same as $(x + 5)^2$, so we can write

$$(x + 5)^2 = 64$$

Taking the square root of both sides gives

$$x + 5 = 8$$
$$x = 3$$

a Alkarismi's method has only produced one root. This is not surprising, because Alkarismi was not concerned with negative numbers and the other root is -13. How can this other root be obtained from Alkarismi's solution to the problem?

b Draw diagrams and use Alkarismi's method to solve the following equations.

- $x^2 + 18x = 20$
- $x^2 + 14x = 32$
- $x^2 + 6x = 6$

c Can you use Alkarismi's method to solve the equation

$$x^2 + 5x - 7 = 0?$$

d Are the diagrams absolutely necessary? Can you use Alkarismi's method to solve the equation

$$x^2 + 7x = 8$$

without drawing a diagram?

e Can you use Alkarismi's method to solve the equation

$$3x^2 + 21x - 5 = 0?$$

f Experiment with other quadratic equations. Make some up and solve them by factorisation, formula and Alkarismi's technique.

g Can Alkarismi's method be used to solve any quadratic equation? If it can, write down a set of instructions that can be used to solve **any** equation of the form $ax^2 + bx + c = 0$ by Alkarismi's method.

h What happens if you draw a diagram and apply Alkarismi's method to the general equation $ax^2 + bx + c = 0$? That is to say, apply the method using only a, b and c, without taking any particular values for the letters.

2 a Investigate the values of these three expressions as n takes the values 1, 2, 3, . . . (Use fractions rather than decimals to write down the values of the expressions.)

$$(n+1)\times\left(1+\frac{1}{n}\right)$$

$$(n+1)+1+\frac{1}{n}$$

$$(n+2)+\frac{1}{n}$$

b This pattern of calculations suggests that there really is no difference between multiplication and subtraction. Investigate and explain this strange result.

$$1 \times \frac{1}{2} = 1 - \frac{1}{2} = \frac{1}{2}$$

$$2 \times \frac{2}{3} = 2 - \frac{2}{3} = 1\frac{1}{3}$$

$$3 \times \frac{3}{4} = 3 - \frac{3}{4} = 2\frac{1}{4}$$

$$4 \times \frac{4}{5} = 4 - \frac{4}{5} = 3\frac{1}{5}$$

c This pattern of calculations suggests that there really is no difference between division and addition. Investigate and explain this strange result.

$$1\frac{1}{3} \div \frac{2}{3} = 1\frac{1}{3} + \frac{2}{3} = 2$$

$$2\frac{1}{4} \div \frac{3}{4} = 2\frac{1}{4} + \frac{3}{4} = 3$$

$$3\frac{1}{5} \div \frac{4}{5} = 1\frac{1}{5} + \frac{4}{5} = 4$$

$$4\frac{1}{6} \div \frac{5}{6} = 4\frac{1}{6} + \frac{5}{6} = 5$$

d Can you discover any other patterns of calculations which seem to suggest a strange result.

3 Investigate the following results. Demonstrate that they are true for a range of numbers. Can you prove that they are true for any number?

a The product of any three consecutive whole numbers is always a multiple of 6.
For example, $7\times8\times9=504$, which is a multiple of 6.

b The product of any four consecutive whole numbers is always one less than a square number.
For example, $2\times3\times4\times5=120$ and $120+1=11^2$.

c If the sum of the digits of any number can be divided exactly by 9, then the number itself can be divided exactly by 9. For example, the sum of the digits in the number 70785

is $7+0+7+8+5$ or 27, and both 27 and 70785 can be divided exactly by 9.

d $(1+2+3+ \ldots +n)^2=1^3+2^3+3^3 \ldots +n^3$.

For example, $(1+2+3)^2=36$ and $1^3+2^3+3^3=36$.

e Try to discover, by investigation or research, some other facts about numbers. (For example, what are the rules to determine if a number will divide by 5 or by 3?) Demonstrate that the results are true for a range of numbers and try to prove that they are true for any number.

4 The outside faces of a 3 cm cube are painted red. It is then cut up into individual centimetre cubes.
a How many of the centimetre cubes will hve no red painted faces?
b How many of the centimetre cubes will have one red painted face?
c How many of the centimetre cubes will have two red painted faces?
d How many of the centimetre cubes will have three red painted faces?
e What happens if you start with a 4 cm cube?
f What happens if you start with an n cm cube?
g What happens if you start with an m by n by p cuboid?

5 a Four people meet in a pub. If each person each shakes hands with the other three people, how many handshakes will there be? How many handshakes would there be if n people met?
b Six people work in an office. If everybody buys everybody else a Christmas present, how many presents are given altogether? How many presents would be given if n people worked in the office?
c Twenty-two football teams play in the English First Division. Every season each team plays every other team twice, once at 'home', once 'away'. How many first division games are played each season? How many games would be played in a league with n teams?
d A 'mystic rose' is the name given to the pattern produced when a number of points are marked around a circle and every point is joined to every other point. This diagram shows a mystic rose formed with 6 points.

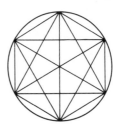

How many lines have been drawn in the circle to form this mystic rose? How many lines must be drawn to form a mystic rose with n points marked on the circle?

6 The extract below is reproduced from 'A Course in Mathematics' by Charles Hutton, written in 1836 for the use of the Royal Military Academy.

OF COMPUTING SHOT OR SHELLS IN A FINISHED PILE

Shot and Shells are generally piled in three different forms, called triangular, square, or oblong piles, according as their base is either a triangle, a square, or a rectangle.

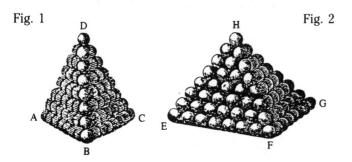

Fig. 1

Fig. 2

ABCD, fig. 1, is a triangular pile.
EFGH, fig. 2, is a square pile.

Fig. 3

ABCDEF, fig. 3, is an oblong pile.

A triangular pile is formed by the continual laying of triangular horizontal courses of shot one above another, in such a manner, as that the sides of these courses, called rows, decrease by unity from the bottom row to the top row, which ends always in 1 shot.

A square pile is formed by the continual laying of square horizontal courses of shot one above another, in such a manner, as that the sides of these courses decrease by unity from the bottom to the top row, which ends also in 1 shot.

The oblong pile may be conceived as formed from the square pile ABCD, to one side or face of which, as AD, a number of arithmetical triangles equal to the face have been added.

Investigate piles of cannonballs of different heights.

a Draw up some tables that could be used by gunners showing the total number of cannonballs in piles of different heights and shapes.

b Can you discover a formula for the number of cannonballs in a particular shape and height of pile?

c Are any other shapes possible for piling cannonballs? Why

not experiment with marbles or ball bearings, use plasticine to hold the bottom layer in place? Take photographs of your results.

d What about piles of cans in supermarkets?

7 Before the invention of reliable calculators, the **method of differences** was often used to calculate successive values of a function. For example, suppose we wish to calculate the value of the function

$$f: x \rightarrow 5x^2 - 3x + 7$$

for values of x from 1 to 100.
We start by working out the value of the function for the first few values of x, as follows.

x	1	2	3	4	5
$f(x)$	9	21	43	75	117

We now find the difference between each pair of values in the sequence for $f(x)$.

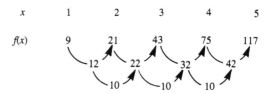

We now find the difference between each term in this new sequence.

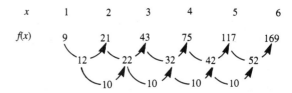

You can see that we have obtained a sequence which simply repeats a difference of 10. If we assume that this pattern continues, we can use it to generate all the other values of $f(x)$. For example, to generate a value for $f(6)$, we add an extra difference of 10, this gives us a difference of 52 in the row above and a value of 169 for $f(6)$.

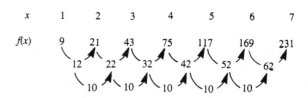

To generate a value for $f(7)$, we add another difference of 10; this gives us a difference of 62 in the row above and a value of 231 for $f(7)$.

So, using this method of differences, we have reduced the difficult arithmetic involved in calculating the values of $5x^2-3x+7$ to a process of simple addition.

a Experiment with the method of differences, using some simple linear functions like $f: x \rightarrow 3x+2$ or $g: x \rightarrow 2x+3$. Can you predict in advance what the constant difference will be for any linear function? (A linear function is any function of the form $f: x \rightarrow ax+b$, where a and b can take any values.)

b Experiment with the method of differences, using some simple quadratic functions like $f: x \rightarrow 3x^2+2x-5$ or $g: x \rightarrow 2x^2-7x+13$. Can you predict in advance what the constant difference will be for any quadratic function? (A quadratic function is any function of the form $f: x \rightarrow ax^2+bx+c$, where a, b and c can take any values.)

c Experiment with the method of differences, using some more complicated functions like $f: x \rightarrow x^3+2x^2-3x+11$ or $g: x \rightarrow x^4-2x^3$. Can you predict in advance what the constant difference will be for any function? Can you predict how many sequences of differences you will have to write down before you reach a constant sequence?

d Can the method of differences be used to calculate the values that result when a function is applied to a sequence of negative numbers?

e Can the method of differences be used to calculate the values that result when a function is applied to a sequence of decimal numbers?

f During the nineteenth century, several people tried to build mechanical calculators called **'difference engines'** which used the method of differences to calculate long sequences of values automatically. The Englishman Charles Babbage designed one which never worked properly but the Swede George Scheutz built two successful machines. These machines were the forerunners of modern computers. Do some library and/or museum research on these and other early calculating devices.

8 Obtain an up-to-date copy of one of the magazines which gives a table of values for second-hand cars. Investigate the ways that the value of a car decreases with age.

a Find an approximate formula to fit the sequence of values quoted for different ages of a particular make and model of car.

b Does your formula work with different models and makes? Can it be adjusted to give better approximations?

c Which cars lose value quickly, which lose value more slowly?

d If somebody regularly changes their car for a new model, what advice would you give them about how long to keep the car before they trade it in? Does it cost less to trade it in each year or to keep it for 2, 3 or more years? What about running costs; do they have an effect on your advice?

9 When a diagonal is drawn in a 2 by 3 rectangle, it cuts through 4 of the unit squares inside the rectangle.

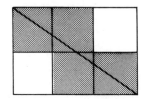

a How many unit squares are cut by the diagonal in a 4 by 5 rectangle?

b Investigate other rectangles. Can you find a general rule for an n by m rectangle, where m and n are two numbers with **no** common factors? Can you find a general rule for an n by m rectangle, where m and n are two numbers **with** common factors?

Algebra – Past paper questions

1 a $S=180n-360$.
Find the value of S when $n=10$.

b $T= \dfrac{a+m}{2}$.
Find the value of T when $a=6$ and $m=81$.

2 The power, P watts, consumed by an electric light bulb of resistance R ohms when a current of I amps is passed through it is given by

$$P=I^2R.$$

a Find the value of P when $R=50$ and $I=4$.

b Express I in terms of P and R.

(MEG)

3 A formula connecting T, f and g is $T=4f-5g$.

Work out the value of T when $f=6.4$ and $g=3.9$.

(MEG)

4 Lilian asked her uncle how old he was. 'In 13 years, I'll be twice as old as I was 7 years ago,' he replied.

a Taking his age now to be x years, write down

(i) his age in 13 years, in terms of x.

(ii) an equation in x.

b Solve your equation and find Lilian's uncle's age.

(MEG)

5 The cost, C pence, of a newspaper advertisement of n words is given by the formula

$$C = 12n + 32$$

Find the cost of an advertisement of 16 words.

(MEG)

6 The price £P, charged by 'Motif Shirts' for making sweat shirts of your own design is given by the formula $P = 3N + 20$, where P is the price in pounds and N is the number of shirts ordered.

a Work out the price of 40 shirts.

b Work out the price per shirt when 40 shirts are ordered.

(LEAG)

7 The total weight of a box of sweets is given by the following formula.

Total weight of a box of sweets = Weight of box + number of sweets × weight of one sweet

An empty box weighs 80 grams and can hold 40 sweets.
Each sweet weighs 3½ grams.
Find the total weight of the box and the sweets.

(WJEB)

8

	Won	Drawn	Lost	Points
Army	6	4	2	......
Navy	...	3	5	18
RAF	X	Y	3	11

This table shows the positions of 3 service hockey teams one weekend during the season.
They get 3 points for a win, 1 point for a draw and no points if they lose.

a Copy the table and fill in the two blanks.

b How many games have the Army played?

c Copy this table and list all the possible values of X and Y. (Remember, there are 3 points for a win).

You may not need all the answer spaces.

X	Y

The RAF has played 10 games.

d What are the values of X and Y?

(MEG)

9

1	2	3	4	5	6	7	8	9	10
11	12	13	14	15	16	17	18	19	20
21	22	23	24	25	26	27	28	29	30
31	32	33	34	35	36	37	38 ....

This table shows part of a pattern which goes on for ever.
The cross with 13 in the middle has a value of 65 because $3 + 13 + 23 + 12 + 14 = 65$.

a What is the value of the cross at 27?

b Copy this cross and fill in the blank spaces using x's.

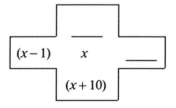

c Copy and complete this addition to the cross:

$$(x-1) + x + (x+10) + (............) + (............) = ...$$

d Tracey draws a cross with a value of 125.

What is the middle number in Tracey's cross?

(MEG)

10 Electricians sometimes use this formula to calculate the value of resistances:

$$\frac{1}{R} = 1 - \frac{1}{A} + \frac{1}{B}$$

When $A = 2.4$ and $B = 1.5$,

a find $\dfrac{1}{R}$.

b find R.

(MEG)

11 Here are three mathematical statements **a**, **b**, **c**.

In each part, give an example which shows that the statement is not **always** true, for instance:

Statement

'If you join three points with straight lines, you get a triangle.'

Example

a 'If we add together two numbers p and q, the answer is bigger than p.'

b 'If $\dfrac{p}{q} = \dfrac{s}{t}$, then $p = s$ and $q = t$.'

c 'If you divide a quadrilateral with one straight cut, then there will be two pieces.'

(MEG)

12

A rescue harpoon is fired horizontally from a cliff-top. The horizontal distance, x metres, it has travelled after t seconds is given by

$$x = 250t$$

The distance of the harpoon below the cliff-top, y metres, is given by $y = 5t^2$.

a (i) Write t in terms of x.

  (ii) Write an equation which connects y and x, but does not include t, in the form $y = \ldots\ldots$

b How many centimetres below the cliff-top will the harpoon be when it is 50 metres horizontally from the firing gun?

(WJEB)

13 Given that $y = 4a - 2b^2$, $a = -1$ and $b = -2$, then $y =$

A	-20
B	-12
C	-4
D	4
E	12

(LEAG)

14 The formula for the surface area, A, of a closed circular cylinder of radius r and height h is

$$A = 2\pi r(r + h)$$

a Make h the subject of the formula.

b Find the radius, in cm to one decimal place, of a cylinder whose surface area is 120π cm² and whose height is 12 cm.

(LEAG)

15 The cost, £C, of making n articles is given by the formula

$$C = a + bn$$

where a and b are constants.

The cost of making 4 articles is £20 and the cost of making 7 articles is £29.

Write down two equations in a and b.

Solve these equations to find the values of a and b.

(LEAG)

16

$$\frac{1}{f} = \frac{1}{u} + \frac{1}{v}$$

Find f, correct to three significant figures, when $u = 2.50$ and $v = 1.25$.

(LEAG)

17 The voltage, V volts, available from a 12 volt battery of internal resistance r ohms when connected to apparatus of resistance R ohms is given by

$$V = \frac{12R}{(r+R)}$$

a Find V when $r = 1.5$ and $R = 6$.

b Express R in terms of V and r.

(MEG)

18 A temperature can be measured as $F°$ Fahrenheit or $C°$ Celsius. The exact relationship between F and C is given by

$$F = \frac{9}{5}C + 32 \ .$$

a Find the value of F when $C = 20$.

b Find the value of C when $F = 14$.

An approximate relationship between F and C is given by the following rule.

'To find F, add 15 to C and double your answer.'

c Write this relationship as a formula.

d Use this relationship to find an approximate value of F when $C = 20$.

(MEG)

19 W. Morgan's 'East Africa' gives the formula

$$T = 24.5 - 0.69H$$

for the mean minimum temperature $T°C$ at a height H measured in hundreds of metres above sea level in Uganda.

a The maximum recommended height for growing coffee is 1800 m. What is the mean minimum temperature given by the formula for this height?

b Above what height could you expect a mean minimum temperature of less than $0°C$?

c Give a formula for H in terms of T.

(MEG)

20 Factorise completely $2\pi rh + \pi r^2$.

(MEG)

21 Multiply out the brackets and collect together like terms.

$$3(x + 2y) + 4(3x - 2y)$$

(SEG)

22 Factorise $14x + 49y$.

(SEG)

23 a Solve the simultaneous equations

$$x - 4y = 29$$

$$3x + 2y = 17$$

b Multiply out

(i) $2p(p - 3)$ (ii) $(2q - 1)(2q + 5)$

c Simplify

(i) $\dfrac{2n}{n^2}$ (ii) $\dfrac{r^2 - r}{r}$

d Solve the inequality

$$7 - 3t < 4 + 2t$$

(MEG)

24 The sides of a triangle are a cm, $(a-2)$ cm and $(a+3)$ cm, as shown.

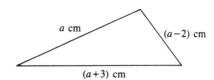

a What is the perimeter of the triangle in terms of a?

b The triangle has a perimeter of 19 cm. Calculate the value of a.

(MEG)

25 a Factorise completely:

(i) $5x^2 - 20y^2$ (ii) $x^2 + 8x - 20$

b Solve the following equations:

(i) $\dfrac{1}{4}x - \dfrac{1}{3}(x-2) = 1$ (ii) $x^{1/2} = 9$ (iii) $x^{-2} = 4$

(MEG)

26 a It is known that $x = 2.8$, correct to one decimal place, and

$$y = \frac{4x}{3-x}$$

(i) State the least possible value of x and the greatest possible value of x.

(ii) Find the least possible value of y.

(iii) Find the greatest possible value of y.

b Make x the subject of the formula $y = \frac{4x}{3-x}$.

(MEG)

27 a Factorise $x^2 + 11x + 24$.

b Solve $y^2 + y - 6 = 0$.

(LEAG)

28 a Complete the second bracket so as to make

$$p^2 - q^2 = (p - q)\,(\quad\quad)$$ a true statement.

b Use your answer to (a) to help you calculate the exact value of

$$10\,000\,000\,001^2 - 9\,999\,999\,999^2$$

(MEG)

29 Solve

a $3x - 4 = 11$ **b** $4p^2 = 9$

(LEAG)

30 a When $x + y = 5$ and $3x - 2y = 4$ find the values of x and y.

b The organisers for a charity concert sold 500 tickets. There were two prices: £3 for adults and £2 for children. The money received from the sale of adult tickets was £400 more than the money received from the sale of children's tickets. How many adult tickets were sold?

(SEG)

31 Cans of soup are delivered to a supermarket in **closed** rectangular cardboard boxes. Each box is 30 cm high and x cm wide. The length is 20 cm more than the width (inside measurements).

Write down expressions for

a (i) the length,

(ii) the area of each of the two shorter sides,

(iii) the area of each of the two longer sides,

(iv) the area of the base.

b From your answers, write down as far as possible an expression for the total inner surface area of the box (including the top).

c The total inner surface area is 10 800 cm². Show that

$$x^2 + 80x - 4800 = 0$$

One solution of this equation is

$$x = -120$$

Find the other solution.

d The cans are 10 cm high and have a diameter of 5 cm. How many cans does each box contain when full?

(MEG)

32 a Given that $1 - \frac{x}{3} = 4$, then $x =$

    A -9
    B -3
    C 3
    D 6
    E 9

b $2(3x - 5) - 3(x - 2) =$

    A $3x - 16$
    B $3x - 12$
    C $3x - 7$
    D $3x - 4$
    E $3x - 3$

(LEAG)

33 Nelson decides to plant vegetables in a piece of garden which is rectangular in shape. He uses a long cane to measure the land and finds that it is 5 cane lengths plus one stride by 3 cane lengths plus one stride. The plan of the land and the proposed vegetable plots is shown below. The unshaded area represents a path.

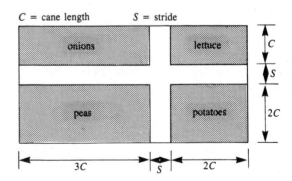

a Find, in terms of C, the total area of land used for growing vegetables.

b Find, in terms of C and S, the area of the path.

c The area of the potato plot is 216 square feet. Find C.

(SEG)

123

34

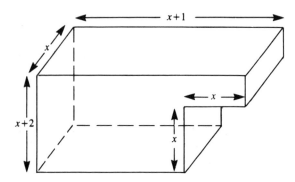

A firm of body-builders designs furniture removal vans to meet customers' requirements. The figure above illustrates the general design of these vans. All measurements are in metres and the value of x is calculated to give the customer the volume he requires.

a Obtain, and simplify, an expression in x for the volume of the van.

b A customer, Mr Smith, requires a van with a volume of 8 m³. To obtain this volume show that x has to be calculated from the equation

$$3x^2 + 2x - 8 = 0$$

c Solve this equation and select the appropriate value of x.

d To satisfy the requirements of another customer, Mr Hamid, the value of x has to be 1. Calculate the area of sheet metal required to build this van, neglecting any overlaps.

(SEG)

35 Sid decides to invest £240 in British Gas Shares.

a If each share costs x pence write down an expression for the number of shares received.

b If each share had been 10p less, Sid could have bought another 80 shares. Form an equation for x and show that it reduces to

$$x^2 - 10x - 3000 = 0$$

c Calculate the price which Sid paid for each share.

(SEG)

36 At $f(x) = 3 - 2x$

a Calculate $f(4)$.

b Calculate $ff(4)$.

c Obtain and simplify an expression for $ff(x)$.

d Calculate $f^{-1}(x)$.

(MEG)

37 a A hexagon has 6 sides and 9 diagonals. A heptagon has 7 sides and 14 diagonals.

A pentagon has 5 sides. How many diagonals does it have?

b f is a function defined by $f(n) = \dfrac{n(n-3)}{2}$ where $n \in$ {positive numbers}.

Find

    (i) $f(2)$,

    (ii) $f(6)$,

    (iii) $f(7)$.

    (iv) Draw the graph of $f(n)$ for values of n from 0 up to 8.

    (v) What is the value of n if $f(n) = 10$?

c The formula $d = \dfrac{n(n-3)}{2}$ can be used to find the number of diagonals (d) in a polygon with n sides.

Give a domain for f such that $f(n)$ will give the number of diagonal of a polygon with n sides.

(WJEB)

38 A sequence is defined by $u_1 = 1$, $u_{n+1} = \dfrac{1}{1 + u_n}$.

a Calculate u_2.

b Calculate u_4.

(MEG)

39 a In a sequence of fractions, the next term after $\dfrac{x}{y}$ is $\dfrac{y+x}{y+2x}$. For example, the term which follows

124

$\frac{5}{7}$ is $\frac{12}{17}$, i.e. $\frac{7+5}{7+10}$.

(i) Write down the next three terms in the sequence

$$\frac{2}{3} , \frac{5}{7} , \frac{12}{17} , \dots$$

(ii) Copy and complete the following table for the first six terms in the sequence, giving their decimal values to as many decimal places as your calculator will give.

		Decimal value
1st term	$\frac{2}{3}$	
2nd term	$\frac{5}{7}$	
3rd term	$\frac{12}{17}$	
4th term		
5th term		
6th term		

(iii) What do you notice about the decimal values of these terms?

b In another sequence of fractions, the next term after

$\frac{x}{y}$ is $\frac{y-x}{y+x}$.

(i) Write down the first six terms of the sequence which starts with $\frac{2}{3}$.

(ii) What do you notice about the values of these terms?

(MEG)

40 The diagram shows part of the graph of $f: x \to x^3 - 2x - 1$ and the solution $x = w$ of the equation $x^3 - 2x - 1 = 0$.

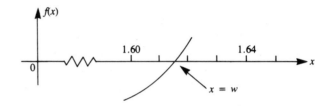

a From this diagram, estimate the value of w correct to **two** decimal places.

b Show that $x^3 - 2x - 1 = 0$ may be written as

$$x = \sqrt{2 + \frac{1}{x}}$$

c Using

$$x_{n+1} = \sqrt{2 + \frac{1}{x_n}}$$

and taking x_1 to be the value you obtained as your estimate for w in part **a**, calculate x_2, x_3, and x_4. In each case, write down all the digits shown on your calculator.

d Continue this iteration until you can give the value of w correct to 5 decimal places.

Write down this value of w.

(LEAG)

125

Graphs

How Graphs Began

For four centuries, the mathematicians of the rather primitive countries of Northern Europe learnt and used the techniques of the great Hindu and Muslim mathematicians but added little new knowledge of their own. Then, during the sixteenth century, three developments set the scene for a rapid expansion in mathematics. These three developments were:

- The invention of accurate mechanical clocks. This stimulated an interest in the mathematics of time and functions which change as time passes.

- The increasing use of artillery in warfare. This stimulated an interest in the mathematics of projectiles.

- The need to discover ways to navigate long distances out of sight of land. This stimulated an interest in the mathematics of map making and also had an effect on clock design because navigation is very difficult without an accurate sea-going clock.

One of the first major contributions by Northern Europeans to mathematics was the development of graphs. In some ways, however, the groundwork that led to their discoveries was laid many centuries earlier. For example, the Alexandrian mathematician Ptolemy had in 150 A.D. drawn maps with lines of longitude and latitude (see below).

Cartesian graphs and co-ordinates

The great Muslim mathematician Omar Khayyam had in the twelfth century demonstrated that an accurate sketch of a curve could be used to solve an equation.

In the sixteenth century, the French mathematician René Descartes drew these ideas together and developed a new form of mathematics in which algebra was applied to geometry. This branch of mathematics has been named in his honour and is called **Cartesian geometry**.

Descartes developed a grid of numbers on which pictures of mathematical functions could be plotted. You will have certainly already met this basic Cartesian grid (or graph) in earlier maths lessons.

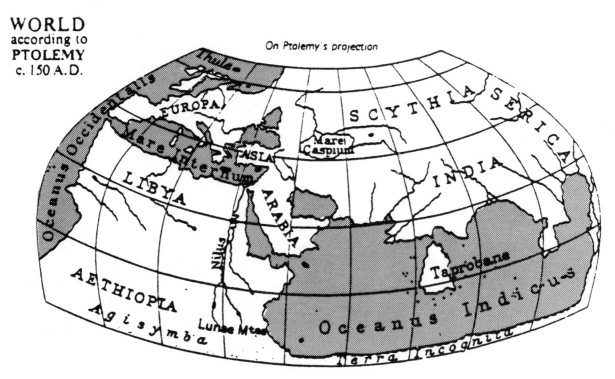

WORLD according to PTOLEMY c. 150 A.D.

On Ptolemy's projection

126

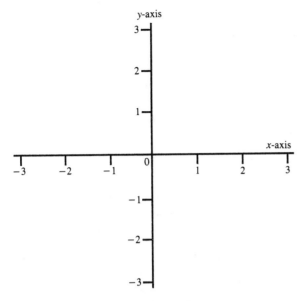

The Cartesian graph

A is the point $(3,2)$ F is the point $(-2,2)$
B is the point $(2,3)$ G is the point $(-2,0)$
C is the point $(5,0)$ H is the point $(-2,-3)$
D is the point $(0,3)$ I is the point $(0,-4)$
E is the point $(-1,4)$ J is the point $(4,-3)$

Descartes called the horizontal number line the **x-axis** and the vertical number line the **y-axis**. To establish the position of any particular point on the graph we write down two numbers. If you draw a straight line from the point perpendicular to the x-axis, then the number where this line meets the x-axis is called the **x co-ordinate** of the point. Similarly, if you draw a straight line from the point perpendicular to the y-axis, then the number where the line meets the y-axis is called the **y co-ordinate** of the point. The co-ordinates are usually written in a bracket. To avoid any possible confusion between points like (3,2) and (2,3), the **x co-ordinate is always the first number in the bracket.**

Examples

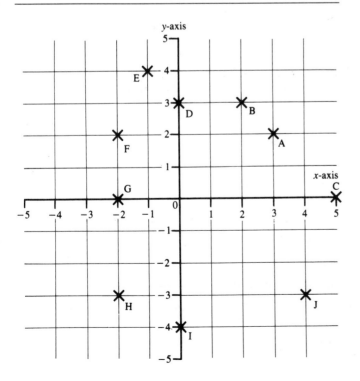

CHECKPOINT 1

1 Draw a graph with x- and y- axes from -5 to 5. Plot each of the following sets of points on your graph, joining them in the order they are plotted.

a $(0,4)$, $(2,1)$, $(3,-3)$, $(-1, -2)$, $(-4,0)$, $(-1,-1)$, $(-3,3)$, $(1,1)$
b (0.4), $(4,0)$, $(4,-4)$, $(0,-4)$, $(-4,0)$, $(-4,1)$, $(-3,1)$, $(-5,2)$, $(-5,0)$, $(0,-5)$, $(5,-5)$, $(5,0)$, $(0,5)$, $(-2,5)$, $(-1,3)$, $(-1,4)$

3D co-ordinates

We can extend the system of Cartesian co-ordinates into three dimensions. To do this, we add a third axis, the **z-axis**, at right angles to both the x-axis and the y-axis. Our co-ordinate system now looks like this.

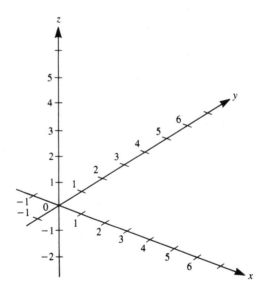

Any point in the three-dimensional space of the graph can now be located by giving three numbers, an x co-ordinate, a y co-ordinate and a z co-ordinate. These co-ordinates are given in a bracket, just like two-dimensional co-ordinates, always giving first the x, then the y, then the z co-ordinate. For example, in the diagram overleaf, a cube ABCDEFGH with an edge length of 4 units has been drawn on our three-dimensional grid.

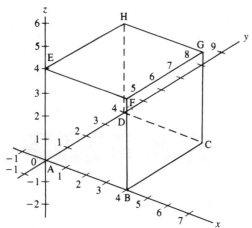

On the grid
A has co-ordinates (0,0,0)   B has co-ordinates (4,0,0)
C has co-ordinates (4,4,0)   D has co-ordinates (0,4,0)
E has co-ordinates (0,0,4)   F has co-ordinates (4,0,4)
G has co-ordinates (4,4,4)   H has co-ordinates (0,4,4)

CHECKPOINT 2

1 The following diagrams show a cube ABCDEFG with an edge length of 3 units drawn in different positions on a three-dimensional grid. In each case give the co-ordinates of the vertices A, B, C, D, E, F, G and H of the cube.

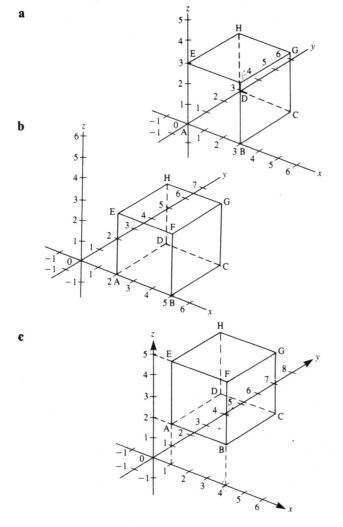

a

b

c

2 The centre of a cube is at (0,0,0). One vertex is at (3,3,3). Give the co-ordinates of the other seven vertices of the cube.

3 This diagram shows a cuboid ABCDEFG. A has co-ordinates (6,0,3) and C has co-ordinates (6,4,0). Give the co-ordinates of the other six vertices of the cuboid.

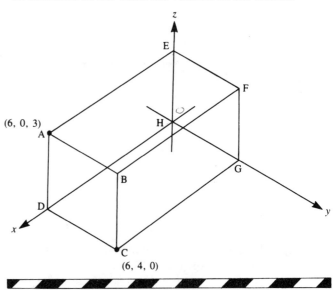

Lines parallel to the axes

We have seen that a Cartesian graph consists of two number lines, set at right angles, called the x-axis and the y-axis. If a line parallel to the y-axis is drawn on a graph, all the points on the line will share a common x co-ordinate. For example, if a line is drawn parallel to the y-axis and passing through the number 4 on the x-axis, then every point on the line must have an x co-ordinate of 4. For this reason, we describe the line as **the line with the equation $x = 4$**.

If a line parallel to the x-axis is drawn on a graph, all the points on the line will share a common y co-ordinate. For example, if a line is drawn parallel to the x-axis and passing through the number -1 on the y-axis, then every point on the line must have a y co-ordinate of -1. For this reason, we describe the line as **the line with the equation $y = -1$**.

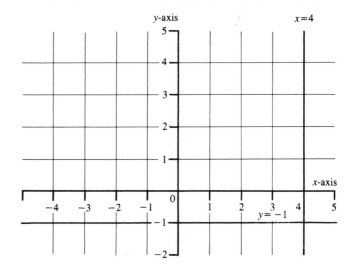

CHECKPOINT 3

1 Draw a graph and mark on it the lines with equation

a $x=3$ **b** $x=-2$ **c** $x=0$ **d** $x=4.5$ **e** $x=-3.5$

2 Draw a graph and mark on it the lines with equation

a $y=4$ **b** $y=-3$ **c** $y=0$ **d** $y=-2.5$ **e** $y=-5$

3 Draw a graph and mark on it the lines with equation

a $x=1$ **b** $y=1$ **c** $x=-3$ **d** $y=-2$

4 Write down the equation of the line which passes through each of the following pairs of points:

a $(2,-2)$ and $(5,-2)$ **b** $(2,-2)$ and $(2,5)$
c $(0,7)$ and $(0,-7)$ **d** $(0,7)$ and $(-5,7)$
e $(-5,0)$ and $(5,0)$ **f** $(-5,0)$ and $(-5,5)$

Gradients

If a straight line which is not parallel to either axis is drawn on a graph, the points on the line will share neither a common x co-ordinate nor a common y co-ordinate. There will however be a common **slope or gradient** between any two points on the line. The slope or gradient of a line joining two points measures how 'steep' the line is and is defined as the fraction;

$$\frac{\text{difference between the } y \text{ co-ordinates of the points}}{\text{difference between the } x \text{ co-ordinates of the points}}$$

Suppose we take this straight line.

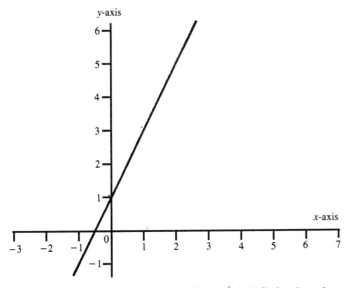

The gradient between the points $(0,1)$ and $(1,3)$ is given by

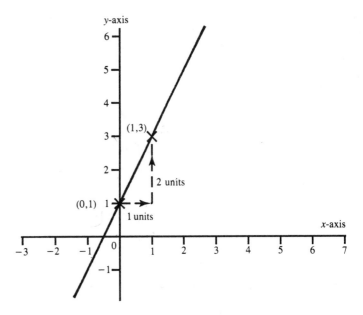

$$\text{gradient} = \frac{3-1}{1-0} = \frac{2}{1}$$

An identical gradient would be obtained between any other two points on the line. For example

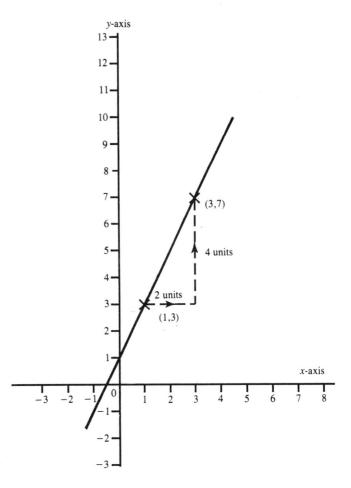

$$\text{gradient} = \frac{7-3}{3-1} = \frac{4}{2} = \frac{2}{1}$$

129

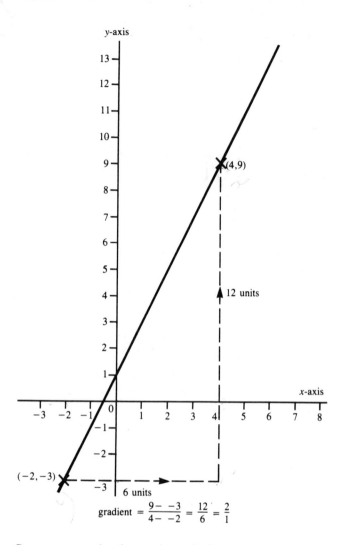

$$\text{gradient} = \frac{9 - -3}{4 - -2} = \frac{12}{6} = \frac{2}{1}$$

So, we can make the mathematical statement

'The line has a constant gradient of $\frac{2}{1}$.'

Or, in simpler words,

'The line climbs 2 squares up the graph for every 1 square across the graph.'

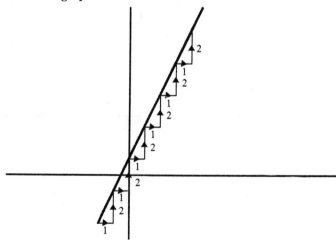

Examples

1 Find the gradient of the line which connects the points (1,1) and (5,3).

By drawing a graph we find

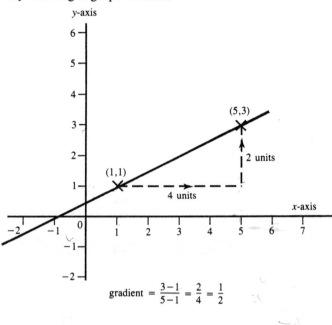

$$\text{gradient} = \frac{3-1}{5-1} = \frac{2}{4} = \frac{1}{2}$$

2 Find the gradient of the line which connects the points $(-2, 3)$ and $(4, -2)$.

By drawing a graph we find

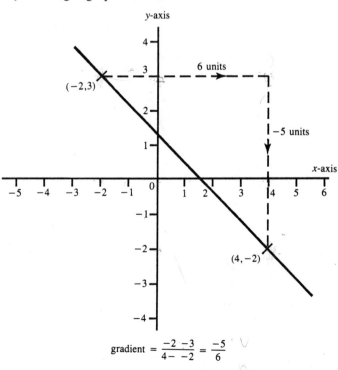

$$\text{gradient} = \frac{-2-3}{4--2} = \frac{-5}{6}$$

130

It is of course possible to calculate the gradient of the line connecting two points without drawing a graph. A graph should, however, always be drawn to check your calculations. Also, if preferred, calculations can be avoided and the gradient can be read directly from the graph, as the horizontal and vertical lines marked on the graphs have shown. Many students find this an easier approach, simply taking any pair of points and finding the horizontal and vertical distances between them. Then

$$\text{gradient} = \frac{\text{vertical distance}}{\text{horizontal distance}}$$

The only difficulty is in remembering that a distance 'down' the graph must be considered negative.

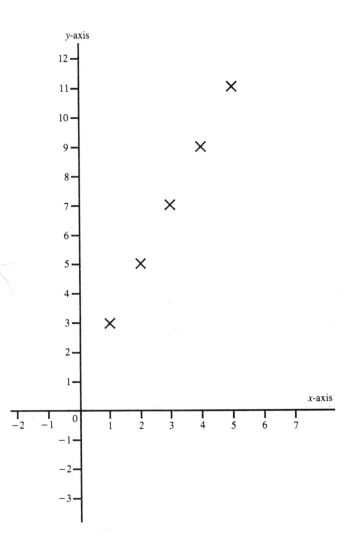

CHECKPOINT 4

Draw a graph and find the gradient of the line which connects each of the following pairs of points.

a (0,0) and (3,6)   b (0,0) and (2,6)
c (0,0) and (4,4)   d (−2,−1) and (2,1)
e (−4,−1) and (6,1)   f (−3,1) and (3,5)
g (−1,1) and (1,4)   h (−4,4) and (3,−3)
i (−5,−2) and (−3,−6)   j (1,6) and (2,4)
k (−1,5) and (1,−5)   l (−4,−3) and (4,−5)

Equations for lines

We have already seen that mathematical relationships like $y = 2x + 1$, $T_n = 4n - 1$ or $x \rightarrow 3x^2 + 2x - 1$ transform one sequence of numbers into another sequence of numbers. We have investigated the behaviour of these relationships and illustrated their effects with mapping diagrams.

Cartesian graphs can also be used to illustrate mathematical relationships. For example, the equation $y = 2x + 1$ is a rule for transforming a value for the number x into a value for the number y. If we select a sequence of values for x, the equation produces a sequence of values for y. If we start with the sequence of x values 1, 2, 3, 4, 5, the equation produces the sequence of y values 3, 5, 7, 9, 11. Putting these values into pairs gives us (1,3), (2,5), (3,7), (4,9), (5,11). These pairs of values can now be plotted as co-ordinates on a graph as shown in the next column.

The points all lie on a straight line. This raises two questions:

• Should the points be connected simply by a straight line, using a ruler?

• If the points are connected, what does the line joining them represent?

It will help us to answer these questions if we obtain and plot some more pairs of values. Values obtained from an equation are often organised into a table. This table shows a larger set of possible x and y values which fit the equation $y = 2x + 1$.

x	−5	−4.5	−4	−3.5	−3	−2.5	−2
$y = 2x + 1$	−9	−8	−7	−6	−5	−4	−3

x	−1.5	−1	−0.5	0	0.5	1	1.5
$y = 2x + 1$	−2	−1	0	1	2	3	4

x	2	2.5	3	3.5	4	4.5	5
$y = 2x + 1$	5	6	7	8	9	10	11

131

Adding all these extra values to our graph gives us this diagram.

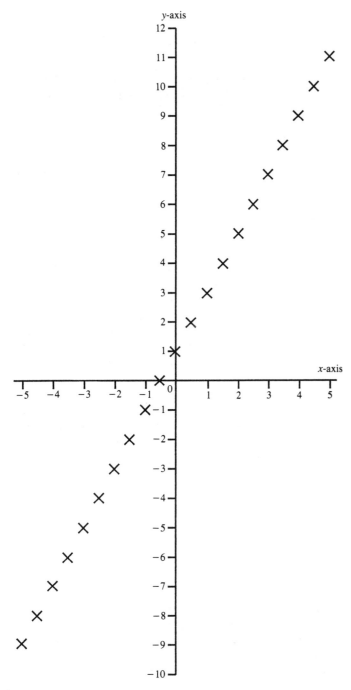

It now starts to become clear that **any** pair of values which fits the relationship $y = 2x + 1$ will plot as a point **somewhere** along the same straight line. So, we can answer the two questions raised by our first graph.

• Yes, the points should be connected using a ruler.

• The line joining the points represents **all** possible pairs of values connected by the equation $y = 2x + 1$.

Draw up a table of values for each of the following equations, using all the whole number x values from -3 to 3. Plot the pairs of values you obtain as co-ordinates on a graph and, if it seems sensible to do so, connect the points with a straight line.

a $y = x + 4$ **b** $y = x - 4$ **c** $y = 2x$ **d** $y = \dfrac{x}{2}$

e $y = 2x + 4$ **f** $y = \dfrac{x}{2} - 4$ **g** $y = 4 - x$ **h** $y = x^2$

Equations for straight lines

The solution to the last part of Checkpoint 43 demonstrates that some equations do not produce straight line graphs. This leads us to ask, which types of equation produce a straight line graph and which do not?

The next checkpoint will help us to answer this question.

CHECKPOINT 6

1 Construct a table of values and draw the graph of $y = 3x + 2$, using values of x from 0 to 5.

a What is the difference between each term in the sequence of y values in the table?

b What is the gradient of the line which represents the equation $y = 3x + 2$?

c At what point does the graph cross the y-axis?

2 Construct a table of values and draw the graph of $y = 5x - 1$, using values of x from 0 to 5.

a What is the difference between each term in the sequence of y values in the table?

b What is the gradient of the line which represents the equation $y = 5x - 1$?

c At what point does the graph cross the y-axis?

3 Construct a table of values and draw the graph of

$$y = \frac{x}{2} + 1$$

using values of x from 0 to 5.

a What is the difference between each term in the sequence of y values in the table?

b What is the gradient of the line which represents the equation

$$y = \frac{x}{2} + 1?$$

c At what point does the graph cross the y-axis?

4 Construct a table of values and draw the graph of $y = 6 - x$, using values of x from 0 to 5.

a What is the difference between each term in the sequence of y values in the table?
b What is the gradient of the line which represents the equation $y = 6 - x$?
c At what point does the graph cross the y-axis?

$y = mx + c$

The general equation

$$y = mx + c$$

where m and c represent any selected numbers, produces this table of values.

x	0	1	2	3	4	5
$y = mx + c$	c	$m + c$	$2m + c$	$3m + c$	$4m + c$	$5m + c$

The y values form a sequence, starting with c and with a constant difference of m. It is clear that the graph drawn from this table will produce a straight line with a gradient equal to m, passing through $(0,c)$ on the y-axis.

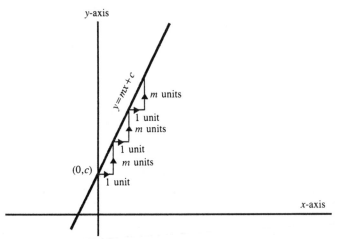

So, we can state the general rule:

> Any equation which can be expressed in the form $y = mx + c$, where m and c are any selected numbers, will produce a straight line graph with a gradient equal to m and an intersection with the y-axis at the point $(0,c)$.

This rule enables us to predict in advance that, for example, the graph drawn from the equation $y = 4x - 5$ will have a gradient equal to $\frac{4}{1}$ and will cross the y-axis at the point $(0, -5)$.

Equipped with this knowledge, it is possible to draw the graph of an equation like $y = 4x - 5$ without constructing a table of values. We can simply draw a line with the correct slope passing through the correct point on the y-axis. In practice most people still prefer to complete a table of values and use their knowledge of slope and y-axis cutting point to check their results. Knowing that the result should be a straight line does, however, mean that we can reduce the number of values included in the table. The minimum number of points necessary to fix a straight line is two, but usually at least three are plotted (the third serves as a check).

Example

Draw a graph to illustrate the equation $y = 11 - 2x$, using x values from -3 to 3.

(We know that the graph will be a straight line, so we only need 3 points. It is a good idea to use the two extreme values of x and one other value. This will tell us in advance what values need to be covered on the y-axis of our graph.)

A suitable table of values is

x	-3	0	3
y	17	11	5

which produces the graph on the next page.

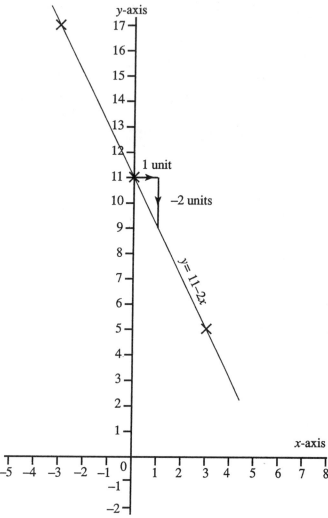

From the graph, we see that the line has a slope of $\frac{-2}{1}$ and cuts the y-axis at $(0,11)$. This checks with the predicted result of a slope equal to m and a cutting point of $(0,c)$.

CHECKPOINT 7

1 Draw a graph to illustrate each of the following equations using x values from -4 to 4 and write down the gradient of the graph and the co-ordinates of the point where the graph cuts the y-axis.

a $y=y+3$ **b** $y=x-3$ **c** $y=3x$

d $y=\frac{x}{4}$ **e** $y=3x-3$ **f** $y=\frac{x}{4}+3$

g $y=4-2x$ **h** $y=\frac{3x}{4}+3$ **i** $y=2(x-1)$

j $y=8-\frac{x}{2}$

2 Write down the equations of the lines which have the following gradients and cutting points on the y-axis.

a gradient 2, cutting point $(0,3)$
b gradient 3, cutting point $(0,2)$

c gradient $\frac{1}{2}$, cutting point $(0,-1)$

d gradient -1, cutting point $(0,0)$
e gradient -2, cutting point $(0,12)$

Conversion graphs

Many relationships can be expressed in the form $y=mx+c$ and illustrated with straight line graphs. For example, the relationship between a temperature measured in Fahrenheit degrees and a temperature measured in Centigrade can be expressed in the form.

$$F = \frac{9C}{5} + 32$$

If we are interested in temperatures between 0°C and 100°C, we can construct this table of values.

C	0	50	100
F	32	122	212

and draw the graph shown on the next page. (2 mm graph paper is used for reasons that will become apparent later.)

This graph illustrates the relationship between the two different systems of temperature measurement and can also be used as a **conversion graph**. Conversion graphs were once widely used as a quick calculation device. The introduction of cheap calculators has made them far less important but they are still sometimes used (and set as examination questions!). To illustrate their use, we will perform the following conversions with our temperature graph.

1 Convert 75°C into a Fahrenheit temperature.

2 Convert 100°F into a Celsius temperature.

To answer the first conversion, we start at the 75 on the Celsius axis, draw a vertical line up to the graph and then a horizontal line across to the Fahrenheit axis. The temperature at this point is our answer, 167°F (approximately). To answer the second conversion, we start at the 100 on the Fahrenheit axis, draw a horizontal line out to the graph and then a vertical line down to the Celsius axis. The temperature at this point is our answer, 38°C (approximately). The second graph shows both conversions completed.

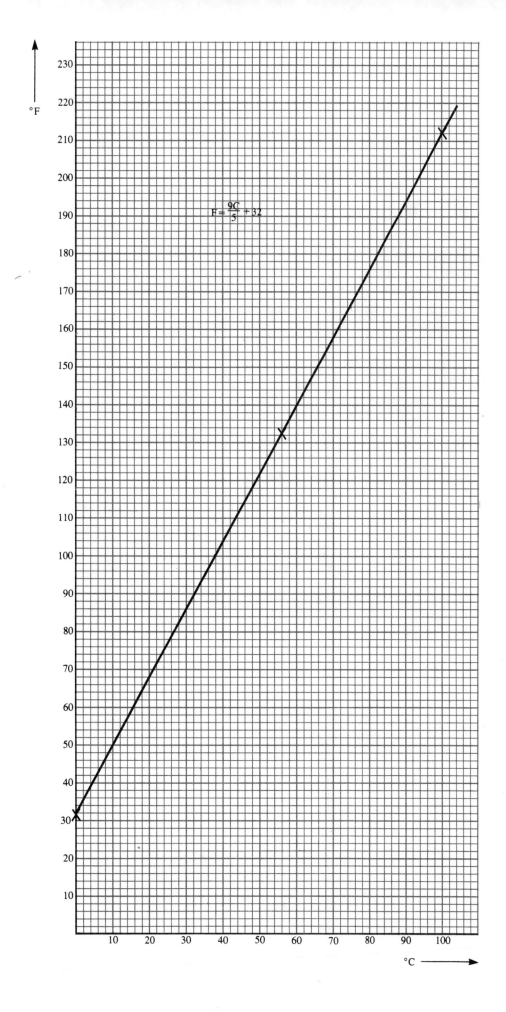

$$F = \frac{9C}{5} + 32$$

°F

°C

135

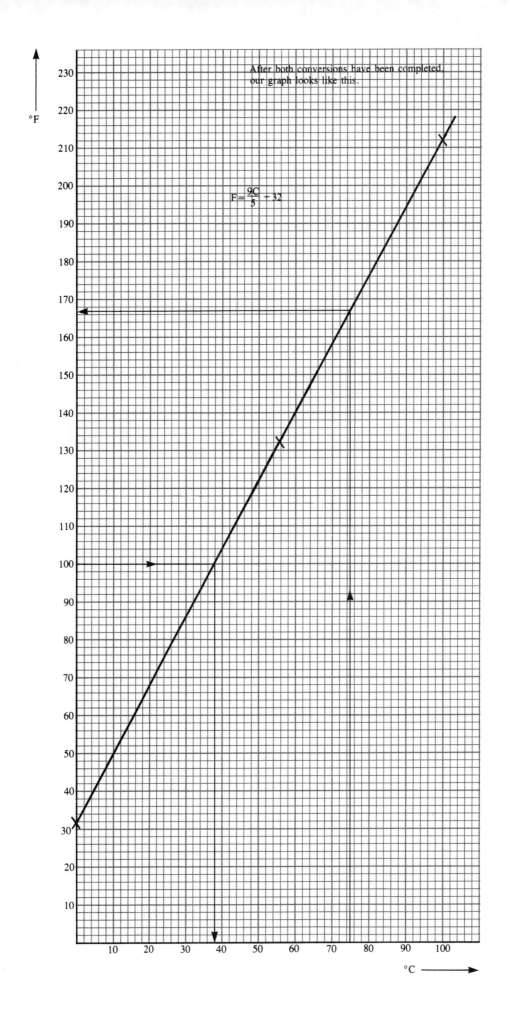

After both conversions have been completed, our graph looks like this.

$$F = \frac{9C}{5} + 32$$

136

It is now apparent why 2 mm graph paper was used for the graph. 10 mm or 5 mm graph paper would not have allowed us to read off conversion answers with any degree of accuracy.

When drawing such graphs, it is difficult to give any hard and fast rules for deciding the scales to be used on the axes. In the last example, the decision to let 1 cm equal 10 degrees on both the axes was made by 'common sense', in order to use the graph paper sensibly. The aim was to produce a graph which fitted the sheet of graph paper well and had axes that were easy to read values from. In practice, you will find that many examination questions contain precise details of the scales to be used when drawing a graph.

CHECKPOINT 8

1 The Rick Dastardly Detective Agency charges £40 a day for the hire of one of their detectives. This can be expressed as the equation

$$C = 40d$$

where C is the total cost and d is the number of days the detective is hired for.

a The Purple Panther Detective Agency charges a fixed fee of £80 plus a charge of £20 a day to hire one of their detectives. Express this as an equation.

b Prepare a graph on 2 mm graph paper, with a horizontal axis from 0 to 7 days and a vertical axis from 0 to £280. Use 2 cm to represent 1 day on the horizontal axis and 2 cm to represent £40 on the vertical axis.

c Plot lines to represent the cost equations for both companies. What advice would you offer to somebody who intended to hire a detective from one of the two companies?

2 The cost of building a stretch of motorway is estimated at £5 million per kilometre, plus a fixed cost of £15 million. Express this as an equation.

a Draw a graph to illustrate the cost equation, with a horizontal axis from 0 to 15 km and a vertical axis from 0 to £120 million. Use a scale of 1 cm to represent 1 km on the horizontal axis and 1 cm to represent £5 million on the vertical axis.

b Use your graph to calculate the cost per kilometre of building a 12 km stretch of motorway.

c Use your graph to calculate the cost per kilometre of building a 4 km stretch of motorway.

3 Tulip bulbs are offered for sale on the following terms:

- 10p each for orders of up to 20 bulbs

- 9p each for orders of more than 20 bulbs

- 8p each for orders of more than 40 bulbs

a Prepare a graph with a horizontal axis from 0 to 80 bulbs and a vertical axis from 0 to 650 pence. Use a scale of 1 cm to represent 10 bulbs on the horizontal axis and 1 cm to represent 50 pence on the vertical axis.

b Plot lines to represent the cost of buying between 1 and 20 bulbs, between 21 and 40 bulbs and between 41 and 80 bulbs.

c What advice would you offer to somebody buying either 20 bulbs or 40 bulbs?

4 The Hire-A-Heap Car Hire Company offer an executive saloon at three different daily hiring rates.

Scheme A: £20 per day plus 4 pence per mile

Scheme B: £25 per day plus 2 pence per mile

Scheme C: £33 per day with no mileage charges

a The daily cost of hiring a car under Scheme A can be expressed as the equation

$$C=20+0.04m$$

where C is the daily cost and m is the number of miles covered. Write down an equation to express the daily cost of hiring a car under Scheme B.

b Prepare a graph with a horizontal axis from 0 to 500 miles and a vertical axis from 0 to £50. Use a scale of 1 cm to represent 50 miles on the horizontal axis and 1 cm to represent £5 on the vertical axis.

c Plot lines to represent the daily hire costs under each of the three schemes.

d Jeff Collinson wants to hire a car for a holiday during which he anticipates he will travel an average of 150 miles each day. Which hiring scheme will be the cheapest for Jeff?

e Susan Taylor wants to hire a car for a holiday during which she anticipates she will travel an average of 300 miles each day. Which hiring scheme will be the cheapest for Susan?

f Aruna Patel wants to hire a car for a day to make a business trip of 500 miles. Which hiring scheme will be the cheapest for Aruna?

Equations not expressed in the form $y=mx+c$

Relationships expressed with equations like $4y-3x=12$ or $2y=x+5$ will produce straight line graphs because they can be rearranged into the form $y=mx+c$, using the rules of algebra. It is, however, preferable to obtain the graph of such equations without going to all the trouble of rearranging them. Remember, because we know the result will be a straight line, we only need two points to draw the graph (plus one extra point as a check). A quick way to obtain two points from these equations is to let first x and then y take the value 0. A third point can be obtained by selecting one other x value that gives the easiest possible calculations. For example, to obtain two points that fit $4y - 3x = 12$, we can use this table.

x	0		4
y		0	

This is easily completed, giving

x	0	-4	4
y	3	0	6

Plotting these points gives us this graph.

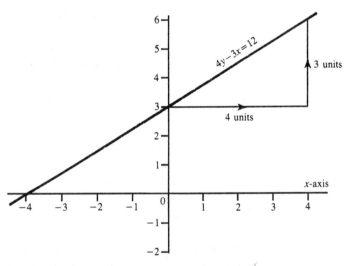

The line has a gradient of $\dfrac{3}{4}$ and cuts the y-axis at $(0,3)$.

This is of course exactly the result we would have obtained if we had started by rearranging $4y - 3x = 12$ into $y = \dfrac{3x}{4} + 3$.

Examples

1 Draw the graph of $2y = x + 5$.

Starting with this table

x	0		1
y		0	

gives us these points

x	0	-5	1
y	2.5	0	3

and this graph.

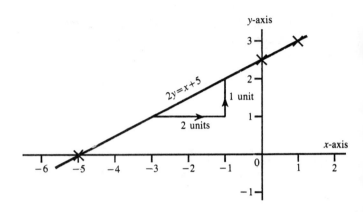

The line has a gradient of $\frac{1}{2}$ and cuts the y-axis at $(0,2\frac{1}{2})$. This is of course exactly the result we would have obtained if we had started by rearranging $2y = x + 5$ into $y = \frac{1}{2}x + 2\frac{1}{2}$.

2 Draw the graph of $3x + 5y = 30$.

Starting with this table

x	0		5
y		0	

gives us these points

x	0	10	5
y	6	0	3

and this graph.

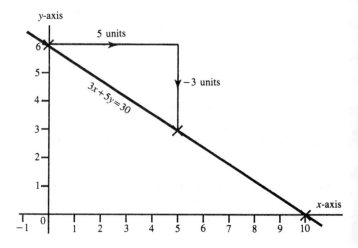

138

The line has a gradient of $\dfrac{-3}{5}$ and cuts the y-axis at $(0,6)$.

This is of course exactly the result we would have obtained if we had started by rearranging $3x + 5y = 30$ into $y = 6 - \dfrac{3x}{5}$.

CHECKPOINT 9

Draw a graph to illustrate each of the following equations.

a $4y = x + 1$ **b** $3y = 6x - 12$ **c** $2x + 3y = 24$
d $2x - 3y = 24$ **e** $2y - x = 8$ **f** $5x + 4y = 20$
g $x - y = 7$ **h** $x + y = 10$ **i** $3y = 21 - 7x$
j $40x + 60y = 240$

Using graphs to solve simultaneous equations

Simultaneous equations can be solved by drawing a graph. For example, suppose we wish to solve the equations

$$2y + x = 8$$

$$4y - x = 4$$

We can construct these tables

x	0	8	2
y	4	0	3

x	0	-4	8
y	1	0	3

and draw this graph.

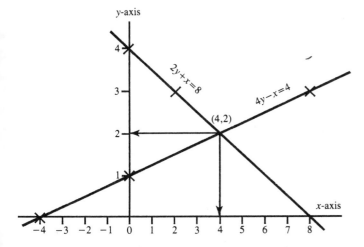

From the graph we can see that the lines intersect at $(4,2)$. This must mean that $x = 4$ and $y = 2$ are values that satisfy **both** equations. So, these values are the solution to our simultaneous equations.

CHECKPOINT 10

1 Solve each of the following pairs of simultaneous equations by drawing a graph.

a $y = x - 3$ **b** $y = 2x + 2$ **c** $y + 2x = 6$
    $x + 3y = 6$ $2y = x - 2$ $2y + x = 6$
d $2y - 2x = 7$ **e** $2y = x - 8$
    $4y + 3x = 0$ $4y = 20 - x$

2 The relationship between a temperature measured in Fahrenheit degrees and a temperature measured in Celsius degrees can be expressed in the form

$$F = \frac{9C}{5} + 32$$

Is there a temperature which is numerically the same in both Celsius and Fahrenheit? In other words, can you solve these simultaneous equations?

$$F = \frac{9C}{5} + 32$$

$$F = C$$

Solving simultaneous equations by drawing a graph illustrates situations in which there may be either no solution or many solutions to a particular problem.

Examples

1 Solve the equations

$$2x + 5y = 10$$

$$4x + 10y = 30$$

We produce these tables

x	0	5	2.5
y	2	0	1

x	0	7.5	5
y	3	0	1

and this graph.

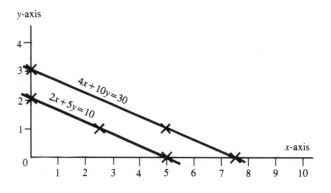

The lines representing the equations are parallel. There is no point which is common to both lines and therefore no solutions to the simultaneous equations. These equations cannot be true at the same time; they cannot be **simultaneously** true. If you rearrange the equations, you will see that this is because the equations produce lines with identical gradients but different cutting points on the y-axis.

2 Solve the equations:

$$5y = 2x + 10$$

$$10y - 4x = 20$$

We produce these tables:

x	0	-5	5
y	2	0	4

x	0	-5	5
y	2	0	4

and this graph.

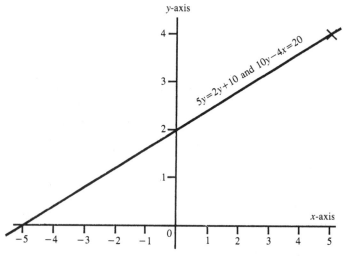

The equations are represented by the same line. Any point on this line represents a 'solution' to the equations. Thus, $x = 0$, $y = 2$ is a 'solution', $x = -5$, $y = 0$ is a 'solution', $x = 5$, $y = 3$ is a 'solution' and so are the co-ordinates of any other point selected from the line. If you experiment with the equations, you will see that this is because the equations are in fact identical, one being a simple rearrangement of the other.

CHECKPOINT 11

Draw graphs to solve each of the following pairs of simultaneous equations and state whether the equations have one solution, no solution or many solutions. If the equations have one solution, find that solution. If the equations have many solutions, give three possible solutions.

a $x + y = 5$
  $8x + 8y = 64$

b $y = 3x + 2$
  $7y - 21x = 148$

c $3x + 2y = 12$
  $x + 3y = 24$

d $2y = x - 8$
  $7x = 56 - 14y$

e $3x + 5y = 30$
  $15x = 75 - 25y$

f $x + y = 0$
  $x - y = 0$

The graph of a quadratic expression

One of the questions in Checkpoint 43 asked you to draw a graph to illustrate the equation

$$y = x^2$$

This equation produces the table:

x	-3	-2	-1	0	1	2	3
y	9	4	1	0	1	4	9

When these points are plotted on a graph, it is obvious that they do not lie on the same straight line.

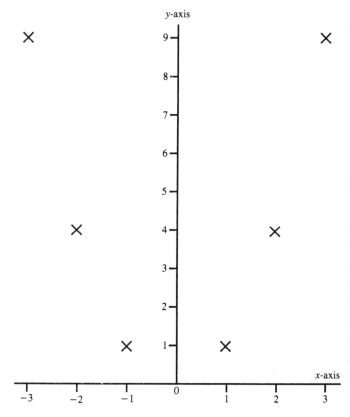

This raises three questions.

- Can the points be connected?

- If we do connect them, how do we connect them? Do we use a series of straight lines or perhaps a curved line?

- If the points are connected, what will the line(s) joining them represent?

It will help us to answer these questions if we obtain and plot some more pairs of values. This table shows a larger set of possible x and y values which fit the equation $y = x^2$.

x	-3	-2.5	-2	-1.5	-1	-0.5	0
y	9	6.25	4	2.25	1	0.25	0

x	0.5	1	1.5	2	2.5	3
y	0.25	1	2.25	4	6.25	9

Adding all these extra values to our graph gives us this diagram.

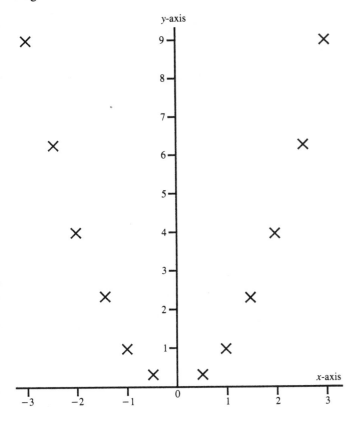

It now starts to become clear that **any** pair of values which fit the relationship $y = x^2$ will plot as a point somewhere along the same curve. So, we can answer the three questions raised by our first graph.

• Yes, the points should be connected.

• The points should be connected with a smooth curve, not with a series of straight lines.

• The line joining the points represents **all** possible pairs of values connected by the equation $y = x^2$.

Drawing a smooth curve through a set of points is not easy, but with practice and patience you should be able to produce a graph like this.

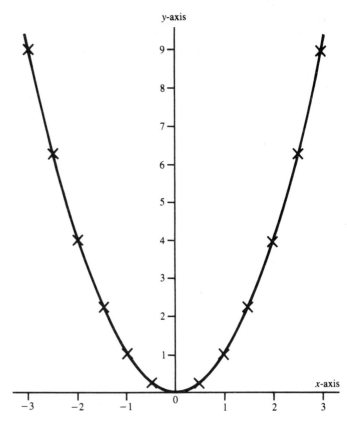

The graph we have just drawn is the simplest example of a type of curve called a **parabola**. The parabola always has this 'bowl' shape and is produced by any equation of the form $y = ax^2 + bx + c$, where a, b and c are any selected numbers. To draw a curved graph accurately we obviously need as many points as possible. The table of values always includes all the whole number values of x and, if the shape of the graph is not clear, may also include decimal values of x.

Example

Draw a graph to illustrate the equation $y = x^2 - 2x - 8$, as x takes values from -5 to 5.

As the equation is quite complicated, the possibility of mistakes can be reduced by setting out the calculations in a table like this.

x	-5	-4	-3	-2	-1	0	1	2	3	4	5
x^2	25	16	9	4	1	0	1	4	9	16	25
$-2x$	10	8	6	4	2	0	-2	-4	-6	-8	-10
-8	-8	-8	-8	-8	-8	-8	-8	-8	-8	-8	-8
y	27	16	7	0	-5	-8	-9	-8	-5	0	7

This gives us the following graph.

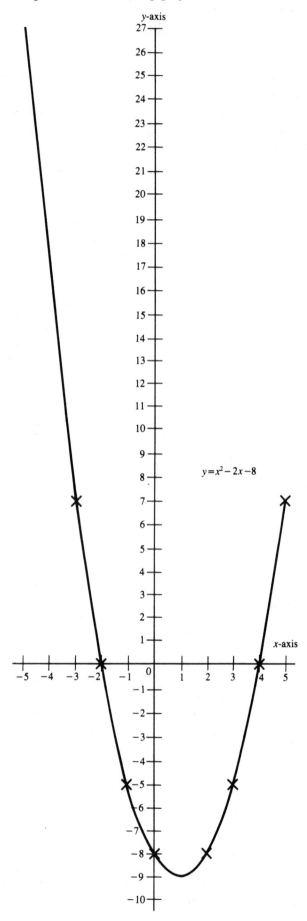

$y = x^2 - 2x - 8$

1 a Copy and complete this table of values for $y = x^2 + x - 6$.

x	-4	-3	-2	-1	0	1	2	3
x^2	16	9	4	1	0	1	4	9
$+x$	-4	-3	-2	-1	-0	1	2	3
-6	-6	-6	-6	-6	-6	-6	-6	-6
y	6	0	-4	-6	-7	-4	0	6

b Use the table to draw the graph of $y = x^2 + x - 6$ as x takes values from -4 to 3.

2 a Copy and complete this table of values for

$$y = \frac{x^2}{2} - 5$$

x	-5	-4	-3	-2	-1	0	1	2	3	4	5
$\frac{x^2}{2}$	12.5	8	4.5	2	$\frac{1}{2}$	0	0.5	2	4.5	8	$12\frac{1}{2}$
-5	-5	-5	-5	-5	-5	-5	-5	-5	-5	-5	-5
y	7.5	3	-0.5	-3	$-4\frac{1}{2}$	-5	-4.5	-3	$-\frac{1}{2}$	-3	$7\frac{1}{2}$

b Use the table to draw the graph of $x = \frac{x^2}{2} - 5$ as x takes values from -5 to 5.

3 Wayne and Sharon are camping at the Arrow River Campsite. This is a campsite beside the absolutely straight Arrow River. Campers at the site are given a 16-metre length of rope and four posts to fence off a piece of land for themselves. Sharon wants to fence off the greatest possible area and considers the possibilities. She decides to fence off a rectangle, using the river bank as one side. She draws this sketch.

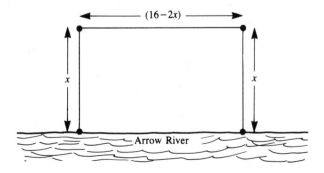

Sharon realises that if she uses x metres of the rope for each side of the rectangle, the area enclosed will be $x(16-2x)$ square metres.

a Copy and complete this table of values in the area enclosed as x takes values from 0 to 8 metres.

x	0	0.5	1	1.5	2	2.5	3	3.5	4
$16-2x$	16		14			11			
Area	0	7.5	14		24				31.5

x	4.5	5	5.5	6	6.5	7	7.5	8
$16-2x$								0
Area						14		0

b Why has the table only been drawn up with values of x from 0 to 8 metres?

c Use your table to draw a graph to illustrate the way that the area enclosed varies as x takes values from 0 to 8 metres. (Make the y-axis an 'area' axis and plot the area values against the x values.)

d What advice would you offer to Sharon?

4 When a body is dropped from a height, the distance it has fallen is given by the equation

$$s = \frac{9.8t^2}{2}$$

where s is the distance dropped (in metres) and t is the time (in seconds) that the body has been falling.

a Copy and complete this table of values for the distance fallen (correct to 1 d.p.) during the first 4 seconds.

t	0	0.5	1	1.5	2	2.5	3	3.5	4
s	0	1.2		11.0			44.1		78.4

b Use your table to draw a graph to illustrate the distance fallen as the time varies from 0 to 4 seconds. (Make the x-axis your 'time' axis and the y-axis your 'distance' axis. Use 2 mm graph paper with a scale of 2 cm to represent 1 second on the time axis and 2 cm to represent 10 metres on the distance axis.

c Wayne drops a stone down a well and times it with his multi-function turbo-injected digital watch. It is 2.8 seconds before he hears a splash. Use your graph to estimate the depth of water in the well.

5 If a car is travelling at v miles per hour, its stopping distance, d metres, is given by the formula

$$d = \frac{v^2 + 20v}{60}$$

This formula calculates a total stopping distance, including the time taken for a driver to react and apply the brakes.

a Draw up a table of values showing the stopping distances for speeds from 10 mph to 70 mph in steps of 6 mph.

b Draw a graph to illustrate your table of values.

c Sid Bozo likes to prove how clever he is by racing through 30 mph speed limits at speeds of 50 mph and more. Over a pint of after-shave he justifies this to his friends, saying, 'Well, you know, it's only 20 mph over the limit innit, you know, I mean, you know, that's nuffin is it, you know.'

Write some comments for Sid to consider about speeds and stopping distances (assume that Sid can read).

Using graphs to solve equations

Having drawn a graph to represent a mathematical relationship, we can use it to solve a range of equations. For example, this is a table of values for the equation

$$y = x^2 + 3x - 10$$

x	-6	-5	-4	-3	-2	-1
x^2	36	25	16	9	4	1
$+3x$	-18	-15	-12	-9	-6	-3
-10	-10	-10	-10	-10	-10	-10
y	8	0	-6	-10	-12	-12

x	0	1	2	3
x^2	0	1	4	9
$+3x$	0	3	6	9
-10	-10	-10	-10	-10
y	-10	-6	0	8

The next two pages show graphs drawn from this table. To illustrate the way that a graph can be used to solve a range of equations, we will use our graphs to solve:

1 $x^2 + 3x - 10 = 0$ **3** $x^2 + 3x - 10 = x$

2 $x^2 + 3x - 10 = 6$ **4** $x^2 + x = 5$

Equation **1** This equation is equivalent to the equation of our graph if $y = 0$. The table of values or the graph can be used immediately to solve

$$x^2 + 3x - 10 = 0$$

The points where the graph cuts the x-axis (or $y = 0$) give us solutions of $x = -5$ or $x = 2$ for the equation.

Equations **2** and **3** To solve equation **1**, we looked for the crossing points of the lines representing $y = x^2 + 3x - 10$ and $y = 0$. In the same way, equation **2** can be solved by looking for the crossing points of $y = x^2 + 3x - 10$ and $y = 6$.

143

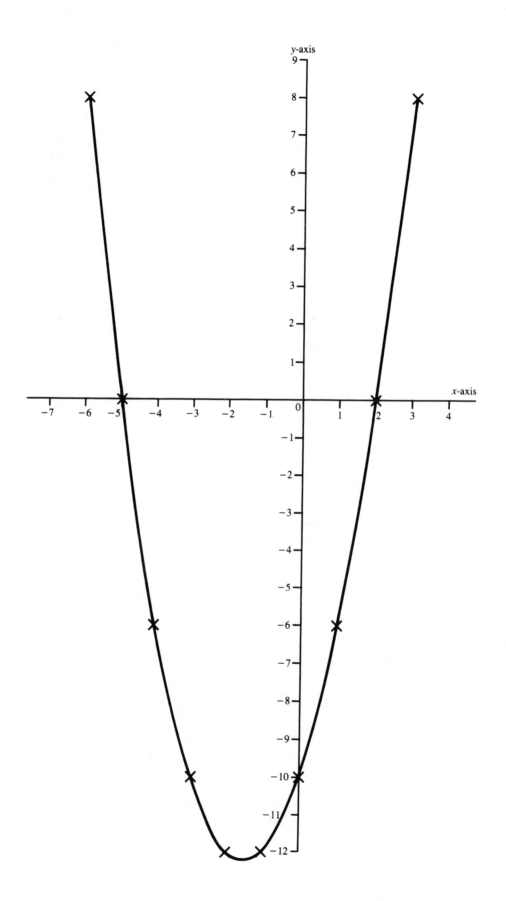

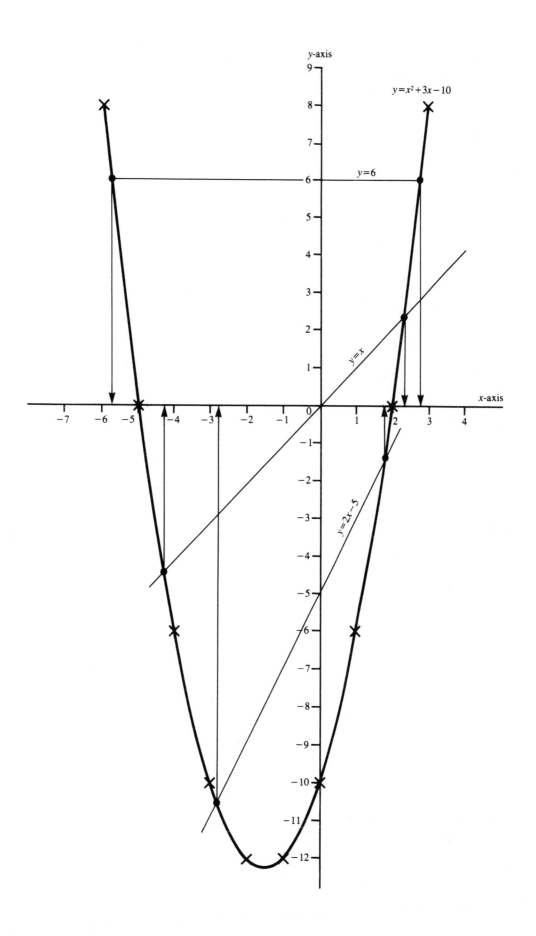

145

Equation **3** can be solved by looking for the crossing points of $y = x^2 + 3x - 10$ and $y = x$.

Equation **4** This is more difficult, because it is not in the form $x^2 + 3x - 10 = g(x)$, where $g(x)$ is some other function of x.

We must start our solution by rearranging the equation to force one side into the form $x^2 + 3x - 10$.

We start with

$$x^2 + x = 5$$

Adding $2x$ to both sides gives

$$x^2 + 3x = 2x + 5$$

Subtracting 10 from both sides gives

$$x^2 + 3x - 10 = 2x - 5$$

We now see that equation **4** can be solved by looking for the crossing points of $y = x^2 + 3x - 10$ and $y = 2x - 5$.

The graph on the previous page shows all the required lines added.

Reading from the graph, our equations have the following solutions;

Equation **2**

$$x^2 + 3x - 10 = 6$$

$$x = 2.8 \text{ or } -5.8$$

Equation **3**

$$x^2 + 3x - 10 = x$$

$$x = 2.3 \text{ or } -4.3$$

Equation **4**

$$x^2 + x = 5$$

$$x = 1.8 \text{ or } -2.8$$

◢◢◢ CHECKPOINT 13 ◣◣◣

1 Draw a graph to illustrate $y = x^2 - 8$, as x takes values from -3 to 3. Use your graph to solve the equations:

a $x^2 - 8 = 0$ **b** $x^2 - 8 = -3$ **c** $x^2 = 7$

2 Draw a graph to illustrate $y = 10 - x^2$ as x takes values from -4 to 4. Use your graph to solve the equations:

a $10 - x^2 = 1$ **b** $10 - x^2 = x$ **c** $x^2 = 2$

3 a Copy and complete this table of values for

$$y = x^2 - 4x.$$

x	-1	0	1	2	3	4	5
x^2	1						25
$-4x$	4	0	-4				-20
y	5		-3			0	

b Use the table to draw the graph of $y = x^2 - 4x$ as x takes values from -1 to 5.

c Use your graph to solve the equations:

- $x^2 - 4x = 0$
- $x^2 - 4x = -2$
- $x^2 - 3x - 4 = 0$

4 Draw a graph to illustrate $y = x^2 - 4x + 3$ as x takes values from -1 to 5.

a Use your graph to solve these equations:

- $x^2 - 4x + 3 = 0$
- $x^2 - 4x + 3 = 3$
- $x^2 - 3x = 0$

b Explain how your graph can be used to demonstrate that there are no real solutions to the equation

$$x^2 - 4x + 3 = -2$$

5 a Copy and complete this table of values for

$$y = (3 - x)(x + 2)$$

x	-3	-2	-1	0	1	2	3	4
$(3-x)$	6	5		3				-1
$(x+2)$	-1		1			4		6
y	-6		4				0	

b Use the table to draw the graph of $y=(3-x)(x+2)$ as x takes values from -3 to 4.

c Use your graph to solve the equations:

- $(3-x)(x+2)=1$

- $(3-x)(x+2)=x+2$

- $(3-x)(x+2)=3-x$

6 These luxury placemats are made from heavy embroidered cloth which costs 0.5 pence per square centimetre. They are stitched along all edges with silver thread, at a cost of 0.8 pence per centimetre of stitching. The designer label which is fixed to the placemats costs 2 pence.

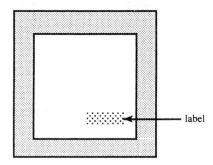

a Write down a formula for the total cost of manufacturing a placemat which is x cm by x cm.

b Draw a graph to illustrate the cost of manufacturing placemats as x takes values from 5 cm to 20 cm.

c Use your graph to estimate the largest placemat which can be produced for a cost of less than £2.

We have now mastered three different techniques for solving quadratic equations. These are

- by Factorisation

- by Formula

- by Drawing a Graph.

Question **4b** of the last checkpoint has demonstrated that some quadratic equations have no real number solutions. We will now look at one such equation and investigate how the three techniques indicate that no real solutions exist.

We will attempt to solve the equation

$$x^2+x+5=0$$

We can draw up this table of values for

$$y=x^2+x+5$$

x	-3	-2	-1	0	1	2	3
x^2	9	4	1	0	1	4	9
$+x$	-3	-2	-1	0	1	2	3
$+5$	5	5	5	5	5	5	5
y	11	7	5	5	7	11	17

From the table we can draw this graph:

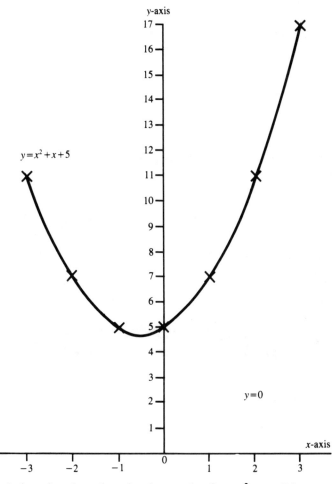

It is quite clear that the the graph of $y=x^2+x+5$ has no intersection with $y=0$ (the x-axis) and therefore there are no real solutions to the equation $x^2+x+5=0$.

If you attempt to solve $x^2+x+5=0$ by factorisation, you will find that you simply cannot factorise x^2+x+5. The start of a factorisation table is:

$\times$	x
x	x^2
	5

147

but you will find there are no numbers which will multiply to produce 5 and also produce the required x term. So, what happens if we attempt to solve $x^2 + x + 5 = 0$ by the formula method?

First, we must compare the equation with the general equation $ax^2 + bx + c = 0$ and carefully write down the values of a, b and c. These are

$$a = 1, \ b = 1 \text{ and } c = 5$$

Substituting these values for a, b and c in the formula for the roots gives

$$x = \frac{-1 + \sqrt{1^2 - 4 \times 1 \times 5}}{2 \times 1} \text{ or } x = \frac{-1 - \sqrt{1^2 - 4 \times 1 \times 5}}{2 \times 1}$$

or

$$x = \frac{-1 + \sqrt{1 - 20}}{2} \text{ or } x = \frac{-1 - \sqrt{1 - 20}}{2}$$

or

$$x = \frac{-1 + \sqrt{-19}}{2} \text{ or } x = \frac{-1 - \sqrt{-19}}{2}$$

This is as far as we can go with the formula. The square of a positive number is a positive number and the square of a negative number is also a positive number. Therefore, no number can be squared and produce a negative answer. So, -19 does not have a square root and we cannot obtain real solutions to the equation from the formula.

CHECKPOINT 14

Attempt to solve each of the following equations by using first a graphical technique, then factorisation and finally the formula. Explain in each case how your graph demonstrates clearly that the equation has two, one or no real roots.

a $x^2 + x - 6 = 0$
b $x^2 - 4x + 4 = 0$
c $x^2 + 2x + 2 = 0$

So far, we have looked at two types of function and the shape of the graph that each produces. These are:

• Functions of the form $y = mx + c$. Functions of this type always produce a straight line graph.

• Functions of the form $y = ax^2 + bx + c$. Functions of this type always produce a symmetrical 'bowl'-shaped curve called a **parabola**.

Reciprocal graphs

We will now turn our attention to graphs produced by **reciprocal** functions. A reciprocal function is one which involves a division by an x term. Examples are:

$$y = \frac{12}{x} \text{ or } y = 3 + \frac{3}{x} \text{ or } y = \frac{6}{x^2}$$

As a first example, we will plot the graph of the function

$$y = \frac{6}{x}$$

as x takes values from -6 to 6.

This is a table of values for $y = \frac{6}{x}$ as x takes values from 1 to 6.

x	1	2	3	4	5	6
y	6	3	2	1.5	1.2	1

From the table we can draw this graph.

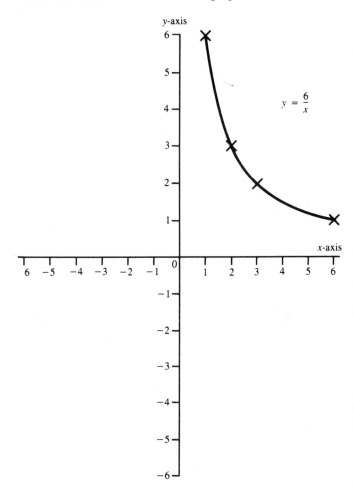

This is a table of values for $y = \frac{6}{x}$ as x takes values from -6 to -1.

x	-6	-5	-4	-3	-2	-1
y	-1	-1.2	-1.5	-2	-3	-6

Using the table we can now extend our graph like this:

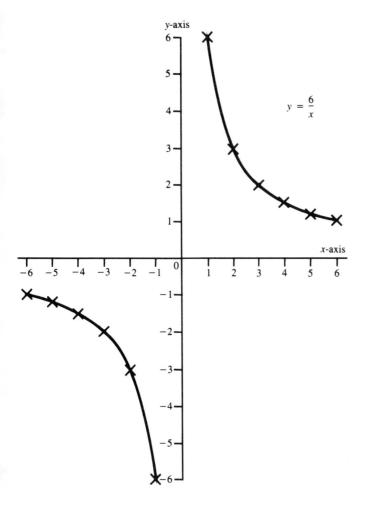

What happens to the graph as x takes values from -1 to 1? Do we connect the two 'halves' of our graph like this?

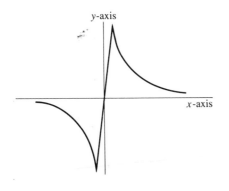

Or, perhaps like this?

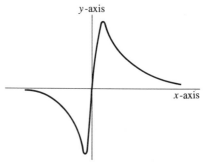

The sensible way to answer this question is by extending our tables to include more values of x.

This is a table of values for $y = \frac{6}{x}$ as x takes values from 0.1 to 0.9.

x	0.1	0.2	0.3	0.4	0.5	0.6	0.7	0.8	0.9
y	60	30	20	15	12	10	8.6	7.5	6.7

This is a table of values for $y = \frac{6}{x}$ as x takes values from -0.1 to -0.9.

x	-0.1	-0.2	-0.3	-0.4	-0.5	-0.6	-0.7	-0.8	-0.9
y	-60	-30	-20	-15	-12	-10	-8.6	-7.5	-6.7

Adding these values to a graph re-drawn on 2 mm graph paper gives us the graph on the next page.

It now becomes clear that the two 'halves' of our graph are not connected at all. As x goes from 1 to 0, taking smaller and smaller decimal values, y becomes a larger and larger positive number. As x goes from -1 to 0, taking smaller and smaller decimal values, y becomes a larger and larger negative number.

This can be illustrated by extending our tables even further with these values:

x	0.01	0.001	0.0001	0.00001
y	600	6000	60 000	600 000

x	-0.01	-0.001	-0.0001	-0.00001
y	-600	-6000	$-60 000$	$-600 000$

149

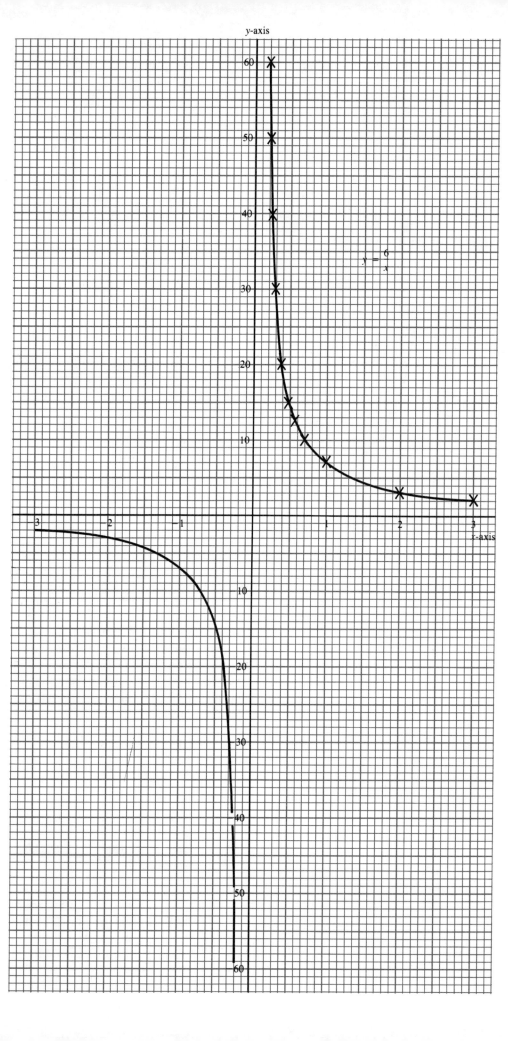

150

So, as x becomes a smaller and smaller positive number, y becomes a bigger and bigger positive number. As x becomes a smaller and smaller negative number, y becomes a bigger and bigger negative number. When x actually becomes 0, y is equal to 6 divided by 0.

But division by zero is impossible, so we cannot plot any point on the graph when x is zero.

So, we are left with a graph which is in two distinct parts, with a boundary line on which no point can be plotted. This is typical of all reciprocal graphs. From the point of view of a student determined to do well in examinations this need cause no problems; the essential thing is to remember this fact and to never fall into the temptation of joining the two parts with a straight line or a curve.

CHECKPOINT 15

1a Draw a graph to illustrate $y = x + \dfrac{6}{x}$ as x takes values from 1 to 6.

b Use your graph to solve the following equations:

- $x + \dfrac{6}{x} = 5.5$
- $x^2 + \dfrac{6}{x} = 7x$

2 When a battery is connected to a circuit, it makes an electric current flow through the components of the circuit. The components in the circuit resist the flow of this current. The resistance of each component depends on several factors and is measured in **ohms**. The more powerful a battery is, the more electricity it can force through a component with a given resistance. The force a battery can develop is measured in **volts**. The current that is forced through a component is measured in **amps**. The connection between the current, voltage and resistance is, where I is the current, V the voltage of the battery, R the resistance of the component,

$$I = \frac{V}{R}$$

So, if a 9 volt battery is connected to a component with a resistance of 18 ohms, it will force a current of $\dfrac{9}{18}$ or 0.5 amps through the component.

Draw a graph to illustrate the the current that will flow through components with resistances from 1 to 12 ohms if they are connected to a 12 volt battery.

3 Draw a graph to illustrate $y = x^2 + \dfrac{12}{x}$ as x takes values from -4 to 4. Use steps of 0.5 in your table, i.e. $-4, -3.5, -3, -2.5$, etc.

4 a Zapper Plastics has an order for 2400 plastic moulded dashboards. One worker can make 100 dashboards each day.

Copy and complete this table to show how many days the order will take to complete with different numbers of workers.

Number of workers	1	2	3	4	5	6
Number of days to complete order	24	12	8	6	4.8	4

Number of workers	7	8	9	10	11	12
Number of days to complete order		3		2.4		

b Use your table to draw a graph.

c What advice would you give to Zapper's Production Manager if she wants the order completed in less than 10 days?

Cubic graphs

A **cubic** function of x is one which contains an x^3 term. For example,

$$y = 2x^3 + 3x^2 - x + 7$$

Questions involving the graphs of cubic functions are not common in examination but may sometimes crop up on the highest level papers. The next checkpoint gives practice in drawing graphs of cubic functions.

CHECKPOINT 16

1 a Copy and complete this table of values for $y = x^3 - 2x^2 - 24x$ as x takes values from -4 to 6.

x	-4	-3	-2	-1	0	1
x^3	-64	-27	-16	-4		1
$-2x^2$	-32	-18		-2		
$-24x$	96	72	48	24	0	24
y	0		32			-25

x	2	3	4	5	6
x^3	8			125	
$-2x^2$			-96		-144
$-24x$	-48			-120	
y		-63			-45

b Use your table to draw the graph of $y = x^3 - 2x^2 - 24x$ as x takes values from -4 to 6. Use 2 mm graph paper with a

151

scale of 2 cm to represent 1 unit on the x-axis and 2 cm to represent 10 units on the y-axis.

c Use your graph to solve the equations;

- $x^3 - 2x^2 - 24x = 0$
- $x^3 - 2x^2 - 24x = 5x$

2 An open box is made from a sheet of aluminium 20 cm by 20 cm. To do this, a square x cm by x cm is cut from each corner of the sheet and the resulting projections are then folded up to make the sides of the box. This is the construction plan.

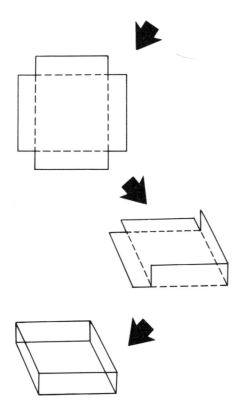

a Write down an expression for the side length of the box.
b Write down and simplify an expression for the volume of the box.
c Draw up a table of values showing the volume of the box as x takes values from 1 cm to 9 cm, in steps of 1 cm.
d Use your table to draw a graph.
e Which value of x should be selected to produce a box with the maximum possible volume?

Growth curves

We live in a world in which almost everything is constantly changing. Plants spring from seeds, grow, flower and die back. Animals follow similar patterns of growth and decay. The wealth of individuals, organisations and countries grows or declines as circumstances change. Many of these patterns of growth or decay closely resemble **geometric sequences**. You will remember that a geometric sequence is one in which each new term is obtained by multiplying the previous term by a constant amount. For example, Emma Lawrence started breeding rabbits 3 years ago and now has 24 rabbits. Experience has shown her that the number of rabbits doubles every year. The number of rabbits she will own after successive years is shown in this table.

Years	0	1	2	3	4	5
Rabbits	24	48	96	192	384	768

The number of rabbits Emma will own in successive years is the geometric sequence 24, 48, 96, 192, 384, 768, ... This is the sequence produced by the equation $y = 24 \times 2^x$ as x takes values from 0 to 5.

If we draw a graph to illustrate the information in the table, we produce this typical growth curve.

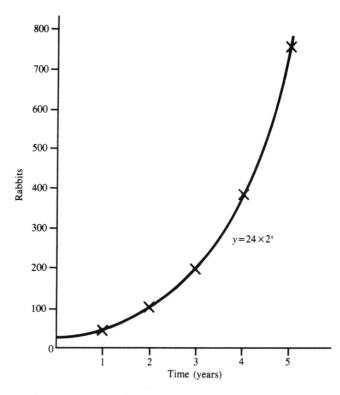

At first glance, this growth curve looks very like the 'bowl'-shaped curves produced by equations of the form $y = ax^2 + bx + c$. It is in fact a totally different type of curve, the general form of which is

$$y = ax^b$$

where a and b are any selected numbers.

You will remember that the definition of a negative power of a number is

$$x^{-n} = \frac{1}{x^n}$$

For example

$$2^{-3} = \frac{1}{2^3} = \frac{1}{8}$$

So, we can apply the equation $y = 24 \times 2^x$ with negative values of x to predict, backwards in time, the number of rabbits Emma owned 1, 2 and 3 years ago. Adding these results to our table gives us:

Years	−3	−2	−1	0	1	2	3	4	5
Rabbits	3	6	12	24	48	96	192	384	768

Adding the extra points to our growth curve gives us this graph, which is now quite clearly different from the typical 'bowl'-shape of a parabola.

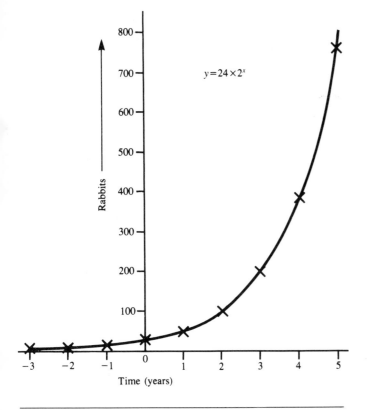

Example

The population of the town of Ginpeed is falling by 10% each year. If it is currently 5000, estimate the number of years that will pass before the population falls to 3000.

A reduction of 10% is equivalent to a multiplication by 0.9.

So;

after 1 year the population will be 5000×0.9

after 2 years the population will be 5000×0.9^2

after 3 years the population will be 5000×0.9^3

after 4 years the population will be 5000×0.9^4

after x years the population will be 5000×0.9^x

We can construct this table of values for $y = 5000 \times 0.9^x$ (correct to the nearest inhabitant).

x	0	1	2	3	4	5	6
y	5000	4500	4050	3645	3281	2952	2657

We can now draw this graph, from which we can estimate that the population will fall to 3000 in approximately 4.9 years.

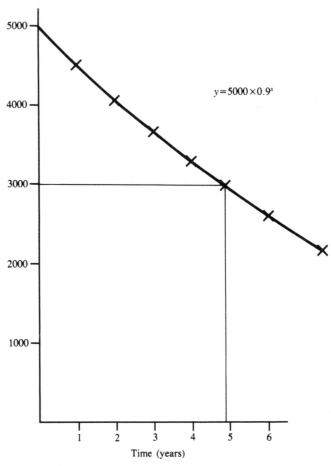

CHECKPOINT 17

1 Draw a graph to illustrate the function $y = 2^x$ as x takes values from −3 to 3.

153

2 The city of Minas Troney has a population of 90 000, but this is falling by 8% each year. The town of Chikken Noodul has a population of 40 000, but this is increasing by 5% each year.

a Draw a graph to illustrate the populations of Minas Troney and Chikken Noodul for the next ten years, if these population trends continue.
b Estimate from your graph the number of years that will pass before Chikken Noodul has a greater population than Minas Troney.

3 The value of a sum of money, after a number of years invested at a given rate of compound interest can be calculated with the formula

$$\text{value} = \text{sum} \times \left(\frac{100 + \text{rate}}{100} \right)^{\text{time}}$$

For example, if £80 is invested for 4 years at a rate of compound interest of 5% we have

$$\text{value} = 80 \times \left(\frac{100 + 5}{100} \right)^4$$

$$\text{value} = 80 \times (1.05)^4$$

$$\text{value} = 80 \times 1.2155$$

$$\text{value} = £97.24 \text{ (to the nearest penny)}$$

a Draw a graph to illustrate the value that £50 will have at the end of each year for 10 years invested at a rate of compound interest of 20%.
b Add to your graph a series of growth curves to illustrate the value that £50 will have each year for 10 years if it is invested at rates of compound interest of:

• 5%   • 10%   • 15%

c How long would £40 need to be invested at a rate of 10% before it was worth more than £50 invested for the same time at a rate of 5%?

4 A shopkeeper buys chocolate bars for 20p and sells 500 of them each week for 30p. As an experiment, he increases the selling price of the bars by 5p each week for 6 weeks. He discovers that when he does this he sells 20% fewer bars each week.

a Copy and complete this table showing the shopkeeper's results over the six week trial period.

Selling Price	30	35	40	45	50	55	60
Profit per Bar	10	15	20	25			40
Number Sold	500	400			205	164	131
Total Profit	5000	6000			6150		

b Draw a bar graph from your table to illustrate the shopkeeper's total profit each week over the trial period.
c What conclusions do you think the shopkeeper will draw from the trial?

5 The island of Great Britain has a land area of approximately 230 000 km^2. Suppose a new plant disease is currently only affecting wheat crops in a 100 km^2 area of Norfolk, but that observations have shown that this area is doubling each year. Draw a graph to illustrate this rate of increase for the next 10 years and state how many years it would take for the whole of Great Britain to be affected by the disease if its rate of increase continued unchecked.

6 The table below shows times that were simultaneously world records for various events. Copy and complete the table.

Event	Time (seconds)	Average speed (metres per second)
100 metres	9.95	10.05
200 metres	19.72	10.14
400 metres	43.86	9.12
800 metres	102.4	
1500 metres	212.1	
5000 metres	788.4	
10 000 metres	1642.4	6.09

a Using 2mm graph paper, draw a graph to illustrate the change in running speed with the distance run. On the distance axis, which must extend from 0 to 10 000 metres, use a scale of 2 cm to represent 1000 metres. On the speed axis, which must extend from 0 to 11 metres per second, use a scale of 2 cm to represent 1 metre per second. Lay your graph out like this:

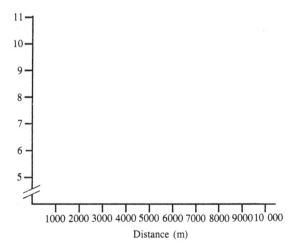

b Comment on your graph.

Graphs of inequalities

We have used graphs to illustrate many different functions, all of which produced either straight lines or curves. Graphs can also be used to illustrate **inequalities**.

Remember, an inequality is a statement such as

$$x > 2 \text{ or } y \leqslant -1$$

and we have already illustrated these inequalities with simple number lines, like this.

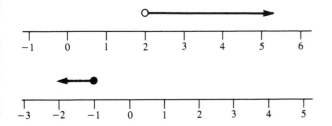

On a co-ordinate grid, all the points with an x co-ordinate equal to 2 lie on a straight line. All the points with an x co-ordinate which is greater than 2 lie to the right of this line. So, using a graph, the inequality $x > 2$ is illustrated like this.

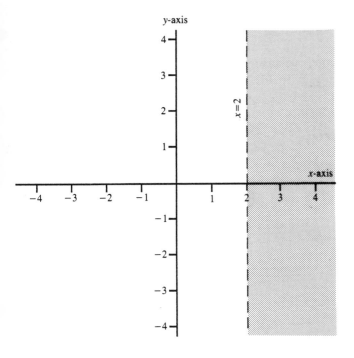

Our illustration can be interpreted as saying there is a region in which each and every point has an x co-ordinate greater than 2.

A dotted line is used for the boundary of the region because points which are on the line $x = 2$ cannot be included in the region.

We can illustrate the inequality $y \leqslant -1$ with this graph.

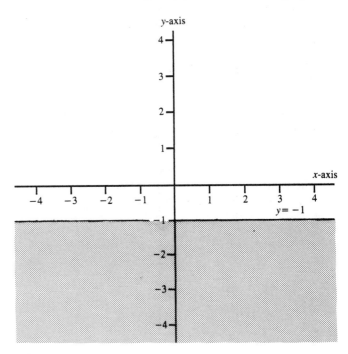

In this case a solid line is used for the boundary of the region because points which are on the line $y = -1$ can be included in the region.

CHECKPOINT 18

1 Illustrate each of the following inequalities with a graph.

a $x < 2$ **b** $y > -1$ **c** $x > 0$ **d** $y < 0$

e $x \geqslant -2$ **f** $y \leqslant -3$

2 Write down the inequality illustrated by each of the following graphs.

a

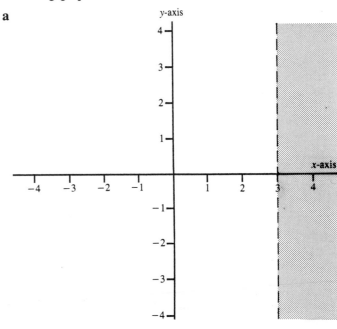

155

b

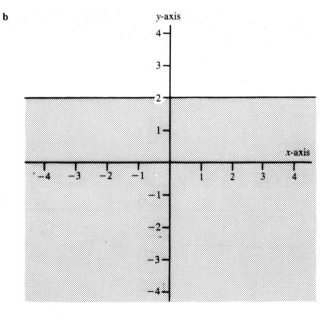

c

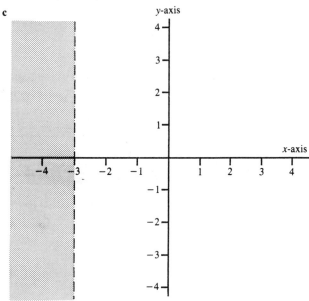

d

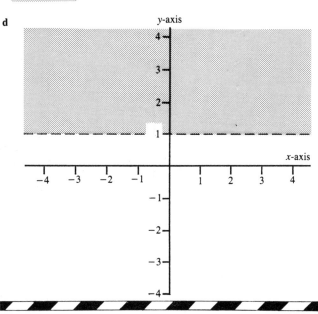

Two or more combined inequalities can be illustrated on one graph.

Examples

1 Illustrate on a graph the region where $x \leqslant 2$ **and** $y > -1$.

First, we draw a graph and mark on the lines $x = 2$ and $y = -1$.

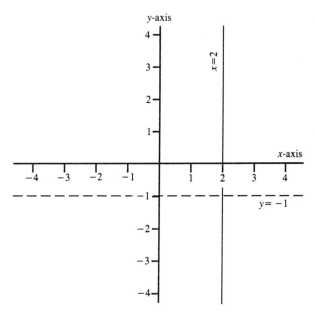

Now, we shade in the region of the graph where **both** inequalities are true.

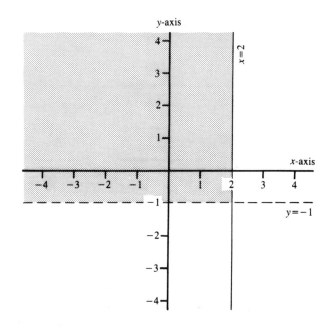

2 Illustrate on a graph the region where $x \geqslant -3$, $x < 0$, $y \geqslant -2$ and $y < 3$.

156

First, we draw a graph and mark the lines $x = -3$, $x = 0$, $y = -2$ and $y = 3$.

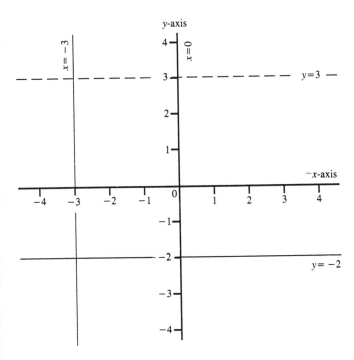

Now, we shade in the region of the graph where **all** the inequalities are true.

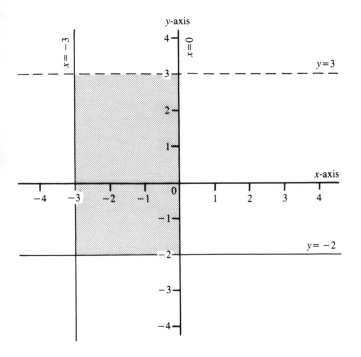

A double inequality like $x > -2$ and $x < 2$ means that x can be any number which is both greater than -2 and less than 2. This can be written as the single combined inequality $-2 < x < 2$. In the same way, the double inequality $y < 0$ and $y > -3$ can be written as the single combined inequality $-3 < y < 0$.

1 Illustrate on a graph the regions where the following inequalities hold.

a $x > -1$ and $x \leqslant 1$ **b** $y > -4$ and $y < -2$
c $x \geqslant 1$ and $y \leqslant 1$ **d** $x \geqslant 0$ and $y > 0$
e $x \leqslant -2$ and $y \leqslant 2$ **f** $x < -1$ and $y > -3$
g $x \geqslant 0$, $x < 3$ and $y \geqslant -2$
h $-3 < x \leqslant -1$ and $1 < y < 3$

2 Write down the combined inequalities illustrated by each of the following graphs.

a

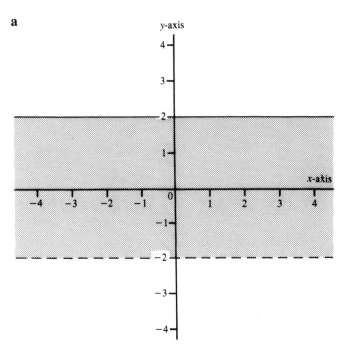

b

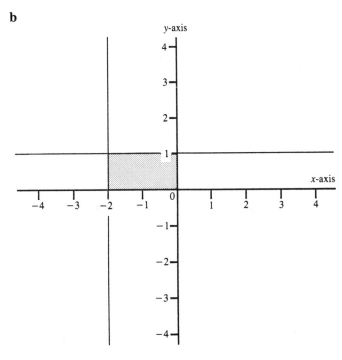

c

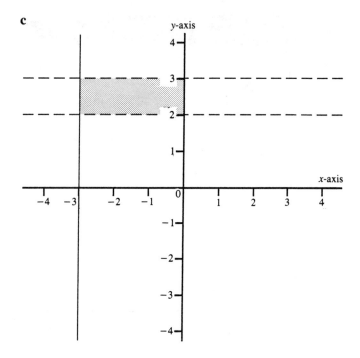

d

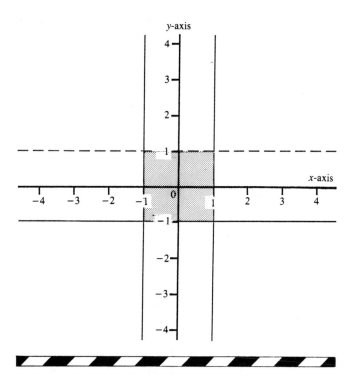

It is quite obvious that any line parallel to either axis must divide the graph into two regions representing two inequalities. It is perhaps less obvious that the graph of **any** function will also divide the graph in this way. For example, this co-ordinate grid shows the line representing the function $y = x$.

If you examine the co-ordinates of the points above the line, you will find that in every case they fit the inequality $y > x$.

If you examine the co-ordinates of the points below the line, you will find that in every case they fit the inequality $y < x$. So, the line with equation $y = x$ divides the graph into the two regions $y > x$ and $y < x$.

Examples

1 Illustrate on a graph the region where $2x - 3y \geqslant 12$.

The boundary line for the region will be $2x - 3y = 12$, so we start by constructing a table and drawing the graph of this function.

x	0	6	3
y	-4	0	-2

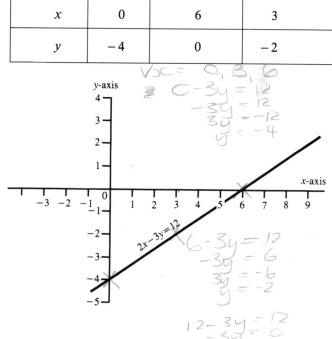

The region we have been asked to illustrate will consist of all the points on one side of this line. Our only problem is in deciding **which** side of the line.

The strategy is quite simple. We select any point which is not actually on the line and test to see if the inequality applies at this point. If it does, then we shade the side of the line which includes that point. If it does not, we shade the side of the line which does **not** include that point.

For example, if we select (1,1) as a test point and apply the inequality at this point we have

$$(2 \times 1) - (3 \times 1) \geqslant 12$$

or

$$-1 \geqslant 12$$

which is clearly **not** true. So, we shade the side of the line which **does not** include (1,1) to illustrate the region $2x - 3y \geqslant 12$.

This is our completed graph.

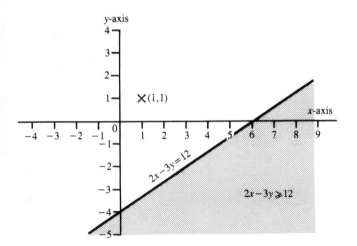

2 Illustrate the region where $x > -2$, $y \geqslant -1$ and $y \leqslant 8 - 2x$.

We can construct this table of values for $y = 8 - 2x$:

x	-2	0	4
y	12	8	0

and draw this graph.

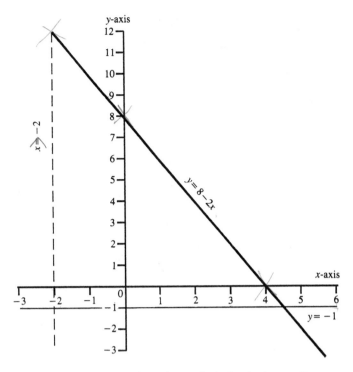

If we select (1,1) as a test point and apply the inequality at this point, we have

$$1 \leqslant 8 - (2 \times 1)$$

or

$$1 \leqslant 6$$

which is clearly true. So, we shade the side of the line which **does** include (1,1) to illustrate the region.

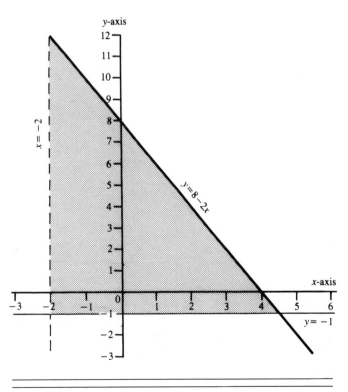

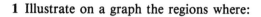

CHECKPOINT 20

1 Illustrate on a graph the regions where:

a $y > x + 1$ **b** $y < 2x - 1$
c $x + y > 5$ **d** $5x + 4y < 20$
e $x > 0$, $y < 0$ and $y > 2x - 5$
f $-1 < x < -4$, $y < 4$ and $x + 2y > 4$

2 Anita has £2 pocket money to spend on sweets. Her favourites are Jupiter bars at 16p each and Frittles at 25p a packet.

a Write down an expression for the cost of x Jupiter bars at 16p each.
b Write down an expression of the cost of y packets of Frittles at 25p each.
c Explain why Anita's spending decisions can be represented by the inequality

$$16x + 25y \leqslant 200$$

d Draw a graph to illustrate all the combinations of different numbers of Jupiter bars and packets of Frittles that Anita can buy.
e Can Anita spend the whole £2 on Jupiter bars and Frittles?

3 Write down the inequalities illustrated by each of the following graphs.

a

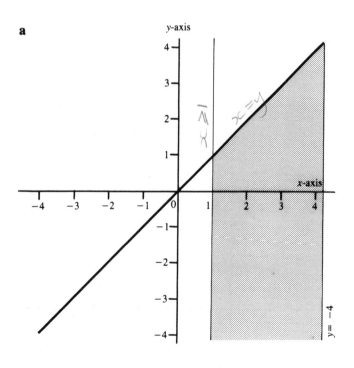

b

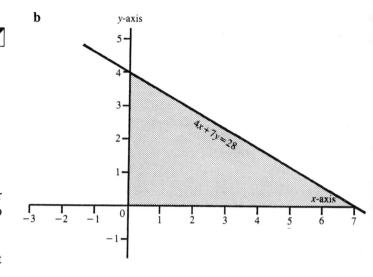

c

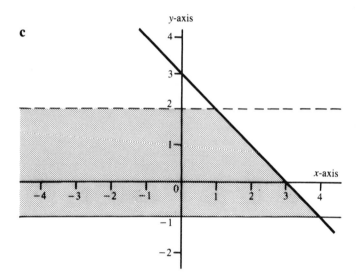

d

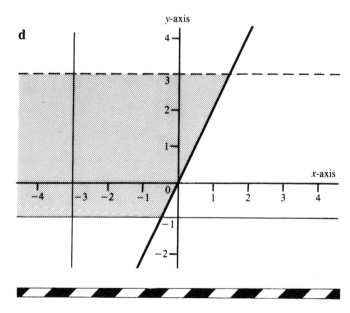

160

More complicated problems may require us to find regions which illustrate a combination of several inequalities. In these cases, we first draw a graph and mark on all the boundary lines. Each line must then be tested in turn until the region is identified that satisfies all the inequalities.

Example

Illustrate on a graph the region where $x \geqslant 0$, $y \geqslant 2$, $x + y \leqslant 12$ and $y < x + 4$.

We can draw the following graph.

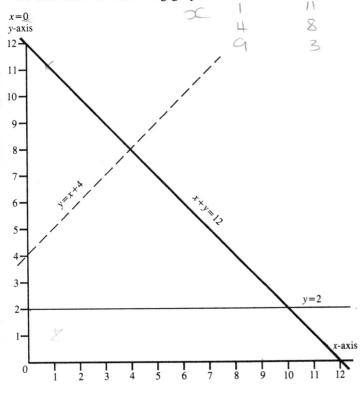

Testing $y < x + 1$ at (1,1) we have

$$1 < 1 + 4$$

or

$$1 < 5$$

which is clearly true. So, we shade the side of the line which **does** include (1,1) to illustrate the region $y < x + 4$. Testing $x + y \leqslant 12$ at (1,1) we have

$$1 + 1 < 12$$

or

$$2 \leqslant 12$$

which is clearly true. So, we shade the side of the line which **does** include (1,1) to illustrate the region $x + y \leqslant 12$.

Shading on the correct side of both $y = x + 4$, $x + y = 12$ and also $x = 0$ and $y = 2$ produces this graph:

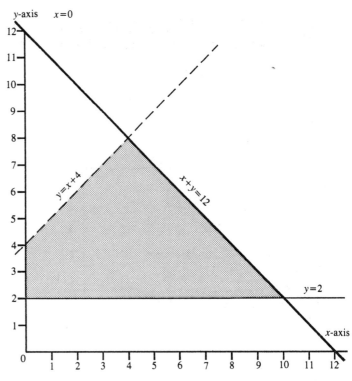

CHECKPOINT 21

1 Illustrate on a graph the regions where:
a $1 < x < 4$, $y > x - 1$ and $y < x + 3$
b $3x + 7y < 21$, $y > x - 2$ and $y > 0$
c $y > -1$, $2y + x < 6$ and $2y + 3x > 6$
d $-3 < x < 1$, $4y > x - 10$ and $3y < 4x + 12$

2 Write down the inequalities illustrated by each of the following graphs.

a

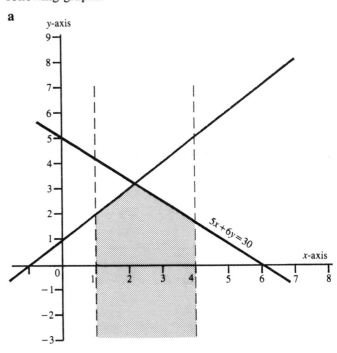

161

b

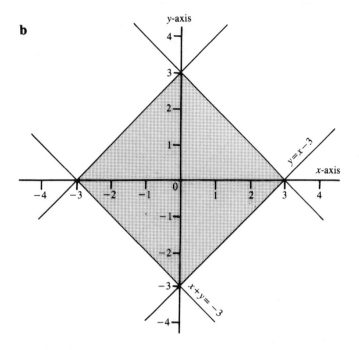

3 Ms Patel has decided to buy a solid oak fitted kitchen. She wants to fit a combination of two different types of unit against a wall 5 metres long. One type of unit is 50 cm long, the other 80 cm long. Ms Patel may decide to fill the whole length of the wall with units or she may decide to leave some gaps for other equipment.

a Write down an expression for the length of x units, each 80 cm long.

b Write down an expression for the length of y units, each 50 cm long.

c Explain why Ms Patel's decision about her kitchen arrangement can be represented by the inequality

$$80x + 50y \leqslant 500$$

d Draw a graph to illustrate all the combinations of different units that Ms Patel could fit to the wall.

e Are there any combinations which will fill the whole wall without gaps?

f The 80 cm units cost £800 each and the 50 cm units cost £700 each. Ms Patel wants to spend no more than £5600 on this part of the design. Explain why this spending constraint can be represented by the inequality

$$800x + 700y \leqslant 5600$$

g Add this inequality to your graph.

h Are there any combinations which will fill the whole wall without gaps and cost less than £5600?

162

Distance and time graphs

We have used cartesian graphs to illustrate many different functions. A function, remember, is a transformation which changes one set of numbers into another set of numbers. Often, we write an equation linking the letters x and y to express the rules for transforming the numbers. Examples of typical 'rules' are:

$$y = 3x + 2$$

$$y = 3x^2 + 2x + 1$$

$$y = \frac{6}{x}$$

$$y = 5^x$$

Many real-life situations also produce functions which transform one set of numbers into another set of numbers, but there may not be simple rules to describe the transformation. For example, suppose a journey of 12 km from home to work takes 40 minutes. Each time within the 40 minutes will correspond to a certain distance from home and, in mathematical language, we can say there is a function which transforms time into distance. This function will probably not have a single fixed rule to describe the transformation, since the distance might not be covered at the same speed all the way. Instead, we may have some information linking particular times and distances. For example, we may know that:

- the journey started with a 5-minute walk to a bus stop 600 metres from the house.

- there was a 10-minute wait for a bus.

- the bus then travelled 8 km in 10 minutes.

- there was a 5-minute wait for a second bus.

- the second bus completed the journey in the remaining 10 minutes.

From this information, we can can draw up this table of known times and distances.

Time	5	15	25	30	40
Distance	0.6	0.6	8.6	8.6	12

We could then draw this graph.

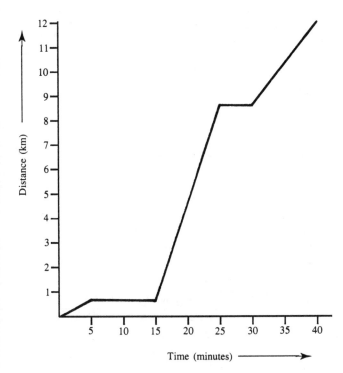

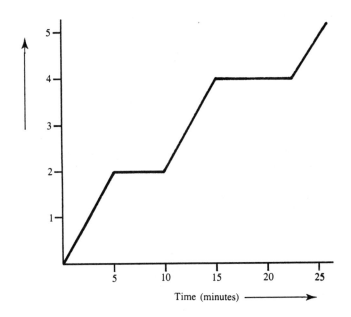

The points on the graph have been connected with straight lines. Common sense tells us that the progress of a walk or a bus ride would probably not be as smooth as these straight lines imply. Any bus is certainly likely to start and stop several times along its route. The graph is only an approximation to the actual journey, the best illustration we can draw from the available information.

CHECKPOINT 22

1 Mary Walker cycles to school each day. Leaving home she rides alone to the Co-op where she waits for her friend Benny Shaw. They then ride on together to the end of Pascal Drive, where they wait for their friend Lac Tran. The three then cycle together to school. This graph illustrates Mary's journey one day last week.

a How far is the Co-op from Mary's House?

b How long does Mary wait for Benny?

c How far is the end of Pascal Drive from the Co-op?

d How long do Mary and Benny wait for Lac Tran?

e How far is it from Mary's house to her school?

f What is Mary's average speed in kilometres per hour for the journey from:

- home to the Co-op,

- the Co-op to the end of Pascal Drive,

- home to school?

2 Two teams of soldiers race each other over a 50 km course to raise money for charity. There are 5 soldiers in each team and each runs one 10 km leg of the course. The graph below shows the two teams' progress.

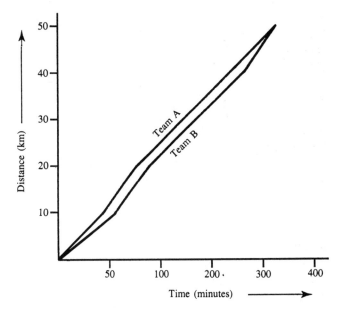

a Write down the time that each soldier in Team A took to run his leg of the race.

b Write down the time that each soldier in Team B took to run his leg of the race.

c What is the greatest distance by which Team A were ahead of Team B?

d How long had Team A's second runner been running when Team B's second runner started?

e What was the average speed in kilometres per hour of the last runner in Team A?

f What was the average speed in kilometres per hour of the last runner in Team B?

g The race ended in a dead heat, so both teams had the same overall average speed. Calculate this average speed in kilometres per hour, correct to one decimal place.

3 Peterborough is approximately 80 miles from London, via the M11, A604 and A1. Gillian Harrison leaves London at 9.30 am and drives to Peterborough. Gurdev Singh leaves Peterborough 30 minutes later and drives to London. Gillian drives non-stop, but Gurdev stops for petrol just south of Peterborough. This graph illustrates the two journeys.

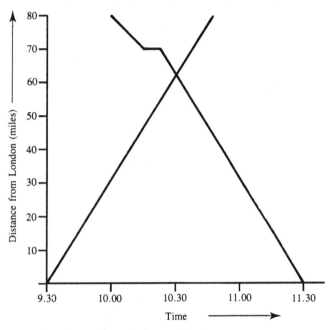

a At what time does Gillian arrive in Peterborough?

b At what time does Gurdev arrive in London?

c How long does it take Gurdev to stop for petrol?

d At what time and at what distance from Peterborough does Gillian pass Gurdev going in the opposite direction?

e What is Gillian's average speed for the journey?

f What is Gurdev's average speed:

• from Peterborough to the petrol station,

• from the petrol station to London,

• for the whole journey?

4 Billy Brag and Hugh Steady race each other over a 1000 metre course. Hugh runs at a constant pace of 125 metres per minute. Billy runs the first 300 metres in a 1 minute, rests for 1 minute, runs 200 metres in the next minute, rests for another minute, runs 200 metres in the next minute, rests for 2 minutes and completes the course in 2 more minutes.

a Prepare a graph on 2 mm paper with a time axis from 0 to 9 minutes and a distance axis from 0 to 1000 metres. Use 2 cm to represent 1 minute on the time axis and 2 cm to represent 100 metres on the distance axis.

b Draw a distance–time graph to illustrate the race.

c How far is Billy ahead of Hugh after one minute?

d After how many minutes does Hugh first catch up with Billy?

e After how many minutes does Hugh overtake Billy?

f Who wins the race and how many metres and how many minutes is he ahead of his rival?

5 Susan Gregson and Helen Speechley live in house 20 km apart. At 9.00 am, Susan starts to cycle from her house to Helen's house at a speed of 20 km per hour. Ten minutes later, Helen leaves her house and cycles towards Susan's house at a speed of 30 km per hour. Draw a graph to illustrate this information and estimate the time and the distance from Helen's home at which Helen and Susan meet.

Distance and velocity graphs

In the last section we have looked at graphs which illustrate connections between distance and time. We can also draw graphs to illustrate connections between velocity and time. Before we do this, however, we need to clarify some definitions.

Velocity is the rate of change of distance with time. For example, if an object has a velocity of 5 metres per second, this means that it is increasing its distance from a fixed point by 5 metres every second. 5 metres per second can be written $5 \, \mathrm{m \, s^{-1}}$. Velocity can be negative as well as positive. A velocity of $-5 \, \mathrm{m \, s^{-1}}$ means that the distance from a fixed point is **decreasing** by 5 metres every second.

Acceleration is the rate of change of velocity with time. For example, if an object has an acceleration of 5 metres per second per second, this means that it is increasing its velocity by 5 metres per second every second. 5 metres per second per second can be written $5 \, \mathrm{m \, s^{-2}}$. Acceleration can be negative as well as positive. An acceleration of $-5 \, \mathrm{m \, s^{-2}}$ means that the velocity is **decreasing** by 5 metres per second every second.

The word **speed** is often interchanged with the word **velocity** as if both words had the same meaning. There is in fact a difference between speed and velocity. The word **velocity** means **speed in a fixed direction**. When we say that a body has a certain **speed**, we imply nothing about the direction the body is moving in. The body could be moving in a circle, a spiral or in a random manner. When we say that a body has a certain **velocity** we imply that it is moving along a straight line in a definite direction.

High speed   High velocity

Example

A car pulls away from some traffic lights and accelerates to a velocity of 50 miles per hour in 20 seconds. It then continues to travel at this velocity for 20 seconds before braking to a stop in 10 seconds at another set of traffic lights. Draw a graph to illustrate the car's changes in velocity.

We can draw this graph.

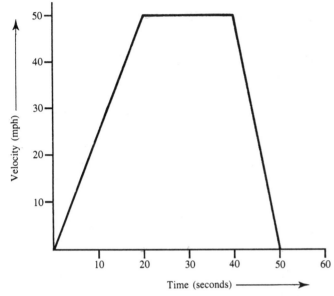

This graph of **velocity against time** must not be confused with a graph of **distance against time**. The diagrams below indicate some essential differences and possible points of confusion.

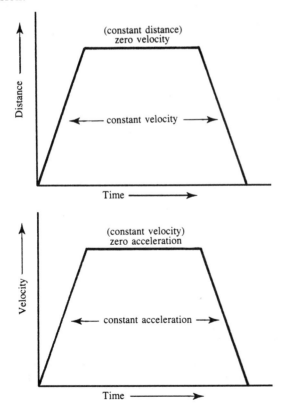

In the distance–time graph, a sloping line indicates increasing or decreasing distance, that is a constant velocity. A horizontal line indicates constant distance, that is zero velocity.

In the velocity–time graph, a sloping line indicates increasing or decreasing velocity, that is a constant acceleration. A horizontal line indicates constant velocity, that is zero acceleration.

In a real-life situation, acceleration is almost never constant. Many factors such as air resistance and friction increase as velocity increases and this in turn reduces acceleration. This is a more life-like graph for a vehicle travelling between two sets of traffic lights.

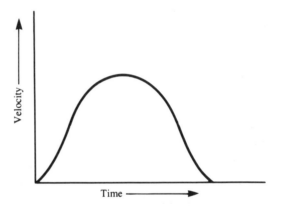

CHECKPOINT 23

1 This graph shows the velocity of a car as it travels between two sets of traffic lights.

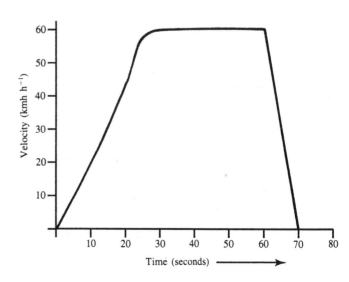

Which of the following statements are true and which are false?

a The rate of acceleration was constant during the first 20 seconds.

b The maximum velocity of the car was 60 km h^{-1}.

c The car stops after 30 seconds and remains motionless for 20 seconds.

d The car decelerates (brakes) for 20 seconds, losing velocity at a constant rate of 3 km h^{-1} every second.

e The car has zero acceleration for a 20-second period during its journey.

2 A motorbike is racing round this race track.

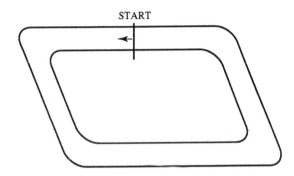

This is the speed–time graph for the first circuit of the course.

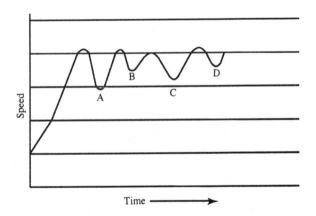

a Explain, in your own words, the information that the graph illustrates, paying particular attention to the parts of the graph labelled A, B, C and D.

b Draw a speed-time graph for a motorcycle racing round these courses.

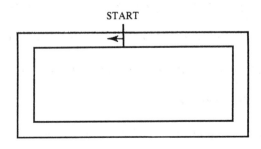

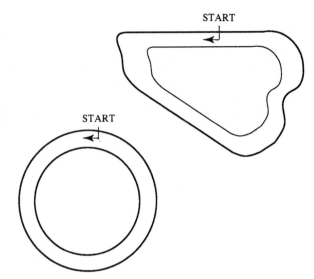

3 This table gives acceleration times (seconds) to various velocities (miles per hour) for four cars.

	TIME			
Speed	Austin Montego 2.0 BBD	Volkswagen Passat 1.8i GL	BMW M3	Ford Sierra RS Cosworth
0–30	3.4	3.9	2.5	2.3
0–40	5.1	6.0	3.6	3.2
0–50	7.1	8.7	5.3	4.5
0–60	9.9	12.4	6.8	5.8
0–70	13.3	16.8	9.0	7.9
0–80	17.4	22.7	11.3	9.9

a Draw a velocity-time graph on 2 mm graph paper. Use 1 cm to represent 1 second on the time axis and 1 cm to represent 10 miles per hour on the velocity axis. Lay your axes out like this.

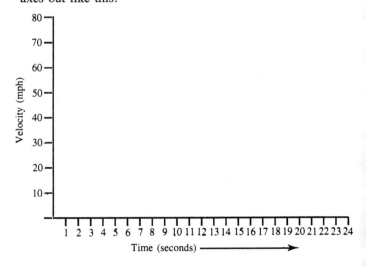

166

b Plot sets of points on your graph to illustrate each car's performance and connect each set with the best smooth curve you can draw through the points.

c If these four cars raced each other from a standing start, estimate the velocity with which each would be travelling after 10 seconds of the race had elapsed.

Graphs which illustrate practical situations

If an electrician has a fixed charge of £10 to call at a house plus a charge of £12 for each hour of work done, we can draw this graph to illustrate the cost of up to 10 hours work.

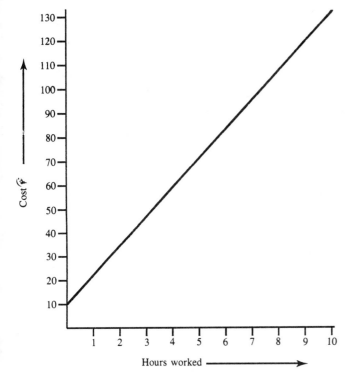

The gradient of the graph is $\frac{120}{10}$ or $\frac{12}{1}$. The physical meaning of this gradient is that labour costs increase by £12 per hour. Mathematically we say **the rate of change of labour costs is £12 per hour.** The gradients of other 'real-life' graphs also represent physical quantities.

CHECKPOINT 24

1 This graph shows the cost of using various amounts of electricity.

a What is the cost of using 500 units of electricity?
b Why does the graph start at £10 on the cost axis?
c The graph passes through the points (0,10) and (500, 40).

- What is the horizontal change between these points?
- What is the vertical change between these points?
- What is the gradient of the graph?

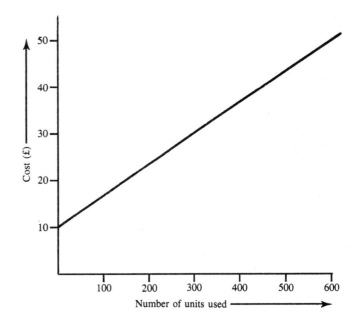

d What is the physical meaning of this gradient?

2 This graph shows the length of a spring as it is loaded with various weights.

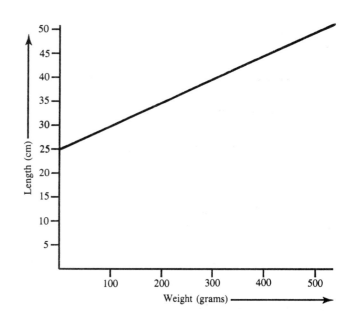

a How long is the unstretched spring?
b What weight is required to stretch the spring to a length of 38 cm?
c The graph passes through the points (0,25) and (500, 50).

- What is the horizontal change between these points?
- What is the vertical change between these points?
- What is the gradient of the graph?

d What is the physical meaning of this gradient?

3 This graph shows the change in height of a candle as it burns.

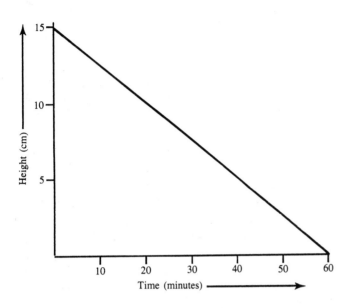

a How high is the un-lit candle?

b How long does it take the candle to burn down to a height of 8 cm?

c The graph passes through the points (0,15) and (60,0).

- What is the horizontal change between these points?

- What is the vertical change between these points?

- What is the gradient of the graph?

d What is the physical meaning of this gradient?

The tangent of a graph

Many graphs, drawn from either real-life information or mathematical equations, produce graphs which are curved. For example, this graph shows the average weights of males and females in the USA at ages from 1 to 18 years of age.

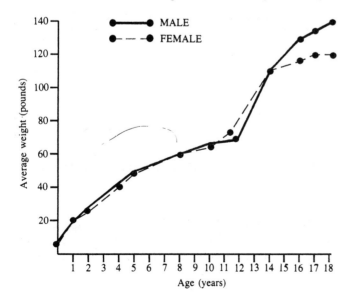

This real-life information does not produce either the perfect straight line or smooth curve of an abstract mathematical equation. As you can see from the graph, for the first 11 years of life, male and female average weights are almost identical, with males only slightly heavier than females. Between the ages of 11 and 14, the average female weighs a few pounds more than the average male. By the age of 18 this has been reversed and the average male now weighs approximately 23 pounds more than the average female.

It is obvious from the graphs that there is no single value for the gradient or rate of change of weight. The rate of change of weight varies with the age of the person. We can use the graph to estimate the rate of change of weight at any particular age. We do this by drawing a **tangent** to the graph and finding its gradient. To draw a tangent at any point on a graph, you imagine what the graph would look like if it suddenly stopped curving at that point and continued as a straight line. Drawing in this straight line with a ruler produces the required tangent.

This graph shows the weight increase of a USA female from ages 1 to 18 years. Tangents have been drawn in at 1 year of age and 14 years of age.

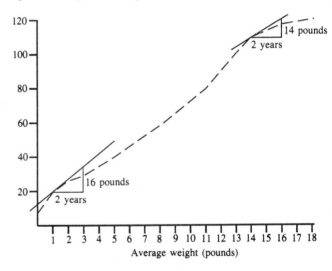

The gradients of these tangents are $\frac{8}{1}$ and $\frac{7}{1}$. The physical meaning of these gradients is that at 1 year of age the average weight is increasing at a rate 8 pounds per year and at 14 years of age, the average weight is increasing at a rate of 7 pounds per year.

Example

1 When a stone is dropped down a deep well or mine shaft, the distance in metres it has fallen after t seconds is given by the formula

$$d = 4.9^2$$

a Draw a distance–time graph for the first 5 seconds of a stone's fall.

b Estimate the velocity of a stone after it has been falling for 3 seconds.

We can prepare this table of values.

t	0	1	2	3	4	5
d	0	4.9	19.6	44.1	78.4	122.5

We can then draw this graph.

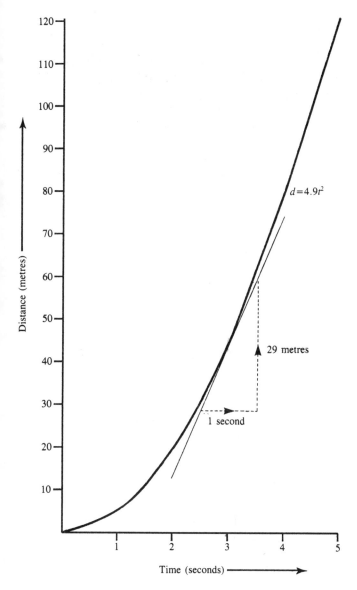

To estimate the velocity of the stone after 3 seconds, we draw a tangent to the curve at the point (3, 44.1). Since velocity is the rate of change of distance with time, the gradient of this tangent is the velocity of the stone after 3 seconds. This produces an estimate of 29 metres per second for the velocity of the stone after 3 seconds.

1 The temperature of the water in an electric kettle is measured every minute and the following results recorded.

Time (minutes)	1	2	3	4	5	6
Temperature (°C)	6	18	41	73	92	100

a Prepare a graph using 2 mm graph paper. Use 2 cm to represent 1 minute on the horizontal axis and 2 cm to represent 10°C on the vertical axis.

b Use your graph to illustrate the information in the table.

c By drawing tangents to your curve, estimate the rate of increase of temperature after 1 minute and 4 minutes.

2 The height of a bean seedling is recorded each day after it first emerges from the earth and the following results recorded.

Day	1	2	3	4	5	6	7	8	9	10
Height (cm)	0.1	0.2	0.4	0.7	1.1	1.6	2.2	2.8	3.7	4.8

a Prepare a graph using 2 mm graph paper. Use 2 cm to represent 1 day on the horizontal axis and 2 cm to represent 1 cm on the vertical axis.

b Use your graph to illustrate the information in the table.

c By drawing tangents to your curve, estimate the rate of increase of height after 2 days and 7 days.

3 This table presents performance data for a Vauxhall Carlton 1.8i GL.

SPEED (mph)	TIME (seconds)
0–30	3.1
0–40	4.9
0–50	7.1
0–60	10.1
0–70	13.7
0–80	18.0

a Draw a graph to illustrate the information in the table.

b By drawing a tangent to the graph, estimate the acceleration of the Carlton (in miles per hour per second) after 6 sections.

4 This table gives the distance in metres covered by a runner during a 1000 metre race.

Time (minutes)	0	1	2	3	4	5
Distance (metres)	0	400	615	780	910	1000

a Draw a graph to illustrate this information.

b By drawing tangents to your graph, estimate the speed of the runner (in metres per second) after 1 minute and 4 minutes.

5 a Draw the graph of the function $y = \dfrac{12}{x}$ as x takes values from 1 to 12.

b Estimate the gradient of tangents down to the curve at the points (3,4) and (6,2).

6 a Draw the graph of the function $y = x^2 + x - 6$ as x takes values from −4 to 3.

b Estimate the gradient of tangents down to the curve at the points (−3,0), (−0.5,−6.25) and (2,0).

The area under a straight line graph

The area enclosed by lines on a graph is often calculated and may represent a physical quantity. For example, this velocity–time graph illustrates the performance of a cyclist in a short race.

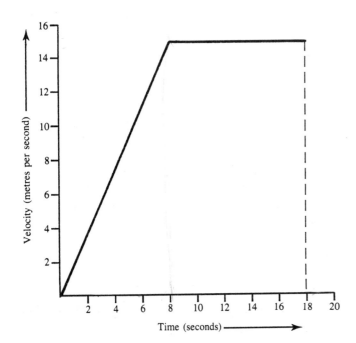

We see from the graph that the cyclist accelerated uniformly to a velocity of 15 metres per second and then held that velocity for the final 10 seconds of the race.

The area enclosed under the graph can be easily calculated

because it is a combination of a triangle and a rectangle. The necessary calculations are as follows:

$$\text{Area of triangle} = \frac{15 \times 8}{2} = 60 \text{ square units}$$

$$\text{Area of rectangle} = 10 \times 15 = 150 \text{ square units}$$

$$\text{Total area} = 210 \text{ square units}$$

The area under a velocity–time curve is equal to the total distance covered. So, in this case the area has a physical meaning and we can state that the cyclist raced over a distance of 210 metres.

CHECKPOINT 26

1 A car starts from rest and accelerates uniformly for 10 seconds to a velocity of 20 metres per second. It then continues at this velocity for 30 seconds before braking uniformly to a stop in a further 6 seconds. Draw a velocity–time graph and calculate the total distance travelled by the car.

2 This velocity–time graph illustrates the motion of a radio controlled car as it executes a manoeuvre.

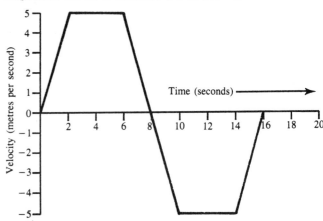

a Describe what happens during the first 8 seconds of the manoeuvre.

b Calculate the total distance covered during the first 8 seconds of the manoeuvre.

c Describe what happens during the second 8 seconds of the manoeuvre (remember that a **negative** velocity means that the distance from a fixed point is **decreasing**).

d Calculate the total distance covered during the second 8 seconds of the manoeuvre.

3 Draw a graph and calculate the area enclosed by the lines $y = 0$, $x = 0$ and $x + y = 12$.

4 Draw a graph and calculate the area enclosed by the lines $y = 0$, $x = 0$, $x = 4$ and $y = x + 3$.

5 Draw a graph and calculate the area enclosed by the lines $x + y = 5$, $x + y = -5$, $y = x + 5$ and $y = x - 5$.

6 When a stone is dropped from a height, its velocity (in metres per second) after it has been falling for t seconds can be calculated from the formula

$$v = 9.8t$$

a Draw a velocity–time graph to illustrate the first 4 seconds after a stone is dropped.

b How far does the stone fall in these 4 seconds?

The area under a curve

We can also estimate the area enclosed by curved lines on a graph. For example, this diagram shows the graph of $y = 4x - x^2$ as x takes values from 1 to 4.

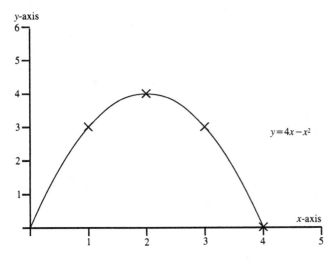

To estimate the area enclosed between the curve and the x-axis, we connect the plotted points with straight lines and divide the area under the curve into strips of equal width like this.

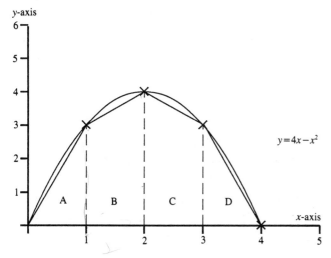

This produces a series of triangles and trapeziums. The total area of these shapes is our estimate for the area under the curve.

You will remember that the formula for the area of a triangle or a trapezium is:

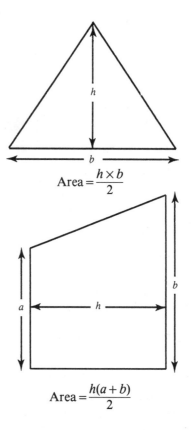

$$\text{Area} = \frac{h \times b}{2}$$

$$\text{Area} = \frac{h(a + b)}{2}$$

The necessary calculations to estimate the area are:

$$\text{Area A} = \frac{3 \times 1}{2} = 1.5 \text{ square units}$$

$$\text{Area B} = \frac{1(3 + 4)}{2} = 3.5 \text{ square units}$$

$$\text{Area C} = \frac{1(4 + 3)}{2} = 3.5 \text{ square units}$$

$$\text{Area A} = \frac{3 \times 1}{2} = 1.5 \text{ square units}$$

These give an estimated area under the curve of 10 square units.

Example

The roof of an aircraft hangar is designed so that it has the same shape as a graph of $y = \frac{2000 - 2x^2}{100}$ as x takes values from -20 to 20.

a Draw the graph of this function.

b Calculate an estimate for the area between the curve and the x-axis.

c This is a sketch of the completed hangar. Calculate an estimate of its volume.

171

$$\frac{2000 - 2x^2}{100}$$

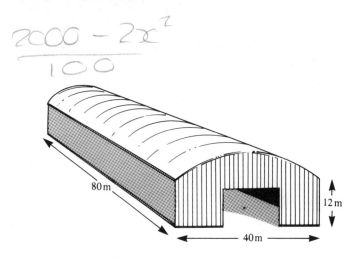

We can prepare this table of values:

x	-20	-15	-10	-5	0	5	10	15	20
y	12	15.5	18	19.5	20	19.5	18	15.5	12

We can then draw this graph:

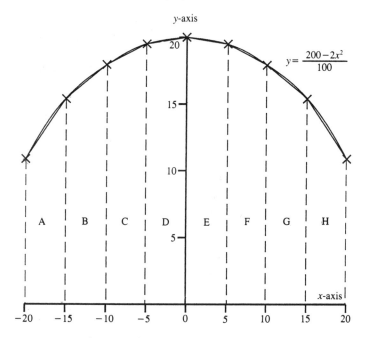

The calculations required to estimate this area are:

$$\text{Area A} = \frac{5(12 + 15.5)}{2} = 68.75 \text{ square units}$$

$$\text{Area B} = \frac{5(15.5 + 18)}{2} = 83.75 \text{ square units}$$

$$\text{Area C} = \frac{5(18 + 19.5)}{2} = 93.75 \text{ square units}$$

$$\text{Area D} = \frac{5(19.5 + 20)}{2} = 98.75 \text{ square units}$$

$$\text{Area E} = \frac{5(20 + 19.5)}{2} = 98.75 \text{ square units}$$

$$\text{Area F} = \frac{5(19.5 + 18)}{2} = 93.75 \text{ square units}$$

$$\text{Area G} = \frac{5(18 + 15.5)}{2} = 83.75 \text{ square units}$$

$$\text{Area H} = \frac{5(15.5 + 12)}{2} = 68.75 \text{ square units}$$

Total area = 690 square units

The sketch indicates that this is the area (in square metres) of one end of the building. Therefore

Volume of building = $690 \times 80 = 55\,200$ cubic metres

In the last example, the area under the curve was divided into strips 5 units wide. It is obvious that a better estimate for the area could be obtained if the area was divided into strips only 1 unit wide. In this case, however, we would need to calculate the area of 40 trapeziums rather than 8! Unless a computer was available the work involved would be far too time consuming. The decision to use strips 5 units wide is thus a compromise between accuracy and number of calculations.

CHECKPOINT 27

1 Estimate the area under this curve.

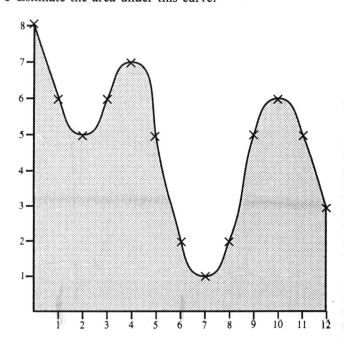

2 a Estimate the area enclosed by the lines $x = 1$, $x = 6$, $y = 0$ and $y = \frac{12}{x}$.

b This sketch shows a decorative polystyrene covering strip designed to fit between the wall and ceiling of a room. The curved face of the coving is in the shape of the graph of $y = \frac{12}{x}$.

Estimate the volume (in cm³) of polystyrene required to make a 1 metre length of the coving.

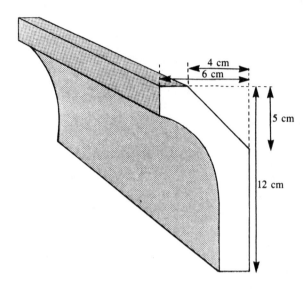

3 a Draw a graph of the function $y = \frac{16 + x^2}{10}$ as x takes values from 0 to 5.

b This sketch shows a machine part which is to be cast in bronze. The curved surface is in the shape of the graph of $y = \frac{16 + x^2}{10}$. Estimate the volume of bronze needed to make the part.

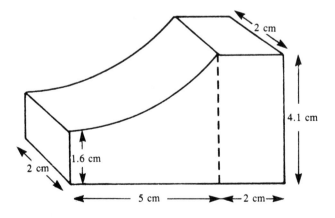

4 A tunnel 100 metres long is to be dug through a hill. The mouth of the tunnel will be in the shape of the graph of the function $y = \frac{x(6-x)}{2}$ as x takes values from 0 to 6.

Estimate the volume of earth and rock that must be dug out to make the tunnel.

Graphs—practice and revision exercise

1 Draw a graph and mark on it the lines with equation

a $x = 3$　**b** $y = -2$　**c** $x = 0$　**d** $y = 0$　**e** $x = -3.5$
f $y = 2.5$

2 Write down the equation of the line which passes through each of the following pairs of points.

a $(2, -3)$ and $(5, -3)$ 　 $y = mx + c$ 　 **b** $(5, -2)$ and $(5, 5)$
　 $y = -3$ 　　　　　　　　　　　　　$x = 5$

3 Draw a graph and find the gradient of the line which connects each of the following pairs of points.

a $(0,0)$ and $(4,8)$　**b** $(0,0)$ and $(8,4)$　**c** $(0,0)$ and $(5,5)$
d $(-3,1)$ and $(1,-3)$　　　**e** $(-6,-2)$ and $(-1,-1)$
f $(-5,2)$ and $(-4,-3)$

4 Draw a graph to illustrate each of the following equations using x values from -4 to 4. Write down the gradient of the graph and the co-ordinates of the point where the graph cuts the y-axis.

a $y = x + 5$　**b** $y = x - 6$　**c** $y = 2.5x + 1.5$　**d** $y = \frac{x}{6}$

e $y = 2x - 7$　**f** $y = \frac{x}{2} + 1$　**g** $y = 6 - 2x$　**h** $y = \frac{2(x-1)}{4}$

5 Write down the equations of the lines which have the following gradients and cutting points on the y-axis.

a gradient 3, cutting point $(0,2)$　$y = 3x + 2$

b gradient $\frac{1}{2}$, cutting point $(0, -5)$

c gradient -2, cutting point $(0,0)$

d gradient $\frac{-1}{4}$, cutting point $(0,5)$

6 Blank computer disks are offered for sale on the following terms:

- £1.40 each for orders of up to 9 disks.
- £1.20 each for orders of 10 or more disks.
- £1.10 each for orders of 20 or more disks.
- A fixed handling charge of £2 is added to all orders.

a Prepare a graph with a horizontal axis from 0 to 30 disks and a vertical axis from 0 to £40. Use a scale of 2 cm to represent 10 disks on the horizontal axis and 2 cm to represent £10 on the vertical axis.

b Plot lines to represent the cost of buying between 1 and 9 disks, between 10 and 19 disks and between 20 and 30 disks.

c What advice would you offer to somebody buying either 9 disks or 19 disks?

7 Draw a graph to illustrate each of the following equations:

a $5y = x + 1$ **b** $6y = 3x - 18$ **c** $9x + 2y = 18$
d $3x - 8y = 24$ **e** $x + y = 0$ **f** $x - y = 0$

8 Solve each of the following pairs of simultaneous equations by drawing a graph.

a $y = 2x + 2$ **b** $4x + 5y = 20$
  $y = 3x + 4$ $6x + 5y = 30$

9 Draw graphs to solve each of the following pairs of simultaneous equations and state whether the the equations have one solution, no solution or many solutions. If the equations have one solution, find that solution. If the equations have many solutions, give three possible solutions.

a $2x + y = 8$ **b** $2y = 3x + 2$ **c** $5x + 6y = 30$
  $4x + 2y = 9$ $2y = x - 2$ $18y = 90 - 15x$

10 a Copy and complete this table of values for

$$y = x^2 + 4x - 5$$

x	-5	-4	-3	-2	-1	0	1	2
x^2	25	16	9	4	1	0	1	4
$+4x$	-20	-16	-12	-8	-4	0	4	8
-5	-5	-5	-5	-5	-5	-5	-5	-5
y	0	-5	-8	-9	-8	-5	0	7

b Use the table to draw the graph of $y = x^2 + 4x - 5$ as x takes values from -5 to 2.

11 If a rectangle is formed from a loop of string 18 cm long, it can take many different shapes. It could for example be a 6 cm high by 3 cm wide rectangle, or a 4 cm high by 5 cm wide rectangle.

a Copy and complete this table showing the dimensions and areas of rectangles formed from an 18 cm loop of string.

Size of rectangle (height × width)	9×0	8×1	7×2	6×3	5×4	4×5	3×6	2×7	1×8	9×0
Area (square centimetres)	0	8	14							

b Draw a graph to illustrate the change in area as the width of the rectangle varies from 0 cm to 9 cm.

c What is the maximum area that can be enclosed by a rectangle formed with an 18 cm loop of string?

12 a Copy and complete this table of values for

$$y = 8 + 2x - x^2$$

x	-3	-2	-1	0	1	2	3	4	5
8	8	8	8	8	8	8	8	8	8
$+2x$	-6	-4	-2	0	2	4	6	8	10
$-x^2$	-9	-4	-1	0	-1	-4	-9	-16	-25
y	-7	0	5	8	9	8	5	0	-7

b Use the table to draw the graph of $y = 8 + 2x - x^2$ as x takes values from -3 to 5.

c Use your graph to solve these equations.

- $8 + 2x - x^2 = 0$ • $8 + 2x - x^2 = 4$
- $8 + 2x - x^2 = x$ • $7 + 3x = x^2$

13 Draw a graph to illustrate the function $y = \dfrac{8}{x}$ as x takes values from -8 to 8.

14 A group of students want to travel from Birmingham to London to visit the Science Museum. A 40-seater coach will cost £120 to hire for the return journey.

a Copy and complete this table to show the cost per student for the trip for different numbers of students sharing the coach hire.

Number of students on coach	5	10	15	20	25	30	35	40
Cost per student (£)	24	12			4.80			

b Use your table to draw a graph.

c What is the minimum number of students who must go on the trip to keep the cost under £5 a head?

15 Draw a graph to illustrate the function $y = 3x$ as x takes values from -3 to 3.

16 There is an estimated stable population of 150 000 rabbits on the island of Grumpling. At the present time, 20 of these rabbits are suffering from a viral disease but this number is doubling every 2 months. Draw a graph to illustrate this rate of increase and estimate how long it will be before the entire rabbit population is infected by the disease.

17 Illustrate each of the following inequalities with a graph.
a $x < 3$ **b** $y > -2$ **c** $x > 0$ **d** $y < 0$

18 Write down the inequality illustrated by each of the following graphs.

a

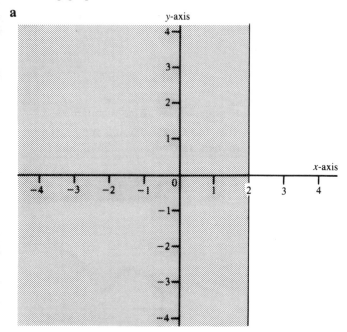

b

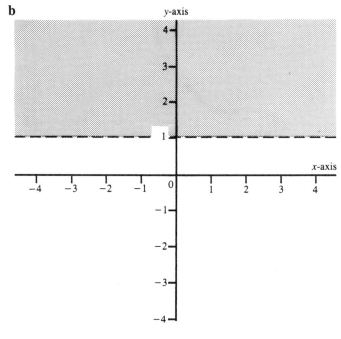

19 Illustrate on a graph the regions where:
a $x > -2$ and $x < 1$ **b** $y > -2$ and $y < -4$
c $x > 0$ and $y < 0$ **d** $x > 4$ and $y > 4$
e $x < 4$ and $y < -3$ **f** $x < -3$ and $y > -1$

20 Write down the combined inequalities illustrated by each of the following graphs.

a

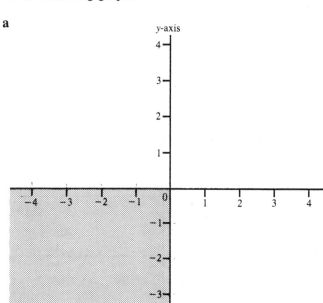

b

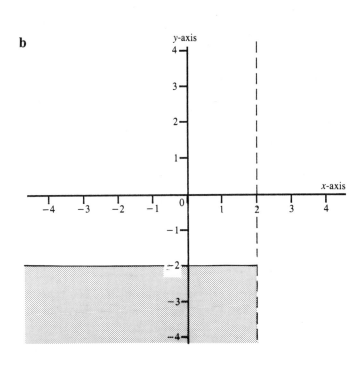

21 Illustrate on a graph the regions where:
a $y > x - 3$ **b** $y < 2x + 1$ **c** $2x + y > 8$
d $x > 0$, $y > 0$ and $y > x + 3$
e $-3 < x < -3$, $y < 3$ and $x + 3y > 1$

22 Illustrate on a graph the regions where
a $1<x<4$, $y>x-3$ and $y<x+1$
b $4x+6y<24$, $y>x-6$ and $y>0$

23 Write down the inequalities illustrated by each of the following graphs.

a

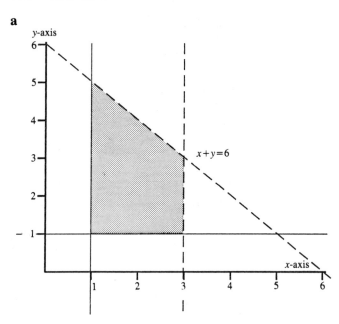

b

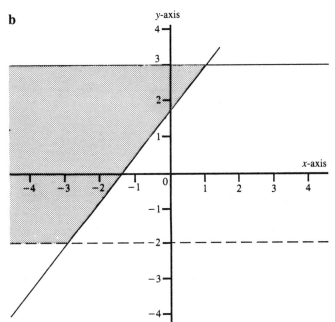

24 The Hire-a-Heap car rental company hire two types of car. The Astrid has 4 seats and costs £30 a day, and the Carlta has 5 seats and costs £40 a day.

a How many seats are provided in:

● 6 Astrids?

● x Astrids?

● 8 Carltas?

● y Carltas?

● x Astrids and y Carltas?

b A party of 40 people want to hire cars to transport them to a wedding. If they hire a mixture of x Astrids and y Carltas, explain why

$$4x+5y\geqslant40$$

c The party does not wish to spend more than £360 on their transport. Explain why

$$30x+40y\leqslant360$$

d The Hire-a-Heap company only has 7 Carltas and 9 Astrids. Explain why

$$y\leqslant7 \text{ and } x\leqslant9$$

e Draw a graph to illustrate all these inequalities.
f How many Astrids and Carltas should the party hire if they wish to obtain their transport at the minimum cost?

25 This simplified map shows the relative locations of Spalding, Market Deeping, Uffington and Stamford.

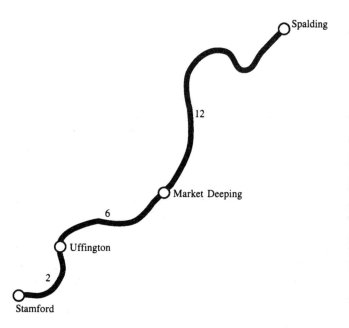

At 9.30 am, the Brown family sets out from Spalding and drives to visit friends who live in Uffington. At the same time, the Green family who live in Stamford set out to drive to visit friends who live in Market Deeping. This distance–time graph illustrates the journeys.

176

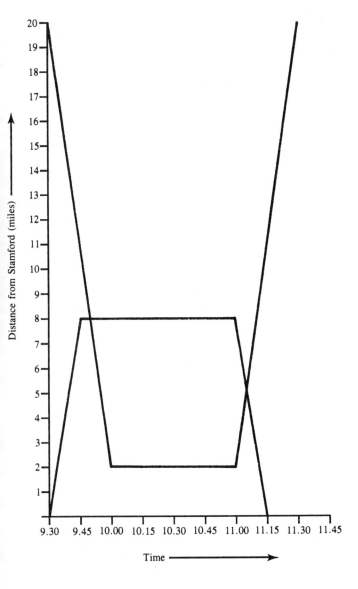

a How long did the Brown family stay in Uffington?

b At what average speed did the Browns drive to Uffington?

c How long did the Green family stay in Market Deeping?

d At what average speed did the Greens drive to Market Deeping?

e At what time did the Greens going home to Stamford pass the Browns going home to Spalding in the opposite direction?

26 At 11.30 am, a lorry travelling at 60 mph passes under a motorway bridge on which a stationary police car is standing. Five minutes later, the police car drives down on to the motorway and starts to travel in the same direction as the lorry at 70 mph. Draw a distance–time graph and estimate the time at which the police car overtakes the lorry and the distance from the bridge when this happens. Use a scale of 2 cm to represent 5 minutes on the time axis and a scale of 2 cm to represent 10 miles on the distance axis. Your time axis should extend from 9.30 am to 10.30 am and your distance axis should extend from 0 to 80 miles.

27 This label gives cooking instructions for a bacon joint. Draw a graph to illustrate the cooking times required for joints from 1 to 4 pounds in weight.

> **PREMIUM TENDERSWEET**
> # LOIN ROAST
> **ENGLISH SMOKED BONELESS**
> Cooking instructions: Remove joint from bag and roast in a pre-heated oven 180°C, 350°F, Gas Mark 4 for 35 minutes per lb, plus 35 minutes.

28 Liquid in a test tube is boiled and then allowed to cool and the following results recorded.

Elapsed time (minutes)	0	5	10	15	20
Temperature (°C)	100	65	52	45	40

a Draw a graph to illustrate the results recorded in the table.

b Estimate the rate at which the liquid was cooling (in degrees Celsius per minute) after

- 5 minutes,

- 15 minutes.

c Estimate the temperature the liquid will cool to in a further 5 minutes.

29 A car accelerates from rest to a velocity of 20 metres per second in 10 seconds. It then travels at this speed for 20 seconds before braking to a stop in a further 10 seconds. Draw a velocity–time graph to illustrate this journey and calculate the total distance travelled by the car.

30 Estimate the area enclosed between the curve $y = (x - 3)(x + 2)$ and the x-axis.

31 This sketch shows a greenhouse tunnel made from plastic. The end is in the shape of the curve $y = \dfrac{8x - x^2}{4}$ as x takes values from 0 to 8.

Estimate the volume of air in the greenhouse.

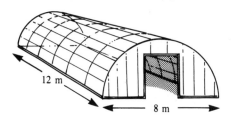

177

Graphs - extended problems for project work

1 In this unit you have used graphs to illustrate many different relationships between pairs of variables. Some of these relationships have produced straight line graphs and others have produced smooth curves. Using simple apparatus, you can investigate many different real-life situations, display your results on a graph and attempt to explain the relationships involved. When you obtain your own data in this way, do not expect to obtain perfect straight lines or curves on your graphs.

For example, if various weights are hung on a spring and its extension measured, we might obtain these results:

Weight (grams)	0	50	100	150	200	250	300	350	400	450	500
Length (cm)	10.0	10.25	10.5	10.75	11.25	11.0	11.5	11.75	12.0	12.0	12.5

You can then draw this graph.

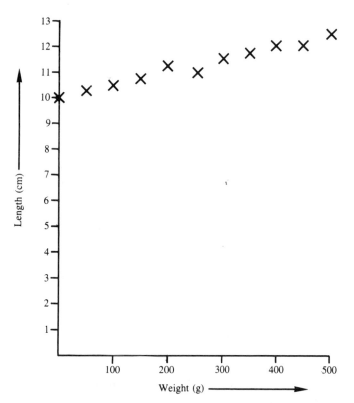

In any experimental situation like this, the question now arises:

'How shall I connect the points?'

First, you must decide whether your points lie approximately on a straight line or a curve.

If, like the results we have plotted, the points appear to lie approximately on a straight line, you draw in the best line you can to fit the points. This is most easily done with a transparent ruler. You should aim to balance the points, so that some are above and some are below your line. A line of 'best fit' drawn through the points we have plotted might look like this.

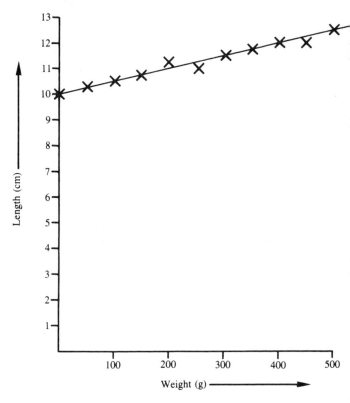

Reading off the slope and *y*-axis cutting point of the straight line produces this equation linking the length (*l*) and the weight (*w*):

$$l = 10 + 0.005w$$

If experimental results, when plotted, clearly lie on a curve rather than a straight line then a 'curve of best fit' is drawn through them.

There are hundreds of suitable relationships which you can experiment with and attempt to find equations to describe. Some suggestions are:

- What is the relationship between the load hung on a spring and its length? How is this relationship applied in the design of spring balances and weighing machines?

- What is the relationship between the height of a candle and the time for which it has been burning? What is a candle clock?

- Some coins are placed on one end of a ruler and it is gradually pushed further and further out over the edge of a table until it is just at the point of tipping.

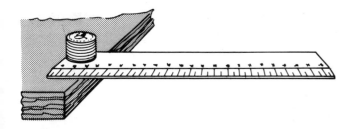

What is the relationship between the number of coins and the distance the ruler can be pushed out over the edge?

- Many different combinations of pulleys can be set up like this one:

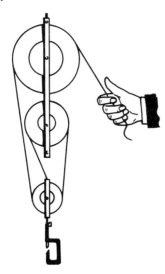

For any given pulley system, what is the relationship between the load lifted and the force needed to lift it? What is the relationship between the distance the load is lifted and the distance the lifting force moves?

- As a liquid is heated or cooled, what is the relationship between the time that has elapsed and the temperature of the liquid? What about substances like wax that change from a solid to a liquid as they are heated? (**Any experiment which involves heating is potentially dangerous and requires safety precautions. Always discuss any experiments with an experienced Science teacher *before* you attempt them.**)

- What is the relationship between the length of a pendulum and the time it takes to complete a single swing? Why are pendulums used in some clocks? What is the history of pendulum clocks?

These are just a few examples of experiments that you can conduct with simple apparatus. Many books are available for you to research other experiments and graphical techniques.

2 The parabola is the curve produced when we plot the graph of any equation of the form

$$y = ax^2 + bx + c$$

This curve appears in many natural situations and also has properties which are very useful for industrial designers. The curve can be drawn in many different ways.

a The diagrams below suggest three different ways to draw parabolas. Experiment with these techniques.

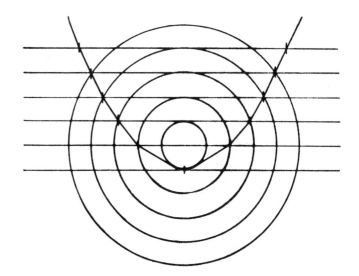

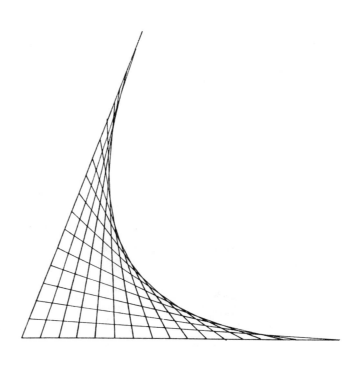

179

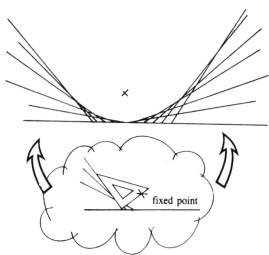

This special property of parabolic surfaces can be used in reverse. If a source of light or heat is placed at the focus of a reflecting surface, a parallel beam of light or heat will be produced. This property is used in torches, searchlights and some electric fires.

b If a reflecting surface is made in the shape of parabola, it has a very important property. Any light or other radiation from a distant source which falls on the surface will be focused at a single point, called the focus. This property is used in solar ovens, radio telescopes and satellite TV 'dish' aerials.

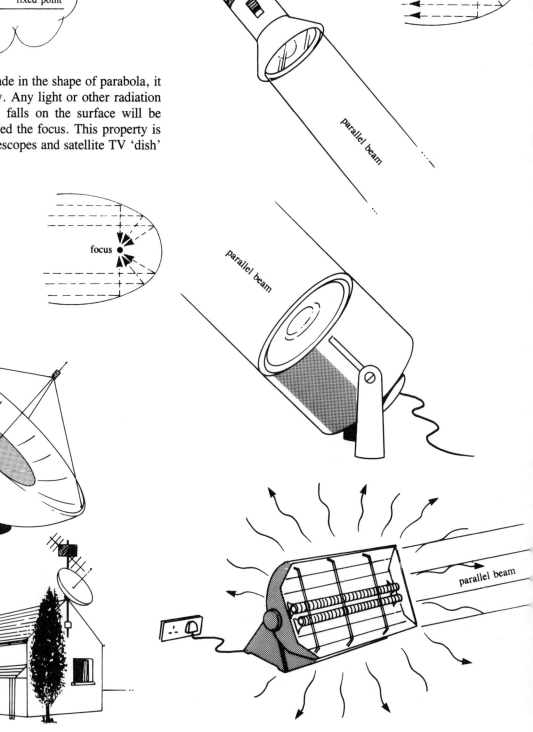

Some suggestions for project work based on this property of the parabola are:

- In a library, find out all you can about parabolas from the books in the mathematics section. Write a report.

- Can you design and build a solar oven from cardboard and aluminium foil? This is a quick design sketch.

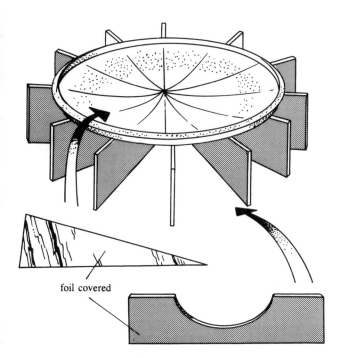

foil covered

foil covered

c When a ball is thrown, the path it follows is approximately a parabola. The study of paths of objects thrown or shot through the air is called the study of 'projectiles'. It is very difficult to follow the path of an object as it flies through the air but similar paths are followed if an object is projected up a smooth sloping surface and these are quite easy to observe and perhaps video. Many simple experiments can be carried out with apparatus like this:

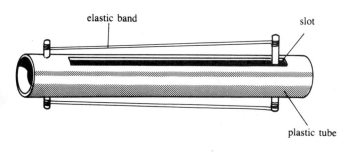

a 'gun' to project marbles, etc.

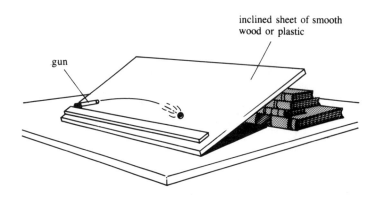

inclined sheet of smooth wood or plastic

gun

3 Sports records are easily researched in any library and offer many opportunities for investigation. Some starting ideas are:

- What was the world record for the mile in 1910, 1920, 1930, etc? Can you illustrate the way in which the world record mile time has been cut over the years? Can you predict what the world record might be in 10 years time?

- What about other running distances?

- What about the world record for putting the shot?

- What about other throwing, lifting or jumping records?

- What about attendances at football matches?

Graphs
Past paper questions

1 a On a grid, plot and label the points

$$P(4,1) \qquad Q(3,-2) \qquad R(-3,-2) \qquad S(-2,1).$$

b Give the geometrical name of quadrilateral *PQRS*.

(LEAG)

181

2

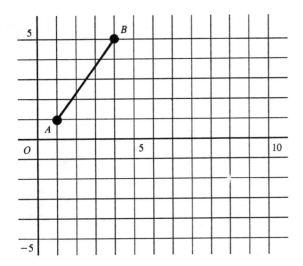

A and *B* are two corners of a quadrilateral.

a Write down the co-ordinates of *A* and *B*.

The corner *C* is at (8,2). The corner *D* is at (2, −6).

b Copy the diagram and plot these two points and complete the quadrilateral *ABCD*.

c What name is given to *ABCD*?

E is a point on *CD*. The line *AE* is perpendicular to *CD*.

d Draw *AE* and write down the co-ordinates of *E*.

(MEG)

3

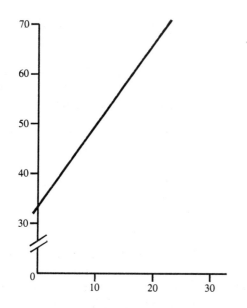

This graph can be used to convert between degrees Celsius and degrees Fahrenheit.

a What is 20°C in °F?

b What is 60°F in °C?

Overnight, the temperature falls by 18°F.

c How many degrees C does it fall?

4

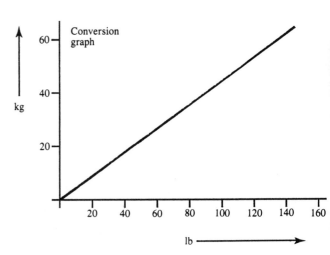

Use the graph to answer the following questions.

a The minimum weight to qualify as an amateur lightweight boxer is 57 kg.

What is this weight in lb to the nearest lb?

b A person lost 12 lb after dieting for 2 weeks. What is the weight loss in kg to the nearest kg?

(LEAG)

5

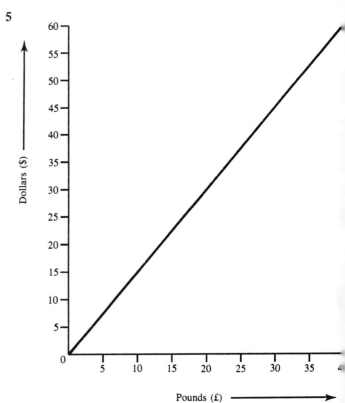

182

The graph is used to convert between pounds (£) and dollars ($).

Use the graph to find

a the price, in dollars, of a watch costing £22,

b the price, in pounds, of a basketball costing 42 dollars.

6

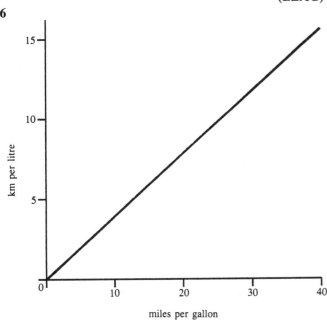

The graph above shows the relationship between 'petrol consumption in miles per gallon' and 'petrol consumption in kilometres per litre'.

a At a steady speed of 50 miles per hour, a British car travels 30 miles per gallon of petrol.

(i) Express the petrol consumption in kilometres per litre.

(ii) How much petrol, in gallons, will this car use if it is driven at 50 miles per hour for 1½ hours?

b A French car, driven at 100 kilometres per hour, has a petrol consumption of 10 kilometres per litre.
Express this petrol consumption in miles per gallon.

c Give a reason why it is not possible to say which of the two cars is more economical with petrol.

7

SYDENHAMS PRINTERS

Personal notepaper, supplied to order, printed with your own name and address.

Two qualities are available.

STANDARD: white paper, black elite print
EXECUTIVE: coloured paper, gold embossed print

The cost consists of a basic charge for the printing block plus a fixed charge per sheet ordered.

Discounts available for bulk purchase.

---

a The graph below shows the cost of ordering standard notepaper.

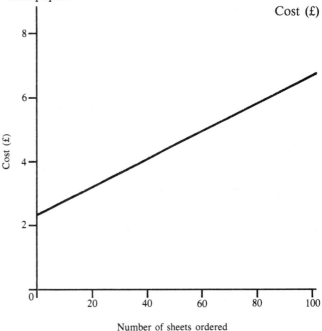

(i) What is the cost of buying 60 sheets of standard notepaper?

(ii) What is the basic charge for the printing block?

(iii) What is the cost per sheet of standard notepaper?

(iv) The cost, C, of an order for STANDARD notepaper can be written as $C = b + pS$ pence, where b is the basic charge for the printing block, p is the price per sheet and S is the number of sheets ordered.

Complete the formula $C = $ .... + ...S pence

(v) Use your formula to calculate the cost of ordering 180 sheets of STANDARD notepaper.

b EXECUTIVE notepaper cost 6 pence per sheet plus a basic charge for the printing block of £3.60. Draw a line on the axes above to show the cost of EXECUTIVE notepaper. The following discounts are available for bulk orders over 200 sheets.

Number of sheets ordered	Discount
201 to 500	10%
501 to 1000	20%
Over 1000	25%

c Calculate the cost of ordering 800 sheets of STANDARD notepaper.

d A small engineering firm orders a quantity of EXECUTIVE notepaper and qualifies for the maximum discount of 25%.

(i) They pay £92.70 for the order. How much would the order have cost without the discount?

(ii) How many sheets did they order?

8

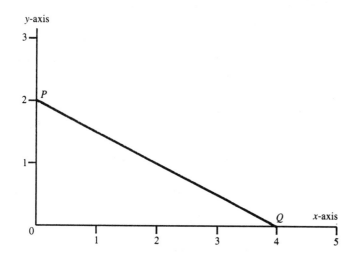

Calculate the gradient of the line *PQ*.

(LEAG)

9 The diagram shows the point *A* with coordinates (2,3).

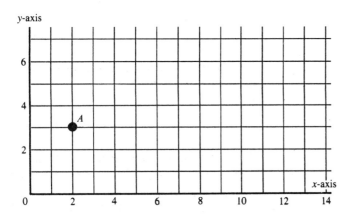

a Copy the diagram and draw in the straight line passing through *A* with gradient $-\frac{1}{2}$.

b Write down the coordinates of the point where your line crosses the *y*-axis.

(MEG)

10 Huw observes a bird flying directly away from a bird box. He starts his watch and finds out how far the bird is from the box at different times.

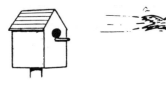

This graph is drawn from his results.

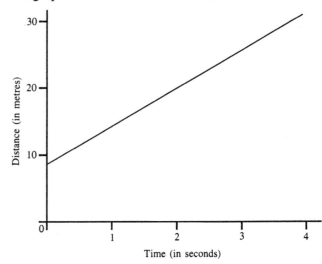

a How far is the bird from the box when Huw starts his watch?

b How fast is the bird flying?

c Write down a formula for the distance, *d*, the bird is from the box in terms of time, *t*.

(WJEB)

11 The number of kilometres (*y*) approximately equivalent to a number of miles (*x*) is given by the formula $y = \frac{8x}{5}$.

a Copy and complete the following table, using the formula to calculate the values of *y*.

x	0	20	40	60
y	0		64	

b (i) Draw a pair of axes using a scale of 2 cm to represent 10 units on each axis. Mark on your graph the points from your table.
(ii) Draw the **straight** line which is the graph of $y = \frac{8x}{5}$.

c Use your graph to find
 (i) the number of kilometres equivalent to 52 miles,
(ii) the number of miles equivalent to 43 kilometres.
d Work out the number of kilometres equivalent to 200 miles.

(MEG)

12 A school inspector uses his own car to visit schools. He can claim travel expenses each week on one or other of two schemes.

Scheme A: For distances up to 100 miles, 40 pence per mile.
For distances over 100 miles, 40 pence per mile for the first 100 miles then 10 pence per mile for each mile after the first 100 miles.

Scheme B: A basic allowance of £10 plus 20 pence per mile travelled.

a Copy and complete the table for Scheme A:

Miles travelled (x)	0	50	100	150	200	250	300	350	400
Expenses claimed (£y)	0		40		50			65	

b On graph paper, using scales of 2 cm to 50 miles travelled and 2 cm to £10 expenses claimed, draw a graph for Scheme A for distances travelled up to 400 miles in one week.

c On the same axes, draw a graph for Scheme B for distances travelled up to 400 miles in one week.

d (i) Use your graph to find the two values of x (miles travelled) for which Scheme A and Scheme B produce equal values of £y (expenses claimed).

(ii) For what range of values of x (miles travelled) does Scheme A produce the greater value of £y (expenses claimed)?

(iii) When the distance travelled is 400 miles, find how much more can be claimed using Scheme B than using Scheme A.

(iv) Find the values of x for which the amount claimed using one Scheme is £10 more than the amount claimed using the other Scheme.

(LEAG)

13 The removal firm of W. E. Shiftman hires out vans at a basic charge of £20 plus a further cost of 30p per kilometre. Some of the charges for given distances are shown below.

Distance (x km)	0	100	200	300
Charge (£C)	20			110

a Copy and complete the table.

b Use the values from the table to draw a graph to show the charges up to a distance of 300 km.

Another firm, D.I.Y. Transport, hires out vans at a basic charge of £35 plus a further cost of 20p per kilometre.

Distance (x km)	0	100	200	300
Charge (£C)				

c Copy and complete this table for D.I.Y. Transport charges.

d Using the same axes as in part (b), draw a graph to show the charges of D.I.Y. Transport up to a distance of 300 km.

e For what distance do both firms charge the same amount?

f (i) Which firm is the cheaper for a journey of 180 km?

(ii) What is the difference in charges between the firms for a journey of 180 km?

g For D.I.Y. Transport, write down a formula giving the value of C in terms of x.

(LEAG)

14 Corks released from Champagne bottles can reach great heights. For a cork leaving a bottle with speed V (in metres per second) the maximum height (in centimetres) is given by

$$h = 5 \times V^2$$

a Complete this table of values.

V	0	1	2	3	4	5
h	0	5			80	

b On a graph plot the points and join them all in a smooth curve.

c Use your graph to find:

(i) the height reached by a cork which leaves the bottle at 3.5 m/s;

(ii) the speed a cork leaves the bottle if it reaches 30 cm.

(MEG)

15 a A rectangular water tank with a capacity of 62.5 m³ has a square base of side 5 m.
Find the depth of water in the tank when it is full.

b A firm manufactures a range of rectangular water tanks of height 4 m with square bases.
The volume, V m³, of a tank with a square base of side x metres is given by the formula $V = 4x^2$.

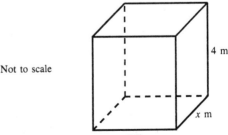

Not to scale

4 m

x m

x m

(i) Copy and complete the following table to calculate the values of V for the given values of x.

185

x	0	1	2	3	3.5
V				36	

(ii) Using a horizontal scale of 2 cm to represent 0.5 m and a vertical scale of 2 cm to represent 5 m³, plot these values and draw a smooth curve through your points.

(iii) Use your graph to estimate
- the volume, in m³, of a tank with a square base of side 1.5 m,
- the length of the side of the base of a tank of volume 25 m³.

(MEG)

16 a Given that $y = x^2$, copy and complete the following table.

x	-3	-2.5	-2	-1.5	-1	-0.5	0	0.5	1	1.5	2	2.5	3
y	9	6.25			1		0		1			6.25	9

b Using a scale of 2 cm to represent 1 unit on each axis, draw the graph of $y = x^2$ for values of x from -3 to 3.

c (i) Using the same scales and axes as in part **b**, draw the straight line $y = 3 - x$.

(ii) Write down the gradient of the straight line.

d Using your graphs of $y = x^2$ and y and making your method clear, find the solutions of the equation $x^2 = 3 - x$.

(MEG)

17 A pebble is thrown upwards from the edge of a sea-side cliff and eventually falls into the sea. The height of the pebble above the sea after t seconds is h metres, where h is given by the formula

$$h = 24 + 8t - 2t^2$$

a Copy and complete the table for the values of h.

t	0	1	2	3	4	5	6
h							

b Using a scale of 2 cm for 5 m on the h-axis and 2 cm for 1 second on the t-axis, draw a graph of h against t for $0 \leqslant t \leqslant 6$.

c Find
(i) the height of the cliff,
(ii) how high the pebble rises above the level of the cliff-top,
(iii) after how many seconds the pebble lands in the sea,
(iv) by drawing a suitable line, an estimate for the speed of the pebble after 5 seconds.

(LEAG)

18 Copper wire is rolled into coils for storage purposes. It is found that the weight of a coil, W tonnes, is related to the diameter, d millimetres, of the copper wire by the formula

$$W = 0.5 \, d^2$$

(The length of copper wire in each coil is the same.)

a Write down the missing values in the following table, which gives the values of W for values of d from 0 to 6:

d	0	1	2	3	4	5	6
W	0	0.5	2			12.5	18

b Use graph paper to draw the graph of $W = 0.5 \, d^2$ for values of d from 0 to 6.

c Use your graph to estimate the weight of a coil of copper wire having a diameter of 2.6 mm.

d Use your graph to estimate the thickness of the wire in a coil weighing 12 tonnes.

(WJEB)

19 A box without a lid is to be made from a sheet of thin metal. The sheet measures 20 cm by 30 cm. Squares of side x cm are cut from each corner and the sides folded up.

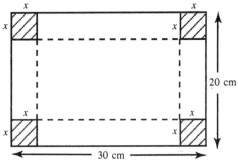

a V cm³ is the volume enclosed by the box when it is made up.
Explain why $V = 4x(10 - x)(15 - x)$.

b Complete a table of volumes for V as x takes values from 1 to 9.

c Draw the graph of (x, V).

d From your graph find
(i) the largest value of V,
(ii) the corresponding value of x, to the nearest whole number.

(MEG)

20

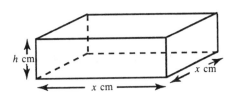

A rectangular block has a square base of side x cm and a height of h cm. The total surface area of the block is 72 cm^2.

a Express h in terms of x.

b Show that the volume, V cm^3, of the block is given by

$$V = 18x - \frac{1}{2}x^3$$

c Copy and complete the following table to show corresponding values of x and V.

x	0	1	2	3	4	5	6
V	0			40.5	40		0

d Using a scale of 2 cm to represent 1 unit on the x-axis and 2 cm to represent 10 units on the V-axis, draw the graph of $V = 18x - \frac{1}{2}x^3$ for values of x from 0 to 6 inclusive.

e A block of this type has a volume of 30 cm^3. Given that $h > x$, find the dimensions of the block.

(MEG)

21 The table shows the temperature, $\theta°C$, of a cup of coffee after it had been cooling for a time t minutes.

t	0	5	10	15	20	25	30	35	40	45	50	55	60
θ	81	70	63	57	52	48	44	41.5	39	37	35.5	34	32.5

a Plot a graph to show this information. Use 2 cm to 10 minutes across the page (with $y=0$ at the left-hand edge) and 2 cm to 10° up the page.

b From your graph estimate
 (i) the temperature after 38 minutes,
(ii) the time at which the temperature would be 28.

c Explain why your answer to **b** (ii) must be treated with caution.

d Estimate the rate at which the cup of coffee was cooling after 20 minutes had elapsed.

e Estimate the room temperature, giving a clear indication of how you arrive at your answer.

(MEG)

22 Describe, using inequalities, the region illustrated in the diagram below.

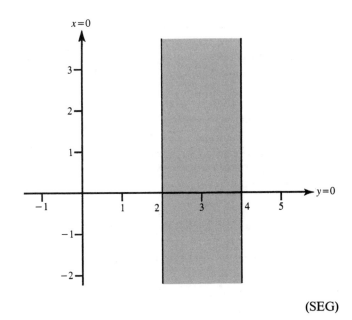

(SEG)

23 A player hits a ball vertically upwards. At a time t seconds later the height of the ball above the ground is y metres, where $y = 1 + 15t - 5t^2$.

Corresponding values of t and y are given in the table:

t	0	0.5	1	2	2.5	3
y	1	7.25	11		7.25	1

a Calculate the height, y, of the ball above the ground 2 seconds after it was hit.

b Using a scale of 2 cm per unit on both axes, draw the graph of $y = 1 + 15t - 5t^2$ for values of t from 0 to 3.

c Use your graph to estimate
 (i) the length of time for which the ball is at least 6 m above the ground,
(ii) the maximum height of the ball above the ground.

d By drawing a straight line on your graph, estimate the speed of the ball 0.5 seconds after it was hit.

(SEG)

24 In an experiment, different weights were attached to a spring and the length of the spring was measured.

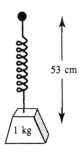

53 cm

1 kg

The following results were obtained:

weight (kg)	1	2	4	5	6
length (cm)	53	58	68	73	78

a (i) Plot these values on a graph,
(ii) join the points with a straight line.
b Find from your graph
(i) the weight needed to stretch the spring to 60 cm,
(ii) the length of the spring when no weight is attached.

(SEG)

25 Katrina is heating a beaker of water and she records the temperature of the water at 20 s intervals. The readings she obtained are given in the table below, but she forgot to record the temperature after 80 s.

Time (*t* seconds)	20	40	60	80	100	120	140
Temperature (*W*°C)	26	35	48		68	79	88

a Plot these points on graph paper and carefully draw a line of best fit for these points.

b From your graph estimate, and write down, the temperature of the water after 80 s.

c The temperature of the water (*W*) and the time (*t*) are connected by the equation

$$W = at + b$$

where *a* and *b* are constants. From your graph estimate, and write down, the values of *a* and *b*.

d When Katrina started to heat the water it was at room temperature. Use your graph to estimate the room temperature.

e Water boils at 100°C. How long did it take Katrina to boil the water? (SEG)

26 Rory joins a Health Club and undergoes a fitness test. After a strenuous workout her pulse rate is recorded every 30 seconds for four minutes. The results are illustrated in the table below. (Pulse rate is the number of heart beats each minute.)

Time (in seconds)	0	30	60	90	120	150	180	210	240
Pulse rate	150	120	100	90	86	84	82	81	80

a Plot this information on graph paper and draw a curve that best fits these points.

b From your graph estimate:
(i) Rory's pulse rate after 45 seconds,
(ii) the number of seconds it takes for Rory's pulse rate to fall to 95.

c The gradient of the tangent drawn at a point on the curve gives the rate at which Rory's pulse rate is decreasing each second. Find the rate at which Rory's pulse rate is decreasing after 60 seconds.

(SEG)

27 Fiona's ride from Luton to Hitchin

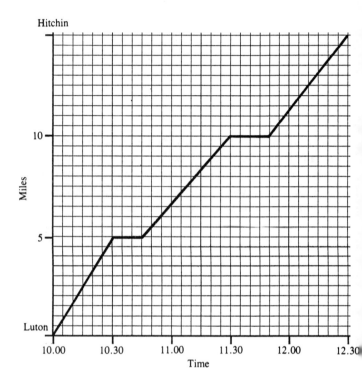

This graph shows Fiona's bike ride from Luton to Hitchin. She set out in the morning and stopped for 2 rests.

a What time did she set out?
b How far is it from London to Hitchin?
c How long was her second rest?
d During which part of her journey was she cycling fastest?
e How fast was she cycling for the first half-hour?
f At what time did she reach Hitchin?
g What was her average speed for the whole journey?

Gary left Hitchin at 10.00 am and raced to Luton, arriving at 11.20 am.

h Show this journey on the graph.
i At what time did he pass Fiona?
j How far from Luton did they pass each other?

(MEG)

28

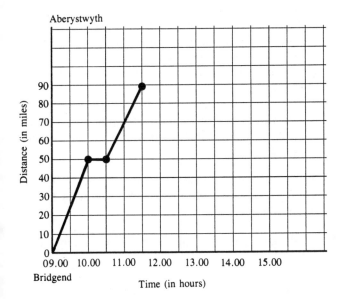

The above graph represents **part** of the journey of a motorist travelling from Bridgend to Aberystwyth and back to Bridgend.

a Describe fully the section of the journey shown in the graph.

b The motorist stays in Aberystwyth for 1½ hours. He then drives back to Bridgend without stopping, arriving at 15.00.

Complete the graph to show this section of his journey.

(WJEB)

29 The graph shows the relationship between the rate of turning of the pedals of Anne's bicycle and the road-speed, for three gears.

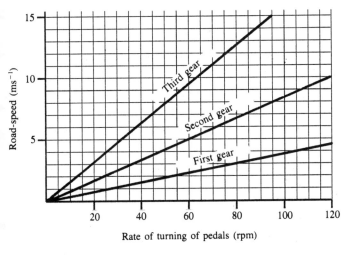

a Anne is in first gear. She is pedalling at 35 r.p.m. What is her speed?

b She now changes to second gear without changing speed. At what rate will she now be pedalling?

c From this speed she accelerates steadily for the next 6 seconds to reach a speed of $8\,\mathrm{m\,s^{-1}}$.
 (i) What is her average speed over this period of time?
(ii) How far does she travel during this time?

d Later, Anne is pedalling at 60 r.p.m. in third gear.
 (i) How far will she travel in 1 minute?
(ii) The diameter of the roadwheels is 66 cm. How many revolutions will the roadwheels make during this minute?

(MEG)

30

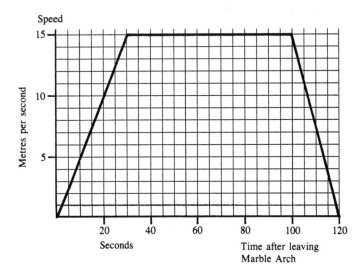

A train runs between two stations, Marble Arch and Bond Street.

The journey takes 2 minutes. The graph above is the speed–time graph for the train during the journey.

Use the graph to find

 (i) the greatest speed of the train,
 (ii) the acceleration during the first 30 seconds,
(iii) the length of time for which the train is slowing down,
(iv) the distance the train moved at its greatest speed,
 (v) the distance between the two stations.

(LEAG)

31 On the grid on the answer sheet indicate, by shading out the region not required, the solution of the inequality $2x + 3y \geqslant 6$.

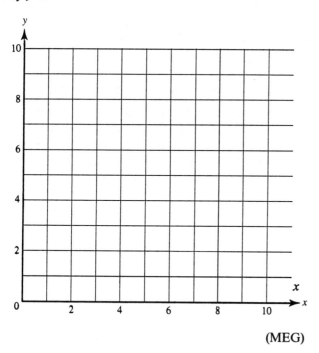

(MEG)

32 An expedition to cross a desert is being planned. The party will travel in landrovers and minibuses.

A landrover has seats for 4 people and has $2\,m^2$ of luggage space.

A minibus has seats for 10 people and has $1\,m^2$ of luggage space.

Suppose that x landrovers and y minibuses are used for the expedition.

a The following four conditions must be satisfied. Express each condition as an inequality involving x and y.

(i) There must not be more than 16 vehicles altogether.
(ii) There must be seats for at least 72 people.
(iii) There must be at least $20\,m^3$ of luggage space.
(iv) For some parts of the journey each minibus may have to be towed by a landrover, so there must be at least as many landrovers as minibuses.

b Illustrate these four inequalities on a graph, using scales of 1 cm for 1 vehicle on each axis, and shading the regions which are **not** required.

Each vehicle (whether a landrover or a minibus) costs £14 000 to buy.

c How many landrovers and how many minibuses should be used if the total cost of buying the vehicles is to be as small as possible?

After the expedition, each landrover can be sold for £11 000, and each minibus can be sold for £5000.

d Write down an expression (in terms of x and y) for the total net cost of the vehicles (i.e. the cost of buying them less the amount received when they are sold).

e How many landrovers and how many minibuses should be used if the total net cost of the vehicles is to be as small as possible?

(MEG)

Shape and Space

Euclidian Geometry

The history of geometry

The Ancient Babylonians, Sumerians and Egyptians began the study of shape and space over 6000 years ago. In these ancient cultures, people stopped relying on hunting and learnt the skills of farming. This meant that an accurate calendar was essential to keep track of the seasons and to predict the correct times for sowing grain and breeding animals. The need for an accurate way to record and predict the passage of time led to the study of star patterns in the night sky. It was soon realised that each morning the rising sun appeared in a slightly different position against the background of stars. In fact the star pattern gradually rotated, taking one full year before the rising sun returned to exactly the same position. The Babylonians measured this year as lasting 360 days, but the Egyptians were more accurate. They knew that a full rotation of the star map took 365 days. The early priest-mathematicians who measured and recorded the movements of the stars invented ways to measure angles and directions. Even today we still divide a full turn into 360 degrees of turning because these early mathematicians thought there were 360 days in a year. As civilisations developed and expanded, more and more practical mathematical knowledge was needed. The construction of large buildings required very accurate measurement of length and angle. The division, ownership and taxation of land required accurate surveying techniques and the measurement of area. The rapid spread of trade required the development of arithmetic and the measurement of weights and volumes.

The discoveries of many different early mathematicians were drawn together by the Greek mathematician Euclid. While living in the Egyptian city of Alexandria, he wrote (in about 300 B.C.) thirteen books on mathematics. These books survived the destruction of the University of Alexandria and were re-published in Venice in 1482. They became an important part of mathematical education and, until the 1900s, were studied by almost all school students. Today we only study some of Euclid's work. Euclid described the mathematics of shape and space as **Geometry**, from the Greek words 'geo' meaning earth and 'metry' meaning to measure.

Angles and lines

We have inherited our system of angle measurement from the Babylonians. The mathematicians of this ancient civilisation, as they mapped the heavens, measured **direction** with a circle divided into 360 parts. These parts of a circle are called **degrees**. There are 360 degrees in a full circle, 180 degrees in half a circle and 90 degrees in a quarter of a circle. The abbreviation for 'degree' is a small circle. So, 180 degrees is abbreviated as 180°. An angle of 90° is often called a **right angle**.

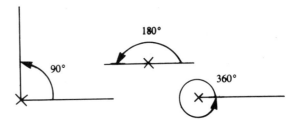

It is obvious that any set of angles which fits together to make a right angle must add to 90°. Any set of angles which fits together to make a straight line must add to 180° and any set of angles which fits together to make a circle must add to 360°.

Examples

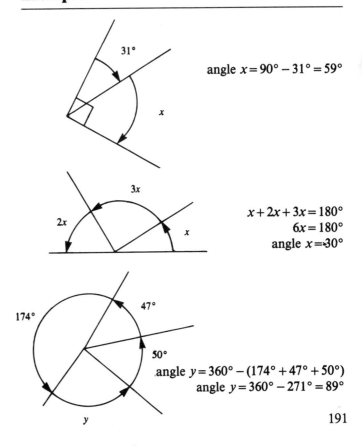

angle $x = 90° - 31° = 59°$

$x + 2x + 3x = 180°$
$6x = 180°$
angle $x = 30°$

angle $y = 360° - (174° + 47° + 50°)$
angle $y = 360° - 271° = 89°$

Find the size of each unknown angle in these diagrams.

a

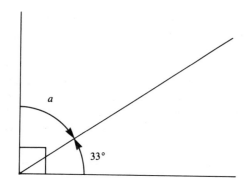

b

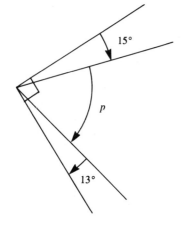

c

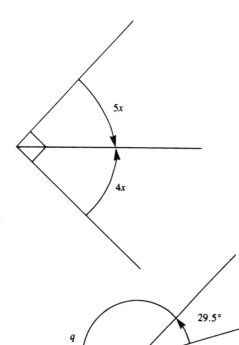

d

e

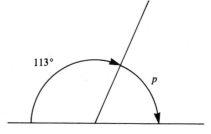

f

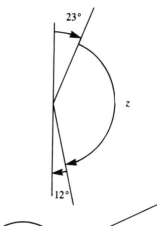

g

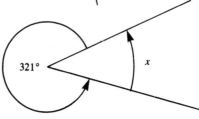

h

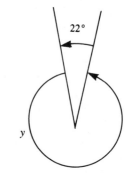

i

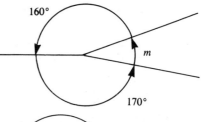

j

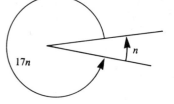

192

Many facts about angles were discovered in a practical way and were well known to craftsmen long before Euclid wrote his books on geometry. For example, suppose two straight rods are supported by tying another rod across them, like this.

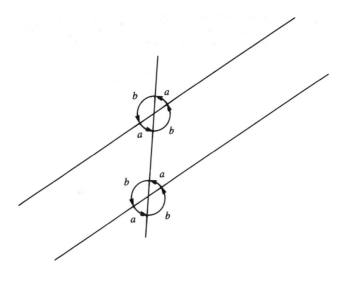

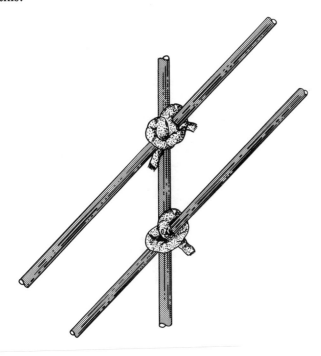

If we want the first two rods to be parallel, it is obvious that the two angles marked A and the two angles marked B must be equal. (To see that this is true, just turn the book through 180° until the diagram appears upside down.)

Examples

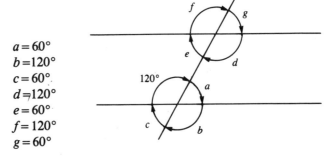

$a = 60°$
$b = 120°$
$c = 60°$
$d = 120°$
$e = 60°$
$f = 120°$
$g = 60°$

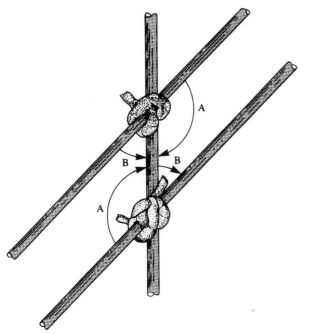

Euclid called these equal angles **alternate angles.** This diagram shows all the equal alternate angles formed when a third line crosses two parallel lines.

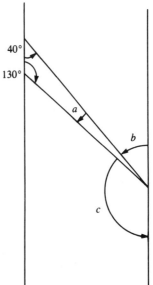

$b = 40°$
$c = 130°$
$a = 180° - (40° + 130°) = 10°$

1 Find the size of each unknown angle in these diagrams.

a

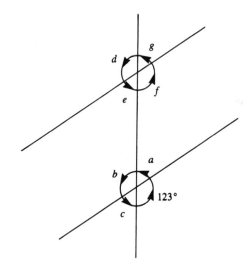

b

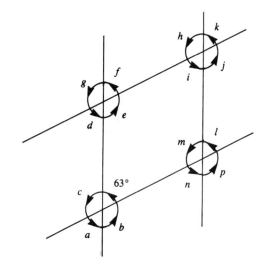

c

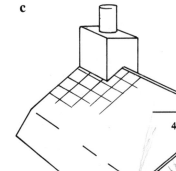

d

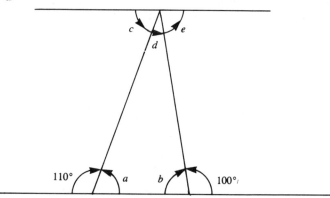

e

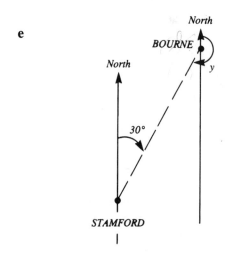

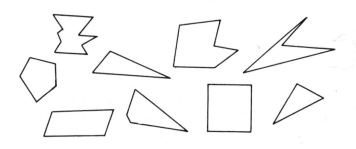

Angles and polygons

A **polygon** is a shape made from straight lines. These are all examples of polygons;

If a polygon has all its sides and all its angles equal, it is called a **regular polygon.** This is a regular eight-sided polygon.

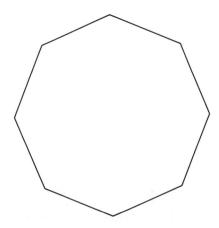

Many polygons have special names.

Polygons with three sides are called triangles.

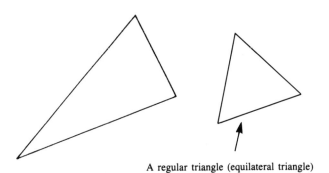

A regular triangle (equilateral triangle)

Polygons with four sides are called quadrilaterals.

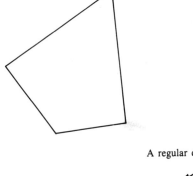

A regular quadrilateral (square)

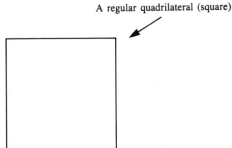

Polygons with five sides are called pentagons.

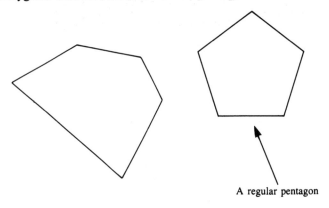

A regular pentagon

Polygons with six sides are called hexagons.

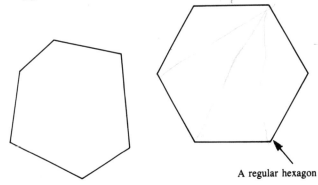

A regular hexagon

Triangles, the simplest form of polygon, have an important angle property.

> Internal angles of a triangle
> The three angles inside a triangle always add up to 180°.

It is very easy to prove this important result. Look at this triangle. A line has been drawn through the top corner of the triangle, parallel to the base.

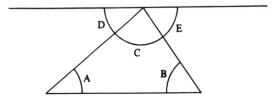

angle A must be equal to angle D (alternate angles)
angle B must be equal to angle E (alternate angles)
angle D + angle E + angle C = 180° (they form a straight line)

Therefore, since angle D + angle E must equal angle A + angle B;

angle A + angle B + angle C = 180°

Because this result is true for any triangle, we can always calculate the size of one angle in a triangle if the other two angles are known.

Examples

1 Find angle x.

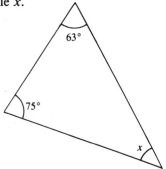

angle $x = 180° - (75° + 63°)$
angle $x = 180° - 138°$
angle $x = 42°$

2 Find the size of each angle in this triangle.

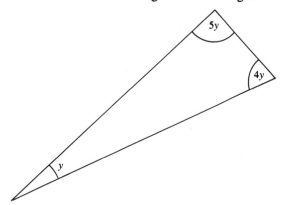

$4y + 5y + y = 180°$
$\qquad 10y = 180°$
$\qquad\quad y = 18°$
The angles are 18°, 90° and 72°.

An **isosceles** triangle has two equal sides. The equal sides are usually marked on a diagram by dashes. The angles formed between the equal sides and the third side are always equal. In this isosceles triangle, AB and AC are the equal sides and angles ABC and ACB are the equal angles.

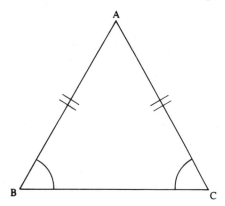

Example

Find angle y.

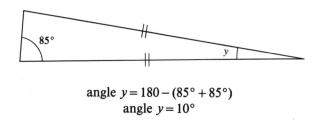

angle $y = 180 - (85° + 85°)$
angle $y = 10°$

Find the size of each unknown angle in these diagrams.

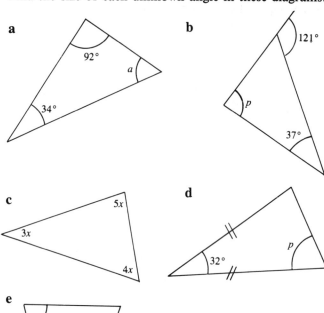

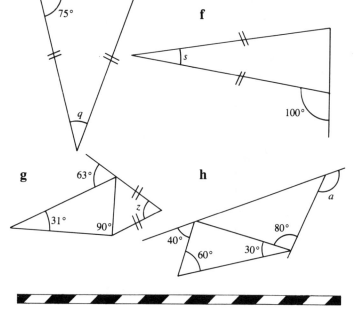

196

Quadrilaterals

Any four-sided polygon is called a **quadrilateral**. There are several different types of quadrilaterals, each with its own name and special properties. You are asked to discover some of these properties in the next checkpoint.

1 A **trapezium** is a quadrilateral with one pair of parallel sides.

Draw three different trapeziums.

2 A **parallelogram** is a quadrilateral with two pairs of parallel sides.

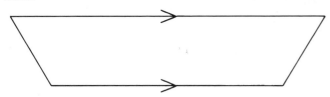

a Draw three different parallelograms.

b By making measurements on your drawings, what can you discover about

- the angles of a parallelogram;
- the diagonals of a parallelogram?

3 A **rhombus** is a quadrilateral with four equal sides.

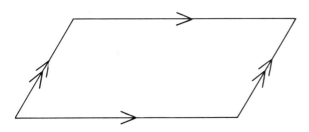

a Draw three different rhombuses.

b By making measurements on your drawings, what can you discover about

- the angles of a rhombus;
- the diagonals of a rhombus?

4 A **rectangle** is a quadrilateral with two pairs of parallel sides and interior angles of 90°.

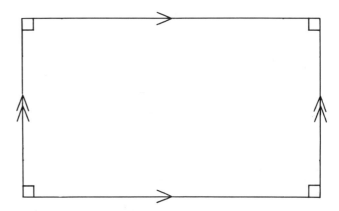

a Draw three different rectangles.

b By making measurements on your drawings, what can you discover about the diagonals of a rectangle?

5 A **square** is a quadrilateral with four equal sides and interior angles of 90°.

a Draw three different squares.

b By making measurements on your drawings, what can you discover about the diagonals of a square?

6 A **kite** is a quadrilateral with two pairs of equal sides arranged in opposite pairs.

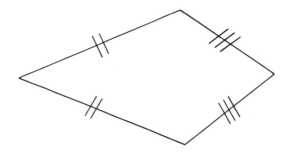

a Draw three different kites.

b By making measurements on your drawings, what can you discover about

- the angles of a kite;
- the diagonals of a kite?

The angles formed inside a polygon are called **interior** angles. If each side of a polygon is extended, the angles formed are called the **exterior** angles of the polygon.

197

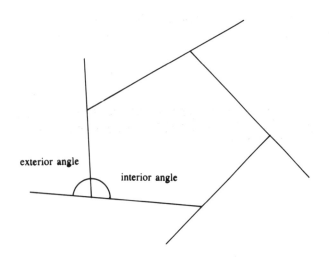

exterior angle

interior angle

We know that the three interior angles of any triangle always add up to 180°. The interior angles of any other type of polygon also always add up to a fixed total. We could learn these totals by heart, but they can quickly and easily be worked out, so there is little point in remembering them. For example, suppose we wish to know what the angles inside any pentagon add up to. First, we draw any pentagon.

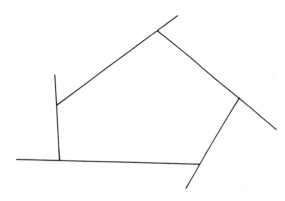

Then, starting at any corner point, we divide the pentagon into triangles.

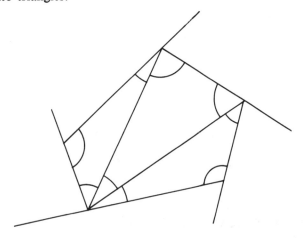

We see that the interior angles of the pentagon are now divided into the angles of three triangles. Since the angles in each of these triangles must add up to 180°, the interior angles of the pentagon must add up to 180° × 3 or 540°. So,

the interior angles of any pentagon add to 540°. Now, each **pair** of interior and exterior angles of the pentagon form an angle of 180°

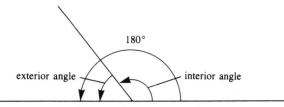

180°

exterior angle — interior angle

So, the total of all five interior angles plus all five exterior angles must be 180° × 5 or 900°.

The interior angles add up to 540°, so the exterior angles must add up to 900° − 540° = 360°.

In a regular pentagon each angle is equal, so in a regular pentagon, each interior angle must equal or $\frac{540°}{5}$ or 108° and each exterior angle must equal $\frac{360°}{5}$ or 72°.

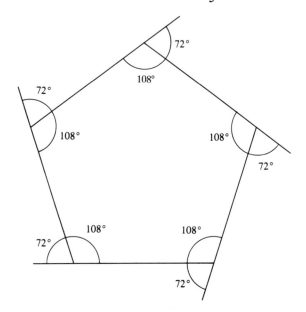

72°
108°
72°
108°
108°
72°
108°
108°
72°
108°
108°
72°
72°

CHECKPOINT 5

1 Find,

a the total of the interior angles of a quadrilateral

b the total of the exterior angles of a quadrilateral

c the size of the interior angles of a regular quadrilateral

d the size of the exterior angles of a regular quadrilateral.

2 Repeat Question **1** for:

a a triangle   **b** a hexagon   **c** an octagon (8 sides).

3 What do you notice about the total of the exterior angles for each shape? Can you prove that this result must always be true?

4 If the interior angles of a polygon add to 2160°, how many sides does it have?

5 If a regular polygon has interior angles of 162°, how many sides does it have?

6 ABCDEFGHIJKL is a regular 12-sided polygon with centre O.

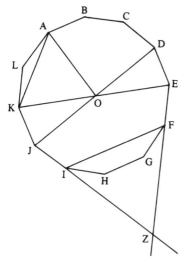

Find the angles;

a ALK   **b** AKO   **c** JKO   **d** AKJ
e DJI   **f** HIZ   **g** FIH   **h** IZF

Tessellations

A **tessellation** is a pattern of recurring shapes which covers a flat surface leaving no gaps or overlaps. For example, it is possible to fit regular hexagons together in this way to form a tessellation.

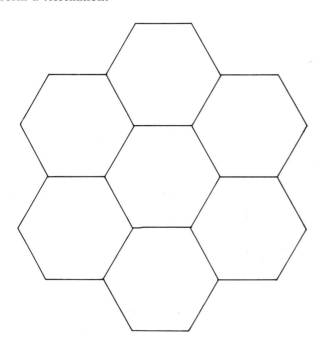

If we examine any point in the tessellation where the vertices (corner points) of the hexagons meet, we see that three hexagons, each with an interior angle of 120°, fit together to form a complete angle of 360°.

CHECKPOINT 6

1 This is an regular triangle (equilateral triangle).

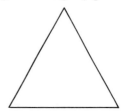

Trace the triangle onto card and then cut it out to form a template. Draw round your template to form a tessellation of equilateral triangles. Can you discover more than one possible tessellation of equilateral triangles?

2 This is a regular quadrilateral (square).

Trace the triangle onto card and then cut it out to form a template. Draw round your template to form a tessellation of squares. Can you discover more than one possible tessellation of squares?

3 Can you discover a tessellation which uses a combination of squares and equilateral triangles?

4 This is a regular pentagon.

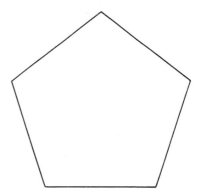

Trace the triangle onto card and then cut it out to form a template. Can you discover a tessellation of regular pentagons? If you cannot discover a tessellation, can you prove that it is not possible to tesselate with regular pentagons?

5 This is a regular hexagon.

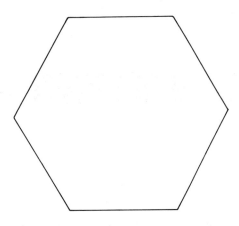

Trace the hexagon onto card and then cut it out to form a template. Can you discover a tessellation of equilateral triangles and regular hexagons? Can you discover a tessellation of equilateral triangles, squares and regular hexagons?

6 This diagram shows a tessellation formed from an irregular triangle. Investigate some other tessellations with irregular triangles. Do you think a tessellation can be formed from **any** irregular triangle?

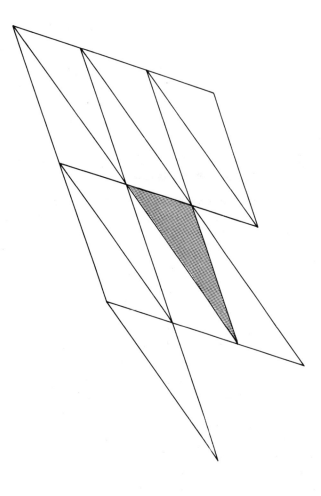

7 This diagram shows a tessellation formed from an irregular quadrilateral. Investigate some other tessellations with irregular quadrilaterals. Do you think a tessellation can be formed from **any** irregular quadrilateral? What about a trapezium, a parallelogam, a rhombus, a rectangle or a kite?

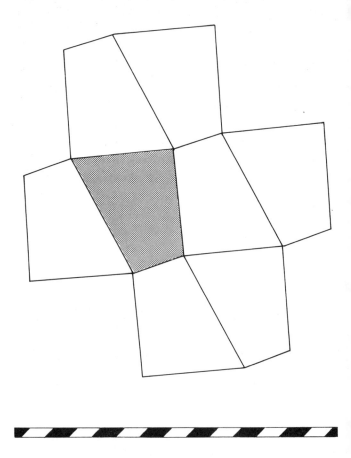

An infinite number of tessellations can be formed, many of a very striking artistic quality. The **Alhambra** is a palace built by the Moors in Southern Spain in the thirteenth century. The Moors were Muslims and stricly observed their second commandment:

"Thou shalt not make thee any graven image"

Consequently their artists used only abstract designs and decorated the walls of the Alhambra (see next page) with many examples of ingenious tessellations, for which the palace is still famous. The Dutch artist Maurits Escher is said to have found the Alhambra a source of inspirations for some of his famous illustrations, although, unlike the Moors, Escher used people and animals as the basis for many tessellations.

Tessellations are used to decorate many Muslim buildings, such as the Alhambra palace in Spain.

CHECKPOINT 7

These are some examples of more complex shapes which form tessellations. Use tracing paper and card to make copies of these shapes and use them to draw tessellations.

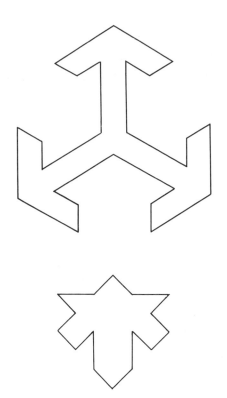

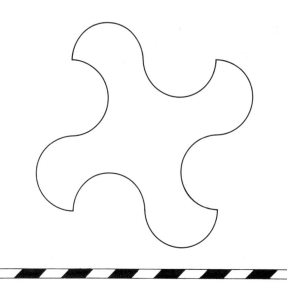

Angles and circles

A line which joins two points on the circumference of a circle is called a **chord**. A chord which passes through the centre of the circle is called a **diameter.** This diagram shows some chords and a diameter drawn in a circle.

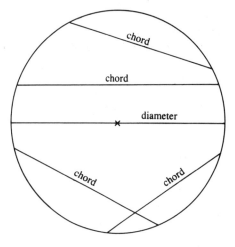

From the ends of any given chord, it is possible to construct one angle at the centre of the circle and many different angles on the circle itself.

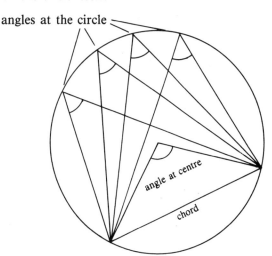

There is an important relationship between the angle drawn at the centre from a chord and an angle drawn at the circle. To prove this result, we must first prove a simple fact about isosceles triangles. Look at this isosceles triangle.

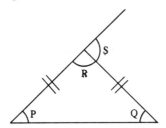

angle P = angle Q (PQR is an isosceles triangle).
angle R + angle P + angle Q = 180° (angles of a triangle).
So, angle R + (2 × angle P) = 180°
But, angle R + angle S = 180° (they form a straight line), therefore, angle S = 2 × angle P

So, we have proved that

The exterior angle drawn opposite to the equal angles of an isosceles triangle is exactly twice the size of the equal angles.

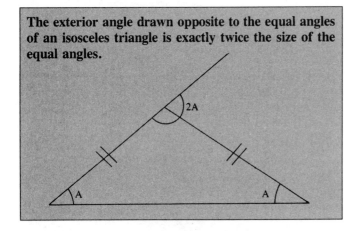

We can now use this result to prove an important connection between angles drawn on a chord. Look at this diagram.

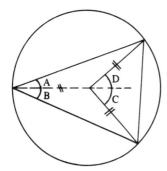

angle D = 2 × angle A
angle C = 2 × angle B
Therefore, angle C + angle D = 2 × (angle A + angle B) and we have proved that

The angle drawn from a chord to the centre of a circle is twice as large as an angle drawn from the chord to the circle.

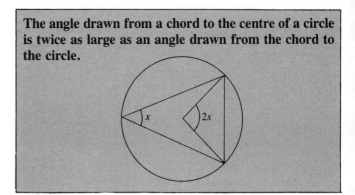

Example

Find angles
a QPR   **b** OQR

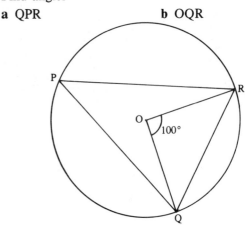

a Angle QPR = ½ of angle QOR. So, angle QPR = 50°
b angle OQR = ½ of (180° − 100°), because triangle QOR is isosceles. So, angle OQR = 40°

CHECKPOINT 8

1 Find angles   **a** YOZ   **b** OZY

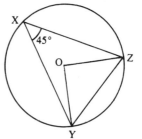

2 Find angles   **a** AOB   **b** ACB

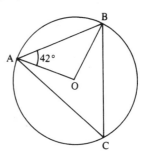

3 Find angles **a** POQ   **b** OPQ

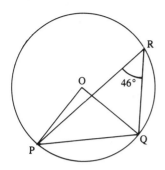

4 Find angles **a** OPN   **b** OMN

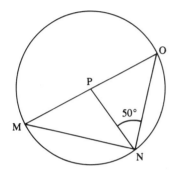

5 Find angles **a** AOB   **b** ACB

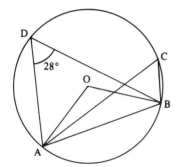

6 Find angles **a** ACB   **b** CAB.

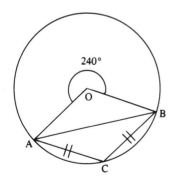

Two further angle relationships can be deduced directly from the results we have proved.

1 Since any angle drawn from a chord to the circle must be half the size of a fixed angle at the centre,

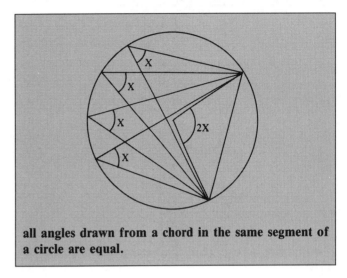

all angles drawn from a chord in the same segment of a circle are equal.

2 Since all the angles drawn in a semi-circle must be half of an angle of 180° at the centre,

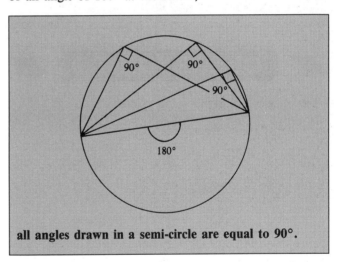

all angles drawn in a semi-circle are equal to 90°.

Examples

1 Find angles
a PRS   **b** PSR   **c** QXR

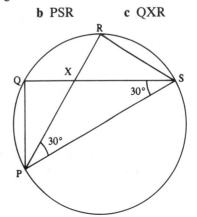

a Angle PRS = 90° (angle in a semicircle).

b Angle PSR = 180° − (30° + 90°) = 60°

c Angle QXR = angle PXS = 180° − (30° + 30°) = 120°.

2 Find angles **a** FEG **b** EGF **c** EFG

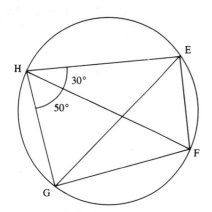

a Angle FEG = angle FHG = 50° (both angles are on the chord FG).

b Angle EGF = angle EHF = 30° (both angles are on the chord EF).

c Angle EFG = 180° − (50° + 30°) = 100°.

CHECKPOINT 9

1 Find angles **a** ACB **b** ADB

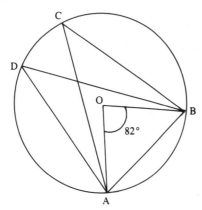

2 Find angles **a** MON **b** MRN **c** MQN **d** MPN

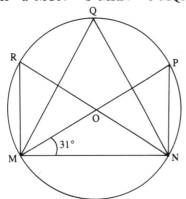

3 Find angles **a** QPR **b** PQR **c** QOR **d** QSR

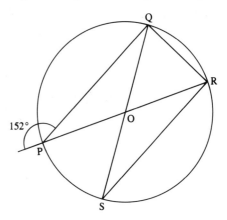

4 Find angles **a** ABD **b** BCD **c** DBC **d** ABC

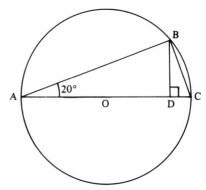

5 Find angles **a** SPQ **b** SQP **c** RPQ **d** PRQ

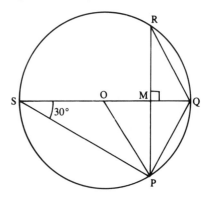

6 Find angles **a** XZY **b** WXZ **c** XOY **d** XUY

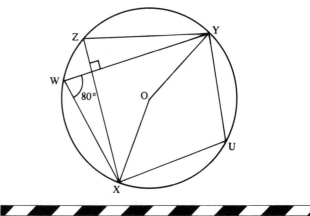

Maps, plans and drawings

The achievements of the architects of Babylon and Egypt are truly astonishing. For example, the four-sided Pyramid of Cheops was built so that the sides faced North, South, East and West with an error of less than 1° and the base was almost perfectly square and level. The plans for these great constructions were laid out using only simple geometrical instruments like a straight edge and a pair of compasses. Here are some of the techniques that were used.

To bisect a straight line.

1   2

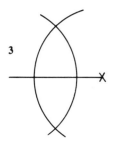
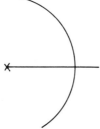

3   4

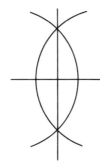

To bisect an angle.

1   2

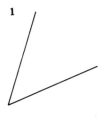
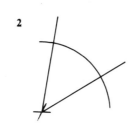

3

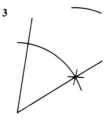

4   5

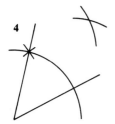

To connect a point to a line so that an angle of 90° is formed.

1   2

3   4

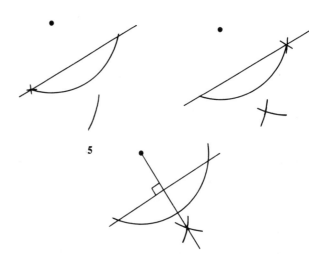

5

Angles of any size can be drawn by using a protractor. Two angles, 90° and 60°, can also be constructed using a pair of compasses.

To construct an angle of 90° at a point on a line.

1   2

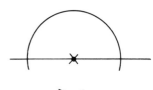

3   4

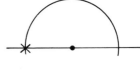
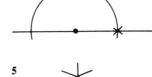

5

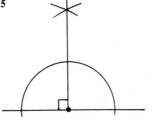

To construct an angle of 60° at a point on a line.

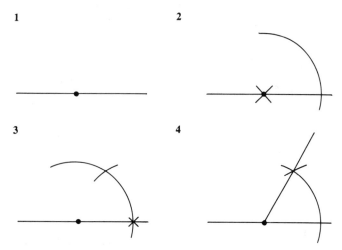

These drawing techniques can be used to solve a variety of practical problems.

Examples

1 Standing 25 metres from the base of a cliff, a student measures the angle of elevation of the top of the cliff as 60°. If the student makes this measurement with an instrument held 1.5 metres from the ground, how high is the cliff?

Using a scale of 1 centimetre = 5 metres, we can draw this diagram.

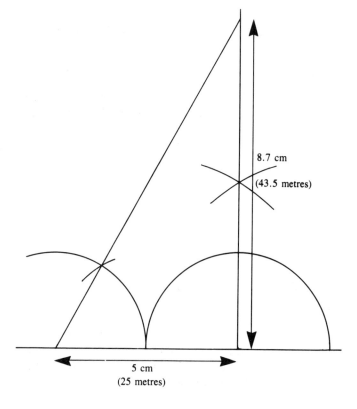

Remembering to add on the 1.5 metres for the height of the instrument, this gives a height for the cliff of 45 metres.

Three towns form a triangle with sides of 12 km, 15 km and 20 km. A supermarket chain wishes to build an out of town superstore. Their planning department suggests that the superstore should be the same distance from each of the three towns. Show the relative positions of the three towns on a diagram and the suggested position for the superstore.

Using a scale 1 centimetre = 2 kilometres, we can draw a base line of 10 cm to represent the 20 km distance. Using a compass, first set at 6 cm and then set at 7.5 cm we can draw arcs to find the relative position of the third town.

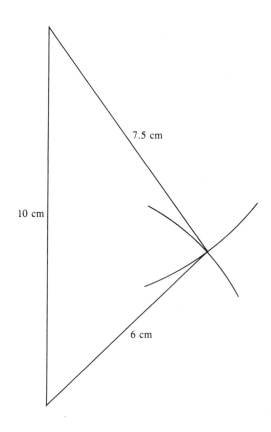

If we bisect one side of the triangle, we will obtain a line on which each point is an equal distance from two of the towns.

Bisecting a second side will give a line on which each point is an equal distance from one of these towns and the third town.

Where these lines cross gives a point that is an equal distance from all three towns. Is this, in fact, the best location for the store? Was the planning department's suggestion a good one?

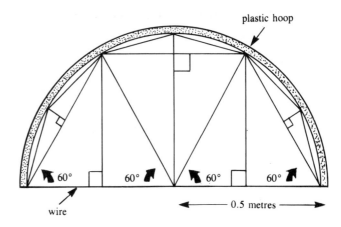

plastic hoop

60°　60°　60°　60°

wire

0.5 metres

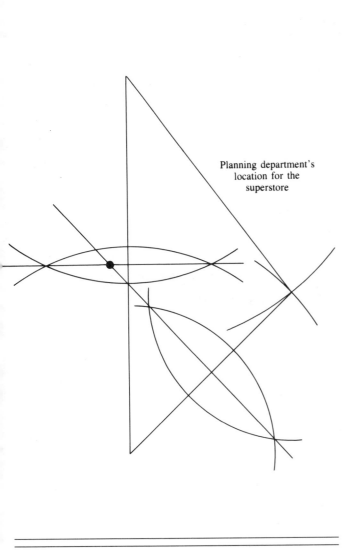

Planning department's
location for the
superstore

1 A ladder 6 metres long rests against a wall with the feet of the ladder 1.5 metres from the base of the wall. How far does the ladder reach up the wall?

2 Construct a triangle with sides 12 cm, 15 cm and 9 cm long. Bisect the interior angles of the triangle. What do you notice? Does this happen in all triangles? What if you bisect the sides rather than the angles?

3 Will an umbrella which is 1 metre long fit inside a suitcase which has inside dimensions of 90 cm by 50 cm?

4 Chelmsford is 30 km to the West and 25 km to the South of Ipswich. Find the direct distance between Chelmsford and Ipswich.

5 This diagram shows a sketch for a framework to be made from steel wire to brace a semi-circular plastic hoop. Find the total length of wire needed to make the framework.

6 Three towns form a triangle with sides 40 km, 50 km and 25 km.

a A TV transmitter is to be built in a position which is as close as possible to being the same distance from each town. Draw a map showing the relative position of the three towns and the ideal location for the transmitter.

7 Amberbridge is 25 km from Beaverbrooke and 50 km from Smidgley. Smidgley is 40 km from Beaverbrooke. A plane flies over Amberbridge on a flight path which bisects the angle formed by Smidgley, Amberbridge and Beaverbrooke. As the plane continues along this flight path, what is the closest that it comes to Smidgley?

8 A camping site is in the form of a triangle with straight sides 100 metres, 150 metres and 180 metres long. Busy roads run along all three sides of the site. Draw a diagram of the site and find the position to pitch a tent so that it is as far away as possible from all three roads.

Bearings

Bearings are used to measure the direction in which one location lies from another. For example, this sketch map shows the locations of Cambridge and Norwich.

Three steps are needed to measure the bearing of Norwich from Cambridge.

● Draw in a line connecting Cambridge to Norwich.
● Draw in a line through Cambridge pointing due North.
● Measure the clockwise angle between the North line and the line connecting the two places.

When these steps have been completed our sketch map looks like this.

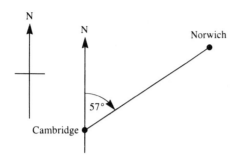

Bearings are always written with three figures, even if the measured angle is less than 100°. So, the bearing of Norwich from Cambridge is 057°.

Notice that the bearing of Cambridge from Norwich is **not** the same as the bearing of Norwich from Cambridge. This map shows the necessary construction to measure the bearing of Cambridge from Norwich.

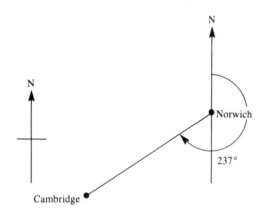

The bearing of Cambridge from Norwich is 237°.

Bearings

Remember, the three steps necessary to measure the bearing of Location B from Location A are:

- draw in a line AB connecting the two locations
- draw in a line through Location A pointing due North
- measure the clockwise angle between the North line and the line connecting the two locations, AB.

Example

Sheffield is 40 miles to the West and 10 miles to the North of Lincoln. What is the bearing of Sheffield from Lincoln?

The sketch was drawn to a scale 1 cm = 5 miles and shows the construction steps necessary to measure the bearing.

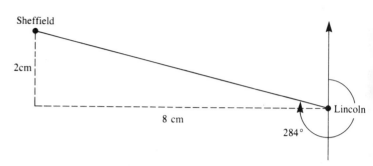

The bearing of Sheffield from Lincoln is 284°.

---

1 Make a copy of this sketch map and measure the bearing of

a Brighton from Gloucester
b Norwich from Luton
c Plymouth from Lowestoft
d Cardiff from Birmingham
e Peterborough from Margate
f Gloucester from Luton
g Peterborough from Brighton
h Margate from Birmingham

2 Newcastle-on-Tyne is 70 miles to the North and 50 miles to the East of Kendal.

a What is the bearing of Newcastle from Kendal?

b What is the bearing of Kendal from Newcastle?

3 Manchester is 40 miles to the North and 40 miles to the West of Nottingham.

a What is the bearing of Manchester from Nottingham?

b What is the bearing of Nottingham from Manchester?

4 Bradford is 150 miles to the North and 40 miles to the West of Chelmsford.

a What is the bearing of Bradford from Chelmsford?

b What is the bearing of Chelmsford from Bradford?

Three-dimensional objects (nets and drawings)

We have already learnt how to find the volumes of common 3-D objects like cubes, cuboids, cylinders, spheres, cones and prisms. We will now consider the **nets** of these basic solids. The net of a solid is the flat shape which, when cut out and folded, would form the outer skin of the solid. For example, this is one possible net for a cube.

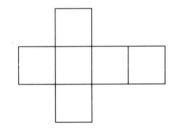

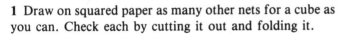

CHECKPOINT 12

1 Draw on squared paper as many other nets for a cube as you can. Check each by cutting it out and folding it.

2 Draw a net for a cuboid which is 4 cm wide, 5 cm high and 8 cm long. Check your net by cutting it out and folding it.

3 This diagram shows three open-topped boxes, A, B and C and three nets, D, E and F. Match each box to one of the nets.

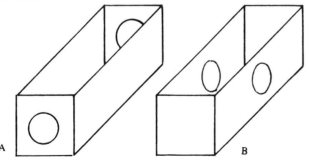

C

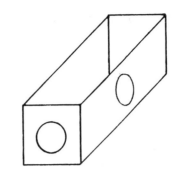

D

E

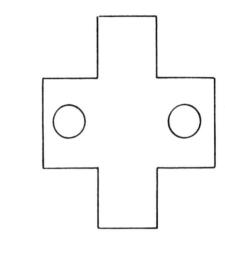

F

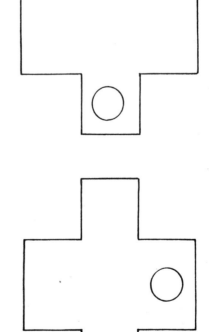

209

4 Draw a net for a cylinder with a radius of 3 cm and a length of 10 cm. Check your net by cutting it out and folding it.

5 Draw a net for a cone. Check your net by cutting it out and folding it.

6 Describe the solids that you think each of the following nets will make. Check your answers by copying the nets, cutting them out and folding them.

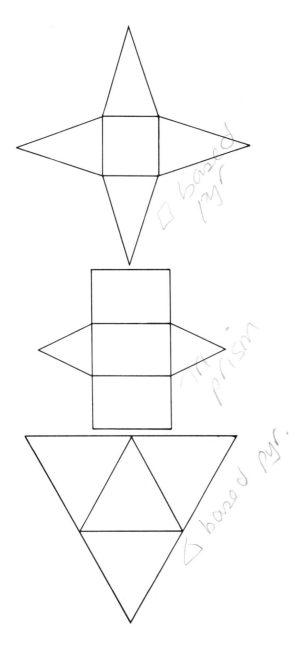

7 Jeff, Mary and Raj are all looking at the same parked car. Jeff is cycling straight towards the car. Mary is directly opposite the car, waiting to cross the road. Raj is looking down from the 12th floor of the building the car is parked in front of. These are the three views of the car. Who sees which picture?

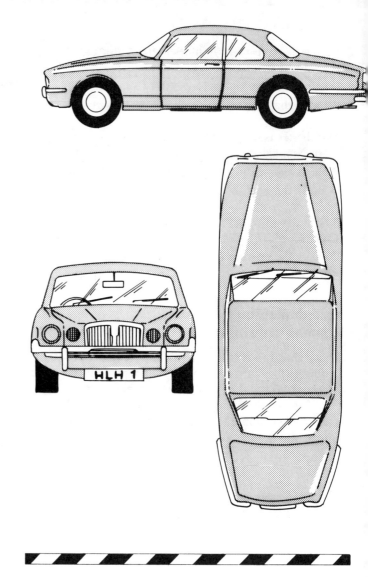

A view from directly overhead is called a **plan view**. A view from the same level as the object is called an **elevation**. This diagram shows a sketch of a pencil sharpener with a plan and two elevations of the same sharpener.

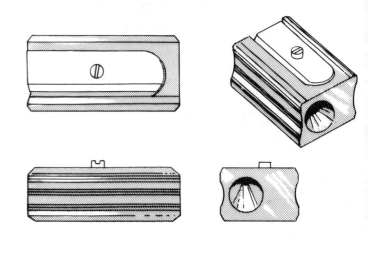

1 These diagrams show sketches, plans and elevations of a cube, a cuboid, a cylinder, a cone, a triangular prism and a square based pyramid. Copy the diagrams, matching the plans and elevations to the correct sketch.

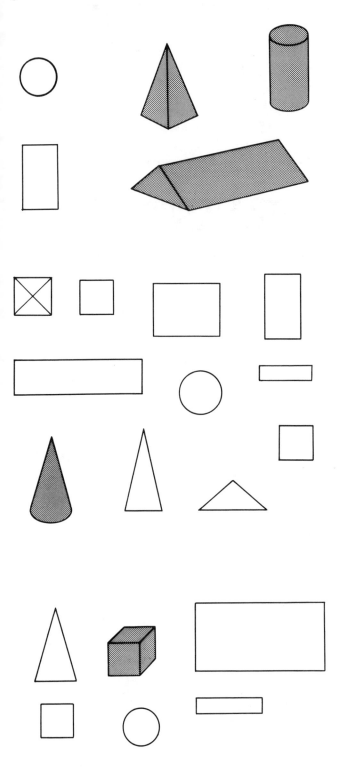

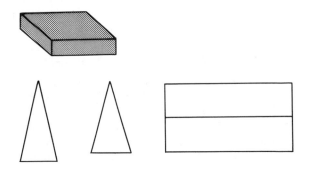

2 This sketch shows a simple model house. Draw a plan of the house and elevations from the directions indicated by the arrows.

3 This sketch shows a pile of 4 centimetre cube building bricks. Draw a plan of the pile and elevations from the directions indicated by the arrows.

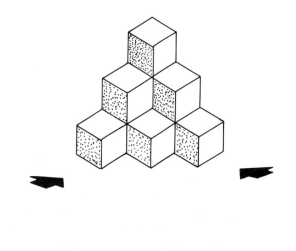

Paths of moving points

A ladder 6 metres long is leaning against a wall with its foot 1.5 metres from the foot of the wall. A window cleaner is standing at a point 4 metres up the ladder. If the foot of the ladder slips away from the wall, what path will the window cleaner follow as he falls with the ladder?

We can answer this question by drawing the ladder in several different positions as it slips away from the wall. This will give us a set of points that the falling window cleaner passes through. Joining this points with a smooth curve will give us the path followed. This is the completed diagram.

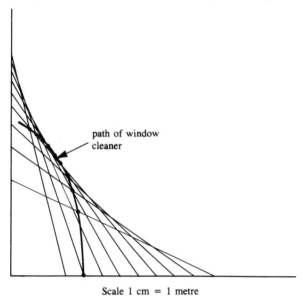

path of window cleaner

Scale 1 cm = 1 metre

The set of points occupied by a body moving under fixed conditions is called a **locus** (locus is the Latin word for place or position).

Sometimes a locus is very simple, for example, when a weight is swung on the end of a string, the locus it traces out is a circle.

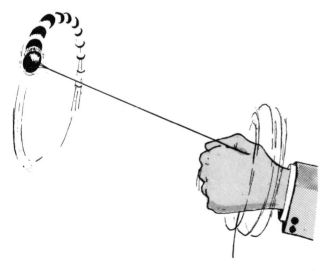

In other cases, a locus can be very complicated. For example,

what would you predict for the locus of the pencil point passed through the hole in this linkage?

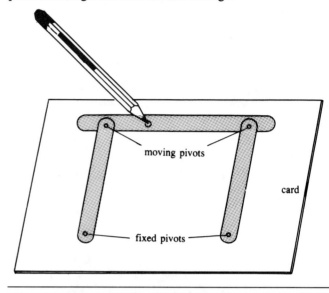

moving pivots

card

fixed pivots

CHECKPOINT 14

1 In this diagram, the point P moves in such a way that it is always 3 cm from the line AB. Copy the diagram and mark on it the locus of the point P.

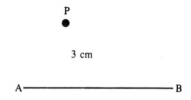

P

3 cm

A ————————— B

2 In this diagram, the point P moves in such a way that its distance from the point A is always equal to its distance from the point B. Copy the diagram and mark on it the locus of the point P.

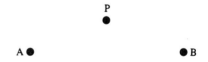

P

A ●   ● B

3 In this diagram, the point P moves in such a way that its distance from the line AC is always equal to its distance from the line AB. Copy the diagram and mark on it the locus of the point P.

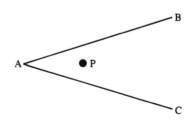

212

4 This diagram shows the square side of a packing case resting on a level floor. The packing case is rolled along the floor, tipping it over each corner in turn. Draw a diagram to show the locus of corner A as the case is moved in this way.

5 A fierce dog is tied to a stake at one end of a 5 metre long passageway which is 2 metres wide. The rope holding the dog is 8 metres long. Copy this diagram (using a scale of 1 cm to 1 m) which shows the passageway seen from above and mark on it the locus of the dog's movements as it strains against the rope.

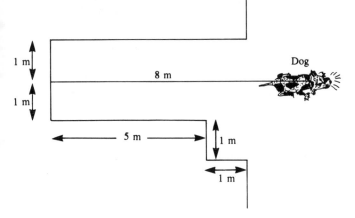

6 ABCD is a parallelogram with AB=8 cm and BC=5 cm. E is a point on AB, 2 cm from A.

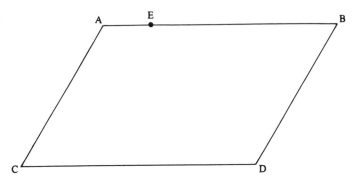

a Using the same base line CD, draw parallelograms ABCD as the angle ADC takes the values; 30°, 45°, 60° and 90°.
b What is the locus of the point E?

7 This diagram shows a point P which is marked on centimetre squared paper 4 cm from a line AB.

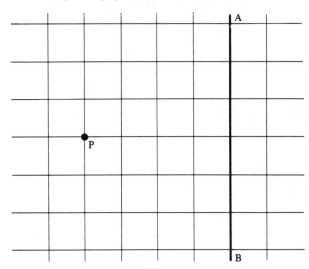

We can use the following construction to find two positions for a moving point which is both 5 cm from the line AB and 5 cm from the point P.

First, we draw an arc on the point P with a radius of 5 cm.

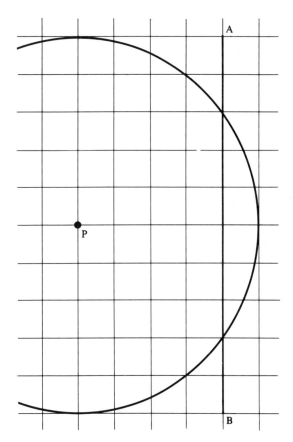

Where this arc cuts the line on the squared paper 5 cm from AB gives two possible positions for a point that is 5 cm from the point P and 5 cm from the line AB.

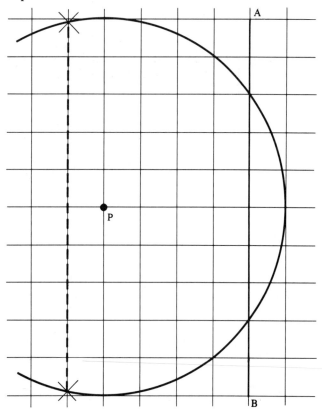

Use this technique to find the locus of a point which moves so that its distance from the point P is always equal to its distance from the line AB.

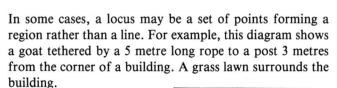

In some cases, a locus may be a set of points forming a region rather than a line. For example, this diagram shows a goat tethered by a 5 metre long rope to a post 3 metres from the corner of a building. A grass lawn surrounds the building.

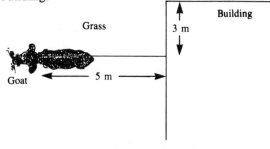

The goat can move about and eat the grass at any point in the shaded region shown below. This region is the **locus** of the goat's movements.

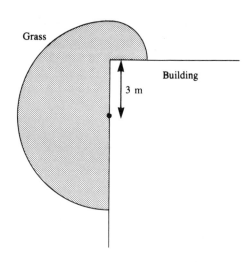

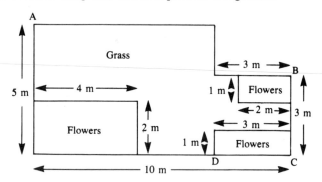

CHECKPOINT 15

1 A goat is kept in a back garden, tied to a post so that she can't eat all the grass at once. The rope that ties the goat is 4 metres long and this is a plan of the garden.

a Draw diagrams to show the locus of the goat's movements if she is tied to a post at points A, B, C or D. Shade the grass and flowers that can be eaten in different colours.
b Draw a diagram to show where the goat should be tied so that she will be able to eat as few flowers as possible.

2 In this diagram, the point P moves in such a way that its distance from the point A is always less than its distance from the point B. Copy the diagram and shade on it the locus of the point P.

3 In this diagram, the point P moves in such a way that is is always less than 3 cm from the line AB. Copy the diagram and shade on it the locus of the point P.

214

4 In this diagram, the point P moves in such a way that its distance from the line AC is always greater than its distance from the line AB. Copy the diagram and shade on it the locus of the point P.

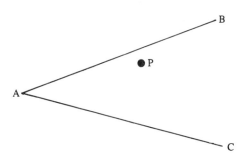

5 A fierce dog is tied to a stake at one end of a 5 metre long passageway which is 2 metres wide. The rope holding the dog is 8 metres long. A cat which enters any part of the area the dog can reach is in great danger. Copy this diagram (using a scale of 1 cm to 1 m) which shows the passageway seen from above and shade on it the danger area for cats.

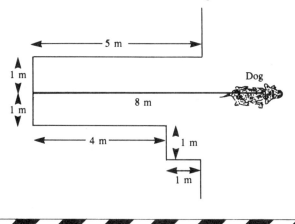

The solution of some locus problems will require a knowledge of the properties of angles drawn in a circle. You will need to remember and use these two results in the box.

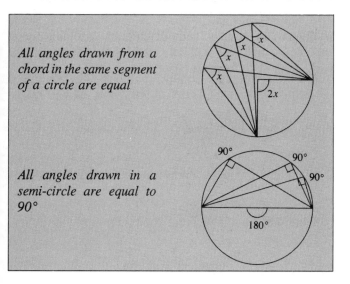

All angles drawn from a chord in the same segment of a circle are equal

All angles drawn in a semi-circle are equal to 90°

The following examples and checkpoint introduce locus problems which depend on these two angle properties.

Examples

1 Two points X and Y are 5 cm apart. A point P moves in such a way that the angle XPY is always equal to 30°. What is the locus of P?

We can answer this question in an experimental way by cutting an angle of 30° from card. If we then mark two points X and Y 5 cm apart, we can use the card angle to find the position of the set of points for which XPY = 30°.

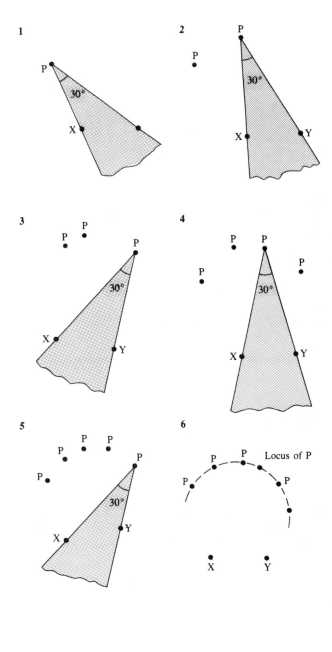

The set of points form an arc of a circle. XY is a chord of this circle. We could have predicted this result because we know that all angles drawn from a chord in the same segment of a circle are equal.

2 This diagram shows a ship C which is sailing on a course 3 km away from and parallel to a straight coastline. Two lighthouses, A and B, stand 10 km apart on the coastline. When the ship reaches the point X, it follows a course which maintains angle ACB equal to 90° until the ship reaches point Y. The ship then continues on its course parallel to the coastline. Using a scale of 1 cm = 1 km, copy the diagram and mark the locus of the ship's movements between points X and Y.

Angle ACB is always equal to 90° as the ship sails between X and Y. This means that any point on the ship's path must lie on a semi-circle with AB as a diameter. By setting a pair of compasses to 5 cm, we can draw in an arc to show the path of the ship between X and Y. This is the completed diagram.

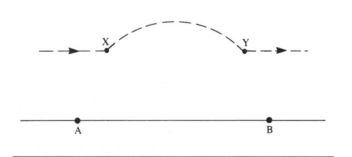

CHECKPOINT 16

1 Using angles cut from card, investigate the locus of a point which maintains a fixed angle with two fixed points. What effect does the distance between the fixed points have on the locus? What effect does the size of the fixed angle have on the locus?

2 Mark two points A and B on plain paper, 8 cm apart. Find one possible position for the point P, so that angle APB = 60°.

a Using compasses, construct the perpendicular bisector of AB.

b Using compasses, construct the perpendicular bisector of AP.

c Using compasses, draw in the locus of the point P if angle APB is always equal to 60°.

3 This is a sketch of a simple bookrack.

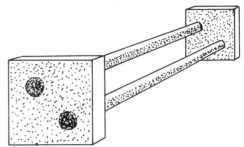

This is an end view of the bookcase, showing one book resting on the rails.

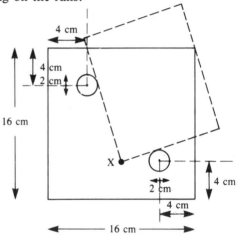

Draw a diagram to show the locus of the corner X of the book. Comment on your diagram.

Transformation Geometry

The geometry of Euclid did not take into consideration the **position** of an object. If two triangles had equal side lengths and angles, they were considered to be identical, even if they were in quite different positions.

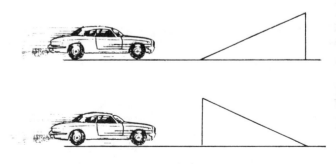

Identical Triangles?

216

During the eighteenth, nineteenth and twentieth centuries, geometries were developed which did take into consideration the position of an object and also the ways in which that position can be changed. **It was discovered that all changes in position could be described in terms of three basic movements: translations, rotations and reflections.**

Translations

A **translation** changes the position of an object by moving every point on the object through the same distance in the same direction.

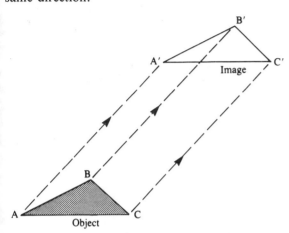

The shape in the new position is usually called the **image** and if the object is lettered ABC, the image is often lettered A′B′C′. Translations are most easily applied or described when objects are drawn on a square grid or a graph. For example, this grid shows a shaded quadrilateral translated to a new position.

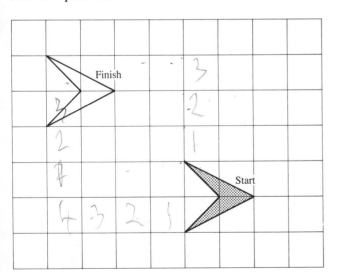

To describe this translation, we break down the complete movement that has taken place into two separate movements. The **horizontal movement** and the **vertical movement**. In this case, a horizontal movement of 4 units to the left and a vertical movement of 3 units upwards. These movements are often written in a vertical bracket using the

normal + and − conventions for left and right and up and down. Our translation would be written like this

$$\begin{pmatrix} -4 \\ +3 \end{pmatrix}$$

This is the general way that translations on a square grid are described.

$$\begin{pmatrix} \overset{-}{\leftarrow}\text{horizontal movement}\overset{+}{\rightarrow} \\ \overset{\uparrow +}{\text{vertical movement}} \\ \downarrow - \end{pmatrix}$$

This diagram shows how seven other translations applied to the shaded quadrilateral are described. Check carefully that you understand this diagram.

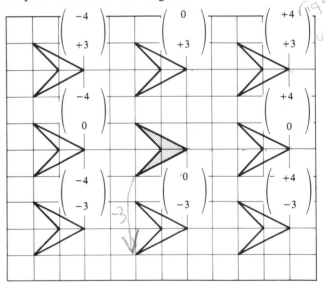

CHECKPOINT 17

1 Copy this diagram and write beside each triangle the translation which moves the shaded triangle to that position.

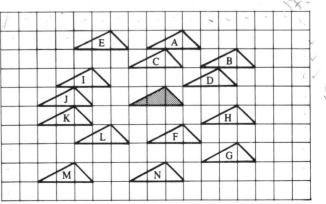

217

2 Draw a graph with *x*- and *y*-axes from −6 to +6. Plot the triangle with corner points at (0,1),(−3,1) and (−3,2). Show on your graph the new position of this triangle after each of the following translations.

a $\begin{pmatrix} +5 \\ +4 \end{pmatrix}$ **b** $\begin{pmatrix} +3 \\ -2 \end{pmatrix}$ **c** $\begin{pmatrix} +5 \\ 0 \end{pmatrix}$ **d** $\begin{pmatrix} 0 \\ -4 \end{pmatrix}$

e $\begin{pmatrix} -4 \\ 0 \end{pmatrix}$ **f** $\begin{pmatrix} -3 \\ +3 \end{pmatrix}$ **g** $\begin{pmatrix} -3 \\ -7 \end{pmatrix}$ **h** $\begin{pmatrix} +4 \\ -8 \end{pmatrix}$

Rotations

A **rotation** changes the position of an object by turning it about a fixed point called the **centre of rotation**.

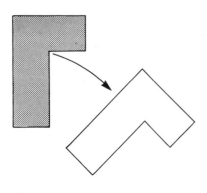

✕
Centre of rotation

We describe a rotation by stating three facts.

- The angle that the object has been rotated through
- The direction of rotation (anticlockwise or clockwise)
- The position of the centre of rotation

This rotation

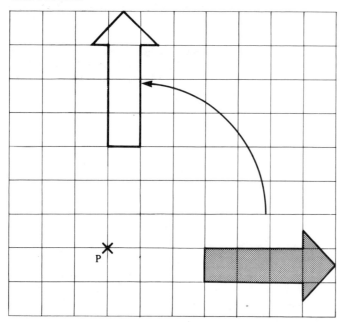

would be described as

- a rotation of 90°
- anticlockwise
- about the point P.

For rotations, anticlockwise is considered the positive direction and clockwise the negative direction.

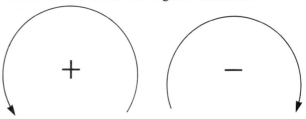

Anticlockwise rotations   Clockwise rotations
are positive   are negative

This diagram shows a rotation of +270° about the point M.

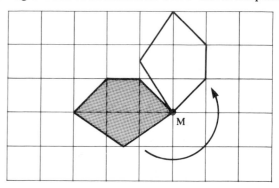

Rotations are most easily completed by using tracing paper to copy the object to be rotated. A pencil point can then be placed on the centre of rotation, the tracing paper turned through the correct angle and the object copied into its new position. Most examination questions are completed on squared paper and involve only angles of 90°, 180° or 270°. It is very easy to judge when the tracing paper has turned through these angles by observing the lines on the squared paper.

CHECKPOINT 18

1 Describe the rotations which move the shaded triangle to each new position in this diagram. Remember these rules.

> **Rules for describing rotations**
>
> - The angle that the triangle has been rotated through
> - The direction of rotation (positive or negative)
> - The position of the centre of rotation

218

+90° around pt P

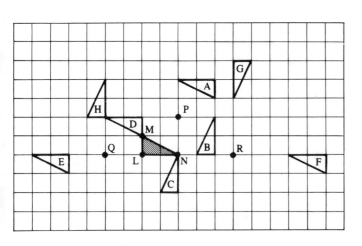

2 Copy each of the following diagrams and draw in the image of the object after the stated rotation about the marked point.

a 180° about P.   **b** −90° about M.

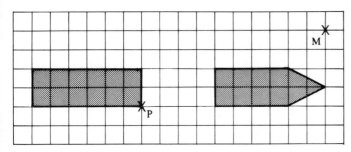

c +90° about Q.   **d** −270° about T.

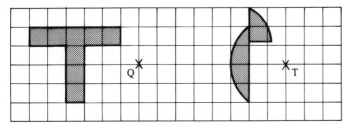

e +270° about R.

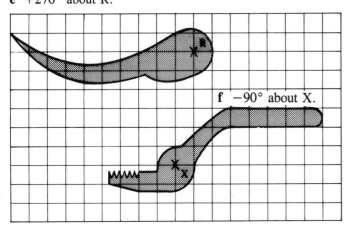

f −90° about X.

3 This diagram demonstrates that a rotation of −90° about a point is equivalent to a rotation of +270° about the same point.

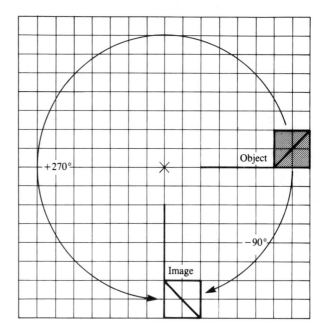

Draw diagrams to illustrate two other pairs of equivalent rotations.

4 Draw a graph with x- and y-axes from −6 to +6. Plot the triangle with corner points at (0,1),(−3,1) and (−3,2). Show on your graph the new position of this triangle after each of the following rotations.

a −90° about (0,0)   **b** +180° about (0,0)
c +90° about (0,0)   **d** +270° about (−3,2)
e −270° about (0,6)   **f** −180° about (−1,2)

Sometimes you may be asked to complete a rotation on plain paper, or through an angle that cannot be easily judged on squared paper. For example, this object is to be rotated through −60° about the point O.

 O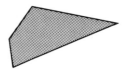

Because there is no background against which we can measure a rotation of −60°, we must construct our own guideline. First, we join the object to the centre of rotation and then, using a protractor, draw in an angle of 60° in the clockwise direction.

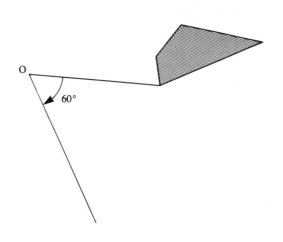

We can now use tracing paper and the guideline we have constructed to complete the required rotation.

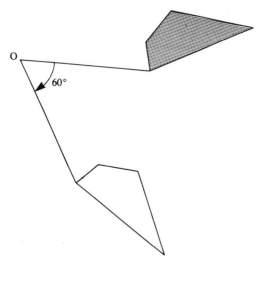

Copy each of the following diagrams and draw in the image of the object after the stated rotation about the marked point.

a +60° about P.   **b** −120° about O.

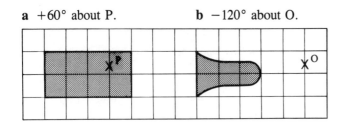

c +200° about X.   **d** −40° about Q.

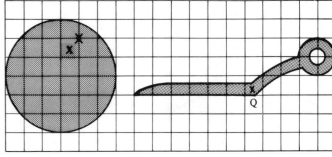

e +300° about A.   **f** −50° about P.

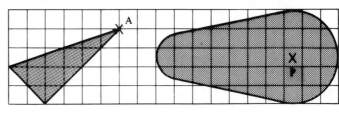

Reflections

A reflection creates an image of an object in the same way that a mirror does. If you place a small mirror along the reflection line in this diagram, you will see an image in the mirror which is identical to the one that has been drawn on the page.

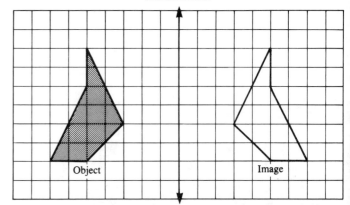

To complete a mathematical reflection

● Each point on the image must be the same distance from the mirror line as the corresponding point on the object
● A line joining a point on the object to the corresponding point on the image must cross the mirror line at right angles.

Examples

1

GCSE   OBJECT

GCƧE   IMAGE

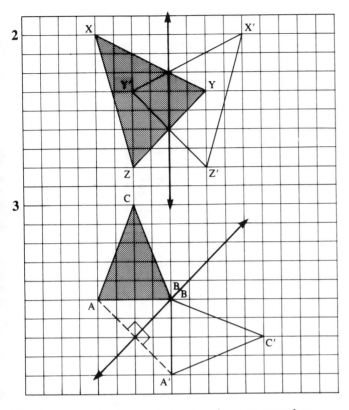

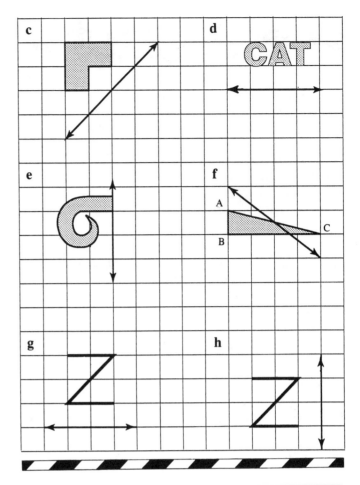

The last example demonstrates two important points.

• The line joining the object point to the image point **must** cross the mirror line at right angles. This is often forgotten when an inclined mirror line is used to reflect an object and is a common cause of incorrect reflections.

• Reflections do not just change the position of a shape. They also make the shape appear to have been picked up and turned over. This can be seen clearly in the third example because if we read A-B-C round the object we are reading anticlockwise. If we read A'-B'-C' round the image we are reading clockwise.

Copy each of the following diagrams and draw in the image of the object after a reflection in the mirror line.

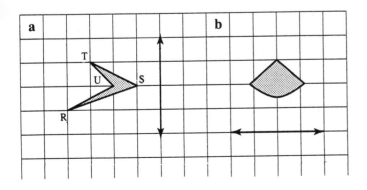

Examples

Draw a graph with x- and y-axes from -6 to $+6$. Plot the triangle with corner points at $(0,1), (-3,1)$ and $(-3,2)$. Show on your graph the new position of this triangle after reflection in each of the following mirror lines.

a The x-axis **b** The y-axis **c** The line with equation $y = 2$
d The line with equation $x = -3$ **e** The line with equation $y = x$

This is the required graph.

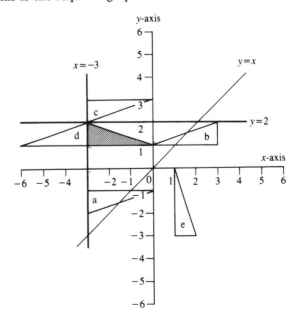

1 Draw a graph with x- and y-axes from -6 to $+6$. Plot the triangle with corner points at $(1,1),(1,2)$ and $(3,1)$. Show on your graph the new position of this triangle after reflection in each of the following mirror lines.

a The x-axis   **b** The y-axis
c The line with equation $y=2$
d The line with equation $x=-1$
e The line with equation $y=x$

2 Draw a graph with x- and y-axes from -6 to $+6$. Plot the rectangle with corner points at $(2,-1),(2,-2),(5,-2)$ and $(5,-1)$. Show on your graph the new position of this rectangle after reflection in each of the following mirror lines.

a The x-axis   **b** The y-axis
c The line with equation $y=-2$
d The line with equation $x=1$
e The line with equation $y=-x$

Enlargements

Translations, rotations and reflections change the position of an object but they do not change the object itself (with the exception that reflection 'flips over' the object).

An **enlargement** changes an object into one with the same **shape** but a different **size**. Enlargements take place about a fixed point called **the centre of enlargement**.

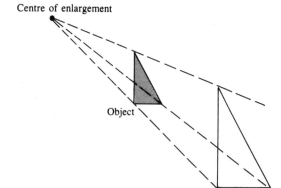

Enlargements

We describe an enlargement by stating two facts.

• The position of the centre of enlargement.

• The scale factor of the enlargement.

This enlargement:

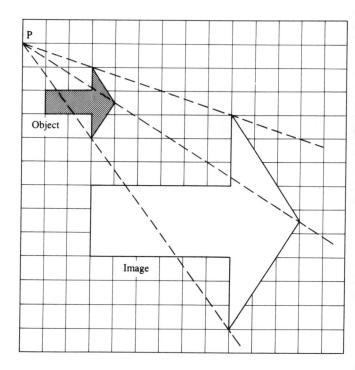

would be described as an enlargement with

• centre P and
• scale factor 3 (because the image is three times bigger than the object).

To complete an enlargement, we draw lines outwards from the centre of enlargement through the main points on the object. Along each of these lines, we first measure the distance of the object point from the centre of enlargement. Multiplying this distance by the scale factor gives us the distance on that line of the image point from the centre of enlargement.

Examples

1 Enlargement, centre P, scale factor 2.

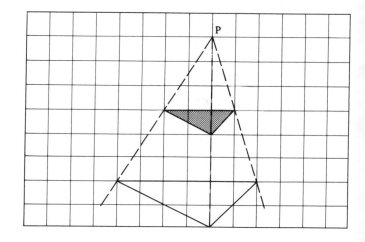

2 Enlargement, centre Q, scale factor 3.

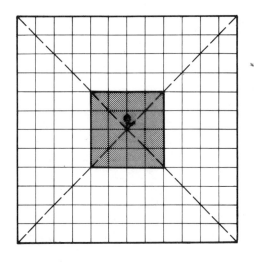

3 Enlargement, centre A, scale factor 4.

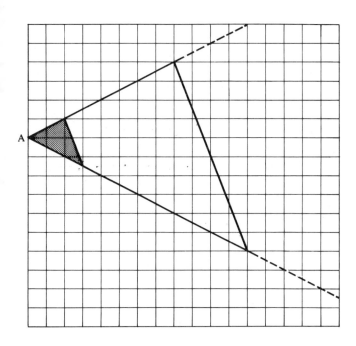

c Centre P, scale factor 2.   **d** Centre P, scale factor 2.

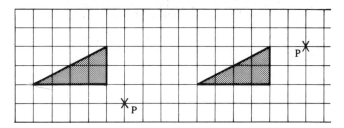

e Centre D, scale factor 2.   **f** Centre M, scale factor 4.

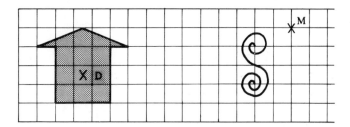

g Centre R, scale factor 4.   **h** Centre P, scale factor 3.

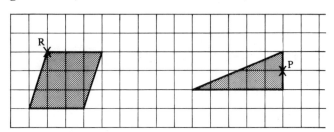

2 Draw a graph with *x*- and *y*-axes from 0 to +12. Plot the triangle with corner points at (1,1),(1,2) and (2,1). Show on your graph the image of this triangle after an enlargement with centre (0,0) and scale factor;

a 2   **b** 3   **c** 4

3 Draw a graph with *x*- and *y*-axes from −12 to +12. Plot the object with corner points at (−2,1),(2,1),(1,−2) and (−1,−2). Show on your graph the image of this object after an enlargement with centre (0,0) and scale factor;

a 2   **b** 3   **c** 4   **d** 5   **e** 6

4 Draw a graph with *x*- and *y*-axes from −6 to +6. Plot the object with corner points at (0,0),(0,1) and (2,0). Show on your graph the image of this object after an enlargement scale factor 2 and centre of enlargement;

a (0,0)   **b** (2,2)   **c** (4,−1)   **d** (0,5)

CHECKPOINT 22

1 Copy each of the following diagrams and draw in the image of the object after the stated enlargement.

a Centre A, scale factor 2.   **b** Centre A, scale factor 3.

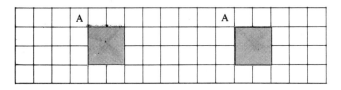

In normal use, the word enlarge means to make something bigger. In maths, enlargements can also make objects smaller! This happens when the scale factor is less than one and consequently the image points are closer to the centre than the object points.

This diagram shows an enlargement, centre P, with scale factor ½.

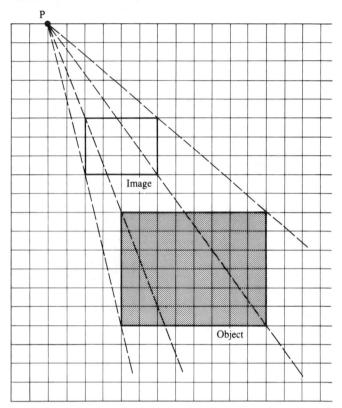

Multiplying all the object point distances by ½ is the same as dividing them by 2. Consequently, all the object point distances are halved and the image is closer to the centre of enlargement and half the size of the object.

Example

This diagram shows enlargements with centre P and scale factors of ½, ⅓ and ¼.

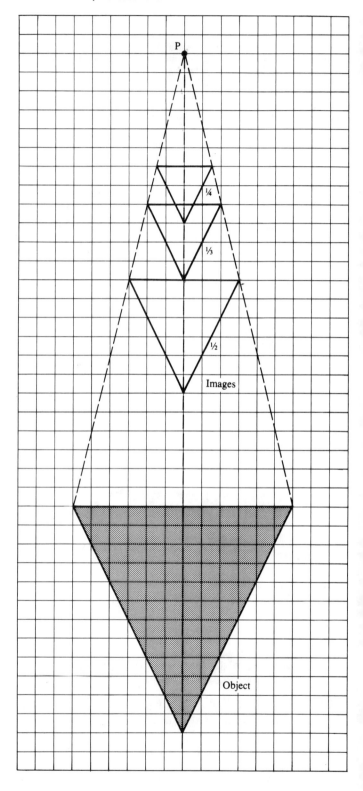

CHECKPOINT 23

1 Copy each of the following diagrams and draw in the image of the object after the stated enlargement.

a Centre M, scale factor ½. **b** Centre A, scale factor ⅓.

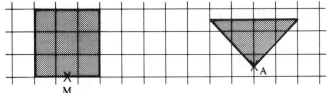

c Centre P, scale factor ½. **d** Centre R, scale factor ⅓.

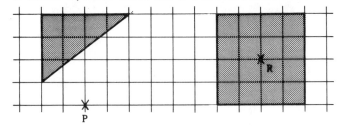

e Centre P, scale factor ½. **f** Centre M, scale factor ¼.

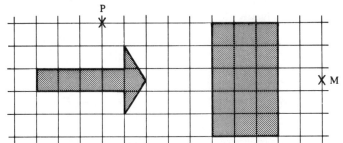

2 Draw a graph with x- and y-axes from 0 to +12. Plot the triangle with corner points at (3,6),(6,3) and (3,3). Show on your graph the image of this triangle after an enlargement with centre (0,0) and scale factor;

a 2 **b** ½ **c** ⅓

This diagram shows an enlargement, centre P, with scale factor −2.

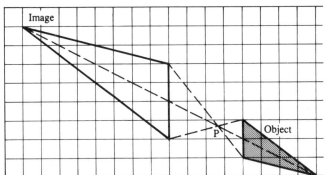

Multiplying the object distances by −2 produces negative distances for the image points. Consequently, all the image point distances are measured on the opposite (negative) side of the centre of enlargement.

Example

This diagram shows enlargements with centre P and scale factors of −2, −3, −1 and −½.

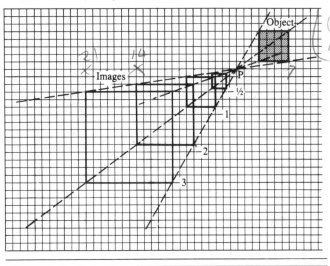

CHECKPOINT 24

1 Copy each of the following diagrams and draw in the image of the object after the stated enlargement.

a Centre P, scale factor −2.

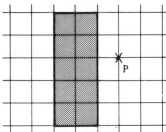

b Centre A, scale factor −1.

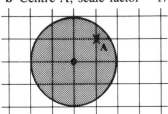

c Centre M, scale factor −3.

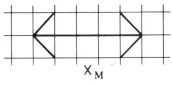

d Centre Q, scale factor −2.

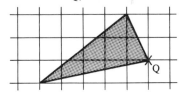

225

e Centre S, scale factor −4.　**f** Centre P, scale factor −5.

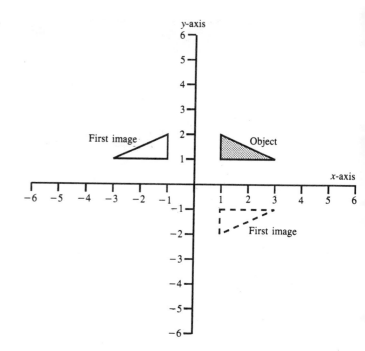

2 Draw a graph with *x*- and *y*-axes from − 12 to + 12. Plot the object with corner points at (2,4),(4,2) and (2,2). Show on your graph the image of this object after an enlargement with centre (0,0) and scale factor

a 2　**b** −2　**c** 3　**d** −3　**e** 1/2　**f** −½

TRANSFORMATIONS

We have now mastered four different ways in which the position and size of an object can be changed. These are;

- Translation ⎫
- Rotation ⎬ (Only position changed)

- Reflection (Position changed and shape 'flipped over')

- Enlargement (Size and position changed)

We call these operations **transformations** because they change or **transform** the object they are applied to.

Sometimes you may be required to apply several transformations in succession to an object.

Example

Draw a graph with *x*- and *y*-axes from − 6 to + 6. Plot the shape at (1,1), (1,2) and (3,1). Show on your graph the image of this shape after it is first reflected in the *x*-axis and then rotated through 180° about the point (0,0). State a single transformation which would have the same effect as this double transformation.

This is the required graph.

We can see from the graph that the single transformation with the same effect as this double transformation is a reflection in the *y*-axis.

The word **equivalent** is used to describe transformations which have the same effect on an object.

So, we can write;

Reflection in the *x*-axis followed by a rotation of 180° about (0,0) is **equivalent** to a reflection in the *y*-axis.

In a problem where several transformations are applied to an object, letters may be used to represent both the transformations and the objects. If the letter P is used to represent a shape and the letters R and T are used to represent transformations then;

- R(P) is the image obtained when R is applied to P
- T(P) is the image obtained when T is applied to P
- RT(P) is the image obtained when *first* T and then R are applied to P
- TR(P) is the image obtained when *first* R and then T are applied to P

Example

P is the object with vertices (corner points) at (1,1), (1,2) and (3,1)

R is a rotation of + 90° about (0,0)

T is the translation $\begin{pmatrix} +3 \\ -3 \end{pmatrix}$

Show in one diagram, P, R(P), T(P), RT(P) and TR(P). State single transformations which are equivalent to RT(P) and TR(P).

This is the required diagram.

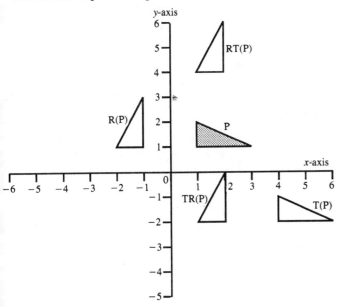

RT(P) is equivalent to a rotation of +90° about the point (0,3)

TR(P) is equivalent to a rotation of +90° about the point (3,0)

CHECKPOINT 25

1 P is the object with vertices (corner points) at (1,1), (1,2) and (3,1)
R is a rotation of +180° about (0,0)
S is a reflection in the *x*-axis
Show in one diagram, P, R(P), S(P), RS(P) and SR(P). State single transformations which are equivalent to RS(P) and SR(P).

2 P is the object with vertices (corner points) at (1,1), (1,2) and (0,1)
R is a reflection in the line with equation *x* = 2
S is a reflection in the line with equation *x* = 4
Show in one diagram, P, R(P), S(P), RS(P) and SR(P). State single transformations which are equivalent to RS(P) and SR(P).

3 P is the object with vertices (corner points) at (1,1), (1,2) and (3,1)
R is a rotation of −90°, about (0,0)
S is a reflection in the *x*-axis
Show in one diagram, P, R(P), S(P), RS(P) and SR(P). State single transformations which are equivalent to RS(P) and SR(P).

4 P is the object with vertices (corner points) at (1,1), (1,2), (2,2) and (2,1).
R is a reflection in *y* = 3
S is a reflection in *x* = 4

Show in one diagram, P, R(P), S(P), RS(P) and SR(P). State single transformations which are equivalent to RS(P) and SR(P).

5 P is the object with vertices (corner points) at (1,1), (1,2), and (3,1).
E is an enlargement with scale factor 2, centre (0,0)
T is the translation $\begin{pmatrix} +3 \\ -3 \end{pmatrix}$

Show in one diagram, P, E(P), T(P), ET(P) and TE(P). State single transformations which are equivalent to ET(P) and TE(P).

6 P is the object with vertices (corner points) at (1,1), (2,1), (4,2) and (3,1)
R is a rotation of +180° about (0,0)
E is an enlargement with scale factor 2, centre (0,0)
Show in one diagram, P, R(P), E(P), ER(P) and RE(P). State single transformations which are equivalent to ER(P) and RE(P).

Coordinate mappings

When transformations are applied to shapes on a graph, the effect on each pair of coordinates often follows a pattern.

For example, this diagram shows the shape with vertices at (1,1), (1,4) and (3,−1) and its image after reflection in the *x*-axis.

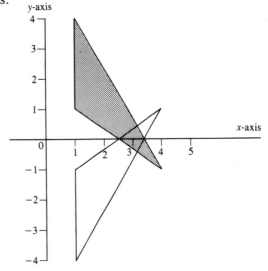

This is the mapping of the vertices of the object onto the vertices of the image

$$(1,1) \to (1,-1)$$
$$(1,4) \to (1,-4)$$
$$(3,-1) \to (3,1)$$

This mapping follows a simple pattern in which the *x* coordinate remains unchanged and the *y* coordinate is multiplied by −1.

A reflection in the *x*-axis is therefore equivalent to the coordinate mapping

$$(x,y) \to (x,-y).$$

Example

Draw a diagram to show the application of the coordinate mapping $(x,y) \rightarrow (y, -x)$ to the shape with vertices at $(1,1)$, $(1,4)$ and $(3, -1)$. Describe the transformation equivalent to this coordinate mapping.

This mapping has the effect of multiplying the x coordinate by -1 and then swapping the x and y coordinates. When applied to the three vertices it gives;

$$(1,1) \rightarrow (1, -1)$$
$$(1,4) \rightarrow (4, -1)$$
$$(3, -1) \rightarrow (-1, -3)$$

So, this is the required diagram.

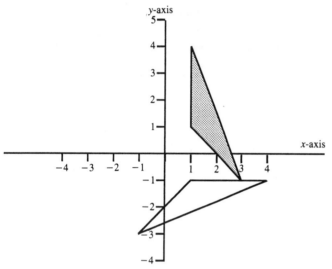

This coordinate mapping is equivalent to a rotation of $-90°$ about $(0,0)$.

CHECKPOINT 26

1 Draw a diagram to show the application of the coordinate mapping $(x,y) \rightarrow (-x, -y)$ to the shape with vertices at $(1,1)$, $(1,4)$ and $(3, -1)$. Describe the transformation equivalent to this coordinate mapping.

2 Draw a diagram to show the application of the coordinate mapping $(x,y) \rightarrow (y,x)$ to the shape with vertices at $(1,1)$, $(1,4)$ and $(3, -1)$. Describe the transformation equivalent to this coordinate mapping.

3 Draw a diagram to show the application of the coordinate mapping $(x,y) \rightarrow (x-4, y+3)$ to the shape with vertices at $(0,0)$, $(2,3)$ and $(3, -1)$. Describe the transformation equivalent to this coordinate mapping.

4 Draw a diagram to show the application of the coordinate mapping $(x,y) \rightarrow (6-x, y)$ to the shape with vertices at $(-1, -1)$, $(-2, -3)$ and $(-3, -1)$. Describe the transformation equivalent to this coordinate mapping.

5 Draw a diagram to show the shape with vertices at $(1,1)$, $(1,4)$ and $(3, -1)$ and its image after reflection in the y-axis. What coordinate mapping is equivalent to this transformation?

6 Draw a diagram to show the shape with vertices at $(1,1)$, $(1, -4)$ and $(3,1)$ and its image after a rotation of $+90°$ about $(0,0)$. What coordinate mapping is equivalent to this transformation?

7 Draw a diagram to show the shape with vertices at $(1,5)$, $(2,3)$ and $(6,1)$ and its image after a reflection in the line with equation $y = -x$. What coordinate mapping is equivalent to this transformation?

8 Draw a diagram to show the shape with vertices at $(-3, -3)$, $(-3, -1)$ and $(-1, -3)$ and its image after an enlargement scale factor 2, centre $(0,0)$. What coordinate mapping is equivalent to this transformation?

Matrix transformations

Matrix transformations are an alternative way to achieve a coordinate mapping. Before a matrix transformation can be completed, the translations from the point $(0,0)$ to each vertex of the object must be recorded in matrix form.

For example, this matrix

$$\begin{pmatrix} 2 & 3 & 7 \\ 4 & 2 & 2 \end{pmatrix}$$

records the translations from $(0,0)$ to each vertex of this object.

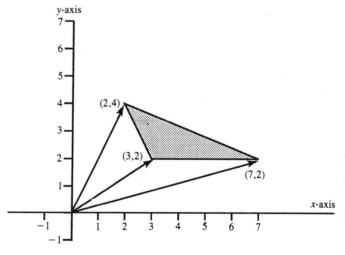

These translations from $(0,0)$ are called the **position vectors** of the shape.

To achieve the matrix transformation, we now multiply this position vector matrix by the transformation matrix. For example, if the transformation matrix is

$$\begin{pmatrix} -1 & 0 \\ 0 & 0 \end{pmatrix}$$

We complete this matrix multiplication

$$\begin{pmatrix} -1 & 0 \\ 0 & 1 \end{pmatrix} \begin{pmatrix} 2 & 3 & 7 \\ 4 & 2 & 2 \end{pmatrix} = \begin{pmatrix} -2 & -3 & -7 \\ 4 & 2 & 2 \end{pmatrix}$$

The answer matrix contains the position vectors for the vertices of the image. Plotting these onto a graph gives us this final diagram.

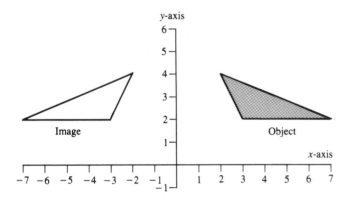

From this diagram we can see that the matrix transformation is equivalent to a reflection in the y-axis.

The steps in applying a matrix transformation to an object on a graph are

- Record the position vectors of the vertices of the object in a matrix.

- Multiply this matrix by the matrix given for the transformation.

- Plot the image of the object from the position vectors in the answer matrix obtained from the multiplication.

Example

Show on a graph the shape with vertices at $(1, -1)$, $(3, -3)$ and $(5, -2)$ and its image after the matrix transformation

$$\begin{pmatrix} 0 & 1 \\ 1 & 0 \end{pmatrix}$$

Describe the effects of the matrix transformation.

This is the position vector matrix for the shape.

$$\begin{pmatrix} 1 & 3 & 5 \\ -1 & -3 & -2 \end{pmatrix}$$

The matrix multiplication produces this answer

$$\begin{pmatrix} 0 & 1 \\ 1 & 0 \end{pmatrix} \begin{pmatrix} 1 & 3 & 5 \\ -1 & -3 & -2 \end{pmatrix} = \begin{pmatrix} -1 & -3 & -2 \\ 1 & 3 & 5 \end{pmatrix}$$

and the transformation can be represented on this graph.

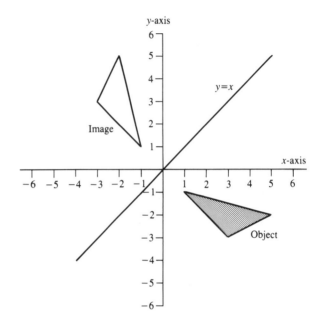

From the graph we can see that the matrix transformation is equivalent to a reflection in the line with equation $y = x$.

CHECKPOINT 27

In each part of this question show the shape with the given vertices on a graph with its image under the given matrix transformation. Describe the effects of the matrix transformation.

a $(3,4)$, $(5,4)$ and $(5,4)$

$$\begin{pmatrix} 1 & 0 \\ 0 & -1 \end{pmatrix}$$

b $(-4,0)$, $(-1,-1)$ and $(-2,-3)$

$$\begin{pmatrix} -1 & 0 \\ 0 & -1 \end{pmatrix}$$

c $(-3,1)$, $(-3,3)$, $(-1,3)$ and $(-1,1)$

$$\begin{pmatrix} 2 & 0 \\ 0 & 2 \end{pmatrix}$$

d $(1,-3)$, $(2,-1)$ and $(3,-3)$ $\begin{pmatrix} 0 & 1 \\ -1 & 0 \end{pmatrix}$

e $(-3,-3)$, $(-1,-1)$ and $(5,-3)$ $\begin{pmatrix} 0 & -1 \\ -1 & 0 \end{pmatrix}$

f $(-1,1)$, $(-1,6)$, $(1,6)$ and $(1,1)$ $\begin{pmatrix} 0 & -1 \\ 1 & 0 \end{pmatrix}$

g $(0,0)$, $(0,1)$, $(1,1)$ and $(1,0)$ $\begin{pmatrix} -5 & 0 \\ 0 & -5 \end{pmatrix}$

h (2 mm graph paper will be needed.)
$(10,10)$, $(10,20)$, $(20,20)$ and $(20,10)$ $\begin{pmatrix} 0.8 & 0.6 \\ -0.6 & 0.8 \end{pmatrix}$

i $(3,2)$, $(2,4)$ and $(6,3)$ $\begin{pmatrix} 2 & 0 \\ 0 & -2 \end{pmatrix}$

j $(0,0)$, $(1,0)$, $(1,1)$ and $(0,1)$ $\begin{pmatrix} 0 & -4 \\ 4 & 0 \end{pmatrix}$

Inverse transformations

The **inverse** of the transformation T is the transformation which reverses the effects of T. For example, if;

T is a rotation of $-90°$ about the point $(0,0)$

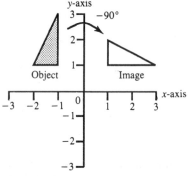

It is obvious that the inverse of T is;

A rotation of $+90°$ about the point $(0,0)$

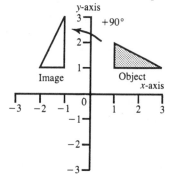

The notation T^{-1} is often used to denote the inverse of the transformation T, so we can write;

If T = A rotation of $-90°$ about the point $(0,0)$

Then T^{-1} = A rotation of $90°$ about the point $(0,0)$

Some general rules for finding inverse transformations are;

- If T = a rotation of about $+R°$ about point P then T^{-1} = a rotation of $-R°$ about point P

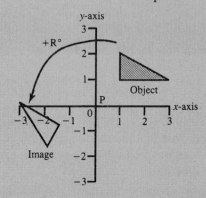

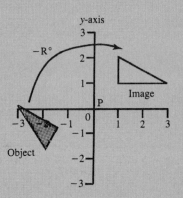

- If T = reflection in the line m then T^{-1} = reflection in the line m

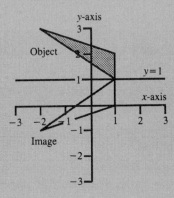

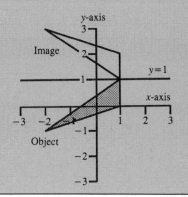

Inverse transformations (continued)

- If T = a translation of $\begin{pmatrix} +a \\ +b \end{pmatrix}$

  then T^{-1} = a translation of $\begin{pmatrix} -a \\ -b \end{pmatrix}$

(This does not, of course, mean that the numbers in the first translation will always be positive and the numbers in the second translation negative. It means that **the numbers in the second translation will have the opposite signs to the numbers in the first translation**.)

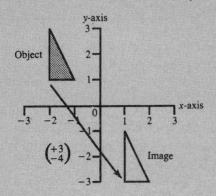

$\begin{pmatrix} +3 \\ -4 \end{pmatrix}$

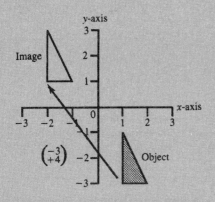

$\begin{pmatrix} -3 \\ +4 \end{pmatrix}$

- If T = an enlargement scale factor n, centre P

  then T^{-1} = an enlargement scale factor $\dfrac{1}{n}$, centre P.

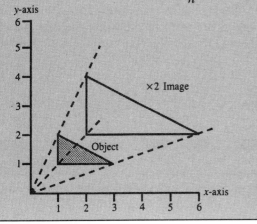

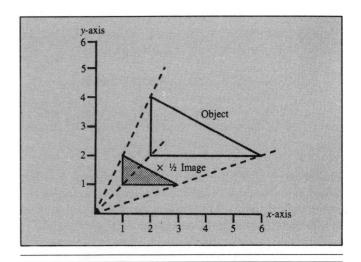

CHECKPOINT 28

1 In each part of this question:

- State the inverse of the given transformation.
- Choose a suitable object and draw diagrams to illustrate the effects of the transformation on your object, and the reverse effects of the inverse transformation.

a T = translation $\begin{pmatrix} +5 \\ -4 \end{pmatrix}$

b R = rotation of $+270°$ about (0,0)

c E = enlargement scale factor 3, centre (0,0)

d R = reflection in the line with equation $x = 0$ (the y-axis)

e R = reflection in the line with equation $y = x$

f M = rotation of $+120°$ about (0,0)

g S = enlargement scale factor 1/4, centre (0,0)

h T = translation $\begin{pmatrix} -7 \\ -7 \end{pmatrix}$

Inverse matrix transformations

If we are asked to find the inverse of a matrix transformation, the required matrix may be found by using our knowledge of inverse transformations. For example, if we are asked to find the inverse of the matrix transformation

$$\begin{pmatrix} 2 & 0 \\ 0 & 2 \end{pmatrix}$$

we may spot that this is the matrix for an enlargement, scale factor 2, centre (0,0).

The inverse of this transformation is an enlargement, scale factor ½, centre (0,0).

So, the required inverse matrix is

$$\begin{pmatrix} ½ & 0 \\ 0 & ½ \end{pmatrix}$$

231

Other inverse matrices may not be so easy, but luckily there is a simple rule which allows us to automatically find the inverse of any matrix transformation (if it exists).

The rule is developed from the **identity matrix**

$$I = \begin{pmatrix} 1 & 0 \\ 0 & 1 \end{pmatrix}$$

This matrix is called the identity matrix because it does not affect any shape to which it is applied (it preserves the **identity** of the shape). Any position vector matrix multiplied by the identity matrix remains completely unchanged.

$$\begin{pmatrix} 1 & 0 \\ 0 & 1 \end{pmatrix} \begin{pmatrix} 3 & 4 & -5 \\ 4 & -7 & -3 \end{pmatrix} = \begin{pmatrix} 3 & 4 & -5 \\ 4 & -7 & -3 \end{pmatrix}$$

Inverse matrices

If the matrix transformation M has an inverse, M^{-1}, these two matrices must combine in such a way that they cancel out each others effects and leave an object unchanged. In other words, M and M^{-1} must combine to produce I, the identity matrix. In symbols we write this as

$$MM^{-1} = I$$

We can demonstrate this is correct with the two enlargement matrices which we have already established are inverses.

$$\begin{pmatrix} 2 & 0 \\ 0 & 2 \end{pmatrix} \begin{pmatrix} \frac{1}{2} & 0 \\ 0 & \frac{1}{2} \end{pmatrix} = \begin{pmatrix} 1 & 0 \\ 0 & 1 \end{pmatrix}$$

So, when asked to find the inverse of a matrix transformation like

$$M = \begin{pmatrix} 0 & -1 \\ 1 & 0 \end{pmatrix}$$

we are really being asked to find a matrix M^{-1} such that

$$\begin{pmatrix} 0 & -1 \\ 1 & 0 \end{pmatrix} M^{-1} = \begin{pmatrix} 1 & 0 \\ 0 & 1 \end{pmatrix}$$

Careful trial and error will show you that the required matrix is

$$M^{-1} = \begin{pmatrix} 0 & 1 \\ -1 & 0 \end{pmatrix}$$

To demonstrate the effects of this matrix and its inverse, we can draw a pair of diagrams with a suitably chosen object. This is a possible pair of diagrams.

$$\begin{pmatrix} 0 & -1 \\ 1 & 0 \end{pmatrix} \begin{pmatrix} 1 & 1 & 3 \\ 1 & 2 & 1 \end{pmatrix} = \begin{pmatrix} -1 & -2 & -1 \\ 1 & 1 & 3 \end{pmatrix}$$

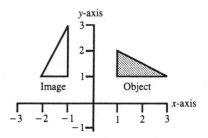

$$\begin{pmatrix} 0 & 1 \\ -1 & 0 \end{pmatrix} \begin{pmatrix} -1 & -2 & -3 \\ 1 & 1 & 3 \end{pmatrix} = \begin{pmatrix} 1 & 1 & 3 \\ 1 & 2 & 1 \end{pmatrix}$$

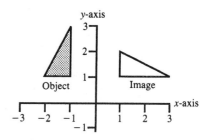

We can see from the diagrams that M is equivalent to a rotation of $+90°$ about (0,0) and M^{-1} is equivalent to a rotation of $-90°$ about (0,0).

CHECKPOINT 29

1 Using a 'trial and error' method, find the inverse of each of the following matrix transformations. Demonstrate that your answers are correct by drawing diagrams showing the application of the matrix and its inverse to a suitable object.

a $\begin{pmatrix} 1 & 0 \\ 0 & -1 \end{pmatrix}$ **b** $\begin{pmatrix} -1 & 0 \\ 0 & -1 \end{pmatrix}$ **c** $\begin{pmatrix} 3 & 0 \\ 0 & 3 \end{pmatrix}$

If the inverse of a matrix cannot be found by trial and error, the following set of rules will find the inverse of **any** 2 by 2 matrix, if an inverse exists.

The inverse of a 2×2 matrix
Starting with the matrix M, where

$$M = \begin{pmatrix} a & b \\ c & d \end{pmatrix}$$

• First we calculate a value called the **determinant** of M. This value, usually shown as $|M|$, is equal to $ad-bc$. If $|M|$ is equal to zero, no inverse exists for the matrix M.

• Having calculated M, the inverse matrix M^{-1} is found using the formula

$$M^{-1} = \begin{pmatrix} \dfrac{d}{|M|} & \dfrac{-b}{|M|} \\ \dfrac{-c}{|M|} & \dfrac{a}{|M|} \end{pmatrix}$$

The formula means that the numbers b and c change their signs and the numbers a and d change their positions. All four numbers are then divided by the value of $|M|$.

Examples

1 Find the inverse of the matrix

$$M = \begin{pmatrix} 0 & 1 \\ 1 & 0 \end{pmatrix}$$

• Step 1, calculating $|M|$

$$|M| = (0 \times 0) - (1 \times 1) = 0 - 1 = -1$$

• Step 2, applying the formula

$$M^{-1} = \begin{pmatrix} \dfrac{0}{-1} & \dfrac{-1}{-1} \\ \dfrac{-1}{-1} & \dfrac{0}{-1} \end{pmatrix}$$

Simplifying,

$$M^{-1} = \begin{pmatrix} 0 & 1 \\ 1 & 0 \end{pmatrix}$$

2 Find the inverse of the matrix

$$P = \begin{pmatrix} -4 & 0 \\ 0 & 4 \end{pmatrix}$$

• Step 1, calculating $|P|$

$$|P| = (-4 \times 4) - (0 \times 0) = -16 - 0 = -16$$

• Step 2, applying the formula

$$P^{-1} = \begin{pmatrix} \dfrac{4}{-16} & \dfrac{0}{-16} \\ \dfrac{0}{-16} & \dfrac{-4}{-16} \end{pmatrix}$$

Simplifying,

$$P^{-1} = \begin{pmatrix} -\dfrac{1}{4} & 0 \\ 0 & \dfrac{1}{4} \end{pmatrix}$$

3 Find the inverse of the matrix

$$A = \begin{pmatrix} 3 & 4 \\ -1 & 2 \end{pmatrix}$$

• Step 1, calculating $|A|$

$$|A| = (3 \times 2) - (4 \times -1) = 6 - -4 = 10$$

• Step 2, applying the formula

$$A^{-1} = \begin{pmatrix} \dfrac{2}{10} & \dfrac{-4}{10} \\ \dfrac{1}{10} & \dfrac{3}{10} \end{pmatrix}$$

Simplifying,

$$A^{-1} = \begin{pmatrix} 0.2 & -0.4 \\ 0.1 & 0.3 \end{pmatrix}$$

4 Find the inverse of the matrix

$$M = \begin{pmatrix} 2 & 8 \\ 1 & 4 \end{pmatrix}$$

• Step 1, calculating $|M|$

$$|M| = (2 \times 4) - (1 \times 8) = 8 - 8 = 0$$

Because $|M|$ is equal to zero, this matrix has no inverse.

Using the formula method, find the inverse of each of the following matrix transformations. Demonstrate that your answers are correct by drawing diagrams showing the application of the matrix and its inverse to a suitable object.

a $\begin{pmatrix} 0 & 1 \\ -1 & 0 \end{pmatrix}$ **b** $\begin{pmatrix} -1 & 0 \\ 0 & 1 \end{pmatrix}$ **c** $\begin{pmatrix} 0 & -1 \\ -1 & 0 \end{pmatrix}$

d $\begin{pmatrix} 0 & 6 \\ -6 & 0 \end{pmatrix}$ **e** $\begin{pmatrix} 1 & 0 \\ 2 & 1 \end{pmatrix}$ **f** $\begin{pmatrix} 3 & 0 \\ 0 & 1 \end{pmatrix}$

Symmetry

When we say that a shape is symmetrical we mean that it contains some kind of repeating pattern. These are all shapes with different kinds of symmetry.

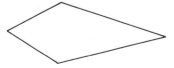

Mathematicians have developed a way to classify the different kinds of symmetry possessed by shapes.

Symmetry is divided into two different types, **rotational symmetry** and **reflectional symmetry**.

Rotational symmetry

Shapes which have rotational symmetry fit back into their original position as they are rotated. For example, this shape

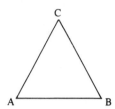

fits back into its original position three times as it is rotated through 360°.

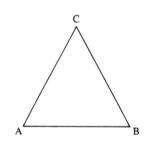
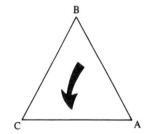

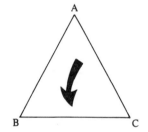
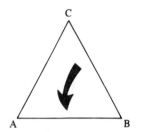

We classify the shape as one with **rotational symmetry of order three**. This is another shape with rotational symmetry of order three.

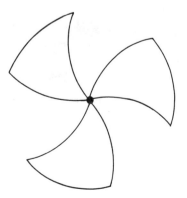

This shape has rotational symmetry of order four.

This shape has rotational symmetry of order two.

All shapes must fit back into their original position after a full rotation of 360°, so all shapes must have an order of rotational symmetry of at least one. Sometimes a shape which has a rotational symmetry of order one may be called a shape with no rotational symmetry.

This shape has rotational symmetry of order one (no rotational symmetry).

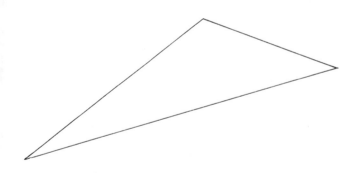

CHECKPOINT 31

What is the order of rotational symmetry of each of the following shapes?

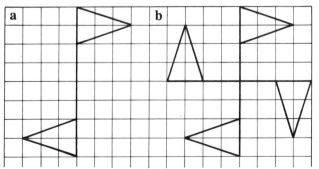

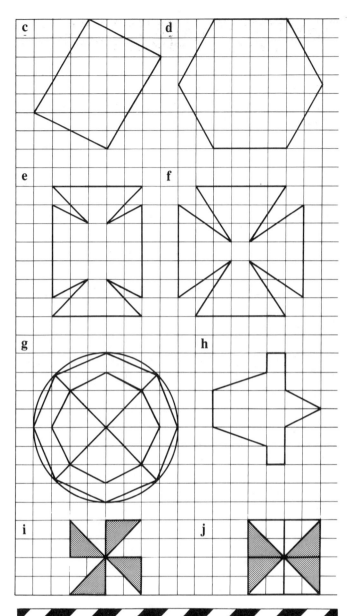

Reflectional symmetry

Shapes which have reflectional symmetry fit back into their original position if they are reflected in a mirror line across the shape. For example, this shape has reflectional symmetry because it fits back into its original position after a reflection in the dotted mirror line.

The mirror line is called **an axis of symmetry** or **line of symmetry**.

Some shapes have several different lines of symmetry. For example, this shape has four lines of symmetry.

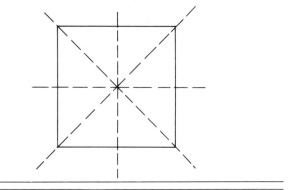

Copy each of the following diagrams and mark on your diagrams all the lines of symmetry of each shape.

a

b

c

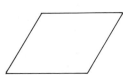

d

e

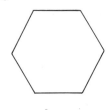

f

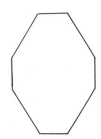

g

h

i

j

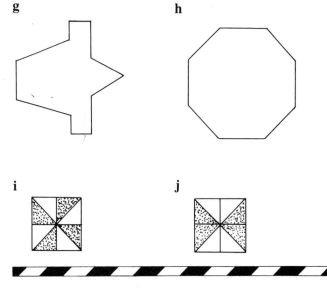

It may be possible to imagine a 'slice' through a solid object leaving two parts which are exact mirror reflections of each other.

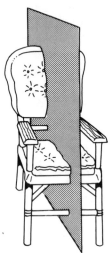

In this case the solid object has reflectional symmetry. The mirror 'slice' is called a **plane of symmetry**.

Example

Draw diagrams to show all the planes of symmetry for this cuboid.

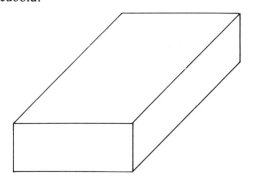

236

These are the required diagrams.

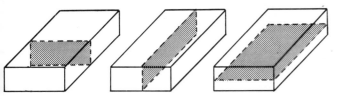

Draw diagrams to show all the planes of symmetry for each of the following objects.

a

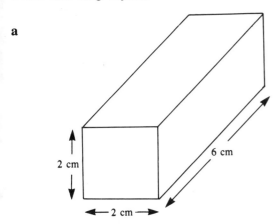

2 cm

6 cm

2 cm

b

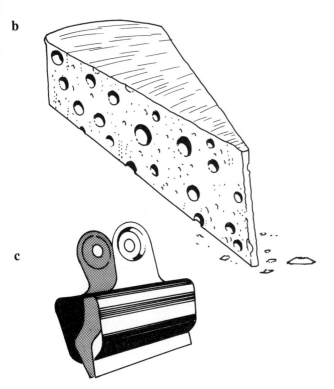

c

d

2

STING

e

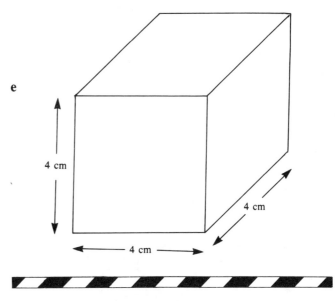

4 cm

4 cm

4 cm

Vector Geometry

Representing vectors

Vector geometry is another geometry which was developed during the nineteenth and twentieth centuries. A **vector** is a quantity which has both magnitude (size) and direction. This is in contrast to a **scalar** quantity which has only a magnitude. For example, if a table costs £50, then this is a **scalar** quantity because it has a magnitude but no associated direction. If, on the other hand, we apply a large force to the table, the force is a **vector** because it has both a magnitude and a direction. The direction in which the force is applied will certainly affect the results on the table!

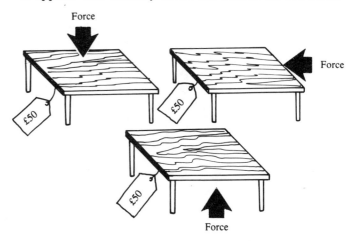

Force

Force

£50

£50

£50

Force

Vectors can be represented by directed arrows. The magnitude and direction of the vector is shown by the length and direction of the arrow. For example, velocities of 50 mph due North and 25 mph due West might be shown by these arrows.

The rules for describing and combining the directed arrows representing vectors form the basis of **vector geometry**.

Basic rules for describing vectors.

● Letters are used to label vectors (usually lower case letters, often in heavy type or underlined, like a, **a** or a)

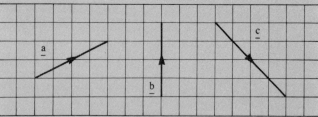

● Any vectors with identical magnitude and direction are equal and are therefore labelled with the same letter.

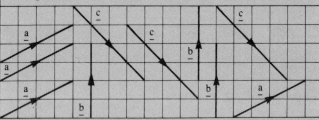

● Any vector quantities with equal magnitude but exactly opposite direction will cancel each other out; consequently they are labelled a and −a, or b and −b, or x and −x.

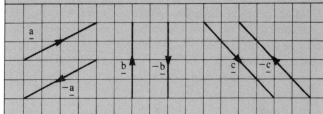

● If one vector has been labelled a, then another vector with the same direction but twice the magnitude will be labelled 2a. A vector with three times the magnitude will be labelled 3a. A vector with half the magnitude will be labelled $\frac{1a}{2}$ or $\frac{a}{2}$.

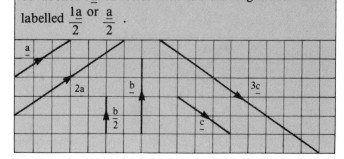

Example

This diagram shows a collection of vectors. Copy the diagram and label each vector using only the letters a, b and c.

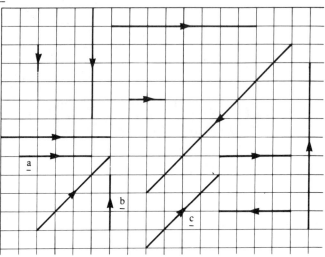

This is the required diagram.

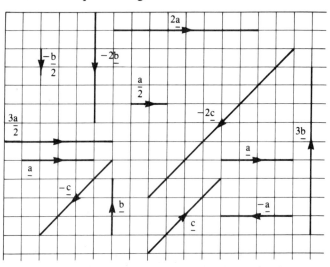

1 This diagram shows a collection of vectors. Copy the diagram and label each vector using only the letters a, b and c.

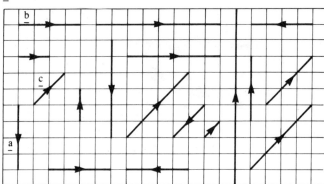

2 This diagram shows a collection of vectors. Copy the diagram and label each vector using only the letters x, y and z.

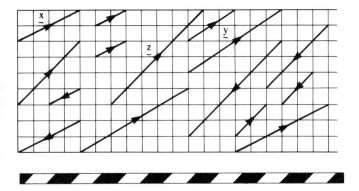

Vector addition

A boat sails between three islands, A, B and C. The boat sails from A to B and then to C. The vector arrows on this map show the boat's journey and the alternative direct route from A to C.

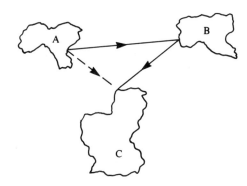

The final result of these two alternative journeys is the same, so in terms of the vector movements we can write

$$AC = AB + BC$$

We do not of course mean that the **distances** AB and BC add up to the **distance** AC. We mean that a **movement** from A to B, followed by a **movement** from B to C is equivalent to a **movement** from A to C.

We call this technique of combining vectors **vector addition** and it can be applied to all vectors, not just those representing movements. However, in order to master the basics of vector geometry, is is often very useful to think of the vectors involved as movements between points. At this stage we must introduce a second form of notation for the directed arrows used to represent vectors.

The end points of a directed arrow may be marked with two capital letters and the vector labelled as a movement between these two letters. This diagram shows the vectors $\overrightarrow{AB}$, $\overrightarrow{BC}$ and $\overrightarrow{AC}$.

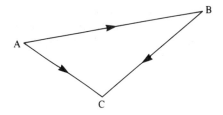

We may use a combination of the two ways to label vectors, and in this diagram $\overrightarrow{AB} = \underline{a}$ and $\overrightarrow{BC} = \underline{b}$.

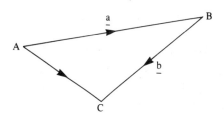

Reversing the capital letters reverses the direction of the vector, so in the same diagram $\overrightarrow{BA} = -\underline{a}$ and $\overrightarrow{CB} = -\underline{b}$

We can also use vector addition to label the third side of the triangle and write

$$\overrightarrow{AC} = \overrightarrow{AB} + \overrightarrow{BC}$$

So,

$$\overrightarrow{AC} = \underline{a} + \underline{b}$$

Examples

1 In this diagram, $\overrightarrow{AB} = 2\underline{x}$ and $\overrightarrow{BC} = 2\underline{y}$. M is the mid-point of $\overrightarrow{AB}$ and N is the mid-point of $\overrightarrow{BC}$. Describe in terms of $\underline{x}$ and $\underline{y}$ the vectors

a $\overrightarrow{AM}$ **b** $\overrightarrow{MB}$ **c** $\overrightarrow{BN}$ **d** $\overrightarrow{AC}$ **e** $\overrightarrow{MN}$

What do your results prove about the lines AC and MN?

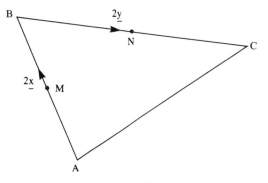

We find the vector descriptions like this.

a $\overrightarrow{AM}$ is half of $\overrightarrow{AB}$, and $\overrightarrow{AB} = 2\underline{x}$, so, $\overrightarrow{AM} = \underline{x}$.

b $\overrightarrow{MB}$ is half of $\overrightarrow{AB}$ and $\overrightarrow{AB} = 2\underline{x}$, so, $\overrightarrow{MB} = \underline{x}$.

c $\overrightarrow{BN}$ is half of $\overrightarrow{BC}$ and $\overrightarrow{BC} = 2\underline{y}$, so, $\overrightarrow{BN} = \underline{y}$.

239

d $\overrightarrow{AC}$ is equivalent to $\overrightarrow{AB}+\overrightarrow{BC}$, so, $\overrightarrow{AC}=2\underline{x}+2\underline{y}$.

e $\overrightarrow{MN}$ is equivalent to $\overrightarrow{MB}+\overrightarrow{BN}$, so, $\overrightarrow{MN}=\underline{x}+\underline{y}$.

If we compare our results for $\overrightarrow{AC}$ and $\overrightarrow{MN}$, we see that

$$\overrightarrow{AC}=2\underline{x}+2\underline{y}$$

$$\overrightarrow{AC}=2(\underline{x}+\underline{y})$$

$$\overrightarrow{AC}=2\overrightarrow{MN}$$

Since both $\overrightarrow{AC}$ and $\overrightarrow{MN}$ are representing vectors, this means that the line AC must be parallel to MN and twice its length.

2 In this diagram, ABCD is a parallelogram with $\overrightarrow{AB}=\underline{a}$ and $\overrightarrow{AC}=\underline{b}$. M is the mid-point of DC and N is the mid-point of BC. Describe in terms of $\underline{a}$ and $\underline{b}$ the vectors

a $\overrightarrow{DC}$ **b** $\overrightarrow{BC}$ **c** $\overrightarrow{AD}$ **d** $\overrightarrow{AM}$ **e** $\overrightarrow{AN}$

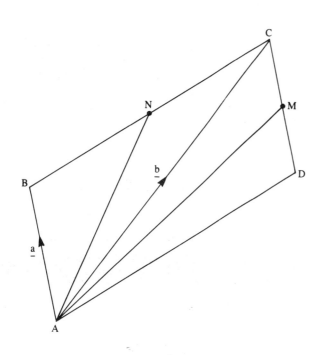

We find the vector descriptions like this.

a $\overrightarrow{DC}$ is parallel to $\overrightarrow{AB}$ and equal in length, so, $\overrightarrow{DC}=\underline{a}$.

b $\overrightarrow{BC}$ is equivalent to $\overrightarrow{BA}+\overrightarrow{AC}$; so,

$$\overrightarrow{BC}=-\underline{a}+\underline{b}=\underline{b}-\underline{a}$$

c $\overrightarrow{AD}$ is parallel to $\overrightarrow{BC}$ and equal in length, so,

$$\overrightarrow{AD}=\underline{b}-\underline{a}$$

d $\overrightarrow{AM}$ is equivalent to $\overrightarrow{AD}+\overrightarrow{DM}$; so,

$$\overrightarrow{AM}=\underline{b}-\underline{a}+\frac{a}{2}=\underline{b}-\frac{a}{2}$$

e $\overrightarrow{AN}$ is equivalent to $\overrightarrow{AB}+\overrightarrow{BN}$; so,

$$\overrightarrow{AN}=\underline{a}+\frac{\underline{b}-\underline{a}}{2}$$

$$\overrightarrow{AN}=\frac{2\underline{a}+\underline{b}-\underline{a}}{2}$$

$$=\frac{\underline{a}+\underline{b}}{2}$$

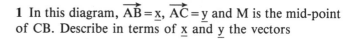

CHECKPOINT 35

1 In this diagram, $\overrightarrow{AB}=\underline{x}$, $\overrightarrow{AC}=\underline{y}$ and M is the mid-point of CB. Describe in terms of $\underline{x}$ and $\underline{y}$ the vectors

a $\overrightarrow{CB}$ **b** $\overrightarrow{CM}$ **c** $\overrightarrow{AM}$

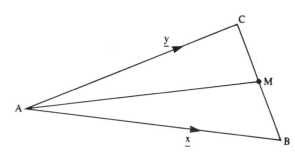

2 In this diagram, $\overrightarrow{XM}=\underline{a}$, $\overrightarrow{MZ}=\underline{b}$ and M is the mid-point of YZ. Describe in terms of $\underline{a}$ and $\underline{b}$ the vectors

a $\overrightarrow{XZ}$ **b** $\overrightarrow{MY}$ **c** $\overrightarrow{XY}$

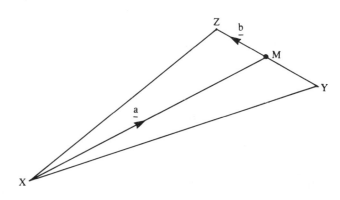

3 In this diagram, OABC is a parallelogram with $\overrightarrow{OA}=2\underline{a}$ and $\overrightarrow{OC}=2\underline{c}$. M is the mid-point of AB, N is the mid-point of BC, P is the mid-point of OA and Q is the mid-point of OC. Describe in terms of $\underline{a}$ and $\underline{c}$ the vectors

a $\overrightarrow{AB}$　　**b** $\overrightarrow{CB}$　　**c** $\overrightarrow{OB}$　　**d** $\overrightarrow{PQ}$　　**e** $\overrightarrow{MN}$

What do your results prove about the lines PQ and MN?

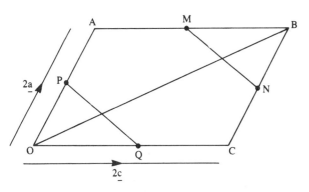

4 In this diagram, OABC is a parallelogram with $\overrightarrow{OA} = \underline{x}$ and $\overrightarrow{OC} = \underline{y}$. AB is extended to the point D and AB = BD. Describe in terms of $\underline{x}$ and $\underline{y}$ the vectors;

a $\overrightarrow{AB}$　**b** $\overrightarrow{CB}$　**c** $\overrightarrow{AD}$　**d** $\overrightarrow{OD}$　**e** $\overrightarrow{OB}$　**f** $\overrightarrow{CD}$

What do your results prove about the lines OB and CD?

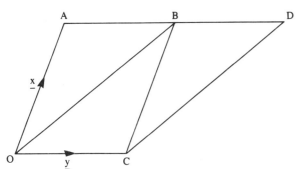

5 In this diagram, $\overrightarrow{OA} = \underline{a}$ and $\overrightarrow{OB} = \underline{b}$. M is the point on OA such that $\overrightarrow{OA} = 4\overrightarrow{OM}$ and N is the point on OB such that $\overrightarrow{OB} = 4\overrightarrow{ON}$. Describe in terms of $\underline{a}$ and $\underline{b}$ the vectors

a $\overrightarrow{OM}$　　**b** $\overrightarrow{ON}$　　**c** $\overrightarrow{AB}$　　**d** $\overrightarrow{MN}$

What do your results prove about the lines AB and MN?

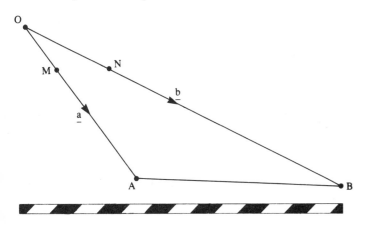

Vectors and translations

When vectors are drawn on a grid or graph, the notation used for translations can be used to describe the vectors. For example, this vector

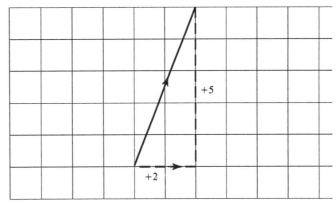

can be described by the translation

$$\begin{pmatrix} +2 \\ +5 \end{pmatrix}$$

Remember, translations are described with two numbers in a vertical bracket using + and − signs to indicate left and right and up and down. The general description is

$$\begin{pmatrix} - \qquad\qquad + \\ \leftarrow\text{horizontal movement}\rightarrow \\ \uparrow + \\ \text{vertical movement} \\ \downarrow - \end{pmatrix}$$

When vectors are described in this way, they are often refered to as **column vectors**.

CHECKPOINT 36

Copy this diagram and beside each vector write its description as a column vector.

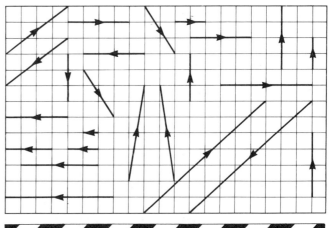

The use of column vectors to describe directed arrows gives us an interesting way to demonstrate the rules of vector addition.

For example, if we have the vectors

$$\overrightarrow{AB} = \begin{pmatrix} +5 \\ -4 \end{pmatrix} \quad \text{and} \quad \overrightarrow{BC} = \begin{pmatrix} -2 \\ +6 \end{pmatrix}$$

we can draw this diagram to demonstrate that $\overrightarrow{AB} + \overrightarrow{BC} = \overrightarrow{AC}$.

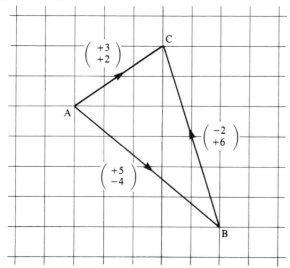

Alternatively, we can just use the rules of matrix addition to obtain the result like this.

$$\overrightarrow{AB} + \overrightarrow{BC} = \begin{pmatrix} +5 \\ -4 \end{pmatrix} + \begin{pmatrix} -2 \\ +6 \end{pmatrix} = \begin{pmatrix} +3 \\ +2 \end{pmatrix}$$

Example

Given the vectors $\underline{a} = \begin{pmatrix} +3 \\ +5 \end{pmatrix}$ and $\underline{b} = \begin{pmatrix} -4 \\ +3 \end{pmatrix}$

Show in a diagram the vectors $\underline{a}$, $\underline{b}$, $\underline{a} + \underline{b}$ and $\underline{a} - \underline{b}$.

Describe $\underline{a} + \underline{b}$ and $\underline{a} - \underline{b}$ as column vectors.

This is the required diagram.

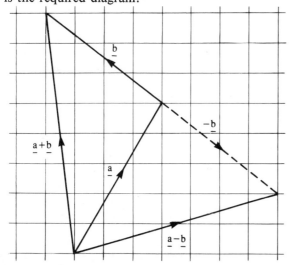

To describe $\underline{a} + \underline{b}$ and $\underline{a} - \underline{b}$ as column vectors, we can either read directly from the diagram or use matrix arithmetic.

From the diagram we read

$$\underline{a} + \underline{b} = \begin{pmatrix} -1 \\ +8 \end{pmatrix} \quad \text{and} \quad \underline{a} - \underline{b} = \begin{pmatrix} +7 \\ +2 \end{pmatrix}$$

Using matrix arithmetic

$$\underline{a} + \underline{b} = \begin{pmatrix} +3 \\ +5 \end{pmatrix} + \begin{pmatrix} -4 \\ +3 \end{pmatrix} = \begin{pmatrix} -1 \\ +8 \end{pmatrix}$$

$$\underline{a} - \underline{b} = \begin{pmatrix} +3 \\ +5 \end{pmatrix} - \begin{pmatrix} -4 \\ +3 \end{pmatrix} = \begin{pmatrix} +7 \\ +2 \end{pmatrix}$$

CHECKPOINT 37

1 In each part of this question you are given the definitions of $\overrightarrow{XY}$ and $\overrightarrow{YZ}$ as column vectors. Draw a diagram to show $\overrightarrow{XY}$, $\overrightarrow{YZ}$ and $\overrightarrow{XZ}$ and describe $\overrightarrow{XZ}$ as a column vector.

a $\quad \overrightarrow{XY} = \begin{pmatrix} +3 \\ +4 \end{pmatrix} \qquad \overrightarrow{YZ} = \begin{pmatrix} +6 \\ +5 \end{pmatrix}$

b $\quad \overrightarrow{XY} = \begin{pmatrix} +2 \\ +7 \end{pmatrix} \qquad \overrightarrow{YZ} = \begin{pmatrix} -6 \\ -1 \end{pmatrix}$

c $\quad \overrightarrow{XY} = \begin{pmatrix} -5 \\ -4 \end{pmatrix} \qquad \overrightarrow{YZ} = \begin{pmatrix} +7 \\ +6 \end{pmatrix}$

d $\quad \overrightarrow{XY} = \begin{pmatrix} +7 \\ +3 \end{pmatrix} \qquad \overrightarrow{YZ} = \begin{pmatrix} +6 \\ -5 \end{pmatrix}$

e $\quad \overrightarrow{XY} = \begin{pmatrix} -7 \\ -4 \end{pmatrix} \qquad \overrightarrow{YZ} = \begin{pmatrix} 0 \\ -5 \end{pmatrix}$

f $\quad \overrightarrow{XY} = \begin{pmatrix} -1 \\ +7 \end{pmatrix} \qquad \overrightarrow{YZ} = \begin{pmatrix} +8 \\ -7 \end{pmatrix}$

2 In each part of this question you are given the definitions of x and y as column vectors. Show in a diagram the vectors x, y, x + y and x − y. Describe x + y and x − y as column vectors.

a $\quad \underline{x} = \begin{pmatrix} -2 \\ +8 \end{pmatrix} \qquad \underline{y} = \begin{pmatrix} +9 \\ -8 \end{pmatrix}$

b $\quad \underline{x} = \begin{pmatrix} -2 \\ +8 \end{pmatrix} \qquad \underline{y} = \begin{pmatrix} +5 \\ -6 \end{pmatrix}$

c $\quad \underline{x} = \begin{pmatrix} -6 \\ +3 \end{pmatrix} \qquad \underline{y} = \begin{pmatrix} +9 \\ -7 \end{pmatrix}$

d $\quad \underline{x} = \begin{pmatrix} -6 \\ +3 \end{pmatrix} \qquad \underline{y} = \begin{pmatrix} +11 \\ -2 \end{pmatrix}$

e $\quad \underline{x} = \begin{pmatrix} -1 \\ +9 \end{pmatrix} \qquad \underline{y} = \begin{pmatrix} +5 \\ -7 \end{pmatrix}$

f $\quad \underline{x} = \begin{pmatrix} 0 \\ +5 \end{pmatrix} \qquad \underline{y} = \begin{pmatrix} +8 \\ -5 \end{pmatrix}$

Geometry – Practice and revision exercise

1 Find the size of each unknown angle in these diagrams.

a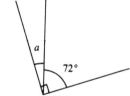

b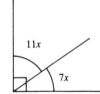

c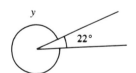

d

e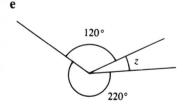

2 Find the size of each unknown angle in these diagrams.

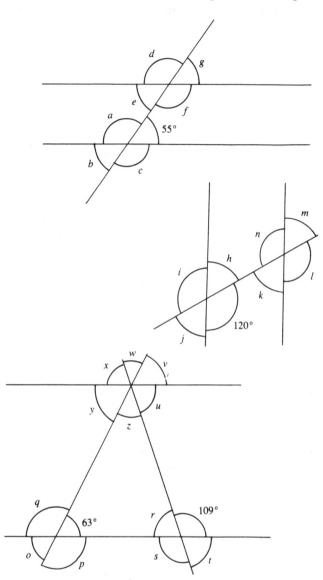

3 Find the size of each unknown angle in these diagrams.

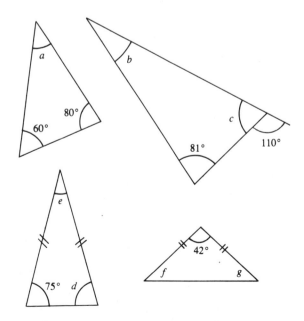

243

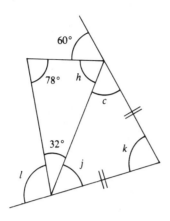

4 Copy this diagram and write the correct name inside each of the quadrilaterals.

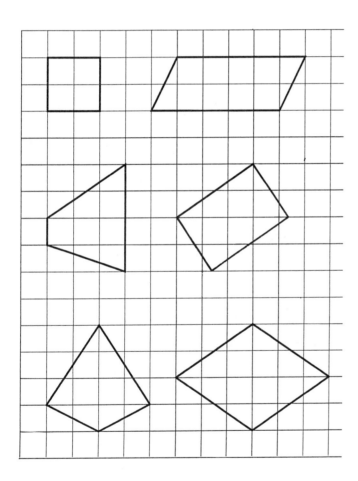

5 A heptagon is a seven-sided polygon. Find
a The total of the interior angles in a heptagon
b The total of the exterior angles in a heptagon
c The size of the interior angles in a regular heptagon
d The size of the exterior angles in a regular heptagon

6 Repeat question 5 for
a A decagon (ten-sided polygon)
b A dodecagon (twelve-sided polygon)

7 If the interior angles of a polygon add to 2880°, how many sides does it have?

8 If a regular polygon has interior angles of 150°, how many sides does it have?

9 Only three of the regular polygons can be used on their own to form a tessellation. Draw diagrams to illustrate tessellations formed with each of these regular polygons.

10 Draw a tessellation formed with three different regular polygons.

11 Find angles
a YOZ **b** OZY

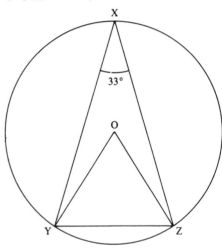

12 Find angles
a AOB   **b** ACB

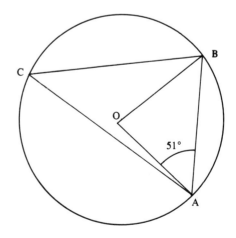

13 Find angles
a POQ   **b** OPQ

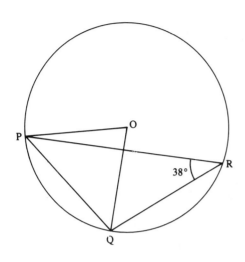

14 Find angles
a OPN   **b** PMN

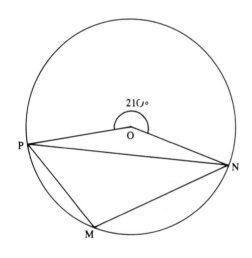

15 Find angles
a ACB   **b** ADB

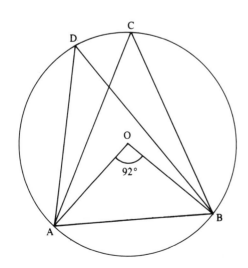

16 Find angles
a MON   **b** MRN   **c** MQN   **d** MPN

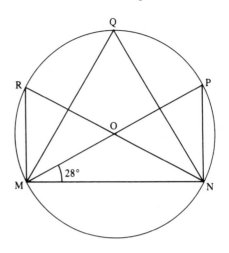

17 Find angles
a QPR   **b** PQR   **c** QOR   **d** QSR

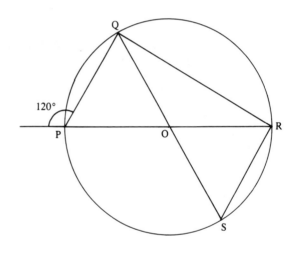

18 Find angles
a ABD   **b** BCD   **c** DBC   **d** ABC

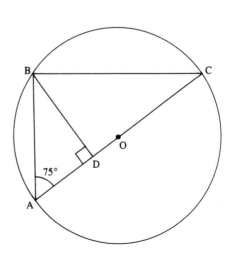

245

19 This diagram shows a design sketch for a lampshade frame which is to be constructed from wire. By making accurate drawings, find the total length of wire required.

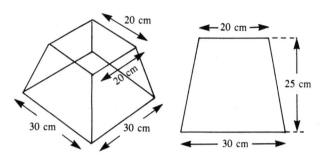

20 Chelmsford is 30 km to the West and 25 km to the South of Ipswich. Find the bearing of Ipswich from Chelmsford and the bearing of Chelmsford from Ipswich.

21 Draw a net for a cuboid which is 6 cm wide, 4 cm high and 7 cm long. Check your net by cutting it out and folding it.

22 Describe the solids that you think each of the following nets will make. Check your answers by copying the nets, cutting them out and folding them.

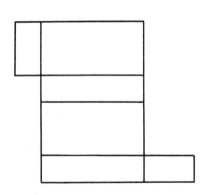

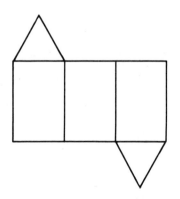

23 These diagrams show a sketch and an elevation of a weight being lifted by a cord. The cord is attached to one hook and passes through a ring on the weight to another hook. It then passes through the second hook to the hand of the person lifting the weight. Make a copy of the elevation and show on your diagram the locus of the weight as it is lifted.

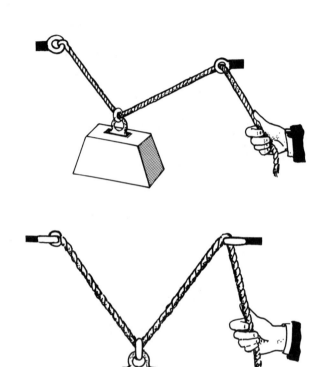

24 This diagram shows a windscreen wiper attached to a car windscreen. Make a tracing of this diagram and shade in the locus of the wiper as it moves across the screen.

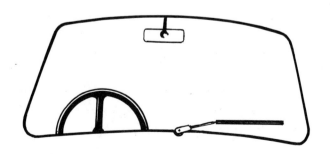

25 A point P moves in such a way that the angle made by P and two fixed points, A and B, 5 cm apart is always 30°. Draw a diagram to show the locus of the point P.

26 Copy this diagram and write beside each triangle the translation which moves the shaded triangle to that position.

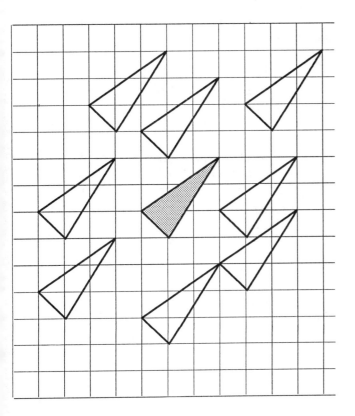

27 Draw a graph with x- and y-axes from −6 to +6. Plot the triangle with corner points at (0,1),(−3,1) and (−3,2). Show on your graph the new position of this triangle after each of the following translations.

a $\begin{pmatrix} +6 \\ 0 \end{pmatrix}$ **b** $\begin{pmatrix} +6 \\ -4 \end{pmatrix}$ **c** $\begin{pmatrix} -3 \\ +4 \end{pmatrix}$ **d** $\begin{pmatrix} 0 \\ +4 \end{pmatrix}$

28 Copy each of the following diagrams and draw in the image of the object after the stated rotation about the marked point.

a +90° about P   **b** −90° about P

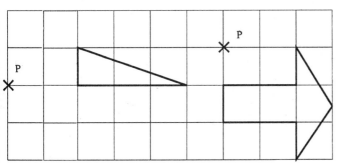

c 180° about P   **d** −60° about P

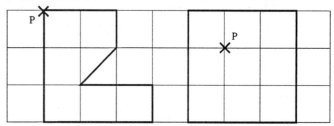

29 Draw a graph with x- and y-axes from −6 to +6. Plot the triangle with corner points at (1,4),(3,4) and (3,1). Show on your graph the new position of this triangle after each of the following rotations.

a −90° about (0,0)   **b** +180° about (0,0)
c +90° about (0,0)   **d** +270° about (1,4)
e −60° about (3,1)

30 Copy each of the following diagrams and draw in the image of the object after a reflection in the mirror line.

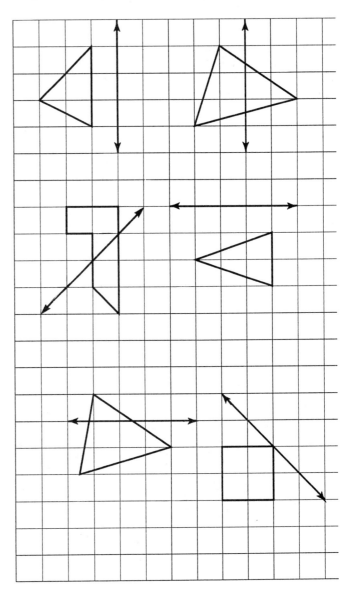

247

31 Draw a graph with x- and y-axes from -6 to $+6$. Plot the triangle with corner points at $(-1,-1),(-2,-1)$ and $(-2,-3)$. Show on your graph the new position of this triangle after reflection in each of the following mirror lines.

a The x-axis　　**b** The y-axis
c The line with equation $y=-2$
d The line with equation $x=1$
e The line with equation $y=-x$

32 Copy each of the following diagrams and draw in the image of the object after the stated enlargement.

a Centre P, scale factor 2.　　**b** Centre P, scale factor 3.

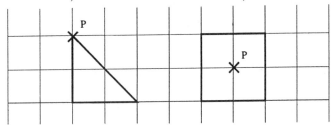

c Centre P, scale factor ½.　　**d** Centre P, scale factor -2.

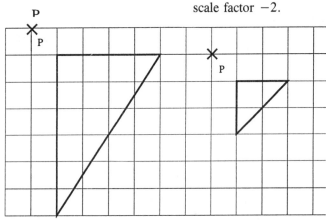

33 Draw a graph with x- and y-axes from -12 to $+12$. Plot the object with corner points at $(2,2),(2,3),(4,2)$. Show on your graph the image of this object after an enlargement with centre $(0,0)$ and scale factor

a 2　　**b** 3　　**c** -3　　**d** $\frac{1}{2}$　　**e** -1　　**f** $-\frac{1}{2}$

34 P is the object with vertices (corner points) at $(1,3),(2,3)$ and $(2,1)$.
R is a rotation of $+180°$ about $(0,0)$.
S is a reflection in the x-axis.
E is an enlargement with scale factor 2, centre $(0,0)$.
T is the translation $\begin{pmatrix} +2 \\ 0 \end{pmatrix}$

Show in one diagram, P, E(P), T(P), ET(P), TE(P)P, R(P), S(P), RS(P) and SR(P). State single transformations which are equivalent to ET(P), TE(P), RS(P) and SR(P).

35 Draw a graph with x and y values from -6 to $+6$. Plot the shape with vertices at $(0,0),(1,3)$ and $(3,1)$. Show on your graph the image of the shape under each of the following coordinate mappings and describe the effects of each mapping.

a $(x,y) \rightarrow (-x,y)$　　**b** $(x,y) \rightarrow (-x,-y)$
c $(x,y) \rightarrow (2x,2y)$　　**d** $(x,y) \rightarrow (3-x,y)$
e $(x,y) \rightarrow (x-6,y-6)$

36 In each part of this question show the shape with the given vertices on a graph with its image under the given matrix transformation. Describe the effects of the matrix transformation.

a $(-3,0),(-3,-2)$ and $(0,0)$　$\begin{pmatrix} 1 & 0 \\ 0 & -1 \end{pmatrix}$

b $(4,0),(1,1)$ and $(2,3)$　$\begin{pmatrix} -1 & 0 \\ 0 & -1 \end{pmatrix}$

c $(0,0),(1,0),(1,1)$ and $(0,1)$　$\begin{pmatrix} 5 & 0 \\ 0 & 5 \end{pmatrix}$

37 In each part of this question

- State the inverse of the given transformation.
- Choose a suitable object and draw diagrams to illustrate the effects of the transformation on your object and the reverse effects of the inverse transformation.

a T = translation $\begin{pmatrix} +7 \\ -3 \end{pmatrix}$

b R = rotation of $+90°$ about $(0,0)$
c E = enlargement scale factor 2, centre $(0,0)$
d R = reflection in the line with equation $y=0$ (the x-axis)

38 Find the inverse of each of the following matrix transformations. Demonstrate that your answers are correct by drawing diagrams showing the application of the matrix and its inverse to a suitable object.

a $\begin{pmatrix} 0 & -1 \\ 1 & 0 \end{pmatrix}$　**b** $\begin{pmatrix} 1 & 0 \\ 0 & -1 \end{pmatrix}$　**c** $\begin{pmatrix} 5 & 0 \\ 5 & 5 \end{pmatrix}$　**d** $\begin{pmatrix} 1 & 0 \\ 4 & 1 \end{pmatrix}$

39 Copy each of the following diagrams. Mark on your diagrams all the lines of symmetry and state the order of rotation of each shape.

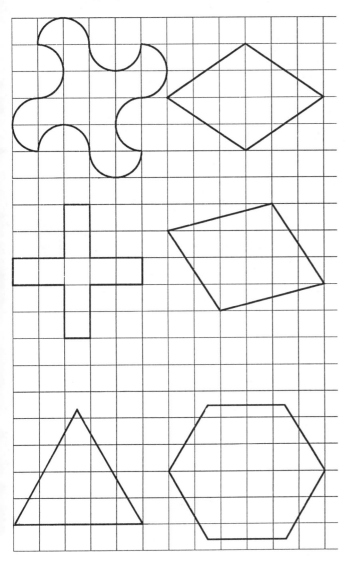

40 This diagram shows a collection of vectors. Copy the diagram and label each vector using only the letters <u>a</u>, <u>b</u> and <u>c</u>.

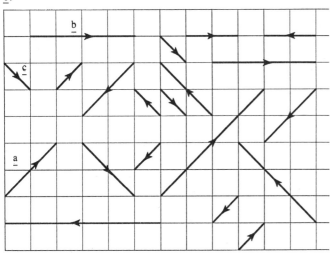

41 In this diagram, $\overrightarrow{OA} = \underline{a}$, $\overrightarrow{OB} = \underline{b}$ and M is the mid-point of AB. Describe in terms of <u>a</u> and <u>b</u> the vectors:

a $\overrightarrow{AB}$ **b** $\overrightarrow{BM}$ **c** $\overrightarrow{OM}$

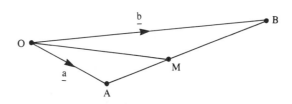

42 In each part of this question you are given the definitions of $\overrightarrow{XY}$ and $\overrightarrow{YZ}$ as column vectors. Draw a diagram to show $\overrightarrow{XY}$, $\overrightarrow{YZ}$ and $\overrightarrow{XZ}$ and describe $\overrightarrow{XZ}$ as a column vector.

a $\overrightarrow{XY} = \begin{pmatrix} +2 \\ +7 \end{pmatrix}$ $\overrightarrow{YZ} = \begin{pmatrix} +3 \\ +1 \end{pmatrix}$

b $\overrightarrow{XY} = \begin{pmatrix} +5 \\ +5 \end{pmatrix}$ $\overrightarrow{YZ} = \begin{pmatrix} -6 \\ -9 \end{pmatrix}$

43 In each part of this question you are given the definitions of <u>x</u> and <u>y</u> as column vectors. Show in a diagram the vectors <u>x</u>, <u>y</u>, <u>x</u> + <u>y</u> and <u>x</u> − <u>y</u>.

Describe <u>x</u> + <u>y</u> and <u>y</u> − <u>x</u> as column vectors.

a $\underline{x} = \begin{pmatrix} -3 \\ +9 \end{pmatrix}$ $\underline{y} = \begin{pmatrix} +8 \\ -7 \end{pmatrix}$

b $\underline{x} = \begin{pmatrix} -1 \\ +7 \end{pmatrix}$ $\underline{y} = \begin{pmatrix} +6 \\ -7 \end{pmatrix}$

Geometry—extended problems for project work

1 Dissection puzzles have been a popular pastime for at least 3000 years. To construct a dissection puzzle, a shape is dissected (cut up) into several smaller pieces. The aim of the puzzle is to reassemble the pieces into either the original shape or into the outlines of birds, animals and other objects. One famous Ancient Chinese dissection puzzle is called a **tangram**. This diagram shows the dissection necessary to create a tangram and some suggestions for possible rearrangements of the pieces.

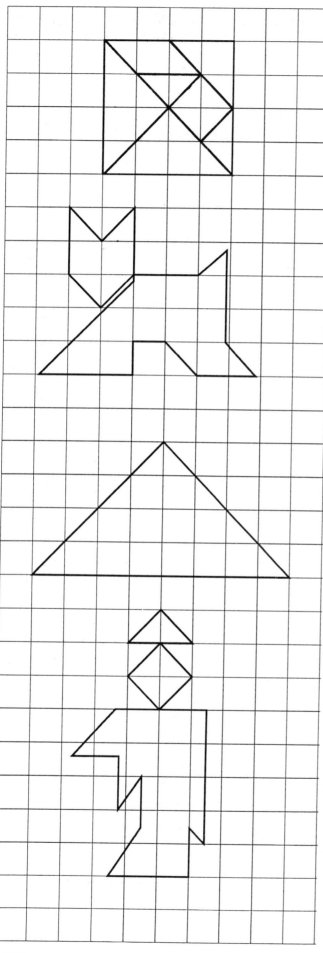

a Make your own tangram puzzle from card or thin plastic. Create some outlines as challenges for friends or relations to complete with the pieces. Try out your puzzle with a range of people and comment on the level of difficulty of the different outlines.

b The diagram which follows shows the construction of a more complex dissection puzzle and one suggestion of a possible rearrangement of the pieces. Make your own version of this puzzle and experiment with it.

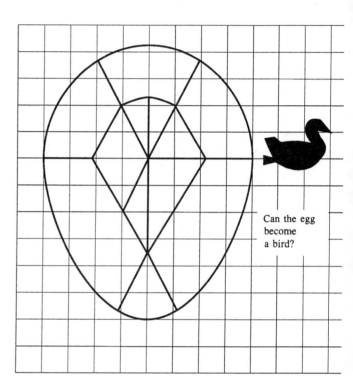

Can the egg become a bird?

c There are several dissection puzzles based on a rearrangement of a Greek cross into a square. This diagram shows one possible dissection by which this can be done. Experiment with this dissection and try to find other ways that the cross can be dissected to form a square.

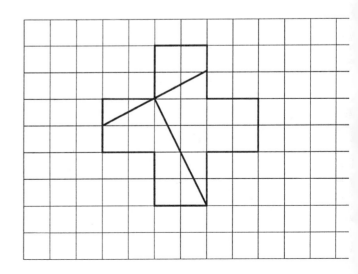

250

d Pentominoes is the name given to a 12-piece puzzle. The twelve pieces represent all the possible patterns that can be made with five squares. The following diagram shows the 12 pieces arranged into a 10 by 6 rectangle. Make your own set of pentominoes and experiment. Can you make an 8 by 8 square? What about a 3 by 20 rectangle?

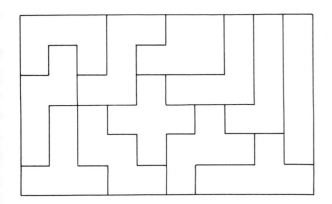

2 A regular tessellation is a tessellation formed from identical regular polygons. In the text you have seen that there are only three regular tessellations. These are based on equilateral triangles, squares and hexagons.

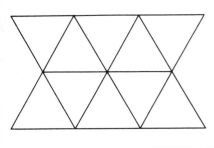

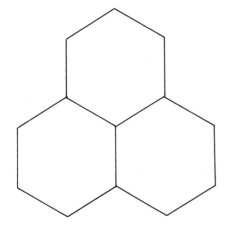

A mathematician called Schlafli invented a way to classify tessellations formed from regular polygons arranged so that the same number and types of polygons meet at every vertex of the tessellation. For example, this tessellation

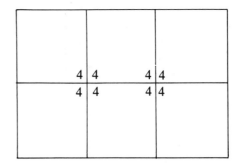

would be classified as 4^4, meaning that 4 four-sided polygons meet at every vertex of the tessellation. This tessellation

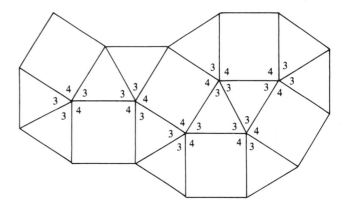

would be classified as $3^2.4.3.4$, meaning that at each vertex we have two equilateral triangles, followed by a square, followed by another equilateral triangle and finally another square.

A tessellation like this one, made from more than one kind of regular polygon is called a **semi-regular tessellation**.
a There are only 8 semi-regular tessellations. Their classifications are:

$$3^4.6$$
$$3^3.4^2$$
$$3^2.4.3.4$$
$$3.6.3.6$$
$$4.8^2$$
$$3.12^2$$
$$4.6.12$$
$$3.4.6.4$$

Draw diagrams of all these semi-regular tessellations.

251

b Many different tessellations can be developed from the regular or semi-regular tessellations. These diagrams show how, by cutting pieces out of regular polygons and then sticking them back on, new tessellations are formed. Experiment with these techniques and produce your own original tessellations.

c It is possible to form tessellations with irregular pentagons. These diagrams show **rough sketches** of some possibilities. Try to turn them into accurate tessellations. (WARNING This question part may require a great deal of experiment or some very careful mathematics to work out the angles and side lengths required in each pentagon!)

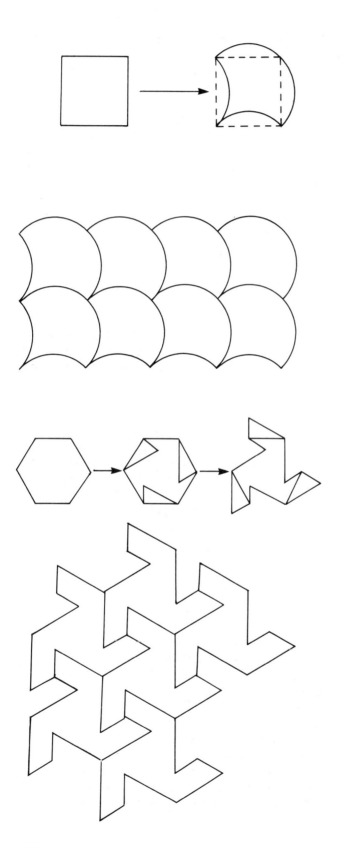

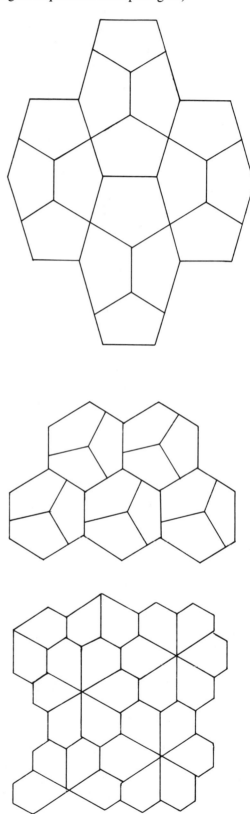

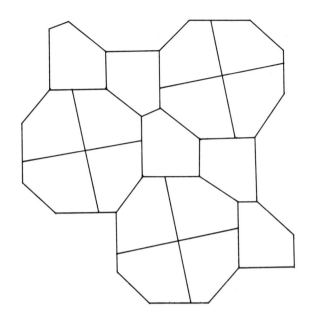

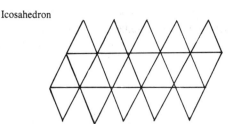

b There are many other irregular solids of interest to mathematicians and scientists. You could follow up your construction work by researching these other solids. Here are two possible starting points.

- There is no net for a sphere. This causes problems both for map makers trying to draw maps of the world on flat surfaces and also for manufacturers trying to cut up flat material to construct spheres (footballs, etc). Investigate solutions to these problems.
- Many naturally occurring crystals take the form of regular or semi-regular polyhedra. Find out all you can about crystals and their shapes.

d Investigate the paving slabs, bricks and floor tiles available at DIY stores. Take photographs and accurate measurements. Make some designs for floors and walls using the construction materials that you find are available.

3 A solid shape with flat faces is called a **polyhedron**. A polyhedron with identical regular polygons forming all its faces is called a **regular polyhedron**. Regular polyhedra were studied by the ancient Greeks and the final part of Euclid's famous book *The Elements* deals with their construction. The Greeks discovered that there are only five regular polyhedra.

a Rough sketches of the nets to construct the five regular solids follow. Drawing these accurately and then constructing the solids could form an interesting practical coursework task.

4 Many machines offer the possibility of research into the locus of a moving point. It is also possible to describe the action of the machine in terms of transformations. You could investigate one or several devices and present a report in the form of

- a general description of the device and its purpose, including drawing and/or photographs.
- a full description of the action of the device. Include photographs and a set of accurate drawings showing various stages of its operation and the locus of several key points.
- a technical description of the device's movements in terms of transformation geometry.

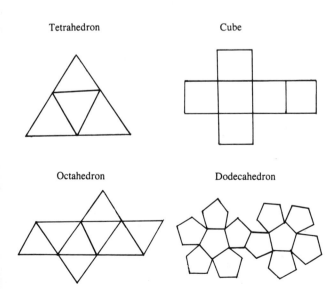

Tetrahedron   Cube

Octahedron   Dodecahedron

Some suggestions for suitable devices are

- a lever action corkscrew
- an ice-cream scoop with an ejector mechanism
- a mechanical drill or kitchen whisk
- a hinge on a kitchen cabinet
- a paper punch
- a pop-up picture book
- a venetian blind
- windscreen wipers
- an 'up and over' garage door
- a car's gear stick (or any other control)
- the gear system on a push bike
- the mechanical system used on a pull-along toy which makes other movements as it is pulled along

Geometry
Past paper questions

1 This is a framework of a gate.

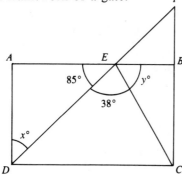

ABCD is a rectangle. Calculate the values of *x* and *y*.

(MEG)

2 The diagram below, **not** drawn to scale, shows a quadrilateral.

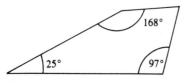

Three of the interior angles are 25°, 168° and 97°. Calculate the size of the fourth angle.

(SEG)

3 a Name the type of triangle shown in Figure A.

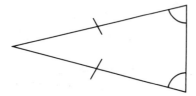

b Figure B shows a parallelogram *WXYZ*.

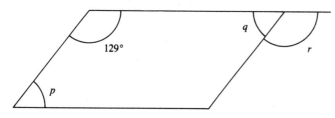

Calculate the value of
(i) *p*,
(ii) *q*,
(iii) *r*.

(LEAG)

4 A square tile has patterns marked on it in the shape of triangles.

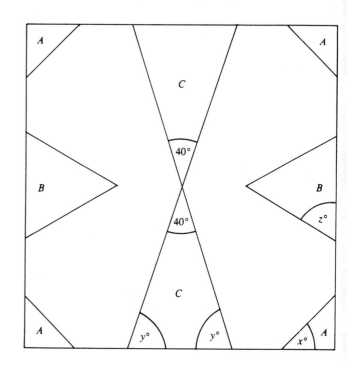

Triangles marked *A* and *C* are isosceles and those marked *B* are equilateral.

Write down the values of *x*, *y* and *z* shown in the diagram.

5

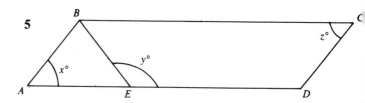

In the diagram (not drawn to scale) *ABCD* is a parallelogram and *ABE* is an equilateral triangle.

Work out the values of *x*, *y* and *z*.

(LEAG)

6 a

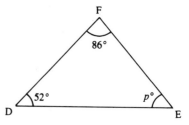

Calculate the value of *p*.

b

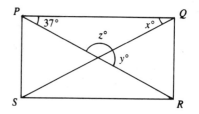

PQRS is a rectangle. Find the value of

(i) *x*,
(ii) *y*,
(iii) *z*.

(LEAG)

7

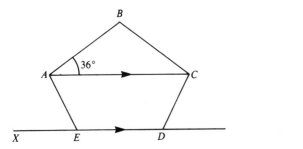

ABCDE represents a swimming pool with all its sides of equal length. A rope joins *A* to *C* and is parallel to *ED*. Given that BAC = 36° calculate:

a ∠*ABC*.
b ∠*CAE*.
c ∠*AEX*.

(SEG)

8 In this question you must give valid reasons for your answers. Numbers on their own will not be sufficient.

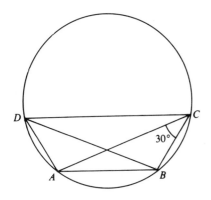

The diagram shows the cross-section of a tunnel. The tunnel is circular with a platform *DC* in it. The platform is held by five rods *AB*, *BC*, *BD*, *AD*, *AC*.

Rods *AB*, *AD* and *BC* are all the same length.

The angle between *AC* and *BC* is 30°.

a Find
(i) ∠*ADB*
(ii) ∠*ABD*,
(iii) ∠*DBC*,
(iv) ∠*BDC*,

b (i) Explain how you know that platform *DC* must be parallel to rod *AB*.
(ii) What does the answer to **a** (iii) tell you about *DC*?

(WJEB)

9 In the diagram below, which is not drawn to scale, *O* is the centre of the circle through the points *B*, *A* and *C*.

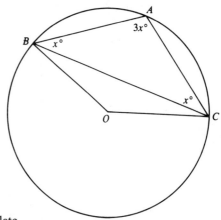

a Calculate
(i) the value of *x*,
(ii) the obtuse angle *BOC*.
b Show that angle *OBC* = ½ angle *ABC*

(SEG)

10 a

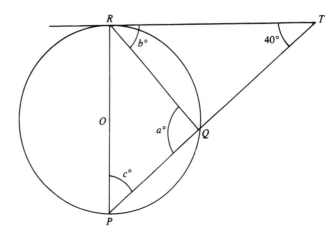

P, Q and *R* are three points on the circumference of a circle with centre *O. POR* is a diameter of the circle and *RT* is a tangent to the circle at *R*.

Write down the values of *a, b* and *c*.

b

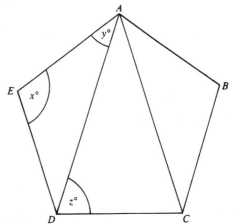

ABCDE is a regular pentagon.

(i) Write down the values x, y and z.

(ii) Show, giving reasons, that ED is parallel to AC.

(WJEB)

11

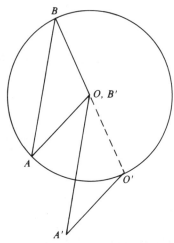

A and B are two points on the circumference of a circle whose centre is O. Triangle ABO is translated to the new position $A'B'O'$, so that B' coincides with O.

a Explain why

(i) O' lies on the circumference,

(ii) $A'B'$ is parallel to AB,

(iii) angle $A'B'A =$ angle $B'AB$,

(iv) angle $B'AB =$ angle $B'BA$.

b State the relationship between the angles $AB'O'$ and ABO.

(LEAG)

12

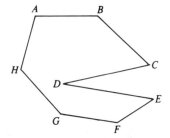

a What is the mathematical name for the shape $ABCDEFGH$?

b Join AD.

(i) What is the mathematical name for the shape $ABCD$?

(ii) What is the mathematical name for the shape $ADEFGH$?

(SEG)

13 The triangle in the diagram below is isosceles, with sides OA and OB each 5 cm long.

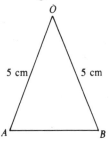

256

a Copy the diagram and draw the line of symmetry on the triangle.

b What angle is equal to angle A?

c Angle AOB is $40°$.

Calculate the size of angle A.

(SEG)

14

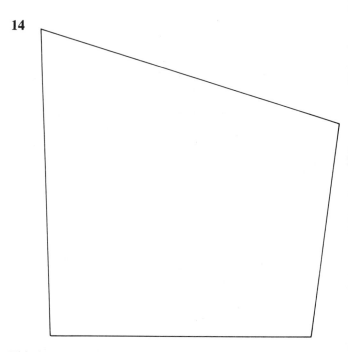

This is a quadrilateral.

a Mark on it the mid-point of each side. Join up the mid-points to make another quadrilateral.

b Measure the angles of the new quadrilateral and write them down.

c What is special about the new quadrilateral?

(MEG)

15 a

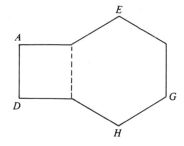

The tile $ABEFGHCD$ is made up of a square $ABCD$ attached to a regular hexagon $BEFGHC$ along their common side BC. What is the size of (i) $A\hat{B}C$ (ii) $E\hat{B}C$ (iii) $A\hat{B}E$?

b Tiles of the same shape as *ABEFGHCD* are placed in the pattern shown below.

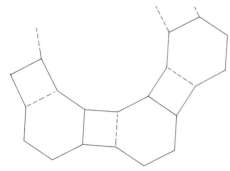

(i) Without drawing the completed figure, explain why the tiles will form a closed shape if the pattern is continued.
(ii) The completed shape encloses a regular polygon.

How many sides has this polygon?

(WJEC)

16 The sum of the exterior angles of any polygon is 260°

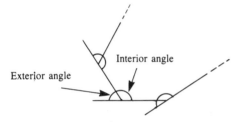

a Calculate the interior angle of a regular

(i) hexagon   (ii) pentagon

b (i) Another regular polygon has *x* sides. Find a formula for *y*, the interior angle, in terms of *x*.
(ii) Rearrange this formula to express *x* in terms of *y*.

c An artist is designing wallpaper patterns. She wants to cover the whole paper with a single repeated regular shape, leaving no gaps. Figure 1 shows her pattern using a regular hexagon. Figure 2 shows that she cannot use a regular pentagon.

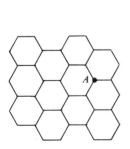

Figure 1   Figure 2

(i) How many hexagons meet at point *A* in Figure 1?
(ii) Use your two answers to the interior angles in part (a) to explain why the artist can use a hexagon but not a pentagon.
(iii) Can she use a regular octagon? Explain your answer.

(SEG)

17

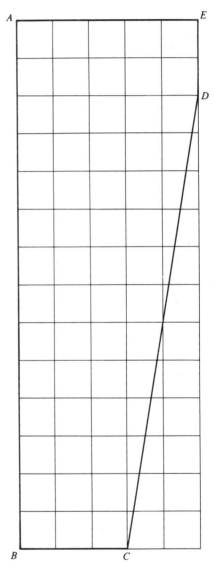

The diagram shows part of the pattern, *ABCDE*, for a pair of jeans. It must be carefully enlarged and placed on the material.

a The length of the side *AB* on the material must be 70 cm. State the scale factor of the enlargement.

b What will be the length, in centimetres, of *AE* on the material?

c What will be the size, in degrees, of angle *BCD* on the material?

(MEG)

18

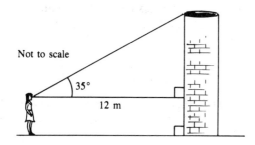

Not to scale

35°

12 m

A girl, whose eyes are 1½ metres above the ground, stands 12 metres away from a tall chimney. She has to raise her eyes 35° upwards from the horizontal to look directly at the top of the chimney.

Using a scale of 1 cm to represent 1 metre, find the height of the chimney by scale drawing.

(MEG)

19 The diagram shows two radar stations *A* and *B* which are 50 km apart.

A plane is at *P* when it is 'picked up' by the radars.

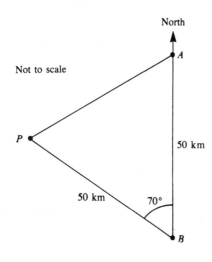

North

A

Not to scale

P

50 km

50 km

70°

B

BP = 50 km and angle *PBA* = 70°.

a What type of triangle is *ABP*?
b Calculate angle *PAB*.
c Work out the bearing of
(i) *P* from *B*,
(ii) *P* from *A*.
d Make a scale drawing of the diagram using a scale of 1 cm to 5 km.
e The plane flies due North from *P* for 30 km to a new position *Q*.
(i) Draw on your diagram the journey *PQ*.
(ii) How far is *Q* from the radar station *A*?

(MEG)

20 Bradford is on a bearing 020° from Huddersfield.

a Draw and label a sketch to show what this means.
b What is the bearing of Huddersfield from Bradford?

(MEG)

21 At an exhibition, one of the buildings is in the shape of a pyramid with a square base.

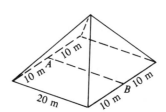

10 m
10 m
A
10 m
20 m
10 m
B 10 m

The height is 8 m. A vertical wall 3 m high is to be built up from *AB*. It touches the sloping sides. Make an accurate drawing of this wall. Use a scale of 1 cm to 2 m.

(MEG)

22 On a map 1 cm represents ½ km on the ground.

a State the distance in kilometres represented by 5 cm on the map.

b Two villages are 7 km apart. How far apart are they on the map?

c This diagram shows three villages and their distances apart on the map. It also shows two bearings. It is **not** drawn accurately. Draw the diagram accurately.

(SEG)

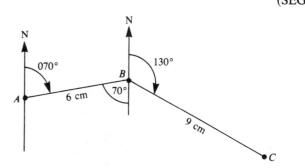

N

N

070°

130°

B

A 6 cm 70°

9 cm

C

23 a (i) Draw a triangle *ABC* with each of its sides 6.0 cm long.
 (ii) Join, with a straight line, vertex *A* to the mid-point, *D*, of the side *BC*.
 (iii) Measure and write down the length of *AD*, correct to the nearest millimetre.
 (iv) Calculate the area of the triangle *ABC*.

CHOCO-BAR

258

b A 'Choco-Bar' is sold in a closed carton with cross-section in the shape of an equilateral triangle with each of its sides 6.0 cm long. The carton is 30 cm long.
(i) **Sketch** a net of this carton.
(ii) Calculate the total surface area of the outside of the carton. Give your answer correct to two significant figures.
(LEAG)

24

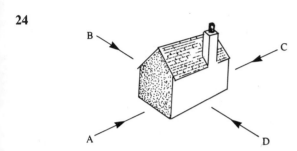

This is a model of a house.
Here are two views of the house.
Which arrow do you look along to see each view?

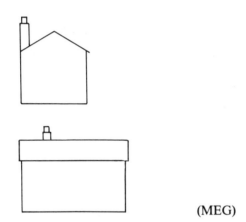

(MEG)

25

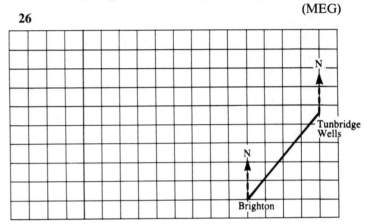

Not to scale

The diagram above shows the junction of two rivers. Some Scouts are asked to estimate the distance between the point

C and the tree, T, on the opposite bank. The Scouts are at the point B and cannot cross either river. They mark the points A and D and make the measurements shown in the diagram. ABC and DBT are straight lines.

$AB = 20$ m, $BD = 15$ m, $AD = 17$ m, angle $TAB = 41°$ and angle $BDC = 36°$

Using a scale of 1 centimetre to represent 5 metres, draw a scale diagram of the situation and find the distance CT, in metres. (The point B is already marked.)

(MEG)

26

The figure above is drawn to a scale of 5 mm to 5 miles. It shows the relative positions of Brighton and Tunbridge Wells.

a (i) Find the distance to the nearest mile from Brighton to Tunbridge Wells.
(ii) Find the bearing of Brighton from Tunbridge Wells.

Guildford is 35 miles from Brighton on a bearing of 326°.

b Plot, as accurately as possible, the position of Guildford on a copy of the grid.
Label this position G.

c Use your completed diagram to find:
(i) the distance to the nearest mile from Guildford to Tunbridge Wells;
(ii) the bearing of Tunbridge Wells from Guildford.

(LEAG)

27

A nurseryman wishes to run a waterpipe from his main water supply P to his two greenhouses G_1 and G_2. The distance

259

from the water supply to each greenhouse is 40 m and angle G_1PG_2 is 60°.

a Draw a scale diagram showing the positions of P, G_1 and G_2. (Use a scale of 1 cm to represent 4 m.)
He wishes to use the least amount of pipe possible and considers two schemes.

b *Scheme 1*
The pipe runs from P to G_1 and then from G_2.
Measure carefully and write down the length of pipe that would be used.

c *Scheme 2*
The pipe runs from P along an axis of symmetry of triangle PG_1G_2 and then along the shortest route from this axis to each of G_1 and G_2.
(i) Draw this axis of symmetry and these shortest routes to this axis of symmetry.
(ii) Hence find the total length of pipe that would be required.

d

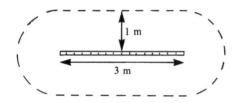

Inside each greenhouse he instals a sprinkler 3 m long, as shown in the diagram. The sprinkler waters all the area within 1 m of the sprinkler.
(i) Using a scale of 2 cm to represent 1 m, draw an accurate scaled diagram of the sprinkler and the area that would be watered.
(ii) Calculate this area. (Take π to be 3.142 or use the π key on your calculator. The area of a circle $= \pi r^2$.)

(SEG)

28 Using a scale of 1 cm to 1 unit, draw coordinate axes Ox and Oy for values of x from 0 to 15 and values of y from 0 to 6. Plot the points E (0,0), B (3,4), H (10,4), and G (12,2). Draw the lines EH and BG, and label their intersection with the letter x.

Treat your diagram as a (simplified) map where 1 cm represents 20 km, and take the line Oy to represent the North direction. Answer the following questions by taking suitable measurements and making suitable calculations as required.

The line EH represents the path of an aircraft which leaves Exeter at 0900 and flies directly to Heathrow at a constant speed of 300 km/h.

a At what time does this aircraft arrive at Heathrow?
The line GB represents the path of a second aircraft, which leaves Gatwick, also at 0900, and flies at a constant speed to Bristol, arriving at 0945.

b What is the speed of this aircraft?

c On what bearing is it flying?

d At what time does the aircraft from Exeter reach the point X?

e How far from Bristol is the Gatwick–Bristol aircraft at this moment?
When the Exeter–Heathrow aircraft is 10 km from Heathrow it is flying at a height of 3500 m.

f Calculate its angle of elevation at this moment as observed from the ground at Heathrow.

(MEG)

29 Using a scale of 1 centimetre to represent 2 metres, mark the positions of 3 boys so that each boy is 12 metres from the other two.

(MEG)

30 Alison Taylor buys an indoor plant and is told to place it more than two metres from the fireplace in her lounge. The diagram below, drawn using a scale of 2 centimetres to represent 1 metre, shows a plan of her lounge, including the front, AB, of the fireplace.

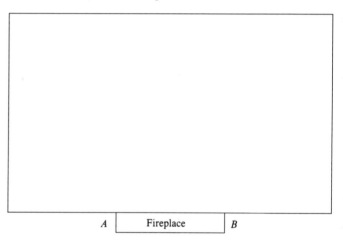

Copy the diagram and show accurately the part of the room which is more than two metres from the front, AB, of the fireplace, where Alison may stand her plant.

(MEG)

31 This is a plan of baby Simon's bedroom.

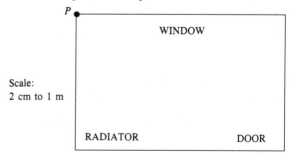

To keep warm, Simon must be within 1½ m of the wall containing the radiator. To be heard on the baby alarm at P he must be within 2 m of it. Copy the diagram and shade the region in which Simon must be if he is to be warm enough and can also be heard on the alarm.

(MEG)

32

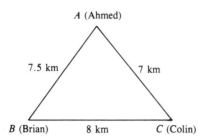

Three police officers, Ahmed, Brian and Colin, each have a radio-transmitter with a range of 5 km. They are on moorland and their positions are shown on the diagram (which is not drawn to scale).

Using a scale of 1 cm to represent 1 km, draw an accurate diagram and, by drawing a circle, show the region X where a person must be in order to listen to Colin by radio.

Show the region Y where an inspector must be in order to hear all three policemen by radio. What is the nearest that the inspector can be to Ahmed if he is also able to listen to the other two?

(SEG)

33

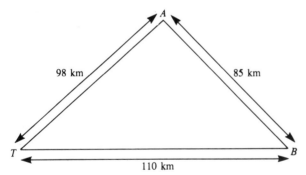

The figure shows the location of a television transmitter (T) in relation to two towns Amburg (A) and Beetown (B).

a Using a scale of 1 cm to represent 10 km, draw an accurate scale diagram of the triangle TAB.
The transmitter has a range of 80 km.

b Draw accurately, on your scale drawing, the curve which represents the limiting range of the transmitter.

It is planned to build a repeater station (R), which is an equal distance from both Amburg and Beetown.

c On your drawing, construct accurately the line on which the repeater station must be built.
The repeater station is to be built at the maximum range of the transmitter.

d (i) Mark, with the letter R, the position of the repeater station on your diagram.
(ii) Find the minimum transmitter range of the repeater station so that programmes can be received in Amburg. Give your answer in km, to the nearest km.

(LEAG)

34

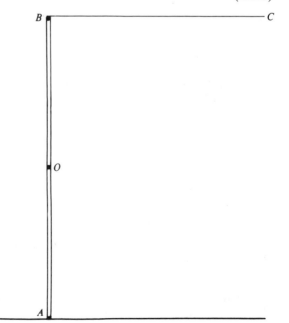

A and B are two landmarks on a straight shore, 3.2 km apart, with A due West of B. C is the point on a bearing of 063° from A and also on a bearing of 322° from B.

a Draw an accurate scale diagram showing A, B, C and the shore line, using a scale of 5 cm to 1 km. Shade the triangle ABC which represents a dangerous sand bank.

b Describe the locus of points P such that angle APB equals 90°.

c A ship P is steaming due East parallel to the shore and 600 m from it. When it is due North of A the Captain measures the angle between PA and PB and finds that it is acute. He continues on his straight course until angle APB is 90°. He then follows the locus of **b** until he is again 600 m from the shore. After this he again sails due East. Draw his course on your diagram.

d How near does he come to the sand bank?

(MEG)

The diagram, which is drawn using a scale of 4 centimetres to represent 1 metre, shows the side view of an up-and-over garage door, *AB*, which is 2 metres high. When the door is opened it moves so that the bottom of the door, *A*, is always 1 metre from the point *O*, which is a fixed point on the garage wall midway between the original positions of *A* and *B*. In addition, the top of the door, B, is constrained to move along the horizontal line *BC*.

Draw accurately, on a copy of the diagram above,

a the locus of the bottom of the door, *A*, as the door is fully opened,

b the position of the door when the bottom of the door, *A*, is 1 metre above the ground.

(MEG)

36 The diagrams below show the working of a shade outside a shop when it is being erected.

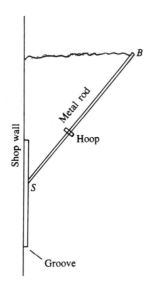

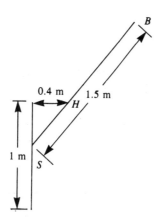

A metal rod *SB* is free to slide in a hoop *H* which is 0.4 m from the wall of the shop. The lower end *S* of the rod slides in a groove which is 1 metre long. The shade is attached at *B* to the rod which is 1.5 m long. Draw on the graph paper a one-tenth size diagram showing two positions of the rod, with *S* at the lowest and highest positions.

a By considering *S* moving 10 cm at a time, or otherwise,

draw the path followed by *B* as *S* goes from the lowest to the the highest position.

b When *S* is halfway between the lowest and highest positions, what is the distance of *B*
 (i) from the shop wall,
(ii) above the horizontal through the hoop?

c When *B* is 1.4 m from the shop wall, how far is it from the hoop?

d The lowest end of the groove is 1.2 m from the ground. How high is *B* above the ground at its highest point?

(SEG)

37 a On each of the quadrilaterals draw in all lines of symmetry. If no lines can be drawn, state on the figure 'no lines possible'.

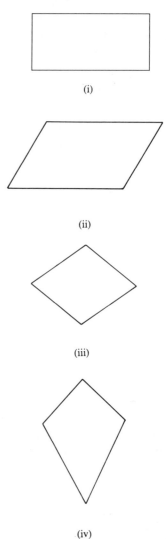

(i)

(ii)

(iii)

(iv)

b Each of the quadrilaterals can be given a distinct name. Give the name of each of the quadrilaterals as precisely as possible.

(LEAG)

262

38 The diagram shows a regular pentagon.

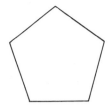

a (i) What is its order of rotational symmetry?
(ii) Copy the diagram and add to the pentagon so that the resulting diagram has only one line of symmetry.

b Calculate the size of an interior angle of a regular pentagon.

c Can a tessellation be formed with tiles in the shape of equally-sized regular pentagons? If so, sketch the tessellation. If not, explain why not.

(MEG)

39 The diagram shows part of a tessellation.

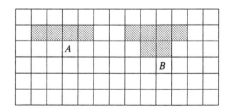

On a copy of this diagram mark

a a line of symmetry, labelling it *m*,

b a point labelled *P* about which the tessellation has rotational symmetry of order 3.

(MEG)

40

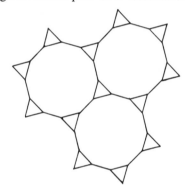

a Use the two shapes *A* and *B* to make one new shape which has only one line of symmetry. Draw the new shape on a piece of graph paper.

b Now use the two shapes *A* and *B* to make another new shape which has two lines of symmetry only. Draw the new shape on a piece of graph paper.

(WJEC)

41

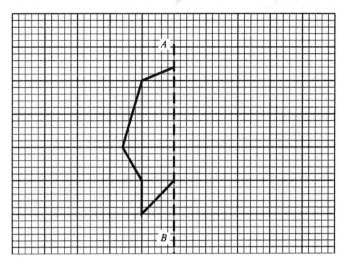

Copy and complete the figure so that the line *AB* is the line of symmetry of the completed shape.

(LEAG)

42 Draw a tessellation of the shape given on the grid below. The shape should be repeated at least eight times.

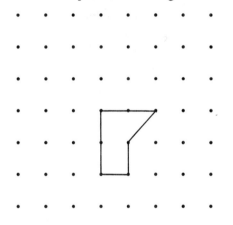

(MEG)

43 The diagram shows the net of a cardboard carton. The carton holds a chocolate bar.

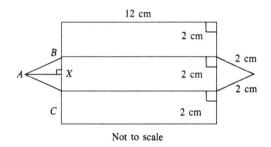

Not to scale

a (i) What type of triangle is *ABC*?
(ii) What is the size of angle *BCA*?

b The length of *AX* is 1.73 cm. Calculate the area of
(i) triangle *ABC*,
(ii) the complete net.

c The chocolate bars (in their cartons) are packed in layers in a box. The box is 10 cm wide, 5.4 cm high and 24 cm long. Some bars are shown in the following full-size diagram.

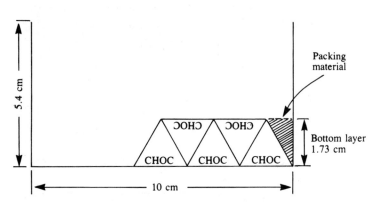

Packing material

5.4 cm

Bottom layer 1.73 cm

10 cm

  (i) How many chocolate bars will there be in the complete bottom layer?
 (ii) How many layers will there be inside the box?
(iii) How many chocolate bars will be packed inside the box?

(MEG)

44 These are the nets of 3 solids. They are not drawn accurately.

(i)

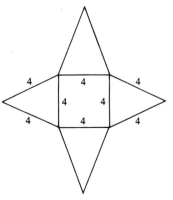

(ii)

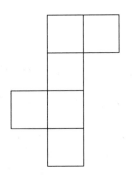

(iii)

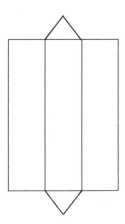

a Copy each net and write under it the name of the shape it will make when it is folded up.

b Draw a full-size copy of net (i). The lengths are marked in cm.

c Measure any lengths you need in your diagram and use them to work out the area of the net. Show clearly all steps of working.

d The net is to be made from a piece of card 12 cm by 12 cm. Find the area of card left over.

(MEG)

45

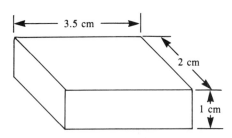

3.5 cm

2 cm

1 cm

a Calculate the volume of a cuboid which has dimensions 3.5 cm by 2 cm by 1 cm.

The diagram below shows part of the net of a cuboid which has dimensions 3.5 cm by 2 cm by 1 cm.

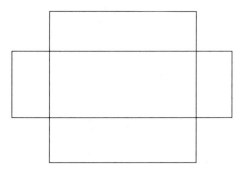

b (i) Copy and complete the net accurately.
(ii) Calculate the surface area of the cuboid.

(SEG)

264

46 Draw a quadrilateral with one and only one line of symmetry.

(SEG)

47

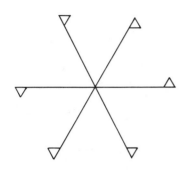

Say whether the figure shown has

A rotational symmetry of order 6
B rotational symmetry of order 3
C line symmetry about exactly three lines
D line symmetry about exactly two lines, or
E line symmetry about exactly one line.

(LEAG)

48 A piece of floor is covered with L-shaped tiles. The design is repeated over its surface. It consists of the 3 colours Red (R), Blue (B) and Yellow (Y) as shown.

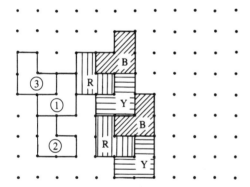

a What fraction of the pattern is coloured yellow?
b What are the colours of the tiles numbered 1, 2, and 3?

(SEG)

49 Three pupils were asked to draw nets for a cube. These were their diagrams.

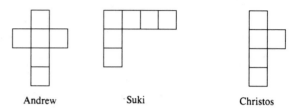

Andrew   Suki   Christos

For each of these, write down whether the net is correct or incorrect.

(SEG)

50 The diagram shows four square tiles with a pattern drawn on the top left-hand tile. Draw the patterns needed on the other three tiles so that the completed picture is symmetrical about the line *AB* and about the line *CD*.

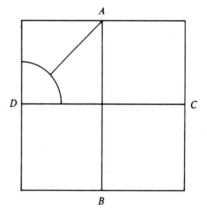

AB and *CD* intersect at the point *O*, which is not labelled in the diagram. Write down a statement that describes the rotational symmetry of the finished pattern about *O*.

Look at the four patterns given below.

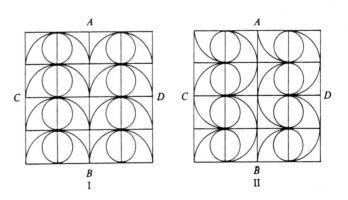

I   II

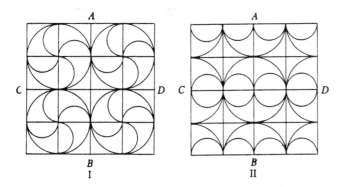

I   II

In each of the above, O is the point of intersection of AB and CD. Pattern IV has a tick in the box for 'Rotational symmetry of 180° about O', because if the pattern is rotated about O through 180° then the pattern would look unchanged.

Pattern	Symmetrical about AB	Symmetrical about CD	Rotational symmetry of 180° about O
I			
II			
III			
IV			✔

For each pattern in turn, place a tick (✔) in the box if the pattern has the property. A pattern may have more than one of the symmetries given in the table.

(WJEC)

50

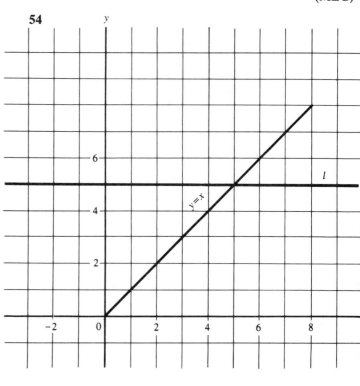

a What is the gradient of the line AE?

b Copy figure $ABCDE$ on to graph paper with the point C near the top centre of the page.

c Draw the enlargement of $ABCDE$ with centre C and scale-factor 2.

(SEG)

52

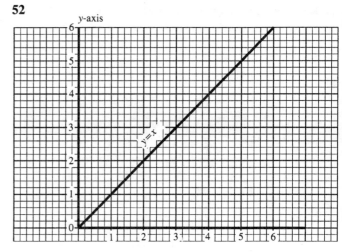

Write down the coordinates of the image of the point with coordinates (4,1) under reflection in the line with equation $y = x$.

(LEAG)

53 The Sky at Night

If you watch the sky on a clear night, the stars appear to rotate anticlockwise about the Pole Star. The 360° rotation takes 24 hours.

The diagram shows the Pole Star (P) and the constellation of stars called Triangulum (T) at 8 p.m. Copy the diagram and draw the position of the constellation at 2 a.m.

P ● T

(MEG)

54

a Write down the equation of line *l*.

b Write down three inequalities satisfied by all points inside the triangle formed by the line *y*=*x*, the line *l* and the *y*-axis.

c Draw the reflection of the line *l* in the line *y*=*x* on your diagram. Label the image *m*.

d Write down the equation of the line *m*.

(MEG)

55

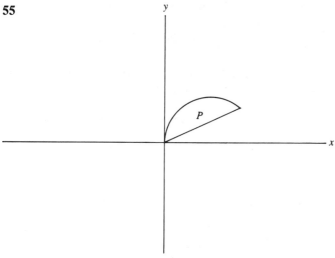

The diagram shows part of a circular disc *P*. *Q* is the reflection of *P* in the *y*-axis. Copy the diagram.

a Draw and label *Q* on your diagram.

R is the result of rotating *P* through 90° clockwise about the origin.

b Draw and label *R* on your diagram.

(SEG)

56 What transformation will move triangle *ABC* to its new position *PQR*?

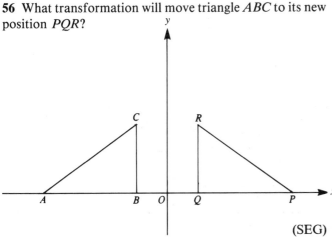

(SEG)

57

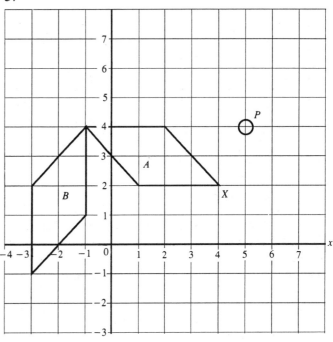

From this diagram,

a describe fully the transformation which maps parallelogram *A* onto parallelogram *B*,

b if parallelogram *A* is enlarged, scale factor 3, with centre of enlargement at *P*, write down the co-ordinates of the point onto which the corner *X* is mapped.

(SEG)

58

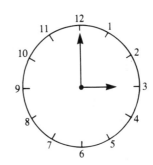

a At 3 p.m. the hour hand of this clock is represented by the vector
$$\begin{pmatrix} 2 \\ 0 \end{pmatrix}$$

What vector will represent the hour hand of the clock at 6 p.m.?

b What is the image of the point (0,1) under the transformation
$$\begin{pmatrix} 0 & 1 \\ -1 & 0 \end{pmatrix} ?$$

(SEG)

59 Draw a diagram which shows the quadrilateral $OABC$ in which the vertices have position vectors

$$\begin{pmatrix} 0 \\ 0 \end{pmatrix}, \begin{pmatrix} 0.5 \\ 0.5 \end{pmatrix}, \begin{pmatrix} 0 \\ 1 \end{pmatrix} \text{ and } \begin{pmatrix} 1.5 \\ 0.5 \end{pmatrix} \text{ respectively.}$$

a The transformation E is an enlargement, centre O and scale factor $+2$. E maps O, A, B, C onto O, X, Y, Z *respectively*
  (i) Write down the position vectors of O, X, Y, Z.
  (ii) Draw the quadrilateral $OXYZ$ on the diagram.
  (iii) Write down the matrix of E.
  (iv) Explain why $ABXC$ is a parallelogram.

b A second transformation F is determined by the matrix

$$\begin{pmatrix} -1 & 1 \\ 1 & -1 \end{pmatrix}$$

Draw the image of $OABC$ under the transformation F and label it $OGHI$.

c The transformation F is equivalent to a rotation followed by an enlargement. Write down
 (i) the angle of rotation,
 (ii) the scale factor of the enlargement.

(SEG)

60 a The points $A (1,1)$, $B (3,2)$ and $C (2,4)$ are the vertices of a triangle ABC. The triangle can be represented in matrix form as:

$$\begin{pmatrix} A & B & C \\ 1 & 3 & 2 \\ 1 & 2 & 4 \end{pmatrix}$$

Triangle ABC is transformed into $A'B'C'$ by the matrix

$$\begin{pmatrix} 2 & 0 \\ 1 & 1 \end{pmatrix}$$

Triangle $A'B'C'$ is then transformed into $A''B''C''$ by the matrix

$$\begin{pmatrix} 1 & 0 \\ -1 & 2 \end{pmatrix}$$

Find the co-ordinates of the points $A''B''C''$.
b What single matrix would perform the combined transformation in part **a**?
c Describe fully the combined transformation in part (a).

(SEG)

61 1 (i) On graph paper plot the following points: (0,0); (0,1); (4,3); (7,3); (3,1); (3,0); (0,0), and join them up in the order given.
(ii) Label the figure P.

(iii) Label the point (7,3), A.
b The figure P is reflected in the y-axis to form the image Q.
  (i) Draw this image and label it Q.
  (ii) Write down the co-ordinates of the image of A.
  (iii) Label this point B.

c The figure Q is enlarged by scale factor 2, with the centre of enlargement the origin, to form the image R.
  (i) Draw this image and label in R.
  (ii) Write down the co-ordinates of the image of B.
  (iii) Label this point C.

d The figure R is translated six units in the negative direction, parallel to the y-axis, to form, the image S.
  (i) Draw the image and label it S.
  (ii) Write down the co-ordinates of the image of C.
  (iii) Label this point D.

e The figure S is enlarged by scale factor ½, with centre of enlargement the origin, to form the image T.
  (i) Draw the image and label it T.
  (ii) Write down the co-ordinates of the image of D.
  (iii) Label this point E.

f Which of the figures is congruent to T?

(SEG)

62

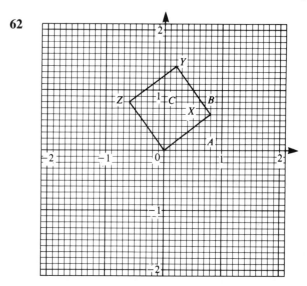

Copy this diagram which shows two squares $OABC$ and $OXYZ$. The points O, A, B, C have position vectors

$$\begin{pmatrix} 0 \\ 0 \end{pmatrix}, \begin{pmatrix} 1 \\ 0 \end{pmatrix}, \begin{pmatrix} 1 \\ 1 \end{pmatrix}, \begin{pmatrix} 0 \\ 1 \end{pmatrix} \text{ respectively.}$$

a A transformation, P, is represented by the matrix

$$\begin{pmatrix} 1 & 0 \\ 0 & -1 \end{pmatrix}$$

P maps O, A, B, C onto O, D, E, F respectively.
  (i) Calculate the position vectors of O, D, E and F.
  (ii) Draw $ODEF$ on your diagram.
  (iii) Describe geometrically the transformation P.
  (iv) Write down the matrix which maps $ODEF$ onto $OABC$.

b The points Z, Y, X have position vectors

$$\begin{pmatrix} 0.8 \\ 0.6 \end{pmatrix}, \qquad \begin{pmatrix} 0.2 \\ 1.4 \end{pmatrix}, \qquad \begin{pmatrix} -0.6 \\ 0.8 \end{pmatrix}$$

A transformation, Q, maps O, A, B, C onto O, X, Y, Z respectively.
 (i) Describe geometrically the transformation Q.
 (ii) Write down the matrix of Q.
c Calculate the matrix representing the transformation which maps $ODEF$ onto $OXYZ$.

(SEG)

63 The matrix **M** is defined as

$$\mathbf{M} \quad \begin{pmatrix} -1 & 3 \\ -1 & 1 \end{pmatrix}$$

a Calculate $\mathbf{M}^2$.
The triangle T has vertices A (1,1), B (4,1) and C (1,2).
b Find the co-ordinates of the vertices of T_1, the image of T under the transformation whose matrix is $\mathbf{M}^2$.

c Using graph paper and taking a scale 1 cm to 1 unit on each axis, draw and label the triangles T and T_1.

d Describe fully, in words, the **single** transformation which maps T onto T_1.

e Find $\mathbf{M}^{-1}$ and hence, or otherwise, find the co-ordinates of the point whose image is the point $(1, -3)$ under the transformation whose matrix is $\mathbf{M}$.

(LEAG)

64 For the matrix $\mathbf{M} = \begin{pmatrix} 2 & 5 \\ 1 & 4 \end{pmatrix}$, find

a the determinant of $\mathbf{M}$,
b the inverse matrix $\mathbf{M}^{-1}$.
The points $(8, -3)$, $(-2, 1)$, $(10, -2)$ and $(20, -6)$ are the vertices of a parallelogram P. Q is the image of P under the transformation represented by $\mathbf{M}$.
c Calculate the co-ordinates of the four vertices of Q.
d Sketch the figure Q.
e State the area of Q.
f Deduce the area of the parallelogram P.
R is the image of the original parallelogram P under rotation through $90°$ anticlockwise about the origin.
g Write down the matrix which transforms P to R.
h Write down a product of two matrices which will transform Q to R, and evaluate this product.

(MEG)

65 Draw the usual x- and y-axes, using a scale of 1 cm to 1 unit on each axis. Label the x-axis from -10 to 8 and the y-axis from -7 to 7. On your diagram draw and label the triangle T whose vertices are at $(-3,2)$, $(-3,2)$, $(-1,2)$.

a (i) A is the image of T under reflection in the line $x=2$. Draw and label A.
 (ii) B is the image of T under reflection in the line $y=x$. Draw and label B.
 (iii) State the angle of the rotation which maps A onto B, and find the co-ordinates of the centre of this rotation.
b E is the enlargement, centre the origin, scale factor 3. F is the enlargement, centre X (1,0), scale factor ½.
 (i) Draw and label the triangle P which is the image of T under E.
 (ii) Draw and label the triangle Q which is the image of P under F.
 (iii) State the scale factor of the enlargement FE, find its centre Y and state the coordinates of Y.

(MEG)

66 The vertices of a rectangle $OABC$ are O (0,0), A (5,0), B (5,2) and C (0,2).
a Taking 1 cm to represent 1 unit on each axis and marking each axis from -6 to 6, draw and label the rectangle $OABC$.
b The rectangle $OABC$ is mapped onto rectangle $OA_1B_1C_1$ by the transformation represented by the matrix $\mathbf{P}$ where

$$\mathbf{P} = \begin{pmatrix} 0 & 1 \\ 1 & 0 \end{pmatrix}$$

Draw and label rectangle $OA_1B_1C_1$ on your diagram, and describe the transformation fully in geometrical terms.
c The original rectangle $OABC$ is mapped onto another rectangle $OA_2B_2C_2$ by reflection in the x-axis. Draw and label the rectangle $OA_2B_2C_2$ on your diagram. Write down the matrix $\mathbf{Q}$ which represents this transformation.
d The rectangle $OA_1B_1C_1$ can be mapped onto the rectangle $OA_2B_2C_2$ by a single transformation represented by matrix $\mathbf{R}$. Describe this transformation represented by matrix $\mathbf{R}$. Describe this transformation fully in geometrical terms and state the relationship between the matrices $\mathbf{P}$, $\mathbf{Q}$, $\mathbf{R}$
e Find the smallest positive integer n for which $\mathbf{R}^n = \mathbf{I}$, where $\mathbf{I}$ is the identity matrix.

(MEG)

67

A, B and C are three points on the circumference of a circle with centre O. The diameters at right angles to AB and BC are m_1 and m_2. M_1 and M_2 are the transformations 'reflect in m_1' and 'reflect in m_2' respectively.

a Identify $M_1(A)$, the image of A under the transformation M_1.

b Identify (i) $M_2(B)$, (ii) $M_2M_1(A)$.

c Explain why, in the figure, the angles marked x and y and equal.

d Describe fully the single transformation equivalent to M_2M_1 and hence express angle AOC in terms of y.

e Comment on the relationship between the angles AOC and ABC.

(MEG)

68 OPQR is a parallelogram. The vectors **x** and **y** are such that

$$\overrightarrow{OP} = \mathbf{x} + \mathbf{y} \text{ and } \overrightarrow{OR} = \mathbf{x} - \mathbf{y}$$

a Express as simply as possible in terms of x and/or **y**
 (i) $\overrightarrow{OR}$,
 (ii) $\overrightarrow{RP}$.
 (b) What special type of parallelogram is OPQR
 (i) when $|\mathbf{x} + \mathbf{y}| = |\mathbf{x} - \mathbf{y}|$,
 (ii) when $|\mathbf{x}| = |\mathbf{y}|$?

(MEG)

69 In the figure, M is the mid-point of PQ. P, Q and M have position vectors **p**, **q** and **m** respectively referred to O as origin.

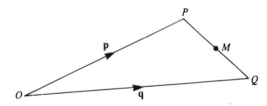

Write down, in terms of **p** and **q** only, expressions for the following vectors:

a $\overrightarrow{PQ}$, **b** $\overrightarrow{PM}$, **c** m.

(MEG)

70

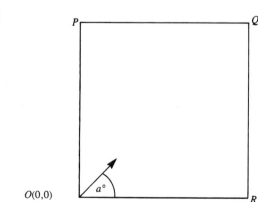

The diagram shows the screen for a game of computer hockey. The 'passes' and 'shots' can be described using vectors, for example the pass from B to A is

$$\begin{pmatrix} -3 \\ 8 \end{pmatrix}$$

a Describe the pass from A to B.

b Describe the pass from B to C.

c C scores a goal. Give the vector of a direct shot which would score.

(MEG)

71 The diagram shows a triangle OAB. M is the mid-point of AB, N is the mid-point of OM.

$$AP = \frac{1}{4} AM \text{ and } OQ = \frac{3}{10} OB.$$

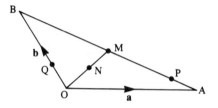

Let $\overrightarrow{OA} = \mathbf{a}$ and $\overrightarrow{OB} = \mathbf{b}$.

Express the following vectors in terms of **a** and **b**, simplifying your answers as much as possible,

a $\overrightarrow{AO}$ **b** $\overrightarrow{OQ}$ **c** $\overrightarrow{AB}$ **d** $\overrightarrow{AM}$ **e** $\overrightarrow{OM}$

Show that
f $\overrightarrow{NQ} = -\frac{1}{4}\mathbf{a} + \frac{1}{20}\mathbf{b}$,

g $\overrightarrow{PN} = -\frac{5}{8}\mathbf{a} + \frac{1}{8}\mathbf{b}$.

h Explain why the results in **f** and **g** show that PNQ is a straight line.

(MEG)

72

In a video game, the screen is 100 units by 100 units.

270

The player has to enter a vector to give the direction the 'ball' will travel.

The ball starts at $O(0,0)$.

John enters the vector $\begin{pmatrix} 1 \\ 2 \end{pmatrix}$ and the ball moves making an angle $a°$ with OR.

a What is the value of a?
b The position of the ball as it moves to the top of the screen PQ can be written as

$$k \begin{pmatrix} 1 \\ 2 \end{pmatrix}$$

What is the value of k when the ball reaches PQ?

c What are the co-ordinates of the point where the ball hits PQ?

d When the ball hits PQ it rebounds so that the 'new' path is at 90° to the 'old' path.

Which vector describes the ball's direction after it rebounds from PQ?

e What are the co-ordinates of the point where the ball hits QR?

(WJEC)

73

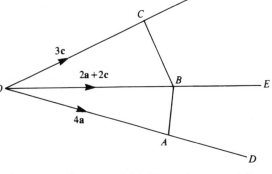

In the above diagram, $OABC$ is a plane quadrilateral with

$$\overrightarrow{OA} = 4\mathbf{a}, \quad \overrightarrow{OB} = 2\mathbf{a} + 2\mathbf{c}, \quad \overrightarrow{OC} = 3\mathbf{c}.$$

a Express the vectors $\overrightarrow{CO}$, $\overrightarrow{CB}$ and $\overrightarrow{AB}$ in terms of $\mathbf{a}$, or $\mathbf{c}$, or $\mathbf{a}$ and $\mathbf{c}$.

The lines OA, OB and OC are produced to D, E and F respectively, where

$$OC = CF \quad \text{and} \quad OB:BE = OA:AD = 2:1.$$

b Find $\overrightarrow{FC}$, $\overrightarrow{BE}$, $\overrightarrow{FE}$ and $\overrightarrow{DE}$ in terms of $\mathbf{a}$, or $\mathbf{c}$, or $\mathbf{a}$ and $\mathbf{c}$.
c Write down two geometrical facts about the points D, E and F.

(LEAG)

Pythagoras and Trigonometry

Pythagoras

Squares and square roots

This section will require some skills in using a calculator. These are practised in this section.

The first skill is the ability to calculate the **square** of a number.

The square of a number is calculated by multiplying the number by itself.

So, we can write:

● the square of 4 is 16.

● the square of 10 is 100.

The word 'square' is used because, when you multiply a number by itself, you are calculating the area of a square.

A square with a side length of 4 units

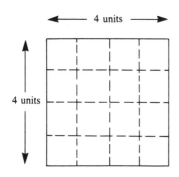

4 units

4 units

has an area of 16 square units.

There is a special way to write the square of a number.

4×4 can be written as 4^2.

10×10 can be written as 10^2.

We read 4^2 as '4 squared' and 10^2 as '10 squared'.

CHECKPOINT 1

Calculate:

1 The square of 5   *25*   **2** 23^2 *529*   **3** 30^2 *900*

4 The area of a square with sides 7 cm long.   *49 cm²*

When the numbers are difficult, a calculator can be used to calculate squares quickly. As usual, we should estimate our answer to check the accuracy of our key pressing.

For example, when calculating 8.73^2, we can estimate that the answer must be between 8^2 and 9^2; that is between 64 and 81.

The actual key pressing required to calculate 8.73^2 will depend on the calculator you are using.

All calculators should allow you to find the answer in the most obvious way by pressing

$$\boxed{8}\ \boxed{.}\ \boxed{7}\ \boxed{3}\ \boxed{\times}\ \boxed{8}\ \boxed{.}\ \boxed{7}\ \boxed{3}\ \boxed{=}$$

Most calculators will allow you to save time by pressing

$$\boxed{8}\ \boxed{.}\ \boxed{7}\ \boxed{3}\ \boxed{\times}\ \boxed{=}$$

Scientific calculators usually have a function button marked x^2. This will allow you to press

$$\boxed{8}\ \boxed{.}\ \boxed{7}\ \boxed{3}\ \boxed{x^2}$$

Whichever method you use, the answer should be 76.2129.

CHECKPOINT 2

1 Experiment with your calculator and find the squares of

4225   166.41   1.69   53361

a 65   **b** 12.9   **c** 1.3   **d** 231

2 Find the area of a square with sides 53.5 cm long.

2862.75 cm²

The second calculator skill that you must practise is the ability to find the **square root** of a number.

The square root of a number *N* is the number which, when squared, is equal to *N*.

So, we can write:

● the square root of 16 is 4, because 4 squared is equal to 16.

In the same way:

● the square root of 100 is 10;

● the square root of 25 is 5.

There is a special way to write the square root of a number.

The square root of 16 is written as $\sqrt{16}$.

So,

$$\sqrt{16} = 4 \qquad \sqrt{100} = 10 \qquad \sqrt{25} = 5$$

We can think of the square root of a number *N* as the side length of a square with an area of *N* square units.

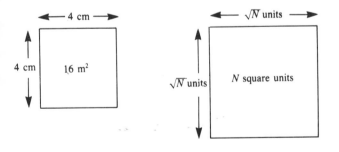

CHECKPOINT 3

Calculate:

1 the square root of 64   **2** $\sqrt{4}$ **3** $\sqrt{81}$

4 the side length of a square with an area of 36 cm².

Unless a number has an obvious square root, the only practical way to find a square root is with a calculator. Most calculators have a square root button marked $\boxed{\sqrt{}}$.

Usually, you enter the number you wish to square root and then press this button.

So, pressing

$\boxed{1}$ $\boxed{6}$ $\boxed{\sqrt{}}$ should produce the answer 4.

Many square roots are long awkward decimals. For example, when I press

$\boxed{2}$ $\boxed{0}$ $\boxed{\sqrt{}}$ on my calculator the result 4.4721359

is produced. Even this long decimal is not completely accurate, because if I use the same calculator to square 4.4721359, the result produced is 19.999999.

As usual when working with a calculator, we should use an estimate to check the accuracy of our key pressing. Suppose, for example, we wish to find the square root of 350. We know that $\sqrt{100} = 10$ and that $\sqrt{400} = 20$. Therefore, $\sqrt{350}$ should be between 10 and 20. My calculator produces 18.708286 as the answer to $\sqrt{350}$, which agrees with my estimate.

CHECKPOINT 4

1 Explain why $\sqrt{60}$ must be between 7 and 8.

7² = 49 and 8² = 64

2 Explain why $\sqrt{734}$ must be between 20 and 30.

20² = 400   30² = 900

3 Experiment with your calculator and find the square roots of

7.745966692 dP = 7.76 to 2 dP   27.09243437 = 27.09 to 2 dP   2.387467277 = 2.39 to 2 dP   30.6022875 to 2 dP = 30.60 to 2 dP

a 60   **b** 734   **c** 5.7   **d** 936.5

4 Find the side length of a square with an area of 45 cm².

6.708203932 = 6.71cm to 2 dP

Pythagoras and the Pythagoreans

Pythagoras was a Greek mathematician and philosopher. He lived in Crotona, a Greek city in what is now Southern Italy, about 2500 years ago.

He was the founder of a secret society called the Pythagoreans whose main interest was social and moral reform. Although they were founded as a political brother-hood, the society also discussed mathematics and astronomy. They made several important discoveries in these areas. They were, for example, the first group to believe and teach that the Earth and other planets revolved round the Sun.

The Pythagoreans were fascinated with numbers. They discovered many different number patterns and relationships and attributed mysterious powers to their discoveries. The Pythagoreans did not like outsiders to know about their discoveries. They even drowned one of their members called Hippasus because he betrayed their secrets!

The most famous discovery of the Pythagoreans is the relationship between the lengths of the sides in any right-angled triangle.

This discovery is known as the **theorem of Pythagoras.**

Look at this right-angled triangle.

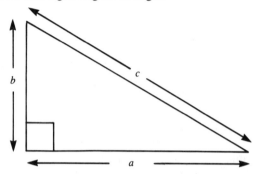

The Pythagoreans proved that in every right-angled triangle like this,

$$c^2 = a^2 + b^2$$

The longest side of a right-angled triangle is called the **hypotenuse**.

So, we can state:

The theorem of Pythagoras
The square of the hypotenuse of a right-angled triangle is equal to the sum of the squares of the other two sides.

If we know the lengths of two of the sides in a right-angled triangle, we can use the theorem of Pythagoras to calculate the length of the third side.

Example

Calculate the length of the side PQ in this triangle.

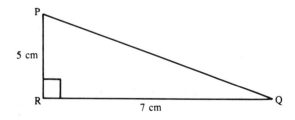

PQ is the hypotenuse of the triangle, so, using the theorem of Pythagoras, we can write

$$PQ^2 = RQ^2 + PR^2$$

$$PQ^2 = 7^2 + 5^2$$

$$PQ^2 = 49 + 25 = 74$$

$$PQ = \sqrt{74}$$

$$PQ = 8.6 \text{ cm, correct to one decimal place}$$

CHECKPOINT 5

1 Find the length of the side RT in this triangle.

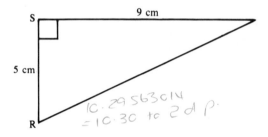

10.29563014
=10.30 to 2 d P.

2 Find the length of the side XZ in this triangle.

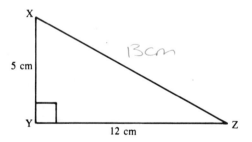

13cm

3 Find the length of the side AB in this triangle.

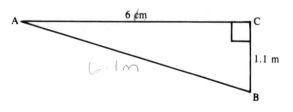

6.1m

4 Find the length of a diagonal in a rectangle 8.4 m long and 1.3 m high.

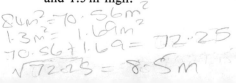

8.4m² = 70.56m²
1.3m² = 1.69m²
70.56 + 1.69 = 72.25
√72.25 = 8.5m

274

5 ABC is the triangle with vertices at $(-1,2),(0,3)$ and $(3,-1)$. Calculate the lengths of the sides AB, BC and CA and hence prove that ABC is an isosceles triangle.

6 A rectangular lawn is 40 m by 15 m. Instead of walking along a path down two sides of the lawn, Sue Naylor takes a short cut across the diagonal. How much shorter is her direct route than the path down two sides of the lawn?

55m   42.72001873 = 42.72m to 2 dp = 12.28m shorter

▰▰▰▰▰▰▰▰▰▰▰▰

In all the calculations in the last checkpoint, the side to be found was the **hypotenuse**. If the hypotenuse is one of the given sides, our calculations are slightly changed.

Example

A ladder 5 m long rests against a wall with its foot 1.5 m from the base of the wall. How far up the wall will the ladder reach?

The first step in any Pythagoras problem set in words is to reduce the information to a sketch of a right-angled triangle. In this case we can make this sketch.

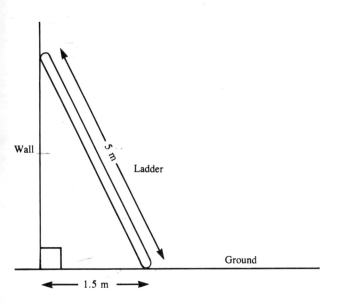

If we call the distance we wish to calculate x, using the theorem of Pythagoras we can write

$$5^2 = x^2 + 1.5^2$$

$$25 = x^2 + 2.25$$

$$x^2 = 25 - 2.25 = 22.75$$

$$x = \sqrt{22.75}$$

$$x = 4.77\,\text{m},\ \text{correct to the nearest centimetre.}$$

---

1 Find the length of the side CD in this triangle.

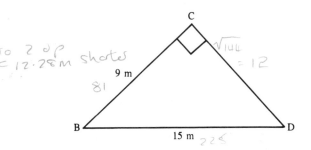

√144 = 12   81   225

2 Find the length of the side JL in this triangle.

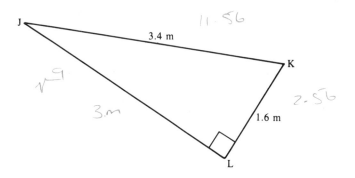

11.56   √9   3m   2.56   1.6 m

3 Find the length of the side HF in this triangle.

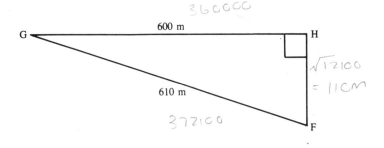

360000   √12100 = 11cm   372100

4 Will an umbrella which is 1 metre long fit inside a suitcase which has inside dimensions of 90 cm by 50 cm?

90² = 8100 cm²   8100 + 2500 = 10600
50² = 2500 cm²   √10600 = 102.95630914 to 2dp
102.96 to 2dp

5 If a square has a diagonal of length 20 cm, what is the side length of the square?   14.14 cm to 2 dp.

6 A support wire 10 m long is to be attached to a television mast and then pegged into the ground. The wire must be attached to the mast at a point 7 m from the base. How far from the base of the mast will the wire be pegged to the ground?

▰▰▰▰▰▰▰▰▰▰▰▰

Pythagoras in 3D *Not on paper*

Some problems will involve three-dimensional objects. For example, we might be asked to calculate the length of the diagonal BH in this cube.

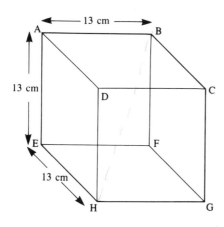

The first step to any Pythagoras solution is:

Find a right-angled triangle that has the required length as one of its sides.

In this diagram, the triangle BFH has the required length, BH, as one of its sides.

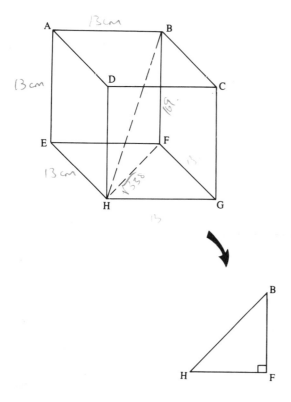

The only problem is we don't know the length of the side FH! We can, however, calculate the length of FH by using the theorem of Pythagoras in the triangle HFG.

Our full solution therefore requires **two** applications of the theorem of Pythagoras.

First, in triangle HFG:

$$HF^2 = FG^2 + GH^2$$

$$HF^2 = 13^2 + 13^2$$

$$HF^2 = 169 + 169 = 338$$

Then, in triangle BHF:

$$BH^2 = BF^2 + HF^2$$

$$BH^2 = 169 + 338 = 507$$

$$BH = \sqrt{507}$$

$$BH = 22.52 \text{ cm, correct to two decimal places}$$

Notice in this calculation, the actual length of HF was not found. The value of HF^2 was simply carried forward into the second part of the calculation. You should do this in **all** two-stage calculations because unnecessary square-rooting involves extra work and can introduce errors.

For example, if we had found the length of HF we might have set our calculations out like this.

First, in triangle HFG:

$$HF^2 = FG^2 + GH^2$$

$$HF^2 = 13^2 + 13^2$$

$$HF^2 = 169 + 169 = 338$$

$$HF = \sqrt{338}$$

$$HF = 18.38 \text{ cm, correct to two decimal places}$$

Then, in triangle BHF:

$$BH^2 = BF^2 + HF^2$$

$$BH^2 = 13^2 + 18.38^2$$

$$BH^2 = 169 + 337.8244 = 506.8244$$

$$BH = \sqrt{506.8244}$$

$$BH = 22.51 \text{ cm, correct to two decimal places}$$

As you can see, a lot of unnecessary extra work has been done and an error has been introduced by the approximation used for $\sqrt{338}$.

1 This diagram shows a cuboid PQRSTUVW in which PQ = 4 cm, PR = 8 cm and PW = 5 cm. Calculate the length of the diagonal PU.

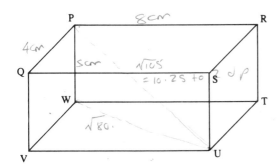

2 A television mast 40 metres high is to be erected at one corner of a small rectangular field which is 50 metres by 30 metres. One of the support wires is fixed to the top of the mast and anchored in the ground at the opposite corner of the field. Calculate the length of this support wire.

3 Ms Smith's garage is 3 metres by 3 metres by 5 metres. Is it possible to fit a yacht mast 6.4 metres long into this garage?

4 In this diagram, ABCDEF is a triangular prism with AB = 1.5 cm, AC = 6.6 cm and CD = 7.1 cm.

Calculate the length of the diagonal CE.

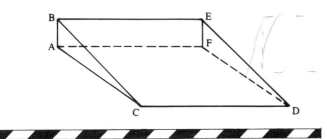

Pythagoras and vectors

The physical length of a vector $\underline{a}$ is called the **modulus of $\underline{a}$ and is written** $|\underline{a}|$ We can use Pythagoras to calculate the modulus of any vector drawn on a square grid.

For example, in this diagram

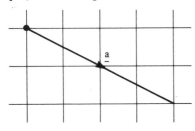

The vector $\underline{a}$ is the hypotenuse of this triangle

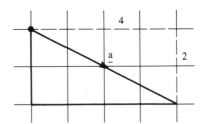

and hence the modulus of $\underline{a}$ can be calculated like this.

$$|\underline{a}|^2 = 4^2 + 2^2$$

$$|\underline{a}|^2 = 16 + 4 = 20$$

$$|\underline{a}| = \sqrt{20}$$

$$|\underline{a}| = 4.47 \text{ cm, correct to one decimal place}$$

Example

$$\underline{a} = \begin{pmatrix} +3 \\ -4 \end{pmatrix} \qquad \underline{b} = \begin{pmatrix} +2 \\ +5 \end{pmatrix}$$

Show in one diagram, $\underline{a}$, $\underline{b}$, $\underline{a} + \underline{b}$ and $\underline{a} - \underline{b}$. Calculate $|\underline{a}|$, $|\underline{b}|$, $|\underline{a} + \underline{b}|$ and $|\underline{a} - \underline{b}|$.

This is the required diagram

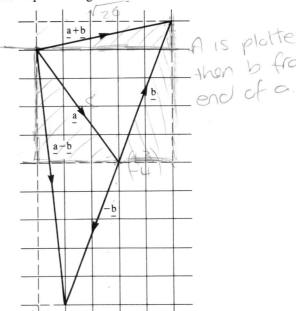

and these are the necessary calculations.

$$|\underline{a}|^2 = 3^2 + 4^2 = 25 \qquad |\underline{b}|^2 = 2^2 + 5^2 = 29$$

$$|\underline{a}| = 5 \qquad\qquad |\underline{b}| = 5.4 \text{, correct to 1 d.p.}$$

$$|\underline{a} + \underline{b}|^2 = 1^2 + 5^2 = 26$$

$|\underline{a} + \underline{b}| = 5.1$ correct to 1 d.p.

$|\underline{a} - \underline{b}|^2 = 9^2 + 1^2 = 82$

$|\underline{a} - \underline{b}| = 9.1$ correct to 1 d.p.

CHECKPOINT 8

1 In each part of this question you are given the definitions of $\overrightarrow{XY}$ and $\overrightarrow{YZ}$ as column vectors. Draw a diagram to show $\overrightarrow{XY}$, $\overrightarrow{YZ}$ and $\overrightarrow{XZ}$ and describe $\overrightarrow{XZ}$ as a column vector. *Calculate* $|\overrightarrow{XY}|$, $|\overrightarrow{YZ}|$ and $|\overrightarrow{XZ}|$.

a $\qquad \overrightarrow{XY} = \begin{pmatrix} +3 \\ -2 \end{pmatrix} \qquad \overrightarrow{YZ} = \begin{pmatrix} +4 \\ -3 \end{pmatrix}$

b $\qquad \overrightarrow{XY} = \begin{pmatrix} +3 \\ +4 \end{pmatrix} \qquad \overrightarrow{YZ} = \begin{pmatrix} +4 \\ +3 \end{pmatrix}$

2 In each part of this question you are given the definitions of $\underline{x}$ and $\underline{y}$ as column vectors. Show in a diagram the vectors $\underline{x}$, $\underline{y}$, $\underline{x} + \underline{y}$ and $\underline{x} - \underline{y}$. Describe $\underline{x} + \underline{y}$ and $\underline{x} - \underline{y}$ as column vectors. Calculate $|\underline{x}|$, $|\underline{y}|$, $|\underline{x} + \underline{y}|$ and $|\underline{x} - \underline{y}|$.

a $\qquad \underline{x} = \begin{pmatrix} -2 \\ +8 \end{pmatrix} \qquad \underline{y} = \begin{pmatrix} +8 \\ -2 \end{pmatrix}$

b $\qquad \underline{x} = \begin{pmatrix} -2 \\ +8 \end{pmatrix} \qquad \underline{y} = \begin{pmatrix} +5 \\ -6 \end{pmatrix}$

Trigonometry

How trigonometry began

The solution of geometrical problems by scale drawing was well known to both the ancient Greeks and Egyptians. The mathematicians of Alexandria made further advances by discovering methods to solve geometrical problems by **calculation**.

The Egyptian city of Alexandria was founded at the mouth of the River Nile by Alexander the Great in 332 BC. The cosmopolitan population of the new city was mainly made up of Jews, Greeks and Egyptians. Alexandria rapidly became a centre of learning when a large university and library were built there by its first ruler, Ptolemy, one of Alexander's generals.

The achievements of the scientists and mathematicians of Alexandria during the next 400 years were simply astonishing. Among them,

- Aristarchus measured the distance from the earth to both the sun and the moon.

- Eratosthenes measured the circumference of the World, obtaining an answer which is only 50 miles different from modern measurements!

- Archimedes established several important scientific and mathematical laws, particularly those concerned with levers and floating bodies. He also invented many new mechanical devices, including irrigation pumps and weapons of war.

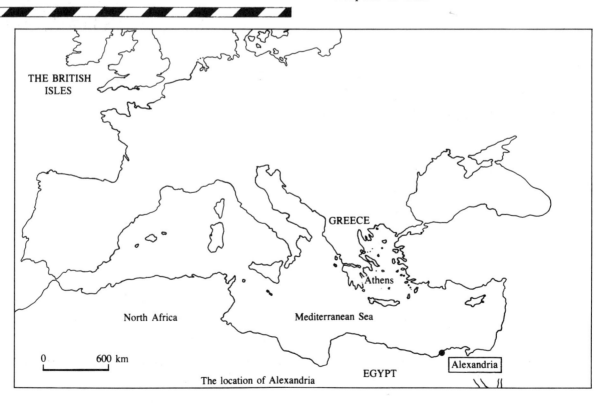

The location of Alexandria

- Hero wrote a book detailing the design of over 100 mechanical devices, including a theodolite, a double action pump and (believe it or not) a steam engine!

- Hipparchus is of particular interest in the context of this chapter because he created the World's first trigonometry tables.

- Hypatia was one of the last great mathematics teachers of Alexandria. She was murdered by Christian Monks—with incredible cruelty they killed her by scraping her skin off with oyster shells. These monks destroyed the 'pagan' schools of science in Alexandria and sadly brought to a close one of history's most dramatic periods of scientific and mathematical advance.

Angles and sides in right-angled triangles

The word **trigonometry** is formed from two Greek words meaning **triangle** and **measure**. Simple trigonometry is concerned with the sides and angles of right-angled triangles. As in all branches of mathematics, there are some new words to learn: first, the names given to the sides of a right-angled triangle. We already know from the Pythagoras section that the longest side is called the **hypotenuse.** The other two sides are named in relation to a selected angle.

In this triangle, angle A is our selected angle.

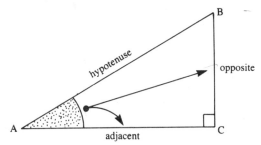

Side AB is called the **hypotenuse.**

Side BC is called the **opposite** because it is directly opposite to the selected angle.

Side AC is called the **adjacent** because it is adjacent to the selected angle. The word 'adjacent' means 'next to'. (Side AB is also 'next to' the selected angle, but we have already given it a special name.)

Notice that if we change our selected angle, the adjacent and opposite side swap over. So, in this triangle where angle B is our selected angle,

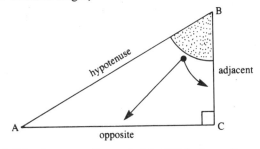

side AC is the opposite and side BC is the adjacent.

Copy each of these triangles and label their sides with the names hypotenuse, opposite and adjacent. The selected angle in each triangle has been shaded.

1

2

3

4

The tangent ratio

Trigonometry is based on very simple concepts. Before the first concept is explained, the next checkpoint tests to see if you already understand it as a matter of 'common sense'.

CHECKPOINT 10

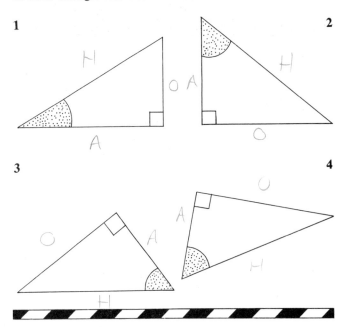

How long is the side YZ?

If you were able to answer the last checkpoint correctly, you already understand two facts.

> **Similar triangles**
>
> **1** If the angles of two triangles are identical, the triangles are **similar**. That is to say, they have the same **shape**.
>
> **2** If two triangles are similar then **the ratios between their sides must be the same.**

That is to say, if the first diagram is accurate, then in any other right-angled triangle with an angle of 42° the opposite side will also be 0.9 times the adjacent side.

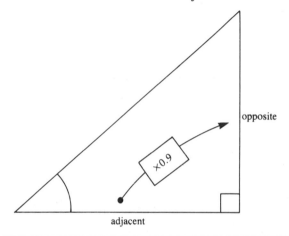

opposite

×0.9

adjacent

CHECKPOINT 11

Use the relationship illustrated in the diagram above to solve each of these problems.

1 These stairs climb at an angle of 42° for a horizontal distance of 10 metres. How high is the top of the stairs?

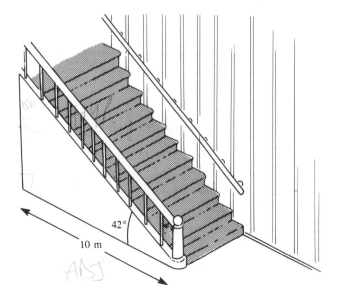

42°

10 m

2 Measured at a point 20 metres from its base, the angle of elevation of the top of a fir tree is 42°. How high is the tree?

42°

20 m

3 The diagram shows three cottages. How far is it along the road from cottage A to cottage B?

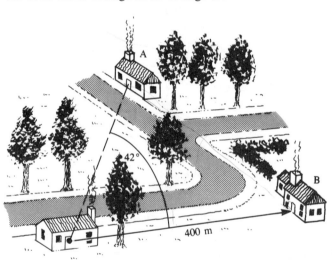

A

42°

B

400 m

The last checkpoint demonstrated that if we know the relationship between the opposite and adjacent sides for a specific angle we can solve many different problems which involve a triangle of similar shape. It was Hipparchus, working in Alexandria about 150 BC, who first realised that if he constructed tables of values for many different angles, they could be used to solve **any** geometrical problem simply and quickly.

One such table is constructed to show the relationship between the opposite and adjacent sides in a right-angled triangle. The value it gives for an angle is called the **tangent ratio** of the angle. This ratio is the value obtained when the length of the opposite side is divided by the length of the adjacent side.

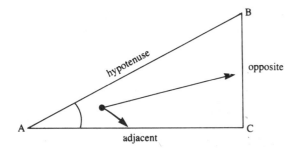

$$\text{Tangent ratio of angle A} = \frac{\text{length of BC}}{\text{length of AC}}$$

The best possible way to fully understand the tangent ratio is to construct a simple table of your own values. You are asked to do this in the next checkpoint.

CHECKPOINT 12

Draw the diagram sketched below **accurately to scale** on a piece of graph paper. Start with the baseline of 10 cm, and draw angles of 10°, 20°, 30° and so on from one end of the baseline. Then use the height opposite each angle to complete this table of values for the tangent ratio.

Angle	10	20	30	40	45	50	60
Tangent ratio	0.18	0.36	0.58	0.84	1.0	1.19	1.73

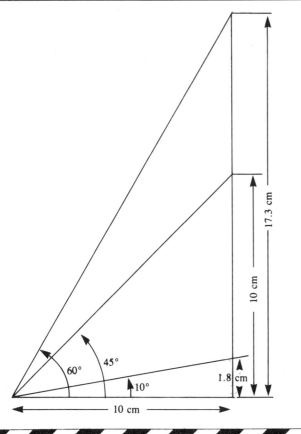

This is a more accurate tangent table.

Angle	10	20	30	40	50	60	70	80
Tangent	0.176	0.364	0.577	0.839	1.192	1.732	2.747	5.671

(To simplify things, the tangent ratio of angle A is usually just written as tan A.)

The example below shows how our table of tangent ratios can be used to solve problems.

Example

From a distance of 15 metres, a surveyor measures the angle of elevation of the top of a building to be 60°. How high is the building?

First, we draw a sketch.

From the sketch we see that the height of the building is the opposite side in a right-angled triangle with an adjacent side 15 metres long.

Therefore

$$\tan 60° = \text{height of building} \div 15$$

$$\text{height of building} = 15 \times \tan 60°$$

$$\text{height of building} = 15 \times 1.732$$

$$\text{height of building} = 25.98 \text{ metres}$$

1 Find the length of the side AB in each of these triangles.

a

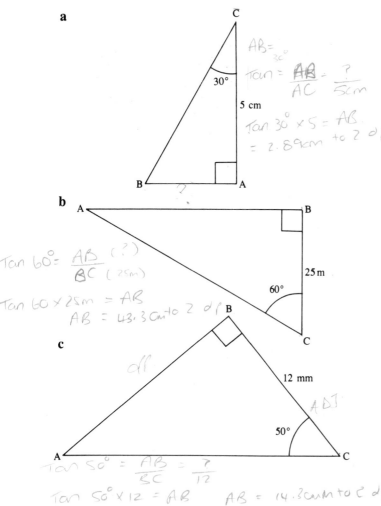

AB=
30°
Tan = $\frac{AB}{AC}$ = $\frac{?}{5cm}$

Tan 30° × 5 = AB
= 2.89km to 2 dp

b

Tan 60°= $\frac{AB}{BC}$ $\frac{(?)}{(25m)}$

Tan 60 × 25m = AB
AB = 43.3 cm to 2 dp

c

dp

Tan 50° = $\frac{AB}{BC}$ = $\frac{?}{12}$

Tan 50° × 12 = AB   AB = 14.3cm to 2 dp.

2 How far will this ladder reach up the wall?

Tan 70° × 1.5m = ?
= 4.12m to 2 dp

3 How far from the ground is the top end of this see-saw?

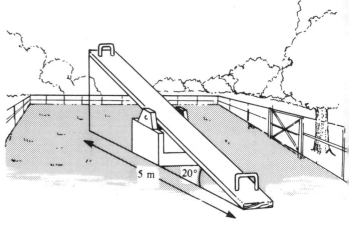

4 After take-off, a plane climbs at an angle of 40° to the ground. How high will it be when it passes over a building 1 kilometre from the end of the runway?

Our simple table only gives the tangent ratio for angles in steps of 10°. A table at the end of this text gives the tangent ratio for each angle from 1° to 90° in steps of 1°. It is, however, preferable to tackle trigonometrical problems with a **scientific calculator**. This will have a button marked **tan**, which can give a very accurate value for the tangent ratio of **any** angle. Most calculators require you to enter the angle before pressing this button. So, to find the tangent ratio of 42°, press

| 4 | | 2 | | tan |

This should give an answer of 0.9004040.

Use your calculator to find

1 tan 15°   **2** tan 76°   **3** tan 37.5°   **4** tan 60.55°

Example

This triangular wooden framework requires a brace fitted halfway along the base (shown with dashed lines). Calculate the length of this brace.

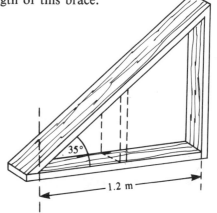

The brace is the opposite side in a right-angled triangle with an adjacent side of 0.6 metres.

Therefore,

$$\tan 35° = \text{length of brace} \div 0.6$$

$$\text{length of brace} = 0.6 \times \tan 35°$$

To calculate this with most calculators we press

| 0 | . | 6 | × | 3 | 5 | tan | = |

This should give an answer of 0.42 metres (to 2 d.p.).

CHECKPOINT 15

1 Find the length of the side AB in each of these triangles.

a

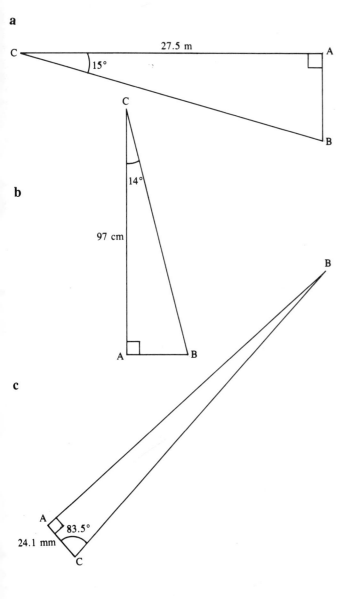

b

c

2 The steepest normal railway in the world, in Guatemala, climbs at an angle of 5.2° to horizontal ground. What is the gain in height of a train travelling a horizontal distance of 900 metres along this line?

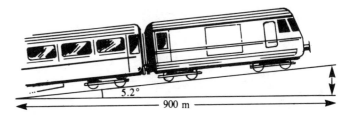

3 On a sunny day, a flagpole casts a shadow 3.7 metres long when the sun rays are at an inclination of 56° to the ground. How high is the flagpole?

4 This diagram shows a sketch for a triangular framework made from steel wire. Calculate the total length of wire needed to make the framework.

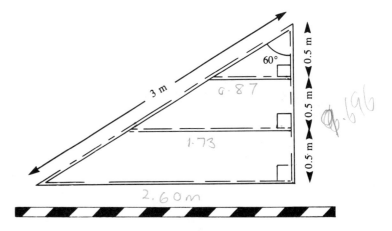

In all the problems we have tackled so far, the side length we have calculated has been the **opposite**. A slightly different technique is required if the side length to be found is the **adjacent** rather than the opposite.

Example

Ms Jones is standing at the top of a cliff which she knows is 35 metres high. She sees a yacht out to sea, with an angle of depression of 12° from where she is standing. How far is the yacht from the base of the cliff?

We can draw this sketch.

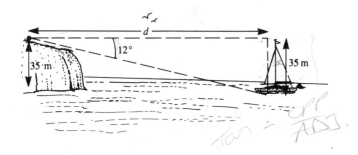

We can see that, if d is the distance of the yacht from the cliff

$$\tan 12° = 35 \div d$$

The problem requires us to calculate d, the **adjacent** side.

If we first multiply both sides of the equation by d we have

$$d \times \tan 12° = 35$$

Now, if we divide both sides of the equation by tan 12° we have

$$d = 35 \div \tan 12°$$

Most calculators will allow us to enter the calculation like this:

$$\boxed{3}\ \boxed{5}\ \boxed{\div}\ \boxed{1}\ \boxed{2}\ \boxed{\tan}\ \boxed{=}$$

which gives

$$d = 164.7 \text{ metres (to 1 d.p.)}$$

CHECKPOINT 16

1 Find the length of the side AB in each of these triangles.

a

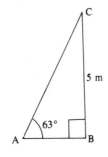

b

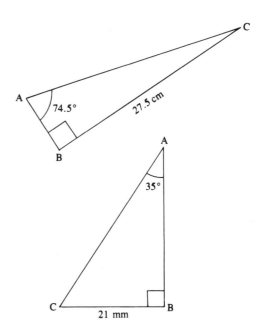

c

2 The wall in a loft conversion slopes at an angle of 60° to the floor. How close to the base of the wall can a wardrobe 2.1 metres high be pushed?

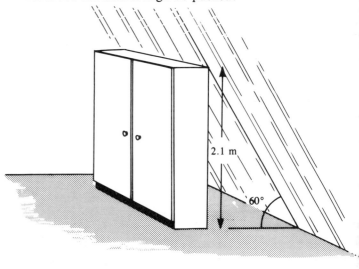

3 A wheelchair ramp is to be built up to a viewing platform 2.3 metres above the ground. How far from the base of the platform must the ramp start if it is designed to climb at an angle of 9° to the ground?

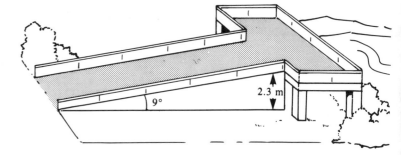

4 Two surveyors are standing at different points on a straight path leading to a church steeple 32.5 metres high. They each measure the angle of elevation of the top of the steeple. One finds it to be 67.5°, the other finds it to be 43.9°. How far apart are the two surveyors?

In all the problems we have tackled so far, we have calculated either the opposite or the adjacent side. With a slightly different technique, we can also calculate a missing angle.

Example

The ramp leading up to the second floor of a car park climbs 3 metres vertically over a horizontal distance of 8.3 metres. What is the angle of slope of the ramp?

We can draw this sketch.

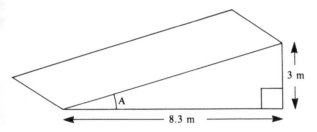

We can see that, if A is the angle of slope,

$$\tan A = 3 \div 8.3$$

So,

$$\tan A = 0.361 \text{ (to 3 d.p.)}$$

If you look back at the table of tangents, you will see that the angle which has a tangent ratio closest to 0.361 is 20°. So, the most accurate value we can give (from the table) for angle A is 20°.

Most scientific calculators can give a more accurate value for angle A. We already know how to start with an angle and use the **tan** button to find its tangent. The calculator usually also has a button marked **INV** (for inverse function). Using this button, we can start with a tangent and find its angle. So, starting with the information

$$\tan A = 3 \div 8.3$$

and pressing

 $\boxed{3}$ $\boxed{\div}$ $\boxed{8}$ $\boxed{.}$ $\boxed{3}$ $\boxed{=}$

gives

$$\tan A = 0.3614458$$

Now, leaving 0.3614458 in the calculator and pressing

$$\boxed{\text{INV}} \quad \boxed{\text{tan}}$$

gives

$$\text{angle } A = 19.872176°$$

1 Use a scientific calculator, or tables, to find the angles which have the following tangent ratios.

a 0.25   **b** 0.745   **c** 1.5   **d** 11.8   **e** 0.0174

2 Calculate the angle ABC in each of these triangles.

a

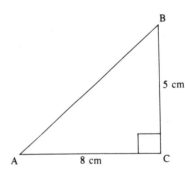

b

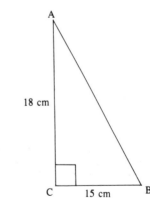

c

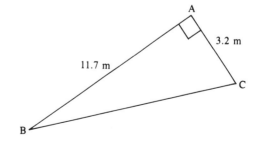

285

3 This cone is 15 cm high and has a base radius of 8 cm. Calculate the angle between the sloping sides of the cone and the base.

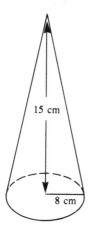

4 The diagonals of a rhombus always cross at an angle of 90°. Calculate the four angles of this rhombus.

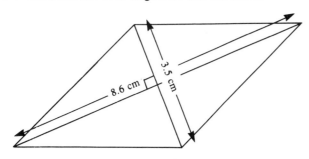

5 This diagram shows a framework made from steel wire. Calculate the angles A and B.

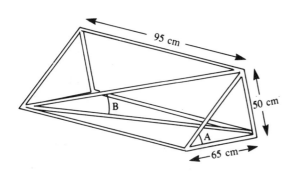

6 Newcastle-on-Tyne is 70 miles to the North and 50 miles to the East of Kendal. Calculate the direct distance and the bearing of Newcastle from Kendal.

The sine ratio

At this point, you might assume that we can solve just about any right-angled triangle problem that is thrown at us. Unfortunately, you would be wrong. Look at this problem.

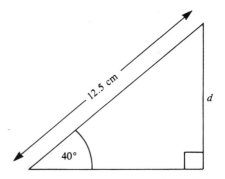

Find the length of side *d*.

We cannot solve this problem at the moment because it involves the **hypotenuse** and the **opposite** and all our previous problems have involved the **adjacent** and the **opposite**.

What we need is a ratio that links the **hypotenuse** and the **opposite** in the same way that the tangent ratio links the adjacent and the opposite. This ratio is called the **sine ratio**.

The sine ratio is the value obtained when the length of the **opposite** is divided by the length of the **hypotenuse.**

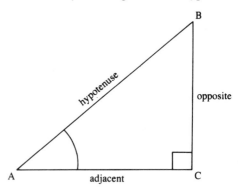

$$\textbf{Sine ratio of angle A} = \frac{\text{length of BC}}{\text{length of AB}}$$

The best possible way to fully understand the sine ratio is to construct a simple table of your own values. You are asked to do this in the next checkpoint.

CHECKPOINT 18

Draw the diagram sketched overleaf **accurately to scale** on a piece of graph paper. Start by drawing a baseline of 10 cm and the arc of a circle with radius 10 cm. By drawing in the radii at angles of 10°, 20°, 30° etc to the baseline, you produce right-angled triangles which all have a **hypotenuse** of 10 cm. The **opposite** is the vertical height from the end of the radius to the baseline. Use the diagram to complete this table of values of the sine ratio.

Angle	10	20	30	40	50	60	70	80	90
Sine	0.17		0.5			0.87			

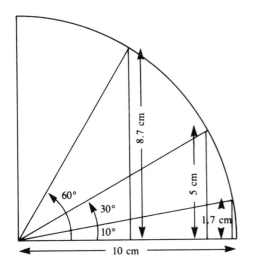

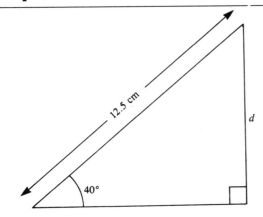

This is a more accurate sine table.

Angle	0	10	20	30	40	50	60	70	80	90
Sine	0	0.174	0.342	0.500	0.643	0.766	0.866	0.940	0.985	1.0

(The sine ratio of angle A is usually just written as sin A.)

We are now in a position to solve the problem at the start of this section.

Example

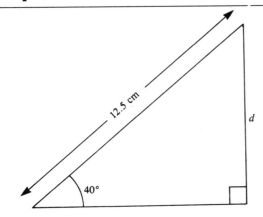

Find the length of side d.

This problem involves the **hypotenuse** and the **opposite**; therefore we can solve it with the **sine ratio**.

Applying this ratio we have

$$\sin 40° = d \div 12.5$$

Multiplying both sides by 12.5 gives

$$d = 12.5 \times \sin 40°$$

Looking up sin 40° in the table gives

$$d = 12.5 \times 0.643$$

$$d = 8.04 \text{ (to 2 d.p.)}$$

Alternatively, we can use a scientific calculator to obtain our answer by pressing

1 Calculate the length of the side AB in each triangle.

a

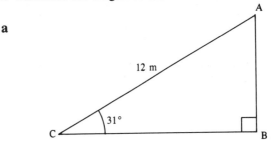

b

c

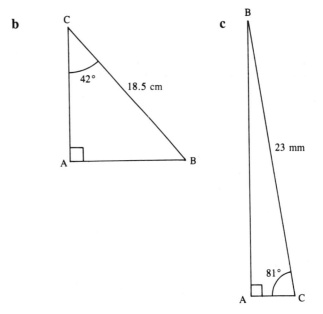

2 A ladder 5 metres long rests against a wall, making an angle of 70° with the ground. How far up the wall does the ladder reach?

3 A plane climbs at an angle of 40° after take off. How high is the plane after it has flown 900 metres through the air?

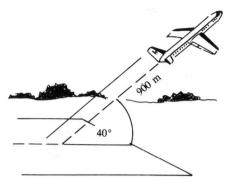

This house roof has sloping sides 8 m long which meet in the centre at an angle of 130°. How wide is the house?

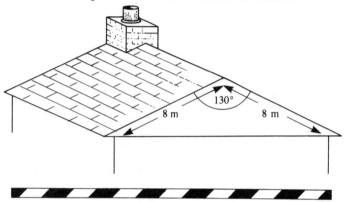

In all the problems we have tackled so far, the side length we have calculated has been the **opposite**. A slightly different technique is required if the side length to be found is the **hypotenuse** rather than the **opposite**.

Example

An aircraft climbs at an angle of 34° to the ground. How far will it have flown through the air before it has increased its height by 500 metres?

We can draw this sketch.

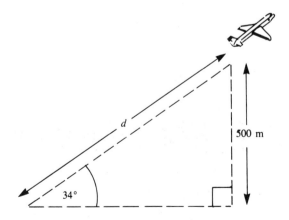

We can now see that, if d is the distance flown,

$$\sin 34° = 500 \div d$$

The problem requires us to calculate d, the **hypotenuse**. If we first multiply both sides of the equation by d, we have

$$d \times \sin 34° = 500$$

Now, if we divide both sides of the equation by $\sin 34°$, we have

$$d = 500 \div \sin 34°$$

Most calculators will allow us to enter the calculation like this:

$$\boxed{5}\ \boxed{0}\ \boxed{0}\ \boxed{\div}\ \boxed{3}\ \boxed{4}\ \boxed{\sin}\ \boxed{=}$$

This gives

$$d = 894 \text{ metres (correct to the nearest metre)}$$

CHECKPOINT 20

1 Calculate the length of the side AB in each triangle.

a

b

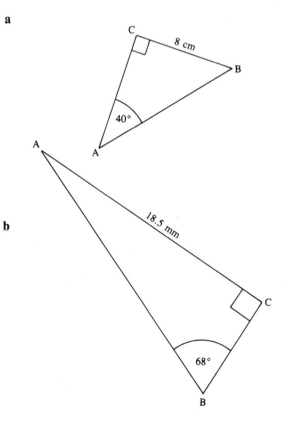

c

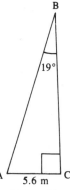

B

19°

A ⌐ C
5.6 m

2 Calculate the length of the side y in this triangle.

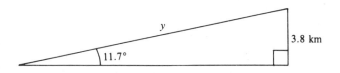

y

3.8 km

11.7°

3 A pendulum swings through an angle of 42° and a width at the bottom of 54 cm. Calculate the length of the pendulum.

42°

◄— 54 cm —►

4 Calculate the slant height of this cone. (The slant height is shown in the diagram by the line AB.)

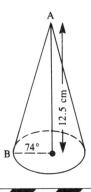

A

12.5 cm

B 74°

In all the problems we have tackled so far, we have calculated either the opposite or the hypotenuse. With a slightly different technique, we can also calculate a missing angle.

Example

A ladder 3.1 m long rests against a wall with its top end resting 1.98 m up the wall. What angle does the foot of the ladder make with the ground?

We can draw this sketch.

3.1 m
1.98 m
A

We can see that if A is the angle required,

$$\sin A = 1.98 \div 3.1$$

So,

$$\sin A = 0.639 \text{ (to 3 d.p.)}$$

If you look back at the table of sines, you will see that the angle which has a sine ratio closest to 0.639 is 40°. So, the most accurate value we can give (from the table) for angle A is 40°.

Most scientific calculators can give a more accurate value for angle A. We already know how to start with an angle and use the **sin** button to find its tangent. The calculator usually also has a button marked **INV** (for inverse function). Using this button, we can start with a sine and find its angle. So, starting with the information

$$\sin A = 1.98 \div 3.1$$

pressing

1 . 9 8 ÷ 3 . 1 =

gives

$$\sin A = 0.6387097$$

Now, leaving 0.687097 in the calculator and pressing

INV   sin

gives

$$\text{angle A} = 39.695671°$$

CHECKPOINT 21

1 Use a scientific calculator, or tables, to find the angles which have the following sine ratios.

a 0.25   **b** 0.745   **c** 0.5   **d** 0.866   **e** 0.015

2 Calculate the size of the angle ABC in each triangle.

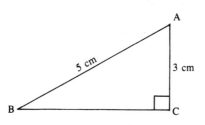

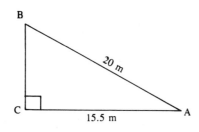

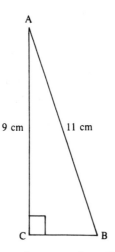

3 The manufacturer of a type of roofing tile recommends that they should not be used on roofs with a slope of less than 21°. With a slope less than 21°, the tiles will allow water to enter the roof in severe weather. Can the tiles be used on this roof design?

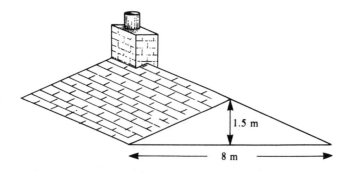

4 Rack and pinion railways can climb steeper slopes than normal railways. They obtain extra 'grip' from toothed wheels which engage a toothed rail. The maximum slope that can be climbed is about 7.1°. Could a rack and pinion railway be built to climb this incline?

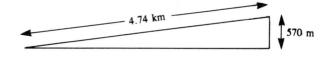

5 Wires 42.5 metres long are used to support a radio mast. If the wires are fixed from ground anchors to a point 32.7 metres up the mast, what angle do they make with the ground?

The cosine ratio

At this point, you might assume that we can solve just about any right-angled triangle problem that is thrown at us. We have after all mastered both the **tangent** and **sine** ratios. Unfortunately, you would be wrong. There is one more ratio to be studied before we really can tackle **any** problem. Look at this example.

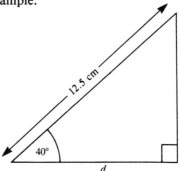

Find the length of side *d*.

We cannot solve this problem at the moment because it involves the **hypotenuse and the adjacent** and all our previous problems have involved either the **adjacent and the opposite** or the **hypotenuse and the opposite**.

What we need is a ratio that links the **hypotenuse** and the **adjacent** in the same way that the sine ratio links the hypotenuse and the opposite. This ratio is called the **cosine ratio**.

The cosine ratio is the value obtained when the length of the **adjacent** is divided by the length of the **hypotenuse**.

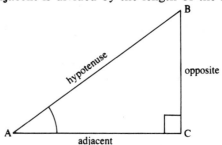

Cosine ratio of angle A = $\dfrac{\text{length of AC}}{\text{length of AB}}$

The best possible way to fully understand the cosine ratio is to construct a simple table of your own values. You are asked to do this in the next checkpoint.

CHECKPOINT 22

Draw the diagram sketched below **accurately to scale** on a piece of graph paper. Start by drawing a 10 cm baseline and the arc of a circle with radius 10 cm. By drawing in the radii at angles of 10°, 20°, 30° etc to the baseline, you produce right-angled triangles which all have a **hypotenuse** of 10 cm. The **adjacent** is the distance along the baseline to the vertical drawn from the hypotenuse. Use the diagram to complete this table of values for the cosine ratio.

Angle	10	20	30	40	50	60	70	80	90
Cosine	0.98		0.87			0.5			

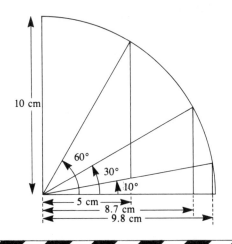

This is a more accurate cosine table.

Angle	0	10	20	30	40	50	60	70	80	90
Cosine	1.0	0.985	0.940	0.866	0.766	0.643	0.500	0.940	0.174	0

(The cosine ratio of angle A is usually just written as cos A.)

We are now in a position to solve the problem at the start of this section.

Example

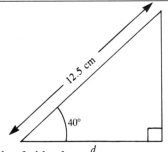

Find the length of side d.

This problem involves the **hypotenuse** and the **adjacent;** therefore we can solve it with the **cosine ratio.**

Applying this ratio, we have

$$\cos 40° = d \div 12.5$$

Multiplying both sides by 12.5 gives

$$d = 12.5 \times \cos 40°$$

Looking up cos 40° in the table gives

$$d = 12.5 \times 0.766$$

$$d = 9.58 \text{ (to 2 d.p.)}$$

Alternatively, we can use a scientific calculator to obtain our answer by pressing

[1] [2] [.] [5] [×] [4] [0] [cos] [=]

CHECKPOINT 23

1 Calculate the length of the side AB in each triangle.

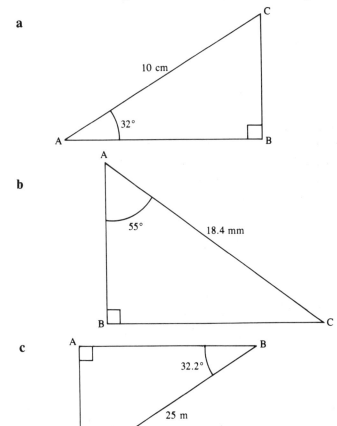

2 A ship leaves harbour and sails for 50 km on a bearing of 050°. How far to the East of the harbour is the ship?

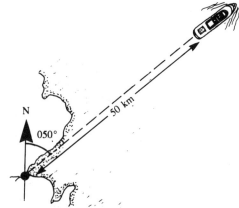

3 A ladder 3.4 m long rests against a wall, making an angle of 35° with the ground. How far is the foot of the ladder from the base of the wall?

4 Calculate the width of this roof.

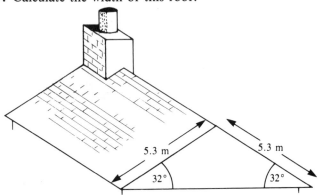

In all the problems we have tackled so far, the side length we have calculated has been the **adjacent**. A slightly different technique is required if the side length to be found is the **hypotenuse** rather than the **adjacent**.

▰▰▰▰▰▰▰▰▰▰▰▰▰▰▰▰

Example

An aircraft climbs at an angle of 34° to the ground. How far will it have flown through the air after it has covered a distance of 500 metres over the ground?

We can draw this sketch.

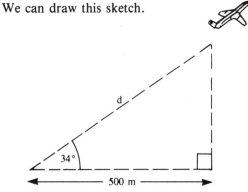

We can now see that, if d is the distance flown,

$$\cos 34° = 500 \div d$$

The problem requires us to calculate d, the **hypotenuse**. If we first multiply both sides of the equation by d, we have

$$d \times \cos 34° = 500$$

Now, if we divide both sides of the equation by $\cos 34°$, we have

$$d = 500 \div \cos 34°$$

Most calculators will allow us to enter the calculation like this

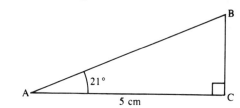

which gives

$$d = 603 \text{ metres (correct to the nearest metre)}$$

▰▰▰ **CHECKPOINT 24** ▰▰▰

1 Calculate the length of the side AB in each triangle.

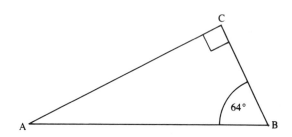

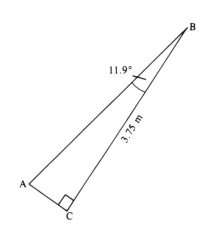

292

2 A ship leaves harbour and sails on a bearing of 050°. How far has the ship sailed when it reaches a point that is 50 km to the East of the harbour?

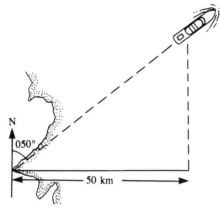

3 A ladder rests against a wall, making an angle of 35° with the ground. The foot of the ladder is 1.35 m from the base of the wall. How long is the ladder?

4 Calculate the length of the slope down this roof.

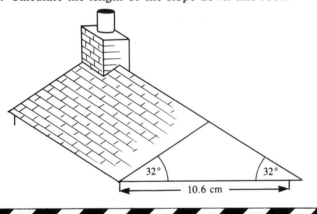

In all the problems we have tackled so far, we have calculated either the adjacent or the hypotenuse. With a slightly different technique, we can also calculate a missing angle.

Example

A ladder 3.1 m long rests against a wall with its bottom end 1.98 m from the base of the wall. What angle does the foot of the ladder make with the ground?

We can draw this sketch.

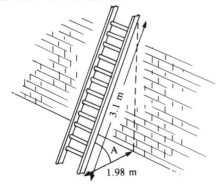

We can see that if A is the angle required,

$$\cos A = 1.98 \div 3.1$$

So,

$$\cos A = 0.639 \text{ (to 3 d.p.)}$$

If you look back at the table of cosines, you will see that the angle which has a cosine ratio closest to 0.639 is 50°. So, the most accurate value we can give (from the table) for angle A is 50°.

Most scientific calculators can give a more accurate value for angle A. We already know how to start with an angle and use the **cos** button to find its cosine. The calculator usually also has a button marked **INV** (for inverse function). Using this button, we can start with a cosine and find its angle. So, starting with the information

$$\cos A = 1.98 \div 3.1$$

pressing

$$\boxed{1}\ \boxed{.}\ \boxed{9}\ \boxed{8}\ \boxed{\div}\ \boxed{3}\ \boxed{.}\ \boxed{1}\ \boxed{=}$$

gives

$$\cos A = 0.6387097$$

Now, leaving 0.687097 in the calculator and pressing

$$\boxed{\text{INV}}\ \boxed{\cos}$$

gives

$$\text{angle A} = 50.304329$$

CHECKPOINT 25

1 Calculate the size of the angle ABC in each triangle.

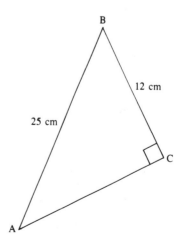

293

b

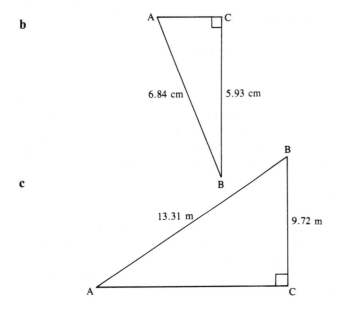

c

2 A ship leaves harbour and sails 50 km. It has then reached a point that is 34.6 km East of the harbour. On what bearing did the ship sail?

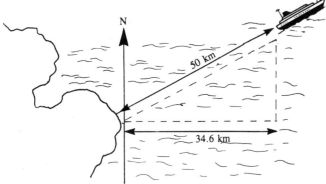

3 A ladder 3.8 m long rests against a wall. The foot of the ladder is 1.35 m from the base of the wall. What angle does the ladder make with the ground?

4 Calculate angle A in the diagram of a roof.

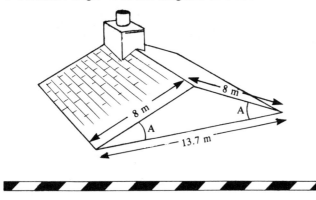

Trigonometrical ratios of angles greater than 90°

For simplicity, the definitions given for the sine and cosine ratios in the previous sections were based on a right-angled triangle. Using these definitions, it is hard to see how we can ever apply these ratios to angles greater than 90°. However, a slight change of definition makes it possible to have a sine or cosine ratio for **any** angle, no matter how large.

The definitions are based on this diagram. It shows a circle with a radius of one unit drawn at the centre of a graph.

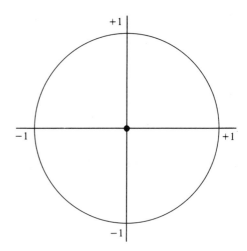

We imagine a rotating arm sweeping round this circle.

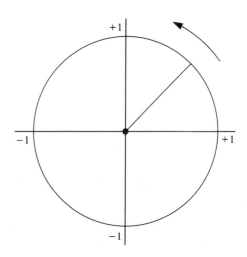

The sine and cosine ratios are defined like this. If you look at the diagram below, the length of the **opposite** for the angle 60° is given by the hypotenuse × sin 60°. But since our hypotenuse is one unit long, the length of the opposite is equal to sin 60°. So

- The sine ratio is the distance of the end of the arm from the x-axis.

In a similar way,

- The cosine ratio is the distance of the end of the arm from the y-axis.

This diagram shows the sine and cosine ratios for 60°.

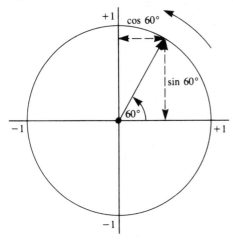

We can now use these definitions to explore angles beyond 90°.

This diagram shows the position of the arm when it has turned through 120°.

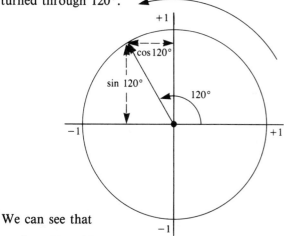

We can see that

- sine 120° will be equal to sine 60°.

- cosine 120° will be **negative** but otherwise equal to cosine 60°.

Tables of sine and cosine ratios only go up to 90°. Before the introduction of scientific calculators, rules derived from diagrams like these were used with the tables to find the sines, cosines and tangents of angles greater than 90°. For example, if the sine and cosine of 210° was needed, a sketch like this

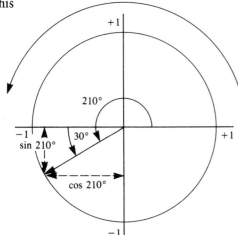

established that

$$\text{sine } 210° = -\text{sine } 30° = -0.5$$

$$\text{cosine } 210° = -\text{cosine } 30° = -0.866$$

These techniques are no longer necessary, because you will find that your scientific calculator will quite happily give you the sines and cosines of large angles. The largest possible angle that can be entered will vary from calculator to calculator; my calculator, for example, can cope up to 1440°.

In many ways this makes obsolete all the techniques that earlier students struggled with to find trigonometrical ratios of angles greater than 90°. The next checkpoint is still worth completing, however, as it will increase your understanding of the ratios.

CHECKPOINT 26

1 Draw a diagram to show the position of the arm after it has turned through 240°. What are the relationships between the trigonometrical ratios for 240° and the trigonometrical ratios for 60°? What are the values of sine 240° and cosine 240°?

2 Draw a diagram to show the position of the arm after it has turned through 330°. What are the relationships between the trigonometrical ratios for 330° and the trigonometrical ratios for 60°? What are the values of sine 330° and cosine 330°?

3 When the arm has turned through 90°, the sine ratio has become 1 and the cosine ratio has become 0, as this diagram shows.

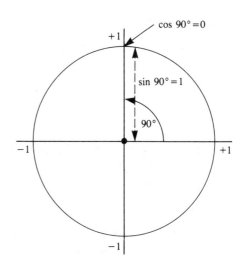

295

Copy and complete this table.

	0°	90°	180°	270°	360°
SINE	0	1			
COSINE	1	0			

Graphs of sin x and cos x

This is a table of values for sin x and cos x as x takes values from 0° to 360°.

Angle	0	30	60	90	120	150	180
sin x	0	0.5	0.866	1	0.866	0.5	0
cos x	1	0.866	0.5	0	−0.5	−0.866	−1

Angle	210	240	270	300	330	360
sin x	−0.5	−0.866	−1	−0.866	−0.5	0
cos x	−0.866	−0.5	0	0.5	0.866	1

From this table we can draw these graphs of sin x and cos x.

sin x

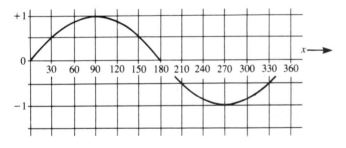

cos x

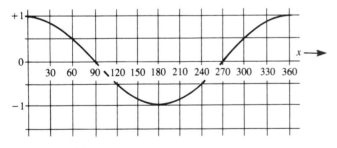

1 Draw your own graphs for sin x and cos x as x takes values from 0° to 360°.

2 Copy and complete this table of values for $2 + \sin x$. Use the table to draw a graph of $y = 2 + \sin x$.

Angle	0	30	60	90	120	150	180
$2 + \sin x$	2	2.5	2.866				

Angle	210	240	270	300	330	360
$2 + \sin x$	1.5		1			

3 Copy and complete this table of values for 3 cos x. Use the table to draw a graph of $y = 3 \cos x$.

Angle	0	30	60	90	120	150	180
3 cos x	3	2.598	1.5	0	−1.5		

Angle	210	240	270	300	330	360
3 cos x						

Problem identification and revision section

At this point, we have mastered **all** the skills we need to solve any right-angled triangle problem. We are familiar with Pythagoras, the tangent ratio, the sine ratio and the cosine ratio. We understand all the following formulas.

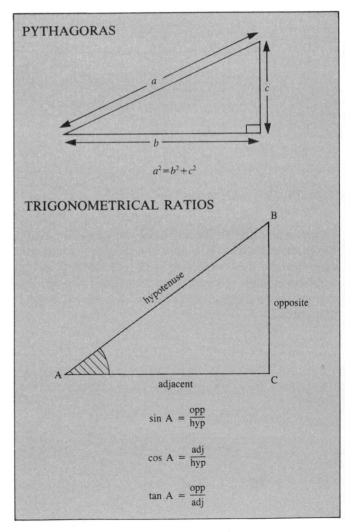

PYTHAGORAS

$a^2 = b^2 + c^2$

TRIGONOMETRICAL RATIOS

$\sin A = \dfrac{opp}{hyp}$

$\cos A = \dfrac{adj}{hyp}$

$\tan A = \dfrac{opp}{adj}$

We must ensure that we always use the correct technique to solve any particular problem. This is quite easy if, at the start of each solution, we carefully list the values we are given or asked to calculate. Having made this list, we can then use the following rules.

Rules for problem identification

• If the problem involves the **three sides** and **no angles**, use **PYTHAGORAS**.

• If the problem involves an angle, the **hypotenuse** and the **opposite**, use the **SINE RATIO**.

• If the problem involves an angle, the **hypotenuse** and the **adjacent**, use the **COSINE RATIO**.

• If the problem involves an angle, the **adjacent** and the **opposite**, use the **TANGENT RATIO**.

The four examples that follow illustrate problem identification and also revise the three different techniques for using the trigonometrical ratios.

Examples

1

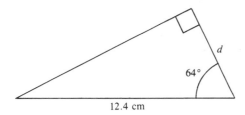

Find the length of side d in this triangle.

PROBLEM IDENTIFICATION

This problem involves **an angle**, the **hypotenuse** and the **adjacent.** Therefore we must use the **cosine ratio**.

SOLUTION

Applying the cosine ratio to this problem, we have

$$\cos 64° = d \div 12.4$$

Multiplying both sides of the equation by 12.4 gives

$$d = 12.4 \times \cos 64°$$

Using a calculator, we press

which gives

$$d = 5.44 \,\text{cm (to 2 d.p.)}$$

2

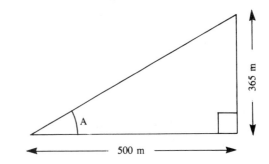

Find the size of angle A in this triangle.

PROBLEM IDENTIFICATION

This problem involves **an angle**, the **opposite** and the **adjacent.** Therefore we must use the **tangent ratio**.

SOLUTION

Applying the tangent ratio to this problem, we have

$$\tan A = 365 \div 500$$

Using a calculator, we press

$$\boxed{3}\ \boxed{6}\ \boxed{5}\ \boxed{\div}\ \boxed{5}\ \boxed{0}\ \boxed{0}\ \boxed{=}$$

which gives

$$\tan A = 0.73$$

Pressing

$$\boxed{\text{INV}}\quad \boxed{\text{tan}}$$

gives

$$\text{angle } A = 36.13° \text{ (to 2 d.p.)}$$

3

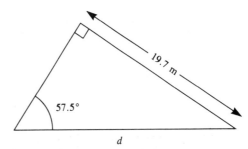

Find the length of side d in this triangle.

PROBLEM IDENTIFICATION

This problem involves **an angle**, the **hypotenuse** and the **opposite.** Therefore we must use the **sine ratio**.

SOLUTION

Applying the sine ratio to this problem, we have

$$\sin 57.5° = 19.7 \div d$$

Multiplying both sides of the equation by d gives

$$d \times \sin 57.5° = 19.7$$

Dividing both sides of the equation by $\sin 57.5°$ gives

$$d = 19.7 \div \sin 57.5°$$

Using a calculator, we press

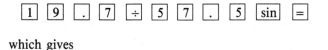

which gives

$$d = 23.36 \text{ m (to 2 d.p.)}$$

4

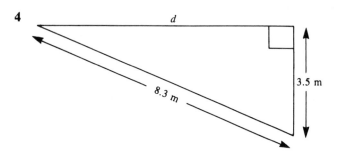

Find the length of side d in this triangle.

PROBLEM IDENTIFICATION

This problem involves **three sides and no angles**; therefore we must use **Pythagoras**.

SOLUTION

Applying the Pythagoras formula to this problem, we have

$$8.3^2 = 3.5^2 + d^2$$

So,

$$68.89 = 12.25 + d^2$$

Subtracting 12.25 from both sides of the equation gives

$$d^2 = 56.64$$

$$d = \sqrt{56.64}$$

$$d = 7.53 \text{ m (to 2 d.p.)}$$

Pythagoras and trigonometry – Practice and revision exercise

1 In this diagram,

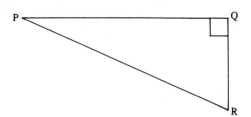

find the length of the side PR of the triangle if

a PQ = 6 m and QR = 8 m
b PQ = 1 cm and QR = 2.4 cm
c PQ = 8.5 mm and QR = 8.5 mm
d PQ = 56 cm and QR = 120 cm

2 In this diagram,

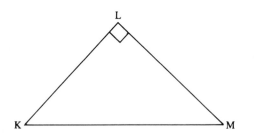

find the length of the side LM if

a KL = 27 cm and KM = 45 cm
b KL = 2.4 cm and KM = 2.5 cm
c KL = 3 cm and KM = 4 cm
d KL = 56 cm and KM = 120 cm

3 Find the length of a diagonal in a square with sides 4 cm long.

4 Find the length of the sides of a square with a diagonal 4 cm long.

5 The diagram below shows a boat moored 3 metres away from a river bank. The top of the bank is 1 metre above the water level and the deck of the boat is 3 metres above the water level. Will a 3.5 metre plank of wood be long enough to make a gang-plank for the boat?

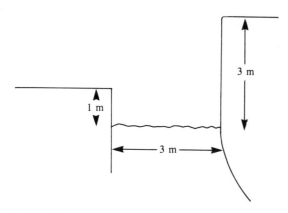

6 The diagram below shows a cuboid made from straws.

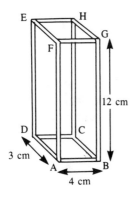

a To what length should a straw be cut to fit exactly from D to B?

b To what length should a straw be cut to fit exactly from B to E?

7 A woman's garage is 6 m long, 2.5 m high and 3 m wide. Can she store a 7 m yacht's mast in her garage?

8 Chelmsford is 30 km to the West and 25 km to the South of Ipswich. Calculate the direct distance between Chelmsford and Ipswich.

9 The following safety advice is often given for working with ladders:

'The distance between the foot of the ladder and the wall should be about one quarter of the height of the ladder.'

Copy and complete this table showing how far different lengths of ladder will reach up a wall if the distance from the foot to the wall is exactly one quarter of the height of the ladder.

Length of ladder (metres)	4	5	6	7	8
Distance of foot from wall (metres)	1				
Reach up the wall (metres)	3.87				

10 An isosceles triangle has two sides of length 7.5 cm and one side of length 12 cm. Calculate the area of the triangle.

11 Find the length of the side d in each triangle.

a

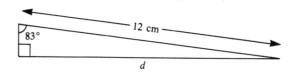

b

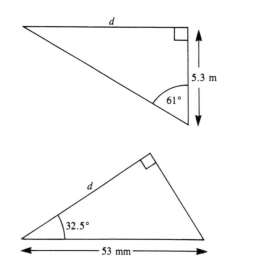

c

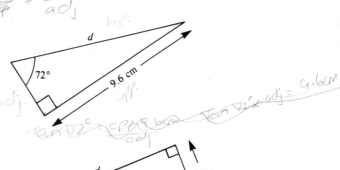

12 Find the length of the side d in each triangle.

a

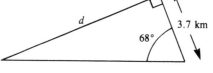

b

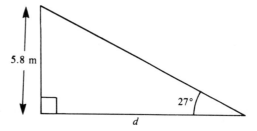

c

299

13 Find angle A in each triangle.

a

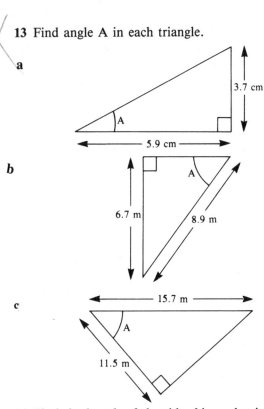

b

c

14 Find the length of the side *d* in each triangle.

a

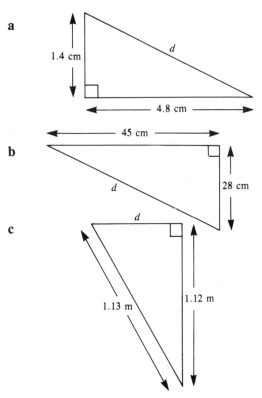

b

c

15 An escalator 12.5 metres long rises at an angle of 37° to the horizontal. How high is the top of the escalator above the bottom?

16 Daventry is 11.4 km to the East and 23 km to the North of Banbury. Calculate the bearing of Daventry from Banbury.

17 An isosceles triangle has two equal sides 8 cm long and a third side 5 cm long. Calculate the sizes of the angles in the triangle.

18 Redditch is 23 km on a bearing of 060° from Worcester. Find the distance that Redditch is to the East of Worcester.

19 A chord of length 6 cm is drawn in a circle. If the chord subtends an angle of 56° at the centre of the circle, what is the radius of the circle?

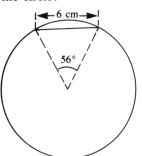

20 This ramp is to be built as part of a bike test track. It will be 3.5 m high and should have an angle of slope of 40°. What will be the total length of the ramp?

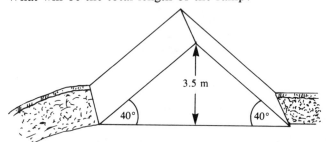

21 A plane climbs at an angle of 55°. Find its gain in height after it has covered a horizontal distance of 850 m.

22 The top of a ladder 12.5 m long rests against a window ledge 11.3 m high. Find the angle that the bottom of the ladder makes with the ground.

23 A hiker walks 3.5 km on a bearing of 125°. How far is she to the South of her starting point?

24 This map shows three triangular building plots. Calculate the area (in square metres) of each plot.

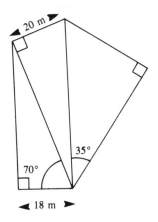

300

25 This lampshade framework is to be constructed from steel wire. The corner points have been labelled ABCDEFGH and the points M, N and P are the mid-points of the edges AB, EF and DC. ABCD is a square of side length 45 cm and EFGH is a square of side length 15 cm. The edges AE, BF, CG and DH are all 38 cm long.

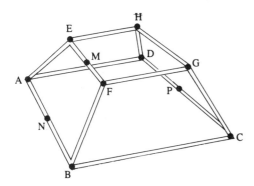

Calculate:

a angle ABF **b** angle CAE **c** angle MNP
d the area of the face ABFE

Pythagoras and trigonometry – extended problems for project work

1 The Pythagoreans studied many different number patterns. One type of number which they found interesting were the **square numbers**.

A square number is a whole number which is formed by multiplying another whole number by itself.

The sequence of square numbers starts:

1, 4, 9, 16, 25, 36, 49, 64, 81, 100 ,..........

One discovery which the Pythagoreans made about square numbers is shown below.

$$1 \qquad = 1 \qquad \bullet$$

$$1+3 \qquad = 4 \qquad \circ \ \bullet$$
$$ \bullet \ \bullet$$

$$1+3+5 \qquad = 9 \qquad \circ \ \circ \ \bullet$$
$$ \circ \ \circ \ \bullet$$
$$ \bullet \ \bullet \ \bullet$$

$$1+3+5+7 \qquad = 16 \qquad \circ \ \circ \ \circ \ \bullet$$
$$ \circ \ \circ \ \circ \ \bullet$$
$$ \circ \ \circ \ \circ \ \bullet$$
$$ \bullet \ \bullet \ \bullet \ \bullet$$

a Copy this diagram and continue it for 4 more lines.
b Write down, in your own words, the discovery which is illustrated in the diagram.
c By studying the diagram, can you state reasons why extending the pattern will always produce more square numbers?
d Any three whole numbers which satisfy the relationship $a^2 + b^2 = c^2$ are called a **Pythagorean triple**. For example, 3, 4 and 5 are a Pythagorean triple because $3^2 + 4^2 = 5^2$. The Pythagoreans used the discovery illustrated in the first part of this question to produce these triples.

This was their technique.

- Add together the sequence of odd numbers until you reach an odd number which is also a square number (the first time this happens is when you reach 9, which is 3^2).

$$\text{e.g. } 1+3+5+7+9 = 25$$

- Divide up the sequence like this:

$$\underbrace{(1+3+5+7)}+9 = 25$$

$$\text{or} \qquad 16 \qquad +9 = 25$$

- This produces the Pythagorean triple 3, 4, 5.

Use this technnique to produce at least five Pythagorean triples.

e Write an explanation of how and why the technique in part **d** works.
f Some of the Pythagorean triples you will have produced in part **d** are shown in the table below.

a	3	5	7		
b	4	12	24		
c	5	13	25		

Copy and continue this table. Can you discover patterns in the table which allow you to continue it without using the technique of part **d**?

2 The technique used in question 1 does not produce all possible Pythagorean triples. For example, the technique fails to discover the triple 8, 15, 17.

A very powerful formula to produce Pythagorean triples is:

$$a = m^2 - n^2$$

$$b = 2mn$$

$$c = m^2 + n^2$$

where m and n can be any pair of whole numbers.

For example, if we select $m = 5$ and $n = 2$, we produce the triple 21, 20, 29 like this:

$$a = 5^2 - 2^2 = 21$$

$$b = 2 \times 5 \times 2 = 20$$

$$c = 5^2 + 2^2 = 29$$

a Experiment with this formula, selecting your own values of m and n.

b Can you explain why the formula works?

c This is a computer program, written in BBC BASIC, designed to print out the triples produced by every possible pair of numbers up to $m = 10$ and $n = 9$.

```
10 FOR M = 2 TO 10

20 FOR N = 1 TO M − 1

30 PRINT M, N, M*M − N*N, 2*M*N, M*M + N*N

40 NEXT N

50 NEXT M
```

Experiment with the program, obtain some printed output and explain how the program works.

3 The diagram below shows a form of car jack called a 'scissors jack'. As the screw is turned, the distance between points X and Y is shortened and the height of the jack is increased. Each time the screw is turned through three complete revolutions, the distance XY is shortened by 2 cm. Each arm of the jack is 25 cm long and in the lowest position the length of XY is 48 cm.

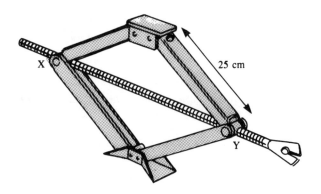

a Calculate the height of the jack in each of the positions shown below.

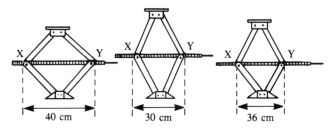

b What is the height of the jack after the handle has been turned 3 times from the lowest position?

c What is the height of the jack after the handle has been turned 6 times from the lowest position?

d Draw a graph to show how the height of the jack changes as the handle is turned through 42 complete revolutions from the lowest position.

e Obtain a car jack of the scissors design.

• With the jack in the lowest position, take all the measurements you need to **predict** how it will behave as the handle is turned.

• Complete any necessary calculations and write down your prediction for the jack's behaviour as the handle is turned.

• Experiment with the jack and obtain actual measurements to compare with your prediction.

4 The geometrical interpretation of the theorem of Pythagoras is shown below.

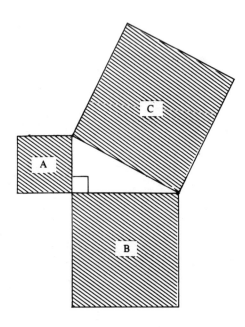

AREA A + AREA B = AREA C

A simple example of this is

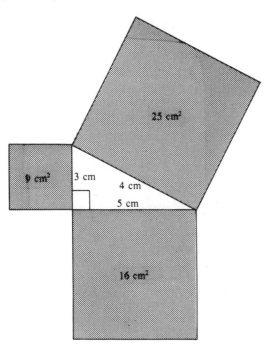

$$9 \text{ cm}^2 + 16 \text{ cm}^2 = 25 \text{ cm}^2$$

What about other shapes drawn on the sides of a right-angled triangle? Will the relationship between their areas also fit the theorem?

What about semi-circles?   Or hexagons?

Or circles?   Or octagons?

Investigate these and other shapes drawn on the sides of a right-angled triangle. In each case:

- Try some simple examples to see if the relationship does fit the theorem.

- Try to prove that the relationship **must** fit the theorem in **any** right-angled triangle.

5 Look at this triangle.

The length of the hypotenuse is $\sqrt{2}$ cm, or approximately 1.414 cm.

The value of $\sqrt{2}$ is not exactly 1.414, because $1.414 \times 1.414 = 1.999396$.

In fact, it is possible to prove that there is no decimal number which when multiplied by itself comes to exactly 2!

All that we can ever obtain is a close approximation to $\sqrt{2}$. Most square roots, unless they are exact whole numbers, can only be found as approximations.

Because these numbers exist but cannot be expressed as exact decimals, they are called **irrational numbers.**

One way to obtain approximations for irrational square roots is by drawing triangles. For example, if we measure the hypotenuse in the diagram above, we will obtain an approximation for $\sqrt{2}$.

The small size of the diagram will not give a very accurate value for $\sqrt{2}$. A better approximation can be found by using 10 cm as the side length of the triangle.

In this triangle

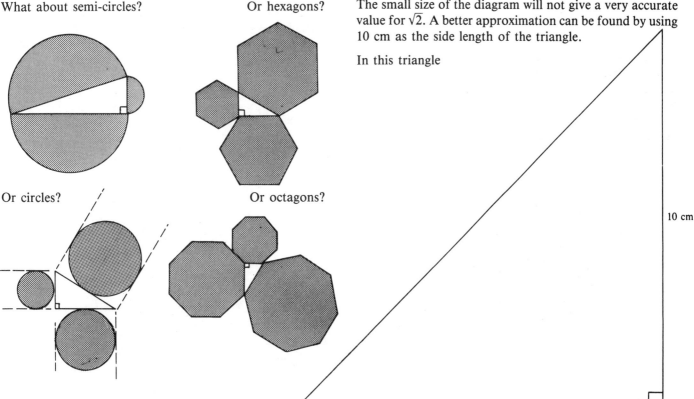

303

because we have used 10 cm instead of 1 cm for the side length, the length of the hypotenuse must be 10 times $\sqrt{2}$.

Measuring the hypotenuse, we obtain an answer of approximately 14.1 cm. This in turns gives us an approximation of 1.41 for $\sqrt{2}$.

The diagram below shows a construction that can be used to find $\sqrt{2}$, $\sqrt{3}$, $\sqrt{4}$ and $\sqrt{5}$.

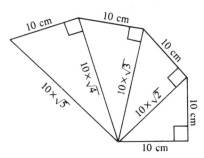

a Explain **how** and **why** this construction allows these estimates to be made.

b Make an accurate copy of the diagram and use it to estimate $\sqrt{2}$, $\sqrt{3}$ and $\sqrt{5}$. (You will need a *large* sheet of paper.)

c Extend the diagram to estimate $\sqrt{6}$, $\sqrt{7}$, $\sqrt{8}$ and $\sqrt{10}$.

d This diagram shows how an estimate for $\sqrt{5}$ and an estimate for $\sqrt{6}$ can be combined to make an estimate for $\sqrt{11}$. Draw a similar diagram to estimate $\sqrt{13}$.

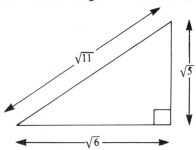

e Is is true that $\sqrt{8} = 2 \times \sqrt{2}$? If it is true, can you explain why? Can you use your explanation to estimate $\sqrt{12}$ and $\sqrt{20}$?

f Obtain, by using the methods of part **d** or part **e**, approximations of the square roots of all the whole numbers from 1 to 30.

g Do some research to discover other methods for finding square roots, including the ways that calculators and computers find square roots.

6 This diagram shows the layout of a typical Rugby pitch.

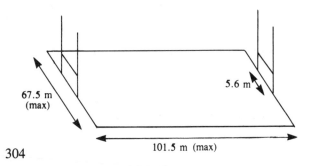

During the game, a 'try' can be scored by touching the ball on the ground at any point behind the opponent's goal line. This is worth 4 points. A kicker can then attempt to add an extra 2 points, 'a conversion', by kicking the ball over the bar and between the two uprights of the goal posts. Before it is kicked, the ball can be placed anywhere along a line at 90° to the goal line through the point where the ball was touched down. This diagram shows the choice available to Chantal Bindley, star kicker of the Market Deeping Maulers ladies team, after Jessica Jellis, their star winger, has scored a try.

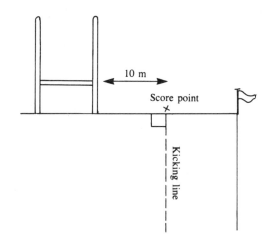

a Most kickers walk back along the kicking line until they reach a point where they think they have the 'best shot' at the goal. By this, they mean that the angle they can kick into and score is made as big as possible. This diagram shows two possible kicking positions for Chantal; the 'scoring angle' for each position is shown with dotted lines. Which position gives the best chance of scoring a conversion?

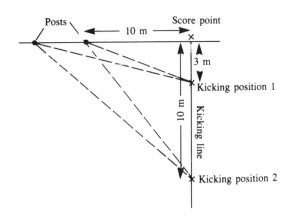

b Calculate the scoring angles (correct to 1 d.p.) for each of the kicking positions shown above.

c Calculate the scoring angles for points along the kicking line from 1 metre to 20 metres from the goal line, in steps of 0.5 metres. Where along the kicking line would you advise Chantal to place the ball to obtain the maximum chance of scoring?

d This computer program, written in BBC BASIC, prints out all the calculations required in part **c**. Explain how it works, using a BBC BASIC manual for reference.

```
10 FOR J=1 TO 20 STEPS 0.5

20 PRINT 180 / PI * (ATN (15.6 / J)−ATN (10 / J))

30 NEXT J
```

e Draw an accurate scale drawing of a Rugby pitch on a large sheet of graph paper. Mark possible kicking lines (at 90° to the goal lines) at 2 metre intervals across the pitch. Along each kicking line, mark the point where a ball should be placed to obtain the maximum chance of scoring. What do you notice?

f Many practical 'real life' problems have not been considered in this investigation. Discuss your findings in the light of a real game of Rugby.

7 The mathematicians of Alexandria used tables of trigonometrical ratios to produce an estimation of π. The method used is explained in the sequence of steps that follow. Work through the steps and you will understand their method.

a Draw a circle of radius 3 cm. You know that the circumference of this circle is 6π cm.

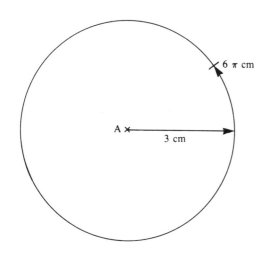

b Sketch a pentagon like this inside the circle (there is no need to be accurate).

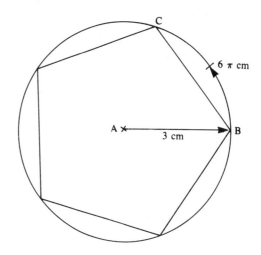

c Calculate the length of the side BC of the pentagon. Use your answer to calculate the perimiter of the pentagon.

d Sketch this pentagon outside the circle (there is no need to be accurate).

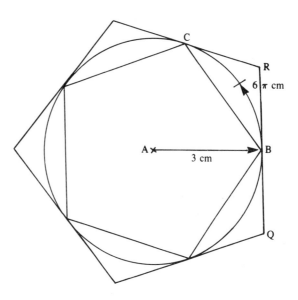

e Calculate the length of the side QR of the pentagon. Use your answer to calculate the perimeter of the pentagon.

f You know that the circumference of the circle must be greater than the perimeter of the inner pentagon but smaller than the perimeter of the outer pentagon. Or, in mathematical terms:

inner perimeter < circumference < outer perimeter

So,

inner perimeter < 6π < outer perimeter

Divide this inequality throughout by 6 and you have an inequality for the value of π:

$$\text{inner perimeter} \div 6 < \pi < \text{outer perimeter} \div 6$$

Write down the inequality for the value of π that is produced by your calculations.

g This estimation for the value of π is not particularly accurate. A better estimation can be obtained by repeating the technique but using a figure with more sides than a pentagon. Investigate this possibility, perhaps using a computer to help with the calculations.

h Some general questions you might like to consider are:

- Does the radius chosen for the circle affect the calculations?

- Can you reduce the calculations to a general formula, expressed in terms of the number of sides in the figure chosen?

- Archimedes used this method and decided that the value of π was somewhere between $3\frac{1}{7}$ and $3\frac{10}{71}$. What kind of shape do you think Archimedes drew in a circle to obtain this degree of accuracy?

- If you take the mean average of each pair of limits for the value of π, a single estimate can be found. If an accurate value for π is taken as 3.1415927, the percentage error in each estimation can then be calculated. How does the percentage error change as the number of sides in the shape used is increased?

- How does the accuracy limits of the calculator or computer you are using affect your investigation?

j Early Japanese and Chinese mathematicians working in about AD 20 had already discovered the theorem of Pythagoras (possibly before Pythagoras had!) and used it to obtain an estimate of π. The method used is just hinted at in the three diagrams below and you are left to investigate the technique for yourselves.

First, draw a quarter-circle with a radius of 1 unit. It has an area of $\pi/4$.

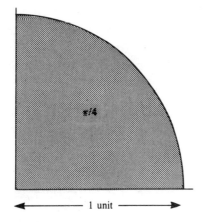

Now, divide the radius into five equal lengths. On each length construct two rectangles, one just inside the circle, one just outside the circle. (The last of the inner rectangles has a height of zero and so disappears.)

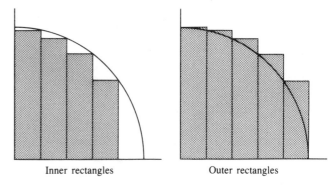

Inner rectangles   Outer rectangles

Calculate the total area of the sets of inner and outer rectangles. The area of the quarter-circle must lie between the areas of the inner and outer rectangles and an inequality for the value of π can thus be found.

8 If the two additional trigonometrical topics, the **sine rule** and the **cosine rule** are included on your syllabus, you should delay this project until you have worked through the two sections dealing with them (p 306).

The most common practical application of trigonometry is in surveying. Surveyors use various instruments to measure some of the angles and distances required to draw up plans of buildings, etc., and then use trigonometry to calculate all the other angles and distances they need. As a coursework project you could select a building or group of buildings and carry out all the necessary measurements and calculations to draw up an accurate plan of the building(s) and grounds. A strategy for approaching this task might be as follows.

- Draw a rough sketch showing the layout of the building(s), judging distances, heights, etc., by eye. Photographs could also be taken to illustrate the site chosen for your survey.

- Mark on your sketch all the values you intend to measure and all those you intend to calculate. As a general principle, measurements should be kept to the minimum number necessary to calculate all other distances, etc.

- Obtain the necessary equipment to make your measurements and complete the survey.

- Draw an accurate plan to an appropriate scale, showing all distances, heights, areas, etc.

9 The introduction to this Unit mentioned the astonishing achievements of the Alexandrian mathematicians in measuring the circumference of the Earth and the distance to the Sun and the Moon. Do some research to find out how these measurements were made and write an account of your findings.

The sine rule and the cosine rule

Check your syllabus. If it does not include a study of the sine rule and the cosine rule you can leave out this section. All the trigonometry you have studied so far has been concerned with right-angled triangles. This section looks at the trigonometry of triangles that **do not** contain a right angle.

For example, a triangle like this:

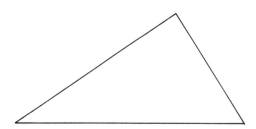

These are the stages in labelling the sides and angles of a triangle that does not include a right angle.

1 Label the corner points with three (normally consecutive) capital letters. These letters also label the angles at each corner. That is, the angle at corner A is called angle A and so on.

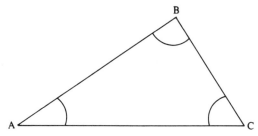

2 Label the sides opposite each angle with the corresponding small letter of the alphabet. That is, label the side opposite to angle A with the small letter *a* and so on.

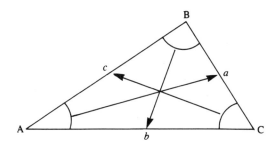

Copy each of these triangles and complete the labelling of all sides and angles.

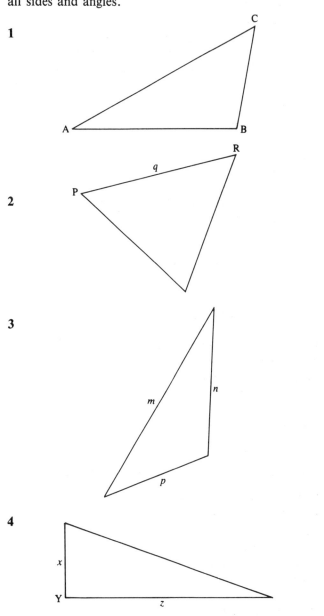

The sine rule

The formula known as the **sine rule** is developed by applying simple trigonometry to a triangle that does not contain a right angle. Look at this diagram:

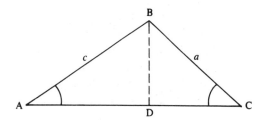

A line perpendicular to AC has been drawn from corner B. The point where the perpendicular meets AC has been labelled D.

Applying simple trigonometry in triangle BCD, we have

$$BD = a \times \sin C$$

Applying simple trigonometry in triangle BAD, we have

$$BD = c \times \sin A$$

Therefore, since both are equal to BD,

$$a \times \sin C = c \times \sin A$$

This is usually rearranged to read

$$\frac{a}{\sin A} = \frac{c}{\sin C}$$

It should be obvious that we could start with slightly different diagrams and show that either

$$a \times \sin B = b \times \sin A \qquad \text{or} \qquad b \times \sin C = c \times \sin B$$

Therefore, the general formula called the **sine rule** is normally expressed as:

The sine rule

$$\frac{a}{\sin A} = \frac{b}{\sin B} = \frac{c}{\sin C}$$

The sine rule is used when our problem involves:

• A triangle that does not contain a right angle.

• Two sides and two angles.

Example

The Coastguard station at Mull's Point is 20 km due North of the Coastguard station at Wrecking Rocks. A yacht in distress at sea is seen from both stations. From Mull's Point, the bearing of the yacht is 125° and from Wrecking Rocks it is 078°. How far is the yacht from Mull's Point?

We can draw this sketch, since we know the angle sum of any triangle is 180°. We can also fill in the third angle, 47°.

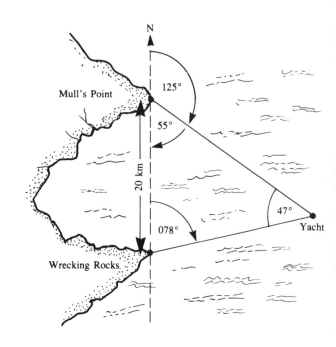

PROBLEM IDENTIFICATION

This problem involves a triangle without a right angle. We must therefore use either the **sine rule** or the **cosine rule**. Since two sides and two angles are involved, we must use the **sine rule**.

SOLUTION

If we call the distance to be calculated d, applying the sine rule to the triangle gives

$$\frac{d}{\sin 78°} = \frac{20}{\sin 47°}$$

Multiplying both sides of the equation by sin 78° gives

$$d = \sin 78° \times \frac{20}{\sin 47°}$$

Using a calculator, we press

| 7 | 8 | sin | × | 2 | 0 | ÷ | 4 | 7 | sin | = |

which gives

$$d = 26.75 \text{ km (to 2 d.p.)}$$

When we are working with triangles that do not contain right angles, we may sometimes encounter angles greater than 90°. Using a calculator, this need cause us no problems. Suppose, for example, in the last example, the bearing of the yacht from Wrecking Rocks had been given as 108°. Our sketch would then have shown

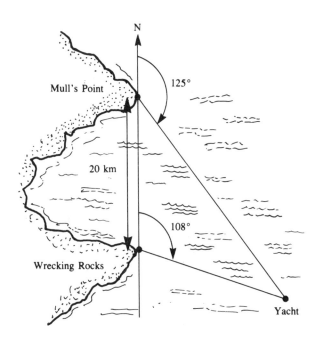

Our calculations would then have been

$$\frac{d}{\sin 108°} = \frac{20}{\sin 17°}$$

Multiplying both sides of the equation by sin 108° gives

$$d = \sin 108° \times \frac{20}{\sin 17°}$$

Using a calculator, we press

| 1 | 0 | 8 | sin | × | 2 | 0 | ÷ | 1 | 7 | sin | = |

which gives

$$d = 65.06 \text{ km (to 2 d.p.)}$$

CHECKPOINT 29

1 Calculate the length of the side d in this diagram.

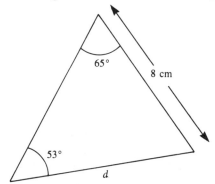

2 Calculate the length of the side d in this diagram.

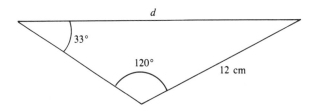

3 A surveyor who wishes to measure the height of a church steeple cannot reach a point directly below the top because of the building's design. Consequently she measures a line 20 m long on the path to the church and then measures the angle of elevation of the steeple from each end of the line. Her theodolite which she uses to measure these angles is 1.8 m high. This diagram illustrates these measurements.

a Calculate the distance AB in the diagram.
b Calculate the height of the steeple.

4 Bradford is approximately 215 miles due North of Bournemouth. The bearing of Norwich from Bradford is 120° and the bearing of Norwich from Bournemouth is 045°. Calculate the direct distances from Norwich to Bradford and Bournemouth.

5 A stepladder has two unequal sides of length 2.5 m and 2.4 m. When fully open, the longer side makes an angle of 70° with the ground. How far apart are the feet of the stepladder when it is fully open?

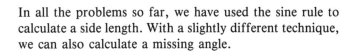

In all the problems so far, we have used the sine rule to calculate a side length. With a slightly different technique, we can also calculate a missing angle.

Example

This ramp has been designed as part of a cycle test track. What angle does the second part of the ramp make with the ground?

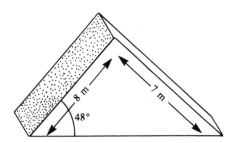

PROBLEM IDENTIFICATION

This problem involves a triangle without a right angle. We must therefore use either the **sine rule** or the **cosine rule.** Since two sides and two angles are involved, we must use the **sine rule**.

SOLUTION

If we call the angle to be calculated A, applying the sine rule to the triangle, we have

$$\frac{8}{\sin A} = \frac{7}{\sin 48°}$$

Multiplying both sides of the equation by sin A gives

$$8 = \frac{7 \times \sin A}{\sin 48°}$$

Multiplying both sides of the equation by sin 48° gives

$$8 \times \sin 48° = 7 \times \sin A$$

Dividing both sides of the equation by 7 gives

$$\frac{8 \times \sin 48°}{7} = \sin A$$

Using a calculator, we press

which gives

$$A = 58.1° \text{ (to 1 d.p.)}$$

CHECKPOINT 30

1 Calculate the size of angle A in this triangle.

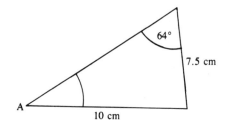

2 This diagram shows a Roman war catapult designed for dropping large rocks on your enemies' heads. It has been wound back so that 3 m of rope are left between the catapult head and the pulley. In this position, the rope makes an angle of 53° with the horizontal. The catapult arm is 4 m long, from the pivot. What angle does it make with the horizontal?

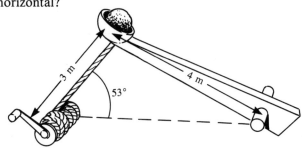

3 This diagram shows a design for a bike frame. Calculate the size of angle A.

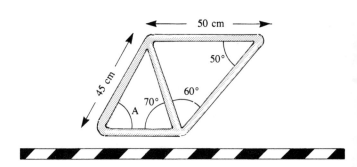

The cosine rule

The formula known as the **cosine rule** is developed by applying simple trigonometry and Pythagoras to a triangle that does not contain a right angle. The algebra is a little 'heavy' and you do not need to understand it as part of your syllabus. It is, however, shown below for interest.

Look at this diagram.

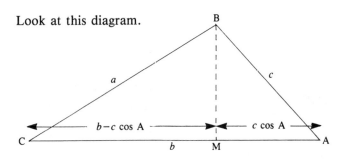

Simple trigonometry tells us that AM = c cos A.

Therefore, CM = $b - c$ cos A.

Applying Pythagoras in the triangle ABM, we can write

$$BM^2 = c^2 - (c \cos A)^2$$

Applying Pythagoras in the triangle CBM, we can write

$$BM^2 = a^2 - (b - c \cos A)^2$$

Since both are equal to BM², we can write

$$a^2 - (b - c \cos A)^2 = c^2 - (c \cos A)^2$$

or

$$a^2 - b^2 + 2bc \cos A - (c \cos A)^2 = c^2 - (c \cos A)^2$$

So,

$$a^2 - b^2 + 2bc \cos A = c^2$$

or, in a final rearrangement,

> **The cosine rule**
>
> $$a^2 = b^2 + c^2 - 2bc \cos A$$

The cosine rule is used when our problem involves:

- A triangle that does not contain a right angle.

- Three sides and one angle.

Example

A pair of stepladders has unequal legs. One is 2.5 m long, the other is 2.4 metres long. How far apart are the bottoms of the legs when there is an angle between the tops of the legs of 24°?

We can draw this sketch.

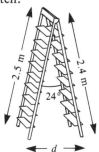

PROBLEM IDENTIFICATION

This problem involves a triangle without a right angle. We must therefore use either the **sine** rule or the **cosine** rule. Since three sides and one angle are involved, we must use the **cosine** rule.

SOLUTION

If we call the distance to be calculated d, applying the cosine rule to the triangle, we have

$$d^2 = 2.4^2 + 2.5^2 - (2 \times 2.4 \times 2.5 \times \cos 24°)$$

Using a calculator we have

$$d^2 = 5.76 + 6.25 - 10.96$$

$$d = \sqrt{1.05}$$

$$d = 1.02 \text{ metres}$$

You will remember that the sine ratio of an angle is positive from 0° to 180°. The cosine ratio, on the other hand, is only positive from 0° to 90°. From 90° to 180° the cosine ratio is negative. Angles greater than 90° thus cause more problems with the cosine rule than the sine rule. In fact, using a good calculator most of the values take care of themselves, but we must just be very careful with the subtraction of negative quantities. Suppose, for example, in our last problem the stepladder was slipping and the angle between the legs had opened up to 110°. Our sketch would then have been:

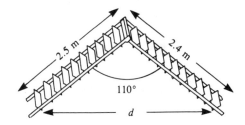

Our calculations would then have been:

$$d^2 = 2.4^2 + 2.5^2 - (2 \times 2.4 \times 2.5 \times \cos 110°)$$

Using a calculator we have

$$d^2 = 5.76 + 6.25 - (-4.10)$$

Subtracting a negative results in an addition, so

$$d^2 = 5.76 + 6.25 + 4.10$$

$$d = \sqrt{16.11}$$

$$d = 4.01 \text{ metres (to 2 d.p.)}$$

CHECKPOINT 31

1 Calculate the length of the side d in this diagram.

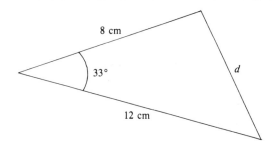

311

2 Calculate the length of the side d in this diagram.

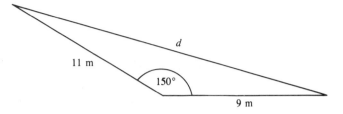

3 James Slofoot and Sally Qikfeet are taking part in an orienteering competition. After reaching the first checkpoint together, they set off in different directions. Sally takes the correct route and runs 0.8 km on a bearing of 030°. In the same time, James runs 0.5 km on a bearing of 085°. How far apart are Sally and James at this point in the competition?

4 A golfer is 120 m from the hole. She slices the ball and hits it 90 m at an angle of 30° to the correct line of flight. How far from the hole does the ball land?

In all the problems so far, we have used the cosine rule to calculate a side length. With a slightly different technique, we can also calculate a missing angle. In this case, the cosine formula is rearranged as in the following steps:

$$a^2 = b^2 + c^2 - 2bc \cos A$$

Adding $2bc \cos A$ to both sides of the equation gives

$$2bc \cos A + a^2 = b^2 + c^2$$

Subtracting a^2 from both sides of the equation gives

$$2bc \cos A = b^2 + c^2 - a^2$$

Dividing both sides of the equation by $2bc$ gives

The cosine rule to find an angle
$$\cos A = \frac{b^2 + c^2 - a^2}{2bc}$$

This rearranged formula should be learnt. You will not have time to rearrange the formula during the examination.

Example

A parallelogram has sides of 8 cm and 14 cm. One diagonal is 12 cm long. Calculate the sizes of the angles in the parallelogram.

We can draw this sketch.

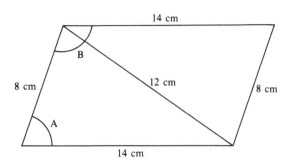

PROBLEM IDENTIFICATION

This problem involves a triangle without a right angle. We must therefore use either the **sine rule** or the **cosine rule**. Since three sides and one angle are involved, we must use the **cosine rule**.

SOLUTION

Applying the rearranged cosine rule to this problem, we have

$$\cos A = \frac{8^2 + 14^2 - 12^2}{2 \times 8 \times 14}$$

So,

$$\cos A = \frac{64 + 196 - 144}{224}$$

Using a calculator we press

| 6 | 4 | + | 1 | 9 | 6 | − | 1 | 4 | 4 | = | ÷ | 2 | 2 | 4 |

Giving
$$\cos A = 0.5178571$$

Finally, with this value left in the calculator, we press

| INV | cos |

which gives

$$A = 58.8° \text{ (to 1 d.p.)}$$

Simple geometry gives us the other angle in the parallelogram.

$$B = 180 - A$$

Therefore

$$B = 121.2°$$

---

1 Calculate the size of angle A in this diagram.

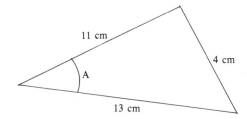

2 Calculate the size of angle A in this diagram.

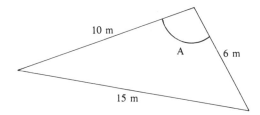

3 The sides of a triangle are 4 cm, 5 cm and 6 cm. Find the sizes of the angles in the triangle.

4 The sides of a triangle are 2 cm, 5 cm and 6 cm. Find the size of the largest angle in the triangle.

5 A golfer is 120 m from the hole. He hits the ball a distance of 65 m, to a point 70 m from the hole. At what angle to the correct line did the golfer hit the ball?

Pythagoras and trigonometry
Past paper questions

1 A surveyor is finding the height BC of a tower. The point A is on horizontal ground at a distance of 100 metres from the foot of the tower. The angle of elevation of the top of the tower from A is 16.7°. Calculate the height of the tower correct to the nearest metre.

Not to scale

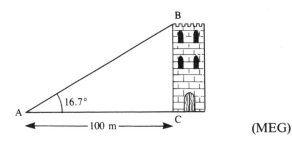

(MEG)

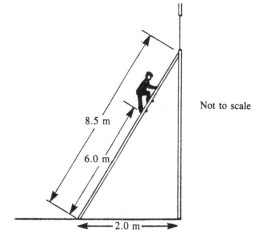

A window cleaner uses a ladder 8.5 m long. The ladder leans against the vertical wall of a house with the foot of the ladder 2.0 m from the wall on horizontal ground.

a Calculate the size of the angle which the ladder makes with the ground.

b Calculate the height of the top of the ladder above the ground.

c The window cleaner climbs 6.0 m up the ladder (see diagram). How far is his lower foot from the wall?

(MEG)

3 Gareth marks out a rectangular plot ABCD measuring 6 m by 4 m.

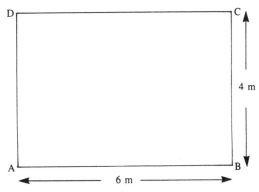

One of the checks a building inspector makes on Gareth's work is to measure the length of AC after first calculating what it should be.

Calculate the value of AC in metres, correct to 1 decimal place.

(WJEC)

4 The diagram shows a drink carton which is a tetrahedron with base ABC. The vertex D is vertically above A.

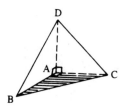

$$AB = AC = AD = 8 \text{ cm}$$

Angles BAC, BAD and CAD are all 90°.

a On graph paper draw the net of the carton using 1 cm to represent 2 cm.

b Calculate (do not measure) the lengths of DC and BC.

c Calculate (do not measure) angle BDC.

d Calculate the total surface area of the carton.

(SEG)

5

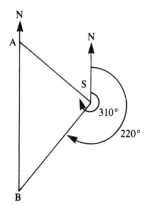

The diagram shows two navigation lights A and B with A due North of B. From a ship, S, the bearing of A is 310° and the bearing of B is 220°.

a Calculate

(i) angle ASB.

(ii) angle ABS.

b The distance AB is 2000 m; calculate the distances SA and SB.

(SEG)

6

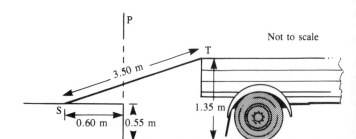

In the diagram, ST represents a ramp, 3.50 m long, used when goods are moved from a warehouse on to a lorry. The end T rests on the lorry and is 1.35 m above the horizontal ground. The end S is 0.60 m inside the warehouse and is on the horizontal floor of the warehouse, 0.55 m above ground level.

a Write down the vertical distance between S and T.

b Calculate the angle which ST makes with the horizontal.

c Calculate the horizontal distance between T and the vertical wall PQ of the warehouse.

(MEG)

7

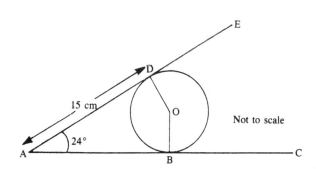

The diagram shows a tennis ball, centre O, resting on a table top, ABC. A ruler, ADE, touches the ball at D.

The distance AD = 15 cm and angle DAB = 24°.

a Write down the length of AB.

b Write down the size of angle ABO.

c Calculate the radius, OB, of the tennis ball, correct to the nearest millimetre.

(MEG)

8 The diagram below shows four points A, B, C, and D, all on a horizontal parade ground with the straight line BAD running due North. There is a vertical flagpole at the point A and the length of BA is 32.4 m.

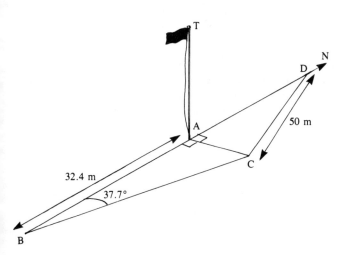

a From the point B the angle of elevation of the point T, the top of the flagpole, is 10.5°. Calculate the height, AT, of the flagpole.

b The point C is due East of A and the bearing of C from B is 037.7°. Calculate.

  (i) the distance AC,

  (ii) the angle of elevation of T from C,

  (iii) the distance BC.

c The length of CD is 50 m. Calculate

  (i) the angle CDA,

  (ii) the bearing of C from D.

(SEG)

9

Brighton is due South of London and Le Havre is due South of Brighton. Portsmouth is due West of Brighton.

a Use the Pythagoras theorem to calculate the distances required to complete this table. Give your answers to the nearest mile.

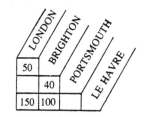

DISTANCE IN MILES	LONDON	BRIGHTON	PORTSMOUTH	LE HAVRE
	50			
		40		
	150	100		

b Calculate, giving your answers to 1 decimal place,

  (i) angle LPB,

  (ii) the bearing of London from Portsmouth,

  (iii) the bearing of Le Havre from Portsmouth.

c A hot air balloon is vertically above Brighton and is seen from London at an angle of elevation of 2.5°. Calculate

  (i) the height of the balloon above the ground,

  (ii) the angle of elevation at which it will be seen from Portsmouth.

(SEG)

10

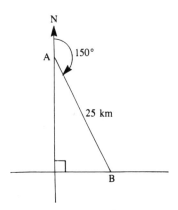

Beckthorpe House (B) is 25 km from Appletree Inn (A) on a bearing of 150°.

a What is the bearing of Appletree Inn from Beckthorpe House?

b Calculate how far, in km correct to three significant figures, Beckthorpe House is South of Appletree Inn.

(LEAG)

11 (*In this question, give all distances to the nearest 0.01 km.*)

315

This figure represents three villages A, B and C on a hillside. A, C and N are at the same height above sea level and N is vertically below B. Angle CAB is 90° and angle BAN is 2.5°. The villages are linked by three straight roads AB, AC and CB, where

$$AB = 8 \text{ km} \quad \text{and} \quad AC = 12 \text{ km}$$

Calculate

a the horizontal distance AN,

b the length of the road CB.

(LEAG)

12 The box for a chocolate mint is a square-based pyramid with its point vertically above the middle of the base. The sides of the box are 6 cm long and the box is 6 cm tall.

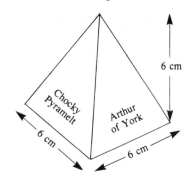

a (i) Calculate the diagonal distance across the base.

(ii) Calculate the length of a sloping edge.

b Sketch a net for the box, indicating the lengths of the sides.

(WJEC)

13

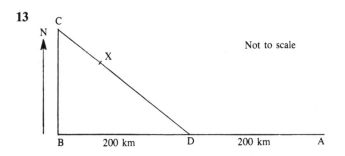

Not to scale

Airport A is 400 km due East of airport B. An aircraft leaves A at 2155 hours to fly to B. Its speed over the ground is 320 km/h.

a (i) Calculate the time the aircraft takes to fly 400 km.

(ii) At what time is the aircraft expected to arrive at B?

b When the aircraft is at D, halfway between A and B, it is diverted to airport C because of fog at airport B. Airport C is 120 km due North of B.

(i) Calculate the bearing of C from D.

(ii) Calculate the distance from D to C.

(iii) The point on the aircraft's path nearest to B is X. Calculate the distance of X from B.

(MEG)

14 Jack is at sea in a boat which is travelling directly towards an island where there is a vertical cliff-face. When the boat is at point A, the angle of elevation of the top T of the cliff from the boat is 17°. A short time later the boat has reached the point B, where AB = 565 m, and the angle of elevation of T from the boat is then 22°.

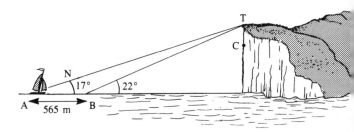

Calculate

a the angle ATB,

b the perpendicular distance BN from B to the line at AT,

c the distance BT,

d the height of T above sea level.

Later still, when the boat is closer to the island, Jack sees that there is a climber C on the cliff-face vertically below T. From the boat at this moment, the angle of elevation of T is 54°, and the angle of elevation of C is 51°. Calculate

e the distance of the boat from the bottom of the cliff at this moment,

f how far, to the nearest metre, the climber is from the top of the cliff.

(MEG)

15 The sketch below shows the positions of two ships Q and R three hours after they left the port P.

The bearing of Q from P is 016.7°.

The bearing of R from P is 075.75°.

The ship R is 65 km from P.

The points L and M are due South of Q, and the distance QM is 50 km. The point L is due West of R and the point N is due South of R.

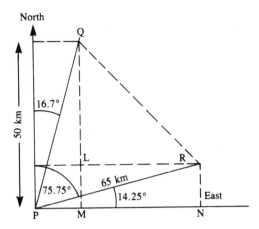

Calculate

a the distance RN,

b the distance PN,

c the distance PM,

d the angle QRL,

e the bearing of Q from R.

(SEG)

16 The diagram is a sketch of the Swansea Bay area showing Mumbles, Baglan and Porthcawl.

Mumbles is 13 km due West of Baglan and 20 km on a bearing of N 50° W (310°) from Porthcawl.

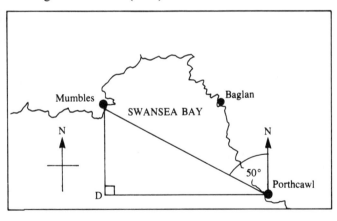

A ship sails from Porthcawl due West and arrives at a point D, which is directly due South from Mumbles.

Calculate

a how far the ship has sailed from Porthcawl,

b how far is the ship from Mumbles,

c the bearing of Baglan from the ship.

(WJEC)

17

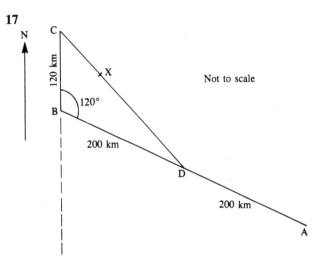

Airport A is 400 km from airport B on a bearing 120°. An aircraft leaves A at 2155 hours to fly to B. Its speed over the ground is 320 km/h.

a Calculate the time at which the aircraft is expected to arrive at B.

b When the aircraft is at D, halfway between A and B, it is diverted to airport C because of fog at airport B. Airport C is 120 km due North of B.

(i) Calculate the distance from D to C.

(ii) Calculate the bearing of C from D.

(iii) The point on the aircraft's path nearest to B is X. Calculate the distance of X from B.

(MEG)

18

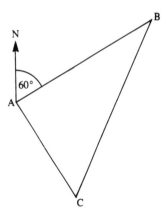

This sketch shows the flight paths between three airports at Appleton (A), Berriton (B) and Cherriton (C).
Berriton is 60 km from Appleton on a bearing 060°.
Cherriton is 80 km from Appleton on a bearing 170°.

a (i) What is the size of angle BAC?

(ii) Calculate the distance from Berriton to Cherriton.

(iii) By finding angle ACB, find the bearing of Berriton from Cherriton.

b Find the area of land enclosed by the three flight paths.

(WJEC)

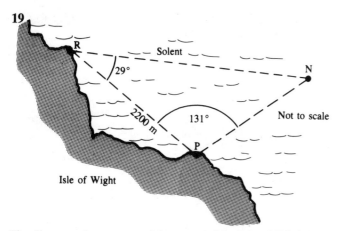

19

The diagram shows part of the coast of the Isle of Wight and the Solent. The point R represents the position of Ryde, point P the position of Puckpool Point and point N the position of No Man's Land Fort.

RP=2200 metres, angle NRP=29° and angle RPN=131°.

a Calculate the distance RN, correct to the nearest 10 metres.

b A boat sails directly from Ryde to No Man's Land Fort. Calculate, correct to the nearest 10 metres, its closest distance to Puckpool Point.

(MEG)

20

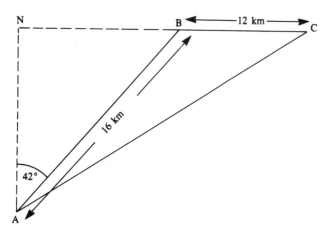

This figure shows the route taken by a boat on a fishing trip. The boat starts from a port A and sails 16 km on a bearing of 042° to its first stop at the point B. In the figure, N is the point which is due North of A and due West of B.

a Calculate, to the nearest 0.01 km,

(i) the distance AN,

(ii) the distance BN.

The boat then sails 12 km due East to its second stop at the point C.

b Calculate

(i) the distance AC, in km, to the nearest 0.01 km,

(ii) the bearing of C from A, to the nearest degree.

c What is the bearing of A from C?

The boat travels at 6.4 km/h.

d Find the time it takes to return directly to A from C.

(LEAG)

21

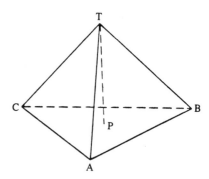

ABCT is a pyramid with its triangular base, ABC, on horizontal ground. The top, T, of the pyramid is 40 m above the ground. The point on the ground vertically below T is P, so that TP=40 m.

The positions of A, B and C are as shown on the plan:

North

A is 30 m South of P.
B is 30 m East of P.
C is on a bearing of 315° from P.

a *Sketch* the triangle PBT and calculate the length of the edge BT.

The edge CT is the same length as the edge BT.

b Write down the distance CP.

c Calculate the size of angle PAC.

d Calculate the length of the edge AC.

Give your answer in metres correct to three significant figures.

(LEAG)

318

22 Jasmine is asked to calculate the height of a tower.

From a point A she finds the angle of elevation of the top of the tower C to be 40°.

She walks 50 metres towards the tower and finds the new angle of elevation of the top of the tower to be 60°.

Her results are illustrated in the diagram below.

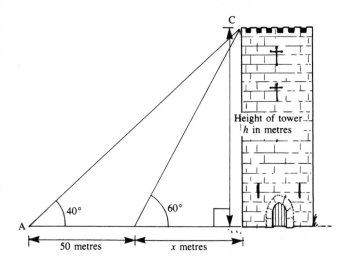

a Express, in terms of x and h,

(i) tan 60,

(ii) tan 40.

b Using the two equations in part **a**, show that

$$x(\tan 60 - \tan 40) = 50 \tan 40$$

c Use Jasmin's results to find the height of the tower, in metres, to 3 significant figures.

(SEG)

23 The table shows the depth of water, in metres, at the mouth of Sheringport harbour at various times of a day.

Time (number of hours after midnight)	0	1	2	3	4	5	6
Depth of water (metres)	12.0	11.7	11.0	10.0	9.0	8.3	8.0

a (i) On a grid, plot the points representing the information in the table.

(ii) Join these points to form a smooth curve.

b From your graph, estimate the depth of water at 4.15 a.m.

c A ship needs at least 9.2 metres of water to be able to leave the harbour.

What is the latest time before 6.00 a.m. that the ship could leave?

d The formula for finding the depth of water is

$$D = 10 + k \cos (30t)°$$

where D is the depth of water in metres, t is the number of hours after midnight and k is a constant. Using the values $t = 0$ and $D = 12.0$, find the value of k.

(MEG)

Statistics, the mathematics of data handling

Why use Statistics?

Statistics is a branch of mathematics which has been developed over the past 150 to 200 years. It is a systematic, mathematical way to answer questions about the world we live in. Questions like

- What is the average height of English women?
- How much extra money will be raised by a 2p rise in the rate of income tax?
- Is the new breakfast cereal Zappo Flakes likely to be successful?
- Do more females than males pass their driving test at the first attempt? Do younger applicants stand more chance of passing first time?
- Which party is most likely to win the next election?
- In which area of the country is it most expensive to buy a house?
- Who was the most successful pop singer of all time?

To answer questions like these, we work through three stages.

- First, we **collect** data about the question.
- Second, we **organise** our data and present them in a clear way.
- Third, we **interpret** our data and attempt to answer the original question.

Collecting Data

Primary and secondary data

We start any work in statistics by collecting data about the questions we wish to answer. If we collect the data ourselves, specifically to answer the original question, what we have are called **primary data**.

Some ways to collect primary data are

- BY COUNTING. For example, by counting the number of cars passing a given spot for every 15 minute interval between 7 am and 9 am.
- BY MEASURING. For example, by measuring the length of 100 earthworms.
- BY QUESTIONNAIRE. For example, by asking 200 people to answer a set of questions designed to discover their opinions about a proposed change in the law.

In some cases, we may work with data that have been already collected by others. For example, we might use the data in a football encyclopedia to answer a question like

'Has the change to 3 points rather than 2 for winning affected the number of goals scored in football matches?'

Data obtained in this way from existing records are called **secondary data**.

Variables

Statistical data are collected about **variables**. A variable is an attribute of an individual or object that can change and take different values. Examples of variables are

- a pig's weight
- the number of children in a family
- a person's favourite pop singer
- the daily sales of a newspaper.

We distinguish between two types of variable and the type of data that each produces. These variables are called **qualitative** variables and **quantitative** variables.

A **qualitative** variable is a **non-numerical** attribute of an individual or object. Examples are the favourite pop singer, above; social class; religion and where people live.

Some qualitative variables, like 'gender', simply divide individuals into groups. There is no implication that one group is better than another, simply that they are different. Other qualitative variables, like 'army rank', both divide and **order** individuals or objects. The groups produced by the variable are in an order of merit or magnitude.

Some examples of qualitative variables which divide individuals or objects into groups are

- race
- religion
- political party voted for
- newspaper taken
- colour of paintwork.

Some examples of qualitative variables which divide **and order** individuals or objects into groups are

- social class
- educational qualifications
- type of accommodation
- beauty
- resistance to disease.

This diagram illustrates the use of quantitative variables to divide individuals or objects into groups.

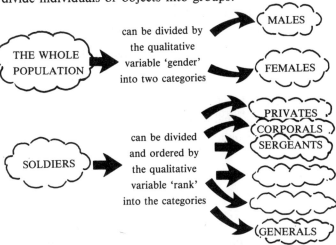

A **quantitative** variable is a **numerical** attribute of an individual or object. Examples are age, height, number of children, income, top speed and fuel consumption.

Quantitative variables are divided into **discrete** quantitative variables and **continuous** quantitative variables.
A **discrete** quantitative variable can only take one of a range of distinct values between the start and end of a scale. For example, a suitable range for the number of children in a family might be from 1 to 6 children. Between the start and end of this scale, the variable can only take the values 0, 1, 2, 3, 4, 5 and 6. Values like 1.3 children or 5.6 children are impossible.

A **continuous** quantitative variable can take any value between the start and end of a scale. For example, a suitable

range for the weight of an adult might be from 30 kg to 150 kg. Between the start and end of this scale, any value of the variable is possible. We can have an adult who weighs 45 kg, or one who weighs 45.6 kg or one who weighs 45.63 kg and so on, with increasingly more accurate measurement.

Some examples of discrete quantitative variables are

- the number of seats in a bus
- the number of goals scored in a hockey game
- the number of bedrooms in a house
- the number of marks scored in a test.

Some examples of continuous quantitative variables are

- a person's height
- a vehicle's fuel consumption
- a person's income
- the time taken by somebody to run 100 metres.

This diagram illustrates the use of quantitative variables to place individuals or objects on to a scale of values.

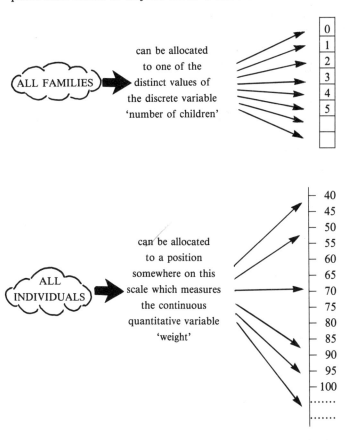

In practice, there is considerable blurring of these definitions. For example, you might be prepared to argue that 'income' is a discrete variable because any income must be one of a distinct range of values listed in pennies. There are, however, so many different possibilities when incomes are taken down to the exact penny that 'income' is almost always considered to be a continuous variable.

In the same way, 'weight' is certainly a continuous variable. If, however, we are measuring 'weight' with a set of scales which is only accurate to the nearest tenth of a kilogram, our results will be from the distinct range of values, 0.1, 0.2, 0.3, 0.4 and so on.

The difference between quantitative and qualitative variables

The difference between qualitative and quantitative variables is that all the operations of arithmetic can be applied to quantitative variables.

For example, by studying this **quantitative** scale

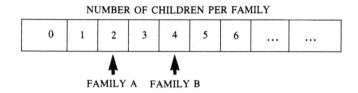

NUMBER OF CHILDREN PER FAMILY

we can make statements like

- family B has twice as many children as family A.

By studying this **quantitative** scale

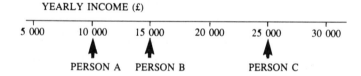

YEARLY INCOME (£)

we can make statements like

- the income of person C is equal to the income of person A plus the income of Person B.

By studying this **qualitative** scale

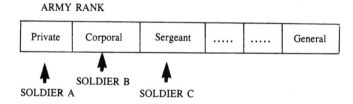

ARMY RANK

we cannot make any mathematical statements. We certainly cannot say

- soldier B has three times as much rank as soldier A, or
- the rank of A plus the rank of B equals the rank of C.

This box summarises some of the types of variable that we could collect data on for any individual.

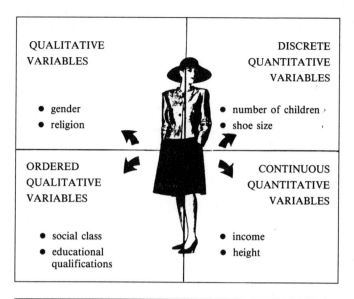

QUALITATIVE VARIABLES	DISCRETE QUANTITATIVE VARIABLES
• gender • religion	• number of children • shoe size
ORDERED QUALITATIVE VARIABLES	CONTINUOUS QUANTITATIVE VARIABLES
• social class • educational qualifications	• income • height

CHECKPOINT 1

1 'Religion' is a **qualitative** variable which could be used to divide a group of people into the following set of categories.

- Catholic • Other Christians • Jews • Hindu
- C of E • Muslim • Sikh • Other

Design a set of categories which could be used with each of the following variables.

a 'newspaper taken'
b 'educational qualifications'
c 'type of accommodation'
d 'eye colour'
e 'political party voted for'
f 'social class'

2 'Weight' is a **quantitative** variable which could be measured for most humans on the following scale.

WEIGHT IN KILOGRAMS ——➤

0 10 20 30 40 50 60 70 80 90 100 110 120 130 140 150

Design suitable scales to measure each of the following variables. In each case indicate what you consider to be suitable start and end points for your scale.

a 'height' (in humans)
b 'shoe size'
c 'top speed' (in cars)
d 'dress size'
e 'yearly income'
f 'weight' (oven-ready turkeys)

3 In each case, state whether the variable in question will produce qualitative data, ordered qualitative data, discrete quantitative data or continuous quantitative data. Give examples of at least three possible values for each variable.

a The shoe sizes of the members of a hockey team.

b The state of the garden in each house on an estate, from 'best kept garden' to 'worst kept garden'.

c The type of windows in each house on an estate.

d The value of each house on an estate.

e The colour of the paintwork of each house on an estate.

f The number of people living in each house on an estate.

g The 'value to the team' rating for each of the members of a hockey team, from 'most valuable player' to 'to least valuable player'.

h The heights of the members of a hockey team.

Organising Data

Frequency tables

In this section we will look at the way that data are organised into tables after they have been collected (or during collection). We will start with an example.

Some data have been collected to answer the question

'Do the families on housing estate A have more children than the families on housing estate B?'

The data were collected by conducting a door to door survey on each estate to discover the number of children in 50 families.

This is the 'raw' data.

ESTATE A

Number of children per family

0	1	2	3	2	2	2	1	1	2
1	0	0	0	2	2	3	4	3	1
1	2	1	3	0	4	1	2	1	2
2	3	0	3	2	2	2	4	3	4
3	2	4	0	0	2	2	0	0	2

ESTATE B

Number of children per family

0	2	2	2	4	4	3	5	3	6
5	2	2	4	2	6	2	2	1	2
3	3	1	0	4	3	2	2	2	2
1	4	2	2	3	0	2	2	2	2
5	6	6	6	2	3	5	3	1	3

Raw results like these are normally organised into a table showing the number of times (frequency) with which each value of the variable occurs. This table is called a **frequency table**. The first stage in constructing a frequency table is to consider the range of values taken by the variable. These values are the headings for the table. In this case we have

NUMBER OF CHILDREN PER FAMILY

0   1   2   3   4   5   6

Under each value we record the number of times it occurred in the survey. The whole survey of 100 families gives us this table.

NUMBER OF CHILDREN PER FAMILY	0	1	2	3	4	5	6
FREQUENCY	13	13	38	17	10	4	5

Taking each estate separately gives us this table.

NUMBER OF CHILDREN PER FAMILY	0	1	2	3	4	5	6
FREQUENCY (ESTATE A)	10	9	18	8	5	0	0
FREQUENCY (ESTATE B)	3	4	20	9	5	4	5

This activity of organising results into a **table** is called **tabulating** the data.

Tally charts

A **tally chart** is often used to help complete the table of results. For example, suppose we intend to toss two coins 100 times to discover the frequency with which two heads, two tails or one head and one tail occur. We could collect and organise our results with this table.

RESULT	TALLY	FREQUENCY
TWO HEADS		
TWO TAILS		
ONE HEAD, ONE TAIL		

As each result is obtained, a **tally** mark is made in the correct row of the tally part of the table. When a particular result is obtained for the fifth time, the fifth tally mark is used to cross out the previous four marks. This system makes it very easy to count up the frequencies at the end of the experiment. Our completed table might look like this.

RESULT	TALLY	FREQUENCY
TWO HEADS	LHT LHT LHT LHT III	23
TWO TAILS	LHT LHT LHT LHT LHT IIII	29
ONE HEAD, ONE TAIL	LHT LHT LHT LHT LHT LHT LHT LHT LHT III	48

Grouped tables

Some variables have so many different values that we may need to arrange them into groups in order to produce a table of a sensible size. For example, if we were collecting data on the weekly earnings of a sample of 500 people, we might expect a very large number of different results. A table showing every possible weekly wage, even correct to the nearest pound, is obviously impossible, so we might use a **grouped table** like this.

Earnings per week (£)	Less than 100	101–120	121–140	141–160	161–180	181–200	Over 200
Frequency							

When we collect continuous data by measuring values of a variable, we will always need to decide how accurate these measurements are going to be. For example, in a survey to find the lengths of 200 earthworms, we might decide to measure each earthworm and record the result correct to the nearest centimetre. A table of results could be presented like this.

Length of earthworm (cm)	1	2	3	4	5	6	7	8	9	10
Frequency										

But this table could be considered very misleading, because a recorded length of 4 cm could be any length from 3.5 to 4.5 cm. A better way to organise and present our data would be in a grouped table like this.

Length of earthworm (cm)	0.5–1.5	1.5–2.5	2.5–3.5	3.5–4.5	4.5–5.5	5.5–6.5	6.5–7.5	7.5–8.5	8.5–9.5	9.5–10.5
Frequency										

Technically, the groups shown in the table are not exactly correct. A measurement given as 1 centimetre, correct to the nearest centimetre, actually falls within the limits

$$0.5–1.4\dot{9}$$

It is common practice, however, to round up the recurring decimal and treat the limits as

$$0.5–1.5$$

If any measurements fall exactly on a boundary, like 1.5 or 2.5, we have to make some decision about dealing with them. There are no hard and fast rules, but we can either

- decide to always record the measurement in the longer group
- decide to always record the measurement in the shorter group
- decide to share the measurement and add 0.5 to the frequencies of both groups.

CHECKPOINT 2

This checkpoint contains suggestions for collecting some primary data. Before starting to collect the data, you should design a suitable table in which to organise your results.

1 Make a set of cards, numbered from 1 to 5 (or use cards from a normal deck). Shuffle the cards and then deal two face up. Record the total number of points on the two cards. Repeat this 100 times, recording all your results. Organise your results into a table and comment on any patterns that emerge. (This experiment is best done by dividing into pairs, one dealing, one recording. The data for the whole group can then be collected to produce a large number of results.)

2 Discuss some possible data that you could collect about the cars parked in the nearest car park. Construct tables to record these data and, if it is possible, go and collect them.

3 The cubit was an early form of measurement, based on the length from the elbow to the end of the outstretched fingers. Collect data on the different lengths produced for one cubit by a group of people.

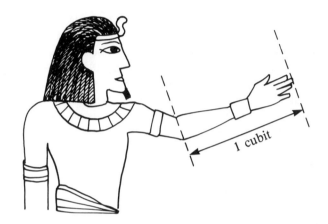

1 cubit

The book of Genesis in the Christian Bible gives the dimensions of Noah's ark like this,

'The length of the ark shall be 300 cubits, the breadth of it 50 cubits and the height of it 30 cubits.'

What measurements would you give for Noah's ark in metric units?

4 Duplicate this questionnaire and ask a group of people to complete it. Consider different ways that your results can be organised and then construct and complete the necessary tables.

Can anything be discovered by subdividing the results?

POLITICAL LEADER SURVEY

If there was an election tomorrow, which party would you like to see gain victory? (tick one box)

Conservative party ☐

Labour party ☐

Social and Liberal Democrats ☐

Do you consider the Prime Minister to be (tick **one** box on each line):

	Very	Fairly	Slightly	Neither	Slightly	Fairly	Very	
Successful								Unsuccessful
Strong								Weak
Friendly								Unfriendly
Hardworking								Lazy
Honest								Dishonest

Do you consider the Leader of the Opposition to be (tick **one** box on each line):

	Very	Fairly	Slightly	Neither	Slightly	Fairly	Very	
Successful								Unsuccessful
Strong								Weak
Friendly								Unfriendly
Hardworking								Lazy
Honest								Dishonest

The next checkpoint gives practice in organising and presenting **secondary** data. Many examination questions will be of this form.

CHECKPOINT 3

1 These are the final scores in some cup matches. Complete a table with tally marks to show the frequency with which teams scored no goals, 1 goal, 2 goals, etc.

Barnsley (3) 4
  Thomas,
  Agnew 2,
  Currie
Birmingham (0) 0
  10,431
Blackpool (0) 0
  5,317
Bradford (1) 1
  Mitchell
Brighton (0) 1
  Curbishly (pen)

Cardiff (1) 1
  Gilligan

Carlisle (0) 0
  18,556

Charlton (1) 2
  Crooks,
  Williams
Crewe (2) 2
  Gardiner,
  Keown (og)
Derby (0) 1
  Hebberd

Hartlepool (0) 1
  Baker (pen)
Huddersfield (0) 0
  15,543
Kettering (0) 1
  Griffith
Manchester City (1) 1
  Mcnab (pen)
Manchester United (0) 0

Middlesboro (1) 1
  Slaven
Millwall (2) 3
  Cascarino,
  Carter,
  Sheringham
Newcastle (0) 0

Nottm Fst (2) 3
  Yallop (og)
  Gaynor, Chapman
Plymouth (0) 2
  Tynan,
  Summerfield
Portsmouth (1) 1
  Quinn
Sheff Wed (2) 5
  Jonsson,
  Hodgson,
  Varadi 2,
  Procter
Shrewsbury (0) 0
  3,982

Stoke (0) 1
  Shaw
Sunderland (1) 1
  Ord
Sutton Utd (1) 2
  Rains, Hanlan
Tranmere (0) 1
  Vickers
Walsall (0) 1
  Pritchard
Weilling (0) 0
  3,850
West Brom (1) 1
  Anderson

Chelsea (0) 0
  13,241

Wimbledon (1) 1
  Gibson
Bournemouth (0) 1
  Blissett
Tottenham (0) 0
  15,917
Leeds (0) 2
  Baird 2
  10,900
Hull (1) 2
  Brown, Edwards
  7,128
Liverpool (1) 3
  Barnes,
  McMahon (2)
Oldham (1) 1
  Milligan
  5,060
Aston Villa (0) 3
  Platt, Gage,
  McInally   5,500
Southampton (0) 1
  Statham (pen)
  17,178
Briston C (0) 0
  4,033
Sheffield Utd (1) 1
  Agana
Halifax (1) 1
  Watson   5,800
Leicester (0) 0
  23,838
QPR (0) 0
  36,222
Grimsby (0) 2
  North 2   19,190
Luton (1) 2
  Black,
  Wilson (pen)
  12,504
Watford (0) 0
  24,086
Ipswich (0) 0
  20,743

Cambridge (0) 0
  8,648

Swindon (0) 1
  Foley   10,582
Torquay (1) 1
  Edwards
  11,381

Colchester (1) 3
  Walsh,
  Pratley (og),
  Allinson (pen)
C Palace (0) 0
  12,294
Oxford (0) 0
  Hill   17,074
Coventry (0) 1
  Phillips   8,000
Reading (0) 1
  Elsey   7,799
Brentford (0) 1
  Jones   5,375
Blackburn (1) 1
  Hildersley
Everton (1) 1
  Sheedy (pen)
  31,186

2 Some letters of the alphabet occur far more frequently in written English than others. The letter e, for example, occurs far more frequently than the letter z. If a large sample of written English is checked, the order of frequency with which each letter occurs is usually

ETOANIRSHDLCWUMFYGPBVKXQJZ

Carry out your own survey to check this order of frequency, using a paragraph selected from any book. Design a tally chart table to collect and organise your results. Comment on your results. How well do they match the predictions?

3 A survey has been completed into the voting intentions of 1000 people. The interviewers conducting the survey were asked to make a judgement about whether the person questioned was a young voter (less than 30), a mature voter (between 30 and 50) or an old voter (over 50). The results obtained were as follows. Of 290 young voters, 178 intended to vote Labour, 32 intended to vote Conservative and 80 intended to vote SLD. Of 334 mature voters, 82 intended to vote SLD, 199 intended to vote Conservative and 53 intended to vote Labour. Of 376 old voters, 189 intended to vote Conservative, 83 intended to vote SLD and 104 intended to vote Labour.

Present these results in a table, with divisions for each political party **and** each age group.

Presenting and Illustrating Data with Diagrams and Graphs

Graphs and diagrams can be used to illustrate data clearly and visually. The following subsections explain the different types of graphs and diagrams that are commonly used.

Bar charts

Bar charts are used to illustrate qualitative data and discrete quantitative data. We will demonstrate the technique by constructing a bar chart to illustrate the data in the following table.

Number of children per family	0	1	2	3	4	5	6
Frequency	10	9	18	8	5	0	0

A bar chart has two axes, one for the variable and one for the frequency. The frequency axis is usually vertical and the variable axis horizontal, like this.

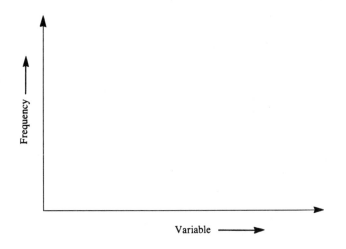

We divide the variable axis into spaces and allocate one space for each value of the variable.

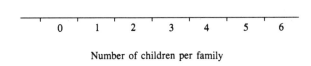

The frequency axis is simply a number line which will allow us to plot all the frequencies. In this example, our frequency axis looks like this.

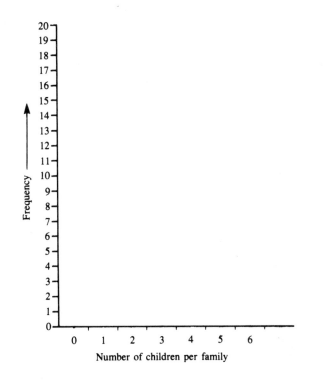

Once this basic layout of the axes has been decided, it is quite easy to draw in the bars of our chart. This is the completed bar graph.

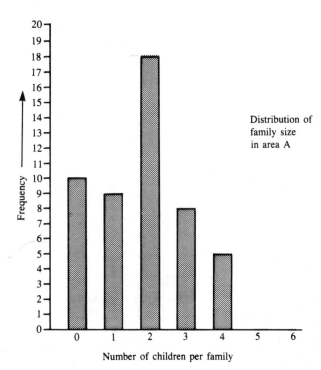

Distribution of family size in area A

The data below are more difficult to illustrate with a bar chart because the large numbers mean that we must use a scale on the frequency axis.

BEST-SELLERS

1.	**Ford Escort**	**144,228**
2.	**Ford Fiesta**	**129,025**
3.	**Ford Sierra**	**111,000**
4.	**Austin/MG Metro**	**91,479**
5.	**Vauxhall Cavalier**	**79,804**
6.	**Vauxhall Astra**	**71,264**
7.	**Ford Orion**	**55,218**
8.	**Austin/MG Montego**	**45,580**
9.	**Rover 200**	**40,525**
10.	**Peugeot 205**	**40,317**

Numbers are those registered in the first nine months of this year.

327

This diagram shows the completed bar graph, which uses a scale of

$$1 \text{ unit} = 10\,000 \text{ cars}$$

on the frequency axis.

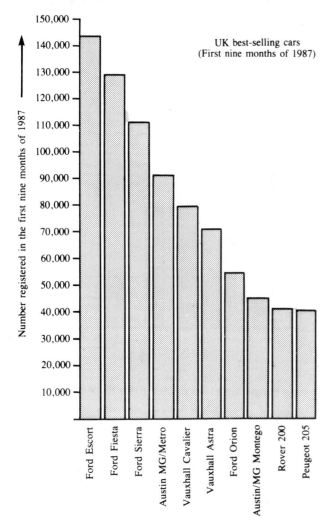

UK best-selling cars
(First nine months of 1987)

Pictograms

A pictogram is a variation of the bar chart, using lines of symbols to replace the solid bar.

For example, these data on the number of drinks sold by a vending machine in a one-hour period

TYPE OF DRINK	NUMBER SOLD
TEA	5
COFFEE	8
SOUP	3
CHOCOLATE	4

could be illustrated with this pictogram.

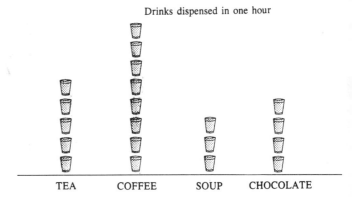

Drinks dispensed in one hour

We can even use a scale with a pictogram. For example, if we were illustrating these data on the number of drinks sold by a vending machine in a one-week period

TYPE OF DRINK	NUMBER SOLD
TEA	120
COFFEE	135
SOUP	63
CHOCOLATE	81

it would be much too tedious to draw lines with 120 or 135 cups. So, we might decide to use a scale and let one cup symbol represent 10 cups of drink sold. The only problem is that some of the actual numbers sold do not divide by 10. In these cases, we draw parts of a cup, judged by eye, to represent the remainder of the drinks sold. This is the completed pictogram.

Drinks dispensed in one week

= 10 cups served

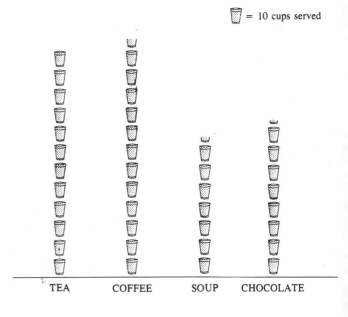

Pictograms are very time-consuming to draw neatly. Unless you have access to a photocopier or, even better, a computer, drawing lots of identical symbols is not easy. Tracing paper or stencils can be used, but unless you spend considerable time and effort, the final results are usually very scruffy. For most of your work the simple bar chart is the best choice and the pictogram is best left to the professional illustrator.

CHECKPOINT 4

1 This bar chart illustrates the price of the mains water supply in eleven different countries for two different years.

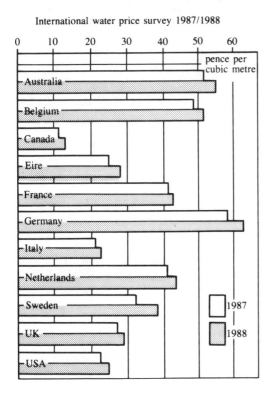

International water price survey 1987/1988

a Estimate the price of water in 1987 in each of the following countries.

- France • UK • Australia • Sweden

b Estimate the price of water in 1988 in each of the following countries.

- Belgium • Italy • Netherlands • Eire

c Estimate the change in the price of water from 1987 to 1988 in each of the following countries.

- Canada • USA • Germany • Sweden

2 Draw a bar chart to illustrate the information in this table.

Number of children per family	0	1	2	3	4	5	6
Frequency	3	4	20	9	5	4	5

3 Draw a bar chart to illustrate the information in this table.

RESULT	FREQUENCY
TWO HEADS	23
TWO TAILS	29
ONE HEAD, ONE TAIL	48

4 This table shows the number of thousands of males and females employed in various occupations. Draw a 'double' bar graph, like the one in question 1, to illustrate this information. Write some comments on the information shown in the graph.

OCCUPATION	(THOUSANDS)	
	MALES	FEMALES
LEGAL PROFESSION	45	8
NATIONAL GOVERNMENT ADMINISTRATORS	40	10
LOCAL GOVERNMENT ADMINISTRATORS	22	11
MEDICAL PROFESSION	60	19
TEACHERS	239	408
NURSES AND NURSING ADMINISTRATION	48	539
SCIENTISTS, ENGINEERS, TECHNOLOGISTS	896	87
MARKETING AND SALES	212	41
SHOP SALES STAFF	130	701
SECRETARIAL STAFF	17	861

Pie charts

Bar charts are very useful for illustrating which categories of a variable are the most frequent or the least frequent. They are less useful for illustrating the 'share' of the values which falls into each category. A better visual impression of the way that a variable is 'shared out' is obtained by drawing a **pie chart**.

A pie chart starts life as a blank circle. Slices of this circle (or pie) are then allocated to each category of the variable. Each category is allocated a slice in proportion to the frequency with which it occurs. For example, this pie chart illustrates the way that the UK government planned to 'share out' its spending for one year.

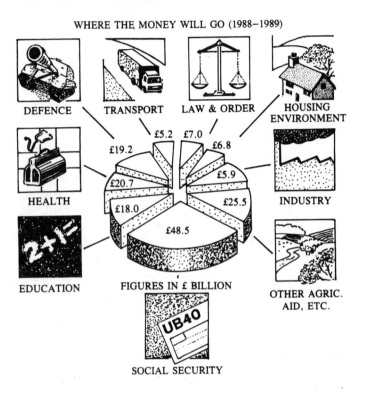

WHERE THE MONEY WILL GO (1988–1989)

DEFENCE · TRANSPORT · LAW & ORDER · HOUSING ENVIRONMENT

£5.2 £7.0 £6.8 £5.9 £19.2 £20.7 £18.0 £25.5 £48.5

HEALTH

EDUCATION · FIGURES IN £ BILLION

INDUSTRY

OTHER AGRIC. AID, ETC.

SOCIAL SECURITY

PLANNING TOTAL: £156.8 bn

Notice that the pie chart in this case was drawn as a real 'pie' and not as a circle. This is quite common and you will find many pie charts in newspapers and magazines are presented in this way.

Pie charts are particularly good at illustrating the way that the distribution or 'share' of a variable changes over a period of time. For example, these pie charts illustrate the way that banks increased their share of the mortgage market over a ten-year period.

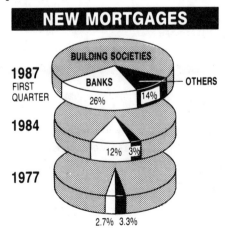

NEW MORTGAGES

BUILDING SOCIETIES

1987 FIRST QUARTER

BANKS 26% — OTHERS 14%

1984

12% 3%

1977

2.7% 3.3%

Sometimes a shape other than a circle is divided up to illustrate the 'share' that falls into each category. These charts are not called pie charts but they serve a similar purpose. This example shows an illustration which divides up a water bottle to show the 'share' that different categories have in the selling price of mineral water.

Mineral water

1 litre-55p

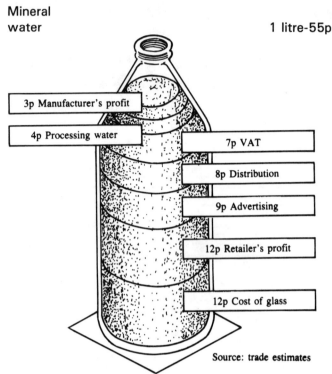

3p Manufacturer's profit

4p Processing water

7p VAT

8p Distribution

9p Advertising

12p Retailer's profit

12p Cost of glass

Source: trade estimates

When we are drawing our own pie charts we usually stick to a simple basic circle, using the technique illustrated in the following example.

Examples

These are the data to be illustrated with a pie chart. An international committee has 18 members, 6 from Great Britain, 7 from America, 3 from France and 2 from Japan.

First, we organise the data into a table like this

COUNTRY	NUMBER OF MEMBERS
GREAT BRITAIN	6
AMERICA	7
FRANCE	3
JAPAN	2
TOTAL	18

In any pie chart, we start with a full circle or **an angle of 360°** to share out between the categories. In this case, our 360° must be shared out between a total of 18 committee members. This means that every committee member is represented by an angle of 20° in the pie chart, because 360 divided by 18 is 20.

Knowing that every committee member is represented by an angle of 20° enables us to add a new column to our table. This column shows the pie chart angle for each country and is obtained by multiplying the number of members by 20°.

COUNTRY	NUMBER OF MEMBERS	PIE CHART ANGLE
GREAT BRITAIN	6	120°
AMERICA	7	140°
FRANCE	3	60°
JAPAN	2	40°
TOTAL	18	360°

We can now draw the pie chart. We draw a circle of a suitable size and starting at any selected point divide it up into slices with the calculated angles. The final diagram, with all labels and a title added looks like this.

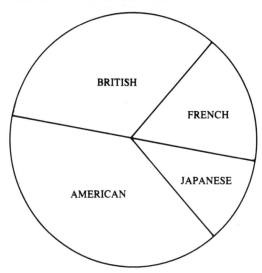

NATIONALITY OF COMMITTEE MEMBERS

Our pie chart is of the simplest and most basic form. Earlier examples have shown that with time, energy and artistic flair, more attractive presentations are possible.

In this first example, the numbers were very simple and all the calculations worked out to perfect whole numbers. In the real world we cannot expect this to happen and we will often need to work with difficult numbers and calculations that lead to approximations. A second example illustrates a more realistic situation.

These are the data to be illustrated with a pie chart.

ROAD ACCIDENT CASUALTIES 1983	
Category	Number killed
Pedestrians	1914
Pedal cyclists	323
Two-wheeled motor vehicles	942
Cars and taxis	2019
Others	226
Total	5424

As you can see, our pie chart angle of 360° must be shared between a total of 5424 casualties. Using a calculator to divide 360 by 5424 gives a result of approximately 0.0664° to represent each casualty. Multiplying the number of each type of casualty by 0.0664 and rounding the results to the nearest degree gives this table.

ROAD ACCIDENT CASUALTIES 1983		
Category	Number killed	Pie chart angle
Pedestrians	1914	127°
Pedal cyclists	323	21°
Two-wheeled motor vehicles	942	63°
Cars and taxis	2019	134°
Others	226	15°
Total	5424	360°

A completed pie chart drawn from this table looks like this.

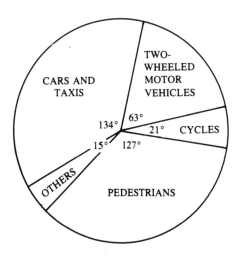

THE DISTRIBUTION OF CASUALTIES BY TYPE OF VEHICLE (OR PEDESTRIANS) IN 1983

We can summarise the rules for drawing a pie chart like this.

> - Organise the data into a table showing the frequency with which each category occurs.
> - Find the total of all the frequencies.
> - Divide 360° by the frequency total to obtain the number of degrees which represent a single unit of the variable.
> - Multiply all the frequencies by this value to obtain the 'slice' angles of your pie chart.

CHECKPOINT 5

1 Study the government expenditure pie chart (p 329).

a Which item did the government plan to spend most on?

b Which item did the government plan to spend least on?

c The pie chart is an artistic representation and may have been distorted from a true mathematical pie chart. Draw up a table showing the angles (correct to the nearest degree) that should have been allocated to each item of government expenditure.

2 Write a short paragraph giving factual information about the changes in the bank's share of mortgage lending during the period 1977 to 1987.

3 Study the following information from Cambridgeshire County Council Reports and Accounts (two figures have been blanked out).

Staffing by Committee
Over 60% of the staff are employed by the Education Committee two thirds of whom are teachers and lecturers at schools and colleges. The Social Services Committee employs social workers, care staff and assistants, and home helps. The Police Committee employs over 1,150 officers plus supporting civilian staff. Transportation employs mainly roadmen. Other committees' employees include firemen, trading standards officers, and professional and administrative support. More details of staff are given below in the section looking at manpower by type of employee.

Education	9,996	63%
Transportation	————	3%
Police	1,584	10%
Social Services	2,532	————
Other	1,557	9%

Manpower by Type of Employee	Number of Staff Employed (FTE)		
	1986–87	1985–86	Difference
Teachers and lecturers	6,604	6,557	+ 47
School support staff	1,359	1,306	+ 53
School meals staff	647	855	− 208
Other education staff	1,387	1,029	+358
Social services staff	2,532	2,287	+245
Police officers	1,147	1,142	+ 5
Firemen	270	266	+ 4
Roadmen	226	233	− 7
Library staff	256	257	− 1
Other service staff	1,807	1,608	+199
Total	**16,235**	**15,540**	**+695**

a Which committee employs 10% of the council's staff?

b What percentage of the county's staff is employed by the social services committee?

c How many staff are employed by the transport committee?

d How many staff are employed by the 'other' committees?

e The slice of the pie chart allocated to the education committee could be divided into separate slices for teachers and lecturers, school support staff, school meals staff and other educational staff. Make a sketch of the pie chart and show on it the way that you think that the education 'slice' should be divided up between these categories of employees. Don't try to be too accurate; a general impression is all that is required.

4 A researcher made a note of 180 cars that passed a road junction one morning. She used this code to write down her results.

F = Ford A = Austin/Rover V = Vauxhall H = French car
I = Italian car   G = German car   J = Japanese car
These are her results.

F A F A V V A F I J G A F F F F I F
F F A H H V J J J H G G F A F F F F
A I H V F V F A J F G G J F J A A V
I A F F F G G J J G G V V V A V V
J V J I H H H A H F F F V F F A H H
F A V H I G J F F A A V V H H I I G
G J J A A F F F V V A J J J V H H H
I I I G G H J H F F F F A A A A A A
J A J A F V F V F V A F F J I J J A
H H H J J A J F I F H I G G A V V I

Organise these results into a table and illustrate them with a pie chart.

5 This table shows the numbers of each type of drink sold from a vending machine in a one-week period. Illustrate this data with a pie chart.

TYPE OF DRINK	NUMBER SOLD
TEA	120
COFFEE	133
SOUP	62
CHOCOLATE	85

6 Draw a pie chart to illustrate the breakdown of the supermarket cost of a bottle of mineral water.

Histograms

Histograms are used to illustrate grouped or continuous data. On first impressions histograms seem very much like bar charts but there are some important differences.

The most obvious difference is the way that the variable axis is constructed.

Bar chart or histogram?

- A bar chart illustrates qualitative or discrete data and therefore the variable axis is just divided into spaces.

- A histogram illustrates grouped or continuous data and therefore the variable axis must be a continuous number line.

We will illustrate the technique of drawing a histogram by drawing one to illustrate this table of data.

Length of earthworm (cm)	0.5–1.5	1.5–2.5	2.5–3.5	3.5–4.5	4.5–5.5	5.5–6.5	6.5–7.5	7.5–8.5	8.5–9.5
Frequency	3	7	12	19	18	18	11	10	2

Remember, a histogram is a suitable choice to illustrate this table because it contains **continuous data**.

The variable axis of our histogram must be a continuous number line, selected to cover the range of possible values for the variable. In this example, the variable axis looks like this.

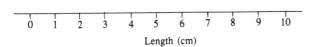

The frequency axis is a number line which will allow us to plot all possible frequencies. In this example, we need to add this frequency axis to our diagram.

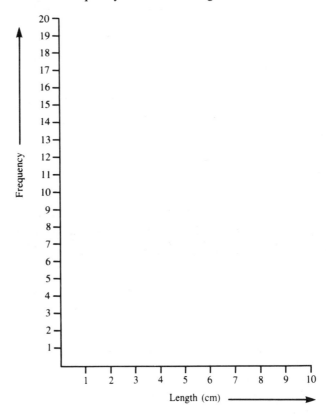

To complete the histogram, we construct a block over each interval on the variable axis. Our completed histogram looks like this.

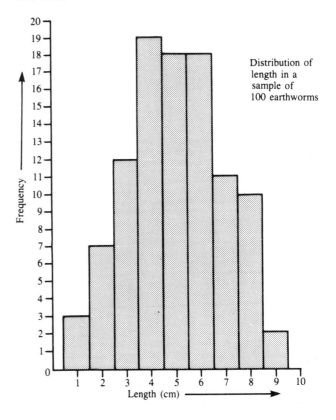

Distribution of length in a sample of 100 earthworms

To emphasise the continuous nature of the variable axis, **gaps must not be left between the blocks of a histogram**. This can cause problems when it is not completely clear where one block ends and the next block starts.

For example, if 100 students take a maths test marked out of 50, the results might be organised into a table like this.

Test mark	1–5	6–10	11–15	16–20	21–25	26–30	31–35	36–40	41–45	46–50
Frequency	1	2	11	17	25	18	13	6	3	4

Remember, a histogram is a suitable choice to illustrate this table because it contains **grouped data**.

When we draw the histogram, there must be no gaps between the bars. We must decide, therefore, where each interval ends and the next one starts.

The most sensible solution in this example is to allow the 1–5 block to extend from 0.5 to 5.5, the 6–10 block to extend from 5.5 to 10.5 and so on.

To justify this, we can argue that in many tests fractions of marks are awarded for some questions and a student's total mark is rounded to the nearest whole number after totalling the marks. In that case, the group 1–5 quite clearly does represent a mark range of 0.5–5.5. So, even if fractions of marks are not awarded, it seems sensible to adopt a similar system to draw the histogram.

This is the completed histogram.

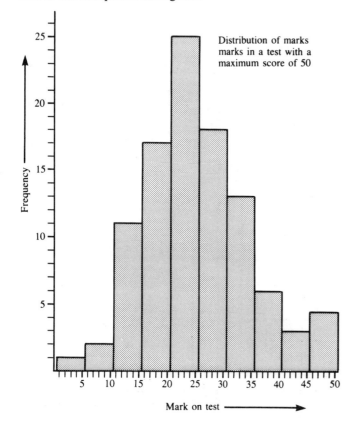

Distribution of marks
marks in a test with a
maximum score of 50

Frequency polygons

A frequency polygon can be used as an alternative to a histogram. The same type of frequency and variable axes are used, but the frequency is plotted as a single point above the **mid-point** of the group or interval.

These points are then connected to form a line graph. The diagram below shows a frequency polygon drawn from the test marks data table.

The histogram and the frequency polygon serve a very similar purpose. The frequency polygon is often preferred when two or more data tables are illustrated on the same pair of axes so that comparisons can be made between them.

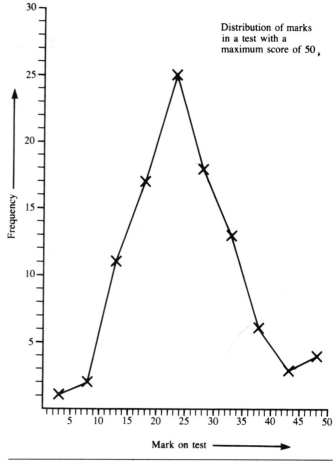

Distribution of marks
in a test with a
maximum score of 50

![CHECKPOINT 6]

1 The weights of two samples of 100 piglets are recorded after the first sample have spent 10 weeks on diet A and the second sample have spent 10 weeks on diet B.

The results are shown in this table.

WEIGHT (kg)	FREQUENCY (Diet A)	FREQUENCY (Diet B)
24.5–26.5	20	17
26.5–28.5	23	20
28.5–30.5	31	30
30.5–32.5	19	23
32.5–34.5	7	8
34.5–36.5	0	2

a Draw histograms to illustrate both frequency distributions.

b Which diet do you consider is the most successful?

2 Two darts players, Maureen and Eric, both throw their three darts 50 times. The 50 total scores for each player are shown in this table.

SCORE	1–30	31–60	61–90	91–120	121–150	151–180
	15.5	*45.5*	*75.5*	*105.5*	*135.5*	*165.5*
FREQUENCY (Maureen)	7	8	10	9	8	8
	108.5	*364*	*755*	*949.5*	*1084*	*1324* *4585*
FREQUENCY (Eric)	0	16	18	14	2.	0
		728	*1359*	*1477*	*271*	*3835*

a Draw histograms to illustrate both frequency distributions.

b Who do you think is the best darts player?

3 Lord Grimby-Dipstick has two woods on his estate, Rooksend and Boggham. He orders a survey to be carried out into the size of the trees in the two woods. The circumferences of 100 selected trees are therefore measured in both woods. The results are shown in this table.

CIRCUMFERENCE (cm)		ROOKSEND	BOGGHAM
0–20	*10*	3	5
20–40	*30*	17	3
40–60	*50*	22	6
60–80	*70*	25	11
80–100	*90*	19	18
100–120	*110*	7	24
120–140	*130*	5	26
140–160	*150*	2	7

a Draw histograms to illustrate both frequency distributions.

b Can we conclude from these results that Boggham Wood contains older trees than Rooksend Wood?

4 Draw, on one graph, two frequency polygons to illustrate the data table shown in question 1.

5 Draw, on one graph, two frequency polygons to illustrate the data table shown in question 2.

6 Draw, on one graph, two frequency polygons to illustrate the data table shown in question 3.

Histograms with unequal class intervals

When data are collected into groups, the spread of values in each group is called the **class interval**. For example, when ages are grouped 1–10 years, 11–20 years and so on, a class interval of 10 years is being used.

Data are sometimes presented in tables using class intervals which are not all equal. For example, the results of a survey of incomes might be presented like this.

WEEKLY INCOME (£)	FREQUENCY
76–100	6
101–125	8
126–150	17
151–200	8
201–300	6

As you can see, the first three class intervals are £25, the third is £50 and the last is £100.

This leads us to consider a second important difference between bar charts and histograms.

Bar chart or histogram?

- In a bar chart, it is the HEIGHT of each bar which represents the frequency.

- In a histogram it is the AREA of each bar which represents the frequency.

This means that if two class intervals have the same frequency, the **areas** of the blocks above them must be equal, even if one class interval is wider than the other.

In our example, the area of the block constructed over the 101–125 interval **must** have the same area as the block constructed over the 151–200 interval. Because the second block will be twice as wide, **it is only drawn to a height of 4 units, even though it represents a frequency of 8.**

In the same way, the area of the block constructed over the 76–100 interval **must** have the same area as the block constructed over the 201–300 interval. Because the second block will be 4 times as wide, **it is only drawn to a height of 1.5 units, even though it represents a frequency of 6.**

This is the completed histogram.

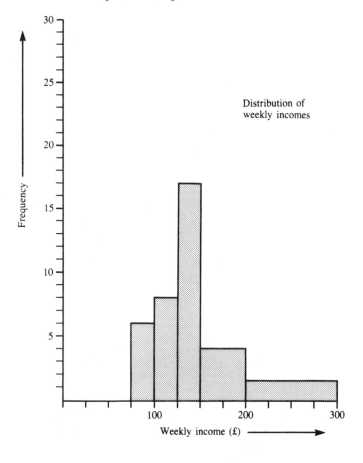

Distribution of weekly incomes

These rules for drawing histograms with unequal class intervals must seem very strange and complicated, so why bother?

The reason is that the histogram is used to illustrate data and, without this rule, would give a false visual impression.

The diagram below shows an **incorrect** histogram drawn from the table with no correction for unequal class intervals. Most people would agree that it creates the false visual impression that the 151–200 and 201–300 intervals have a greater frequency than the 101–125 and 76–100 intervals.

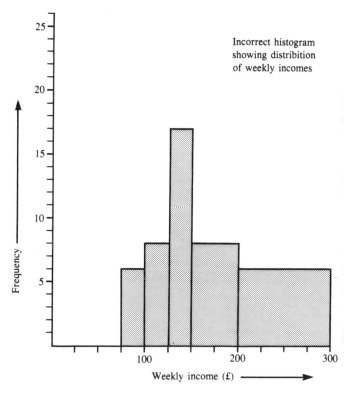

Incorrect histogram showing distribution of weekly incomes

There are three steps in drawing this kind of histogram.

Histograms with unequal class intervals

- Identify the class interval you intend to use as the standard interval for the graph. Usually this is the smallest class interval.

- Establish how many times wider than this standard class interval any non-standard intervals are.

- Divide the frequencies of any non-standard intervals by the results you obtain in the second step, in order to establish the height of their blocks. So, if a class interval is twice as wide divide its frequency by 2, if it is three times as wide divide its frequency by 3 and so on.

Sometimes a distribution will end with an **open-ended** group. For example, a distribution may end with the interval '60 years and over'. This presents a problem when drawing the histogram because we don't know how wide this interval is. To solve the problem, we simply make a sensible decision and give the interval a width which is likely to include almost all of the possible values. For example, if the distribution was for people holding a driving licence, we might decide that an interval of '60 years and over' could be sensibly regarded as a 20-year class interval and treated as the interval '60 years–79 years'.

To illustrate these techniques, we will construct a histogram to illustrate these official data on 1980 road traffic accidents.

KILLED OR SERIOUSLY INJURED	
Age group	Frequency
0–4	1 351
5–9	4 203
10–14	5 255
15–19	21 501
20–24	13 243
25–29	6 741
30–39	9 045
40–49	6 236
50–59	6 027
60 and over	10 806

In the table, the first 6 categories each have a class interval of 5 years. The next 3 categories have a class interval of 10 years and the last category is open.

Our first problem is the open-ended category. It seems sensible to me to call this a 60–79 interval, but you must realise that a different person might make a different decision, perhaps deciding on a 60–89 interval or even a 60–99 interval. Having made this decision, we apply the 3 construction steps and arrive at a table like this.

KILLED OR SERIOUSLY INJURED				
Age group	Frequency	Interval width	Width factor	Block height
0–4	1 351	5	1	1 351
5–9	4 203	5	1	4 203
10–14	5 255	5	1	5 255
15–19	21 501	5	1	21 501
20–24	13 243	5	1	13 243
25–29	6 741	5	1	6 741
30–39	9 045	10	2	4 523
40–49	6 236	10	2	3 118
50–59	6 027	10	2	3 014
60–79	10 806	20	4	2 702

The diagram below shows the final construction of the histogram. You will notice that the blocks are constructed over the intervals 0–5, 5–10, 10–15 and so on. This is a decision made to avoid gaps between the blocks. The justification for this decision is that the 0–4 group contains everybody until just before their 5th birthday, the 5–9 group contains everybody from just after their 5th birthday until just before their 10th birthday and so on.

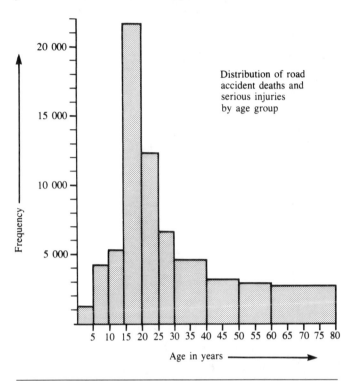

Distribution of road accident deaths and serious injuries by age group

CHECKPOINT 7

1 One hundred people complete a sponsored slim for charity. The distribution of their weights before and after their diets are shown below. Draw histograms to illustrate the weight distributions before and after the sponsored slim.

WEIGHT (kg)	FREQUENCY (BEFORE)	FREQUENCY (AFTER)
31–50	0	2
51–55	2	4
56–60	3	6
61–65	5	9
66–70	8	12
71–75	13	19
76–80	18	23
81–90	24	14
91–100	21	11
101–120	6	0

2 The histogram below illustrates the results of a survey of the 230 vehicles aboard a cross-channel ferry. Copy and complete the frequency distribution shown below the histogram.

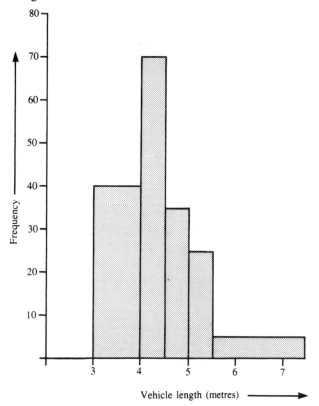

VEHICLE LENGTH (METRES)	FREQUENCY
3.0–4.0	
4.0–4.5	70
4.5–5.0	
5.0–5.5	
5.5–7.5	

3 This table shows the distribution of male and female unemployment by age group in 1981. Draw two histograms to illustrate these data.

	UNEMPLOYED (thousands)	
AGE LAST BIRTHDAY	MALES	FEMALES
Under 20	227	172
20–24	294	157
25–34	399	155
35–44	278	96
45–54	253	95
55–59	149	47
60–64	156	6
65 and over	7	5

Visual Misrepresentation of Data

It is claimed that the nineteenth-century English Prime Minister Disraeli once said,

'There are lies, damned lies and statistics'

Unfortunately Disraeli had a point. It is possible to use statistics to both confuse and delude people.

Sometimes the mistakes in statistical presentations may be just that, genuine mistakes. However, 'mistakes' happen so frequently and in work by such expert statisticians that we can only conclude that the intention is often to deliberately deceive.

We will conclude this section on the presentation of data by looking at some of the techniques that are used to present results in a misleading way.

Graphs drawn without a scale

A graph without a scale is almost meaningless but such graphs are often found in advertising and publicity material. For example, the graph below shows the 'goodness' of Zappo Flakes.

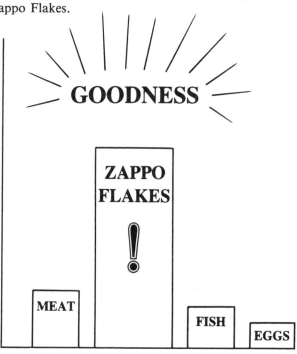

The graph is obviously intended by the manufacturers to convey the message that Zappo Flakes are better for you than meat, fish or eggs. Looking critically at the graph we might ask these questions.

- What is 'goodness'? The graph gives no hint of any units of measurement like calories, vitamin or fibre content.
- Whatever 'goodness' is, were equal quantities of the foods compared? For example, were 2 tons of Zappo Flakes compared with one egg or a single sardine?

- Why is the Zappo Flakes bar twice as wide as the other bars?
- Why is there an exclamation mark on the Zappo Flakes bar?

There are of course no satisfactory answers to any of these questions. The 'graph' is a statistical deception, drawn not to illustrate data but to persuade you to buy the product.

Sometimes numbers may be added to a graph but with no indication as to what they mean. A graph like this is just as worthless as our first example. We can add numbers to the Zappo graph, but it will still be a worthless illustration of data.

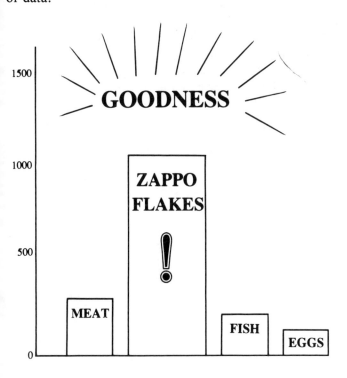

The exaggerated graph

Our previous example was a crude and easily spotted misrepresentation. Graphs like this are usually only found in advertising and publicity material and perhaps few people will take them seriously.

The exaggerated graph, on the other hand, crops up all the time, is just as misleading, harder to spot and is even found in 'serious' material produced by large companies and government departments.

We will illustrate the construction of an exaggerated graph by starting with this honest and fair bar chart drawn to illustrate the sales of Zappo Flakes over a three-year period.

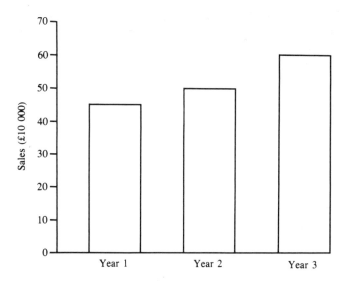

The graph shows that sales have increased from £450 000 in the first year to £600 000 in the third year, a record of steady but not spectacular growth. Now, suppose we wish to exaggerate these figures, perhaps for a presentation to the company shareholders.

The first step is to cut the vertical axis and start it at 35 rather than zero. Our graph now looks like this.

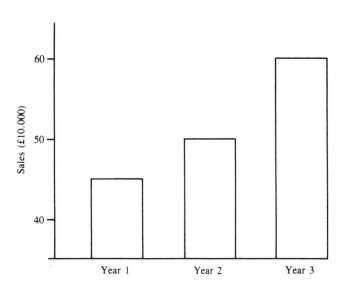

Visually the graph now gives an exaggerated impression of the sales growth. The third bar is over twice as high as the first bar and, at a glance, we may think the sales have more than doubled.

To exaggerate still further, we can now stretch the vertical axis. With another adjustment of the baseline, the graph can be made to look like this.

TASTELESS WONDER
ENGLISH COFFEE

IMPORTED DUTCH
MUD COFFEE

EACH JAR REPRESENTS 1000 JARS SOLD EACH WEEK

As you can see, the best selling brand is 'Tasteless English' which easily outsells the imported Dutch brand.

Now, suppose you were the director of 'Tasteless English Foods PLC' and wanted to present these results in an even better light. Your coffee sells 4 times as many jars as the imported brand, so why not draw a different pictogram, showing just two jars of coffee, one drawn four times as large as the other. This is the graph.

SALES OF COFFEE IN SAINSCO SUPERMARKETS

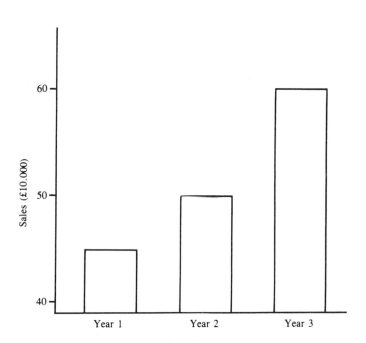

Now that really is dramatic and spectacular sales growth, a company well worth investing in!

So, a respectable sales growth can easily be presented as a really spectacular sales growth by simple adjustment to the frequency axis of the graph. If the axis is correctly labelled, the graph is still 'honest' because it does contain accurate information. There is, however, little justification for using a representation like this unless the intention is deliberately to deceive and exaggerate results.

Remember, if you want to draw a deceptive graph,

- Don't start your frequency axis at zero, select the starting value that shows your results in the best light.

- Exaggerate your results still further by 'stretching' the frequency axis.

Using solid images to deceive the eye

Our third form of visual trickery is developed from the simple pictogram.

To illustrate its use, we will start with this honest representation of the sales of two brands of coffee in a supermarket.

We can argue that since the second jar is drawn four times as wide as the first jar this is a fair representation. There is something wrong, though, because if you look at the diagram, it gives the visual impression that sales of 'Tasteless English' are vastly greater than sales of 'Dutch Mud'.

The trick is in the phrase 'four times as large'. The second jar is certainly four times as wide, but it is also four times as high and four times as thick. This means that it will have **sixty-four** times the volume of the smaller jar. When you look at the illustration, it is this difference in volume that your eye automatically measures. The result is a tremendous exaggeration of the real difference between the sales figures for the two brands.

Remember, if you want to draw a deceptive pictogram,

- use single symbols drawn so that their lengths or heights represent their frequencies;

- turn the symbols into three-dimensional objects. The effect will be to greatly exaggerate any differences represented in the heights or lengths.

CHECKPOINT 8

1 Invent a product. It might be a new brand of washing powder, a new car, a better mouse trap or whatever. Draw a meaningless graph without scales which 'demonstrates' that your new wonder product is far better than its rivals.

2 Look carefully at the graph behind this politician. Comment on the way that the graph represents the jobless figures.

(The Guardian, 13th November, 1987)

3 You are the director of Zapper Cars. In the last 4 years your Supersport model has sold 5400, 5500, 5600 and 5900 cars respectively. Present this information graphically, trying to create the best possible impression for your shareholders.

4 In 1983, the average yearly incomes per head in Switzerland, the UK, Trinidad and Chile were $16 000, $8 000, $4 000 and $2 000 respectively. These data are illustrated in the pictogram below. Re-draw the pictogram using single symbols drawn to a length scale and comment on the results.

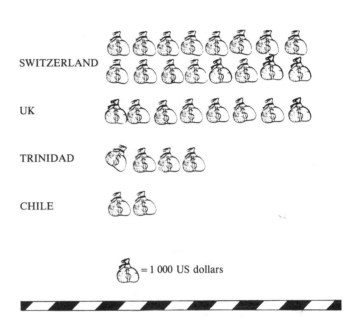

Making comparisons between frequency distributions

Now that we have learnt how to organise, present and illustrate frequency distributions we will turn our attention to the ways that frequency distributions can be compared.

The most obvious way to compare distributions is simply to place them side by side and to look for differences. This is, however, very time-consuming and various techniques have been developed to condense and summarise the data in a frequency distribution so that comparisons can be more easily made.

Selecting a representative value—averages

When making comparisons between distributions, it is obviously very useful if a single typical value can be selected to represent the distribution. Such values are called **measures of location**, or more simply **averages**. An average gives an impression of the type of values to be found in a distribution. For example, if we are told that the **average** test mark of one class is 60% and the **average** test mark for another class (on the same test) is 95%, we are given an impression that a typical student in the second class is likely to have more ability than a typical student in the first class. If a third class

341

has an average mark of 80%, we might expect a typical student in that class to be **located** somewhere in ability between typical students from the other two classes.

TEST SCORE AVERAGES (%)

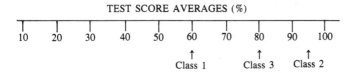

There are three types of average in common use. These are the **mean**, the **median** and the **mode**.

The mean

The mean, more correctly called the **arithmetic mean**, is calculated by adding up all the values in a distribution and then dividing this total by the number of values in the distribution.

Example

Find the arithmetic mean of these values.

1   1   2   2   3   4   4   5   6   6   6   8

First, we find the total of all the values. In this example the total is 48. Second, we divide the total by the number of values. In this example there are 12 values. So, the mean average is

$$\frac{48}{12} = 4$$

CHECKPOINT 9

1 Find the arithmetic mean of each of the following distributions.

a 12   6   7   9   6
b 1   1   1   1   2   2   3   3   3   3   3   4   4   5   6   6
c £1.50   £1.50   £2.00   £3.00
d −2   −1   −2   0   0   0   3   4   1   2   6
e 2.7   3.4   8.9   5.6   6.6   7.3   5.2   2.9   8.0   7.1

2 The test marks of a group of 10 5th-year students are 56, 72, 35, 47, 89, 98, 13, 45, 34 and 73. The test marks of a group of 10 4th-year students who take the same test are 58, 70, 40, 41, 42, 11, 94, 62, 43 and 60. Calculate the mean average of each set of marks.

3 Two players, Maureen and Eric, both throw 9 darts. Maureen's scores are 20, 40, 1, 5, 60, 20, 20, 1 and 60. Eric's scores are 20, 40, 40, 0, 60, 20, 0, 5 and 1. Find the mean average of each set of marks.

4 A group of 5 trees in a garden have a mean average height of 4.5 metres. If a sixth tree with a height of 2.1 metres is planted, what is the new mean average height of the trees?

5 One group of 5 students have a mean average score of 45 on a test. A second group of 11 students have a mean average score of 53 on the same test. Find the mean average score for the whole group of 16 students.

The mean of a frequency table

We may be asked to find the mean average of values presented in a table.

Example

Calculate the mean average number of children per family for this frequency distribution.

NUMBER OF CHILDREN PER FAMILY	0	1	2	3	4	5	6
FREQUENCY	13	13	38	17	10	4	5

Remember, to calculate the mean average, we need to know

- The total number of families

- The total number of children in these families

We can find the number of families by simply adding together all the frequencies.

NUMBER OF CHILDREN PER FAMILY	0	1	2	3	4	5	6	TOTAL
FREQUENCY	13	13	38	17	10	4	5	100

To calculate the total of children, we first multiply each category shown in the table by its frequency. For example, the category '2 children' has a frequency of 38 so we multiply 2 by 38. We can add an extra line to the table to show the results.

NUMBER OF CHILDREN PER FAMILY	0	1	2	3	4	5	6	TOTAL
FREQUENCY	13	13	38	17	10	4	5	100
	0	13	76	51	40	20	30	

By adding all these results together, we can find the total number of children shown in the table.

NUMBER OF CHILDREN PER FAMILY	0	1	2	3	4	5	6	TOTAL
FREQUENCY	13	13	38	17	10	4	5	100
	0	13	76	51	40	20	30	230

We now know that 100 families have a total of 230 children. The mean average number of children per family is therefore

$$\frac{230}{100} = 2.3 \text{ children}$$

CHECKPOINT 10

1 This table shows the results of a survey into the number of children per family on two housing estates. Calculate the mean average number of children per family for each estate.

NUMBER OF CHILDREN PER FAMILY	0	1	2	3	4	5	6
FREQUENCY (Estate A)	10	9	18	8	5	0	0
FREQUENCY (Estate B)	3	4	20	9	5	4	5

2 The cost of a gallon of 4-star petrol was checked at a sample of 50 garages in two different cities. The results are shown in the table below. Calculate the mean average price per gallon in each city.

COST PER GALLON (pence)	CITY A	CITY B
167	2	4
168	5	7
169	12	4
170	21	11
171	7	13
172	3	5
173	0	6

3 This table shows the number of tests taken by some of the students of two different driving schools before they passed. Calculate the mean average number of tests taken for each school.

NUMBER OF TESTS TAKEN	1	2	3	4	5	6
FREQUENCY (School A)	30	15	7	2	4	2
FREQUENCY (School B)	45	23	17	10	5	0

4 In the GCSE Mathematics examination, grades A, B, C, D, E, F, G and U are awarded. This table shows the results for the students entered in the same year from two different schools. Calculate the average grade for each school.

GRADE	A	B	C	D	E	F	G	U
Swotville Comprehensive	3	14	15	23	13	20	9	3
Dipsticks Academy	2	32	18	20	20	0	0	8

The mean of a grouped frequency table

We may be asked to find the mean average of values presented in a grouped table.

Example

Calculate the mean average for the students' test marks shown in this table.

Test mark	1–5	6–10	11–15	16–20	21–25	26–30	31–35	36–40	41–45	46–50
Frequency	1	2	11	17	25	18	13	6	3	4

Remember, to calculate the mean average, we need to know

- The total number of students taking the test

- The total number of marks they scored

To find the total number of students taking the test, we add together all the frequencies.

Test mark	1–5	6–10	11–15	16–20	21–25	26–30	31–35	36–40	41–45	46–50	Total
Frequency	1	2	11	17	25	18	13	6	3	4	100

We now have a problem, because it is impossible to calculate the total number of marks scored by the students. We know, for example, that 18 students scored a mark between 26 and 30, but we have no idea of the exact marks that each of the 18 students scored.

We solve this problem by using an approximation. We assume that 18 students scoring a mark between 26 and 30 is **approximately** equivalent to 18 students scoring a mark of 28 (the middle mark of the class interval).

This is repeated for each interval, using the middle point to represent the class and to be multiplied by the frequency.

The completed table looks like this.

Test mark	1–5	6–10	11–15	16–20	21–25	26–30	31–35	36–40	41–45	46–50	Totals
Mid-value	3	8	13	18	23	28	33	38	43	48	
Frequency	1	2	11	17	25	18	13	6	3	4	100
Mid-point × frequency	3	16	143	306	575	504	429	228	129	192	2525

TOTAL = 100 STUDENTS   TOTAL = 2525 MARKS

We now know that 100 students have scored a total of 2525 marks. The mean average number of marks per student is therefore

$$\frac{2525}{100} = 25.25$$

You must remember, however, that this answer is an **approximation** based on the assumption that the marks are evenly distributed within each class and that therefore each class can be represented by its mid-point.

All mean averages from grouped tables are calculated using this technique. The mid-point of the interval may not be a whole number. The safest way to establish the mid-points is to list at least one interval in full and to then select the mid-point from this list. For example, to establish the mid-point of the interval 0–10 we list

0 1 2 3 4 5 6 7 8 9 10

MID-POINT

To establish the mid-point of the interval 21–24 we list

22.5

21 22 23 24

MID-POINT

These are some more examples of class intervals and their mid-points.

CLASS INTERVAL	MID-POINT
120–130	125
0–9	4.5
1–9	5
1–4	2.5
1–5	3
16–25	20.5
15–25	20

Example

This table shows the results when a player throws 50 sets of 3 darts. Calculate the mean average score for these data.

Score	1–30	31–60	61–90	91–120	121–150	151–180
Frequency	8	7	9	10	9	7

These are the completed calculations.

Score	1–30	31–60	61–90	91–120	121–150	151–180	Totals
Mid-point	15.5	45.5	75.5	105.5	135.5	165.5	
Frequency	8	7	9	10	9	7	50
Mid-point × frequency	124	318.5	679.5	1055	1219.5	1158.5	455.5

$$\text{MEAN AVERAGE PER SET} = \frac{4555}{50} = 91.1$$

$$\text{MEAN AVERAGE SCORE PER DART} = \frac{91.1}{3} = 30.4$$

CHECKPOINT 11

1 Lord Grimby-Dipstick has two woods on his estate, Rooksend and Boggham. He orders a survey to be carried out into the size of the trees in the two woods. The circumferences of 100 selected trees are therefore measured in both woods. The results are shown in this table. Calculate the mean average circumference of the trees in each wood.

Take the mid point of each group.

CIRCUMFERENCE (cm)	ROOKSEND	BOGGHAM
0–20	3	5
20–40	17	3
40–60	22	6
60–80	25	11
80–100	19	18
100–120	7	24
120–140	5	26
140–160	2	7

2 Two darts players, Maureen and Eric, both throw their three darts 50 times. The 50 total scores for each player are shown in this table. Calculate the mean average score (per three-dart throw) for each player.

Score	1–30	31–60	61–90	91–120	121–150	151–180
Frequency (Maureen)	15·5 7	45·5 8	75·5 10	105·5 9	135·5 8	165·5 8
Frequency (Eric)	0	16	18	14	2	0

3 The weights of two samples of 100 piglets are recorded after the first sample have spent 10 weeks on diet A and the second sample have spent 10 weeks on diet B. The results are shown in this table. Calculate the mean average weight for each sample of piglets.

WEIGHT (kg)	FREQUENCY (Diet A)	FREQUENCY (Diet B)
24.5–26.5	20	17
26.5–28.5	23	20
28.5–30.5	31	30
30.5–32.5	19	23
32.5–34.5	7	8
34.5–36.5	0	2

4 One hundred people complete a sponsored slim for charity. The distribution of their weights before and after their diets are shown below. Calculate the mean average weight of the group both before and after the sponsored slim.

WEIGHT (kg)	FREQUENCY (before)	FREQUENCY (after)
31–50	0	2
51–55	2	4
56–60	3	6
61–65	5	9
66–70	8	12
71–75	13	19
76–80	18	23
81–90	24	14
91–100	21	11
101–120	6	0

The median and the quartiles

The mean is a very commonly used average and is sometimes thought of as the **only** type of average. Sometimes it is even confusingly referred to as 'the average', as if no other type of average existed. There are in fact several alternative types of average, one of which is the **median**.

The median of a set of values is simply the **middle value when the values are placed in order**.

Example

Find the median average of

1   4   7   5   6   3   3   2   1   5   1

First, we arrange the values into order.

1   1   1   2   3   3   4   5   5   6   7

Then we pick out the **middle** value.

1   1   1   2   3   ③   4   5   5   6   7

The median = 3

If there is an even number of values, there will be no value in the exact middle position. In this case, we select a value which is halfway between the two values on either side of the exact middle position.

Example

Find the median average of

£4.00   £5.00   £4.50   £6.00   £5.50   £6.00

First, we arrange the values into order.

£4.00   £4.50   £5.00   £5.50   £6.00   £6.00

The **middle** position is between £5.00 and £5.50.

£4.00   £4.50   £5.00 ↑ £5.50   £6.00   £6.00

The median = £5.25

CHECKPOINT 12

1 Find the median of each of the following distributions.

a 12   6   7   9   6

b 1   2   1   3   4   5   5   3   4   1   3   5   2   2   5

c £5.00   £1.50   £4.00   £5.50   £4.50   £6.00   £2.00

d £5.00   £1.50   £4.00   £5.50   £4.50   £6.00   £2.00
    £1.50

e −2   3   0   −1   0   2   0   0   −3   1   1   1   1   2
    −1   −2   3   3   0   −1   −1

f 2.7   3.4   8.9   5.6   6.6   7.3   5.2   2.9   8.0   7.1

2 The test marks of a group of 10 5th-year students are 56, 72, 35, 47, 89, 98, 13, 45, 34 and 73. The test marks of a group of 10 4th-year students who take the same test are 58, 70, 40, 41, 42, 11, 94, 62, 43 and 60. Find the median of each set of marks.

3 Two players, Maureen and Eric, both throw 9 darts. Maureen's scores are 20, 40, 1, 5, 60, 20, 20, 1 and 60. Eric's scores are 20, 40, 40, 0, 60, 20, 0, 5 and 1. Find the median of each set of scores.

4 The set of 5 values

1   2   5   7   20

has a median of 5 and a mean of 7.

Find a set of values which meets each of the following conditions.

a Number of values = 5, median = 9, mean = 10
b Number of values = 7, median = 5, mean = 4
c Number of values = 10, median = 7.5, mean = 8
d Number of values = 10, median = 10, mean = 10

The **quartiles** of a distribution are very closely related to the median. A distribution has two quartiles, a lower **quartile** and an **upper quartile**.

We already know that the median is the halfway point in a distribution of values.

The **lower quartile** is the **quarter way** point in a distribution of values. The **upper quartile** is the **three-quarter way** point in a distribution of values.

Example

Find the median and the quartiles of

1   4   7   5   6   3   3   2   1   5   1

First, we arrange the values into order.

1   1   1   2   3   3   4   5   5   6   7
       LQ   M   UQ

Then we pick out the **middle, quarter way and three-quarter way** values.

1   1   ①   2   3   ③   4   5   ⑤   6   7

The lower quartile = 1

The median = 3

The upper quartile = 5

When distributions contain a large number of values, or if you find it difficult to establish the position of the median and the quartiles, these formulas can be used to establish the positions.

Median and quartile positions

If there are n numbers in a distribution of values,

● The median position is given by $\dfrac{n+1}{2}$.

● The lower quartile position·is given by $\dfrac{n+1}{4}$.

● The upper quartile position is given by $\dfrac{3(n+1)}{4}$.

Example

Find the median and the quartiles of this distribution.

32   33   37   45   56   65   67   34   31   45   47   50   48

First, we arrange the values into order.

31 32 33 34 37 45 45 47 48 50 56 65 67

There are 13 values in this distribution, so, using the formulas gives

$$\text{Median position} = \frac{13+1}{2} = 7\text{th}$$

$$\text{Lower quartile position} = \frac{13+1}{4} = 3.5$$

So, the lower quartile is between the 3rd and 4th values.

$$\text{Upper quartile position} = \frac{3(13+1)}{4} = 10.5$$

So, the upper quartile is between the 10th and 11th values.

31 32 33 34 37 45 (45) 47 48 50 56 65 67

The lower quartile = 33.5

The median = 45

The upper quartile = 53

CHECKPOINT 13

1 Find the median and the quartiles of each of the following distributions.

a 1 1 2 3 1 2 3 5 4 6 7 4 3 2 1 1 0
0 1 0 2 0 3
b 1 2 1 3 4 5 5 3 4 1 3 5 2 2 5
c £5.00 £1.50 £4.00 £5.50 £4.50 £6.00 £2.00
d 34 56 75 68 92 90 83 38 71 17 65
e 201 297 256 289 201 234 254 271 199 231
297 249 300 222 218
f −2 3 0 −1 0 2 0 0 0 −3 1 1 1 1 2
−1 −2 3 3 0 −1 −1

The median and the quartiles of a frequency distribution

We may be asked to find the median and the quartiles of values presented in a table.

Example

Calculate the median and the quartiles for this frequency distribution.

NUMBER OF CHILDREN PER FAMILY	0	1	2	3	4	5	6
FREQUENCY	13	13	38	17	10	4	5

Remember, to find the median and the quartiles, we need to know

- The value which represents the mid-point of the distribution

- The values which represent the quarter-points of the distribution

To discover these values we add an extra line to the table, called the **cumulative frequency**. This line records the number of values of the variable that are included up to that point in the table. So, for example, in this table

NUMBER OF CHILDREN PER FAMILY	0	1	2	3	4	5	6
FREQUENCY	13	13	38	17	10	4	5
CUMULATIVE FREQUENCY	13	26	64	81	91	95	100

the **cumulative frequencies** record that there are 13 families with 0 children per family, 26 families with 0 or 1 children per family, 64 families with 0, 1 or 2 children per family, 81 families with 0, 1, 2 or 3 children per family and so on.

With 100 values, the positions of the median and the quartiles are

Median position is $\frac{100+1}{2}$ (between the 50th and 51st)

Lower quartile position is $\frac{100+1}{4}$ (between the 25th and 26th)

Upper quartile position $\frac{3(100+1)}{4}$ (between the 75th and 76th)

We use the cumulative frequencies to pick out the values that occupy these positions. For example, the cumulative frequencies tell us that there were 26 families with 0 or 1 child and 64 families with 0, 1 or 2 children. This means that the 50th and 51st families in the distribution must both have had 2 children.

In the same way, the cumulative frequencies tell us that there were 13 families with 0 children and 26 families with 0 or 1 child. This means that the 25th and 26th families in the distribution must both have had 1 child.

In the same way, the cumulative frequencies tell us that there were 64 families with 0, 1 or 2 children and 81 families with 0, 1, 2 or 3 children. This means that the 75th and 76th families in the distribution must both have had 3 children.

So, for this frequency distribution

Lower quartile = 1

Median = 2

Upper quartile = 3

NUMBER OF CHILDREN PER FAMILY	0	1	2	3	4	5	6
FREQUENCY	13	13	38	17	10	4	5
CUMULATIVE FREQUENCY	13	26	64	81	91	95	100

LOWER QUARTILE = 1   UPPER QUARTILE = 3

MEDIAN = 2

This diagram shows the necessary steps to find the median and the quartiles from a different table.

Cost per gallon (pence)	Frequency in City A	Cumulative Frequency	
167	2	2	
168	5	7	
169	12	19	Lower quartile = 169 (between the 12th and 13th values)
170	7	26	Median = 170 (between the 25th and 26th values)
171	10	36	
172	10	46	Upper quartile = 172 (between the 38th and 39th values)
173	4	50	

We can summarise the steps in finding the median and the quartiles from a table of data like this.

To find median and quartile values

- **Add the cumulative frequencies to the table.**
- **Establish the positions of the median and quartiles in a distribution with this number of values.**
- **Use the cumulative frequencies to pick out from the table the values in the median and quartile positions.**

CHECKPOINT 14

1 This table shows the results of a survey into the number of children per family on two housing estates. Find the median and the quartiles for both frequency distributions.

NUMBER OF CHILDREN PER FAMILY	0	1	2	3	4	5	6
FREQUENCY (Estate A)	10	9	18	8	5	0	0
FREQUENCY (Estate B)	3	4	20	9	5	4	5

2 The cost of a gallon of 4-star petrol was checked at a sample of 50 garages in two different cities. The results are shown in the table below. Find the median and the quartiles for both frequency distributions.

COST PER GALLON (pence)	CITY A	CITY B
167	2	4
168	5	7
169	12	4
170	21	11
171	7	13
172	3	5
173	0	6

3 This table shows the number of tests taken by some of the students of two different driving schools before they passed. Find the median and the quartiles for both frequency distributions.

NUMBER OF TESTS TAKEN	1	2	3	4	5	6
FREQUENCY (School A)	30	15	7	2	4	2
FREQUENCY (School B)	45	23	17	10	5	0

4 In the GCSE Mathematics examination, grades A, B, C, D, E, F, G and U are awarded. This table shows the results for the students entered in the same year from two different schools. Find the median and the quartiles for both frequency distributions.

GRADE	A	B	C	D	E	F	G	U
SWOTVILLE COMPREHENSIVE	3	14	15	23	13	20	9	3
DIPSTICKS ACADEMY	2	32	18	20	20	0	0	8

The median and the quartiles of a grouped frequency distribution

We may be asked to find the median and the quartiles of values presented in a grouped table.

Example

Find the median and the quartiles for the students' test marks shown in this table.

Test mark	1–5	6–10	11–15	16–20	21–25	26–30	31–35	36–40	41–45	46–50
Frequency	1	2	11	17	25	18	13	6	3	4

We can only **estimate** the median and the quartiles when data are presented in a grouped table.

We make our estimates by drawing a graph called a **cumulative frequency curve (sometimes called an ogive)**.

We start by adding the cumulative frequencies to our table.

Test mark	1–5	6–10	11–15	16–20	21–25	26–30	31–35	36–40	41–45	46–50
Frequency	1	2	11	17	25	18	13	6	3	4
Cumulative frequency	1	3	14	31	56	74	87	93	96	100

We now draw a graph, plotting each cumulative frequency against its class interval. We always plot the cumulative frequencies over the **end** of the class interval. A cumulative frequency graph drawn from this table looks like this.

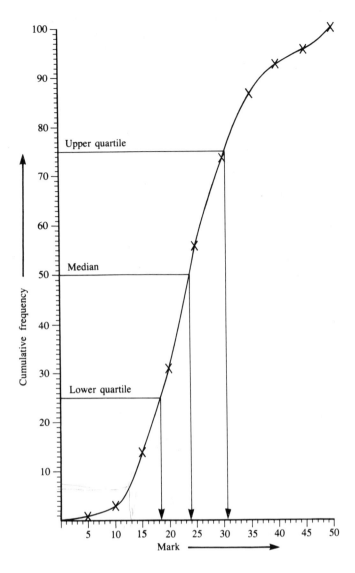

The arrows on the graph show how the median and the quartiles have been estimated. Taking 25, 50 and 75 as the approximate positions for the lower quartile, median and upper quartile in a distribution of 100 values, the marks which correspond with these cumulative frequencies have been read from the graph. Our results are

Lower quartile = 18.5 marks

Median = 23.5 marks

Upper quartile = 30.25 marks

In many examination questions you will also be asked to use the cumulative frequency graph to answer other questions about the distribution.

For example, if asked,

'How many pupils scored 13 or less marks?'

we can add an arrow from the mark of 13 up on to the cumulative frequency axis and estimate that

'8 students scored 13 or less marks'.

Or, if asked,

'What pass mark will allow 65 students to pass the test?'

If 65 students are to pass, 35 must fail, so we can add an arrow from the 35th student down onto the mark axis and estimate that

'A pass mark of 21 will allow 65 students to pass the test'.

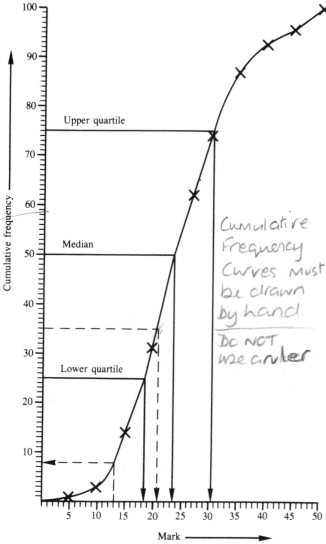

Cumulative Frequency Curves must be drawn by hand.

DO NOT use a ruler

Drawing a cumulative frequency curve is quite straightforward. The only point that can cause problems is that you must remember to plot each cumulative frequency above the **end** of each class interval. This is because the cumulative frequency is the 'frequency up to this point in the distribution'. Only at the exact end of each interval can we be certain that all the values in that class are included in the cumulative total.

Use frequencies to plot frequency polygon

350

Use cumulative frequency to plot a cumulative frequency curve.

CHECKPOINT 15

1 Lord Grimby-Dipstick has two woods on his estate, Rooksend and Bog, ham. He orders a survey to be carried out into the size of the trees in the two woods. The circumferences of 100 selected trees is therefore measured in both woods. The results are shown in this table.

CIRCUMFERENCE (cm)	ROOKSEND	BOGGHAM
0–20	3	5
20–40	17	3
40–60	22	6
60–80	25	11
80–100	19	18
100–120	7	24
120–140	5	26
140–160	2	7

0 – 6.36

a Draw, on the same graph, cumulative frequency curves for the data from each wood and estimate the median and the quartiles for both distributions.

b How many trees in the Boggham sample were between 70 cm and 130 cm in diameter?

2 Two darts players, Maureen and Eric, both throw their three darts 50 times. The 50 total scores for each player are shown in this table.

Score	1–30	31–60	61–90	91–120	121–150	151–180
	15·5	45·5	75·5	105·5	135·5	165·5
Frequency (Maureen)	7	8	10	9	8	8
Cumulative Freq.	7	15	25	34	42	50
Frequency (Eric)	0	16	18	14	2	0
Cumulative Freq	0	16	34	48	50	50·

use top end of each group for plotting on graph (upper class boundary).

a Draw, on the same graph, cumulative frequency curves for the data of each player and estimate the median and the quartiles for both distributions.

b How many times did Maureen score 100 or more with her three darts?

c How many times did Eric score 100 or more with his three darts?

3 One hundred people complete a sponsored slim for charity. The distribution of their weights before and after their diets are shown below.

WEIGHT (kg)	FREQUENCY (before)	FREQUENCY (after)
31–50	0	2
51–55	2	4
56–60	3	6
61–65	5	9
66–70	8	12
71–75	13	19
76–80	18	23
81–90	24	14
91–100	21	11
101–120	6	0

a Draw, on the same graph, cumulative frequency curves for the 'before' and 'after' data and estimate the median and the quartiles for both distributions.

b How many of the slimmers weighed over 85 kg before they started their diet?

c How many of the slimmers weighed over 85 kg after they completed their diet?

4 The Headteacher of Minastroney High School decided to make a survey of the time spent talking to each set of parents at a parents' evening. The interview times of two teachers, Ms Salt and Ms Pepper, were recorded as they each spoke with 30 sets of parents. This table shows the data that were collected.

INTERVIEW TIME (minutes)	FREQUENCY Ms SALT	Ms PEPPER
0–1	0	0
1–2	2	0
2–3	3	0
3–4	6	1
4–5	9	7
5–6	5	10
6–7	3	8
7–8	2	4

a Draw, on the same graph, cumulative frequency curves for the data on each teacher and estimate the median and the quartiles for both distributions.

b How many interviews of less than 5.5 minutes did Ms Pepper have?

c How many interviews of between 3.5 and 6.5 minutes did Ms Salt have?

The mode (modal average)

The third type of average which we will study is called the **mode** (or **modal average**). The mode of a set of values is simply the value that occurs most frequently.

Example

Find the mode of

$$1 \quad 4 \quad 7 \quad 5 \quad 6 \quad 3 \quad 3 \quad 2 \quad 1 \quad 5 \quad 1$$

First, we sort the values into groups.

$$1 \quad 1 \quad 1 \quad 2 \quad 3 \quad 3 \quad 4 \quad 5 \quad 5 \quad 6 \quad 7$$

Then we pick out the value which occurs most frequently. In this case, 1 occurs most frequently so,

$$\text{The mode} = 1$$

In small distributions, where many (or all) values occur the same number of times there is no sensible modal average.

Example

Find the mode of

$$11 \quad 11 \quad 12 \quad 12 \quad 13 \quad 13 \quad 14 \quad 14 \quad 15 \quad 16 \quad 16$$

There is no value that can be selected as a sensible mode for this distribution.

If data are organised into a frequency distribution table, we simply select the value of the variable which has the greatest frequency.

Example

What is the modal number of children per family for the data in this frequency distribution?

NUMBER OF CHILDREN PER FAMILY	0	1	2	3	4	5	6
FREQUENCY	13	13	38	17	10	4	5

The modal number of children per family is 2, because it occurs with the greatest frequency.

In a grouped table, the modal average becomes a **modal group**, and we simply pick out the **group of values** which occurs most frequently. In a large distribution, if two or more values of the variable each occur with the same frequency, they may be stated as alternative values for the mode.

Example

Find the modal group for the students' test marks shown in this table.

Test mark	1-5	6-10	11-15	16-20	21-25	26-30	31-35	36-40	41-45	46-50
Frequency	1	2	11	17	25	18	25	6	3	4

Two groups each occur with a frequency of 25, which is greater than any other group's frequency.

So, the modal group is either 21-25 or 31-35.

CHECKPOINT 16

1 Find the mode of each of the following distributions.

a 12 6 7 9 6
b 1 1 1 1 2 2 3 3 3 3 3 4 4 5 6 6
c £1.50 £1.50 £2.00 £3.00 £3.00 £2.00 £2.50 £1.50 £1.50 £1.50
d −2 −1 −2 0 0 0 3 4 1 2 6
e 2.7 3.4 8.9 5.6 6.6 7.3 5.2 2.9 8.0 7.1

2 The cost of a gallon of 4-star petrol was checked at a sample of 50 garages in two different cities. The results are shown in the table below. Find the modal price in each of the cities.

COST PER GALLON (pence)	CITY A	CITY B
167	2	4
168	5	7
169	12	4
170	21	11
171	7	13
172	3	5
173	0	6

3 Lord Grimby-Dipstick has two woods on his estate, Rooksend and Boggham. He orders a survey to be carried out into the size of the trees in the two woods. The circumferences of 100 selected trees are therefore measured in both woods. The results are shown in this table. Find the modal group for each wood.

CIRCUMFERENCE (cm)	ROOKSEND	BOGGHAM
0-20	3	5
20-40	17	3
40-60	22	6
60-80	25	11
80-100	19	18
100-120	7	24
120-140	5	26
140-160	2	7

A comparison between the mean, the median and the mode

To illustrate the differences between the three types of average we have studied, we will consider a simplified example.

Yasmin Newsom has just left school and is applying for a job in a small electronics factory. The factory was started 2 years ago by Henry Zap who, after a great deal of hard work, has built the business into one employing 17 people, including himself. Henry Zap tells Yasmin that the average income for the factory's employees is £15 000 a year. The assembly workers she talks to tell her she can expect to earn £9 000 a year. Mrs Singh, the factory supervisor, tells Yasmin that she earns £12 000 per year as a supervisor and that this is the average for the factory.

Yasmin is baffled. How can all these people be telling the truth?

This is a bar graph showing the frequency with which different salaries are earned in the factory.

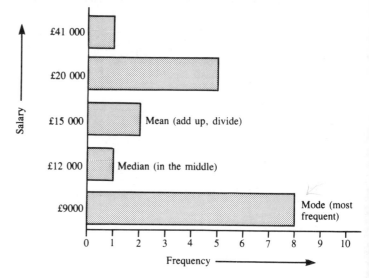

As you can see from the graph, each person was telling Yasmin the truth! The confusion was caused because each person used the word **average** without saying exactly which type of average they were talking about.

● Henry Zap was using a **mean average**, obtained by adding up all the salaries and then dividing by the number of salaries. Mean averages are easily changed by one or two very large or very small values and, in this example, Henry's salary of £41 000 and the 5 salaries of £20 000 paid to the sales staff increase the mean average considerably.

● Mrs Singh was using a **median average**, the 9th largest salary in an ordered distribution of 17 salaries. The median is not so easily changed by one or two very large or very small values. In this example, Henry's salary could have been £80 000 or even £180 000 but the median would have still been £12 000.

● The £9 000 is the **modal salary**; most people earn this salary. In this example, this figure is the most useful for Yasmin because this is the salary she is likely to start on.

The characteristics of the three types of average can be summarised like this.

Averages

● The **mean** average is the most commonly used average. It is calculated by adding all the individual values in the distribution together, and dividing by the number of values.

The mean has two disadvantages, firstly it is the hardest average to calculate and secondly it can be easily changed by one or two very large or very small values. Its main advantages are that it takes into consideration **all** the values of a variable and that it can be used in more advanced statistical work. For example, if we know the mean averages of two distributions (and the number of values in each distribution), we can calculate the mean average of the combined distribution directly from the two means without going back to the original values.

● The **median** average is also quite frequently used in statistical work. It is found by putting all the values in the distribution in order, and choosing or calculating the value exactly in the middle of the sequence of values.

The main advantages of the median are that it is easy to calculate and is easy to understand (it is the middle value). It does not, however, take all the values in the distribution into consideration (only their **positions**). Also, if we know the median averages of two distributions, it is not possible to calculate the median average of the combined distribution directly from the two medians without going back to the original values. This reduces its value in more advanced statistical work.

● The **mode**, or **modal average**, is the least used in serious statistical work.

It is simply the value (or values) which occurs most frequently in a distribution.

The mode has some use with qualitative data, for example, to state the 'most popular' flavour, colour, etc., but it is of little use in comparing two frequency distributions.

CHECKPOINT 17

1 Henry Zap is about to start pay negotiations with his workers. He is offering them a 5% rise; they want a 10% rise.

a Which average wage do you think Henry will use in his arguments for a 5% increase?

b Which average wage do you think the workers will use in their arguments for a 10% increase?

2 Amy Smart sells ice-cream. She sells '99' cones in five sizes, 50p, 60p, 70p, 80p and £1.00. This table shows her weekly sales of '99' cones.

PRICE (pence)	50	60	70	80	100
NUMBER SOLD	101	154	29	146	70

a Find the mean, median and modal average cost per ice-cream.

b Comment on your results.

3 This table shows the number of visits which 100 patients made to a doctor each year.

Number of visits	0	1	2	3	4	5	43
Frequency	10	23	21	14	17	14	1

a Find the mean, median and modal average number of visits per patient.

b Comment on your results.

The spread of a distribution

Comparing two distributions using only an average value can be misleading. For example, suppose you were offered a job by two different companies and told that for each the median wage was £170 per week. You might assume that there was nothing to choose between the wages offered by the two companies. The distributions of wages in the two companies might, however, be like this.

Wage (nearest £10)	£140	£150	£160	£170	£180	£190	£200	£210	£220
Frequency (Company A)	40	220	110	206	150	80	0	90	94

Wage (nearest £10)	£150	£160	£170	£180	£190
Frequency (Company B)	120	170	402	265	43

In the first company, there is a very wide spread of wages and, from a starting wage of £140, it is eventually possible to earn £220 per week. In the second company, there is a much narrower spread of wages and, from a starting wage of £150, the maximum wage possible is £190.

Any measurement which helps us to compare the **spread** of values in a distribution is called a **measure of dispersion**. Two simple measures of dispersion are **the range** and the **interquartile range**.

> Measures of dispersion
>
> - The **range** of a distribution is simply the difference between the greatest and the least values of the variable.
> - The **interquartile range** of a distribution is the difference between the upper quartile and the lower quartile.

Example

Find the range and the interquartile range of this distribution.

$$1 \quad 4 \quad 7 \quad 5 \quad 6 \quad 3 \quad 3 \quad 2 \quad 1 \quad 5 \quad 1$$

First, we arrange the values into order.

$$1 \quad 1 \quad 1 \quad 2 \quad 3 \quad 3 \quad 4 \quad 5 \quad 5 \quad 6 \quad 7$$

The range $= 7 - 1 = 6$

The interquartile range $= 5 - 1 = 4$

We will now use these two different measures of dispersion to compare the wage distributions.

For our wage distributions we have

Range (company A's wages) $= £220 - £140 = £80$

Range (company B's wages) $= £190 - £150 = £40$

To find the interquartile ranges we add a cumulative frequency line to each table. Then the quartiles and the median are in the 250th, 500th and 750th positions.

Wage (nearest £10)	£140	£150	£160	£170	£180	£190	£200	£210	£220
Frequency (Company A)	40	220	110	206	150	80	10	90	94
Cumulative frequency	40	260	370	576	726	806	816	906	1000

Lower quartile   Median   Upper quartile

Wage (nearest £10)	£150	£160	£170	£180	£190
Frequency (Company B)	120	170	402	265	43
Cumulative frequency	120	290	692	957	1000

Lower quartile   Upper quartile
Median

So, for our wage distributions we have

Interquartile range (company A's wages) $= £190 - £150 = £40$

Interquartile range (company B's wages) $= £180 - £160 = £20$

When comparing the wages in the two companies we can now summarise like this.

COMPANY A	COMPANY B
MEDIAN = £170	MEDIAN = £170
RANGE = £80	RANGE = £40
INTERQUARTILE RANGE = £40	INTERQUARTILE RANGE = £20

The two range values tell us that the distribution of wages in company B is 'tighter' than the distribution of wages in company A.

The two interquartile ranges also tell us that the distribution of wages in company B is 'tighter' than the distribution of wages in company A.

The interquartile range is often preferred to the range when making a comparison between two distributions. This is because the range is more easily affected by a very large or very small value. For example, if just one person in company B earned £300 per week, the range would change from £40 to £150 but the interquartile range would still be £20.

1 Most people would agree that 21°C is an almost ideal temperature for a pleasant summer day. The mean average annual temperature in Minastroney is 21°C. Do the inhabitants of this city have pleasant summer days all year long?

2 Find the range and the interquartile range of each of the following distributions.

a 1 1 2 3 1 2 3 5 4 6 7 4 3 2 1 1
   0 0 1 0 2 0 3

b 1 2 1 3 4 5 5 3 4 1 3 5 2 2 5

c £5.00 £1.50 £4.00 £5.50 £4.50 £6.00 £2.00

d 34 56 75 68 92 90 83 38 71 17 65

e 201 297 256 289 201 234 254 271 199 231
   297 249 300 222 218

f −2 3 0 −1 0 2 0 0 0 −3 1 1 1 1
   2 −1 −2 3 3 0 −1 −1

3 Find the range and the interquartile range of the two distributions shown in this table.

Number of children per family	0	1	2	3	4	5	6
Frequency (Estate A)	10	9	18	8	5	0	0
Frequency (Estate B)	3	4	20	9	5	4	5

(handwritten: range between 0 & 4 = 4)
(handwritten: Range between 0 & 6 = 6)

4 The times taken for 60 runners to complete a race are shown in this table. Find the range and the interquartile range of this distribution.

TIME (minutes)	NUMBER OF RUNNERS
18–19	0
19–20	8
20–21	21
21–22	14
22–23	6
24–25	5
25–26	6

Ways to compare frequency distributions

In order to condense and summarise the data in a frequency distribution, we now know how to find

- The mean average
- The median average
- The quartiles
- The modal average
- The range
- The interquartile range

In three different types of distribution

- A simple list of values
- A frequency distribution table
- A grouped frequency distribution table

The following examples revise all these techniques.

Examples

1 Find the mean, median, quartiles, mode, range and interquartile range for this list of values

1 2 4 5 3 3 3 1 1 6 7 10 4 1 1 1 6
1 1 2 2 2 2

There are 23 values, with a total of 69.

$$\text{Mean} = \frac{69}{23} = 3$$

Arranging the values into order,

1 1 1 1 1 1 1 1 2 2 2 2 2 2 3 3 3 4
4 5 6 6 7 10

There are 23 values, so the median is in the 12th position, the lower quartile is in the 6th position and the upper quartile is in the 18th position.

Lower quartile = 1

Median = 2

Upper quartile = 4

The mode = 1

The range = 10 − 1 = 9

The interquartile range = 4 − 1 = 3

2 Six dice are thrown together 1000 times and the number of sixes obtained on each throw is recorded. The table below shows the results. Find the mean, median, quartiles, mode, range and interquartile range for this frequency distribution.

NUMBER OF SIXES	FREQUENCY
0	335
1	402
2	201
3	54
4	7
5	1
6	0

To calculate the mean, we make these additions to the table.

NUMBER OF SIXES	FREQUENCY	NUMBER × FREQUENCIES
0	335	335
1	402	402
2	201	402
3	54	162
4	7	28
5	1	5
6	0	0
TOTALS	1000	1334

$$\text{Mean} = \frac{1334}{1000} = 1.334 \text{ sixes per throw}$$

To find the median and the quartiles we make these additions to the table.

NUMBER OF SIXES	FREQUENCY	CUMULATIVE FREQUENCY	
0	335	335	◄—Lower quartile (250th)
1	402	737	◄———Median (500th)
2	201	938	◄—Upper quartile (750th)
3	54	992	
4	7	999	
5	1	1000	
6	0	1000	

Lower quartile = 0 sixes per throw

Median = 1 six per throw

Upper quartile = 2 sixes per throw

The mode = 1 six per throw

The range = 5 − 0 = 5 sixes per throw

The interquartile range = 2 − 0 = 2 sixes per throw

3 This table shows the lengths of a sample of 80 earthworms. Find the mean, median, quartiles, modal group, range and interquartile range for this frequency distribution.

LENGTH OF EARTHWORM (cm)	FREQUENCY
0.5–1.5	3
1.5–2.5	5
2.5–3.5	6
3.5–4.5	7
4.5–5.5	10
5.5–6.5	13
6.5–7.5	12
7.5–8.5	10
8.5–9.5	8
9.5–10.5	6

We make these additions to the table.

Length of earthworm (cm)	Frequency	Mid-point	Mid-point × frequency	Cumulative frequency
0.5–1.5	3	1	3	3
1.5–2.5	5	2	10	8
2.5–3.5	6	3	18	14
3.5–4.5	7	4	28	21
4.5–5.5	10	5	50	31
5.5–6.5	13	6	78	44
6.5–7.5	12	7	84	56
7.5–8.5	10	8	80	66
8.5–9.5	8	9	72	74
9.5–10.5	6	10	60	80
TOTALS	80		483	

Mean $= \dfrac{483}{80} = 6$ cm (to the nearest cm)

To estimate the median and the quartiles, we draw this cumulative frequency graph.

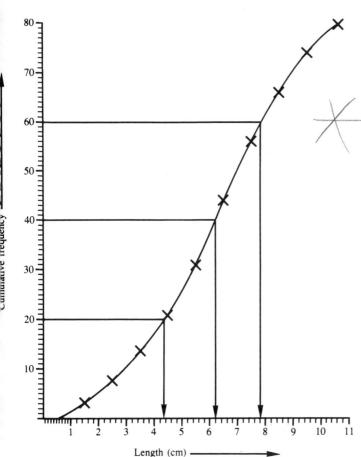

Length (cm) ⟶

From the graph we can estimate

Lower quartile = 4.3 cm

Median = 6.2 cm

Upper quartile = 7.8 cm

Also, we can state

The modal group is the 5.5–6.5 group

The range = 10.5 − 0.5 = 10 cm

The interquartile range = 7.8 − 4.3 = 3.5 cm

1 Find the mean, median, quartiles, mode, range and interquartile range for each list of values.

a 1 1 2 3 3 4 4 5 8 7 6 5 4 4 3 3
  2 1

b 12 23 11 19 11 12 12 5 18 19 13

c 36 36 37 36 38 41 39 40 37 37 38
  39 37 38 40

d 102 101 102 101 102 100 100 100 102
  100 101 100 99

2 In order to test the manufacturers' claims of 'average content 40 matches', two samples of 100 match boxes are opened and their contents counted. The first sample are 'Burners' matches and the second sample are 'Flames'. The table below shows the results. Find the mean, median, quartiles, mode, range and interquartile range for each frequency distribution. Comment on your results, comparing and contrasting the two distributions.

NUMBER OF MATCHES PER BOX	FREQUENCY 'BURNERS'	FREQUENCY 'FLAMES'
36	2	0
37	5	0
38	7	12
39	13	24
40	24	38
41	26	17
42	13	9
43	8	0
44	2	0

3 Each year, a game warden in East Anglia checks on the contents of 60 nests of the Egyptian goose, a bird introduced from Africa in the eighteenth century. The table below shows her results for two successive years. Find the mean, median, quartiles, mode, range and interquartile range for each frequency distribution. Comment on your results, comparing and contrasting the two distributions.

Number of eggs	0	1	2	3	4	5	6	7	8	9
Number of nests (Year 1)	12	0	0	3	0	12	17	12	4	0
Number of nests (Year 2)	17	0	1	5	0	19	12	6	0	0

357

4 A games teacher starts a ten-week training programme for a health and fitness club. She times the students over a one-mile race both before and after they complete the programme. The table below shows her results. Find the mean, median, quartiles, modal group, range and inter-quartile range for each frequency distribution.

TIME (seconds)	FREQUENCY (before)	FREQUENCY (after)
260–280	0	6
280–300	2	12
300–320	4	15
320–340	14	16
340–360	16	8
360–380	11	3
380–400	8	0
400–420	5	0

a How many club members ran the race in less than 350 seconds before the training programme?

b How many club members ran the race in less than 350 seconds after the training programme?

c Comment on your results, comparing and contrasting the two distributions.

5 A comparison test is carried out between the batteries produced by two rival companies. Fifty pairs of batteries from each company are tested, each pair being used to power a personal stereo until they fail. The results obtained are shown in the table below. Find the mean, median, quartiles, modal group, range and interquartile range for each frequency distribution.

TIME BEFORE FAILING	FREQUENCY (Duraready)	FREQUENCY (Evercell)
40–50	0	0
50–60	2	0
60–70	4	0
70–80	6	0
80–90	8	10
90–100	12	28
100–110	17	11
110–120	1	1

a What percentage of the Evercell batteries lasted for more than 100 minutes?

b What percentage of the Duraready batteries lasted for more than 100 minutes?

c What percentage of the Evercell batteries lasted for less than 80 minutes?

d What percentage of the Duraready batteries lasted for less than 80 minutes?

e Comment on your results, comparing and contrasting the two distributions. Which batteries would you recommend and why?

The standard deviation

The standard deviation is not included in many GCSE examinations and you should consult your syllabus before you study this section.

We have already mastered two simple measures of dispersion, the **range** and the **inter-quartile range**.

The **standard deviation** is a more complicated measure of dispersion. It has the same advantages and disadvantages as the mean average, and like the mean, is frequently used in more advanced statistical work.

We will illustrate the calculation of the standard deviation by comparing the homework marks of a group of ten students in Maths and Science. The table below shows the marks, with A, B, C, etc. being used as a code to represent the ten different students.

INDIVIDUAL	MATHS MARK	SCIENCE MARK
A	3	2
B	9	3
C	3	4
D	6	6
E	5	3
F	10	10
G	7	5
H	4	1
I	8	8
J	5	6

We will start with the Maths marks.

First, we calculate the **mean average** in the normal way, by adding all the marks together and then dividing by the number of marks. For our maths homework marks this gives

$$\text{mean average} = \frac{60}{10} = 6$$

We now add a column to our table, showing the **deviation** (difference) of each mark from this mean value. Our table looks like this.

INDIVIDUAL	MATHS MARK	DEVIATION
A	3	−3
B	9	+3
C	3	−3
D	6	0
E	5	−1
F	10	+4
G	7	+1
H	4	−2
I	8	+2
J	5	−1
TOTALS	60	0

Notice that the total of the deviations from the mean is zero, which is what we should expect for any distribution, because the mean is calculated as the arithmetical centre of the distribution of values.

A value that is zero for any distribution is useless for making comparisons between distributions so, to produce a value that differs from distribution to distribution, we now square the deviations.

This has the effect of making all the quantities positive. Our table now looks like this.

INDIVIDUAL	MATHS MARK	DEVIATION	SQUARED DEVIATION
A	3	−3	9
B	9	3	9
C	3	−3	9
D	6	0	0
E	5	−1	1
F	10	4	16
G	7	1	1
H	4	−2	4
I	8	2	4
J	5	−1	1
TOTALS	60	0	54

So our 10 marks have a total squared deviation of 54 from the mean average. We now calculate the mean average of these squared deviations. This value is called the **variance** of a distribution. For our maths mark we have

$$\text{variance} = \frac{54}{10} = 5.4$$

Finally, we calculate the **standard deviation**. This is defined as the **square root of the variance**. So, for our maths marks, standard deviation $= \sqrt{5.4} = 2.3$ (to 1 d.p.). Here is a summary of the calculation in the example.

The standard deviation

The standard deviation is a **measure of dispersion**, that is to say, a measure of how widely the values in a distribution are spread. We calculate it by

1 Finding the mean average of the distribution.
2 Finding the deviation of each value from the mean average.
3 Squaring the deviations from the mean.
4 Finding the total of the squared deviations.
5 Dividing this total by the number of values in the distribution to find the variance.
6 Square rooting the variance to find the standard deviation.

It should be obvious that a distribution in which the values are widely spread will produce a high value for the standard deviation and a distribution in which the values are closely grouped will produce a low value for the standard deviation. The standard deviation is thus a useful way to compare the spread of values in two or more distributions.

These are the required calculations to find the standard deviation of our Science marks.

INDIVIDUAL	SCIENCE MARK	DEVIATION	SQUARED DEVIATION
A	2	−2.8	7.84
B	3	−1.8	3.24
C	4	−0.8	0.64
D	6	1.2	1.44
E	3	−1.8	3.24
F	10	5.2	27.04
G	5	0.2	0.04
H	1	−3.8	14.44
I	8	3.2	10.24
J	6	1.2	1.44
TOTALS	48	0	69.60

$$\text{mean average} = \frac{48}{10} = 4.8 \qquad \text{variance} = \frac{69.6}{10} = 6.96$$

$$\text{standard deviation} = \sqrt{6.96} = 2.6 \text{ (to 1 d.p.)}$$

So, for our two mark distributions, we have

MATHS   mean = 6   standard deviation = 2.3
SCIENCE   mean = 4.8   standard deviation = 2.6

From these calculations we can compare the mark distributions and conclude that

The Maths marks tended to be higher and more tightly grouped than the Science marks.

Many scientific calculators have built-in statistics functions which allow you to enter a set of values and automatically obtain the mean and standard deviation. If your calculator does have these functions, do not use them until you are sure that you thoroughly understand the way that a standard deviation is calculated from a set of data.

CHECKPOINT 20

1 This table shows the scores that Bob and Sue made when they each threw nine darts. Calculate the mean and standard deviation for each set of scores. Comment on your answers.

BOB	SUE
20	20
2	20
5	0
20	20
40	20
1	20
2	0
60	20
3	6

2 The cost (in pence) of a gallon of 4-star petrol was checked at a sample of 10 garages in Leeds and London. The results are shown in the table below. Calculate the mean average and the standard deviation of the results for each city. Comment on your answers.

LEEDS	LONDON
190	205
195	199
197	199
195	199
197	205
198	209
205	205
199	199
195	180
199	190

3 The number of children in 10 families living on two different housing estates is recorded in the table below. Calculate the mean and the standard deviation of the results for each estate. Comment on your answers.

HERON LEA ESTATE	CHERRY TREES ESTATE
3	4
0	2
2	2
1	0
0	3
2	2
0	1
2	4
2	0
1	1

The final question in the last checkpoint demonstrates that finding the standard deviation when the mean is not a whole number value can involve tiresome calculations.

The most sensible way to solve this problem is to use a calculator or computer software which can calculate the standard deviation automatically. If this is not possible, the variance and standard deviation of a distribution can be found by an alternative calculation that avoids these problems (the rather complicated algebra that proves the alternative calculation works will not be shown here).

We will demonstrate the technique by calculating the standard deviation of the data for the Heron Lea Estate from the last checkpoint.

The first step is to add a column to the table showing the square of every value, like this

HERON LEA ESTATE	SQUARED VALUES
3	9
0	0
2	4
1	1
0	0
2	4
0	0
2	4
2	4
1	1
TOTALS 13	27

It can be shown that the variance of the distribution is equal to the mean of the squared values minus the square of the mean of the normal values. So we can calculate the variance like this

$$\text{mean of normal values} = \frac{13}{10} = 1.3$$

$$\text{square of mean of normal values} = (1.3)^2 = 1.69$$

$$\text{mean of squared values} = \frac{27}{10} = 2.7$$

$$\text{variance} = 2.7 - 1.69 = 1.01$$

Which gives up this value for the standard deviation

$$\text{standard deviation} = \sqrt{1.01} = 1.0 \text{ (to 1 d.p.)}$$

It is usual to take the letter x to represent any value that a variable can take and to use the letter n to represent the number of values the variable takes in the distribution. The symbol Σ stands for a summation or total of all possible values of a variable. So, Σx means the total of all possible values of the variable x. Σx^2 means the summation or total of all possible values of x^2. Using this notation, our last example becomes

x	x^2
3	9
0	0
2	4
1	1
0	0
2	4
0	0
2	4
2	4
1	1
$\Sigma x = 13$	$\Sigma x^2 = 27$

$$\text{standard deviation} = \sqrt{\frac{\Sigma x^2}{n} - \left(\frac{\Sigma x}{n}\right)^2}$$

$$\text{standard deviation} = \frac{27}{10} - \left(\frac{13}{10}\right)^2$$

$$\text{standard deviation} = \sqrt{2.7} - 1.69 = 1.0 \text{ (to 1 d.p.)}$$

CHECKPOINT 21

1 Find the mean and the standard deviation for each of the following sets of values for the variable x.

a	b	c
x	x	x
12	2.3	34
13	5.7	27
15	3.4	21
17	1.2	23
15	2.2	25
	3.4	31
	1.9	23
	2.7	34
		26
		30

2 The numbers of ice-creams Ms Russo sold each day during the first week of July were 185, 210, 217, 133, 59, 456 and 391. The corresponding sales for the last week of July were 210, 236, 310, 327, 103, 327 and 409. Calculate the mean and the standard deviation of the data for each week. Comment on your answers.

3 The weights (in kilograms) of twelve piglets after 10 weeks on Diet A are 22.6, 23.7, 24.3, 25.2, 26.9, 27.3, 29.7, 31.3, 32.5, 34.1, 35.6 and 36.4. The weights (in kilograms) of twelve piglets after 10 weeks on Diet B are 26.3, 26.6, 27.5, 28.1, 28.2, 28.4, 30.1, 31.3, 31.5, 31.7, 32.3 and 32.3. Calculate the mean and the standard deviation of the data for each week. Comment on your answers.

Correlation and scatter diagrams

All the work we have done to this point has involved values of a **single** variable. Many of the questions that are asked and answered by more advanced statistical work involve **more than one variable**. For example, we might ask

• Do people with large incomes tend to live in large houses?

• Do parents with high intelligence tend to have children of high intelligence?

• How is the amount that is spent on advertising a new product related to its sales success?

• Do taller than average people tend to be heavier than average?

• Are people who are good at Maths also good at Geography?

All these questions involve the idea that the values of two variables may be **correlated**. This means that the values are linked in some way. For example, if we say that height and weight in children are **correlated**, we mean that tall children tend to be heavier than short children. Of course, some children are lighter than other, much shorter children. The relationship is not an exact one; it is simply a loose connection which applies in the majority of cases. There are many different ways to test for correlations between variables but we will only study one simple technique, the **scatter diagram**. The following example demonstrates the construction of a scatter diagram.

Jamie and Jessica wonder if there is a correlation between a person's homework marks in Maths and Science. They collect the following data from 20 friends who have just had homework from both subjects marked out of 10.

Individual	A	B	C	D	E	F	G	H	I	J	K	L	M	N	O	P	Q	R	S	T
Maths mark	1	9	3	6	5	10	7	4	8	5	5	3	3	4	10	7	7	4	5	6
Science mark	2	3	4	6	3	10	5	1	8	6	5	2	3	3	8	6	7	5	4	5

To construct a **scatter diagram** from these data, the values are plotted on a graph with one axis for the Maths marks and one axis for the Science marks. Each individual plots as a single point on the graph, using their two marks as *x* and *y* coordinates. This is a scatter diagram drawn from Jamie and Jessica's results. The arrow on the scatter diagram points to individual E, plotted at the point (5,3) because his Maths mark is 5 and his Science mark is 3.

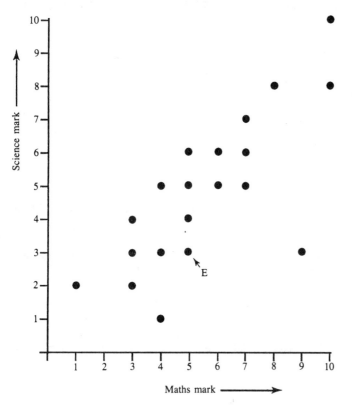

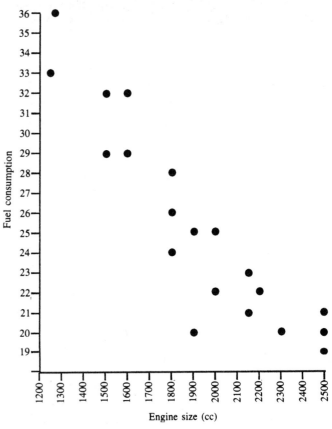

The scatter diagram shows that there is a **positive correlation** between the individuals' homework marks in Maths and Science. This means that the diagram shows that students who get a good mark for Maths tend to also get a good mark for Science. Students who get a poor mark for Maths tend to also get a poor mark for Science.

There are of course exceptions to this rule. Individual B, for example, scores 9 for Maths but only 3 for Science. Remember however that when we say that two variables are correlated we do not mean that they are linked by hard and fast rules; their values just tend to be related.

We can have **negative** correlations as well as **positive correlations.** For example, this scatter diagram shows the relationship between the engine sizes of 20 cars and their average fuel consumption in miles per gallon. It is clear that as the engine size **increases,** the fuel consumption tends to **decrease.** We say that the two variables in this case are **negatively correlated.**

We can of course have instances where two variables are not correlated at all. In this case we would expect to see a random distribution of dots in the scatter diagram, with no noticeable trends at all.

These diagrams illustrate variables with positive correlation, negative correlation and no correlation.

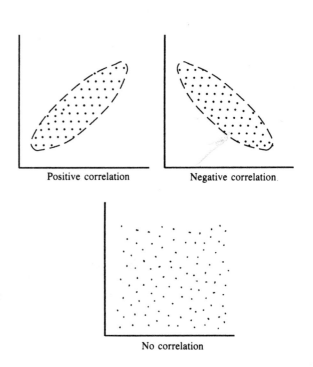

Positive correlation   Negative correlation

No correlation

1 In each of the following cases, say whether you would expect the two variables to have a positive correlation, negative correlation or no correlation. Explain your answers, indicating the likely exceptions there would be to any expected correlation.

a An adult's height and weight.

b A person's income and the value of the house they live in.

c A person's height and the height of their mother.

d The price of a stereo system and the number sold.

e The age of a student and the number of times they are absent from school.

f The age of an adult and the distance they can run without stopping to rest.

g The length of a person's hair and their shoe size.

h The age of a child and the distance they can run without stopping to rest.

i Students' test scores in Maths and English.

j The age of a used car and its value.

2 A shopkeeper makes a record of the temperature each day in September and the number of ice-creams she sells. The table below shows her results. Draw a scatter diagram for these data and comment on any correlation you think they demonstrate.

DATE	NUMBER SOLD	TEMPERATURE (C°)
1	20	21
2	15	16
3	25	24
4	35	27
5	30	27
6	20	18
7	15	18
8	25	24
9	20	24
10	35	29
11	15	16
12	20	18
13	30	21
14	25	18
15	20	21
16	40	29
17	20	21
18	5	10
19	20	13
20	10	10
21	25	21
22	15	18
23	30	27
24	0	16
25	10	16
26	15	16
27	20	18
28	25	24
29	10	10
30	5	7

3 This table shows the latitude of 15 cities and their average highest annual temperature. Draw a scatter diagram for these data and comment on any correlation you think they demonstrate.

CITY	LATITUDE (nearest degree)	HIGHEST TEMPERATURE (nearest °C)
Algiers	37	58
Amsterdam	52	12
Berlin	53	13
Bombay	19	31
Copenhagen	56	11
Hong Kong	22	25
Karachi	25	31
Leningrad	60	8
London	52	14
Madrid	40	19
Manila	15	32
Paris	49	15
Phnom Penh	12	32
Rangoon	17	32
Saigon	11	32

Probability

We have already learnt how to collect, organise, present and compare data. **Probability** is the name given to the branch of statistics which allows us to evaluate how **likely** a given result is. This enables us to compare our experimental results against theoretical 'perfect' results and to draw conclusions about their reliability.

For example, probability predicts that when you roll a normal die you have as much chance of scoring a 6 as you have of scoring a 1, 2, 3, 4 or 5. If, in an experiment, you rolled a die 600 times and recorded 300 sixes, comparing these results with the theoretical 'perfect' result of 100 sixes will lead you to suspect that something is wrong with either the die or the experiment.

The mathematics of probability has been developed over the past 400 years. It had its beginning in the sixteenth century as mathematicians turned their attention to the problems of gambling and insurance (which in those days was little more than a form of gambling anyway). Two famous French mathematicians, Pascal and Fermat, established many basic principles in a series of letters they exchanged to discuss the best strategies to adopt in gambling games. In 1693, the

Royal Society of London published a life table, the results of a statistical survey of births and deaths in the city of Breslau. This allowed insurers to base their life insurance rates on the probabilities of life expectancy contained in the table.

Simple probability (single event)

An **event** is something which happens, like tossing a coin or rolling a die.

Most events have more than one possible outcome. For example, when a die is rolled, there are six possible outcomes, 1, 2, 3, 4, 5 or 6.

Several of these outcomes may give the same result. For example, the scores 2, 4 and 6 on a die all give the result 'an even number'.

The **probability** that any particular result will be obtained in an event is the fraction

the number of outcomes that contain the desired result
the total number of all possible outcomes

So, when a die is rolled, the probability of obtaining an even score is

$$\frac{3}{6} = \frac{1}{2}$$

Examples

1 What is the probability of cutting a deck of cards and obtaining an ace?

The number of outcomes that includes the result is 4.

The total number of all possible outcomes is 52.

The probability of obtaining an ace is $\frac{4}{52} = \frac{1}{13}$.

2 What is the probability of selecting a letter from the word 'probability' and obtaining a vowel?

The number of outcomes that includes the result is 4.

The total number of all possible outcomes is 11.

The probability of obtaining a vowel is $\frac{4}{11}$.

3 A bag contains 3 red, 2 blue and 7 white beads. What is the probability of selecting a bead from the bag at random and obtaining one that is either red or white?

The number of outcomes that includes the result is 10.

The total number of all possible outcomes is 12.

The probability of obtaining a red or white bead is $\frac{10}{12} = \frac{5}{6}$.

If any result is certain to happen because it is included in all the possible outcomes it has a probability of 1. For example, the probability of cutting a deck of cards and obtaining a red or black card is 1 (52 out of 52).

If any result cannot happen because it is not included in any of the possible outcomes it has a probability of 0. For example, the probability of cutting a deck of cards and obtaining a green card is 0 (0 out of 52).

Probabilities are usually written as fraction but may sometimes be written as decimals. For example, the probability of a tossed coin landing as a head can be written as 0.5 (1 out of 2).

It is obvious that all our probability answers are only correct if the outcomes of an event are equally likely. For example, if there are 15 toffees and 7 mints in a bag, the probability of selecting a sweet at random and obtaining a mint is 7/22.

If, however, the selection is not made at random it is impossible to say what the probability of selecting a mint is. The outcomes are not equally likely because they depend on the preference of the person choosing a sweet.

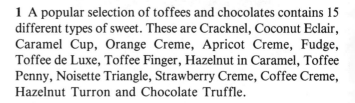

CHECKPOINT 23

1 A popular selection of toffees and chocolates contains 15 different types of sweet. These are Cracknel, Coconut Eclair, Caramel Cup, Orange Creme, Apricot Creme, Fudge, Toffee de Luxe, Toffee Finger, Hazelnut in Caramel, Toffee Penny, Noisette Triangle, Strawberry Creme, Coffee Creme, Hazelnut Turron and Chocolate Truffle.

The Bradshaw family always buys a large tin of these chocolates at Christmas and the tin contains an equal quantity of each type of sweet. The Bradshaws have a rule that selections from the tin must be made with eyes closed so that nobody is allowed to eat up all their favourite centres. When selecting like this, what is the probability that a family member will obtain

a a fruit creme   **b** any creme centre
c a toffee   **d** a noisette triangle
e a sweet with a caramel centre
f a coconut eclair, a cracknel, a fudge, a toffee penny or a hazelnut turron?

2 A card is cut from a normal deck of 52 cards. What is the probability that the card is

a a picture card **b** not a picture card
c a 5 of spades **d** a 5
e a red 5 **f** a red picture card
g a red card or a king **h** a club or a queen
i a diamond or a club **j** a card higher than a 7?

3 A bag contains 3 red, 5 yellow and 4 green beads. If one bead is selected at random from the bag, what is the probability that it is

a red **b** yellow
c green **d** red or green
e red or yellow **f** yellow or green
g not green **h** purple
i red, yellow or green **j** not yellow?

4 In a maths class of 30 students, 15 hate the subject, 7 dislike it, 5 like it and 3 love it. If a student is selected at random from the group, what is the probability that they will

a hate maths **b** dislike maths
c like maths **d** love maths
e either hate or dislike maths
f either like or love maths
g either love or hate maths?

5 This table shows the number of children per family in 50 families on each of two housing estates.

NUMBER OF CHILDREN PER FAMILY	0	1	2	3	4	5	6
FREQUENCY (Estate A)	10	9	18	8	5	0	0
FREQUENCY (Estate B)	3	4	20	9	5	4	5

a What is the probability of selecting a family at random on estate A and obtaining one with

i no children
ii 4 children
iii less than the median average number of families for that estate?

b What is the probability of selecting a family at random on estate B and obtaining one with

i 2 children
ii 1 child
iii more than the mean average number of families for that estate?

6 The weights of two samples of 100 piglets are recorded after the first sample have spent 10 weeks on diet A and the second sample have spent 10 weeks on diet B. The results are shown in this table.

WEIGHT (kg)	FREQUENCY (Diet A)	FREQUENCY (Diet B)
24.5–26.5	20	17
26.5–28.5	23	20
28.5–30.5	31	30
30.5–32.5	19	23
32.5–34.5	7	8
34.5–36.5	0	2

a What is the probability that a pig selected at random from the distribution for diet A will

i weigh less than 28.5 kg
ii weigh more than 28.5 kg
iii weigh between 26.5 and 30.5 kg?

b What is the probability that a pig selected at random from the distribution for diet B will

i weigh less than 28.5 kg
ii weigh more than 28.5 kg
iii weigh between 26.5 and 30.5 kg?

7 Two darts players, Maureen and Eric, both throw their three darts 50 times. The 50 total scores for each player are shown in this table.

Score	1–30	31–60	61–90	91–120	121–150	151–180
Frequency (Maureen)	7	8	10	9	8	8
Frequency (Eric)	0	16	18	14	2	0

a If we assume that these scores are typical of the players' performances, what is the probability that on her next throw Maureen will score

i more than 90
ii less than 61
iii between 31 and 150?

b If we assume that these scores are typical of the players' performances, what is the probability that on his next throw Eric will score

i more than 90
ii less than 61
iii between 31 and 150?

c Comment on your answer to this question. Can we be certain that the probabilities are accurate, or are they just estimates?

Problems with more than one event

We may be asked to find the probability of obtaining a particular result when two or more events are combined. For example, we may be asked to find the probability of obtaining two heads when two coins are tossed or of obtaining five sixes when five dice are rolled.

When **two** events are combined we often draw a small graph or **sample space** to illustrate clearly all the possible outcomes that can be obtained.

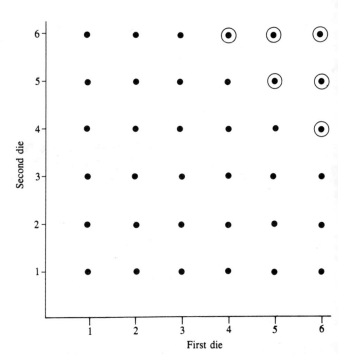

Examples

1 Two coins are tossed. Find the probability that the result obtained is two heads.

To illustrate all the outcomes that are possible, we draw this diagram.

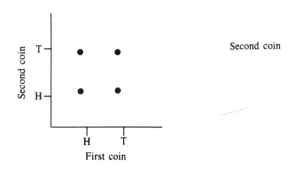

A diagram like this is called a **sample space**. It is simply a graph with all the outcomes of one event listed on the *x* axis and all the outcomes of the other event listed on the *y* axis. All the possible **combined outcomes are illustrated by the dots on the graph**.

Our sample space shows that there are four possible combined outcomes, HH, HT, TH and TT. Of these, only one gives the required result of two heads.

So, the probability of obtaining two heads $= \frac{1}{4}$.

2 Two dice are rolled. Find the probability that the score will be greater than 9.

We can draw this sample space.

From the sample space we see that there are 36 possible outcomes. Of these, 6 (circled in the diagram) give a score greater than 9.

So, the probability of a score greater than $9 = \frac{6}{36} = \frac{1}{6}$.

3 A man buys a packet of 6 eggs, two of which happen to be bad. If he makes a cake using two of the eggs, what is the probability that the cake contains at least 1 bad egg?

We can draw this sample space. The middle line of dots is left out because the same egg cannot be used twice.

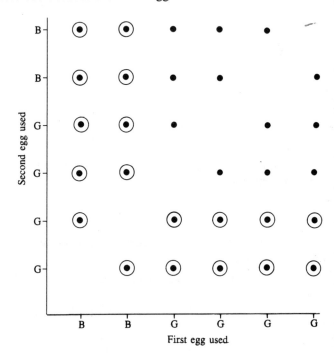

From the sample space we see that there are 30 possible outcomes. Of these, 18 (circled in the diagram) contain at least 1 bad egg.

So, the probability of a bad egg in the cake $= \dfrac{18}{30} = \dfrac{3}{5}$.

CHECKPOINT 24

1 Find the probability that when two coins are tossed the result will be

a two tails   **b** a head and a tail.

2 If two coins are tossed 2000 times, how many of the results would you predict will be

a two heads   **b** two tails   **c** a head and a tail?

Would you expect an actual experiment to exactly match your predictions?

3 If two dice are rolled together, what is the probability that the total score will be

a 8	**b** 7	**c** 4	**d** 5
e 10	**f** 12	**g** an even number	
h a prime number	**i** greater than 5	**j** less than 7	
k 36	**l** greater than 1 but less than 13?		

4 If two dice are rolled 1800 times, how many of the total scores would you predict will be

a 9	**b** 2	**c** 3	**d** 6
e 11	**f** a square number?		

5 A deck of cards is cut twice, the first card being replaced before the second is cut. What is the probability that the cards cut will be

a two spades   **b** two black cards
c one red and one black card   **d** both of the same suit
e one club and one diamond?

6 A group of 7 people, James, Gurmit, Sally, Brian, Tammi, Jason and Melanie, have to elect a manager and an assistant manager for a Young Enterprise company they are forming. They cannot however reach a decision. They decide to put 7 snooker balls in a bag, 5 red balls, one green ball and one black ball. They will take turns to draw; the person drawing the black ball will be director and the person drawing the green ball will be the assistant manager. Find the probability that Gurmit will be the manager and either Sally or Brian the assistant manager.

7 Two spinners are made, one numbered from 1 to 5 and the other from 6 to 10. Find the probability that when the spinners are spun together the total score will be greater than 12.

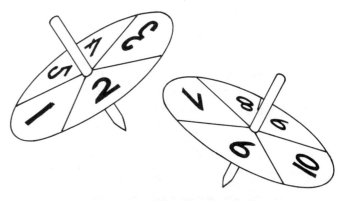

8 Two special dice are made. One has the set of numbers 0, 1, 1, 2, 2, 3 and the other the set of numbers 0, 0, 1, 2, 4, 5. If Bill rolls the first dice and Anthea rolls the second dice, what is the probability that Anthea beats Bill?

If more than two events are combined, a sample space cannot be drawn. In simple cases, the required result may depend on one specific outcome in each of the separate events. If this is so, the required combined probability can be found by **multiplying** the probabilities for each of the separate events.

Examples

1 Find the probability of rolling 3 dice and scoring 18.

To score 18, we must score a 6 on each die. The separate probabilities of doing this are

$$\frac{1}{6}, \frac{1}{6} \text{ and } \frac{1}{6}.$$

The probability of obtaining 3 sixes is

$$\frac{1}{6} \times \frac{1}{6} \times \frac{1}{6} = \frac{1}{216}.$$

2 Find the probability of tossing 5 coins and obtaining 5 heads. The separate probabilities are all $\frac{1}{2}$.

The probability of obtaining 5 heads is

$$\frac{1}{2} \times \frac{1}{2} \times \frac{1}{2} \times \frac{1}{2} \times \frac{1}{2} = \frac{1}{32}.$$

3 Four cards are dealt face up from the top of a full pack. Find the probability that they are all queens.

The probability of obtaining the first queen is $\dfrac{4}{52}$.

If this queen is obtained, there are now three queens left in a deck of 51 cards. So,

The probability of obtaining the second queen is $\frac{3}{51}$.

The probability of obtaining the third queen is $\frac{2}{50}$.

The probability of obtaining the fourth queen is $\frac{1}{49}$.

The probability of obtaining 4 queens is

$$\frac{4}{52} \times \frac{3}{51} \times \frac{2}{50} \times \frac{1}{49} = \frac{1}{270725}.$$

CHECKPOINT 25

1 Find the probability of rolling 8 dice and scoring 8 sixes.

2 Five cards are dealt face up from the top of a full deck of 52 cards. Find the probability that they are all clubs.

3 If 10 coins are tossed, find the probability that 10 tails will be obtained.

4 A bag contains 3 red, 4 green and 5 black beads. 3 beads are drawn from the bag in succession, each bead being returned before the next is selected. Find the probability that the three beads are

a all red   **b** all green   **c** all black
d a red followed by a green followed by a black
e a black followed by a red followed by a green.

5 A bag contains 3 red, 4 green and 5 black beads. 3 beads are drawn from the bag in succession. The selected beads are **not** returned to the bag. Find the probability that the three beads are

a all red   **b** all green   **c** all black
d a red followed by a green followed by a black
e a black followed by a red followed by a green.

6 If you hold 20 tickets in a raffle for which 1000 tickets were sold, what is the probability that you will win 1st, 2nd and 3rd prize?

Tree diagrams

In more complicated cases, we draw a **tree diagram** to illustrate all the possible outcomes in multi-event problems. A tree diagram starts with a dot to represent the first event. From this dot, 'branches' are drawn to represent all the possible outcomes from the event. The probability of each outcome is written on its 'branch'. For example, if we are

drawing a tree diagram to illustrate the tossing of three coins we start with this diagram which shows that the first event can result in a Head or a Tail.

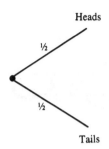

Since the second event can follow any one of these outcomes, dots are placed at the end of all the branches to represent the second event. From these dots branches are drawn to represent all the outcomes of the second event. Adding the branches for the second coin to our tree diagram gives us this diagram.

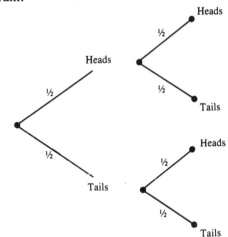

This process continues until all the successive events have been dealt with. This is our tree diagram when all three coins have been dealt with.

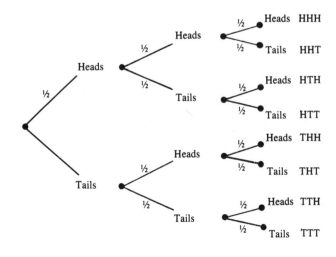

The probabilities on the branches are multiplied together to obtain the probabilities of obtaining each possible combined outcome. It looks quite complicated, but remember it is just a pictorial way to say, 'When you toss three coins you can obtain eight different results, HHH, HHT, HTH, HTT, THH, THT, TTH or TTT.'

We can use the diagram to answer many different probability questions. If a required result is obtained in several different combined outcomes we **add** the probabilities of the separate outcomes together.

These are examples of some questions that can be answered from the diagram.

The probability of obtaining 2 heads is

$$\frac{1}{8} + \frac{1}{8} + \frac{1}{8} = \frac{3}{8}.$$

The probability of obtaining at least 2 heads is

$$\frac{1}{8} + \frac{1}{8} + \frac{1}{8} + \frac{1}{8} = \frac{1}{2}.$$

The probability of obtaining at least 1 tail is

$$\frac{1}{8} + \frac{1}{8} + \frac{1}{8} + \frac{1}{8} + \frac{1}{8} + \frac{1}{8} + \frac{1}{8} = \frac{7}{8}.$$

Tree diagrams are more difficult to draw when selections without replacement are involved.

Example

A bag contains 3 red, 4 green and 5 black beads. Two beads are drawn from the bag in succession. The selected beads are **not** returned to the bag. Draw a tree diagram and find the probability that at least one of the beads is green.

This is the tree diagram. Study the probabilities that have been written on the second event branches very carefully. Remember that the bead selected first is not replaced and this changes the probabilities for the second bead.

COMBINED
OUTCOMES

Red	Red	Red	$\frac{6}{132}$
Red	Green	Red	Green	$\frac{12}{132}$
	Black	Red	Black	$\frac{15}{132}$
	Red	Green	Red	$\frac{12}{132}$
Green	Green	Green	Green	$\frac{12}{132}$
	Black	Green	Black	$\frac{20}{132}$
	Red	Black	Red	$\frac{15}{132}$
Black	Green	Black	Green	$\frac{20}{132}$
	Black	Black	Black	$\frac{20}{132}$

The probability that at least one bead is green is

$$\frac{12}{132} + \frac{12}{132} + \frac{12}{132} + \frac{20}{132} + \frac{20}{132} = \frac{76}{132} = \frac{19}{33}.$$

You may well have noticed that the last example could have been answered by drawing a sample space. This is true of most **two-event** problems, but problems that involve **more than two events** cannot be solved with sample spaces. Even where there is a possible choice of method, most examination questions will indicate which is to be used.

CHECKPOINT 26

1 A bag contains 3 red and 2 white beads. A bead is selected from the bag, it is replaced and then a second bead is selected. Draw a tree diagram and find the probability that

a at least one red bead is selected

b two beads of the same colour are selected.

2 Repeat question 1, but this time assume that the first bead selected is **not** replaced in the bag.

3 Three dice are rolled. Copy and complete this tree diagram and find the probability that at least 2 sixes are obtained.

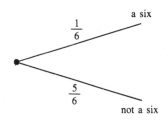

4 A bag of sweets is almost empty. Only 2 mints and 3 toffees are left. If Cindy takes three of these sweets without looking, find the probability that all the sweets left are toffees.

5 A combination lock on a briefcase has three wheels, each numbered from 0 to 9. Copy and complete this tree diagram and find the probability that, if a combination is selected at random, at least one digit is correct.

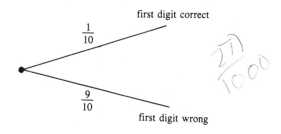

369

6 An electronics factory buys television tubes from a components supplier in batches of 20. A quality control inspector checks each batch of 20 by selecting 3 tubes at random from the batch and testing them. If the inspector finds a single faulty tube in her test sample, the whole batch is sent back to the supplier. If a batch has been received with four faulty tubes, what is the probability that the inspector will reject the batch?

7 Experience has shown that Chantal beats Jean-Luc in six snooker games out of 10. Find the probability that Chantal will win their next three games.

8 One bag contains three red beads and four white beads. A second bag contains five red beads and six white beads. A bead is selected from the first bag and placed in the second bag. A bead is then selected from the second bag and placed in the first bag. Find the probability that the first bag still contains three red beads and four white beads.

Decision maths

Decision maths describes the use of mathematical techniques to reach decisions. We will look in the next sections at **flowcharts** and **critical path networks**.

Flowcharts and algorithms

An **algorithm** is a set of instructions which, if followed exactly, will always produce a solution to a given problem. For example, we can write an algorithm to find the area of any rectangle.

   1 Input the base of the rectangle

   2 Input the height of the rectangle

   3 Calculate the area by multiplying the base by the height

   4 Output the area

The words **input** and **output** are general terms which cover a wide range of possibilities.

The word **input** means to receive data about the problem. The word **output** means to supply the answer. Input could be by listening to a teacher, reading a question in a book or by measuring an actual rectangle. Output could be spoken or written.

A **flowchart** is often used to illustrate an algorithm. A flowchart is a diagram which uses special symbols to show the sequence of steps in a problem solution. These are some of the shapes used.

The symbol	What it is used for
⬭	Start or stop the flow of data
▱	Whenever data is input or output
▭	Whenever the data is processed
◇	Whenever a decision is made

This is a flowchart for the algorithms to find the area of a rectangle.

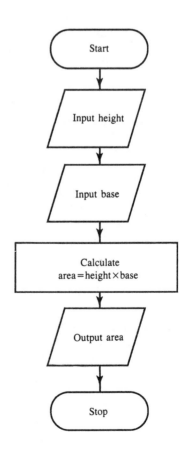

Flowcharts are particularly useful to illustrate an algorithm which requires a decision to be made between two alternatives. For example, suppose we want a computer to search through a long list of car owner details and print out a list of the names and addresses of all the owners of red Metros.

Computers must be given a precise algorithm in order to complete even a simple task. It is the job of computer programmers to find algorithms to solve problems. They use flowcharts to illustrate their solutions.

This is a possible algorithm for the red Metro search and the flowchart which illustrates it.

1 If the list is finished, stop.

2 Read the next name, address and car details.

3 If the car is not red, go to instruction 6.

4 If the car is not a Metro, go to instruction 6.

5 Print the name and address.

6 Go to instruction 1.

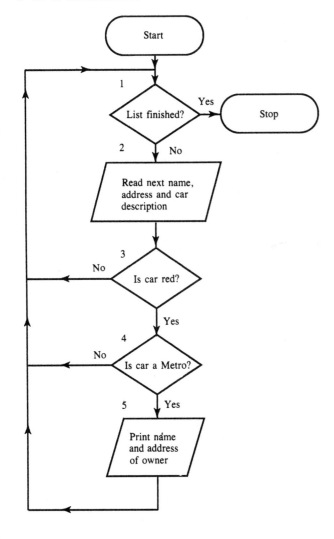

1 The following steps can, when placed in order, be used to make a cup of coffee. Draw a flowchart to illustrate these steps arranged into the correct order to make a cup of coffee.

Step 1. Add some sugar.

Step 2. Stir contents of the cup.

Step 3. But some coffee powder in the cup.

Step 4. Boil some water.

Step 5. Top up the cup with milk.

Step 6. Pour boiling water into cup leaving room for the required amount of milk.

2 To change a mark out of a total of 60 a percentage, you first divide the mark by 60 and then multiply this result by 100. Draw a flowchart that inputs a pupil's name followed by a test mark out of a total of 60. The pupil's percentage mark should then be calculated. Finally, the pupil's name and percentage mark should be output.

3 A box contains a mixture of plastic shapes, each of which is either a rectangle, a triangle or a circle. Three empty boxes and labelled rectangles, triangles or circles. Your task is to draw a flowchart for an automatic process to sort the shapes into the correct empty boxes using the following rules:

Rule 1. If the shape has 4 sides, it is a rectangle.

Rule 2. If the shape has 3 sides, it is a triangle.

Rule 3. If the shape is not a rectangle or a triangle, it is a circle.

To help you the start of the flowchart is shown below.

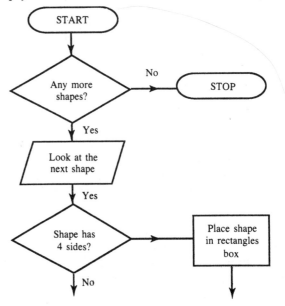

371

4 The flowchart below shows how a code may be broken.

By working through the flowchart for the chosen number, a **new number** can be calculated. Use the following table to find the letter corresponding to the **new number.**

New number:	1	2	3	4	5	6	7	8	9	10	11	12	13
Letter represented:	A	B	C	D	E	F	G	H	I	J	K	L	M
New number:	14	15	16	17	18	19	20	21	22	23	24	25	26
Letter represented:	N	O	P	Q	R	S	T	U	V	W	X	Y	Z

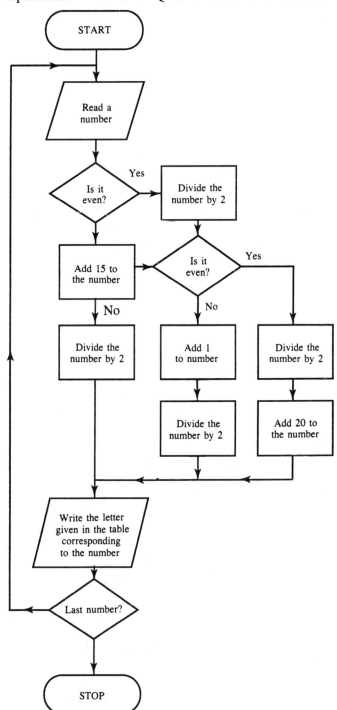

a Decode the following into characters: 4, 13, 3, 8, 2, 10.

b What number entered in the flowchart would produce the number used in the code to represent H?

Critical path networks

Critical path networks are used to find the best schedule for tasks that can be broken down into several separate actions or activities. These activities can be illustrated with a **network**. This is simply a diagram which shows all the separate activities and the relationships between them. For example, three of the activities involved in making a fish and chip supper are

- heat the oil
- chip the potatoes
- fry the chips

We cannot fry the chips before we have heated the oil **and** chipped the potatoes, so this activity depends on the other two. We can however heat the oil either before, during or after chipping the potatoes so these activities are independent and do not depend on each other. This is a critical path network showing all the activities necessary to make a fish and chip supper.

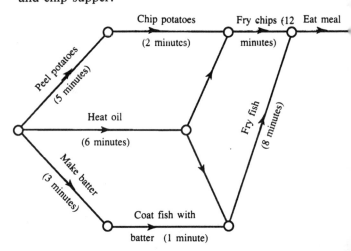

By studying the diagram, we can see that the shortest possible time to make the meal is 26 minutes. This diagram shows how we must plan our activities to achieve this minimum time.

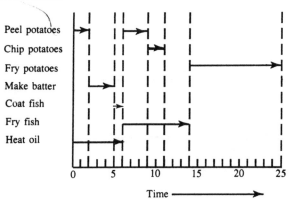

Our example was a very simple one. In industry, a critical path network might be constructed for an activity like building a new road. This could involve hundreds or thousands of separate activities. Computers are used to analyse large networks like this and to produce the most efficient schedule to build the road in the least time at the least cost.

CHECKPOINT 28

1 I am very fond of cheese and tomatoes on toast. The activities I complete to enjoy my toast are (not in order)

- Sprinkle cheese over tomatoes (30 seconds)

- Slice some tomatoes (1 minute)

- Toast the first side of the bread (3 minutes)

- Grate some cheese (2 minutes)

- Toast the cheese on top of the tomatoes and bread (1 minute)

- Partly toast the second side of the bread (2 minutes)

- Finish toasting second side with the tomatoes (2 minutes)

- Place tomatoes on partly toasted side (30 seconds)

Draw a critical path network and find the least time to make the cheese and tomatoes on toast.

2 Each morning when he gets up, Bill Clean goes through all the following activities.

- fill sink with hot water (1 minute)

- fill bath with hot water (5 minutes)

- shave (3 minutes)

- brush teeth (2 minutes)

- take bath (15 minutes)

- towel dry (4 minutes)

- get dressed (5 minutes).

The diagram below shows a possible critical path network for these activities. Copy the network and label it with the activities. Find the least possible line for Bill to complete all these activities.

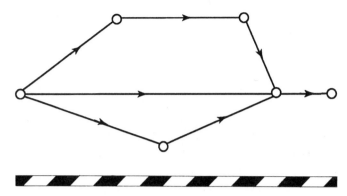

Statistics Practice and revision exercise

1 Explain the differences between qualitative variables, ordered qualitative variables, discrete quantitative variables and continuous quantitative variables. Give some examples of each type.

2 These are the test scores of 100 students in a Maths test. Use a tally chart to organise the results into a table.

2	7	8	9	3	4	1	9	10	2
6	6	5	7	8	9	2	6	4	9
3	4	9	10	6	7	8	4	5	3
2	5	6	7	8	7	6	5	9	10
9	8	7	4	5	6	7	2	8	7
10	1	9	2	8	3	7	4	6	5
5	5	5	6	6	7	8	9	9	4
5	4	3	6	6	6	7	8	9	1
10	10	9	5	6	6	8	8	2	2
9	9	3	7	7	7	7	8	9	5

3 Illustrate the 100 test marks in question 2 with a bar chart.

4 This bar chart illustrates a serious problem in British prisons. Estimate from the bar chart the average daily overcrowding for each year from 1977 to 1987.

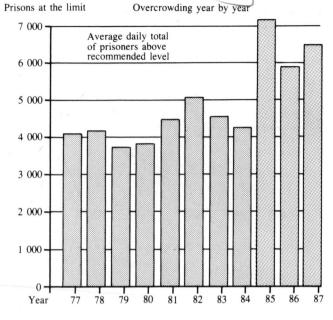

Prisons at the limit   Overcrowding year by year

Average daily total
of prisoners above
recommended level

Year 77 78 79 80 81 82 83 84 85 86 87

5 Draw a pie chart to illustrate the data in this table.

ACTIVITY	TIME SPENT IN ONE DAY (hours)
WORKING	9
TRAVEL	1
LEISURE	4
SLEEPING	8
MEALS	2

6 Draw a histogram to illustrate the data in this table.

Height of seedling (mm)	0–5	5–10	10–15	15–20	20–25	25–30
Frequency	5	11	20	26	12	6

7 Draw

a a histogram to illustrate the data in this table.
b a frequency polygon to illustrate the data in this table.

LENGTH OF VEHICLE (metres)	FREQUENCY
3.0–4.0	36
4.0–4.5	85
4.5–5.0	49
5.0–6.0	21
6.0–7.0	6
7.0–12.0	3

8 Find the mean, median, quartiles, mode, range and interquartile range of each of these sets of numbers.

a 2 2 4 6 7 4 2 6 1 2 6 8 2 3 1
3 5 7 7
b 21 22 23 24 22 22 21 23 25 23 22 21
21 24 21
c −1 0 −1 2 3 −3 2 1 1 1 1
d 200 300 200 400 500 600 200 300 300 400
500 200 200

9 Find the mean, median, quartiles, mode, range and interquartile range of the data shown in each of the following tables.

a

Number of matches per box	36	37	38	39	40	41	42	43
Frequency	3	12	18	27	23	12	5	0

b

Number of children per family	0	1	2	3	4	5	6
Frequency	45	67	124	33	17	12	2

10 Find the mean, median, quartiles, modal group, range and interquartile range of the data shown in each of the following tables.

a

Height of seedling (mm)	0–5	5–10	10–15	15–20	20–25	25–30
Frequency	5	11	20	26	12	6

b

LENGTH OF VEHICLE (metres)	FREQUENCY
3.0–4.0	36
4.0–4.5	85
4.5–5.0	49
5.0–6.0	21
6.0–7.0	6
7.0–12.0	3

11 There is growing concern about the difficulty of recruiting teachers, particularly in Science subjects and in areas of the country where houses are very expensive. This diagram appeared in the 'Times Educational Supplement', a special newspaper for teachers. Write a summary of the information illustrated by the diagram.

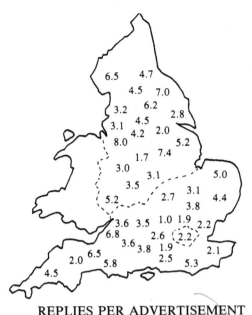

REPLIES PER ADVERTISEMENT

The average number of replies to TES advertisements for physics teachers received by local authorities against the average price of a semi-detached house in that region

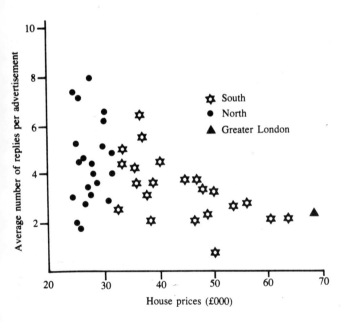

12 If a single die is rolled, what is the probability that the score will be

a even   **b** a factor of 12   **c** less than 5   **d** a 3?

13 If a single card is cut from a deck of 52 cards, what is the probability that it will be

a a club   **b** a red card   **c** the king of diamonds
d a picture card   **e** not a spade   **f** a queen or a red card
g a queen and a red card   **h** a five or a black card?

14 Two dice are rolled together. Draw a sample space for the results and find the probability that the final score will be

a a prime number   **b** 12   **c** greater than 8
d a 7   **e** a factor of 12   **f** 13
g 1   **h** a 2 or a 12.

15 The letters of the word ANIMAL are written on separate cards and placed in a bag. Two cards are withdrawn, one after the other without replacement. Draw a sample space for the results and find the probability that the letters drawn will be

a two vowels   **b** an N and an M   **c** two consonants.

16 Find the probability of

a dealing 4 red cards from the top of a normal deck.
b tossing 15 pennies and getting 15 heads.
c rolling 10 dice and getting a total score of 60.

17 There are two sets of traffic lights on the route that Mr Grimby takes on his way to work each morning. Experience has shown that the first lights are red on four mornings out of 10 and the second lights are red on six mornings out of 10. Draw a tree diagram and find the probability that

a Mr Grimby meets at least one red light on his way to work.
b Mr Grimby meets two green lights on his way to work.

18 An operation has a 70% success rate the first time it is attempted. If it fails, it can be repeated but with only a 30% chance of success. If the operation fails twice it is not repeated. Draw a tree diagram and find the probability that a patient about to have the operation for the first time will eventually have a successful operation after either one or two attempts.

19 A bag contains three toffees, five mints and four fruit lumps. Two sweets are taken at random from the bag and eaten. Draw a tree diagram and find the probability that at least one of the sweets is a fruit lump.

20 Work through the flowchart below, and produce a table showing clearly the values of the printed output C, and the values for A, B and D, as the process is followed.

values of printed output C & values for A, B, & D.

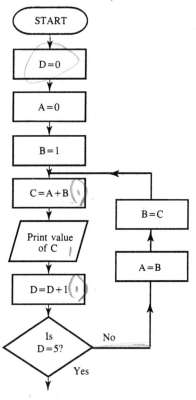

(i) What is the purpose of the variable D?

(ii) What change would you make to the flowchart to obtain TEN printed values of C?

21 (i) Trace through this flowchart to find what the output would be if A is 14 and B is 4.

(ii) Describe in general terms what this flowchart does.

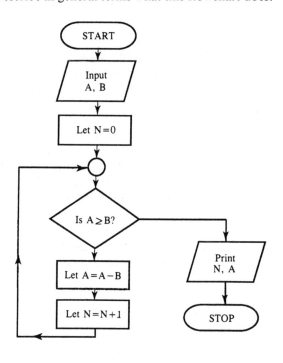

22 Here is a detailed flowchart for finding the average of five numbers:

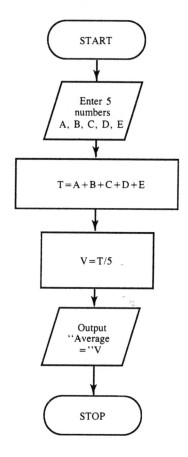

a Explain why this approach is satisfactory for 5 numbers but not for 50 numbers.

b Draw a flowchart to find the average of 500 numbers.

Statistics – extended problems for project work

The most sensible type of project for the Statistics Unit is the completion of an investigation of your own. This should involve

- Deciding on an area of investigation and some suitable questions that you can try to answer.

- Collecting either primary data or secondary data (or both) to help you answer your questions. You should design a data collection form to record any primary data you collect.

- Organising and presenting your data in helpful ways.

- Interpreting your data and making conclusions.

Ideally the investigation should be an entirely original idea. It may, however, be difficult to decide on a suitable investigation so here are a list of possible 'starters'.

1 You could carry out an investigation into used car or motor bike prices. A great deal of secondary data is readily available in newspapers and magazines. Some possible questions might be

- What are the average prices for a particular make and model for a 1 year old car, a 2 year old car and so on?

- What is the range of prices for a particular make and model of a given age?

- Which cars lose their value most quickly?

- Do all the models made by one manufacturer tend to lose value at the same rate?

2 You could carry out a traffic flow investigation. (This is obviously potentially dangerous and needs careful supervision.) Some possible questions might be

- Does the number of vehicles passing a certain point depend on the time of day?

- Does the number of vehicles flowing in each direction depend on the time of day?

- What is the distribution of vehicles into cars, vans, lorries, buses, motor bikes and pedal cycles? Does this depend on the time of day?

- How and why do Government road engineers carry out traffic surveys?

- What is the average number of occupants of a car? Does this depend on the time of day?

- Where are the lorries and commercial vehicles using the road going?

3 You could design and carry out a questionnaire survey. You will first need to decide exactly what you intend to enquire about. This might be people's opinions on TV programs, pop stars, food, shops, books, magazines, politicians or just about anything. Alternatively you could collect numerical data on things like the hours of TV watched each week, weekly income, time spent on homework, smoking or drinking habits (hopefully none), and so on. You should try to design a questionnaire that will collect data that can be organised in different ways. For example, if you decide to conduct a survey into the time spent watching TV, also collect data on gender, age and time spent on homework. You can then organise your data in different ways, for example by dividing the female answers from the male answers, and look for differences between the two groups. You could also try to answer questions like

- Is there a negative correlation between the time spent watching TV and time spent on homework?

4 You could put the theory of probability to the test by carrying out some investigations and comparing theoretical results with actual experiments. Coins, dice and cards are all good starting points.

5 You could carry out investigations into the applications of probability theory in commercial games. Some examples of games that are well worth investigating if you can obtain them are the following:

- Scrabble, to discover the logic behind the letter scores.

- Pass the Pigs, to discover the experimental probability of the pigs landing in each position and to discover playing strategies.

- Hotel, to investigate the relative value to a player of each property and to discover playing strategies.

- Any one of the many board games which use dice or spinners, to discover experimental probabilities and to discover playing strategies.

Statistics
Past paper questions

1 State which of the following are continuous, as opposed to discrete, variables:

a the temperature in a room,
b the number of people in a room,
c the height of trees measured to the nearest metre,
d the speed of a car.

2 During one month at a Driving Test Centre, 140 males took the Driving Test for the first time: 81 of them were successful. During the same month 110 females took the Driving Test for the first time: 62 were successful.

In addition, of the 90 males repeating the Driving Test, 60 passed and of the 70 females, 45 passed.
Present all this information in the form of a table. Include under the main headings, "First time Test" and "Repeat Test" the number of passes and failures for both male and female candidates and the total number of passes and failures for all candidates.

(LEAG)

3 The three main costs of a factory are shown in the pie chart as wages, overheads and raw materials. Two angles at the centre of the circle are given.

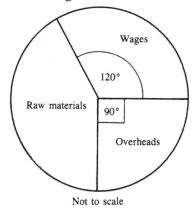

Not to scale

a Calculate the angle which represents 'raw materials'.

b What fraction of the total cost is 'wages'? Give your fraction in its lowest terms.

(NEA)

4 A group of 160 children are asked how they come to school. Their answers are as follows.

How they come to school	Bus	Car	Cycle	Walk
Number of pupils	60	20	20	70

Complete a pictogram to represent the above information.

(WJEC)

5 25 golfers played in a competition. Their scores were

```
 82  88   85   86   92
101  82   86   92   85
 83  86   87   87   82
 94  92  100   96   94
 81  86   89   90   86
```

a Copy and complete the table.

Score	Tally	Frequency
80–84	////	5
85–89		
90–94		
94–99		
100–104		

b How many of the golfers scored less than 90?

c Draw a bar chart to show the information in your table.

d What percentage of the golfers scored less than 85?

(LEAG)

6 In the Fourth Year at Broomswood School, 150 pupils took a mathematics test. The following results were obtained.

Marks in test	Number of pupils
1–20	16
21–40	35
41–60	60
61–80	24
81–100	15

a Draw a bar chart to illustrate this information.

b If the pass mark is 41, how many pupils passed?

c A pie chart is to be drawn to illustrate this information. What size should the angle be of the sector which represents pupils marks 41−60?

(LEAG)

7 The table shows the number of tonnes of fish caught in the English Channel during a certain period:

Fish	Tonnes
Herring	2000
Mackerel	800
Pilchards	5000
Sprats	1200

Using a radius of 6 cm for the circle, draw a pie chart to illustrate these data.

(WJEC)

8

Type of crisp	Tally	Frequency	Angle
Plain	⊮ IIII		
Salt and vinegar	⊮ ⊮ ⊮ I		
Cheese and onion	⊮ ⊮ I		
Beef	⊮ I		
Crispy bacon	III		
	Total	45	

The table shows the result of a survey taken on the sale of crisps one day in a School Tuckshop.

a Copy the table and complete the Frequency column.

The information is to be shown on a pie chart.

b Calculate the size of the angle of each sector of this pie chart.

Write your answers in the Angle column in the table.

c Draw and accurate pie chart to show this information.

Label the sectors clearly.

(LEAG)

9 The speeds of 200 cars passing a certain point subject to an 80 km/h speed limit were checked by the police. They are as shown in the table below:

Speeds (km/h)	0–55	55–60	60–65	65–70	70–75
Frequency	0	1	4	8	15

Speeds (km/h)	75–80	70–85	85–90	90–95	95–100	100–105	105–110
Frequency	20	35	50	40	21	5	1

a On graph paper draw a histogram representing this information.

b State, with a reason, whether or not the majority of motorists broke the law.

(SEG)

10 The table below shows how each £1 of expenditure of Derbyshire County Council was divided up in 1987/8.

How spent	Amount
Day-to-day business	47p
Repaying loans and interest	23p
Investing in assets	30p

Draw a pie chart to illustrate this information, showing clearly how you calculated the angles required. Record them, correct to the nearest degree, on your diagram.

(MEG)

11 A class in a junior school conducted a survey on how they each travelled to school that morning.

The table shows the results.

Method of travel	Number of pupils
Walk	10
Parents' car	4
Friend's car	2
Bus	8

a How many pupils took part in the survey?

b What fraction of the class came to school by bus?

c (i) Find how many pupils came to school by car.
(ii) What fraction of the class is this?

A pie chart is to be drawn to represent the result of the survey.

d (i) Copy and complete the table showing the angle for each sector.

Method of travel	Angle
Walk	150°
Parents' car	
Friend's car	
Bus	

(ii) Using a circle of radius 6 cm, draw and label this pie chart.

(MEG)

12 A baker sells white bread, brown bread, cakes, pies and biscuits. The pie chart shows what proportion of his average daily takings is gained from these sales.

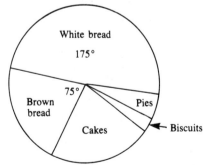

The baker's average daily takings amount to £720.

a How much does he take on his sales of white bread?

b Express his takings on sales of white bread to sales as a ratio in its simplest form.

(MEG)

13 Out of every £180 received from the rates a district council spent as follows:

Highways and planning	£13
Sports and recreation	£29
Environmental health	£37
Housing	£24
Administration	£49
Emergency fund	£28

Illustrate this expenditure by means of a pie chart of radius 5 cm.

(SEG)

14 Tracey asked 50 pupils how they travelled to school. Here are the results.

Type of travel	Number	Percentage
Special bus	23	
Public transport	14	
Walked	8	
Car	5	
TOTAL	50	

She wants to draw a pie chart.

a Work out the percentages and fill them in on a copy of the table.

b Draw the pie chart.

(MEG)

15 a Give two criticisms of this graph.

b From the graph, estimate the number of building societies in 1980.

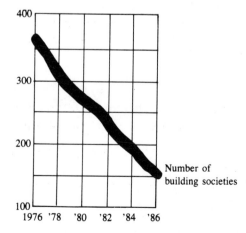

(MEG)

16 The distances travelled by a number of children on their way to school each day are shown on the histogram below:

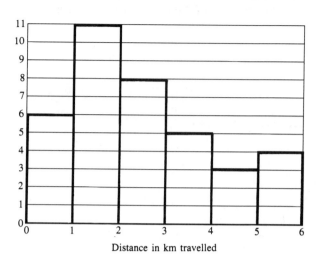

Distance in km travelled

a How many children live between 3 and 4 kilometres from the school?

b Those living more than 3 km from the school qualify for a free bus pass. How many children qualify for a free bus pass?

c What is the median of the distances travelled by the children?

(SEG)

17 The number of goals scored in each of the eleven First Division Football League matches one Saturday last season was

0, 0, 1, 1, 2, 2, 4, 5, 6, 6, 6.

Find

a the mode,

b the median,

c the mean.

(MEG)

18 Samantha and Teresa both did ten Mathematics home-works. Here are their marks out of ten.

Samantha	10	10	7	4	9	8	5	2	9	8
Teresa	5	7	6	8	6	8	7	8	7	6

a Work out the mean mark for each of them.

b Work out the range for each of them.

c Say who you think was better at maths. Give a reason for your answer.

(MEG)

19 In Bhupinder's year group at school, there are 120 boys. She asked each of the boys how many sisters he has. Four was the highest number. She made the following table but forgot to show how many of the boys have no sisters.

Number of sisters	0	1	2	3	4
Number of boys		38	34	20	8

a Work out how many of the boys have no sisters.

b On graph paper, draw a bar chart to represent the information.

c Calculate the total of the numbers of sisters of these 120 boys.

d Calculate the mean number of sisters per boy.

(MEG)

20 Nocane school keeps a record of how many fifth year pupils are absent each day. The numbers include pupils absent either through illness or because they are on school trips. For one week the results were:

Class	Monday	Tuesday	Wednesday	Thursday	Friday
5A	3	8	0	2	2
5B	0	12	2	4	4
5C	2	14	1	0	0
5D	2	10	15	1	2
Daily Totals	7		18	7	8

a (i) How many pupils in 5B were absent on Wednesday?
 (ii) What was the total number of absences on Tuesday?
(iii) Which class had full attendance for two days in that week?

b The pie chart illustrates the number of absences on each day. Copy it and fill in the missing labels.

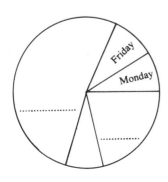

c Which *class* had the smallest total number of absences for the week?

d On one day pupils from all four classes were absent because they went on a trip to a factory. Which day was this?

e On another day pupils from only one class went on a theatre trip. Some were also absent through illness.
 (i) Which class was this?
 (ii) Which day was this?
(iii) Write down an estimate of the number of pupils who went on the theatre trip.
(iv) Describe how you worked out your estimate.

f (i) Calculate the total number of absences for the week for the whole fifth year.
(ii) Calculate the mean number of absences per day.

g What was the median number of absences per day?

h There are no trips planned for the following week. The headteacher decides to use either the mean or the median to estimate the total number of absences for that week.
 (i) Which of these two gives the better estimate?
 (ii) What is the reason for your answer?

(SEG)

21 After a games lesson at Haste School, a teacher recorded to the nearest minute the time taken by each fifth year boy to get changed. The results were as follows:

Time (minutes)	0	1	2	3	4	5	6
Number of boys	15	0	0	5	15	20	4

a (i) How many fifth year boys were present for that lesson?
(ii) How many of these boys did not do games?

b State the median time for **all** the boys.

c (i) Calculate the mean time for **all** the boys.
(ii) Explain why your answer is only an estimate.

d The teacher wants to compare the time taken by the boys to get changed with the time taken by the girls to get changed. he is not sure whether to use the mean or the median.
 (i) Which of these averages represents more accurately the time taken by the boys to get changed?
 (ii) Explain your answer to **d** (i).
(iii) Describe a more accurate way to calculate the average time taken by the boys to get changed. (Do not actually carry out this calculation.)

(SEG)

22 A greengrocer takes delivery of 200 grapefruit. The graph shows the cumulative frequency distribution of their weights.

a From the graph estimate (i) the median, (ii) the interquartile range.

b The greengrocer classifies the fruit as follows:

less than 200 grams:	small
between 200 and 250 grams:	medium
over 250 grams:	large

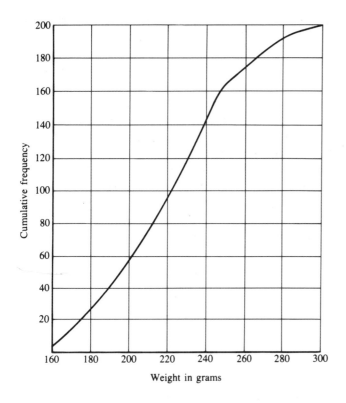

Weight in grams

Estimate the number of medium-sized grapefruit in the consignment.

(MEG)

23 a In the heats of a one hundred metres freestyle swimming competition, the times of the 80 competitors were as follows:

Time (seconds)	56 –	60 –	64 –	68 –	72 –	76 –	80 –	84–88
Frequency	11	25	16	10	7	5	4	2

Calculate an estimate of the mean time.

b Sharon is a javelin thrower. For each throw, the probabilities that she will achieve certain lengths are given in the (incomplete) table below.
(A 'no throw' is counted as 0 m, and is therefore included in '0–'.)

Length of throw (metres)	0 –	40 –	45 –	50 –	55 –
Probability	0.25	0.35	0.2	0.15	

Find the probability that a throw is
(i) shorter than 50 m,
(ii) at least 55 m long.
In a competition Sharon has 3 throws, and the results of the competition is determined by the length of her longest

throw. Assuming that her throws are independent, find the probability that
(iii) her longest throw is shorter than 50 m,
(iv) her longest throw is shorter than 45 m,
 (v) her longest throw is between 45 m and 50 m long.
In another competition Sharon has 6 throws.
(vi) Find, correct to 3 decimal places, the probability that her longest throw is at least 55 m long.

(MEG)

24 Mrs. Tyson, an agent for a firm, kept a record of the time she spent (including travelling time) on each customer she saw.

During one particular 5 day week, she saw 80 customers and the record of the times spent on them is summarised in the following table.

Time (t minutes)	$20<t\leqslant25$	$25<t\leqslant30$	$30<t\leqslant35$	$35<t\leqslant40$	$40<t\leqslant45$	$45<t\leqslant50$
Number of customers	8	10	10	30	18	4

a Find the mean number of customers Mrs. Tyson saw per day during this week.

b Mrs. Tyson's normal working week is 40 hours. Calculate an estimation of the number of hours overtime which she worked during this week.

c Calculate an estimate of the mean length of time Mrs. Tyson spent per customer.

d On graph paper, draw a cumulative frequency diagram for this distribution. (Use a scale of 2 cm to represent 5 minutes on the time axis and 2 cm to represent 10 customers on the cumulative frequency axis.)

e Use your diagram to estimate
 (i) the interquartile range for this distribution,
(ii) the number of customers on each of whom Mrs. Tyson spent more than the mean length of time found in part **c**.

(MEG)

25 A school entered 50 candidates for GCSE Mathematics. There are two papers, each marked out of a maximum of 50. The marks obtained in Paper 1 are shown in the table and illustrated by the frequency diagram.

Mark range	0–4	5–9	10–14	15–19	20–24	25–29	30–34	35–39	40–44	45–49
Number of candidates	0	0	1	1	2	8	19	14	4	1

a Calculate an estimate of the mean mark obtained in Paper 1.

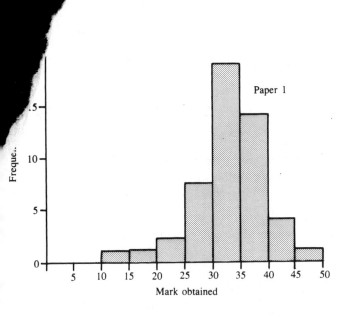

The marks obtained in Paper 2 are shown below.

27	18	31	12	16	37	24	42	15	23
27	27	42	21	3	12	27	24	34	13
9	29	19	32	24	26	33	15	24	25
24	30	23	13	17	6	39	19	18	38
12	18	18	26	31	24	49	12	23	29

b Complete a frequency table for the marks in Paper 2. Use the same classes 0–4, 5–9, etc. as for Paper 1.

c On your graph paper illustrate the data for Paper 2 using the same scales as the frequency diagram for Paper 1.

d Comment briefly on the difference between the candidates' performances in the two papers. (You may like to use the fact that the mean mark for Paper 2 is 23.6.)

(MEG)

26 The pupils of 5A were asked to say how far they travelled to school every day. Their answers were grouped into 2 km intervals. For example, three pupils travelled between 10 and 12 km each day.

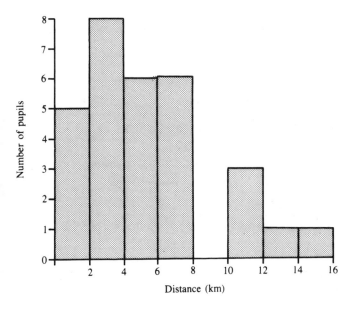

The diagram is a histogram of the distances travelled to school each day by the pupils of class 5A.

a Into which 2 km interval was the greatest number of pupils' answers placed?

b Which 2 km interval contained no answers?

c Gwen said she walked about 7.5 km every day. In which 2 km interval was her answer placed?

d Using the mid-points of the class interval, for example using 13 km as the value for the interval 12 km to 14 km, calculate the mean (average) distance travelled to school each day by the pupils of 5A

(WJEC)

27 Janine throws an ordinary dice.

a What is the probability she gets a 3?

To win a game she needs a 3 or a 5.

b What is the probability that she wins?

(MEG)

28 The sides of a new hexagonal pencil are marked with the numbers one to six.

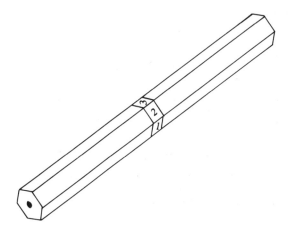

The pencil is rolled across a table and the score is read from the top face. Write down, as a fraction in its lowest terms, the probability of scoring

a a six,

b an odd number,

c a number greater than four.

(MEG)

29 Pupils in a certain class play hockey or tennis but not both. The numbers playing each sport are shown in the table.

	Hockey	Tennis
Boys	8	7
Girls	5	9

A member of the class arrives in the classroom. What is the probability that this pupil plays hockey?

(SEG)

30 Each letter of the word

C A E R O N N E N

is written on identical squares of cardboard, one letter per card, and the cards placed in a bag.

a The cards are well shuffled and a card is taken out of the bag.
(i) What is the probability that the letter on the card is R?
(ii) Which letter is most likely to be chosen?
What is the probability of this letter being chosen?

b A card is taken out of the bag and not replaced. Another card is then taken out of the bag.
What is the probability that the two cards have the letter E on them?

(WJEC)

31 John has bought five of the 500 tickets in a raffle.

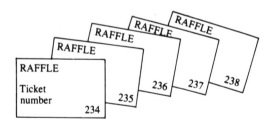

To win the prize you must be present when the tickets are drawn, so John goes along.

Three tickets are drawn.

In each case no-one is there to claim the prize.

What is the probability that one of John's tickets will be drawn next?

(MEG)

32 Chris taped five pop broadcasts, each on a separate tape.

The broadcasts lasted for 40 minutes, 55 minutes, 30 minutes, 42 minutes and 48 minutes.

a Chris picks a tape at random.

What is the probability that the chosen broadcast w
for more than ¾ hour?

b Find the mean length of time of the five recordings.

(LEA

33 John cycles to school on average 3 days out of 5. Otherwise he goes by bus. Bill cycles to school on average 2 days out of 5. Otherwise the walks. Find the probability that, on a certain school day

a they both will cycle to school,

b only one of them will cycle to school.

(LEAG)

34 Mr. Jones travels to work by car on five days each week. He has to cross three busy junctions. He finds that he is delayed three times a week at the first junction, twice a week at the second junction, and once a week at the third junction. A delay at one junction does not affect a delay at any other junction.

a Copy and complete the figure using D for delay and N for no delay in the Outcome column.

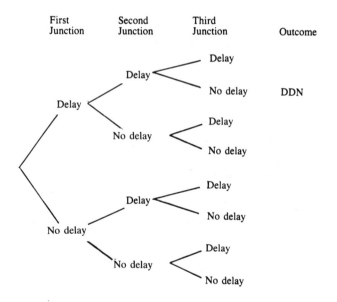

b Find the probability that, on any morning, he will arrive at work without being delayed.

c Find the probability that, on any morning, he will be delayed at only *one* of the three junctions.

(LEAG)

35 A bag contains 5 red discs, 4 white discs and 1 blue disc.

Two discs are to be chosen at random, without replacement.

a Copy and complete the probability tree diagram.

44

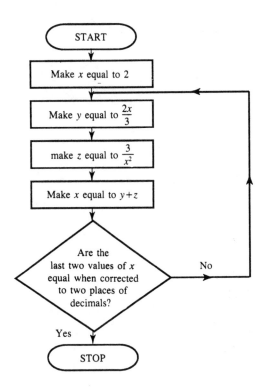

START

Make x equal to 2

Make y equal to $\frac{2x}{3}$

make z equal to $\frac{3}{x^2}$

Make x equal to $y+z$

Are the last two values of x equal when corrected to two places of decimals?

No

Yes

STOP

a Work through the flow diagram, writing down the values of x, y and z in a table, as shown, recording only the first three decimal places of your answers.

x	y	z
2	1.333	

b Cube the last value of x and comment on the result.

c Give the last value of x correct to two decimal places.

(MEG)

Answers

Numbers and Measures

1 1, 8, 2, 4   **2** 1, 25, 5   **3** 1, 13
4 2, 4, 6, 8, 10, 12, 14, 16, 18, 20
5 1, 3, 5, 7, 9, 11, 13, 15, 17, 19
6 2, 3, 5, 7, 11, 13, 17, 19, 23, 29
7 6, 12, 18, 24, 30, 36, 42
8 7, 14, 21, 28, 35, 42

CHECKPOINT 2

1 1, 50, 2, 25, 5, 10   **2** 2, 5   **3** 2×5^2 **4** $2^4 \times 5^2$ **5** $2 \times 3^2 \times 7$

CHECKPOINT 3

1 9   **2** 8   **3** 56   **4** 70   **5** 18   **6** 50
7 1260   **8** 6300   **9** HCF=9, LCM=990
10 HCF=21, LCM=2940

CHECKPOINT 4

1 1, 4, 9, 16, 25, 36, 49, 64, 81, 100
2 4, 6, 8, 9, 10, 12, 14, 15, 16, 18, 20, 21, 22, 24, 25, 26, 27, 28, 30, 32
3 1, 3, 6, 10, 15, 21, 28, 36, 45, 55   **4** Pentagonal numbers?
5 –
6 Numbers whose representation by dots (or in this case, small balls or spheres) could be arranged into a three-dimensional cube. For example, 8 could be arranged into a cube 2 high by 2 wide by 2 deep. The first five cube numbers would be 1, 8, 27, 64, 125.
7 Numbers whose representation by dots (or in this case, small balls or spheres) could be arranged into a three-dimensional pyramid. There could, however, be many types of pyramid number. For example, if a square-based pyramid was used as a model, the pyramid numbers would be 1, 5, 14, 30, etc; if a triangular-based pyramid was used as a model, the pyramid numbers would be 1, 4, 10, 20, etc. These are just two examples, because other shapes like rectangles, pentagons and hexagons could be used to build pyramids.

CHECKPOINT 5

1
a 78   b 12.3   c 7.8   d 57.3   e 5.3   f 26.0
g 6.35   h 1.85   i 1.4   j 19.9   k 1.7   l 3.5
m 3.68   n 13.69   o 42.49   p 45.67   l 101.1   r 2.6
s 5.03   t 50.3

2
a 58.56   b 190.9   c 269.63   d 51.29
e 1579.56   f 248.01   g 2480.1   h 23 457.345
i 24.801   j 1065.66   k 19.57   l 106.13
m 88.72   n 8.872   o 119.977   p 106.6
q 8353.9   r 1.6333   s 2.06   t 67.7

3
a 292.8   b 1369.9   c 705.23   d 7991.53
e 13.342 94   f 128.1103   g 590.384   h 137.147
i 509.7   j 1238.387   k 3221.9   l 110.78
m 60.366   n 1.76   o 329.55   p 1353.05
q 60.017   r 9000.68   s 67.67   t 79.81

CHECKPOINT 6

1
a 0.9   b 2.5   6 1.6   d 5.6   e 0.08
f 5.4   g 3.2   h 40   i 100   j 0.5
k 3.4   l 34   m 0.34   n 55.67   0 556.7
p 55 670   q 556.7   r 5.645   s 0.5645   t 0.056 45
u 0.045   v 2.34   w 0.879   x 5.309   y 0.5309

2
a 103.5   b 1698.6   c 19 049.1   d 10.35   e 169.86
f 190.491   g 2.46   h 22.825   i 15.875   j 114.9
k 69.196   l 0.125

3
a 797.41   b 2551.5   c 94.6192   d 11.5   e 3.412 857
f 6.427 027   g 44.25   h 0.684 210 5   i 0.0909   j 0.8

CHECKPOINT 7

1
a 1.3   b 65.7   c 1.9   d 2.1   e 10.1
f 138.4   g 36.6   h 10.0

2
a 1.3   b 66   c 1.9   d 2.1   e 10
f 140   g 37   h 10

3
a 1070.96   b 3.29   c 0.07   d 0.88   e 3.38
f 39.30   g 1.59   h 0.91

4
a 1000   b 3   c 0.07   d 0.9   e 3
f 40   g 2   h 1

5
a £22.16   b £13.56   c 23 grams   d 2.3 cm^2 e 1.95 cm^3

6 18 000, 22 000, 26 000, 34 000 and 45 000

CHECKPOINT 8

1
a 45, 47   b 21, 23   c 385.25, 431.25
d 2.68, 3   e 41, 43   f 7, 9
g 404.25, 446.25   h 1.4, 1.54   i 5.89, 6.34
j 0.158, 0.191   k 35.36, 38.34   l 2.796, 3.734

2
a 4.5, 4.7   b 2.1, 2.3   c 3.8525, 4.3125
d 2.68, 3   e 83.9, 84.1   f 23.3, 23.5
g 1622.9125, 1631.1325   h 1.7677, 1.7769   i 35.6, 60.67
j 2.863, 3.061   k 1.671, 1.775   l 49.817, 160.65

3 £32, £80

4 Perimeter 34.4, 34.8   Area 58.8225, 60.0875

5 Volume 1.929 781 125, 1.976 656 375   Surface Area 9.300 15, 9.450 15

CHECKPOINT 9

1
a $4\frac{3}{5}$ b $1\frac{2}{7}$ c $7\frac{1}{2}$ d $5\frac{2}{3}$ e $4\frac{3}{4}$ f $5\frac{2}{5}$

g $1\frac{8}{11}$ h $3\frac{3}{8}$ i $2\frac{9}{12}$ j $19\frac{4}{5}$ k $16\frac{3}{4}$ l $2\frac{2}{99}$

2
a $\frac{15}{4}$ **b** $\frac{19}{2}$ **c** $\frac{26}{3}$ **d** $\frac{5}{4}$ **e** $\frac{31}{4}$ **f** $\frac{77}{8}$

g $\frac{45}{16}$ **h** $\frac{165}{32}$ **i** $\frac{35}{3}$ **j** $\frac{43}{4}$ **k** $\frac{39}{20}$ **l** $\frac{202}{99}$

3 The missing numbers are
a 4 **b** 15 **c** 21 **d** 9 **e** 36 **f** 3
g 44 **h** 28 **i** 25 **j** 40 **k** 70 **l** 11

4
a $\frac{5}{7}$ **b** $\frac{5}{12}$ **c** $\frac{2}{3}$ **d** $\frac{4}{5}$ **e** $\frac{4}{5}$ **f** $\frac{7}{13}$

g $\frac{13}{18}$ **h** $\frac{5}{7}$ **i** $\frac{1}{3}$ **j** $\frac{2}{3}$ **k** $\frac{1}{2}$ **l** $\frac{3}{4}$

CHECKPOINT 10

1
a $\frac{1}{3}$ **b** $\frac{4}{5}$ **c** $\frac{5}{6}$ **d** $\frac{5}{9}$ **e** $\frac{4}{6}$ **f** $\frac{5}{7}$

g $\frac{7}{10}$ **h** $\frac{1}{2}$ **i** $\frac{2}{3}$ **j** $\frac{5}{11}$ **k** $\frac{9}{11}$ **l** $\frac{3}{5}$

2 Maths **3** Biology **4** Second bag **5** Susan
6 5B **7** Arsenal **8** The first batch **9** John

CHECKPOINT 11

1
a $\frac{8}{24}$ or $\frac{1}{3}$ **b** $\frac{6}{24}$ or $\frac{1}{4}$ **c** $\frac{3}{24}$ or $\frac{1}{8}$ **d** $\frac{1}{24}$

e $\frac{4}{24}$ or $\frac{1}{6}$ **f** $\frac{18}{24}$ or $\frac{3}{4}$ **g** $\frac{14}{24}$ or $\frac{7}{12}$ **h** $\frac{9}{24}$ or $\frac{3}{8}$

i $\frac{15}{24}$ or $\frac{5}{8}$ **j** $\frac{6}{24}$ or $\frac{1}{4}$

2
a $\frac{1}{6}$ **b** $\frac{5}{12}$ **c** $\frac{1}{5}$ **d** $\frac{2}{3}$ **e** $\frac{1}{2}$ **f** $\frac{1}{4}$

3
a $\frac{1}{10}$ **b** $\frac{5}{6}$ **c** $\frac{7}{10}$ **d** $\frac{7}{12}$ **e** $\frac{3}{4}$ **f** $\frac{1}{3}$

4
a $\frac{1}{24}$ **b** $\frac{1}{6}$ **c** $\frac{1}{4}$ **d** $\frac{1}{3}$ **e** $\frac{1}{12}$ **f** $\frac{1}{2}$

g $\frac{2}{3}$ **h** $\frac{3}{4}$ **i** $\frac{9}{16}$ **j** $\frac{7}{32}$

5
a $\frac{1}{4}$ **b** $\frac{2}{5}$ **c** $\frac{1}{10}$ **d** $\frac{1}{2}$ **e** $\frac{17}{20}$ **f** $\frac{3}{4}$

g $\frac{12}{25}$ **h** $\frac{1}{25}$ **i** $\frac{1}{50}$ **j** $\frac{27}{100}$

6
a 100 **b** 45 **c** 36 **d** 39 **e** 80 **f** 16
g 9 **h** 63 **i** 140 **l** $121\frac{1}{2}$

7 3125 (approximately 3000) **8** Approximately 42

CHECKPOINT 12

1
a $\frac{1}{4}$ **b** $\frac{3}{5}$ **c** $\frac{17}{25}$ **d** $\frac{9}{10}$ **e** $\frac{16}{25}$ **f** $\frac{99}{100}$

g $\frac{2}{5}$ **h** $\frac{3}{20}$ **i** $\frac{8}{25}$ **j** $\frac{19}{20}$

2
a 50% **b** 85% **c** 70% **d** 55% **e** 48% **f** 10%
g 24% **h** 12% **i** 50% **j** 44%

3 $\frac{3}{10}$

390

CHECKPOINT 13

1
a 39 **b** 87 **c** 187 **d** 769.5 **e** 40.96 **f** 2475
g 22.72 **h** 6.75 **i** 14.4 **j** 114

2 £243.60 **3** 12 320 **4** £10 260

5 £27.60 **6** £48.62

CHECKPOINT 14

1
a 174 **b** £57.50 **c** £400.20 **d** £47 250 **e** £19 440

2 £208.69 **3** £30.40, £33.12, £36.48 **4** £21.56

5
a 116 **b** £42.50 **c** £278.40 **d** £42 750 **e** £16 560

6 3080 **7** £138.60 **8** 7707.3, 2175.7, 813.1, 310.1

CHECKPOINT 15

1
a 30% **b** 40% **c** 2.5% **d** 35% **e** 15% **f** 75%
g 34% **h** 75% **i** 80% **j** 40% **k** 12.5% **l** 75%

2 43=36%, 56=47%, 78=65%, 89=74%, 94=78%, 102=85%,
112=93%, 65=54%, 105=87.5%, 84=70%, 22=18%, 17=14%,
68=57%, 72=60%, 118=98%, 88=73%, 71=59%, 59=49%, 60=50%

3 The percentages of rotten potatoes are 15%, 16.7% and 17.5%. Therefore the first bag has the best potatoes.

4 The percentages of female teachers are 60%, 56% and 44%. Therefore the first school has the largest percentage of female staff.

5 Car seat, 17.9% Microwave, 6.9% Camera, 18.2%

CHECKPOINT 16

1
a 75% **b** 80% **c** 87.5% **d** 90% **e** 50% **f** 20%
g 25% **h** 18.75% **i** 66.7% **j** 8.3% **k** 83.3% **l** 55.6%

2
a 0.75 **b** 0.8 **c** 0.875 **d** 0.9 **e** 0.5 **f** 0.2
g 0.25 **h** 0.1875 **i** 0.6 (recurring) **j** 0.083 (recurring)
k 0.83 recurring) **l** 0.5 (recurring)

3
a $\frac{1}{10}$ **b** $\frac{4}{5}$ **c** $\frac{3}{10}$ **d** $\frac{7}{20}$ **e** $\frac{16}{25}$ **f** $\frac{2}{25}$

g $\frac{1}{200}$ **h** $\frac{1}{20}$ **i** $\frac{1}{2}$ **j** $\frac{3}{8}$ **k** $\frac{9}{20}$ **l** $\frac{1}{4}$

4
a 10% **b** 80% **c** 30% **d** 35% **e** 64% **f** 8%
g 0.5% **h** 5% **i** 50% **j** 37.5% **k** 45% **l** 25%

5
a $\frac{4}{5}$ **b** $\frac{8}{25}$ **c** $\frac{1}{4}$ **d** $\frac{7}{10}$ **e** $\frac{49}{50}$ **f** $\frac{11}{20}$

g $\frac{2}{5}$ **h** $\frac{12}{25}$ **i** $\frac{13}{20}$ **j** $\frac{1}{2}$ **k** $\frac{3}{4}$ **l** $\frac{99}{100}$

6
a 0.8 **b** 0.32 **c** 0.25 **d** 0.7 **e** 0.98 **f** 0.55
g 0.4 **h** 0.48 **i** 0.65 **j** 0.5 **k** 0.75 **l** 0.99

CHECKPOINT 17

1
a 2:3 **b** 3:4 **c** 1:5 **d** 5:6 **e** 6:7 **f** 7:4
g 3:5 **h** 2:7 **i** 1:10 **j** 8:17 **k** 1:100 **l** 5:6
m 5:7 **n** 8:73 **o** 1:4 **p** 1:5

2 91:73 **3** 45:205 or 9:41 **4** 84:12 or 7:1

CHECKPOINT 18

1 (all answers in kilograms)
a 12 and 24 **b** 27 and 9 **c** 30 and 6
d 20 and 16 **e** 8 and 28 **f** 32 and 4
g 3 and 33 **h** 15 and 21 **i** 34 and 2
j 10 and 26

2
a £75 and £25 **b** £40 and £60 **c** £20 and £80
d £62.50 and £37.50 **e** £87.50 and £12.50 **f** £50 and £50
g £10 and £90 **h** £70 and £30 **i** £95 and £5
j £15 and £85

3 £9375 and £15 625

4 £6.20 and £9.30. Opinions will vary on the fairness of this distribution. One point worth making is that the division ratio only reflects costs. If both girls worked on the stall for, say, four hours, it could be argued that the cost-based ratio is unfair to Jane and that a more complicated ratio involving both costs and labour should be used (eg £1 per hour each, remainder divided on a costs ratio). The extreme alternative to a strict cost-based division is a simple 50:50 split, perhaps taking out the £1.20 and £1.80 first.

5 See previous answer. Cost-based shares are 9, 12 and 15 sweets.

CHECKPOINT 19

1
$8 + 5 = 13$ $8 + -5 = 3$
$-8 + 5 = -3$ $-8 + -5 = -13$
$8 - 5 = 3$ $8 - -5 = 13$
$-8 - 5 = -13$ $-8 - -5 = -3$

2
$3 + 7 = 10$ $3 + -7 = -4$
$-3 + 7 = 4$ $-3 + -7 = -10$
$3 - 7 = -4$ $3 - -7 = 10$
$-3 - 7 = -10$ $-3 - -7 = 4$

3
$13 + 9 = 22$ $13 + -9 = 4$
$-13 + 9 = -4$ $-13 + -9 = -22$
$13 - 9 = 4$ $13 - -9 = 22$
$-13 - 9 = -22$ $-13 - -9 = -4$

4
$11 + 11 = 22$ $11 + -11 = 0$
$-11 + 11 = 0$ $-11 + -11 = -22$
$11 - 11 = 0$ $11 - -11 = 22$
$-11 - 11 = -22$ $-11 - -11 = 0$

5
$5 + 23 = 28$ $5 + -23 = -18$
$-5 + 23 = 18$ $-5 + -23 = -28$
$5 - 23 = -18$ $5 - -23 = 28$
$-5 - 23 = -28$ $-5 - -23 = 18$

CHECKPOINT 20

1
$10 \times 5 = 50$ $10 \div 5 = 2$
$-10 \times 5 = -50$ $-10 \div 5 = -2$
$10 \times -5 = -50$ $10 \div -5 = -2$
$-10 \times -5 = 50$ $-10 \div -5 = 2$

2
$12 \times 8 = 96$ $12 \div 8 = 1.5$
$-2 \times 8 = -96$ $-12 \div 8 = -1.5$
$12 \times -8 = -96$ $12 \div -8 = -1.5$
$-12 \times -8 = 96$ $-12 \div -8 = 1.5$

3
$6.5 \times 5 = 32.5$ $6.5 \div 5 = 1.3$
$-6.5 \times 5 = -32.5$ $-6.5 \div 5 = -1.3$
$6.5 \times -5 = -32.5$ $6.5 \div -5 = -1.3$
$-6.5 \times -5 = 32.5$ $-6.5 \div -5 = 1.3$

4
$1.2 \times 0.4 = 0.48$ $1.2 \div 0.4 = 3$
$-1.2 \times 0.4 = -0.48$ $-1.2 \div 0.4 = -3$
$1.2 \times -0.4 = -0.48$ $1.2 \div -0.4 = -3$
$-1.2 \times -0.4 = 0.48$ $-1.2 \div -0.4 = 3$

CHECKPOINT 21

1
a 15 625 **b** 7776 **c** 100 **d** 1000 **e** 10 000 **f** 128

g $\frac{1}{16}$ **h** $\frac{1}{5}$ **i** 10 **j** 1 **k** $\frac{1}{64}$ **l** 1

m 1 **n** 35 **o** $\frac{1}{256}$ **p** $\frac{1}{216}$ **q** $\frac{1}{1000}$ **r** $\frac{1}{100\,000}$

2
a 2^5 **b** 3^9 **c** 4^{10} **d** 2^{11} **e** 10^5 **f** 10^6
g 3^4 **h** 5^5 **i** 3^0 **j** 4^0 **k** 2^3 **l** 10^1
m 10^5 **n** 10^0 **o** 10^{-2} **p** 10^5

CHECKPOINT 22

1
a 3.7×10^4 **b** 3.7×10^3 **c** 3.7×10^5
d 1.5×10^5 **e** 6.5×10^8 **f** 6.5×10^7
g 6.5×10^6 **h** 6.5×10^5 **i** 6.5×10^4
j 6.5×10^3 **k** 6.5×10^2 **l** 6.5×10^1

2
a 200 000 **b** 300 000 000 **c** 17 000
d 3 450 000 000 **e** 1 600 000 000 **f** 3800
g 8300 **h** 472 000 **i** 6 730 000
j 1 990 000 000 000 **k** 730 **l** 80 900 000 000

3
a 3.7×10^{-1} **b** 4.0×10^{-3} **c** 4.5×10^{-6}
d 5.6×10^{-8} **e** 5.78×10^{-4} **f** 1.0×10^{-7}
g 6.5×10^{-1} **h** 6.5×10^{-2} **i** 6.5×10^{-3}
j 6.5×10^{-4} **k** 6.5×10^{-5} **l** 6.5×10^{-6}

4
a 0.000 02 **b** 0.000 000 03 **c** 0.000 17
d 0.000 000 003 45 **e** 0.000 000 001 6 **f** 0.0038
g 0.0083 **h** 0.000 047 2 **i** 0.000 006 73
j 0.000 000 000 001 99 **k** 0.073 **l** 0.000 000 000 809

5
a The lifetime of an omega particle is 1.1×10^{-10} seconds.
b The mass of the Earth is 5.967×10^{24} kg.
c The average distance of Uranus from the Sun is 2.869×10^9 km.
d A large orange contains 1.6×10^{-2} grams of vitamin C.
e The moon orbits at an average distance of 3.84×10^5 km from the Earth.
f A light-year, which is the distance travelled by light in one year is equal to 9.4605×10^{15} metres.

CHECKPOINT 23

a 8.5×10^4 **b** 2.25×10^8 **c** 4.875×10^7
d 1.12×10^{-2} **e** 4.615×10^{-4} **f** 6.08×10^{13}
g 3.4532×10^8 **h** 4.75×10^3 **i** 8.3×10^5
j 3.6855×10^{-10} **k** 1.6842×10^1 **l** 9.1753×10^3
m 1.3158×10^7 **n** 8.3×10^{-11} **o** 9.6923×10^{-5}

CHECKPOINT 24

1
a $\begin{pmatrix} 8 & 6 \\ 6 & 4 \end{pmatrix}$ **b** $\begin{pmatrix} 2 & 6 \\ 0 & 0 \end{pmatrix}$ **c** $\begin{pmatrix} 15 & 18 \\ 9 & 6 \end{pmatrix}$ **d** $\begin{pmatrix} 15 & 0 \\ 15 & 10 \end{pmatrix}$

e $\begin{pmatrix} 30 & 18 \\ 24 & 16 \end{pmatrix}$ **f** $\begin{pmatrix} 30 & 0 \\ 30 & 20 \end{pmatrix}$ **g** $\begin{pmatrix} 10 & 12 \\ 6 & 4 \end{pmatrix}$ **h** $\begin{pmatrix} 20 & -12 \\ 24 & 16 \end{pmatrix}$

2
a $\begin{pmatrix} 15 \\ -2 \\ 6 \end{pmatrix}$ **b** $\begin{pmatrix} 3 \\ 20 \\ 11 \end{pmatrix}$ **c** $\begin{pmatrix} 4 \\ 8 \\ 17 \end{pmatrix}$ **d** $\begin{pmatrix} 11 \\ 13 \\ 17 \end{pmatrix}$

e $\begin{pmatrix} -1 \\ 12 \\ -6 \end{pmatrix}$ **f** $\begin{pmatrix} -12 \\ 45 \\ 33 \end{pmatrix}$ **g** $\begin{pmatrix} 200 \\ -175 \\ 150 \end{pmatrix}$ **h** $\begin{pmatrix} 3 \\ 145 \\ 88 \end{pmatrix}$

3
a $\begin{pmatrix} 9 & 11 & 4 \\ 6 & -1 & 2 \\ 2 & 5 & 0 \end{pmatrix}$ **b** $\begin{pmatrix} -9 & -7 & -3 \\ -1 & 3 & 0 \\ 8 & 4 & 9 \end{pmatrix}$

c $\begin{pmatrix} -10 & 5 & -15 \\ 5 & 10 & 15 \\ 25 & 35 & 45 \end{pmatrix}$ **d** $\begin{pmatrix} 12 & 18 & 24 \\ 24 & 0 & -6 \\ 30 & 12 & 0 \end{pmatrix}$ **f** $\begin{pmatrix} 0 & 1 \\ 1 & 0 \end{pmatrix}$ **g** $\begin{pmatrix} 0 & -1 \\ -1 & 0 \end{pmatrix}$ **h** $\begin{pmatrix} 0 & -1 \\ -1 & 0 \end{pmatrix}$

e $\begin{pmatrix} 16 & 24 & 32 \\ 32 & 0 & -8 \\ 40 & 16 & 0 \end{pmatrix}$ **f** $\begin{pmatrix} 25 & 30 & 8 \\ 14 & -3 & 7 \\ 1 & 13 & 0 \end{pmatrix}$

5
a $\begin{pmatrix} -29 & 54 & -12 \\ 12 & 6 & 0 \\ 36 & -6 & 8 \end{pmatrix}$ **b** $\begin{pmatrix} 27 & -18 & -6 \\ 26 & -34 & 31 \\ 1 & 6 & -8 \end{pmatrix}$

g $\begin{pmatrix} 10 & 22 & -5 \\ 11 & 4 & 14 \\ 14 & 29 & 27 \end{pmatrix}$ **h** $\begin{pmatrix} -14 & -1 & -23 \\ -3 & 10 & 17 \\ 15 & 31 & 45 \end{pmatrix}$

CHECKPOINT 26

Answers will vary.

CHECKPOINT 27

1
a 36 cm and 32 cm²   **b** 166 m and 1380 m²
c 556 mm and 18 645 mm²   **d** 25.8 cm and 35.6 cm²
e 13.2 m and 9.45 m²   **f** 21.4 cm and 24.82 cm²
g 7.9 m and 3.375 m²   **h** 226 cm and 2136 cm²

2 Answers will vary with the accuracy of each individual's measurements of the shapes.

3
a 25 cm and 30 cm²   **b** 16 m and 9.25 m²
c 28.2 m and 28.72 m²   **d** 40.4 m and 49.31 m²
Part **d** raises some interesting questions about the minimum data necessary to calculate area and perimeter. You cannot be certain from the diagram of the width of either leg of the ''H'' shape, but you can be certain that they have a total width of 5.6 m (8.7 m − 3.1 m) and hence their total area can be calculated.

4
a 6 m   **b** £239.76   **c** 4 m²   **d** £39.96

CHECKPOINT 28

a 40 cm²   **b** 50.76 m²   **c** 32.93 mm²
d 5.076 m²   **e** 4058.4 cm²

2 Answers will vary with the accuracy of an individual student's measurement of the shapes.

CHECKPOINT 29

1
a 20 cm²   **b** 25.38 m²   **c** 16.465 mm²
d 2.538 m²   **e** 2029.2 cm²

2 Answers will vary with the accuracy of an individual student's measurement of the shapes.

CHECKPOINT 30

1
a 12.5 cm²   **b** 55.935 m²   **c** 25.2 mm²
d 14.25 cm²   **e** 99.715 m²

2 Answers will vary with the accuracy of each individual's measurements of the shapes.

3
a 34.5 cm²   **b** 544 mm²   **c** 50 m²
d 162 cm²   **e** 17.1 m²   **f** 30.175 cm²

CHECKPOINT 31

1
a 25.1 cm and 50.2 cm²   **b** 50.2 cm and 201.0 cm²
c 11.0 m and 9.7 m²   **d** 67.8 mm and 366.3 mm²
e 753.6 m and 45 216.0 m²   **f** 270.0 mm and 5805.9 mm²

2
a 31.42 cm and 78.55 cm²   **b** 77.29 cm and 475.35 cm²
c 41.16 m and 134.8 m²   **d** 202.97 mm and 3278.02 mm²
e 45.56 mm and 165.15 mm²   **f** 74.78 mm and 444.94 mm²

4
a $\begin{pmatrix} 14 & -2 & -4 & 0 \\ 11 & 0 & 5 & -4 \end{pmatrix}$ **b** $\begin{pmatrix} -4 & -6 & 2 & 0 \\ -5 & 4 & -5 & 6 \end{pmatrix}$

c $\begin{pmatrix} 4 & 6 & -2 & 0 \\ 5 & -4 & 5 & -6 \end{pmatrix}$ **d** $\begin{pmatrix} 50 & -40 & -10 & 0 \\ 30 & 20 & 0 & 10 \end{pmatrix}$

e $\begin{pmatrix} 33 & -8 & -9 & 0 \\ 25 & 2 & 10 & -7 \end{pmatrix}$ **f** $\begin{pmatrix} -2 & -26 & 4 & 0 \\ -9 & 16 & -15 & 20 \end{pmatrix}$

g $\begin{pmatrix} 11 & -18 & -1 & 0 \\ 4 & 10 & -5 & 9 \end{pmatrix}$ **h** $\begin{pmatrix} 88 & -6 & -26 & 0 \\ 71 & -4 & 35 & -30 \end{pmatrix}$

5
a $\begin{pmatrix} 156 & 33 \\ 167 & 22 \end{pmatrix}$ **b** $\begin{pmatrix} 118 & 54 \\ 133 & 64 \end{pmatrix}$ **c** $(300 \quad 86)$

d $(274 \quad 87)$ **e** $\begin{pmatrix} 274 & 87 \\ 300 & 86 \end{pmatrix}$ **f** £8732

CHECKPOINT 25

1
a $\begin{pmatrix} 15 & 20 \\ 10 & 5 \end{pmatrix}$ **b** $\begin{pmatrix} 15 & 20 \\ 10 & 5 \end{pmatrix}$ **c** $\begin{pmatrix} 30 & 33 \\ 15 & 12 \end{pmatrix}$ **d** $\begin{pmatrix} 24 & 27 \\ 21 & 18 \end{pmatrix}$

e $\begin{pmatrix} 20 & 15 \\ 5 & 10 \end{pmatrix}$ **f** $\begin{pmatrix} 10 & 5 \\ 15 & 20 \end{pmatrix}$ **g** $\begin{pmatrix} 30 & 15 \\ 15 & 30 \end{pmatrix}$ **h** $\begin{pmatrix} 30 & 15 \\ 15 & 30 \end{pmatrix}$

i $\begin{pmatrix} 0 & 25 \\ 25 & 0 \end{pmatrix}$ **j** $\begin{pmatrix} 0 & 25 \\ 25 & 0 \end{pmatrix}$ **k** $\begin{pmatrix} 15 & 30 \\ 30 & 15 \end{pmatrix}$ **l** $\begin{pmatrix} 15 & 30 \\ 30 & 15 \end{pmatrix}$

2
a $\begin{pmatrix} 6 & 13 \\ 0 & 1 \end{pmatrix}$ **b** $\begin{pmatrix} 6 & 14 \\ 0 & 1 \end{pmatrix}$ **c** $\begin{pmatrix} 8 & 11 \\ 0 & 1 \end{pmatrix}$ **d** $\begin{pmatrix} 8 & 16 \\ 0 & 1 \end{pmatrix}$

e $\begin{pmatrix} 7 & 8 \\ 1 & 2 \end{pmatrix}$ **f** $\begin{pmatrix} 4 & 7 \\ 2 & 5 \end{pmatrix}$ **g** $\begin{pmatrix} 12 & 17 \\ 0 & 1 \end{pmatrix}$ **h** $\begin{pmatrix} 12 & 24 \\ 0 & 1 \end{pmatrix}$

i $\begin{pmatrix} 11 & 13 \\ 1 & 2 \end{pmatrix}$ **j** $\begin{pmatrix} 6 & 11 \\ 3 & 7 \end{pmatrix}$ **k** $\begin{pmatrix} 12 & 12 \\ 1 & 2 \end{pmatrix}$ **l** $\begin{pmatrix} 8 & 9 \\ 4 & 6 \end{pmatrix}$

3
a $\begin{pmatrix} 6 & -9 \\ 0 & 1 \end{pmatrix}$ **b** $\begin{pmatrix} 6 & -12 \\ 0 & 1 \end{pmatrix}$ **c** $\begin{pmatrix} 2 & -3 \\ 0 & -1 \end{pmatrix}$ **d** $\begin{pmatrix} 2 & -3 \\ 0 & -1 \end{pmatrix}$

e $\begin{pmatrix} 7 & 6 \\ -1 & -2 \end{pmatrix}$ **f** $\begin{pmatrix} 4 & -6 \\ -2 & 1 \end{pmatrix}$ **g** $\begin{pmatrix} 3 & 3 \\ 0 & -1 \end{pmatrix}$ **h** $\begin{pmatrix} 3 & -3 \\ 0 & -1 \end{pmatrix}$

i $\begin{pmatrix} 9 & 6 \\ -1 & -2 \end{pmatrix}$ **j** $\begin{pmatrix} 6 & -6 \\ -3 & 1 \end{pmatrix}$ **k** $\begin{pmatrix} 2 & 0 \\ 1 & 2 \end{pmatrix}$ **l** $\begin{pmatrix} 2 & 0 \\ -1 & 2 \end{pmatrix}$

4
a $\begin{pmatrix} -3 & 2 & -1 \\ 1 & 3 & 0 \end{pmatrix}$ **b** $\begin{pmatrix} -1 & -3 & 0 \\ 3 & -2 & 1 \end{pmatrix}$

c $\begin{pmatrix} -1 & -3 & 0 \\ -3 & 2 & -1 \end{pmatrix}$ **d** $\begin{pmatrix} 3 & -2 & 1 \\ 1 & 3 & 0 \end{pmatrix}$

e not possible

3
a 10 cm and 5 cm
c 8 m and 4 m
b 100 cm and 50 cm
d 33 mm and 16.5 mm

4
a 10.1 cm and 5.0 cm
c 2.6 m and 1.3 m
b 18.9 cm and 9.5 cm
d 11.8 mm and 5.9 mm

5 Aproximately 19.5 metres
6 Approximately 11 kilograms

CHECKPOINT 32

1
a 9.8 cm^2 and 13.9 cm
c 1130.4 m^2 and 157.7 m
e 14 179.1 cm^2 and 503.6 cm
b 126.6 cm^2 and 45.3 cm
d 19 625 mm^2 and 564 mm
f 348.6 m^2 and 76.7 m

2
a 22.57 m^2 and 19.28 m
c 44.56 cm^2 and 34.85 cm
e 1.51 cm^2 and 15.08 cm
g 29.34 cm^2
b 906.26 m^2 and 232.12 m
d 26.14 cm^2 and 19.43 cm
f 9.14 cm^2 and 12.57 cm
h 96.34 cm^2 and 37.42 cm

CHECKPOINT 33

1
a 9 cm^3 and 31 cm^2
c 4500 mm^3 and 2100 mm^2
e 384.65 cm^3 and 296.73 cm^2
g 588.75 cm^3 and 464 cm^2
b 336 000 cm^3 and 46 900 cm^2
d 870 cm^3 and 687 cm^2
f 0.4823 m^3 and 3.6575 m^2
h 128.52 m^3 and 149.94 m^2

2 72.9 cm^3 and 1406.241 grams
3 140 000 cm^3 and 308 000 grams = 308 kg = 0.308 tonnes

4
a 1250 m^2 b 1500 m^3 c 300 minutes or 5 hours

5
a 0.8831 m^3 (to 4 d.p.)   b 2331 kg (to nearest kg)   c Helicopter

CHECKPOINT 34

1
a 160 cm^3
d 2571.14 mm^3
b 39.936 cm^3
e 284.65 cm^3
c 648.53 cm^3
f 1.83 m^3

2 16m^3

3
a 3.925 m^3 b 5.652 m^3 c 1.727 m^3 d 3730 kg

4
a 9.42 m^3
b 1 m^3 = 1000 litres, so the cone has a volume of 9420 litres and will take 628 seconds to empty.

Numbers and Measures – Practice and revision exercise (Arithmetic)

1 –

2
a 1, 24, 2, 12, 3, 8, 4, 6   b 1, 51, 3, 17
c 1, 100, 2, 50, 4, 25, 5, 20, 10

3
a 2, 3, 5   b 2, 3, 7   c 3, 5, 7

4
a 2×2×3×5   b 2×3×5×7   c 2×2×2×3×3×3×13

5
a HCF = 2 LCM = 40   b HCF = 2 LCM = 72
c HCF = 13 LCM = 130

6 1, 4, 9, 16, 25, 36, 49, 64, 81, 100, 121, 144
7 4, 6, 8, 9, 10, 12, 14, 15, 16, 18, 20, 21
8 1, 3, 6, 10, 15, 21, 28, 36, 45, 55, 66, 78

9
a 92   b 11.9   c 9.2   d 38.9   e 3.3   f 6.5   g 10.9
h 2.5

10
a 118.53   b 620.9   c 190.63   d 20.49   e 621.44
f 4954.89

11
a 807   b 1053.9   c 7287.066   d 51.75

12
a 2.1   b 3.2   c 0.36   d 1.8   e 0.1   f 2   g 20
h 500   i 0.0347   j 0.096   k 4.73   l 0.803   m 2.794
n 0.00012

13
a 166.5   b 444.6   c 1412.35   d 12.478
e 2.1875   f 4.9   g 0.0694   h 58.525

14
a 797.41   b 2551.5   c 94.6192   d 11.5
e 3.364 788 7   f 6.427 027 0

15
a 33.1   b 19.4   c 0.3   d 3.7

16
a 1561.15   3 33.14   c 1.06   d 0.73

17
a 15.75, 24.75   b 887.75, 948.75   c 4.68, 5.35
d 44.46, 100.04

18
a 25.5025, 26.5225   b 2.7358, 2.8824   c 6.8669, 7.4342

19 Perimeter: 35.8 cm, 36.2 cm   Area:. 79.8525 cm^2, 81.6525 cm^2

20
a $2\frac{2}{5}$ b $3\frac{1}{10}$ c $3\frac{6}{7}$ d $1\frac{3}{4}$

21
a $\frac{7}{4}$ b $\frac{11}{3}$ c $\frac{15}{2}$ d $\frac{133}{11}$ e $\frac{41}{6}$

22
a $\frac{2}{5} = \frac{6}{15}$ b $\frac{5}{8} = \frac{10}{16}$ c $\frac{7}{6} = \frac{28}{24}$ d $\frac{3}{7} = \frac{12}{28}$
e $\frac{12}{17} = \frac{48}{68}$ f $\frac{1}{9} = \frac{2}{18}$ g $\frac{11}{12} = \frac{55}{60}$ h $\frac{4}{5} = \frac{52}{65}$

23
a $\frac{5}{6}$ b $\frac{5}{14}$ c $\frac{2}{5}$ d $\frac{2}{3}$ e $\frac{2}{3}$ f $\frac{7}{15}$ g $\frac{13}{15}$

24
a $\frac{3}{8}$ b $\frac{3}{5}$ c $\frac{5}{60}$

25 Biology

26
a $\frac{1}{8}$ b $\frac{5}{24}$ c $\frac{1}{4}$ d $\frac{3}{8}$ e $\frac{5}{12}$ f $\frac{1}{2}$
g $\frac{7}{12}$ h $\frac{5}{6}$ i $\frac{19}{48}$ j $\frac{11}{16}$

27
a $\frac{1}{4}$ b $\frac{1}{2}$ c $\frac{19}{20}$ d $\frac{3}{4}$ e $\frac{21}{25}$ f $\frac{2}{25}$

28
a 150   b 35   c 108   d 9   e 200   f 32
g 36   h 84

29
a $\frac{1}{4}$ b $\frac{1}{2}$ c $\frac{14}{25}$ d $\frac{47}{50}$ e $\frac{8}{25}$

30
a 50%   b 75%   c 30%   d 85%   e 72%

31
a 36   b 138   c 221   d 540   e 51.84   f 9900
g £19.84

32
a 360 **b** £92 **c** £341.55 **d** £26 250 **e** £19 972.44

33
a 304 **b** £80.75 **c** £248 **d** £37 050 **e** £43 240

34
a 64% **b** 60% **c** 24.5% **d** 30% **e** 7%
f 93.75% **g** 45.2% **h** 25% **i** 40% **j** 60%

35

FRACTION	PERCENTAGE	DECIMAL
$\frac{1}{2}$	50%	0.5
$\frac{1}{4}$	25%	0.25
$\frac{3}{4}$	75%	0.75
$\frac{1}{5}$	20%	0.2
$\frac{1}{10}$	10%	0.1
$\frac{3}{20}$	15%	0.15
$\frac{3}{5}$	60%	0.6
$\frac{13}{25}$	52%	0.52
$\frac{1}{25}$	4%	0.04
$\frac{1}{20}$	5%	0.05

36
a 2:5 **b** 2:3 **c** 1:6 **d** 5:7 **e** 4:7
f 9:4 **g** 1:2 **h** 11:21 **i** 1:10 **j** 3:17

37
a 10 kg and 30 kg **b** 32 kg and 8 kg **3** 25 kg and 15 kg
d 35 kg and 5 kg **e** 28 kg and 12 kg

38
a £90 and £30 **b** £48 and £72 **c** £24 and £96
d £75 and £45 **e** £75, £30 and £15

39

$$8 + 15 = 23$$
$$-8 + 15 = 7$$
$$8 - 15 = -7$$
$$-8 - 15 = -23$$

$$8 + -15 = -7$$
$$-8 + -15 = -23$$
$$8 - -15 = 23$$
$$-8 - -15 = 7$$

$$7 + 12 = 19$$
$$-7 + 12 = 5$$
$$7 - 12 = -5$$
$$-7 - 12 = -19$$

$$7 + -12 = -5$$
$$-7 + -12 = -19$$
$$7 - -12 = 19$$
$$-7 - -12 = 5$$

40

$$2 \times 5 = 10$$
$$-2 \times 5 = -10$$
$$2 \times -5 = -10$$
$$-2 \times -5 = 10$$

$$2 \div 5 = 0.4$$
$$-2 \div 5 = 0.4$$
$$2 \div -5 = -0.4$$
$$-2 \div -5 = -0.4$$

$$2.5 \times 10 = 25$$
$$-2.5 \times 10 = -25$$
$$2.5 \times -10 = -25$$
$$-2.5 \times -10 = 25$$

$$2.5 \div 10 = 0.25$$
$$-2.5 \div 10 = -0.25$$
$$2.5 \div -10 = -0.25$$
$$-2.5 \div -10 = 0.25$$

41
a 4096 **b** 32 **c** 100 000 **d** 10 000 **e** 0.1
f $\frac{1}{128}$ **g** $\frac{1}{9}$ **h** $\frac{1}{10\,000}$ **i** 10 **j** 1
k $\frac{1}{64}$ **l** 1

42
a 2^7 **b** 3^9 **c** 4^5 **d** 2^{-2} **e** 10^9 **f** 10^8 **g** 5^0
h 10^0 **i** 2^3 **j** 10^1

43
a 3×10^3 **b** 4.5×10^4 **c** 3.46×10^2 **d** 3.679×10^2
e 2.34×10^{10}

44
a 3 100 000 **b** 56 700 **c** 191 000 000
d 50 670 000 000

45
a 3.0×10^{-5} **b** 1.7×10^{-2} **c** 1.0×10^{-6} **d** $5.3 \times 10^{--5}$
e 9.009×10^{-3}

46
a 0.000 003 1 **b** 0.000 567 **c** 0.000 000 019 1
d 0.000 000 000 506 7

47
a 6.9×10^{-3} **b** 6.321×10^{-3} **c** 5.7×10^{-5}
d 5.81×10^{-11} **e** 1.724×10^{-5}

48
a $\begin{pmatrix} 16 & 2 \\ 5 & 14 \end{pmatrix}$ **b** $\begin{pmatrix} -10 & 2 \\ -5 & 0 \end{pmatrix}$ **c** $\begin{pmatrix} 9 & 6 \\ 0 & 21 \end{pmatrix}$ **d** $\begin{pmatrix} 65 & 0 \\ 25 & 36 \end{pmatrix}$
e $\begin{pmatrix} 74 & 6 \\ 25 & 56 \end{pmatrix}$

49
a $\begin{pmatrix} 11 & 13 & 6 \\ 4 & -3 & 0 \\ 2 & 3 & 0 \end{pmatrix}$ **b** $\begin{pmatrix} -11 & -9 & -5 \\ -1 & 5 & 2 \\ 10 & 8 & 8 \end{pmatrix}$
c $\begin{pmatrix} -15 & 0 & -20 \\ 0 & 15 & 20 \\ 30 & 40 & 35 \end{pmatrix}$ **d** $\begin{pmatrix} 18 & 24 & 30 \\ 18 & -6 & -12 \\ 36 & 18 & 6 \end{pmatrix}$
e $\begin{pmatrix} 24 & 32 & 40 \\ 24 & -8 & -16 \\ 48 & 24 & 8 \end{pmatrix}$ **f** $\begin{pmatrix} 30 & -35 & 13 \\ 9 & -8 & 2 \\ 0 & 6 & -1 \end{pmatrix}$
g $\begin{pmatrix} 10 & 22 & -5 \\ 5 & 4 & 14 \\ 16 & 27 & 20 \end{pmatrix}$ **h** $\begin{pmatrix} -21 & -8 & -30 \\ -6 & 17 & 24 \\ 18 & 34 & 33 \end{pmatrix}$

50
a $\begin{pmatrix} 6 & 10 \\ 9 & 4 \end{pmatrix}$ **b** $\begin{pmatrix} 6 & 15 \\ 6 & 4 \end{pmatrix}$ **c** $\begin{pmatrix} 13 & 39 \\ 14 & 20 \end{pmatrix}$
d $\begin{pmatrix} 14 & 24 \\ 23 & 19 \end{pmatrix}$ **e** $\begin{pmatrix} 39 & 9 \\ 20 & 8 \end{pmatrix}$ **f** $\begin{pmatrix} 10 & 14 \\ 17 & 37 \end{pmatrix}$
g $\begin{pmatrix} 12 & 6 \\ 2 & 14 \end{pmatrix}$ **h** $\begin{pmatrix} 12 & 4 \\ 3 & 14 \end{pmatrix}$ **i** $\begin{pmatrix} 6 & 6 \\ 14 & 2 \end{pmatrix}$
j $\begin{pmatrix} 6 & 4 \\ 21 & 2 \end{pmatrix}$ **k** $\begin{pmatrix} 22 & 10 \\ 51 & 9 \end{pmatrix}$ **l** $\begin{pmatrix} 10 & 18 \\ 29 & 21 \end{pmatrix}$

51
a $\begin{pmatrix} 15 & -14 \\ 0 & 4 \end{pmatrix}$ **b** $\begin{pmatrix} 15 & -26 \\ 0 & 4 \end{pmatrix}$ **c** $\begin{pmatrix} 9 & -4 \\ 0 & -4 \end{pmatrix}$
d $\begin{pmatrix} 9 & -14 \\ 0 & -4 \end{pmatrix}$ **e** $\begin{pmatrix} 5 & 10 \\ -4 & 20 \end{pmatrix}$ **f** $\begin{pmatrix} 3 & -2 \\ -3 & -18 \end{pmatrix}$
g $\begin{pmatrix} 15 & -6 \\ 0 & -1 \end{pmatrix}$ **h** $\begin{pmatrix} 15 & -14 \\ 0 & -1 \end{pmatrix}$ **i** $\begin{pmatrix} 9 & 20 \\ 1 & 5 \end{pmatrix}$
j $\begin{pmatrix} 5 & -4 \\ -5 & 9 \end{pmatrix}$ **k** $\begin{pmatrix} 5 & 10 \\ 1 & 5 \end{pmatrix}$ **l** $\begin{pmatrix} 3 & -2 \\ -3 & 7 \end{pmatrix}$

52
a $\begin{pmatrix} -4 & 3 & 0 \\ 0 & -2 & -5 \end{pmatrix}$ **b** $\begin{pmatrix} 0 & 2 & 5 \\ 4 & -3 & 0 \end{pmatrix}$
c $\begin{pmatrix} 0 & 2 & 5 \\ -4 & 3 & 0 \end{pmatrix}$ **d** $\begin{pmatrix} 4 & -3 & 0 \\ 0 & 2 & 5 \end{pmatrix}$
e not possible
f $\begin{pmatrix} 0 & -1 \\ -1 & 0 \end{pmatrix}$ **g** $\begin{pmatrix} 0 & 1 \\ -1 & 0 \end{pmatrix}$ **h** $\begin{pmatrix} 0 & 1 \\ -1 & 0 \end{pmatrix}$

Area and volume

1 –
2 23 cm and 32.5 cm²   **3** 12 m and 5.24 m²
4 Answers will vary with the accuracy of each individual's measurements of the shape.
5 40.015 cm²   **6** 22 cm and 26 cm²
7 Answers will vary with the accuracy of each individual's measurements of the shape.
8 30 m²   **9** 18 cm and 12 cm²
10 Answers will vary with the accuracy of each individual's measurements of the shape.
11 41.075 cm²
12 Answers will vary with the accuracy of each individual's measurements of the shape.
13 87.08 cm² and 32.86 cm   **14** 14.18 m² and 13.35 m
15 13 mm and 78 mm   **16** 12 cm and 113.04 cm²
17 4.24 m and 1.09 m²   **18** 25.2 cm and 32.17 cm²
19
a 64 cm³ and 112 cm²   **b** 31.4 cm³ and 69.08 cm²
c 17.3 m³ and 63.46 m²   **d** 53.2 cm³ and 95.16 cm²
20
a 20.25 m³   **b** 102.57 cm³   **c** 4186.67 cm³

Numbers and Measures – Past paper questions (numbers)

1
a (i) 34 and 144   (ii) 144   (iii) 13 and 89
b (i) 34   (ii) 55
c (i) 233   (ii) Each new number in the sequence is obtained by adding the previous two numbers, $144 + 89 = 233$
d (i) 1.618 1818   (ii) 1.617 9775   They are approximately equal, ie 1.618 (to 3 d.p.)

2
a 8 (add two previous numbers to get next in sequence)
b 16 (descending square numbers)

3
a (i) $2 \times 3 \times 3 \times 7$ (ii) $2 \times 2 \times 3 \times 5 \times 7$ **b** 1260

4
a 1, 24, 2, 12, 3, 8, 4, 6   **b** 1, 60, 2, 30, 4, 15, 5, 12, 6, 10   **c** 12

5
a 9   **b** 9   **c** 12   **d** 11

6
a 19   **b** 16   **c** 21   **d** 8   **e** 15   **f** 18

7
a 37   **b** 289   **c** 444

8
a 11   **b** Prime   **c** 25   **d** 121

9
a 15   **b** 25   **c** 66

10
a 503   **b** (i) $x - 10$ and $x + 1$ (ii) $x(x + 1)(x - 10)$ **c** 36L

11
a 169   **b** 289

12
a 9 times   **b** any values of x and $9x$
c They are connected by the relationship: number of teeth on large wheel = 9 times the number of teeth on small wheel.

13
a –   **b** 15   **c** 4 metres   **d** –   **e** 6

Decimals, fractions and percentages

1
a £55   **b** £367   **c** £45   **d** £360

2 0.625

3
a £126.12   **b** £12.12   **c** 23p   **d** £322

4
a 57.803 882   **b** 57.8

5
a £7.80   **b** 6 hours 30 minutes   **c** £1.48

6 £147.35

7
a £2.25   **b** £3.30   **c** £3.00

8 50 kg

9
a 3.16   **b** 2   **c** £24.50   **d** 151.50
e £49.5   **f** 201.00   **g** 231.15

10 $\frac{1}{5}$

11
a 1.75   **b** 8.75 pints

12
a 0.875   **b** 12.5%

13
a 252   **b** 25%

14
a $\frac{2}{3}, \frac{5}{7}, \frac{12}{17}, \frac{29}{41}, \frac{70}{99}, \frac{169}{239}$
b 0.444 444 4, 0.510 204 1, 0.498 269 9, 0.500 297 4, 0.499 948 9, 0.500 008 8   The values are closing on 0.5 alternately from above and below.
c $\frac{985}{1393}$ **d** $\frac{q-p}{2p-q}$

15 The blanks should be filled with, 184, 41.4, 225.4, 76.36, 149.04

16
a $\frac{5}{8}$ **b** $\frac{3}{8}$ **c** 6

17 15p

18 250 minutes

19
a 515   **b** 3261   **c** 22.62, 30.77

20 The car has travelled 280 miles using 8 gallons. It has therefore averaged 35 miles per gallon.

21
a 48 kilometres per hour   **b** 37.5 miles per hour

22
a £161   **b** £136   **c** £208   **d** 35 cm by 40 cm by 20 cm

23 12.5 minutes

24 £27

25
a $\frac{3}{8}$ **b** $\frac{1}{8}, \frac{1}{4}, \frac{3}{8}, \frac{1}{2}$

26
a £3   **b** 50p

27
a £76   **b** £1026

28
a 20.88, 1.45   **b** 65.61, 2.733 75

29
a 73.75   **b** £14.24

30
a $\frac{1}{15}$　**b** 90p

31
a (i) 0.1　(ii) 1.4142136　(iii) 3.1415927
b (i) 2 and $\sqrt{9}$　(ii) 2 and π

32
a £21.25　**b** 200

33
a (i) 12 000　(ii) 20 000　**b** (i) $\frac{12\,000}{20\,000}$　(ii) 60%

34　£360

35　£40.25

36
a 11.3%　**b** (i) £2205　(ii) £2950
c 68.6 miles per hour (173.75 miles in 2.5333 hours)

37
a £105　**b** £28.35 and £76.65　**c** 7.665%

38　£120

39
a £7.99　**b** 20%

40　£55 935

41
a Values in table are: £108.75, £118.27, £128.62, £139.87 and £152.12. This is equivalent to 52.12% over the five years.
b £675

42
a £8640　**b** £5240　**c** £1414.80

43　£2012.50

44
a £286　**b** £26　**c** £59　**d** £236　**e** £274.94
f £24.99　**g** Buy the Beovision. If these TVs are bought on instalments, the Beovision only costs £11.11 more than the Flan.

45
a £16　**b** (i) £85.60　(ii) £17.12

46
a £60　**b** £180　**c** £30

47　£26.55

48
a 1 400 000, 600 000　**b** 1 000 000

49　£66

50　6 people

51
a many possibilities　**b** many possibilities　**c** £4.77

52
a 19p　**b** 0.48p　**c** (i) 50 gallons　(ii) 0.38p
d (i) £73.00　(ii) 38 gallons

53
a 57.1%
b A decrease from 38.6 mph to 24.6 mph (this is a decrease of approximately 36%).

54　£2593.74

55
a £276　**b** 26　**c** £6.91

Ratio

1 660 g, 240 g, 210 ml and 135 ml
2 9 grams
3 12 cm and 24 cm
4 200

5
a 6, 18　**b** 14, 9　**c** 9:6

6 80 girls
7 4 tins
8 Jill has 12, Dave has 18.
9 39 for coursework, 26 for the exam.

10
a 64:125
b The 5 cm oranges, having approximately 2.0 times the volume of the 4 cm oranges are the better value because they cost only approximately 1.7 times as much as the 4 cm oranges.

11
a 3 metres　**b** 4

12
a $\frac{1}{15}$　**b** $\frac{1}{5}$

13 1:0.7 Obviously, one of the reduction ratios must be used: a length ratio of 1:0.5 will produce an area ratio of 1:0.25 and a length ratio of 1:0.7 will produce an area ratio of 1:0.49. The required area reduction of about one-half is most closely met by an area ratio of 1:0.49.

14
a $4x$ coins　**b** $x + 60$　**c** $4x = x + 60$, $x = 20$
d 75

15
a 2 ounces　**b** 3 ounces　**c** 15 pounds 12 ounces

Directed numbers

1
a 5°C　**b** 6°C

2 15°C

3
a 5 am　**b** 7°C

4
a −2°C　**b** 10°C

5
a −6°C　**4** 4°C　**c** 2°C

6
a −7°C　**b** 4°C

7
a −10°C　**b** Thursday　**c** 8°C　**d** 1°C　**e** 3°C

Powers and standard form

1
a 6.3×10^8　**b** 7.326×10^{25}

2
a (i) $2 \times 3 \times 5^2$　(ii) $2 \times 2 \times 3^2 \times 7$　**b** (i) 6　(ii) 6301

3 4.369×10^9

4 2.7 minutes

5
a 2.7　**b** 4.7　**c** £458.85

6 1.4×10^{23}

7
a 3　**b** −3　**c** $-\frac{1}{3}$

8
a 40.1995　**b** 1.3323　**c** −5.3291

9 1.21×10^{-2}

10
a Jupiter　**b** Mercury　**c** Jupiter

Matrix arithmetic

1 $\begin{pmatrix} 10 \\ -9 \end{pmatrix}$

2

a

	P	Q	R	S	T
P	0	9	9	12	7
Q	9	0	6	11	16
R	9	6	0	5	10
S	12	11	5	0	5
T	7	16	10	5	0

b $\begin{pmatrix} 419 \\ 536 \\ 434 \\ 447 \\ 440 \end{pmatrix}$

The warehouses should be located in village P to minimise transport costs.

c A matrix for distances from X is:

$$\begin{array}{c} \quad P \quad Q \quad R \quad S \quad T \\ X\begin{pmatrix} 3 & 12 & 6 & 9 & 4 \end{pmatrix} \end{array}$$

Multiplying N by this matrix gives a transport cost index of 404, so this site is even better than one in village P.

3

a $D = \begin{pmatrix} 2 \\ 1 \\ 8 \end{pmatrix}$

b (i) $\begin{pmatrix} 19 \\ 8 \\ 28 \end{pmatrix}$

(ii) The numbers of straights, points and curves in three Trackpac *C*s and two Trackpac *D*s.

c (i) $\begin{pmatrix} 13.05 & 12.05 \end{pmatrix}$

(ii) The respective costs of Trackpac *C* and Trackpac *D*.

Area and volume

1
a 4 cm² **b** 16 cm²
c Sales have doubled, but the second square has four times as much area and therefore appears 4 times bigger, not 2 times bigger.

2 –

3
a 17.3 m **b** 23.2 m² **c** (i) – (ii) 23.5 m

4
a 5 m **b** 20 m

5
a 57° **b** 147° **c** 2.6 m² **d** 10.4 m²

6
a 22 m² **b** 4 **c** 88

7
a 12 m² **b** 24 **c** 1 m by 2 m

8
a (i) 9.22 m (ii) 4.9824 m² **b** 9 m and 5 m²

9
a 0.8 m by 1.5 m **b** 1.2 m² **c** £8.64

10
a 8 at £2 and 2 at £1 **b** 60

11
a 30 cm × 40 cm × 10 cm **b** 6384 cm³ (the easy way to calculate this answer is to subtract 26 × 36 × 6 from 30 × 40 × 10).
c – **d** 15 200 cm³ **e** many answers possible
f A case 80 cm by 30 cm by 40 cm is the most economical.

12
a (i) 2 × 24, 3 × 16, 4 × 12, 6 × 8 (ii) 6 × 8
b (a) (i) 96 cm (ii) 193 cm

13 –

14 –

15
a 4 cm **b** 36 cm²

16 16 m²

17
a 435.615 m² **b** 10

18
a (i) DE and CB (ii) AE and AB **b** – **c** 39 cm²

19
a – **b** 533.5 m²

20
a 336 cm² **b** 0.0336 m²

21
a 112 m² **b** 1.8 m³ **c** 3.5 m **d** 84 m²

22
a 746 m² **b** 261.1 m³ **c** 39 cm

23
a 57 cm **b** 19 cm

24
a 125.6 cm **b** 63 m

25
a 50.24 m² **b** 50.24 %

26
a 410 cm **b** 110 cm **c** 520 cm

27 –

28 Area $= \pi (R^2 - r^2)$
b The formula above can be written as Area $= \pi (R + r)(R - r)$
Using this formula and the values given, we have:
$1180 = \pi \times 25 \times (R - r)$,
giving $(R - r) = 15$ (nearest whole number)
c $R = 20$, $r = 5$

29
a (i) 37.68 mm (ii) 226.08 mm **b** 6 seconds

30
a 106.76 m **b** 18 m **c** 113 m
d (i) 5 m (ii) £22.60

31 74.2 %
32 6.25 cm²
33 81 m²

34
a $\frac{1}{6}$ **b** 0.204 cm² **c** 1.586 cm²

35
a (i) area $= \dfrac{\pi R^2}{6}$

(ii) The area of sector OAB is $\dfrac{\pi r^2}{6}$

Hence the shaded area is $\dfrac{\pi R^2}{6} - \dfrac{\pi r^2}{6}$

which can be simplified to $\frac{1}{6}\pi (R^2 - r^2)$

b (i) $R - r$ (ii) $\left(\dfrac{R - r}{2}\right)^2$

c 528 mm² **d** 739 mm³

36
a 40 cm³ **b** 480 cm³ **c** 6 cm **d** 576

37
a football **b** cylinder **c** a square pyramid

38
a 50   **b** 2   **c** 24 cm

39 8

40
a 2000 cm^2 **b** 36 litres   **c** 3 cm

41
a (i) 6   (ii) 6   (iii) 4
b (i) 100 cm^3 (ii) 1000 cm^3
c (i) 18   (ii) 6   (iii) 30

42 –

43
a (i) 6.75 m^2 (ii) 7.95 m^2 **b** 1.2 m^2

c The new area formed by the snow is equivalent to the old area slid 40 cm upwards, leaving a 40 cm by 3 m area below it.

44
a 0.525 m^2 **b** 0.66 m^3

45 10

46
a (i) cylinder   (ii) cube   **b** football

47
a (i) 178 cm^3
(ii) The circumference of a 9 cm radius circule is about $2 \times 9 \times 3.14$, or about 57 cm
(iii) 397 cm^3
b 27

48
a 308 cm^3 **b** 5 cm

49
a (i) 13.8 m   (ii) 10   **b** 9.12 m^3 **c** 11 tonnes   **d** £157.30

50 180 cm^2

51 7.5 cm

52
a 455.7 cm^3 **b** 332.3 cm^2

53
a 363 cm^3 **b** (i) 13 cm^3 (ii) 3.6%

54 315

55
a $V = 4r^2$ **b** 36   **c** 3.536   **d** 22.47%

56
a 12.4 cm   **b** 35p

57
a (i) 603 cm^3 (ii) 452 cm^3 **b** 37 or 38 days

58
a 15.8 m   **b** 0.193 m^3

59
a –   **b** 12.5 cm   **c** 100.8°

60
a 535.9 kg (the volumes are: 89 752, 76 930 and 76 930)   **b** 67 kg

61
a 0.5 m   **b** 67.4°   **c** 0.6 m^2 **d** 1.99 m^2
e 1.39 m^2 **f** 6.39 m^3 **g** 25.6 m^3

62
a 509 970 479.2   **b** 5×10^8
Note. These results were obtained with a 10-digit calculator. The question is not possible with an 8-digit calculator!

63
a 2160 g/cm^2 **b** 10 cm

64
a 1.5
b This scale factor represents a length ratio of 2:3, and hence a volume ratio of 8:27.
c 21 cm   **d** 217.5 cm^3

65
a (i) 155 cm^3 (ii) 135 cm^2
b 3.56 cm   **c** 3.70 cm

66
a 502 cm^3 **b** 11.9 cm   **c** (i) 5.25 cm   (ii) 2.76 cm

Algebra

CHECKPOINT 1

a $A = \pi r^2$ **b** $C = \dfrac{5(F - 32)}{9}$
c $p = 3q - 11$ **d** $y = 7x + 23$
e $2j + 3k = 16$ **f** $85f + 40c = 825$
g $7y - 4x > 20$ **h** $25m + 35p + 10n < 2500$
i $5m^2 + 4m - 11 = 0$ **j** $C = 5d^3 + 12d^2 + 75$

CHECKPOINT 2

a 9   **b** 3   **c** 11   **d** 23   **e** 0   **f** 20
g 40   **h** 16   **i** 100   **j** 320   **k** 20   **l** 117
m 28   **n** 22   **o** 28

CHECKPOINT 3

a 1   **b** 7   **c** −1   **d** 7   **e** −20   **f** −20
g 40   **h** 16   **i** −100   **j** −320   **k** 20   **l** −83
m −12   **n** −22   **o** −12

CHECKPOINT 4

1
a

SPEED	10	20	30	40	50	60	70
STOPPING DISTANCE	5	13.3	25	40	58.3	80	105

b No.

2

	Distance round room (metres)							
Height of room (metres)	6	8	10	12	14	16	18	20
3	4	5	6	8	9	10	11	12
3.5		5	6	7	9	10	12	13	14
4		5	7	8	10	12	13	15	16

3

AGE	1	2	3	4	5	6	7	8	9	10	11
DOSE	0.5	1	1.5	2	2.5	3	3.5	4	4.5	5	5.5

4
a 30.6 m   **b** 0.5 m
c 19.6 metres per second

CHECKPOINT 5

a $18x + 17y$ **b** $4x + 17y$
c $18x + 7y$ **d** $18x - 7y$
e $17y - 4x$ or, $-4x + 17y$ **f** $4x - 17y$
g $m^2 + 8m + 15$ **h** $b^2 + 3b - 10$
i $2a^2 - 14a + 12$ **j** $3v^3 + 5v^2 + 2v$
k $12ab^3 + 7a^2b - 10ab$ **l** $5st + 3s^2t + 3st^2$

CHECKPOINT 6

a $12r + 21$ **b** $30g - 45$ **c** $-36r - 36$
d $36 - 36r$ **e** $4m - 3n$ **f** $3n - 4m$
g $s^2 - s$ **h** $s - s^2$ **i** $s^2 - s$
j $15n^2 - 10n^3 + 30n$ **k** $10n^3 - 15n^2 - 30n$
l $10n^4 - 15n^3 + 30n^2$

CHECKPOINT 7

a $16r + 9$ **b** $26g - 73$ **c** -72
d $-72r$ **e** $8m - 6n$ **f** $14n$
g $s^2 - 1$ **h** $2s - s^2 - 1$ **i** $s^2 - 2s + 1$
j $20n^2 - 10n^3 + 30n - 5$ **k** $10n^2 - n - 3$
l $2x^2 - xy - y^2$

CHECKPOINT 8

a $x^2 + 8x + 15$ **b** $x^2 - 2x - 35$ **c** $a^2 - 18a + 81$
d $2w^2 + w - 3$ **e** $a^2 + 2ab + b^2$ **f** $a^2 - 2ab + b^2$
g $2xy - x^2 - y^2$ **h** $3x^2 - 4x - 15$ **i** $2x^2 + x - 6$
j $6x^2 + 5xy - 6y^2$ **k** $6x^2 - 23x + 20$ **l** $4x^2 + 4xy + y^2$

CHECKPOINT 9

a 10 000 **b** 1 002 000 **c** 10 000
d 100 **e** 99 **f** 100
g 1 000 000 **h** 10 000
i 10 000 000 001 600 000 000 000
j 1 000 000 000 000 000 000

CHECKPOINT 10

1
a $\dfrac{5x + 4v}{20}$ **b** $\dfrac{7a - 3b}{21}$ **c** $\dfrac{p - 12}{3}$

d $\dfrac{8 + 3x}{4x}$ **e** $\dfrac{x - 14}{2x}$ **f** $\dfrac{3d + 10c}{2cd}$

g $\dfrac{14f - 15e}{6ef}$ **h** $\dfrac{wz + xy}{yz}$ **i** $\dfrac{4nw - 5rm}{6mn}$

j $\dfrac{ayz + bcx - txy}{xyz}$

2
a $\dfrac{ab}{cd}$ **b** $\dfrac{8}{3a}$ **c** $\dfrac{c^2(a - b)}{4d}$

d $\dfrac{9e^2 + 6e + 1}{a^2d^2}$ **e** $2vxy$

f $\dfrac{ab}{12c}$ **g** $5ef$ **h** $\dfrac{ac}{e}$ **i** $\dfrac{5r^2}{3e}$ **j** $\dfrac{12y}{5xz}$

CHECKPOINT 11

1
a Using a, s, l and b to represent respectively the number of angle brackets, short rods, long rods and base plates, we have:
KIT A $20a + 10s + 20l + 5b$
KIT B $30a + 15s + 30l + 8b$
KIT C $50a + 30s + 40l + 12b$

b $500(20a + 10s + 20l + 5b) + 200(30a + 15s + 30l + 8b)$
$+ 50(50a + 30s + 40l + 12b)$
This can be simplified to
$18\,500a + 9500s + 18\,000l + 4700b$

2
a 11 **b** $\dfrac{6(x + 9) + 12}{6} - x = x + 11 - x = 11$

3
a $200 - 2x$ **b** $x(200 - 2x)$
c

x	10	15	20	25	30	35	40	45	50	55
AREA	1800	2550	3200	3750	4200	4550	4800	4950	5000	4950

x	60	65	70	75	80	85	90	95	100
AREA	4800	4550	4200	3750	3200	2550	1800	950	0

4
a $24 - 2x$ **b** $x(24 - 2x)(24 - 2x)$
c

x	1	2	3	4	5	6	7	8	9	10	11
VOLUME	484	800	972	1024	980	864	700	512	324	160	44

d 4 cm

5
a $\dfrac{\pi x^2}{4}$ **b** $x^2 - \dfrac{\pi x^2}{4} = \dfrac{4x^2 - \pi x^2}{4}$

c $x^2 - \dfrac{2(4x^2 - \pi x^2)}{4} = \dfrac{\pi x^2 - 2x^2}{2}$

6
a $x + y$ **b** $x - y$ **c** $\dfrac{6}{x + y}$

d $\dfrac{6}{x - y}$ **e** $\dfrac{6}{x + y} + \dfrac{6}{x - y} = \dfrac{12x}{(x + y)(x - y)}$

CHECKPOINT 12

a $15(2p + 1)$ **b** $3(9 - 4e)$ **c** $q(1 + 3r)$
d $m(6n - 1)$ **e** $e(13e - 5)$ **f** $f^2(9 - 7f)$
g $pq(q + p + 1)$ **h** $cd(ab + a + b)$ **i** $2mn(6m - 2n + 3)$
j $5f^2g^2(5g + 3 - 2f)$

CHECKPOINT 13

1 $V = \pi l(R^2 - r^2)$ **2** $\dfrac{4\pi(m^3 - n^3)}{3}$

3
a $\dfrac{bh}{2}$ **b** $\dfrac{ah}{2}$ **c** $\dfrac{bh}{2} + \dfrac{ah}{2} = \dfrac{h(a + b)}{2}$

4 Area of sector $= \dfrac{\pi r^2}{6}$ Area of triangle $= \dfrac{r^2\sin60°}{2}$

Area of segment $= \dfrac{\pi r^2}{6} - \dfrac{r^2\sin60°}{2} = \dfrac{r^2(\pi - 3\sin60°)}{6}$

CHECKPOINT 14

1
a $(x + 5)$ **b** $(x + 4)$ **c** $(x + 4)$
d $(x - 2)$ **e** $(x - 7)$ **f** $(x - 5)$
g $(x + 3)$ **h** $(2x - 1)$ **i** $(2x - 3)$
j $(3x - 5)$

2
a $(x + 3)(x + 6)$ **b** $(x + 5)(x + 1)$ **c** $(x + 5)(x - 1)$
d $(x - 5)(x + 1)$ **e** $(x - 5)(x - 1)$ **f** $(x - 7)(x - 4)$
g $(2x + 3)(x + 1)$ **h** $(3x + 1)(x + 4)$ **i** $(2x - 1)(x + 6)$
j $(2x - 4)(x - 5)$

CHECKPOINT 15

1
a $m = 5$ **b** $t = 3$ **c** $x = -9$ **d** $t = 20$
e $r = 21$ **f** $r = -13$ **g** $x = 12$ **h** $t = -25$
i $v = -72$ **j** $w = 1$ **k** $m = 4$ **l** $m = -4$
m $x = 70$ **n** $x = 16$ **o** $x = 1.5$ **p** $x = \dfrac{2}{3}$

2 $x + (x + 2) + (x + 5) = 17$, giving $x = 3.33$ cm

3 $\dfrac{2x - 10}{2} = 4$, giving $x = £9.00$

4 $x + (x + 5) + 2(x + 5) = 60$, giving prices of £11.25, £16.25, £32.50.

CHECKPOINT 16

1
a $p = -7$ **b** $x = 8$ **c** $p = 11$ **d** $e = 2$
e $w = 3$ **f** $m = 11$ **g** $x = -4$ **h** $a = 19.5$

i $x = 6$ **j** $x = 4$ **k** $p = 8$ **l** $x = 5$
m $s = 0.5$ **n** $x = \frac{5}{18}$

2 $39 + n = 3(7 + n)$, giving $n = 9$.

3 $N + (N + 1) + (N + 2) = N + 85$, giving 41, 42, 43.

4 $\frac{x}{2} - 10 = 2(x - 6) - 35.5$, giving $x = 25$.

CHECKPOINT 17

1
a $x = 3.72$ **b** $c = 2.46$ **c** $x = 2.90$ **d** $y = 6.30$
e $p = 17.11$ **f** $y = 8.09$ **g** $u = 7.15$ **h** $s = 11.43$
i $w = 1.50$ **j** $e = 1.20$

2 $\frac{9(100\,000)}{10} = 2.5s$, giving $s = £36\,000$ a year.

3 $\frac{x}{7} = \frac{x - 6}{6}$, giving $x = 42$ years.

4 $500 = 3.14 \times 3.6 \times 3.6 \times h$, giving $h = 12.29$ cm.

CHECKPOINT 18

1
a $x \leq 3$ **b** $y > -3$ **c** $e < -7$ **d** $y \geq 12$
e $x > 8$ **f** $w < -5.6$ **g** $e \geq 16$ **h** $x \leq 10.5$
i $x > -2.5$ **j** $x \geq 10$

2 The end area of the greenhouse is $2x + 0.4x = 2.4x$
The volume of the greenhouse is $4 \times 2.4x = 9.6x$
This gives the inequality $9.6x \geq 24$ or, $x \geq 2.5$

CHECKPOINT 19

1
a $x \geq -8$ **b** $x \leq 2$ **c** $x > -3$
d $y > -2$ **e** $x \geq 0.25$
2 After buying the chocolates, Gurmit has £7.80 left. If x is the number of bars of chocolate he buys, we have the inequality, $780 - 45x \geq 600$, which simplifies to $x \leq 4$.

CHECKPOINT 20

1
a $e = t - 5$ **b** $r = m + 4$ **c** $d = \frac{C}{\pi}$

d $x = \frac{y - 3}{2}$ **e** $r = tx - y$ **f** $v = \frac{s - u}{t}$

g $x = \frac{2y}{3}$ **h** $h = \frac{2A}{a + b}$ **i** $v = \frac{2s - tu}{t}$

j $V = RI$ **k** $u = \frac{2s - at^2}{2t}$ **l** $a = \frac{2s - 2ut}{t^2}$

m $s = \sqrt{\frac{v^2 - u^2}{2a}}$ **n** $u = v^2 - 2as$ **o** $r = \sqrt{\frac{s}{4\pi}}$

p $R = \sqrt{\frac{V}{\pi l} + r^2}$

2
a $t_{\text{total}} = 110w + 110$ **b** $w = \frac{t_{\text{total}} - 110}{110}$

c t_{total} is 22 hours, or 1320 minutes. The heaviest turkey that can be defrosted and cooked is therefore 11 pounds.

CHECKPOINT 21

a $V = \pi r^2 H$ **b** $v = \sqrt{u^2 + 2as}$ **c** $E = \frac{mV^2}{2} + mgh$

d $g = \frac{4\pi^2 l}{t^2}$

CHECKPOINT 22

a $I = \frac{V}{D^2 - d^2}$ **b** $h = \frac{3V}{R^2 - r^2}$ **c** $a = \frac{-fb}{f - 1}$

d $p = \frac{q + T^2 q}{T^2 - 1}$

CHECKPOINT 23

a $x = 5.7, y = 2.3$ **b** $x = 6, y = 5$ **c** $p = 2, q = 3$
d $n = 4, m = 1$ **e** $x = 2, y = -3$ **f** $p = 7, q = 6$
g $a = 4, b = 4$ **h** $a = 1, b = -1$ **i** $x = 2, y = 0$
j $m = 4, q = 7$

CHECKPOINT 24

1
a $a = 2, b = 3$ **b** $x = 4, q = 5$ **c** $t = 2.5, w = -1.5$
d $x = 0, y = -7.5$ **e** $e = 7, f = 5$ **f** $r = 6, s = 3$
g $m = -3, n = -4$ **h** $x = -7, y = 1.6$ **i** $q = 3, p = -5$
j $x = 4, y = -1$

2 The equations are $3b + 2s = 510$ and $5b + 2s = 730$, giving $b = £1.10$ and $s = £0.90$.

3 The equations are $200x - 7y = 65$ and $300x - 7y = 115$, giving $x = £0.50$ and $y = £5.00$.

CHECKPOINT 25

1
a $m = 3, n = 2$ **b** $m = 5, n = 1$
c $x = 6, y = -2$ **d** $t = -3, m = 4$
e $e = 11.5652, f = -6.17391$ **f** $x = 4, y = 2.5$
g $m = -1, n = 1$ **h** $x = 3, y = 5$
i $t = 6, s = 5$ **j** $a = 0, b = -7$

2 The equations are $4a + 2c = 640$ and $2a + 5c = 640$, giving $a = £1.20$ and $c = £0.80$.

3 The equations are $2x - 3y = 150$ and $3x - 2y = 250$, giving $x = £90$ and $y = £10$. This means that Arthur earns £90 and saves £10, Pete earns £180 and saves £30 and Dennis earns £270 and saves £20.

CHECKPOINT 26

1
a $x = -1$ or $x = -3$ **b** $x = 0$ or $x = 7$
c $x = -3$ or $x = -6$ **d** $x = 5$ or $x = -1$
e $x = 5$ or $x = 1$ **f** $x = 4$ or $x = -3$
g $x = 2.5$ or $x = -6$ **h** $x = 2$ or $x = -6$
i $x = 1.5$ or $x = 1$ **j** $m = 4$ or $m = -2$

2 The equation is $\frac{x(x + 3)}{2} = 14$ which can be re-arranged into

$x(x + 3) = 28$, or $x^2 + 3x - 28 = 0$, giving $x = 4$ or $x = -7$. Since x cannot be negative, only the first solution is valid.

3 The equation is $4 + 36t - 16t^2 = 12$, which can be re-arranged into $16t^2 - 36t + 8 = 0$, giving $t = 0.25$ s or $t = 2$ s.

4
a $(2x + 3)(x + 5)$
b $2x^2 + 13x + 15 = 49$, giving $x = 2$ or -8.5. Since x cannot be negative, only the first solution is valid.

CHECKPOINT 27

1 (All solutions have been given correct to 2 decimal places.)
a $x = -1.27$ or -4.73 **b** $x = 4.79$ or $x = 0.21$
c $x = 0.54$ or -5.54 **d** $x = -2$ or $x = -5$
e $x = 7.65$ or -0.65 **f** $x = -0.43$ or -1.18
g $x = 1.68$ or 0.12 **h** $x = 2.26$ or -0.59
i $x = 1$ or -1.75 **j** No solutions exist

2 The equation is $(x + 5)^2 = (x + 4)^2 + x^2$ which can be re-arranged into $x^2 - 2x - 9 = 0$, giving $x = 4.16$ or $x = -2.16$. Since x cannot be negative, the side lengths are 4.16 cm, 8.16 cm and 9.16 cm.

3 If the 'hint' is followed, it produces the equation
$$14(x + 4) + 15(x + 3) = 6(x + 3)(x + 4),$$
which can be re-arranged into $6x^2 + 13x - 29 = 0$, giving $x = 1.37$ or -3.53.

4 The area equation is $(15 + 2x)(12 + 2x) - 12 \times 15 = 150$, which can be re-arranged into $4x^2 + 54x - 150 = 0$, giving $x = 2.36$ or -15.86. Since x cannot be negative, only the first solution is valid, and the path is 2.36 metres wide.

CHECKPOINT 28

a 20   **b** 100   **c** 99   **d** 17

CHECKPOINT 29

a 1, 3, 5, 7 and 19   **b** 8, 13, 18, 23 and 53
c 1, 4, 9, 16 and 100   **d** 2, 6, 12, 20 and 110
e 1, 3, 6, 10 and 55   **f** 100, 98, 96, 94 and 82
g 1, 2, 4, 8 and 512   **h** 5, 20, 80, 320 and 1 310 720

CHECKPOINT 30

1
a $T_n = 2n - 1$ **b** $T_n = 12n - 7$
c $T_n = 128 - 8n$ **d** $T_n = 2 \times 5^{n-1}$
e $T_n = 3 \times 4^{n-1}$ **f** $T_n = 4000 \times 2^{1-n}$

2 The number of each plant required is $n + 3$.
3
a Number of grains on nth square $= 2^{n-1}$.
b The number of grains required on just the 64th square (let alone the 63rd, 62nd etc) is 9.22×10^{18}, an impossibly large number of grains to count, even if they could be collected.

CHECKPOINT 31

1
a 10 + 10 gives a 4 × 5 rectangle,
   15 + 15 gives a 6 × 5 rectangle
b 10 dots high, 11 dots wide.
c It will be a 50 by 51 rectangle, and therefore contain 2550 dots. The 50th triangular number is therefore 1275.

d Number of dots $= n(n + 1)$, giving the formula $\dfrac{n(n + 1)}{2}$

for the nth triangular number.

2
a $T_n = \dfrac{3n^2 - n}{2}$ **b** $T_n = 3n^2 - 2n$

CHECKPOINT 32

1
a 8, 12, 16, 20   **b** 5, 25, 125, 625
c 50, 25, 12.5, 6.25   **d** 5, 13, 29, 61
e 2, 3, 5, 8

2
a $U_{n+1} = U_n + 3$; 26 and 29   **b** $U_{n+1} = U_n - 2$; 93 and 91

c $U_{n+1} = 2U_n$; 16 and 32   **d** $U_{n+1} = \dfrac{U_n}{3}$; 18 and 6

e $U_{n+1} = 2U_n + 1$; 127 and 255
f $U_{n-1} = U_n + U_{n-1}$; 26 and 42

CHECKPOINT 33

Parts *a–c*. Answers will depend on the starting guess adopted by each student.

d 5, 6.1, 6.000 819 7, 6.000 000 1

CHECKPOINT 34

a 1, 2, 3, 4, 5, 6, 7   **b** −6, −4, −2, 0, 2, 4, 6
c −4, −3, −2, 2, 8   **d** −1.5, −1, −0.5, 0, 0.5, 1, 1.5
e 0, 1, 4, 9   **f** −12, −6, −4, −, 4, 6, 12
          (12 cannot be divided by 0)

CHECKPOINT 35

1
a 7   **b** 5   **c** 3   **d** 1   **e** −1
2
a 9   **b** 6   **c** 5   **d** 6   **f** 9
3
a 6   **b** 1   **c** 0   **d** 3   **e** 10

CHECKPOINT 36

1
a 15   **b** 14   **c** 3   **d** 0   **e** −8
f −2   **h** 47   **i** 72   **j** −0.75

2
a 15   **b** −2   **c** 1.667   **d** 0.6   **e** −15
f 8   **h** −0.6   **i** 0.2   **j** 5

CHECKPOINT 37

1
a 80   **b** 30   **c** 1.5   **d** 33   **e** −18
f −4.5   **g** 3   **h** −20   **i** 15   **j** 18

2
a −6   **b** −12   **c** 0.2   **d** 1.8   **e** −0.2
f −1.8   **g** 2.667   **h** 4.667   **i** 0.0667   **j** 0.6

CHECKPOINT 38

1
a $fg(x) = 2x + 2$ **b** $gf(x) = 2x + 4$
c $hf(x) = x^2 + 4x + 4$ **d** $kf(x = x^2 + 8x + 16$
e $gk(x = 2x^2 + 8x + 8$

2
a $rs(x) = 9 - 3x$ **b** $sr(x) = 3 - 3x$

c $ss(x) = x$ **d** $st(x) = 3 - \dfrac{x}{3}$

e $uu(x) = x$

CHECKPOINT 39

a $\dfrac{x + 2}{3}$ **b** $\dfrac{x}{3} + 2$ **c** $\dfrac{3x}{2}$

d $6x + 7$ **e** $6(x + 7)$ **f** $\dfrac{4x + 5}{3}$

g $\dfrac{3x - 5}{4}$ **h** $\dfrac{x + 21}{6}$

CHECKPOINT 40

a $2 - x$ **b** $\dfrac{8 - x}{2}$ **c** $\dfrac{2}{3x}$

d $7 - 6x$ **e** $6(7 - x)$ **f** $\dfrac{6}{7 - x}$

g $1 - \dfrac{1}{x}$ **h** $\dfrac{12 - \dfrac{36}{x}}{4}$

1
a $y = x + 5$ **b** $3t - 4s = r$ **c** $F = \dfrac{9C}{5} + 32$

d $v = u + at$

2
a 9   **b** -2 **c** 21   **d** 19   **e** 18   **f** 18
g 54   **h** 648   **i** 107   **j** 48

3
a -3 **b** -6 **c** -7 **d** 29   **e** 2   **f** -22
g -2 **h** 8   **i** 27   **j** -8

4 $36p$

5
a $20x + 6y$ **b** $x + 8y$ **c** $8x - 3y$
d $6x + 7y$ **e** $2m^2 + 3m + 27$ **f** $2a^2 - 16a + 14$
g $9v^3 + 2v^2 + 2v$ **h** $7s^2t - st^2$

6
a $12x + 20$ **b** $20 - 28r$ **c** $5n - 3m$
d $ab - a$ **e** $12r^2 - 8r^3 + 36r$ **f** $52r - 2$
g $8m - 6n$ **h** $1 - a$ **i** $12n^2 - 22n - 5$
j $3xy - x^2 - 2y^2$

7
a $x^2 + 5x + 4$ **b** $x^2 + 6x - 27$ **c** $5x^2 - 12x - 9$
d $b^2 - 2b + 1$ **e** $x^2 - y^2$ **f** $x^2 + 6xy - 9y^2$

8
a $\dfrac{6x + 5y}{30}$ **b** $\dfrac{35 + 3x}{5x}$ **c** $\dfrac{2x + 9}{3x}$

d $\dfrac{7y + 5x}{yz}$ **e** $\dfrac{5w + xf}{5ef}$ **f** $\dfrac{10a}{7b^2}$

g $\dfrac{4vy}{3u}$ **h** $\dfrac{pq}{33c}$ **i** $\dfrac{er}{fp}$

j $b + ac$

9
a 10   **b** $\dfrac{5(x + 8) + 10}{5} - x = x + 10 - x = 10$

10
a 58 feet   **b** length (feet) $= 2n - 2$

c length (metres) $= \dfrac{12(2n - 2)}{39} = \dfrac{8n - 8}{13}$

11 Oil left $= 12\,000 - 800t$

12
a $5(4x + 7)$ **b** $b(1 - 6a)$ **c** $5e(3e - f)$
d $xy(y + x + 1)$ **e** $cd(ab + a + b)$ **f** $7mn(2m - 3n + 1)$

13 area of path $= (x + 4)(y + 4) - xy = 4x + 4y + 16$

14
a $(x + 2)(x + 7)$ **b** $(x - 6)(x + 7)$ **c** $(x - 8)(x - 5)$
d $(2x + 8)(x + 3)$ **e** $(x - 2)(3x + 4)$

15
a $(x + 2)(x + 9)$ **b** $(x + 12)(x - 1)$ **c** $(x - 9)(x + 1)$
d $(2x + 1)(x + 7)$ **e** $(2x + 1)(x - 8)$ **f** $(2x - 10)(x + 1)$

16
a $m = 6$ **b** $t = 9$ **c** $x = -2.167$
d $t = 59$ **e** $r = 25$ **f** $r = -10$
g $x = 50$ **h** $t = -65$ **i** $v = -6$
j $x = 2$ **k** $m = 5$ **l** $m = -5$
m $x = 24$ **n** $x = 9$ **o** $x = -0.5$
p $x = -6$

17 The equation is $2(x + 2) + 13 = 43$, giving $x = 13$

18
a $p = -4$ **b** $x = 5$ **c** $m = -36$
d $x = 12.5$ **e** $a = 32$ **f** $x = 1$
g $p = 0$ **h** $x = -4$

19
a $x = 5$ **b** $y = 5.4$ **c** $p = 48$
d $y = 14.85$ **e** $u = 3$ **f** $e = 2$

20
a $x < 6$ **b** $y > -15$ **c** $e \leq -8$
d $y \geq 26$ **e** $x > 12$ **f** $w < -15$
g $e \geq -6.6$ **h** $x \leq 3.5$ **i** $x > 2$
j $x > 6$ **k** $x \geq -8$ **l** $x \leq 7$
m $x > -10$ **n** $y < 0$ **o** $x > -2$

21
a $x = y - 5$ **b** $t = p + 7$ **c** $r = \dfrac{C}{2\pi}$

d $C = \pi d$ **e** $x = \dfrac{y + 1}{4}$ **f** $r = \dfrac{tx - m}{t}$

g $u = s - vt$ **h** $x = \dfrac{8y}{7}$ **i** $a = \dfrac{2A}{h} - b$

j $t = \dfrac{2s}{u + v}$ **k** $c = \sqrt{\dfrac{E}{m}}$ **l** $d = \sqrt{\dfrac{kI}{p}}$

m $a = \dfrac{v^2 - u^2}{2s}$ **n** $n = \dfrac{360}{180 - A}$ **o** $r = \sqrt[3]{\dfrac{3V}{4\pi}}$

p $R = \dfrac{3V}{4\pi} + r^2$

22
a $s = Q^2t$ **b** $e = \dfrac{b^2d}{a^2}$ **c** $n = F^2m - m$

d $d = \dfrac{st^2}{2R^2}$

23
a $h = \dfrac{2A}{a - b}$ **b** $m = \dfrac{n}{Tn - 1}$ **c** $a = \dfrac{p - qy}{1 - y}$

d $m = \dfrac{-F^2n}{F^2 - 1}$

24
a $x = 5, y = 4$ **b** $x = 3, y = 4$ **c** $p = 17, q = 10$
d $a = 2, b = -1$ **e** $p = 5, q = 7.5$

25
a $a = 3, b = 2$ **b** $t = 2, w = 5$ **c** $e = 2, f = -2$
d $m = 5, n = 17$ **e** $q = 7.5, p = 10.5$

26
a $m = 4, n = 1$ **b** $m = -2, n = 3$ **c** $x = 3, y = -1$
d $x = 5, y = 2.5$ **e** $t = -2, s = -5$

27 The equations are $7b + 2s = 1718$ and $3b + 5s = 1047$, giving $b =$ £2.24 and $s =$ £0.75.

28
a $x = -1$ or $x = -4$ **b** $x = 5$ or $x = -7$
c $x = 4$ or $x = 3$ **d** $x = -2.5$ or $x = -3$
e $x = 3.5$ or $x = -3$ **f** $x = 4$ or $x = 2.33$

29
a $x = -0.298$ or $x = -6.702$ **b** $x = 0.541$ or $x = -5.541$
c $x = 4.414$ or $x = 1.586$ **d** $x = -0.5$ or $x = -1$
e $x = 2.264$ or $x = 0.736$

30
a cost $= 0.5x^2 + 3.2x + 2$
b The equation is $0.5x^2 + 3.2x + 2 = 84$, giving $x = 10$ or $x = -16.4$. Since x cannot be negative, the solution is $x = 10$ cm.

31
a 22   **b** 4000   **c** 3999   **d** 29

32
a 2, 5, 8, 11, 14 and 29   **b** 9, 13, 17, 21, 25 and 45
c 360, 180, 120, 90, 72 and 36   **d** 1, 8, 27, 64, 125 and 1000
e 1, 3, 6, 10, 15 and 55   **f** 995, 990, 985, 980, 975 and 950
g 1, 3, 9, 27, 81 and 19 683   **h** 4, 20, 50, 500, 2500 and 7 812 500

33
a $T_n = 4n - 3$ **b** $T_n = 11n - 5$ **c** $T_n = 220 - 15n$
d $T_n = 9 \times 2^{n-1}$

34
a £3.20   **b** $20 \times 2^{n-1}$

35
a 3, 5, 7, 9   **b** 2, 4, 8, 16
c 0.1, 0.01, 0.001, 0.000 1   **d** 4, 6, 4, 6
e The sequence is 1, -1, -1, 1, -1, -1, 1 . . .

36
a $U_{n+1} = U_n + 3$; 36 and 39   **b** $U_{n+1} = \dfrac{U_n}{2}$; 22.5 and 11.25

c $U_{n+1} = \dfrac{2}{U_n}$; 2 and 1   **d** $U_{n+1} + 1; = 2U_n + 1$; 445 and 1336

e $U_{n+1} = U_n + U_{n-1}$; 29 and 47

37   –

38
a 17   **b** 84   **c** 1   **d** -24 **e** -14 **f** -3
g 9   **h** 23   **i** 24   **j** 13.5

39
a 75   **b** 13   **c** 3.67   **d** 4   **e** 75   **f** -7
g 0.33   **h** 64   **i** 2.2   **j** 5.76

40
a 600   **b** 100   **c** -6 **d** 6   **e** -30 **f** -1.2
g 0   **h** -125 **i** 3   **j** 6

41
a 48   **b** -8 **c** 9.5   **d** 8.97   **e** 7.5   **f** 32
g 9.25   **h** 0.25   **i** 9.25   **j** 8.5

42
a $5x + 5$ **b** $5x + 25$ **c** $x^2 + 10x + 25$
d $x^2 + 20x + 100$ **e** $5x^2 + 50x + 125$

43
a $8(8 - x)$ **b** $8 - 8x$ **c** x

d $8 - \dfrac{x}{8}$ **e** x

44
a $\dfrac{x + 3}{2}$ **b** $\dfrac{x}{2} + 3$ **c** $\dfrac{4x}{5}$

d $7x + 8$ **e** $9(x - 13)$ **f** $\dfrac{9x + 7}{2}$

g $\dfrac{11x - 3}{7}$ **h** $\dfrac{x + 117}{63}$

45
a $8 - x$ **b** $\dfrac{10 - x}{5}$ **c** $\dfrac{5}{4x}$

d $1 - 2x$ **e** $2(1 - x)$ **f** $\dfrac{2}{1 - x}$

g $12 - \dfrac{12}{x}$ **h** $2 - \dfrac{1}{3x}$

Algebra – Past paper questions

1
a 1440   **b** 43.5

2
a 800 watts   **b** $I = \sqrt{\dfrac{P}{R}}$

3   45.1

4
a (i) $x + 13$ (ii) $x + 13 = 2(x - 7)$
b 27 years

5   £2.24

6
a £140   **b** £3.50

7   220 grams

8
a 22, 5   **b** 12
c Possible pairs of values for X, Y are (1, 8), (2, 5), (3, 2)
d 2 and 5

9
a 135   **b** Blanks are $(x - 10)$ and $(x + 1)$
c $5x$ **d** 25

10
a 1.25   **b** 0.8

12
a (i) $t = \dfrac{x}{250}$ (ii) $y = \dfrac{5x^2}{62\,500}$

b 20

13   **B**

14
a $h = \dfrac{A}{2\pi r} - r$ **b** 3.8 cm

15   The equations are $a + 4b = 20$ and $a + 7b = 29$, giving $a = 8$ and $b = 3$.

16   0.833

17
a 9.6 volts   **b** $R = \dfrac{Vr}{12 - V}$

18
a 68   **b** -10 **c** $F = 2(C + 15)$
d 70

19
a 12.08 °C   **b** 3550 metres   **c** $H = \dfrac{24.5 - T}{0.69}$

20 $\pi r(2h + r)$

21 $15x - 2y$

22 $7(2x + 7y)$

23
a $x = 9$, $y = -5$
b (i) $2p^2 - 6p$ (ii) $4q^2 + 8q - 5$
c (i) $\dfrac{2}{n}$ (ii) $r - 1$
d $t > 0.6$

24
a $3a + 1$ **b** 6 cm

25
a (i) $5(x + 2y)(x - 2y)$ (ii) $(x + 10)(x - 2)$
b (i) $x = -4$ (ii) $x = 81$ (iii) $x = 0.5$

26
a (i) 2.75 and 2.85   (ii) 44   (iii) 76

b $x = \dfrac{3y}{4 + y}$

27
a $(x + 3)(x + 8)$ **b** $y = 2$ or $y = -3$

28
a $(p + q)$ **b** $40\,000\,000\,000$

29
a $x = 5$ **b** $p = 1.5$

30
a $x = 2.8$, $y = 2.2$
b The equations are $a + c = 500$ and $3a = 2c + 400$, giving $a = 280$ and $c = 220$. 280 adult tickets are sold.

31
a (i) $x + 20$ (ii) $30x$ (iii) $30x + 600$ (iv) $x^2 + 20x$
b $2x^2 + 160x + 1200$
c If $2x^2 + 160x + 1200 = 10800$, then dividing by 2 we have $x^2 + 80x + 600 = 5400$, and subtracting 5400 from each side we have $x^2 + 80x - 4800 = 0$. The other solution is $x = 40$.
d 288

32
a A **b** D

33
a $15C^2$ **b** $S^2 + 8SC$ **c** $C = 6$ feet

34
a $3x^2 + 2x$
b We require a volume of $8\ m^3$, therefore $3x^2 + 2x$ must equal 8, or $3x^2 + 2x - 8 = 0$
c $x = -2$ or 1.3333, the appropriate value being $x = 1.3333$
d $20\ m^2$

35
a $\dfrac{24\,000}{x}$

b The equation is $\dfrac{24\,000}{x - 10} = \dfrac{24\,000}{x} + 80$

Multiplying through by $x(x - 10)$ gives,
$24\,000x = 24\,000(x - 10) + 80x(x - 10)$
or, expanding brackets,
$24\,000x = 24\,000x - 240\,000 + 80x^2 - 800x$
or, subracting $24\,000x$ from both sides,
$0 = 80x^2 - 800x - 240\,000$
or, dividing both sides by 80
$0 = x^2 - 10x - 3000$
c 60p

36
a -5 **b** 13   **c** $4x - 3$ **d** $\dfrac{3 - x}{2}$

37
a 5   **b** (i) -1 (ii) 9   (iii) 14   (v) $n = 6.217$ or -3.217
c Positive whole numbers greater than 2.

38
a 1/2   **b** 3/5

39
a (i) $\dfrac{29}{41}, \dfrac{70}{99}, \dfrac{169}{239}$

(ii) $0.666\,666\,6,\ 0.714\,285\,7,\ 0.705\,882\,4,\ 0.707\,317\,1,\ 0.707\,070\,7,$
$0.707\,113$
(iii) They seem to be approaching a value of about 0.7.

b (i) $\dfrac{2}{3}, \dfrac{1}{5}, \dfrac{2}{3}\, \dfrac{1}{5}, \dfrac{2}{3}, \dfrac{1}{5}$ (ii) They repeat, $\dfrac{2}{3}, \dfrac{1}{5}$

40
a 1.62
b Dividing by x gives,

$$x^2 - 2 - \frac{1}{x} = 0$$

or, adding $2 + \dfrac{1}{x}$ to both sides,

$$x^2 = 2 + \frac{1}{x}$$

Square rooting gives the required result.

c $1.617\,802\,2,\ 1.618\,061\,4,\ 1.618\,030\,8$
d $1.618\,03$

Graphs

CHECKPOINT 2

1
a

A(0,0,0)	B(3,0,0)	C(3,3,0)	D(0,3,0)
E(0,0,3)	F(3,0,3)	G(3,3,3)	H(0,3,3)

b

A(2,0,0)	B(5,0,0)	C(5,3,0)	D(2,3,0)
E(2,0,3)	F(5,0,3)	G(5,3,3)	H(2,3,3)

c

A(1,0,2)	B(4,0,2)	C(4,3,2)	D(1,3,2)
E(1,0,5)	F(4,0,5)	G(4,3,5)	H(1,3,5)

2 The full set of eight vertices is:

(3,3,3)	(−3,3,3)	(−3,−3,3)	(3,−3,3)
(3,3,−3)	(−3,3,−3)	(−3,−3,−3)	(3,−3,−3)

3

A(6,0,3)	B(6,4,3)	C(6,4,0)	D(6,0,0)
E(0,0,3)	F(0,4,3)	G(0,4,0)	H(0,0,0)

CHECKPOINT 3

4
a $y = -2$ **b** $x = 2$ **c** $x = 0$ **d** $y = 7$
e $y = 0$ **f** $x = -5$

CHECKPOINT 4

a $\dfrac{2}{1}$ **b** $\dfrac{3}{1}$ **c** $\dfrac{1}{1}$ **d** $\dfrac{1}{2}$ **e** $\dfrac{1}{5}$ **f** $\dfrac{2}{3}$

g $\dfrac{3}{2}$ **h** $\dfrac{-1}{1}$ **i** $\dfrac{-2}{1}$ **j** $\dfrac{-2}{1}$ **k** $\dfrac{-5}{1}$ **l** $\dfrac{-1}{4}$

CHECKPOINT 6

1
a 3   **b** 3   **c** $y = 2$
2
a 5   **b** 5   **c** $y = -1$
3
a $\dfrac{1}{2}$ **b** $\dfrac{1}{2}$ **c** $y = 1$
4
a -1 **b** -1 **c** $y = 6$

CHECKPOINT 7

1
a $\dfrac{1}{1}$, (0,3)   **b** $\dfrac{1}{1}$, (0,−3)   **c** $\dfrac{3}{1}$, (0,0)

d $\dfrac{1}{4}$, (0,0)   **e** $\dfrac{3}{1}$, (0,−3)   **f** $\dfrac{1}{4}$, (0,3)

g $\frac{-2}{1}$, (0,4)   **h** $\frac{3}{4}$, (0,3)   **i** $\frac{2}{1}$, (0,−2)

j $\frac{-1}{2}$, (0,8)

2
a $y = 2x + 3$ **b** $y = 3x + 2$ **c** $y = \frac{x}{2} - 1$

d $y = -x$ **e** $y = 12 - 2x$

CHECKPOINT 8

1 a $C = 20d + 80$ **b** –
c For up to three days work, the Rick Dastardly Agency is cheaper. For four days work the agencies charge the same price, £160. For any work of more than four days, the Purple Panther Agency is cheaper.
2 $C = 5d + 15$, where C is the cost in millions of pounds and d is the length of motorway in kilometres.
a –   **b** £6 250 000 per km   **c** £8 750 000 per km
3
a –   **b** –
c 20 bulbs cost £2.00 but 21 bulbs cost £1.89 and 22 bulbs cost £1.98. Obviously, anyone buying 20 bulbs might just as well buy 21 or 22 and save money. In the same way, orders of 41, 42, 43 or 44 bulbs actually cost less than an order for 40 bulbs (45 bulbs cost the same as 40 bulbs).
4
a $C = 25 + 0.02m$ **b** –   **c** –   **d** A **e** B **f** C

CHECKPOINT 10

1
a $x = 3.75$, $y = 0.75$ **b** $x = -2$, $y = -2$
c $x = 2$, $y = 2$ **d** $x = -2$, $y = 1.5$
e $x = 12$, $y = 2$

2 $-40°C = -40°F$

CHECKPOINT 11

a no solutions   **b** many solutions

c $x = 1\frac{5}{7}$, $y = 3\frac{3}{7}$ **d** $x = 8$, $y = 0$

e no solutions   **f** $x = 0$, $y = 0$

CHECKPOINT 12

1

x	−4	−3	−2	−1	0	1	2	3
x^2	16	9	4	1	0	1	4	9
$+ x$	−4	−3	−2	−1	0	1	2	3
−6	−6	−6	−6	−6	−6	−6	−6	−6
y	6	0	−4	−6	−6	−4	0	6

2

x	−5	−4	−3	−2	−1	0	1	2	3	4	5
$\frac{x^2}{2}$	12.5	8	4.5	2	0.5	0	0.5	2	4.5	8	12.5
−5	−5	−5	−5	−5	−5	−5	−5	−5	−5	−5	−5
y	7.5	3	−0.5	−3	−4.5	−5	−4.5	−3	−0.5	3	7.5

3
a

x	0	0.5	1	1.5	2	2.5	3	3.5	4
$16-2x$	16	15	14	13	12	11	10	9	8
Area	0	7.5	14	19.5	24	27.5	30	31.5	32

x	4.5	5	5.5	6	6.5	7	7.5	8
$16-2x$	7	6	5	4	3	2	1	0
Area	31.5	30	27.5	24	19.5	14	7.5	0

b Negative values of x are obviously impossible. Since the rope is 16 m long, any value of x greater than 8 is also obviously impossible.
c –
d The greatest area is obtained when $x = 4$ metres.

4
a

t	0	0.5	1	1.5	2	2.5	3	3.5	4
s	0	1.2	4.9	11.0	19.6	30.6	44.1	60	78.4

5
a

v	10	15	20	25	30	35	40
d	5	8.8	13.3	18.8	25	32.1	40

v	45	50	55	60	65	70
d	48.8	58.3	68.8	80	92.4	105

CHECKPOINT 13

1
a $x = 2.8$ or -2.8 **b** $x = 2.2$ or -2.2
c $x = 2.6$ or -2.6

2
a $x = 3$ or -3 **b** $x = 2.7$ or -3.7
c $x = 1.4$ or -1.4

3
c $x = 0$ or 4, $x = 3.4$ or 0.6, $x = 4$ or -1

4
a $x = 3$ or 1, $x = 0$ or 4, $x = 0$ or 3
b There is no intersection between the line $y = x^2 - 4x + 3$ and the line $y = -2$.

5
c $x = 2.8$ or -1.8, $x = 2$ or -2, $x = 3$ or -1.

6
a $C = 0.5x^2 + 3.2x + 2$ **c** Approximately 16.9 cm square.

CHECKPOINT 14

a $x = 2$ or -3 **b** $x = 2$ **c** No real roots

CHECKPOINT 15

1
b $x = 4$ or -1.5, $x = 6$ or -1
4
c Use at least 3 workers

1
a

x	-4	-3	-2	-1	0	1	2	3	4	5	6
x^3	-64	-27	-8	-1	0	1	8	27	64	125	216
$-2x^2$	-32	-18	-8	-2	0	-2	-8	-18	-32	-50	-72
$-24x$	96	72	48	24	0	-24	-48	-72	-96	-120	-144
y	0	27	32	21	0	-25	-48	-63	-64	-45	0

c (i) $x = -4$ or 0 or 6 (ii) $x = 0$ or -4.5 or 6.5

2
a $20 - 2x$ **b** $x(20 - 2x)(20 - 2x) = 4x^3 - 80x^2 + 400x$
c

x	1	2	3	4	5
$4x^3$	4	32	108	256	500
$-80x^2$	-80	-320	-720	-1280	-2000
$-400x$	400	800	1200	1600	2000
V	324	512	588	576	500

x	6	7	8	9
$4x^3$	864	1372	2048	2916
$-80x^2$	-2880	-3920	-5120	-6480
$-400x$	2400	2800	3200	3600
V	384	252	128	36

d A value for x of approximately 3.3 cm produces the maximum volume.

2
a $16x$ **b** $25y$ **e** No

3
a $80x$ **b** $50y$
e Yes, when $x = 5$, $y = 2$ and when $x = 0$, $y = 10$.
h Yes, when $x = 5$, $y = 2$.

1
a £40
b There is a standing charge of £10 which must be paid even if no electricity is used.
c 500, 30, $\frac{3}{50}$

d The cost per unit of electricity is £$\frac{3}{50}$, or 6p.

2
a 25 cm   **b** 260 grams   **c** 500, 25, $\frac{1}{20}$

d Each increase of 20 grams in weight extends the spring by 1 cm.

3
a 15 cm   **b** 28 minutes   **c** 60, -15, $-\frac{1}{4}$

d The candle burns down at a rate of 1 cm every 4 minutes.

3 72 square units   **4** 20 square units
5 50 square units   **6** 78 metres

1 55.5 square units

2
a 22.4 square units
b End area $= 22.4 + 12 - 10 = 24.4$ cm^2.
   Volume $= 2440$ cm^3

3
b The area under the curve is 12.25 square units. The end area of the machine part is 20.45 cm^2 and its volume is 40.9 cm^3.
4 1750 m^3

Graphs – Practice and revision exercise

2
a $y = -3$ **b** $x = 5$

3
a $\frac{2}{1}$ **b** $\frac{1}{2}$ **c** $\frac{1}{1}$ **d** $\frac{-1}{1}$ **e** $\frac{1}{5}$ **f** $\frac{-5}{1}$

4
a $\frac{1}{1}$, (0.5)   **b** $\frac{1}{1}$, $(0,-6)$ **c** $\frac{2.5}{1}$, $(0,1.5)$
d $\frac{1}{6}$, $(0,0)$ **e** $\frac{2}{1}$, $(0,-7)$ **f** $\frac{1}{2}$, $(0,1)$
g $\frac{-2}{1}$, $(0,6)$ **h** $\frac{1}{2}$, $(0,-0.5)$

5
a $y = 3x + 2$ **b** $y = \frac{x}{2} - 5$ **c** $y = -2x$

d $y = 5 - \frac{x}{4}$

6
c It is cheaper to buy 10 or 20 discs rather than 9 or 19 discs.

8
a $x = -2$, $y = -2$ **b** $x = 5$, $y = 0$

9
a No solutions   **b** $x = -2$, $y = -2$ **c** Many solutions

10
a

x	-5	-4	-3	-2	-1	0	1	2
x^2	25	16	9	4	1	0	1	4
$+4x$	-20	-16	-12	-8	-4	0	4	8
-5	-5	-5	-5	-5	-5	-5	-5	-5
y	0	-5	-8	-9	-8	-5	0	7

11
a

Size of Rectangle (height × width)	9×0	8×1	7×2	6×3	5×4
Area (square centimetres)	0	8	14	18	20

b

Size of Rectangle (height × width)	4×5	3×6	2×7	1×8	9×0
Area (square centimetres)	20	18	14	8	0

c 20.25 cm^2, when the height and width are both equal to 4.5 cm

12
a

x	-3	-2	-1	0	1	2	3	4	5
8	8	8	8	8	8	8	8	8	8
$-2x$	-6	-4	-2	0	2	4	6	8	10
$-x^2$	-9	-4	-1	0	-1	-4	-9	-16	-25
y	-7	0	5	8	9	8	5	0	-7

c (i) $x = -2$ or 4 (ii) $x = 3.2$ or -1.2 (iii) $x = 3.4$ or -2.4
(iv) $x = 4.5$ or -1.5

14

a

Number of students on coach	5	10	15	20	25	30	35	40
Cost per student (£)	24	12	8	6	4.80	4	3.43	3

c 25

24

a (i) 24 (ii) $4x$ (ii) 40 (iv) $8y$ (v) $4x+8y$

30 20 square units

31 The end area is 21 m² and the volume 252 m².

Graphs – Past paper questions

1 Parallelogram

2
a A (1,1), B (4,5) **c** Trapezium **d** E (5,−2)

3
a 68°F **b** 15.5°F **c** 10°C

4
a 128 lb **b** 5 kg

5
a $33 **b** £28

6
a (i) 10.7 km per litre (ii) 2.5 gallons
b (i) 28 mpg
c The cars are not travelling at the same speed. The English car is travelling at 50 mph, but the French car is travelling at 62.5 mph (100 kph).

7
a (i) £4.80 (ii) £2.40 (iii) 4p (iv) $C = 240 + 4S$ pence (v) £9.60
c £27.52 **d** (i) £123.60 (ii) 2000

8 $\dfrac{-1}{2}$

9 (8,0)

10
a 8 m **b** 6 m/s **c** $d = 8 + 6t$

11
a Missing values are 32 and 96
c (i) 83.2 km (ii) 27 miles **d** 320 km

12
a Missing values are 20, 45, 55, 60 and 70
d (i) 50 and 200 (ii) From 50 miles to 200 miles (iii) £20
(iv) 100 and 300

13
a Missing values are 50 and 80
c Missing values are 35, 55, 75 and 95
e 150 miles
f (i) DIY Transport (ii) £3
g $C = 35 + 0.2x$

14
a Missing values are 20, 45, and 125.
c (i) 61 cm (ii) 2.4 m/s

15
a 2.5 m
b (i) Missing values are 0, 4, 16 and 49
(iii) • 9 m³ • 2.5 m

16
a Missing values are 4, 2.25, 0.25, 2.25 and 4.
c (ii) $\dfrac{-1}{1}$

d $x = 1.3$ or -2.3 (these are the x co-ordinates of the points of intersection of $y = x^2$ and $y = 3 - x$)

17
a Missing values are 24, 30, 32, 30, 24, 14 and 0
c (i) 24 m (ii) 8 m (iii) 6 secs (iv) 12 m/s

18
a Missing values are 4.5 and 8.
c 3.4 tonnes **d** 4.9 mm

19
a The measurements of the box are x cm, $(20 - 2x)$ cm and $(30 - 2x)$ cm. This gives a volume of $x(20 - 2x)(30 - 2x)$ which, by extracting a factor of 2 from each bracket, can be written as $4x(10 - x)(15 - x)$

b

x	1	2	3	4	5	6	7	8	9
V	504	832	1008	1056	1000	864	672	448	216

d (i) 1056 cm³ (ii) 4 cm

20
a $h = \dfrac{36 - x^2}{2x}$

b Volume $= hx^2 = \dfrac{(36 - x^2)x^2}{2x} = \dfrac{36x - x^3}{2} = 18x - \dfrac{x^3}{2}$

c Missing values are 17.5, 32 and 27.5.
e 1.85 cm by 1.85 cm by 8.77 cm

23
a 11 **c** (i) 2.2 secs (ii) 12.25 metres **d** 10 metres per second

24
b (i) 2.4 kg (ii) 48 cm

27
a 10.00 **b** 15 miles **c** 30 minutes
d The first part **e** 10 mph **f** 12.30
g 6 mph

29
a 1.5 ms⁻¹ **b** 20 revs/min
c (i) 4.75 ms⁻¹ (ii) 28.5 m
d (i) 570 m (ii) 276

30
(i) 15 ms⁻¹ (ii) 0.5 ms⁻² (iii) 20 s
(iv) 1050 m (v) 1425 m

32
a
(i) $x + y \leq 16$ (ii) $4x + 10y \geq 72$
(iii) $2x + y \geq 20$ (iv) $x \geq y$
c 8 landrovers and 4 minibuses
d $3000x + 9000y$
e 14 landrovers and 2 minibuses

Shape and Space

a 57° **b** 62° **c** 10° **d** 150.5° **e** 67° **f** 145°
g 39° **h** 338° **i** 30° **j** 20°

a $b = f = d = 123°$, $a = c = e = g = 57°$
b $a = d = f = i = k = n = l = 63°$, $b = c = e = g = h = j = m = p = 117°$
c 160°
d $a = 70°$, $b = 80°$ $c = 70°$, $d = 30°$, $e = 80°$
e 210°

CHECKPOINT 3

a 54°   b 84°   c 45°, 60, 75°   d 74°   e 30°
f 20°   g 64°   h 130°

CHECKPOINT 4

2 The opposite angles in a parallelogram are in two equal pairs. The diagonals of a parallelogram bisect each other.
3 As for a parallelogram, but also, the diagonals bisect at a right angle.
4 As for a parallelogram, but also the diagonals are equal.
5 As for a parallelogram, but also, the diagonals are equal and bisect at a right angle.
6 The angles between the two pairs of non-equal sides are equal. The diagonals do not bisect each other but do cross at a right angle.

CHECKPOINT 5

1
a 360°   b 360°   c 90°   d 90°

2a
a 180°   b 360°   c 60°   d 120°

2b
a 720°   b 360°   c 120°   d 60°

2c
a 1080°   b 360°   c 135°   d 45°

3 The total of the exterior angles of any polygon is always 360°. The easiest way to prove this result is to argue as follows.
• Suppose a polygon has n sides.
• The interior will divide into $(n-2)$ triangles and therefore the total of the interior angles must be $180(n-2)°$.
• There are n pairs of interior and exterior angles, therefore, the total of the interior angles plus the exterior angles must be $180n°$.
• The total of the exterior angles must therefore be $180n° - 180(n-2)°$, which simplifies to 360°.

4 14

5 20

6
a 150°   b 60°   c 75°   d 135°   e 75°   f 30°
g 30°   h 60°

CHECKPOINT 8

1
a 90°   b 45°

2
a 96°   b 48°

3
a 92°   b 44°

4
a 80°   b 40°

5
a 56°   b 28°

6
a 120°   b 30°

CHECKPOINT 9

1
a 41°   b 41°

2
a 118°   b 59°   c 59°   d 59°

3
a 28°   b 90°   c 56°   d 28°

4
a 70°   b 70°   c 20°   d 90°

5
a 90°   b 60°   c 30°   d 30°
6
a 80°   b 10°   c 160°   d 100°

CHECKPOINT 19

1 A is the result of a rotation of 180° about the point P
B is the result of a rotation of +90° about the point P
C is the result of a rotation of +90° about the point N
D is the result of a rotation of 180° about the point M
E is the result of a rotation of 180° about the point Q
F is the result of a rotation of 180° about the point R
G is the result of a rotation of −90° about the point R
H is the result of a rotation of +90° about the point Q

CHECKPOINT 26

1 Rotation of 180° about (0, 0)
2 Reflection in the line $y = x$

3 Translation $\begin{pmatrix} -4 \\ +3 \end{pmatrix}$

4 Reflection in the line with equation $x = 3$
5 $(x, y) (-x, y)$
6 $(x, y) (-y, x)$
7 $(x, y) (-y, -x)$
8 $(x, y) (2x, 2y)$

CHECKPOINT 27

1
a Reflection in the x-axis.
b Rotation of 180° about (0, 0).
c Enlargement, scale factor 2, centre (0, 0).
d Rotation of −90° about (0, 0).
e Reflection in $y = -y$.
f Rotation of +90° about (0, 0).
g Enlargement, scale factor −5, centre (0, 0).
h Rotation of −37° about (0, 0).
i A reflection in the x-axis, followed by an enlargement scale factor 2, centre (0, 0).
j A rotation of +90° about (0, 0) followed by an enlargement scale factor 4, centre (0, 0).

CHECKPOINT 28

1

3 Translation $\begin{pmatrix} -5 \\ +4 \end{pmatrix}$

b Rotation of −270° about (0, 0).

c Enlargement, scale factor $-\frac{1}{3}$, centre (0, 0).

d Reflection in the line with equation $x = 0$.
e Reflection in the line with equation $y = x$.
f Rotation of −120° about (0, 0).
g Enlargement scale factor 4, centre (0, 0).

h Translation $\begin{pmatrix} +7 \\ +7 \end{pmatrix}$

CHECKPOINT 29

a $\begin{pmatrix} 1 & 0 \\ 0 & -1 \end{pmatrix}$ b $\begin{pmatrix} -1 & 0 \\ 0 & -1 \end{pmatrix}$ c $\begin{pmatrix} \frac{1}{3} & 0 \\ 0 & \frac{1}{3} \end{pmatrix}$

CHECKPOINT 30

a $\begin{pmatrix} 0 & -1 \\ 1 & 0 \end{pmatrix}$ b $\begin{pmatrix} -1 & 0 \\ 0 & 1 \end{pmatrix}$ c $\begin{pmatrix} 0 & -1 \\ -1 & 0 \end{pmatrix}$

d $\begin{pmatrix} 0 & -\frac{1}{6} \\ \frac{1}{6} & 0 \end{pmatrix}$ **e** $\begin{pmatrix} 1 & 0 \\ -2 & 1 \end{pmatrix}$ **f** $\begin{pmatrix} \frac{1}{3} & 0 \\ 0 & 1 \end{pmatrix}$

CHECKPOINT 35

1
a $\underline{x} - \underline{y}$ **b** $\dfrac{\underline{x} - \underline{y}}{2}$ **c** $\dfrac{\underline{x} + \underline{y}}{2}$

2
a $\underline{a} + \underline{b}$ **b** $-\underline{b}$ **c** $\underline{a} - \underline{b}$

3
a $2\underline{c}$ **b** $2\underline{a}$ **c** $2\underline{a} + 2\underline{c}$ **d** $\underline{c} - \underline{a}$ **e** $\underline{c} - \underline{a}$
Answers **d** and **e** demonstrate that PQ is parallel to MN and of equal length.

4
a $\underline{y}$ **b** $\underline{x}$ **c** $2\underline{y}$ **d** $\underline{x} + 2\underline{y}$ **e** $\underline{x} + \underline{y}$
e $\underline{x} + \underline{y}$
Answers **d** and **e** demonstrate that OB is parallel to CD and of equal length.

5
a $\dfrac{\underline{a}}{4}$ **b** $\dfrac{\underline{b}}{4}$ **c** $\underline{b} - \underline{a}$ **d** $\dfrac{\underline{b}}{4} - \dfrac{\underline{a}}{4}$

Answers **c** and **d** demonstrate that MN is parallel to AB and that AB = 4MN.

CHECKPOINT 37

1
a $\begin{pmatrix} +9 \\ +9 \end{pmatrix}$ **b** $\begin{pmatrix} -4 \\ +6 \end{pmatrix}$ **c** $\begin{pmatrix} +2 \\ +2 \end{pmatrix}$

d $\begin{pmatrix} +13 \\ -2 \end{pmatrix}$ **e** $\begin{pmatrix} -7 \\ -9 \end{pmatrix}$ **f** $\begin{pmatrix} +7 \\ 0 \end{pmatrix}$

2
a $\underline{x} + \underline{y} = \begin{pmatrix} +7 \\ 0 \end{pmatrix}$ $\underline{x} - \underline{y} = \begin{pmatrix} -11 \\ +16 \end{pmatrix}$

b $\underline{x} + \underline{y} = \begin{pmatrix} +3 \\ +2 \end{pmatrix}$ $\underline{x} - \underline{y} = \begin{pmatrix} -7 \\ +14 \end{pmatrix}$

c $\underline{x} + \underline{y} = \begin{pmatrix} +3 \\ -4 \end{pmatrix}$ $\underline{x} - \underline{y} = \begin{pmatrix} -15 \\ +10 \end{pmatrix}$

d $\underline{x} + \underline{y} = \begin{pmatrix} +5 \\ +1 \end{pmatrix}$ $\underline{x} - \underline{y} = \begin{pmatrix} -17 \\ +5 \end{pmatrix}$

e $\underline{x} + \underline{y} = \begin{pmatrix} +4 \\ 0 \end{pmatrix}$ $\underline{x} - \underline{y} = \begin{pmatrix} -6 \\ +10 \end{pmatrix}$

f $\underline{x} + \underline{y} = \begin{pmatrix} +8 \\ 0 \end{pmatrix}$ $\underline{x} - \underline{y} = \begin{pmatrix} -8 \\ +10 \end{pmatrix}$

Geometry – Practice and revision exercise

1
a 18° **b** 5° **c** 148.5° **d** 338° **e** 20°

2 $a = c = d = f = 125°$ $\qquad$ $b = e = g = 55°$
$\quad j = h = k = m = 60°$ $\qquad$ $i = n = l = 120°$
$\quad o = y = v = 63°$ $\qquad$ $p = q = 117°$ $\qquad s = 109°$
$\quad r = t = u = x = 71°$ $\qquad$ $v = z = 46°$

3
a = 40° **b** = 29° **c** = 70° **d** = 75° **e** = 30° **f** = 69°
g = 69° **h** = 70° **i** = 50° **j** = 50° **k** = 80° **l** = 98°

5
a 900° **b** 360° **c** 128.57° **d** 51.43°

6
a 1440°, 360°, 144°, 36° **b** 1800°, 360°, 150°, 30°

7 18 sides

8 12 sides

11
a 66° **b** 57°

12
a 78° **b** 39°

13
a 76° **b** 52°

14
a 15° **b** 105°

15
a 46° **b** 46°

16
a 124° **b** 62° **c** 62° **d** 62°

17
a 60° **b** 90° **c** 120° **d** 60°

18
a 15° **b** 15° **c** 75° **d** 90°

37

a Translation $\begin{pmatrix} -7 \\ +3 \end{pmatrix}$.

b Rotation of −90° about (0, 0).

c Enlargement scale factor $\frac{1}{2}$, centre (0, 0).

d Refelction in the line with equation $y = 0$.

38
a $\begin{pmatrix} 0 & 1 \\ -1 & 0 \end{pmatrix}$ **b** $\begin{pmatrix} 1 & 0 \\ 0 & -1 \end{pmatrix}$ **c** $\begin{pmatrix} \frac{1}{5} & 0 \\ 0 & \frac{1}{5} \end{pmatrix}$

d $\begin{pmatrix} 1 & 0 \\ -4 & 1 \end{pmatrix}$

41
a $\underline{b} - \underline{a}$ **b** $\dfrac{\underline{a} - \underline{b}}{2}$ **c** $\dfrac{\underline{a} + \underline{b}}{2}$

42
a $\begin{pmatrix} +5 \\ +8 \end{pmatrix}$ $\begin{pmatrix} -1 \\ -4 \end{pmatrix}$

43
a $\underline{x} + \underline{y} = \begin{pmatrix} +5 \\ +2 \end{pmatrix}$ $\underline{x} - \underline{y} = \begin{pmatrix} -11 \\ +16 \end{pmatrix}$

b $\underline{x} + \underline{y} = \begin{pmatrix} +5 \\ 0 \end{pmatrix}$ $\underline{x} - \underline{y} = \begin{pmatrix} -7 \\ +14 \end{pmatrix}$

Geometry – Past paper questions

1 $x = 52°$ $y = 57°$

2 70°

3
a isoceles
b $p = 51°$ $q = 51°$ $r = 129°$

4 $x = 45°$ $y = 70°$ $z = 60°$

5 $x = 60°$ $y = 120°$ $z = 60°$

6
a $p = 42°$ **b** $x = 37°$ $y = 74°$ $z = 106°$

7
a ABC = 108° **b** CAE = 72° **c** AEX = 72°

8
a (i) ADB = 30° (i) ABD = 30° (iii) DBC = 90° (iv) BDC = 30°

9
a (i) $x = 36$ (ii) 144° **b** Angle OBC $= \dfrac{(180 - 144)}{2} = 18°$

10
a $a = 90$ $b = 60$ $c = 60$
b (i) $x = 108$ $y = 36$ $z = 72$

12
a Octagon **b** (i) Quadrilateral (ii) Hexagon

13
b B **c** 70°

15
a (ii) 90° (ii) 120° (iii) 150°
b (i) The shape is regular, with an interior angle of 150° and an exterior angle of 30°. Therefore it will be a regular 12-sided shape, ie (ii) a dodecagon.

16
a (i) 120° (ii) 108°
b (i) $y = 180 - \dfrac{360}{x}$ (ii) $x = \dfrac{360}{180 - y}$
c (i) 3
(ii) No. An octagon has an interior angle of 135°, which is not a factor of 360.

17
a 5 **b** 25 cm **c** 100°

19
a Isosceles **b** 55° **c** (i) 290° (ii) 235°

20
b 200°

22
a 2.5 km **b** 14 cm

24 C and B

37
b (i) Rectangle (ii) Parallelogram (iii) Rhombus (iv) Kite

38
a (i) 5 **b** 108°

43
a (i) Equilateral (ii) 60° **b** (i) 1.73 cm² (ii) 75.46 cm²
c (i) 9 (ii) 3 (iii) 54

45
a 7 cm³ **b** (ii) 25 cm²

47 E

49 Only Andrew's is correct.

51
a $\dfrac{2}{5}$

52 (1, 4)

56 Reflection in the y-axis

57
a Rotation of −90° about (−1, 4) **b** (1, −4).

58 **a** $\begin{pmatrix} 0 \\ -2 \end{pmatrix}$ **b** (1, 0)

60
a A''(2, 2), B''(6,4), C''(4, 80) **b** $\begin{pmatrix} 2 & 0 \\ 0 & 2 \end{pmatrix}$

c Enlargement scale factor 2, centre (0, 0)

62
a (i) $\begin{matrix} O & D & E & F \end{matrix}$ (iii) Reflection in the x-axis
$\begin{pmatrix} 0 & 1 & 1 & 0 \\ 0 & 0 & -1 & -1 \end{pmatrix}$

(iv) $\begin{pmatrix} 1 & 0 \\ 0 & -1 \end{pmatrix}$

b (i) Rotation of +36.9° about (0, 0)
(ii) $\begin{pmatrix} 0.8 & -0.6 \\ 0.6 & 0.8 \end{pmatrix}$

c $\begin{pmatrix} 0.8 & 0.6 \\ 0.6 & -0.8 \end{pmatrix}$

63
a $\begin{pmatrix} -2 & 0 \\ 0 & -2 \end{pmatrix}$ **b** (−2, −2), (−8, −2), (−2, −4)

d Enlargement, scale factor −2, centre (0, 0).

e $\begin{pmatrix} 0.5 & -1.5 \\ 0.5 & -0.5 \end{pmatrix}$ (5, 2)

64
a 3 **b** $\begin{pmatrix} \frac{4}{3} & -\frac{5}{3} \\ -\frac{1}{3} & \frac{2}{3} \end{pmatrix}$ **c** $\begin{pmatrix} 1 & 1 & 10 & 10 \\ -4 & 2 & 2 & -4 \end{pmatrix}$

e 54 square units **f** 18 square units

g $\begin{pmatrix} 0 & -1 \\ 1 & 0 \end{pmatrix}$ **h** $\begin{pmatrix} 0 & -1 \\ 1 & 0 \end{pmatrix} \begin{pmatrix} -\frac{4}{3} & -\frac{5}{3} \\ -\frac{1}{3} & \frac{2}{3} \end{pmatrix} = \begin{pmatrix} \frac{1}{3} & -\frac{2}{3} \\ \frac{4}{3} & -\frac{5}{3} \end{pmatrix}$

67
a B **b** (i) C (i) C
d Rotation anticlockwise about O through the obtuse angle AOC, which is equal to ''x or $2y$
e Angle AOC = 2 times Angle ABC

68
a (i) $2x$ (ii) $2y$ **b** (i) Rhombus (ii) Square

69
a $q - p$ **b** $\dfrac{q - p}{2}$ **c** $\dfrac{q + p}{2}$

70
a 3 **b** −10 **c** −2
   −8   5   −2

71
a $-a$ **b** $\dfrac{3b}{10}$ **c** $b - a$ **d** $\dfrac{b - a}{2}$ **e** $\dfrac{a + b}{2}$

f NO $= \dfrac{-OM}{2} = \dfrac{-a - b}{4}$

NQ $= \dfrac{-a - b}{4} + \dfrac{3b}{10} = \dfrac{-5a - 5b + 6b}{20} = \dfrac{-a}{4} = \dfrac{b}{20}$

g PM $= \dfrac{3AM}{4} = \dfrac{3a - 3b}{8}$ MN $= \dfrac{-a - b}{4}$

PN $=$ PM $+$ MN $= \dfrac{3b - 3a}{8} + \dfrac{-a - b}{4} = \dfrac{3b - 3a - 2a - 2b}{8}$

PN $= \dfrac{b - 5a}{8} = \dfrac{-5a}{8} + \dfrac{b}{8}$

h The results show that NQ $= \dfrac{2PN}{5}$

If one vector is a multiple of another they must be parallel, therefore PN and NQ are parallel. But, the lines share a common point, N. Therefore, they are part of the same straight line.

72
a 63.4° **b** 50 **c** (50,100) **d** $\begin{pmatrix} 2 \\ -1 \end{pmatrix}$ **e** (100, 75)

73
a CO $= -3c$ CB $= 2a - c$ AB $= 2c - 2a$
b FC $= -3c$ BE $= a + c$ FE $= 3a - 3c$ DE $= 3c - 3a$
c Since DE $= -$FE, DEF are three points on a straight line and E is the mid-point of FD.

Pythagoras and Trigonometry

1 25
2 529
3 900
4 49 cm²

CHECKPOINT 2

1
a 4225   **b** 166.41   **c** 1.69   **d** 53 361
2 2862.25 cm²

CHECKPOINT 3

1 8
2 2
3 8
4 6 cm

CHECKPOINT 4

1 $7^2 = 49$ and $8^2 = 64$, therefore the square root of 60 must lie between 7 and 8.
2 $20^2 = 400$ and $30^2 = 900$, therefore the square root of 734 must lie between 20 and 30.

3
a 7.745 966 7   **b** 27.092 434   **c** 2.387 467 3   **d** 30.602 29

4 6.708 cm (to 3 d.p.)

CHECKPOINT 5

1 10.30 cm (2 d.p.)
2 13 cm
3 6.1 m
4 8.5 m
5 1.414 cm, 5 cm and 5 cm
6 12.28 m (55 m − 42.72 m)

CHECKPOINT 6

1 12 m
2 3 m
3 110 m
4 The diagonal of a 90 cm by 50 cm rectangle is 102.96 cm long, therefore the umbrella will probably fit in the suitcase.
5 14.14 cm
6 7.14 m

CHECKPOINT 7

1 10.25 cm (to 2 d.p.)
2 70.71 m (to 2 d.p.)
3 The longest diagonal inside the garage will be approximately 6.56 m long, therefore the mast will probably fit.
4 9.81 cm (to 2 d.p.)

CHECKPOINT 8

1
a $\underline{XZ} = \begin{pmatrix} +7 \\ -5 \end{pmatrix}$ $|\underline{XY}| = 3.606$ $|\underline{YZ}| = 5$ $|\underline{XZ}| = 8.602$

b $\underline{XZ} = \begin{pmatrix} +7 \\ +7 \end{pmatrix}$ $|\underline{XY}| = 5$ $|\underline{YZ}| = 5$ $|\underline{XZ}| = 9.899$

2
a $\underline{x} + \underline{y} = \begin{pmatrix} +6 \\ +6 \end{pmatrix}$ $\underline{x} - \underline{y} = \begin{pmatrix} -10 \\ +10 \end{pmatrix}$

$|\underline{x}| = 8.246$ $|\underline{y}| = 8.246$ $|\underline{x} + \underline{y}| = 8.485$ $|\underline{x} - \underline{y}| = 14.142$

b $\underline{x} + \underline{y} = \begin{pmatrix} +3 \\ +2 \end{pmatrix}$ $\underline{x} - \underline{y} = \begin{pmatrix} -7 \\ +14 \end{pmatrix}$

$|\underline{x}| = 8.246$ $|\underline{y}| = 7.810$ $|\underline{x} + \underline{y}| = 3.606$ $|\underline{x} - \underline{y}| = 15.652$

CHECKPOINT 10

The side YZ must be 1.8 m long.

CHECKPOINT 11

1 9m
2 18 m
3 360 m

CHECKPOINT 13

1
a 2.887   **b** 43.301 m   **c** 14.301 mm

2 4.12 m
3 1.820 m
4 0.839 km

CHECKPOINT 14

1 0.267 949 2
2 4.010 780 9
3 0.767 327 0
4 1.771 098 5

CHECKPOINT 15

1
a 7.369 m   **b** 24.185 cm   **c** 211.523 mm

2 81.906 m
3 5.485 m
4 9.696 m

CHECKPOINT 16

1
a 2.548 m   **b** 7.626 cm   **c** 29.991 mm
2 1.212 m
3 14.522 m
4 The distances from the church are 13.462 m and 33.772 m, so the surveyors are 20.31 m apart.

CHECKPOINT 17

1
a 14.036°   **b** 36.686°   **c** 56.310°   **d** 85.156°   **e** 0.997°
2
a 57.995°   **b** 50.194°   **c** 15.297°
3 61.928°
4 44.29° and 135.71°
5 A = 37.569° B = 23.479°
6 86 miles and 0.35.5°

CHECKPOINT 19

1
a 6.180 m   **b** 12.379 cm   **c** 22.717 mm

2 4.698 m
3 578.509 m
4 14.501 m

CHECKPOINT 20

1
a 12.446 cm   **b** 19.953 mm   **c** 17.201 m

2 18.739 km
3 75.342 cm
4 13.004 cm

CHECKPOINT 21

1
a 14.478°   **b** 48.159°   **c** 30°   **d** 59.997°   **e** 0.859°

2

a 36.870° **b** 50.805° **c** 54.903°

3 The angle of the roof's slope is approximately 21° and the tiles can therefore be used.
4 The angle of the slope is approximately 6.89° and a rack and pinion railway can therefore be constructed.
5 50.301°

CHECKPOINT 23

1
a 8.480 cm **b** 10.554 mm **c** 21.155 m

2 38.302 km
3 2.785 m
4 8.989 m

CHECKPOINT 24

1
a 5.356 cm **b** 18.934 cm **c** 3.832

2 65.270 km
3 1.648 m
4 6.250 cm

CHECKPOINT 25

1
a 61.315° **b** 29.893° **c** 43.090°

2 043.79°
3 69.190°
4 31.102°

CHECKPOINT 26

1 sine 240° = −sine 60° = −0.866
   cosine 240° = −cosine 60° = −0.5
2 sine 330° = −sine 30° = −0.5
   cosine 330° = cosine 30° = 0.866
3

	0°	90°	180°	270°	360°
SINE	0	1	0	−1	0
COSINE	1	0	−1	0	1

Pythagoras and trigonometry –
Practice and revision exercise

1
a 10 m **b** 2.6 cm **c** 12.021 mm **d** 132.424 cm

2
a 36 cm **b** 0.7 cm **c** 2.646 cm **d** 106.132 cm

3 5.657 cm

4 2.828 cm

5 No, the minimum distance from the bank to the boat is 3.606 m.

6
a 5 cm **b** 13 cm

7 The longest diagonal inside the garage will be approximately 7.16 m long, therefore the mast will probably fit.

8 39.051 km
9

Length of ladder (metres)	4	5	6	7	8
Distance of foot from wall (metres)	1	1.25	1.5	1.75	2
Reach up the wall (metres)	3.87	4.84	5.81	6.78	7.75

10 The height of the triangle is 4.5 cm and the area is 27 cm^2.

11
a 11.911 cm **b** 9.561 m **c** 44.700 mm

12
a 10.094 cm **b** 9.158 km **c** 11.383 m

13
a 32.093° **b** 48.834° **c** 42.905

14
a 5 cm **b** 53 cm **c** 0.15 m

15 7.523 m
16 026.4°
17 71.8°, 71.8°, 36.4°
18 19.919 km
19 6.390 cm
20 8.342 m
21 1213.926 m
22 64.689
23 2.008 km
24 445.1 m^2, 526.3 m^2, 744.6 m^2
25
a 66.750° **b** 56.066° **c** 64.556° **d** 1047.425 cm^2

Pythagoras and trigonometry –
Optional section

CHECKPOINT 29

1 9.079 cm
2 19.081 cm

3
a 105.49 m **m** 57.45 m

4 Norwich to Bradford, 157.4 miles.
   Norwich to Bournemouth, 192.8 miles
5 1.346 m

CHECKPOINT 30

1 42.384°
2 36.797°
3 67.453°

CHECKPOINT 31

1 6.854 cm
2 19.325 m
3 0.66 km
4 61.59 m

CHECKPOINT 32

1 16.656°
2 137.874°
3 55.8°, 41.4°, 82.8°
4 110.487°
5 28.4°

Pythagoras and trigonometry –
Past paper questions

1 30 m
2
a 76.39° **b** 8.26 m **c** 0.59 m

3 7.2 m
a — **b** DC = BC = 11.31 cm **c** 60° **d** 151.39 cm²

5
a (i) 90° (ii) 40° **b** 1285.6 m and 1532.1 m

6
a 0.8 m **b** 13.2° **c** 2.8 m

7
a 15 cm **b** 90° **c** 3.2 m

8
a 6.0 m
b (i) 25.0 m (ii) 13.5° (iii) 40.9 m
c (i) 30° (ii) 150°

9
a 64 miles and 108 miles
b (i) 51.3° (ii) 038.7° (iii) 158.2°
c (i) 2.2 miles (ii) 3.1°

10
a 330° **b** 12.5 km

11
a 7.99 km **b** 14.42 km

12
a (i) 8.49 cm (ii) 7.35 cm **b** —

13
a (i) 1.25 hours (ii) 2310 hours
b (i) 301° (ii) 233.2 km (iii) 102.9 km

14
a 5° **b** 165.2 m **c** 1895.3 m **d** 710.0 m
e 515.8 m **f** 637.0 m

15
a 16.00 km **b** 63.00 km **c** 15.00 km
d 35.31° **e** 305.31°

16
a 15.32 km **b** 12.86 km **c** 45.3°

17
a 2310
b (i) 280 km (ii) 321.8° (iii) 74.2 km

18
a (i) 90° (ii) 100 km (iii) 29.9°
b 2400 km²

19
a 4850 m **b** 1070 m

20
a (i) 11.89 km (ii) 10.71 km
b (i) 25.63 km (ii) 062°
c 242° **d** 4 hours

21
a 50 m **b** 30 m **c** 22.5° **d** 55.4 m

22
a (i) $\tan 60° = \dfrac{h}{x}$ (ii) $\tan 40° = \dfrac{h}{50 + x}$

b Equation (i) can become $x \tan 60° = h$.
Equation (ii) can become $(50 + x) \tan 40° = h$
Therefore, since both are equal to h, we have
$$x \tan 60° = (50 + x) \tan 40°$$

Or,
$$x \tan 60° = 50 \tan 40° + x \tan 40°$$
Subtracting $x \tan 40°$ from both sides gives
$$x \tan 60° - x \tan 40° = 50 \tan 40°$$

Or,
$$x (\tan 60° - \tan 40°) = 50 \tan 40°$$

c 81.4 m

23
d $k = 2$

Statistics

3
a Discrete quantitative **b** Ordered qualitative
c Qualitative or perhaps ordered qualitative
d Continuous quantitative **e** Qualitative
f Discrete quantitative **g** Ordered qualitative
h Continuous quantitative

1

Number of goals scored	0	1	2	3	4	5
Number of teams	17	28	8	5	1	1

2

	YOUNG	MATURE	OLD
LABOUR	178	53	104
CONSERVATIVE	32	199	189
SLD	80	82	83

1
a 41p, 47p, 51p, 32p **b** 51p, 22p, 43p, 28p
c 2p, 2p, 4p, 6p

1
a Social Security **b** Transport
c

EXPENDITURE	£ BILLION	ANGLE
Social Security	48.5	111°
Education	18.0	41°
Health	20.7	47°
Defence	19.2	44°
Transport	5.2	12°
Law & Order	7.0	16°
Housing Environ	6.8	16°
Industry	5.9	14°
Other	25.5	59°

3
a Police **b** 16% **c** 487
d 1557

2

Vehicle length (metres)	Frequency
3.0–4.0	80
4.0–4.5	70
4.5–5.0	35
5.0–5.5	25
5.5–7.5	20

1
a 8 **b** 3 **c** £2
d 1 **e** 5.77
2 56.2 and 52.1 **3** 25.2 and 20.7 **4** 4.1 metres
5 50.5

CHECKPOINT 10

1 Estate A, 1.78 children per family, Estate B, 2.82 children per family.
2 City A, 169.7p per gallon, City B, 170.22p per gallon.
3 School A, 2.0167 tests per pupil, School B, 2.07 tests per pupil.
4 Using a code of $A = 1$, $B = 2$, $C = 3$ etc., the averages work out at Swotville, 4.4, Dipsticks 3.64. This gives an average of grade D-E for Swotville and C-D for Dipsticks. It is interesting to note that taken to the nearest grade, both averages are Grade D.

CHECKPOINT 11

1 Rooksend, 68.2 cm; Boggham, 9.9 cm
2 Maureen 91.7; Eric 76.7
3 Diet A, 28.9 kg; Diet B, 29.32 kg
4 Before 82.125 kg; after, 74.525 kg

CHECKPOINT 12

1
a 7   b 3   c £4.50   d £4.25   e 0   f 6.1
2 5th Years, 51.5, 4th Years 50.5
3 Maureen, 20, Eric, 20

CHECKPOINT 13

a Lower Quartile = 1, Median = 2, Upper Quartile = 3
b Lower Quartile = 2, Median = 3, Upper Quartile = 5
c Lower Quartile = £2.00, Median = £4.50, Upper Quartile = £5.50
d Lower Quartile = 38, Median = 68, Upper Quartile = 83
e Lower Quartile = 218, Median = 249, Upper Quartile = 289
f Lower Quartile = −1, Median = 0, Upper Quartile = 1.25

CHECKPOINT 14

1 Estate A, Q1 = 1, M = 2, Q2 = 3
  Estate B, Q1 = 2, M = 2, Q2 = 4
2 City A, Q1 = 169, M = 170, Q2 = 170
  City B, Q1 = 169, M = 170, Q2 = 171
3 School A, Q1 = 1, M = 1.5, Q2 = 2.75
  School B, Q1 = 1, M = 2, Q2 = 3
4 Swotville, Q1 = C, M = D, Q2 = F
  Dipsticks, Q1 = B, M = C, Q2 = E

CHECKPOINT 15

1
a Rooksend, Q1 = 42 cm, M = 63 cm, Q2 = 84 cm
  Boggham, Q1 = 80 cm, M = 103 cm, Q2 = 123 cm
b 62 trees

2
a Maureen, Q1 = 50, M = 90, Q2 = 132
  Eric, Q1 = 54, M = 76, Q2 = 93
b 28 times   c 9 times

3
a Before, Q1 = 72 kg, M = 83 kg, 93 kg
  After, Q1 = 66.5 kg, M = 74.5 kg, 80 kg
b 45   c 18

4
a Ms Salt, Q1 = 3.5 mins, M = 4.4 mins, Q2 = 5.4 mins
  Ms Pepper, Q1 = 4.95 mins, M = 5.65 mins, Q2 = 6.5 mins
b 13   c 19

CHECKPOINT 16

1
a 6   b 3   c £1.50   d 0
e No sensible mode

2 City A, 170p, City B, 171p

3 Rooksend, 60–80 cm, Boggham, 120–140 cm

CHECKPOINT 17

1
a Mean   b Mode

2 Mean = 70p, Median = 60p, Mode = 60p

3 Mean = 2.88 visits, Median = 2 visits, Mode = 1 visit

CHECKPOINT 18

1 Obviously, the mean average does not indicate this. It is possible that not one single day has this 'ideal temperature'. Days may range from very hot to very cold, only *averaging* out to 21°.

2
a Range = 7 − 0 = 7   Interquartile range = 3 − 1 = 2
b Range = 5 − 1 = 4   Interquartile range = 5 − 2 = 3
c Range = £6.00 − £1.50 = £4.50
  Interquartile range = £5.50 − £2.00 = £3.50
d Range = 92 − 17 = 75
  Interquartile range = 83 − 38 = 45
e Range = 300 − 199 = 101
  Interquartile range = 289 − 218 = 71
f Range = 3 − −3 = 6
  Interquartile range = 1.25 − −1 = 2.25

3 Estate A, Range = 4 − 0 = 4,
  Interquartile range = 3 − 1 = 2
  Estate B, Range = 6 − 0 = 6,
  Interquartile range = 4 − 2 = 2

4 Range = 26 − 18 = 8 minutes
  Interquartile range = 23 − 20 = 3 minutes

CHECKPOINT 19

	Mean	Median	Q1	Q2	Mode	Range	IQR
1a	3.63	3	2	5	3	7	3
1b	14.09	12	11	19	12	18	8
1c	37.93	38	37	39	37	5	2
1d	100.77	101	101	102	100	3	2
2a	40.34	40	39	41	41	8	2
2b	39.87	40	39	41	40	6	5
3a	4.783	6	4	7	6	8	3
3b	3.767	5	2	6	5	7	4

4

	Mean	Median	Q1	Q2	Mode	Range	IQR
Before	354.7	352	334	376	340–360	140	42
After	315.7	316	296	334	320–340	120	38

a 28   b 54

5

	Mean	Median	Q1	Q2	Mode	Range	IQR
Duraready	90.8	95	81	103	100–110	70	22
Evercell	95.6	98	91	104.5	90–100	50	13.5

a 44%   b 36%   c 24%   d 0%

CHECKPOINT 20

1 BOB Mean = 17 Standard Deviation = 19.6
  SUE Mean = 14 Standard Deviation = 8.6

2 LEEDS   Mean = 197 Standard Deviation = 3.7
  LONDON Mean = 199 Standard Deviation = 8.1

3 HERON LEA ESTATE   Mean = 1.3 Standard Deviation = 1.0
  CHERRY TREES ESTATE Mean = 1.9 Standard Deviation = 1.4

CHECKPOINT 21

1
a Mean = 14.4   Standard Deviation = 1.7
b Mean = 2.85   Standard Deviation = 1.28
c Mean = 27.4   Standard Deviation = 4.4

2 FIRST WEEK   Mean = 235.9   Standard Deviation = 129.8
LAST WEEK   Mean = 274.6   Standard Deviation = 92.5

3 DIET A   Mean = 29.13   Standard Deviation = 4.61
DIET B   Mean = 29.53   Standard Deviation = 2.15

CHECKPOINT 23

1
a $\frac{1}{15}$ **b** $\frac{4}{15}$ **c** $\frac{1}{5}$ **d** $\frac{1}{15}$ **e** $\frac{2}{15}$ **f** $\frac{4}{15}$

2
a $\frac{3}{13}$ **b** $\frac{10}{13}$ **c** $\frac{1}{52}$ **d** $\frac{1}{13}$ **e** $\frac{1}{26}$ **f** $\frac{3}{26}$
g $\frac{7}{13}$ **h** $\frac{4}{13}$ **i** $\frac{1}{2}$ **j** $\frac{6}{13}$

3
a $\frac{1}{4}$ **b** $\frac{5}{12}$ **c** $\frac{1}{3}$ **d** $\frac{7}{12}$ **e** $\frac{2}{3}$ **f** $\frac{3}{4}$
g $\frac{2}{3}$ **h** 0   **i** 1   **j** $\frac{7}{12}$

4
a $\frac{1}{2}$ **b** $\frac{7}{30}$ **c** $\frac{1}{6}$ **d** $\frac{1}{10}$ **e** $\frac{11}{15}$ **f** $\frac{4}{15}$
g $\frac{3}{5}$

5
a (i) $\frac{1}{5}$ (ii) $\frac{1}{10}$ (iii) $\frac{19}{50}$
b (i) $\frac{9}{25}$ (ii) $\frac{2}{25}$ (iii) $\frac{23}{50}$

6
a (i) $\frac{43}{100}$ (ii) $\frac{57}{100}$ (iii) $\frac{27}{50}$
b (i) $\frac{37}{100}$ (ii) $\frac{63}{100}$ (iii) $\frac{1}{2}$

7
a (i) $\frac{1}{2}$ (ii) $\frac{3}{10}$ (iii) $\frac{7}{10}$
b (i) $\frac{8}{25}$ (ii) $\frac{8}{25}$ (iii) 1

c The answers are simply estimates based on past performances. The final answer demonstrates this clearly, because it is obvious that we cannot be certain (probability = 1), that Eric will score between 31 and 150!

CHECKPOINT 24

1
a $\frac{1}{4}$ **b** $\frac{1}{2}$

2
a 500   **b** 500   **c** 1000

3
a $\frac{5}{36}$ **b** $\frac{1}{6}$ **c** $\frac{1}{12}$ **d** $\frac{1}{9}$ **e** $\frac{1}{12}$ **f** $\frac{1}{36}$
g $\frac{1}{2}$ **h** $\frac{7}{18}$ **i** $\frac{13}{18}$ **j** $\frac{5}{12}$ **k** 0   **l** 1

4
a 200   **b** 50   **c** 100   **d** 250   **e** 100   **f** 350

5
a $\frac{1}{16}$ **b** $\frac{1}{4}$ **c** $\frac{1}{2}$ **d** $\frac{1}{2}$ **e** $\frac{1}{8}$

6 $\frac{1}{21}$ **7** $\frac{6}{25}$ **8** $\frac{4}{9}$

CHECKPOINT 25

1 1/1 679 616   **2** 33/66 640   **3** 1/1024

4
a $\frac{1}{64}$ **b** $\frac{1}{27}$ **c** $\frac{125}{1728}$ **d** $\frac{5}{84}$ **e** $\frac{5}{84}$

5
a $\frac{1}{220}$ **b** $\frac{1}{55}$ **c** $\frac{1}{22}$ **d** $\frac{1}{22}$ **e** $\frac{1}{22}$

6 19/2 769 450

CHECKPOINT 26

1
a $\frac{21}{25}$ **b** $\frac{13}{25}$

2
a $\frac{9}{10}$ **b** $\frac{2}{5}$

3 $\frac{2}{27}$ **4** $\frac{3}{10}$ **5** $\frac{271}{1000}$ **6** $\frac{29}{57}$
7 $\frac{27}{125}$ **8** $\frac{23}{42}$

CHECKPOINT 27

4
a U, N, I, V, A, C   **b** 1

Statistics – Practice and revision exercise

1 See Text

2

SCORE	1	2	3	4	5	6	7	8	9	10
FREQUENCY	3	8	6	8	12	15	15	12	15	6

3 77, 4100   78, 4150   79, 3700   80, 3800   81, 4450   82, 5050
83, 4500   84, 4250   85, 7200   86, 5800   87, 6500

	Mean	Median	Q1	Q2	Mode	Range	IQR
8a	4.105	4	2	6	2	7	4
8b	22.33	22	21	23	21	4	2
8c	0.545	1	−1	2	1	6	3
8d	330.77	300	200	450	200	400	250
9a	39.11	39	38	40	39	7	2
9b	1.847	2	1	2	2	6	1
10a	15.438	15.5	11.5	19.5	15–20	30	8
10b	4.515	4.4	4.1	4.8	4.0–4.5	9	0.4

12
a $\frac{1}{2}$ **b** $\frac{5}{6}$ **c** $\frac{2}{3}$ **d** $\frac{1}{6}$

13
a $\frac{1}{4}$ **b** $\frac{1}{2}$ **c** $\frac{1}{52}$ **d** $\frac{3}{13}$ **e** $\frac{3}{4}$ **f** $\frac{7}{13}$
g $\frac{1}{26}$ **h** $\frac{4}{13}$

415

14
a $\frac{7}{18}$ **b** $\frac{1}{36}$ **c** $\frac{5}{18}$ **d** $\frac{1}{6}$ **e** $\frac{1}{3}$ **f** 0

g 0 **h** $\frac{1}{18}$

15
a $\frac{1}{5}$ **b** $\frac{1}{15}$ **c** $\frac{1}{5}$

16
a $\frac{46}{833}$ **b** 1/32 768 **c** 1/60 466 176

17
a $\frac{19}{25}$ **b** $\frac{6}{25}$

18 $\frac{79}{100}$

19 $\frac{1}{3}$

20

A	B	D	C
		0	
0		0	
0	1	0	
0	1	0	1
0	1	1	1
1	1	1	1
1	1	1	1
1	1	1	2
1	1	2	2
1	1	2	2
1	2	2	2
1	2	2	3
1	2	3	3
2	2	3	3
2	3	3	3
2	3	3	5
2	3	4	5
3	3	4	5
3	5	4	5
3	5	4	8
3	5	5	8

(i) The variable D is 'counting' the number of times the loop is repeated.
(ii) Change the question to 'Is $D = 10$?'

21
(i) Output is 3, 2 (ii) The flowchart inputs two numbers, it then calculates and outputs the number of times that the second number divides into the first number and the remainder that is left.

22
a This flowchart deals with five numbers and uses the 'names' A, B, C, D and E to represent them. A flowchart of this design to find the average of 500 numbers would need 500 'names' written in both the input and output boxes. This would be very time-consuming and, since the alphabet would be rapidly used up, more complicated 'names' like $A1$, $A2$, $A3$, etc would have to be used.
b The flowchart should be drawn with a loop (see question 20).

Statistics – past paper questions

1
a Continuous **b** Discrete **c** Discrete
d Continuous

2

	FIRST TEST		REPEAT TEST	
	PASS	FAIL	PASS	FAIL
MALES	81	59	60	30
FEMALES	62	48	45	25
TOTAL	151	107	105	55

3
a 150° **b** $\frac{1}{3}$

5
a

Score	80–84	85–89	90–94	94–99	100–04
Frequency	5	11	4	3	2

b 16 **c** 20%

6
a – **b** 99 **c** 144°

8

TYPE OF CRISP	PLAIN	S AND V	C AND O	BEEF	BACON
FREQUENCY	9	16	11	6	3
ANGLE	72	128	88	48	24

11
a 24 **b** $\frac{1}{3}$ **c** (i) 6 (ii) $\frac{1}{4}$

d Angles are 150°, 60°, 30° and 120°.

12
a £350 **b** 35:72

14 Percentages are 46%, 28%, 16% and 10%.

15
a The vertical axis does not start at zero and the line is much too thick.
b 275

16
a 5 **b** 12 **c** 2.6 km

17
a 6 **b** 2 **c** 3

18
a Samantha 7.2, Teresa 6.8 **b** Samantha 8, Teresa 3

19
a 20 **b** – **c** 198 **d** 1.65

20
a (i) 2 (ii) 44 (iii) 5C **c** 5A **d** Tuesday
e (i) 5D (ii) Wednesday (iii) 12–15
(iv) Total absence for Wednesday – approximate daily absence
f (i) 84 (ii) 16.8 **g** 8
h (i) Median (ii) Mean has been distorted by trip absence.

21
a (i) 59 (ii) 15
b 4 minutes
c (i) 3.4 mins (ii) The table shows a grouped variable. All we know is that, for example, 15 boys took between 3.5 and 4.5 minutes. We do not know the exact times for each boy.
d (i) Median (ii) The mean is distorted more than the median by the 15 boys recorded under 0. These boys did not do games and therefore should have been excluded from the table rather than recorded as super-fast changers.
(iii) A description of finding the median by graphical techniques should be given.

22
a (i) 222 g (ii) 48 g **b** 60

23
a 66.9 seconds **b** (i) 0.8 (ii) 0.05 (iii) 0.512 (iv) 0.216 (v) 0.296 (vi) 0.143

24
a 16 **b** 7 hours 40 minutes **c** 37.75 **d** –
e (i) 9.5 (ii) 39

25
a 32.6
b

MARK	0–4	5–9	10–14	15–19	20–24
FREQ	1	2	6	10	10

MARK	25–29	30–34	35–39	40–44	45–49
FREQ	9	6	3	2	1

26
a 2–4   **b** 8–10   **c** 6–8   **d** 5.4 km

27
a $\frac{1}{6}$ **b** $\frac{1}{3}$

28
a $\frac{1}{6}$ **b** $\frac{1}{2}$ **c** $\frac{1}{3}$

29 $\frac{13}{29}$

30
a (i) $\frac{1}{9}$ (ii) N, $\frac{1}{3}$ **b** $\frac{1}{36}$

31 $\frac{5}{497}$

32
a $\frac{2}{5}$ **b** 43 minutes

33
a $\frac{6}{25}$ **b** $\frac{13}{25}$

34
b $\frac{24}{125}$ **c** $\frac{58}{125}$

35
b (i) $\frac{2}{9}$ (ii) 0   (iii) $\frac{16}{45}$ (iv) $\frac{29}{45}$

36
a (i) $\frac{2}{3}$ (ii) $\frac{1}{3}$ (iii) $\frac{2}{9}$ **b** $\frac{1}{9}$

37
a (i) $\frac{1}{6}$ (ii) $\frac{5}{6}$ (iii) $\frac{5}{6}$ **b** $\frac{25}{36}$

c (i) $\frac{125}{216}$ (ii) $\frac{1}{216}$ (iii) $\frac{5}{72}$

38
a (i) 5°C   (ii) $\frac{x - 30}{2}$ (iii) 100°F

b (i) 20°C   (ii) −40°C

39
a 380 minutes   **b** 5.20 am

40 £950

41 50, 25, 12.5, 6.25, 3.125, 1.562 5, 0.781 25

42
a 4   **b** 5 or 6

43 Kite, B; Rhombus, C; Rectangle, D; Equilateral Triangle, A.

44
a

x	y	z
2	1.333	0.75
2.083	1.388	0.691
2.079		

b The result is approximately 9   **c** 2.08

Table of roots and trigonometrical values

x	sin x°	cos x°	tan x°	√x	x	sin x°	cos x°	tan x°	√x
0	0	1	0	0	51	.777	.629	1.235	7.141
1	.017	1	.017	1	52	.788	.616	1.28	7.211
2	.035	.999	.035	1.414	53	.799	.602	1.327	7.28
3	.052	.999	.052	1.732	54	.809	.588	1.376	7.348
4	.07	.998	.07	2	55	.819	.574	1.428	7.416
5	.087	.996	.087	2.236	56	.829	.559	1.483	7.483
6	.105	.995	.105	2.449	57	.839	.545	1.54	7.55
7	.122	.993	.123	2.646	58	.848	.53	1.6	7.616
8	.139	.99	.141	2.828	59	.857	.515	1.664	7.681
9	.156	.988	.158	3	60	.866	.5	1.732	7.746
10	.174	.985	.176	3.162	61	.875	.485	1.804	7.81
11	.191	.982	.194	3.317	62	.883	.469	1.881	7.874
12	.208	.978	.213	3.464	63	.891	.454	1.963	7.937
13	.225	.974	.231	3.606	64	.899	.438	2.05	8
14	.242	.97	.249	3.742	65	.906	.423	2.145	8.062
15	.259	.966	.268	3.873	66	.914	.407	2.246	8.124
16	.276	.961	.287	4	67	.921	.391	2.356	8.185
17	.292	.956	.306	4.123	68	.927	.375	2.475	8.246
18	.309	.951	.325	4.243	69	.934	.358	2.605	8.307
19	.326	.946	.344	4.359	70	.94	.342	2.747	8.367
20	.342	.94	.364	4.472	71	.946	.326	2.904	8.426
21	.358	.934	.384	4.583	72	.951	.309	3.078	8.485
22	.375	.972	.404	4.69	73	.956	.292	3.271	8.544
23	.391	.921	.424	4.796	74	.961	.276	3.487	8.602
24	.407	.914	.445	4.899	75	.966	.259	3.732	8.66
25	.423	.906	.466	5	76	.97	.242	4.011	8.718
26	.438	.899	.488	5.099	77	.974	.225	4.331	8.775
27	.454	.891	.51	5.196	78	.978	.208	4.705	8.832
28	.469	.883	.532	5.292	79	.982	.191	5.145	8.888
29	.485	.875	.554	5.385	80	.985	.174	5.671	8.944
30	.5	.866	.577	5.477	81	.988	.156	6.314	9
31	.515	.857	.601	5.568	82	.99	.139	7.115	9.055
32	.53	.848	.625	5.657	83	.993	.122	8.144	9.11
33	.545	.839	.649	5.745	84	.995	.105	9.514	9.165
34	.559	.829	.675	5.831	85	.996	.087	11.43	9.22
35	.574	.819	.7	5.916	86	.998	.07	14.301	9.274
36	.588	.809	.727	6	87	.999	.052	19.081	9.327
37	.602	.799	.754	6.083	88	.999	.035	28.636	9.381
38	.616	.788	.781	6.164	89	1	.017	57.29	9.434
39	.629	.777	.81	6.245	90	1	0		9.487
40	.643	.766	.839	6.325	91				9.539
41	.656	.755	.869	6.403	92				9.592
42	.669	.743	.9	6.481	93				9.644
43	.682	.731	.933	6.557	94				9.695
44	.695	.719	.966	6.633	95				9.747
45	.707	.707	1	6.708	96				9.798
46	.719	.695	1.036	6.782	97				9.849
47	.731	.682	1.072	6.856	98				9.899
48	.743	.669	1.111	6.928	99				9.95
49	.755	.656	1.15	7	100				10
50	.766	.643	1.192	7.071					

28/3/95
- Left to do:- H/work Checkpoint 7.
                                   a tof & al
                                   no. 2

Complete Graphs section

Do Shape & Space
HWK 28/3/95
P197 Chk 6 No 4
P199 Chk 6&7, 8, 9, 11, 12, 13, 14, 15